WORLD CERAMICS

An illustrated history edited by Robert J. Charleston

John Ayers
David Boston
Rollo Charles
Robert J. Charleston
P. E. Corbett
Dr. F. A. Dreier
Dr. S. Ducret

Dr. Géza Fehérvári
Alice W. Frothingham
Jeanne Giacomotti
Dr. J. Basil Hennessy
John Hurst
Dr. G. Liverani
Dr. A. H. S. Megaw

J. Bruce Palmer
Anthony Ray
Barrie Reynolds
Donald Towner
Oliver Van Oss
Hugh Wakefield

PAUL HAMLYN

LONDON · NEW YORK · SYDNEY · TORONTO

EDITOR
R. J. Charleston
Keeper, Department of Ceramics and Glass,
Victoria and Albert Museum, London

AUTHORS
John Ayers
Deputy Keeper, Department of Ceramics and Glass,
Victoria and Albert Museum, London; authority on Oriental
ceramics

David Boston
Curator of the Horniman Museum and Library,
London; authority on pre-European American culture

Rollo Charles
Keeper of the Department of Art, National Museum of Wales,
Cardiff; authority on Continental porcelain

P. E. Corbett
Yates Professor of Classical Art and Archaeology
at the University of London

Dr. F. A. Dreier
Staatliche Kunstsammlungen,
Kassel; authority on German pottery

Dr. S. Ducret
authority on German porcelain

Dr. Géza Fehérvári
Lecturer in Islamic Art and Archaeology, School of Oriental
and African Studies, University of London

Alice W. Frothingham
Hispanic Society of America;
authority on Spanish pottery

Jeanne Giacomotti
Assistante au Département des Objets d'Art,
Musée du Louvre; authority on medieval French pottery

Dr. J. Basil Hennessy
Director of the British School of
Archaeology in Jerusalem

John Hurst
Inspector of Ancient Monuments, Ministry of Public Building
and Works, in charge of rescue excavations on medieval sites in
Britain; special interest in medieval British ceramics

Dr. G. Liverani
Director of the Museo Internazionale delle Ceramiche, Faenza

Dr. A. H. S. Megaw
Director of the British School of Archaeology, Athens

J. Bruce Palmer
Director and Secretary of the Fiji Museum

Anthony Ray
Master of Modern Language at Eton College
and authority on English delftware

Dr. Barrie Reynolds
formerly Director of The Rhodes Livingstone Museum, Zambia;
special interest in the material culture of African peoples

Donald Towner
Hon. Secretary of the English Ceramic Circle;
authority on English 18th-century pottery

Oliver Van Oss
Headmaster of Charterhouse, one-time editor of the
Transactions of the English Ceramic Circle; authority on Dutch Delft

Hugh Wakefield
Keeper of the Department of Circulation at the Victoria and
Albert Museum, London; authority on Victorian pottery

THE HAMLYN PUBLISHING GROUP LIMITED
LONDON · NEW YORK · SYDNEY · TORONTO
Hamlyn House, Feltham, Middlesex, England
© The Hamlyn Publishing Group Limited, 1968
Reprinted 1971

ISBN 0 600 03949 8

Phototypeset by BAS Printers Limited
Wallop, Hampshire, England
Printed in Italy by
Arnoldo Mondadori
Officine Grafiche
Verona

Frontispiece:

*Vase with relief decoration in the Art Nouveau style about 1900,
by the French potter, Edmond Lachenal. Hessisches Landesmuseum,
Darmstadt.*

Contents

Colour Plates

Acknowledgments

A.C.I., Brussels 470, 554; A.F.I., Venice 546; Manlio Agodi, Ferrara 74; Alinari, Florence 410, 412, 420, 429, 487, 493, 659; American School of Classical Studies at Athens 296, 305, 309; Amman Museum, Jordan 27, 41; Ernst Amman, Zürich 567, 605, 607, 611, 619, 625, 636, 637, 638; Anderson, Rome 389; Angewandte Kunst, Vienna 893, 894, 895; Archaeological Museum, Ankara 3, 25, 39, 42; Archives Photographiques, Paris 382; Arkeoloji Muzesi, Istanbul 302, 308; Jean Arland, Geneva 152, 161, 191; Arts Council of Great Britain 105, 112, 119, 132, 139; Ashmolean Museum, Oxford 6, 8, 16, 17, 18, 20, 22, 23, 84, 92, 95, 137, 197, 201, 202, 204, 207, 216, 225, 235, 255, 263, 285, 286, 290, 329, 447, 477, 480, 481, 6; Ayasofya Museum, Istanbul 306, 317; Badisches Landesmuseum, Karlsruhe 566; Bandieri, Modena 423; Barrie & Rockliff Limited, London 48; Bavaria Verlag, Munich 35; Bayerisches Nationalmuseum, Munich 563; J. Blauel, Munich 21; Lionel R. Bell 677, 697; Benaki Museum, Athens 310, 319; Bibliothèque Nationale, Paris 70; Bildarchiv Foto Marburg 67; Bodleian Library, Oxford 386, 442; Borchi, Faenza 341, 413, 422, 425, 436, 489, 491, 542, 544, 547, 548, 550, 647, 38; Borel, Marseilles 525; Bristol City Art Gallery 478, 482, 483, 485, 817, 8, 32; British Museum, London 5, 15, 21, 24, 28, 38, 50, 51, 52, 53, 54, 55, 56, 57, 59, 69, 75, 76, 79, 110, 122, 131, 147, 150, 151, 153, 174, 190, 196, 198, 199, 200, 209, 217, 224, 234, 245, 252, 266, 268, 269, 284, 295, 321, 397, 424, 437, 471, 484, 522, 595, 603, 643, 651, 653, 707, 751, 756, 758, 777, 779, 780, 782, 783, 959, 969, 983, 985, 986, 992, 994, 998, 1002, 1005, 1006, 1008, 4, 49, 62, 63; Bulloz, Paris 602; Castle Museum, Norwich 328; Castle Museum, Nottingham 333; Celso, Lodi 541; Christie, Manson & Wood, London 661; Cincinnati Art Museum 920; Cleveland Museum of Art, Ohio 187, 394, 395; Yves Coffin, Fontenay aux Roses 182; Colchester and Essex Museum, Colchester 90, 94; A. C. Cooper, London 48, 49, 51, 83, 91, 125, 129, 149, 150, 160, 169; Cyprus Museum, Nicosia 10, 12, 26, 30, 31, 44, 45, 46, 47, 318, 320; J. E. Dayton, London 19; Decker, Saumur 498; Deutsche Fotothek, Dresden 371, 675; Professor W. Dexel 337, 339; Henri Devos, Boulogne 68; Dorman Memorial Museum, Middlesbrough 917, 923; Dr S. Ducret 562a, 610, 612, 613, 614, 616, 617, 618, 620, 622, 624, 626, 630, 42; Dumbarton Oaks, Harvard University 966, 27; Dyson Perrins Museum, Worcester 854; Josef Ehm, Prague 845, 847; Encyclopaedia Britannica, 23; Thomas Fall, Stanmore 117, 552, 553, 555; Dr G. Fehérvári, London 251; Pierre Feuillade, Limoges 355, 604, 666, 668; Fine Art Engravers, Godalming 85, 86, 93, 96, 154; Fitzwilliam Museum, Cambridge 362, 649, 657, 753, 787, 802, 13; Paul Fox, London 221, 240, 242, 243, 20; John R. Freeman, London 608b; Sir Harry Garner 127, 173; Gasperini, Genoa 494, 495; Germanisches Nationalmuseum, Nuremberg 448, 450, 639; G. M. Gompertz 172, 176, 178; Irmgard Groth-Kimball, Mexico 963; Guildhall Museum, London 359; Haags Gemeentemuseum 101, 463, 557; Hassia, Paris 2; Dr J. B. Hennessy 4; Hermitage Museum, Leningrad 301, 316, 390; Hessisches Landesmuseum, Darmstadt 505, 866, 880, 881, 884, 885, 1; Hans Hinz, Basel 564, 627, 628, 631, 634, 635, 640, 46; Hispanic Society of America, New York 391, 396, 399, 400, 402, 404, 407, 510, 511, 591, 592, 597, 36, 37; Hispanic Society of America Photo Library, New York 401, 403, 453, 455, 456; Michael Holford 89, 156, 159, 179, 181, 188, 203, 205, 211, 212, 214, 215, 219, 222, 223, 227, 228, 230, 233, 236, 237, 238, 239, 244, 250, 253, 254, 256, 257, 259, 260, 267, 271, 273, 279, 287, 292, 360, 361, 374, 384, 642, 652, 700, 716, 743, 744, 745, 746, 747, 748, 749, 750, 754, 755, 759, 762, 763, 764, 766, 767, 768, 769, 770, 772, 775, 776, 778, 784, 785, 786, 788, 789, 790, 791, 792, 793, 794, 795, 796, 797, 798, 799, 800, 801, 803, 804, 805, 807, 816, 818, 823, 830, 832, 834, 837, 838, 839, 841, 843, 844, 846, 848, 849, 850, 851, 852, 853, 855, 856, 857, 858, 863, 865, 867, 869, 873, 874, 876, 878, 879, 883, 888, 891, 897, 898, 899, 900, 901, 902, 903, 909, 914, 919, 922, 924, 926, 927, 931, 933, 940, 945, 951, 952, 973, 974, 975, 7, 9, 14, 15, 16, 24, 25, 26, 29, 31, 33, 34, 40, 43, 45, 51, 52, 53, 54, 55, 56, 57, 58, 59, 60, 61; Horniman Museum, London 962, 981; Albert Huck, Strasbourg 529, 533, 534; Iraq Museum, Baghdad 2, 14; Pierre Joly—Vera Cardot, Bourges 935; Kaiser Wilhelm Museum, Krefeld 369; Kestnermuseum, Hanover 507, 570, 635; Koninklijk Instituut Voor de Tropen, Amsterdam 970; Kunsthistorisches Museum, Vienna 77; Kunstgewerbemuseum, Berlin 877, 886, 889, 892, 911, 913; Kunstgewerbemuseum, Cologne 887; Landesbildstelle Rheinland 336, 373, 378, 379a; Raymond Laniepce, Paris 438, 488, 500, 521, 527, 532, 593, 600, 601, 663, 664, 669, 670, 671, 672, 673, 674, 676, 681, 682, 686, 687, 690, 691, 692, 693, 694, 695, 30, 47; K. M. Lee, Seoul 170, 171; Leeds City Museum 327; Prof G. Liverani 411; Liverpool City Museum 486, 710; Livingstone Museum, Rhodesia 990, 995, 997; London Museum 334, 446; Dr Jane Gaston Mahler, New York 109; Manchester City Art Gallery 479; Martin von Wagner Museum, Würzburg 73; MAS, Barcelona 405, 458, 459, 509, 660; Dr A. H. S. Megaw 307, 312, 313, 314, 315; Peter Macdonald, London 157; Meissener Porzellan-Manufaktur 882; Metropolitan Museum of Art, New York 162, 297, 392, 427, 439, 608a, 820, 822, 861; Toso Mirco, Venice 428; Mr & Mrs R. Joseph Monsen Jr, Seattle 957; Musée des Arts Décoratifs, Paris 518, 519, 536, 538, 539, 665, 896, 906, 908, 932; Musée des Arts et Traditions Populaires, Bourges 840; Musée des Beaux Arts, Rouen 516; Musée Guimet, Paris 111; Musée de l'Homme, Paris 964, 972, 982; Musée National d'Art Moderne, Paris 936, 937, 938; Museo Arqueologico Nacional, Madrid 594, 658; Museo Civico, Bologna 430; Museo Civico, Lucera 409; Museo Civico, Padua 343; Museo Civico, Pavia 342; Museo Gregoriano Etrusco, Vatican 62; Museum of the American Indian, New York 960, 965, 967; Museum Boymans-van Beuningen, Rotterdam 944; Museum für Kunsthandwerk, Frankfurt 561, 565; Museum of Far Eastern Antiquities, Stockholm 102, 140; Museum of Fine Arts, Boston 62, 81, 106, 167; Museum für Kunst und Gewerbe, Hamburg 99, 189, 452, 501, 504, 558, 559, 569, 582, 648, 871, 872, 890, 910, 912, 939, 941, 942, 943, 39; Museo Poldi Pezzoli 545; Museum Rietberg, Zürich 115; Muzea v Brne, Brno 568; National Archaeological Museum, Athens 58, 65, 5; National Museum, Stockholm 571, 572, 573, 574; National Museum of Wales, Cardiff 641, 645, 650, 654, 655; National Museum, Tokyo 193; Newark Museum, New Jersey 821, 860, 862; Susan Newman, New York 953; Nicholas Museum, University of Sydney 29, 3; Nordenfkeldske Kunstindustrimuseum 955; Nordiska Musset, Stockholm 733; Peabody Museum. Harvard University 961; Pflueger Collection, New York 621; Pitt Rivers Museum, Oxford 984, 987, 988, 989, 991, 993, 996, 999, 1000; Osterreiches Museum für angewandte Kunst, Vienna 364; J. Otto, Prague 946, 947, 948, 949; Palestine Archaeological Museum, Jerusalem 9, 11, 13, 32, 33, 35, 37, 40, 43; Pandolfi, Pesaro 549; Colin Penn, London 148; Percival David Foundation, London University 118, 121, 123, 126, 134, 141, 143, 158, 11; Philadelphia Museum of Art 833; Portsmouth City Art Gallery Collections 824; Rampazzi, Turin 543, 644; Réunion des Musées Nationaux, Versailles 71, 80, 303, 323, 324, 345, 349, 350, 351, 353, 354, 497, 499, 515, 517, 524, 526, 530, 540, 685, 678, 679; Reissmuseum, Mannheim 632; Daniel Rhodes, New York 956; Rijksmuseum, Amsterdam 379b, 454, 551, 609, 629; Rijksmuseum van Oudheden, Leiden 87, 338; Rohsska Konstslojdmuseum, Goteborg 576; Rörstrands Porslinsfabriker, Lidköping 814, 859; Royal Copenhagen Porcelain Manufactory 870, 875; Royal Ontario Museum, University of Toronto 114, 116; Richard Sadler, Coventry 331; St Annen Museum, Lubeck 587; Scala, Florence 22, 24, 28, 41; Scarborough Museum 332; Schleswig-Holsteinisches Landesmuseum 588; Seattle Art Museum 180–185; Smithsonian Institution, Freer Gallery, Washington 103, 135, 183, 194, 606, 615, 921, 17; Soprintendenza alle Antichita, Florence 78; Soprintendenza alle Gallerie, Florence 398, 406; Soprintendenza alle Gallerie, Naples 492, 656, 662; Soprintendenza Foro Romano, Rome 322; Sotheby, London 623, 735; South African Museum, Cape Town 1001, 1003, 1004, 1007; Staatliche Antikensammlungen, Munich 63, 72, 82; Staatliche Kunstsammlungen, Kassel 372, 503, 506, 508, 562b; Staatliche Museen, Berlin 311, 365, 416, 449; Staatliche Museen zu Berlin 451; Stickelmann, Bremen 377; Studio Laventon Rueil, Paris 689; Studies Josse-Lalance 347, 348, 352, 356, 357, 383, 514, 520, 528, 531, 537; Suntory Gallery, Tokyo 12; University Museum of Archaeology and Ethnology, Cambridge 325, 330, 335, 968, 971; U.S. Department of the Interior 363; O. Van Oss 460, 464; Vestlandske Kunstindustrimuseum, Bergen 589; Victoria and Albert Museum, London 91, 98, 107, 108, 113, 120, 128, 130, 133, 142, 145, 146, 155, 165, 166, 168, 175, 177, 184, 186, 192, 206, 208, 210, 213, 218, 220, 226, 231, 232, 241, 246, 247, 248, 249, 258, 261, 262, 264, 270, 272, 274, 275, 276, 277, 278, 280, 281, 282, 283, 288, 289, 291, 292, 293, 299, 344, 346, 358, 366, 367, 368, 375, 376, 380, 381, 385, 387, 388, 393, 408, 414, 415, 417, 419, 421, 426, 431, 432, 433, 434, 435, 440, 441, 443, 444, 461, 462, 465, 466, 467, 468, 469, 472, 473, 474, 475, 476, 490, 502, 512, 523, 535, 556, 575, 577, 578, 584, 585, 586, 590, 596, 598, 646, 667, 696, 698, 699, 701, 702, 703, 704, 705, 706, 708, 709, 711, 712, 713, 714, 715, 717, 718, 719, 720, 721, 722, 723, 724, 725, 726, 729, 731, 732, 734, 737, 738, 739, 740, 741, 742, 752, 757, 760, 761, 765, 771, 773, 774, 806, 808, 819, 825, 826, 827, 828, 829, 831, 835, 836, 842, 864, 868, 904, 905, 907, 915, 916, 918, 925, 928, 929, 930, 934, 10, 18; Peter Vouklos, California 954; Wallace Collection, London 163, 683, 684; John Webb, Brompton Studio 1, 7, 34, 36, 370, 976, 977, 978, 979, 980; 64 Wedgwood Museum Josiah Wedgwood & Sons Limited, Stoke-on-Trent 50; William Rockhill Nelson Gallery of Art, Kansas City 104; Ole Woldbye, Copenhagen 97, 560, 580, 583, 583, 594, 728, 730, 960; Rob Wright Jr, Suva, Fiji 1009, 1010, 1011, 1012, 1013, 1014, 1015, 1016, 1017, 1018, 1019; Zambia Information Services 958.

Reading List

GENERAL

Hannover, E. *Pottery and Porcelain*, 3 vols., London, 1925
Honey, W. B. *The Art of the Potter*, London, 1946
 European Ceramic Art from the End of the Middle Ages to about 1815, 2 vols., London, 1952
Lane, Arthur *Style in Pottery*, London, 1948
Leach, Bernard *A Potter's Book*, London, 1940 and later ed.
Savage, George *Porcelain through the Ages*, London, 1954
 Pottery through the Ages, London, 1959
Victoria and Albert Museum, *Guide to the Collection of Tiles* (by Arthur Lane), London, 1960

THE ANCIENT WORLD
PREHISTORIC NEAR EAST
Mellaart, James *The Chalcolithic and Early Bronze Ages in the Near East and Anatolia*, Beiruth, 1966
GREECE
Lane, Arthur *Greek Pottery*, London, new ed., 1963
ROMAN EMPIRE
Charleston, R. J. *Roman Pottery*, London, 1955

THE FAR EAST
CHINA
Garner, Sir Harry *Oriental Blue and White*, London, 1954
Gompertz, G.St.G. M. *Chinese Celadon Wares*, London, 1958
Gray, Basil *Early Chinese Pottery and Porcelain*, London, 1953
Honey, W. B. *Ceramic Art of China and other Countries of the Far East*, London, 1945
Jenyns, Soame *Later Chinese Porcelain*, London, 1965
 Ming Pottery and Porcelain, London, 1953
KOREA
Chewon Kim and Gompertz, G.St. G. M. *The Ceramic Art of Korea*, London, 1961
Gompertz, G.St G. M. *Korean Celadon*, London, 1963
Honey, W. B. *Korean Pottery*, London, 1947
JAPAN
Jenyns, Soame *Japanese Porcelain*, London, 1965
Miller, R. A. *Japanese Ceramics*, Tokyo and Rutland, 1960

THE LANDS OF ISLAM
Dimond, M. S. *A handbook of Muhammadan Art*, Chapter X, New York, 3rd ed. 1958
Hobson, R. L. *A guide to the Islamic pottery of the Near and Far East*, London, 1932
Lane, Arthur, *Early Islamic Pottery*, London, 1947 *Islamic pottery from the 9th–14th centuries. The Eldred Hitchcock collection*, London, 1956 *Later Islamic Pottery*, London, 1957
Wilkinson, Charles K. *Iranian Ceramics*, New York, 1963

EUROPE: LEAD-GLAZE AND STONEWARE
BYZANTINE
Morgan, C. H. *The Byzantine Pottery (Corinth)*, Cambridge, Mass., 1942
Rice, D. Talbot *Byzantine Glazed Pottery*, Oxford, 1930
Stevenson, R. B. K. *The Pottery (1936–7)* in *The Great Palace of the Byzantine Emperors, First Report*, pp. 31 ff. Oxford, 1947
Taylor, J. du P. and Megaw, A. H. S. *Cypriot Medieval Glazed Pottery*, *Report of the Department of Antiquities*, pp. 1 ff. Cyprus, 1937–39
ITALY
Ballardini, G. *L'Eredità ceramistica dell' Antico Mondo Romano*, Rome, 1964
Morazzoni, J. *The Majolicas . . . of Legnago*, Milan, 1950
Victoria and Albert Museum *Catalogue of Italian Maiolica*, 2 vols. (by Bernard Rackham), pp. 423 ff. London, 1940
FRANCE
Ballot, M. J. *La Céramique Française*, 2 vols., 1 Paris, 1925
Fontaine, G. *La Céramique Française*, Paris, 1965
Poncetton, F. and Salles, G. *Les Poteries Françaises*, Paris, 1928
ENGLAND
Charleston, R. J. *Pottery, Porcelain and Glass in Connoisseur Period Guides, Tudor* and *Stuart*, London, 1956 and 1957
Honey, W. B. *English Pottery and Porcelain*, London, revised ed. 1962
Rackham, Bernard *Catalogue of the Glaisher Collection*, Fitzwilliam Museum, 2 vols, Cambridge, 1934 *Medieval English Pottery*, London, 1948

GERMANY
Blümel, F. *Deutsche Ofen*, Munich, 1965
Braat, W. C. *Die frühmittelalterliche Keramik von Burgh in Oudheidkundige Mededelingen*, 41, pp. 98 ff. 1960
Lobbedey, U. *Zur Kunstgeschichte der rheinischen Keramik vom 12. bis 14. Jahrhundert* in *Keramos*, 27, pp. 3 ff. 1965
Plath, H. *Mittelalterliche Keramik vom 12. bis zum 15 Jahrhundert in Hannover in Hannoversche Geschichts-blätter*, N. F. 12, pp. 1 ff. 1959
Schindler, R. *Die hamburgische Keramik des 8.–12. Jahrhunderts als Geschichtsquelle in Hammaburg*, 3, pp. 115 ff. 1951–2
Schmidt, R. *Deutsche Hafnerarbeiten der Gotik und Renaissance*, Frankfurt a.M., 1919
Schultheiss, W. *Nürnberber Hafnergewerbe in 650 Jahren*, Neustadt/Aisch, 1956
Spies, G. *Hafner und Hafnerhandwerk in Sudwestdeutschland*, Tübingen, 1964
Strauss, K. *Alte deutsche Kunsttöpferien*, Berlin, 1923
STONEWARE
Albrecht, R. *Töpferkunst in Kreussen*, Rothenburg (n.d)
Berling, K. *Sächsisches Steinzeug aus Waldenburg und Zeitz*, Berlin, 1934
Falke, O. von *Das Rheinische Steinzeug*, 2 vols., Berlin, 1908
Koetschau, K. *Rheinisches Steinzeug*, Munich, 1924
Kohlhaussen, H. *Geschichte des deutschen Kunsthandwerks*, Munich, 1955
Strauss, K. (see above)

EUROPE: TIN-GLAZE
ITALY
Liverani, G. *Five Centuries of Italian Majolica*, London, 1960
Rackham, Bernard *Catalogue of Italian Maiolica*, pp. 1–421, London, 1940 *Italian Maiolica*, London, 1952

FRANCE
Alfassa, P., Block, J. and Chompret, J. *Répertoire de la Faience française*, Paris, 1935
Connaissance des Arts, *L'Oeuvre des faienciers français du XVIe à la fin du XVIIIe siècle*, Paris, 1966
Giacomotti, J. *Faiences françaises*, Fribourg, 1963
Lane, Arthur *French Faience*, London, 1948

HOLLAND
Hudig, W. *Delfter Fayence*, Berlin, 1929
de Jonge, Jonkvrouwe C. H. *Delfts Aardewerk*, Rotterdam, 1965
Korf, D. *Dutch Tiles*, London, 1963

ENGLAND
Garner, F. H. *English Delftware*, London, 1948
Ray, Anthony *English Delftware Pottery in the R. Hall Warren Collection*, London, 1968
GERMANY
Hüseler, Konrad *Deutsche Fayencen*, 3 vols., Stuttgart, 1956–58
Kohlhaussen, H. *Geschichte des deutschen Kunsthandwerks*, pp. 376 ff. Munich, 1955
Krisztinkovich, B. *Habaner Pottery*, Rotterdam, 1965
Pfeiffer, W. *Beitrage zu Bartholomaus Dill Riemenschneider in Cultura Artesina*, XVI, pp. 19 ff. 1962
Wyss, Robert L. *Der Winterthurer Hafner Ludwig Pfau II . . .* in *Keramos*, 10 pp. 183 ff. 1960
SPAIN
Batllori y Munné, A. and Llubía y Munné, L. M. *Cerámica catalana decorada*, Barcelona, 1949
Romani, Manuel Escrivá de *Historia de la cerámica de Alcora*, Madrid, 1945
Corbacho, Antonio Sancho *La Crámica andaluza . . .* Seville, 1948
Folch y Torres, J. *Noticia sobre la cerámica de Paterna*, Barcelona, 1921
Frothingham, Alice Wilson *Lustreware of Spain*, New York, 1951
 Talavera Pottery, New York, 1944
Martí, Manuel González *Cerámica del Levante español: siglos medievales*, 3 vols., Barcelona, Madrid, 1944–52
SCANDINAVIA
Hernmarck, Carl *Fajans och Porslin*, Stockholm, 1959
Hüseler, K. *Geschichte der Schleswig-Holsteinischen Fayence-Manufakturen im 18 Jahrhundert*, Breslau, 1929
Opstad, L. *Herreboe Fajance Fabrique*, Borregaard, 1959
Uldall, Kai *Gammel Dansk Fajence*, Copenhagen, 1967

EUROPE: PORCELAIN
GENERAL
Charles, Rollo *Continental Porcelain*, London, 1964
ITALY AND SPAIN
Frothingham, Alice Wilson *Capodimonte and Buen Retiro Porcelains*, New York, 1955
Lane, Arthur *Italian Porcelain*, London, 1954
FRANCE
Alfassa, P. and Guerin, J. *Porcelaines françaises du XVIIIe siècle au milieu du milieu du XIXe. siècle*, Paris, 1930
Chavagnac, X. de and Grollier, A. de *Histoire des manufactures françaises de Porcelaine*, Paris, 1906
Connaissance des Arts, *Les Porcelainiers du XVIIIe siècle français*, Paris, 1964.
Honey, W. B. *French Porcelain of the XVIIIth century*, London, 1950
Verlet, P., Grandjean, S. and Brunet, M. *Sèvres*, 2 vols., Paris, 1954
GERMANY
Ducret, S. *German Porcelain and Faience*, London, 1962
Hayward, J. F. *Viennese Porcelain of the Du Paquier Period*, London, 1952
Honey, W. B. *Dresden China*, London, new ed., 1954 *German Porcelain*, London, 1947
Savage, George *18th Century German Porcelain*, London, 1958
ENGLAND
Charleston, R. J. (Ed.) *English Porcelain 1745–1850*, London, 1965
Dixon, J. L. *English Porcelain of the 18th Century*, London, 1952
Honey, W. B. *Old English Porcelain*, London, 2nd ed., 1948
Lane, Arthur *English Porcelain Figures of the 18th Century*, London, 1961
Watney, Bernard *English Blue and White Porcelain of the 18th century*, London, 1963
OTHER EUROPEAN CENTRES
Grandjean, Bredo L. *Kongelig Dansk Porcelain*, Copenhagen, 1962
Hernmarck, V. *Marieberg*, Stockholm, 1946
Lukomsky, G. *Russisches Porzellan*, Berlin, 1924
Schrijver, E. *Hollands Porcelein*, Bussum, 1966

STAFFORDSHIRE AND THE RISE OF INDUSTRIALISM
Honey, W. B. *Wedgwood Ware*, London, 1948
Towner, Donald. C. *English Cream-Coloured Earthenware*, London, 1957
 Leeds Pottery, London, 1963

THE MODERN WORLD
Barber, E. A. *The Pottery and Porcelain of the United States* 3rd ed New York, 1909
Barret, R. C. *Bennington Pottery and Porcelain*, New York, 1958
Birsk, T. *The Art of the Modern Potter*, London, 1967
Faré, M. *La Céramique Contemporaine*, Paris, 1954
Godden, G. A. *Victorian Porcelain*, London, 1961
Hayden, A. *Royal Copenhagen Porcelain*, London, 1911
Hetteš, K. and Rada, P. *Modern Ceramics*, London, 1965
Klein, A. *Moderne Deutsche Keramik*, Daramik, Darmstadt, 1956
Köllmann, E. *Berliner Porzellan*, 2 vols., Braunschweig, 1966
Leistikow-Duchardt, A. *Die Entwicklung eines neuen Stiles im Porzellan*, Heidelberg, 1957
Lukomskij, G. *Russisches Porzellan*, Berlin, 1924
Poche, E. *Bohemian Porcelain*, Prague, 1955
Rose, M. *Artist-Potters in England*, London, 1955
Valotaire, M. *La Céramique Française Moderne*, Paris, 1930
Wakefield, H. *Victorian Pottery*, London, 1962

THE PRIMITIVE WORLD
PRE-EUROPEAN AMERICA
Bushnell, G. H. S. and Digby, A. *Ancient American Pottery*, London, 1955
Bushnell, G. H. S. *Ancient Arts of the Americas*, London, 1965
Coe, M. D. *Mexico*, London, 1962
Lothrop, S. K. *Treasures of Ancient America*, Cleveland, Ohio & London, 1964
Meggers, B. J. *Ecuador*, London, 1956
Reichel-Dolmatoff, G. *Colombia*, London, 1965
Thompson, J. E. S. *The Rise and Fall of Maya Civilization*, Oklahoma, 1964
Wanchope, R. (Ed.) *Handbook of Middle American Indians*, Texas, 1964
AFRICA
Balfet, Helene, *Ethnographic Observations in North Africa and Archaeological Interpretations in Ceramics and Man by Frederick Matson*, 1965
Coart, E. and Haulleville, A. De *La Céramique in Annales du Musée du Congo Belge*, Bruxelles, 1907
Reynolds, Barrie. *The Material Culture of the Peoples of the Gwembe Valley*, Manchester, 1967
Schofield, J. F. *Primitive Pottery, An Introduction to South African Ceramics*, in *Prehistoric and Protohistoric Handbook of the South African Archaeological Society*, No. 3, Cape Town, 1948
Trowell, Margaret and Wachsmann, K. P. *Tribal Crafts of Uganda*, London, 1953

OCEANIA
Cranstone, B. A. L. *Melonesia: a short ethnography*, British Museum, 1961
Roth, Kingsley *Pottery making in Fiji* in *Journal of the Royal Anthropological Institute*, Vol. 65, p. 217, 1935

Introduction

The making of pottery is the longest lived handicraft of which we have continuous knowledge. In some parts of the world, pots are being made today which are not markedly different in technique and general appearance from those excavated in cultural contexts many millennia old. Yet within this space of time, pottery has at various periods and in different places, been the vehicle of the most sophisticated and up-to-the-minute artistry, its technical difficulties bent to serve the subtlest demands which could be made upon it. Its history is therefore not only long, but complicated. It is the object of this book to give a general picture of its development from its earliest days in many parts of the world until the present, including equally the work of primitive communities today, the refined products of China a thousand years ago, and the pottery of modern civilisation in its bewildering complexity. Since such a survey, within the compass of a single volume, must necessarily be selective, it has been the aim to include all that is either aesthetically of merit or historically important for the development of the ceramic art.

Yet although pottery has aesthetic values of its own, it necessarily cannot develop independently of more general artistic movements, or of the social and cultural environment in which it is designed to play its part. Pottery is most commonly made into vessels for use (and the humblest utilitarian wares may possess great beauty); but it may also be fashioned, for example, into architectural details or into cult objects, the form of which is predetermined by esoteric religious demands. These forms may well first have evolved in some other material, and where pottery follows a form traditional in another substance, it not infrequently copies its modes of decoration too, a pot being given, for example, not only the shape but the texture of a basket. Normally the less precious material follows the more precious, and time and again the potter has imitated the forms and the decoration (however inappropriate) of the silversmith.

The potter has usually been a humble craftsman, providing the world with its utilitarian wares, and only occasionally rising to a higher plane of artistic pretention in the execution of some special commission, as when the 17th-century English country potter made a slipware dish to commemorate a wedding or a birth. Such pieces survive when the plainer products which were the staple of his trade have long since been broken and discarded. Sometimes, however, the potter has aspired to the status of an artist, whether as modeller, painter, or (less often) as the maker of a material considered in itself precious by reason of its rarity and beauty. In the High Renaissance the artist had achieved a dignity and status unparalleled in the history of his calling, but Taddeo Zuccaro did not consider it beneath him to design for maiolica; Bernard Palissy, the potter of Saintes, was appointed to make his rustic wares for the king; and Francesco I de' Medici set up a workshop within the confines of the Boboli Gardens to accommodate the master whose precious porcelain bears the Medici name.

Considered in these different lights the potter and his pots may be seen in their various relationships to their environment. The ceramic art, however, also follows independent laws of development imposed upon it by the nature of its techniques. Technical knowledge has grown slowly over millennia, and each stage is impossible without the one that precedes it. In the course of time, various branches of the ceramic family have established themselves, each with advantages and drawbacks peculiar to itself. The virtues of different branches are not readily interchangeable and each can be developed only within the potential of its technical nature. You cannot, for instance, readily paint under a lead-glaze, nor produce a fine turquoise colour in other than alkaline glaze. A proper understanding of merit in ceramics, therefore, depends to a great extent on an appreciation of the techniques involved.

Pottery is essentially clay hardened in a fire. The type of clay used, and the degree of heat to which it is submitted, decide the technical character of the ware. At about 1250° centigrade clay vitrifies, becoming thereby impervious to liquids, a condition to which most pottery aspires. The same end, however, can be achieved at a lower temperature by adding the vitreous sheath of glass known as a 'glaze'. Since not all clays will withstand a high temperature without collapsing in the kiln, glazing may be a technical necessity in producing a water-tight pot: it has the further advantage of producing a sheeny surface capable of being kept clean, and normally one that can be given the added charm of colour. Glazes normally consist of a largish proportion of a fluxing-agent, such as lead, borax, soda or potassium, sometimes mixed with a siliceous substance (sand, ground flint, or quartz, etc.), and are normally applied to the surface of a pot in a liquid condition. A glaze must be suited to the body of the pot which it covers, or it may crack or peel off. Thus, the alkaline-glazed pottery of the Near East (see page 14) was made of a glaze compounded essentially of sand and soda or potash, laid on a pasty body which also contained a high percentage of these elements. The limitations imposed by the lack of plasticity of this body in throwing were perhaps more than compensated for by the brilliant turquoise colour which this type of glaze alone makes possible. A similar balance of advantage and disadvantage may be observed in the process of making salt-glazed stoneware. Here, by a unique technical procedure, common salt was shovelled into the kiln at the height of the firing. The volatilised soda combined with the silica and alumina of the clay to form a thin vitreous coating. This was often pleasantly irregular in texture and therefore to some extent lacking in the glassy quality normally expected of a glaze. On the other hand it fitted so tightly to the surface of the pot that none of its contours became blunted, as sometimes happened in the case of the more fluid applied glazes, which collected more readily in recesses.

The basic techniques of the potter have not varied greatly down the centuries. A pot can, of course, be built up laboriously of coils of clay applied in successive layers and beaten together, the potter turning his work on a board as he progresses. More normally, however, in historic times, he has taken advantage of the natural plastic quality of clay combined with water to squeeze it between finger and thumb on a relatively fast-turning wheel, forcing it to rise under his hand in a desired form, the motion of the wheel guaranteeing the pot's circularity about its vertical axis. Once shaped, the pot may be cut from the wheel and set aside to dry. If a sharper or smoother profile is desired, it may be turned on a lathe when 'leather-hard'. Throwing, however, is not the only shaping technique available. Clay may be pressed into moulds to form open shapes, or in a liquid state it may be poured into multipartite plaster of Paris moulds, so that a thin crust of clay forms on the inside, to be released by dismantling the mould. These moulding processes make possible multiple production, but obviously spontaneity of form is thereby lost.

The pot so made may then be simply fired and left in its native simplicity. If it is to be decorated, however, a number of options are open to the potter. He may add shreds of clay or incise lines (with a blade, a single point, or a comb-like instrument) in the patterns he desires: or he may draw in clay of a contrasting colour, whether applied in a creamy consistency (slip) by means of a spouted can, or painted on with a brush. Alternatively, the whole pot may be dipped in a slip of a contrasting colour and the design then cut or scratched through this to reveal the ground colour of the pot beneath. Since white clays are rarer and less easily thrown than red, this process is usually, but not always, carried out with a white slip on a red body.

Most of these techniques may be practised on an unglazed pot, but, where a glaze is intended, there are further possibilities. A glaze is seldom entirely colourless, and usually transmutes the tone of the clays it covers, a normal lead-glaze, for example, being yellowish and thereby heightening the red-brown clay-colours but deepening the creamy tones of a 'white' slip. A transparent glaze protects and enhances painting under it, but some glazes (lead-glaze is a case in point) flow too easily and carry the painting with them. This may be counteracted, as was done in East Persia in the 9th–10th century, by painting in pigments stabilised by additions of white slip. This thick medium lends itself to different effects from those obtained by painting in thinner pigments. If a glaze is made opaque, however, by the deliberate or involuntary presence of clay particles, dense bubbles or oxide (ashes) of tin, the painting has to be done over the glaze. This may be executed either before the glaze is fired or after. In the former case, the colours used must be such as will stand the relatively high temperature of the glaze-firing, and these are comparatively few in number; in the latter, the colouring-material must be compounded with a glassy substance to enable it to adhere to the glaze in a subsequent firing, but the relatively low temperatures required for such 'enamels' permit a much wider range of colours.

The colours of clays and metallic pigments are greatly affected by the atmosphere within the kiln at the time of firing. For example, an iron-bearing clay will fire to red tones in a bright (oxidising) flame, but will become grey or black in a smoky (reducing) atmosphere. The colour contrasts of early Greek pottery depend on the skilled manipulation of these firing conditions. Copper will fire red in a reducing atmosphere, but green in an oxidising flame; the difficulty of maintaining the reduction accounts for the imperfect reds of some underglaze-copper effects on Chinese porcelains. Another effect of a reducing atmosphere on metallic colours is to endow them with a rainbow-like 'lustre' which may be seen on much Near Eastern, Spanish and Italian pottery.

Throughout history the potter has striven to improve the fineness and whiteness of his wares and the lead in this endeavour has normally come from the Far East. The Chinese preoccupation with the physical quality of materials—epitomised in their appreciation of jade, which formed the touchstone for their judgment of many other materials—ensured that the Chinese potters sooner or later concentrated on the achievement in clay of material qualities comparable with those of jade. Hard stonewares had already been made there before the Christian era had opened in the West, and it was only a matter of time before the Chinese potters chanced upon the refractory white clay which is the body of porcelain (china clay or kaolin) and combined with it the related felspar (china stone or petuntse). These two ingredients constitute the substance of 'true' or 'hard-paste' porcelain, and the petuntse when fluxed with lime and potash formed a compatible glaze. These materials require a very high temperature (about 1300°C) to fuse them, and complete mastery of these complicated procedures was not achieved all at once. Nevertheless, a white porcelain was being made in China in T'ang times (AD 618–906). The secret was rediscovered in Europe in the first decade of the 18th century, but before that time the potters of Europe had attempted successfully to imitate the outward characteristics of porcelain—its whiteness and translucency—by mixing white clays and other substances with what was in essence ground glass, and glazing it with a modified lead-glaze. This substitute evidently lacked the hardness and practicality of the true porcelain. True porcelain, requiring such a high temperature for its realisation, could be decorated under-glaze only with metallic colours capable of withstanding this heat—in practice, cobalt for blue and copper for red—although it might be embellished with enamels fixed in a second firing.

With true porcelain the zenith of the ceramic art may be said to have been reached, but in its wake there also followed improvements to earthenware and stoneware bodies in Europe. Notably in England, the use of light-coloured clays, compounded with ground-up burned flints, produced a fine light-coloured and light-weight body-material capable of being fired either as a stoneware (normally salt-glazed) or as a cream-coloured earthenware.

Such then are the materials and methods of the potter's art, and the chapters which follow will show what different uses were made of them in different places and different times. No single standard will suffice for judging the qualities of a pot, for a simple thrown salt-glazed mug is clearly of a different order of creation from an elaborate porcelain figure put together from a dozen carefully moulded components. Success flows from the potter's understanding and scrupulous observance of the qualities and limitations of the materials at his command.

Note: Numbers in the margins throughout this book refer to black-and-white illustrations; italic numbers refer to illustrations in colour.

I The Ancient World

1 (*previous page*). Sections of an Egyptian wall-painting, showing pottery-making. From Tomb 2, Beni Hasan, about 1900 BC. The scene shows the kneading of the clay and its formation by hand and potters' turntable. The completed pottery was then stacked into the tall kiln for baking.

2. Plate, Tell Halaf period, Arpachiyah, North Iraq, about 4500—4000 BC. Rim diam. 12¾ in. (32 cm.); ht. 3⅝ in. (9 cm.). Polychrome decoration with petals and chequer pattern in red, with a thin line around each petal reserved in the pink-buff body clay of the vessel. The artist relied on strong colour contrast with added white quatrefoil designs against a black background. Iraq Museum, Baghdad.

3. Seated figure of baked clay, Çatal Hüyük, Turkey, about 5500 BC. Ht. 3⅝ in. (9·2 cm.). Clay had been used for modelling figurines for magical or religious purposes long before it was used to manufacture vessels. At both Çatal Hüyük and Hacilar, similar figures were deposited in grain bins, thus ensuring by sympathetic magic the continuity and increase of grain crops. Archaeological Museum, Ankara.

4. Vertical kiln, Tell Far'ah, Palestine. Early Bronze Age II, about 2900—2800 BC. Similar kilns were in use in Mesopotamia before 4000 BC, and allowed the potter not only to separate his baking vessels from immediate contact with the fire, but also to control the heat during firing. The cost of fuel would have made such treatment impractical for normal domestic pottery.

5. Glassmaker's Tablet. Tell 'Umar, Iraq, about 17th century BC. 3¼ × 2 in. (8·3 × 5·2 cm.). The tablet contains the earliest known formula for the making of copper-lead glazes and their application to treated earthenware—anticipating by a thousand years the chemical texts of the Royal Library at Nineveh. British Museum, London.

2

3

4

5

The Prehistoric Near East

The earliest societies for which we have evidence of a ceramic industry are undoubtedly those of the ancient Near East, where there is a tradition of pottery production dating back some seven to eight thousand years.

Long before this, however, in the practice of magic or religion, man had learned to fashion and bake human and animal figurines of clay and was thus already aware of the plastic and durable qualities of the material. Such basic technical knowledge has certainly been the possession of many different societies at varying stages of development, but has only led to a full-scale industry when allied with a social need and favourable economic conditions.

Man, being an acquisitive animal, has always had a need for containers of some kind, even in a nomadic hunting economy, as witness the Australian aborigines of the present day. The mere gathering of food required vessels both for its collection and storage. Among nomadic hunters, the simplest and most readily available material served the purpose, perhaps a tray of wood or bark, a stitched animal skin or the hollowed-out body of a gourd or similar vegetable. That such a situation has often been the inspiration behind the construction of clay vessels can be seen in the forms of much early pottery, where the shapes of earlier containers have been slavishly copied. In Cyprus, for example, both gourds and animal skin vessels first copied as early as 3500 BC, remained as the basic forms of domestic pottery until the end of the Late Bronze Age, about 1000 BC.

Basically, pottery is clay, formed to a required shape and hardened. There are, however, a number of processes necessary for the production of a practical article. All clays contain chemically combined water which must be expelled before the material becomes rigid and incapable of again being made plastic by the addition of water. To effect this change, a baking temperature of between 450–700 degrees is required, attainable, but barely so, in the open fires of early settlements. One early failure in this respect is attested in the Neolithic community of Khirokitia in Cyprus, where first attempts to fire pottery were abandoned soon after 6000 BC, and not again attempted in the life of the society.

However, the generally high quality of many early Near Eastern ceramics suggests that most groups were soon able to master the required techniques of slow and even firing. A vast improvement on the open hearth, and a practice still in use amongst some modern primitives, is to cover both fire and pottery with dung or earth and so dampen the entire process of baking. Such a method would take considerably longer, but the loss of time would be more than compensated for by the greater percentage of pots successfully baked. It is quite likely that this method was the one commonly used for the bulk of domestic pottery throughout the history of the early Near East.

Vertical kilns, in which the pottery was entirely separated from contact with the fire (for which there is evidence in Mesopotamia and Persia before 4000 BC), were apparently widely used in Egypt and Palestine by the 3rd millennium BC. Not only does kiln firing give greater heat, but by altering the draught, the potter is able to control the uniformity of his product and its colour. At Arpachiyah, in Northern Mesopotamia, soon after 4000 BC, the potters of the local Halaf ware, were able to produce a magnificent polychrome pottery, by the application of varying thicknesses of a single pigment before firing. All the early kilns so far discovered have been comparatively small, and it seems most likely that this more sophisticated procedure was reserved, in all but the wealthiest societies, for the production of luxury wares.

In a process where the firing temperature was comparatively low —and this would apply to a great bulk of the earliest ceramics—it was soon discovered that the finished articles were partly porous and pitted on the surface, where impurities had burnt out of the clay. A

6. Copy in clay of stone vessel. The Gerzean ceramic artist of late 4th millennium BC. Naqada. Ht. 4⅞ in. (12·3 cm.) ; and Matmar, Ht. 5 in. (12·6 cm.). Egypt has copied the original even to the graining of the stone. Ashmolean Museum, Oxford.

6

simple method of lessening the porosity was to smooth the surface of the pot while it was still wet, so that any imperfections would be covered over before firing. A somewhat more elaborate treatment, again used very early, was to paint the outside of the vessel with a slip of very highly refined clay. On drying, this additional skin could be burnished with a pebble or bone and perhaps polished after firing. The resultant lustre, in addition to producing a more pleasing article, also considerably enhanced its practical value. Both

required shape. An improvement was early effected by placing the clay on a board or a mat, which could be slowly turned by an assistant, thus leaving the potter free to use both hands in the shaping of the vessel. There is good evidence that the principle of the wheel was understood by Mesopotamian engineers as early as 3500 BC, and certainly the contemporary pottery in the area occasionally shows even striations in the clay, which suggest quick circular motion in the formation of the vessels.

7. Baked clay figurine of a duck. Tomb B.23, Qurney, Egypt. Probably 17th century BC. L. 8 in. (20·5 cm.). The vessel was used for the pouring of libations, in this instance, at the time of burial. The incised decoration and clay are typical of Tell el Yehudiyeh ware, a ceramic possibly connected with the Hyksos groups of the Levant and Egypt. Petrie Collection, University College, London.

7

of these techniques were in use before 5000 BC, in some areas of the Near East.

It is, of course, a considerable step from a simply produced lustrous finish of this type to the highly complicated and technically perfect finish of present day ceramics, but one further advance in surface treatment, a basic one, was made soon after 2000 BC, in Mesopotamia. Some thirty years ago, a clay tablet inscribed in Babylonian cuneiform was discovered in Northern Iraq. After much trouble, it was found to contain secret recipes for the production of copper-lead glazes, and perhaps even more important, an additional recipe for the treatment and greening of earthenware, to enable it to take the glaze of the preceding recipes. Additional proof of the early realisation of this important ceramic process came dramatically to light in 1946, when Sir Leonard Woolley, excavating at Atchana in North Syria, discovered a quantity of earthenware vessels of the 17th–14th centuries BC, covered with a strikingly attractive blue-green glaze; undoubtedly the practical proof of the recipes given in the Mesopotamian Tablet.

Alkaline glazes had been used from pre-Dynastic times in Egypt and the use of glazed frit was common throughout the Near East by the Middle Bronze Age; but until the Mesopotamian discovery of a lead-glaze, it had not been possible to get the known glazes to adhere to the body of a clay pot.

Initially, pottery was formed entirely by hand, the moist clay being slowly revolved as the artist squeezed and pressed it into the

It is possible that the earliest turntables were of wood and so unlikely to have survived; but a large clay disc with a bitumen-lined pivot hole, discovered at Ur, belongs to the period around 3000 BC, and clearly demonstrates that the practice of wheel-turning pottery was already in use. In the following millennium, the practice appears to have become common and a series of matched stone turntables and pivots of this period have been discovered in Palestine. They closely resemble the hand-turned apparatus depicted on an Egyptian wall-painting of about 1900 BC, from Beni Hasan. The considerable centrifugal force generated by such a machine allowed the potter to form his vessel with a minimum of personal effort and no doubt considerably increased his rate of production. With this increased production, however, and a new uniformity of shape, much of the individuality of the earlier Near Eastern ceramics disappeared.

The advance in techniques meant that the ceramic industry came to play a greater part in the economic and social life of the communities. The age old tradition of modelling cult figures, for use in fertility ceremonies, continued with the manufacture of a greater number and variety of forms. These were for the most part undistinguished, but occasionally, as in Cyprus during the latter part of the Early Bronze Age, they were both charming and illustrative of contemporary custom. Thirteen hundred years later, the ceramic artists of the same island entered the field of monumental art, with clay figures of more than life-size, some from a group of as many as

5

1

7

12

10

8. Lamp, Jericho, Palestine. Early Bronze Age—Middle Bronze Age, about 2200 BC. L. 4⅛ in. (10·5 cm.). The four nozzles of the lamps of this period are unusual, the normal Bronze Age forms have only one spout. Late in the Bronze Age the nozzles became more pinched, and by the Hellenistic period completely enclosed forms had become common. Ashmolean Museum, Oxford.

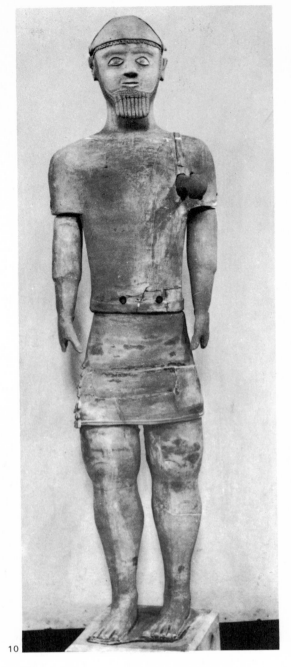

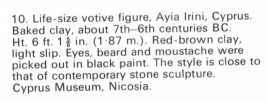

9. Burial urn in form of a house, Hedera, Palestine, about 3500 BC. Ht. 21¼ in. (54 cm.). Coarse buff clay, wet-smoothed and decorated in matt black paint. The bones of the deceased were placed in the ossuary after the flesh had decayed. The shape is probably a copy of contemporary dwellings. Palestine Archaeological Museum, Jerusalem.

10. Life-size votive figure, Ayia Irini, Cyprus. Baked clay, about 7th–6th centuries BC. Ht. 6 ft. 1⅜ in. (1·87 m.). Red-brown clay, light slip. Eyes, beard and moustache were picked out in black paint. The style is close to that of contemporary stone sculpture. Cyprus Museum, Nicosia.

11. Offering stand and bowl. Megiddo 'V A', about 8th century BC. Ht. of stand and bowl, 22⅞ in. (58 cm.) ; w. of stand 5½ in. (14 cm.). Similar fenestrated stands and bowls were normal in cult centres in the Near East from the Chalcolithic period. The stand is well fired, of reddish clay, wet-smoothed and decorated in red, black and white paint. Palestine Archaeological Museum, Jerusalem.

12. Baked clay model of a sanctuary and religious ceremony. Vounous, Cyprus, about 2000 BC. Diam. 14⅝ in. (37 cm.). Red Polished III ware. The scene is that of a small open air shrine, surrounded by a low wall. Inside, a ceremony connected with the worship of snake and bull indicates the fertility aspects of the cult. Cyprus Museum, Nicosia.

13

14

15

13. Small spouted jar, Megiddo, Palestine, Tomb 619, about 2200 BC. Made on wheel; fine, hard, grey clay covered with matt black slip. Painted decoration in matt white. Similar spouted vessels were widely used for drinking in the Ancient Near East and parallel forms remain in use at the present day. Palestine Archaeological Museum, Jerusalem.

14. Samarra ware bowl, Hassuna, North Iraq, about 5000–4500 BC. Diam. 9¾ in. (24·8 cm.). The decoration is in matt red-brown pigment on a light buff background. The quatrefoil arrangement of semi-stylised animal or human forms was a favourite motif of the Samarra artists. Iraq Museum, Baghdad.

15. Model of a brewing scene, Egypt, Middle Kingdom. W. 13½ in. (34·3 cm.). The product was stored in tall earthenware jars and stoppered with clay. The tall narrow shape of the wine and beer jars was found most suitable for storing either in corners of rooms or in holds of ships. British Museum, London.

16

17

18

16. Base-Ring I ware juglet, Cyprus, about 1500 BC. These small vessels were used extensively in the Late Bronze Age Near East for the trade of ointments, drugs and scents. The ware is usually very fine, grey or brown, fired to an almost metallic hardness and covered with a thin polished, black or brown slip. Ashmolean Museum, Oxford.

17. Red lustrous wheel-made ware spindle bottle. Atchana, Syria, about 1500–1450 BC. Ht. 10½ in. (26·8 cm.). These tall, graceful jugs have been found in quantity in Syria, Cyprus and Egypt and possibly served the same purpose as the Base-Ring juglets. The clay is very well refined and hard baked, orange to red-brown in colour. The vessels were finished with a highly polished red to orange-red slip. Ashmolean Museum, Oxford.

18. Kül Tepe jug, Anatolia, about 1800 BC. Ht. 17 in. (43·2 cm.). The decorative panel, typical of the Cappadocian painted ware, is here applied to a shape which was commonly used, without painted ornament, during the succeeding period of the early Hittite Empire. Ashmolean Museum, Oxford.

two thousand, found in place round an open-air shrine at Ayia Irini.
Parallel with this practice, there developed a group of religious clay
11   furniture and vessels used for the offering of incense or goods, the
shapes remaining more or less standard throughout the entire early
history of the area.

The contemporary view of life after death, as a slightly less
harassing continuation of life on earth, led to the placing of large
quantities of clay vessels round the deceased, both as containers for
the food necessary on the dark journey and as articles to be used in
the after life. Burials, themselves, were not uncommon in clay
containers, most often a cooking pot or large storage jar; and in
Palestine during the Chalcolithic period, about 3500 BC, the bones of
9   the deceased were stored in house-shaped urns, possibly a copy in
clay of the shape of contemporary dwellings.

Domestic pottery remained for the most part dull and uninspired;
but there was a great increase in the number and types of vessels
8   used. Lamps became common, a translation into clay of a simple
bowl form first used in stone during the Palaeolithic period about
9th–7th millennium BC. Cooking, eating, drinking and storage
13   vessels of clay became an ordinary part of every household, and
doubtless the increased use in turn suggested new forms.

In industry, clay vessels were used in such processes as the smelting
15   of ores, the brewing and storage of beer and wine and the spinning
of thread.

From the earliest times, the inequality of natural resources
throughout the Near East had forced communities to trade one with
another, and before long pottery was being widely used in trade,
16   both to provide containers for such luxury items as scents, drugs,
17   ointments and wines and, occasionally, in the class of better ceramics,
for their own intrinsic merit. Before the middle of the 3rd
millennium BC, such commercial activity was widespread and
doubtless did much to diffuse both techniques and fashions in art.
Such widespread and increased uses, particularly in growing
industrial and commercial societies, often relegated the ceramic
industry to an unimportant, mass-producing, practical role; but
there were wide areas and periods in the Ancient Near East which
saw the creation of first-class examples of pottery as an art-form.

Throughout the early history of Near Eastern ceramics there were
two major traditions, the one a dark-surfaced burnished or polished
ware, more often than not completely undecorated, but occasionally
using added incision, plastic or light painted ornament; the other a
painted ware, which normally employed a dark decoration on a
light background. The two traditions were not mutually exclusive,
18   often appearing together and occasionally combined in one ware.

Painted Pottery

Evidence from the first Near Eastern settlements (about 6000 BC)
suggests that painted pottery succeeded an initial stage when plain
dark or light wares were exclusively in vogue; but that the time-lag
was not great. The initial inspiration for painted decoration almost
certainly came from earlier art forms. In Anatolia, the earliest
painted pottery emerged in a succession of settlements where there
had been a well-established basketry and weaving industry and,
perhaps more important, where the monumental art-form of wall-
painting had already developed to a remarkable degree. The red
ochre used in the decoration of these earliest Hacilar ceramics was
the same as that employed in the frescos of Çatal Hüyük, where
there now seems some evidence of a ceramic industry ancestral to
6   that of Hacilar. Perhaps the most surprising feature of this fabric is
p. 20)   its extraordinarily high technical quality and advanced design. The
decoration, in red on a cream slip, utilises a great variety of
geometric patterns in bold design; both slip and paint were highly
burnished and the result is pleasing to both eye and touch.

Painted pottery occurs at an equally early stage in the eastern
regions of Persia and Mesopotamia, the former remaining for a long
period the major centre of painted wares in the Ancient Near East.

19   20

19. Cornet-shaped cup, Teleilat Ghassul,
Jordan, about 3400 BC. Ht. 7⅞ in. (19·5 cm.).
Matt cream pigment on a matt red surface.
The use of pastel coloured pigments is
typical of the late Ghassulian period. The
shape is probably a copy of an animal horn
and would have been used as a drinking
vessel. Recently excavated.

20. Susa 'A' painted goblet. Persia, about
4000 BC. Ht. 8½ in. (21·5 cm.). The fabric is
extremely fine and the delicate painted
stylised designs were carefully adapted to the
shape of the vessel. Ashmolean Museum,
Oxford.

In both areas, the first two thousand years of settlement saw the
production of what are probably the finest of all Near Eastern
painted ceramics. Commencing before 5000 BC, the pottery artists of
Northern Mesopotamia developed, by the middle of the millennium,
a luxury fabric which has been named Samarra ware, after the site   14
where it was first isolated. Using a dark paint, varying from red to
black, on a matt cream slip, they covered their vessels with a wide
variety of carefully drawn and arranged geometric patterns,
occasionally relieved with semi-stylised natural motifs. Perhaps the
most successful of all their creations are the quatrefoil designs of
human and animal figures, which grace the inside of shallow bowls
with a vivid sense of motion.

While the artists of the Samarra settlements were still at work,
new groups of people were gradually settling in Northern
Mesopotamia. The founders of the succeeding brilliant Tell Halaf
culture, they were, nevertheless, no doubt impressed by the excellent
ceramic productions of the indigenous Samarra group. The fact that,
in time, their own artists were to surpass the products of their
predecessors must have been due, in no small way, to the period of
initial contact.

Using a highly refined ferruginous clay which was fired in kilns
capable of a heat that often partly vitrified both paint and pot, the
later ceramic artists of the Tell Halaf culture of the 5th millennium
BC reached a technical standard not again witnessed in the Near
East until the arrival of imported Mycenaean Greek fabrics three
thousand years later. Thin-walled bowls, carinate jars with flaring

rims and a variety of round bodied vessels were decorated with red and black pigments in a series of geometric, floral and natural motifs, the latter in time developing through gradual stylisation into completely schematic patterns. Towards the end of the period, experiments with the kiln had taught the Halaf artists the value of controlled firing and a series of polychrome platters from Arpachiyah marks the high point of the industry.

The tradition of painted pottery was to continue in Mesopotamia through the succeeding late pre-Dynastic period of the 4th millennium BC, and although in the painted wares of the 'Ubaid and Eridu cultures, and in those of the Early Dynastic Scarlet ware of the Diyala region, there is much of merit, they can only come as an anti-climax. There can be little doubt that the ceramic industries of Samarra and Halaf had employed the best artists in the community, and it is perhaps significant that the final stage of pre-Dynastic culture saw the rise of the great monumental arts, wall-painting, sculpture and architecture—employment which no doubt weaned the best of the communities' creative spirits away from the ceramic industry.

Meanwhile, the ceramic artists of the earliest settlements (late 6th millennium BC) on the Persian plateau had developed their own particular painted styles. Beginning at a time roughly contemporary with the first painted pottery of Mesopotamia, the earliest products displayed a series of geometric designs on a light slip, setting a style

that was to last through the succeeding millennium; relieved for a time by a new and delicate fabric, with lively animal scenes, painted in black on a polished red background.

Undoubtedly the finest of all the early ceramics, however, are those which were in fashion soon after the beginning of the 4th millennium BC. As in Mesopotamia, the use of wheel and kiln now added new shapes and a new control to the industry, and the potters of Susa and Sialk developed a wide series of jar, bowl, chalice and goblet forms which rival those of the earlier Halaf products. As with the latter, carefully painted and minutely arranged combinations of geometric and semi-stylised natural forms were sympathetically adapted to the shape of the vessel.

From the middle of the 4th millennium, there is evidence of large-scale migrations into Persia, from the North and North East, of a people who brought with them a new style of monochrome red and grey pottery, a movement which eventually spread into Mesopotamia and perhaps as far West as Anatolia. To the west of the Iranian plateau, however, at centres like Giyan, the earlier painted traditions continued without major interruption through the 3rd and 2nd millennia BC. The conservative aspects of the art can be seen in the emergence of a new painted pottery at Tepe Sialk soon after 1000 BC. A completely new series of shapes, many of them possibly intended as ritual vessels, were covered with painted geometric and animal forms. Although the arrangements of patterns

21

22

23

24

21. Large jar with black-painted decoration. From Giyan, near Nihavand, in Iran; 3rd millennium BC. Ht. 8 in. (20 cm.). The ornament on this handsome jar exemplifies the characteristic decoration of a bird's comb-like crest, a stylisation of the well-known Mesopotamian motif of an eagle seizing his prey. British Museum, London.

22. Gerzean jar, Naqada Grave 1873, Egypt, about 3200 BC. Ht. 11½ in. (29·3 cm.). Painted decoration in matt red to brown on a buff surface. The design of reed ships bearing nome standards, and space filling ornament, are paralleled in contemporary wall-painting at Hierakonpolis. Ashmolean Museum, Oxford.

23. Amratian white-line ware goblet. Naqada, Egypt, Grave 1644 about 3500 BC. Ht. 10 in. (25·5 cm.). Decoration in matt or a lightly polished white paint on a polished red surface. The combination of haphazard animal groups and geometric pattern are typical of the fabric. Ashmolean Museum, Oxford.

24. Sialk, Luristan, spouted jar, about 8th century BC. Ht. 14¼ in. (36 cm.). Lustrous red pigment on a polished buff slip. Such elaborate shapes were probably designed for ritual purposes; in the present instance in association with burial rites. British Museum, London.

2. Jug from Phaistos, Crete. Middle Minoan II, 1900–1700 BC. Ht. 10¼ in. (26 cm.). These abstract motifs, executed in white and red on a dark ground, possibly derive ultimately from vegetable forms. Heraklion Museum, Crete.

3

4

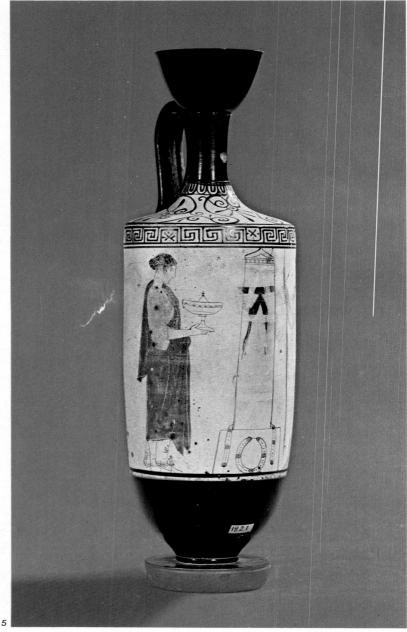

5

6

7

are different, there can be no doubt of the debt to earlier traditions.

To the west, the earliest settlements of Palestine, Egypt and Cyprus were also to develop painted styles peculiarly their own; but for the most part offering very poor comparison with the Eastern fabrics.

In Egypt, a magnificent series of polished monochrome wares were largely replaced, early in the 4th millennium BC, by a painted fabric utilising white decoration on a polished red background; but the ceramic basis of the new style was still that of the monochrome wares. The decorative elements of this new Amratian pottery, often human and animal figures, as well as geometric patterns, were spread over the surface of the vessel in a lively style, but with no attention to arrangement and a disregard for symmetry shared by their successors of the late pre-Dynastic period. Quatrefoil designs on the interiors of bowls recall the similar devices of Samarran and Persian artists; but the ponderous effect of the Amratian creations is not entirely due to the fact that the hippopotamus was so often favoured as chief actor in the scene.

In the latter half of the 4th millennium BC, the Egyptian artists, possibly under the influence of eastern traditions, turned to a light-surfaced ware as the vehicle for their creations. In dark-brown, red or black pigment they covered their buff-surfaced pots with ships, human and animal figures, often embellished with haphazard space-fillers, a decorative device which also appears in the slightly later wall-paintings of a tomb at Hierakonpolis. This painting was to herald, as in Mesopotamia, the birth of other media for artistic expression and the ceramic industry of Dynastic Egypt was for the most part relegated to a utilitarian role. There was a brief revival of painted pottery during the 18th Dynasty (about 1450–1350 BC), but the polychrome decoration and often exaggerated forms do not qualify these pots as major works of art.

To the North, the potters of Palestine were painting their products as early as the middle of the 5th millennium, but there is little of merit in their creations until just before 3000 BC, when local artists developed a painted fabric which probably owes much to the earlier traditions of the area. Neither technically nor artistically as adept as their earlier eastern neighbours, they nevertheless graced a rather dull monochrome scene with simple and charming geometric patterns.

For a considerable time in the Near East painted pottery was comparatively rare. This period, covering the greater part of the 3rd millennium BC, saw mass movements of population into the Near East from the north, groups of people who brought with them a tradition of dark-surfaced burnished pottery, and it was only with the resurgence of eastern influence towards the close of the 3rd millennium that painted ceramics again became popular. From this period, until the end of the Iron Age, painted pottery was well favoured in many areas, and although there were few productions to compare with the earlier fabrics of Anatolia, Persia and Mesopotamia, the finer wares were more common.

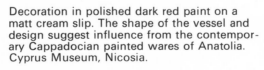

25. Phrygian jug, Gordion, Anatolia, 7th century BC. Ht. 10 in. (25·5 cm.). The carefully drawn decoration of Phrygian pottery marks a return to Eastern painted traditions. The geometric design and animal metopes are typical of the style. Archaeological Museum, Ankara.

26. White Painted I ware jug, Lapithos, Cyprus, about 200 BC. Ht. 12½ in. (31·8 cm.).

Decoration in polished dark red paint on a matt cream slip. The shape of the vessel and design suggest influence from the contemporary Cappadocian painted wares of Anatolia. Cyprus Museum, Nicosia.

27. Proto-Urban 'B'. deep bowl, Jericho, Palestine, about 3200 BC. Diam. 9½ in. (24 cm.). The clay was fairly coarse, but well fired to a pink-brown colour. The decoration

in matt dark red paint possibly copies basketry patterns. Amman Museum, Jordan.

28. Cappadocian painted ware cup, Kül Tepe, Anatolia, about 1800 BC. Ht. 2½ in. (6·4 cm.). Cappadocian pottery was formed by hand, the clay often heavy, but well fired. The painted decoration was in a lightly polished buff slip or straight onto the burnished surface of the clay. British Museum, London.

3. White Slip I ware spouted bowl, Stephania, Cyprus, about 1500 BC. Rim diam. 5⅛ in. (13 cm.); ht. 2⅜ in. (6 cm.). Nicholas Museum, University of Sydney.

4. Bowl, 'red gloss' pottery with moulded relief-decoration; Gaulish (La Graufesenque); 1st century AD. Diam. 9¾ in. (24·8 cm.). British Museum, London.

5. Lekythos (made as a grave offering). Attic white-ground. Eretia, about 440 BC. Ht. 12⅝ in. (32 cm.). National Museum, Athens.

6. Small jar, Hacilar, Turkey, about 5000 BC. Ht. 5⅞ in. (14·8 cm.). The high technical quality of the pottery and bold design mark a high point in the early ceramics of Anatolia. Ashmolean Museum, Oxford.

7. Dish, glazed 'quartz fritware', Egyptian (perhaps Memphis); probably 1st century AD. Diam. 8½ in. (21·5 cm.). Fritware is usually moulded, carved or incised; this piece is painted in manganese-brown, with touches of turquoise on the white ground. The back is covered with brilliant turquoise glaze. Victoria and Albert Museum, London.

29

30

29. White Painted V ware amphora, Stephania, Cyprus, about 1650–1600 BC. Ht. 7¼ in. (18 cm.). Hand-formed. Very finely mixed clay, matt dark cream slip with matt dark brown decoration. The two charming animal handles probably represent dogs. Nicholson Museum, University of Sydney.

30. Bichrome III ware amphora, Vartivounous, Cyprus, about 8th century BC. Ht. 26½ in. (68 cm.). The scene represents a funeral rite. Cyprus Museum, Nicosia.

In Anatolia, a new painted pottery appeared around 2300 BC, when groups from the East established themselves in the region of Cappadocia. The new style, utilising geometric motifs and panelled ornament, immediately recalls earlier Persian wares and shows the origin of the new cultural influences. The pottery was made entirely by hand, without the use of a wheel, and both painted decoration and slip were highly polished. For a brief period wares in the new style existed side by side with the age-old traditional monochrome wares of Anatolia, and a quantity of ceramics showing characteristics of both styles attests to the marriage of the two traditions. It was, however, but a brief episode and shortly after 2000 BC, with the arrival of the people who were to establish the Hittite kingdom of Anatolia, painted ceramics again went out of fashion and were not to reappear until the Phrygian invasions of the 12th century BC again brought in the painted traditions of the East.

Cyprus, long the home of individualists, received much the same ethnic and artistic influences in the later years of the Early Bronze Age (2300–2000 BC); but unlike the Anatolians, the exuberant island ceramic artists kept the painted traditions in full favour during the succeeding millennium and a half and, in the process, produced some of the most pleasant pottery of the Ancient World. For a time, these new influences were treated with respect and culminated in a technically superb and pleasingly painted ware of the 17th and 16th centuries BC. In decoration, much of the White Painted ware of the Middle Bronze Age in Cyprus is closely allied in its decorative elements to Cappadocian painted ware; but the Cypriot artist adapted the design to his own, age-old, ceramic forms. The earlier White Slip wares of the Late Bronze Age (1600–1050 BC) were exported to the mainland in considerable quantities, no doubt on their appeal alone. An interesting feature of this latter ware is the frequent use of bichrome decoration. The technique employed was identical with that used three thousand years earlier by the potters of Tell Halaf; but there can be no doubt as to its separate invention.

After a brief two centuries, when the island potters bowed before the technical superiority of imported Mycenaean Greek fabrics, the Cypriot artists reached their heights in the naturalistic and semi-stylised patterns of the Early Iron Age (1050–700 BC). Rarely bothering with adaptation of design, they created a pottery which exudes freedom. Often humorous, it must then, as now, have fitted well the islanders' temperament.

Elsewhere within the Near East, the painted traditions were kept alive in the restrained work of the Habur artists of Mesopotamia and North Syria, during the early centuries of the 2nd millennium BC. For a century in Palestine, between 1550 and 1450 BC, an exotic bichrome decoration using shades of red and black gave further witness to the age-old Eastern traditions of naturalistic and panel ornament, enclosed by geometric design, and for a time relieved the monochrome traditions of the earlier Middle Bronze Age. The fabric is fairly widely distributed in the coastal regions of the Levant and Cyprus. In both areas, although the particular form of decoration died out quite suddenly, the style of painting continued in the Late Bronze Age Decorated ware of Palestine and was an integral part of the decorative forms used in the final flowering of painted ceramics in Palestine, during the late 13th and 12th centuries BC. Here, a fabric known as 'Philistine ware' embodied Greek and Cypriot as well as local traditions. As in Cyprus, the designs combining natural and geometric forms quite often show a freedom not obvious in the earlier stereotyped fabrics of the Middle and Late Bronze Age. In both areas, something of this freedom was no doubt due to the multi-racial influences of the Iron Age migrations in the Eastern Mediterranean.

Monochrome Pottery

More restrained, and relying much on shape, the monochrome wares of the Ancient Near East were the backbone of the ceramic industry. As with the painted wares, they reached their greatest heights in the simpler societies of the Ancient World. There can be no single origin for these fabrics; but many of the earliest shapes and

31

32

31. Cypro-Archaic I jug, Arnadhi, Cyprus, about 7th century BC. Ht. 11½ in. (29 cm.). The style of ornament with a minimum of subsidiary detail was one of the most successful of all the island ceramic artists' productions. Cyprus Museum, Nicosia.

32. Bichrome wheel-made ware jug, Gaza, Palestine, about 1550–1450 BC. Ht. 11⅖ in. (29 cm.). An example of a highly distinctive and sophisticated ceramic ware. Palestine Archaeological Museum, Jersualem.

33. Interior of Late Bronze Age footed bowl, Palestine, about 1300–1200 BC. Ht. 3¾ in. (9·5 cm.). The painted decoration is crude, but shows an age-old oriental motif of animals grouped around a tree. Palestine Archaeological Museum, Jerusalem.

33

34. Badarian bowl, Egypt, about 4000 BC. Diam. 11 in. (27·9 cm.). The earliest and probably finest of Egyptian ceramic fabrics: fine, hard, with a polished dark surface and light combed decoration. University College, London. Petrie Collection.

34

35. Philistine ware bowl, Ascalon, Palestine, 1200–1100 BC. Ht. 3½ in. (8·9 cm.). Matt red-brown and black paint on a creamy buff slip; stylised natural forms of earlier wares. The shape is from Mycenaean Greek vessels. Palestine Archaeological Museum, Jerusalem.

36. Carinate bowl, Meydum, Egypt, Dynasty IV-V, 2600-2200 BC. Diam. 10⅞ in. (27.7 cm.). Highly polished red-brown surface. Meydum bowls are unusually refined. University College, London. Petrie Collection.

35

36

37. Early Bronze Age II jug, Jericho, Palestine, about 2900 BC. Ht. 10½ in. (26·7 cm.). The clay is somewhat coarse, but well fired, and covered with a polished red slip. Many such vessels were found in tombs of First Dynasty Egypt. Palestine Archaeological Museum, Jerusalem.

38. Early Bronze Age spouted jug, Yortan, Anatolia, about 2500 BC. Ht. 9¾ in. (24·8 cm.). Polished black surface; added decoration in matt white paint. The design and applied lugs possibly copy the stitching and knots of leather vessels. British Museum, London.

39. Early Hittite spouted jug, Kül Tepe, Anatolia, about 18th century BC. Ht. 15¾ in. (40 cm.). Polished red slip. The sharply carinate body, treatment of handle attachment and added lugs are probably derived from metal originals. Archaeological Museum, Ankara.

decorations suggest copies of natural containers, such as hollowed-out vegetables, skin bags, wooden or stone trays.

In Egypt, during the 5th millennium BC, dark-surfaced fabrics, often with incised decoration in geometric motifs, probably copy earlier basketry. The tall goblets of this earliest Egyptian ceramic are extremely graceful, but were soon to give way to what is undoubtedly one of the finest groups of pottery ever produced in the Ancient Near East. The settlers of Badari and Deir Tasa in the Central Nile Valley, using mud from the river, produced vessels of extreme thinness, well baked and highly burnished.

Surface colours of black, brown and red, the latter often used with a black upper body, were highlighted by the lustrous finish. The only form of decoration was the occasional use of a light comb ripple. The forms are basically simple and the entire production gives a sense of restraint and simplicity which has rarely been equalled. It was for Egyptian ceramics, unfortunately, a standard that was never to be surpassed. The traditions of Badarian potting was of minor consequence after about 3750–3500 BC when the painted wares of El Gerzeh were introduced for, as previously mentioned, the rise of the Old Kingdom, with its accent on industry and the major arts, meant a quick decline in the ceramic field; but it is of interest that the only meritorious productions of the succeeding two thousand years in Egypt were vessels produced in the monochrome tradition.

The Meydum bowls of the 4th–5th Dynasties, between about 2600 and 2200 BC, are typical of the better class of late Old Kingdom fabrics. Often carinate, their simple lines and highly polished red-brown surface make an appealing combination. Somewhat later, the Kerma potters of the Sudan returned to almost completely Badarian traditions of the late 5th millennium BC, with an extremely fine red and black ware, often polished to an almost mirror-like surface. Together with a series of somewhat bizarre shapes, there are the clearly recognisable simple deep bowls of the earlier period. Such is the similarity between the two fabrics that it can only be supposed that Badarian traditions had continued in some area which has not been identified. The style then disappeared abruptly, and for the remainder of early Egyptian Dynastic history the ceramic industry was to achieve no further distinction.

On present evidence, the earliest of all pottery-producing centres in the Ancient World is situated in West Central and Southern Anatolia, where monochrome fabrics have been found in association with cave-dwelling communities of the Late Mesolithic period and with the earliest settlements of the central plateau. Both are certainly no later than the middle of the 7th millennium BC. The initial production of both dark and light surfaced burnished wares was to initiate a tradition which remained throughout the entire early history of the country. For a brief time the excellence of the Late Neolithic and Early Chalcolithic (5th millennium BC) painted

40

41

42

43

44

40. Early Iron Age bowl, Beth Shan, Palestine about 11th century BC. Diam. 7¼ in. (18·3 cm.). Extremely fine, hard fabric fired red to grey. Thin, hard, highly polished dark-red slip. Palestine Archaeological Museum, Jerusalem.

41. Middle Bronze Age II painted jar, Citadel, Amman, Jordan, about 17th–16th centuries BC. Ht. 4⅞ in. (12·5 cm.). Very fine, hard fabric fired pink-buff. Burnished pink-white slip. Decoration in faintly lustrous brick-red paint. Both the shape and decoration are close to those of the contemporary Ḥabur fabrics of North Syria and Iraq. Amman Museum, Jordan.

42. Early Bronze Age fluted bowl, Alaca Hüyük, Anatolia, about 2300 BC. The highly polished surface, usually in black or red or a combination of both, and the channelled ornament link these Early Bronze Age fabrics of Anatolia to the contemporary Khirbet Kerak ware of Palestine. Archaeological Museum, Ankara.

43. Late Bronze Age I bowl, Megiddo, Palestine, about 1550–1500 BC. Diam. 7⅞ in. (20 cm.). Extremely fine, well-baked fabric, ring-burnished white slip. The forms of many of the finer Middle Bronze and early Late Bronze Age fabrics in Palestine imitate metal originals. Palestine Archaeological Museum, Jerusalem.

44. Base Ring I ware bowl, Cyprus, about 1550–1450 BC. Ht. 3⅝ in. (9·2 cm.). The Base-Ring products of the early Late Bronze Age, made from highly refined clays, fired at a high temperature and finished with polished brown or black slips are amongst the most successful products of the Cypriot ceramic artists. Cyprus Museum, Nicosia.

fabrics of centres like Hacilar and Cilicia took precedence over the dark-surfaced wares; but the tradition never died out and, doubtless under the influence of the painted fashions, emerged in the Late Chalcolithic period (second half of 4th millennium BC) as a painted dark-surfaced ware.

Typical of the succeeding Bronze Age ceramics was a fluted decoration, possibly copying the popular fluting on contemporary metal vessels, an influence which played a growing part in many Near Eastern societies as the ownership of metal objects became more common. As with the earlier traditions, the fabric relied mainly on a pleasant combination of highly burnished orange to red-brown and black surfaces. A fabric exactly parallel to that of Early Bronze Age Anatolia also appeared in Syria and Palestine at around the same period—in the first quarter of the 3rd millennium BC, and, undoubtedly, the same ceramic tradition lies behind the products of both areas. In Anatolia, the monochrome style reached its height in the technically superb, but often rather overpowering, wares of the early Hittite Empire (16th century BC). Here, sharply carinated forms with such plastic additions as rivet heads and elongated handle bases, attest the influence of metalwork. Hittite pottery, for the most part, employed a highly burnished orange to red slip; but occasionally a yellow slip was used, almost certainly with the aim of copying gold work.

Equally at home with a polished monochrome ware, the potters of Palestine and Syria rarely reached the high technical quality of their more advanced neighbours; but during the Early Bronze Age, the pleasing large jug forms of Palestine were thought worthy of inclusion in the courts and royal tombs of the 1st Dynasty of Egypt (about 3100 BC). The long history of monochrome ceramics in this area, made easy the acceptance of the highly polished fabric known as Khirbet Kerak ware, a ceramic which was imported into Syria and Palestine around 2700 BC. With added fluting, knobs and heavy

plastic ornament, it marks a complete break with the accepted modes of monochrome decoration; but seems not to have been allied with any alien occupation of the area.

It was, however, during the 2nd millennium BC that the Levant produced its finest monochrome ceramics, with the incursion of the Hyksos tribes about 1800 BC. That the invaders were skilled metal-workers is clear from their pottery. Graceful goblets, jugs, chalices and broad carinate bowls (occasionally painted), the early ones covered with highly polished cream, black or orange slips, can only have derived from metallic forms. It would not, however, be too much to suggest that the ceramic artists of this period rose well above their original inspiration, as the grace of many of their products could never have been equalled by the metal objects. The finest period of production undoubtedly lay between 1800 and 1600 BC, and although the traditions continued until the end of the Late Bronze Age, the purity of the earlier creations was lost in commercial competition with the extremely fine fabrics of Greece and Cyprus, which swamped the Levant from the middle of the 15th century. Rarer, but equally fine products at the beginning of the Early Iron Age (1050–700 BC) clearly demonstrate that the ceramic artists of the Levant were capable of highly artistic and technically superb work.

It was only in Cyprus that the relative conservatism inherent in plain pottery was broken, and throughout the history of the island's pottery production the artist embellished his creations with a great variety of added plastic and incised ornament, ranging from completely natural to geometric patterns. Much of the Early Bronze Age pottery of Cyprus (2300–2000 BC) is heavy and technically inferior, but the finished product is still sufficiently appealing to put it amongst the best creations of the time in the Near East. At times, however, the artist in a fit of virtuosity could create such bizarre pieces as that illustrated. The product is completely without use and almost totally without artistic merit; but it did serve to demonstrate

38

42

39

37

41

43

40

45

46

47

the potter's complete mastery of his material. Confident of his own prowess, he scorned the technical advances of the mainland and even as late as the 15th century was still producing mainly hand-formed pottery without a wheel. That his skill was equal to his boasting can be seen in the 'Base Ring' products of the Late Bronze Age (1600–1050 BC), a type of pottery which was extensively used throughout the Near East in connection with the cosmetic and drug trade. The ware is extremely fine, often little more than a millimetre thick, fired to a very high temperature and usually polished to a dull lustre. The forms are graceful and for the most part restrained, and with this ware the island ceramic industry reached its technical high point.

The Ancient Near East was never at any period a unified area, made up as it was of a diversity of peoples, economies and geographical environments. Such differences tended through much of its early history to foster regional development, and only with the widespread international trade and political activity of the 2nd millennium BC, was there any sign of general acceptance and use of the accumulated technical skills of 5000 years of ceramic industry.

It is perhaps significant that the same period saw the first great European interest in the area, under the widespread economic empire of the Mycenaean Greek world. There was almost certainly some exchange of ideas at this period, and the well-recognised orientalising period in Greece, during the 7th and 6th centuries BC, is but a late recognition of a debt that the technical West had owed to the East for a considerable period of time and in many fields.

From a purely practical and utilitarian beginning, the potters and artists of the Ancient Near East came, in time, to serve a variety of human activities and emotions. In the service of religion pottery tended to remain static, retaining the stereotyped shapes and patterns which served their appointed purpose. In the secular field, shapes were changed and refined as need and inspiration dictated; and fabrics, if never really practical by modern standards, were doubtless sufficient for the basically simple needs of the period. Aesthetic qualities cannot readily be measured and the freedom of Cypriot art on the one hand or the minute care and symmetry of the Halaf wares on the other are both valid forms of artistic expression. In any case, one should never lose sight of the fact that these forms of pottery were as much the expression of a society as of an individual.

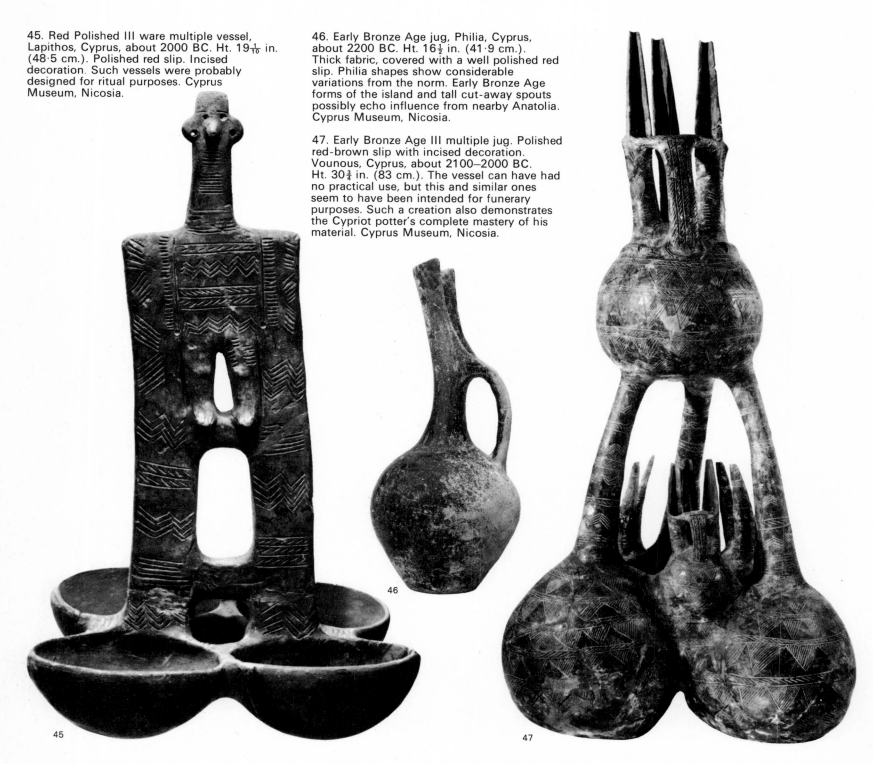

45. Red Polished III ware multiple vessel, Lapithos, Cyprus, about 2000 BC. Ht. 19 1/10 in. (48·5 cm.). Polished red slip. Incised decoration. Such vessels were probably designed for ritual purposes. Cyprus Museum, Nicosia.

46. Early Bronze Age jug, Philia, Cyprus, about 2200 BC. Ht. 16½ in. (41·9 cm.). Thick fabric, covered with a well polished red slip. Philia shapes show considerable variations from the norm. Early Bronze Age forms of the island and tall cut-away spouts possibly echo influence from nearby Anatolia. Cyprus Museum, Nicosia.

47. Early Bronze Age III multiple jug. Polished red-brown slip with incised decoration. Vounous, Cyprus, about 2100–2000 BC. Ht. 30¾ in. (83 cm.). The vessel can have had no practical use, but this and similar ones seem to have been intended for funerary purposes. Such a creation also demonstrates the Cypriot potter's complete mastery of his material. Cyprus Museum, Nicosia.

45

46

47

Prehistoric Europe

48

Pottery first appears in prehistoric Europe with the emergence of the Neolithic stage of culture involving more or less settled agriculture and the domestication of animals. In the communities which this way of life made possible, various crafts began to flourish, pottery being one of the most important. Probably made mostly by the women, prehistoric pots before the Iron Age were built up by hand without benefit of the wheel, and usually decorated by the simplest techniques of impressing and incising. Since these prehistoric wares in Europe had no great significance for the subsequent development of ceramic art in general, they are here merely summarily represented by illustrations showing some of the main, and aesthetically most satisfying, types.

48. Neolithic bowl, conjectural restoration based on fragments; from Whitehawk Hill in Sussex. Early 3rd millennium BC. Ht. 7¼ in. (18·4 cm.). With agriculture and herding, neolithic man, unlike his hunting predecessors, needed containers which could stand heat while preparing his mashes of cereal and milk. Such bowls had remarkably well potted, thinnish walls, a well-smoothed surface and occasional decoration with pricked lines or incisions. Brighton Art Gallery and Museum.

49. Food vessel from Northumberland, of buff clay with small moulded lugs and impressed and incised decoration. Early Bronze Age (1700–1300 BC). Ht. 5¾ in. (14·6 cm.). At

the end of this period the North of Britain was dominated by the 'Food-vessel Folk', who were probably semi-nomadic. They made pottery by building up coils of clay. The handsome finished pots were profusely decorated with incised or impressed herring-bone and zig-zag motifs. British Museum, London.

50. 'Long-necked' beaker from Lambourn, Berkshire, buff clay decorated with vertical lines of circular impressions. 1600 BC. Ht. 7⅜ in. (18·8 cm.). The late neolithic immigrant people, known by their characteristic pottery vessel as the 'Beaker' folk, probably used it as a drinking-vessel,

possibly for fermented liquors. A smooth finish and effective ornament lend this beaker a certain sophistication. British Museum, London.

51. Bowl of dark grey pottery with horizontal cordons turned on the wheel, from Bletchley (Bedfordshire). Early Iron Age (about 75 BC). Ht. 2¾ in. (6·9 cm.). From late 2nd century BC Celtic Belgic tribes invaded Britain, succeeded in the 1st century BC by settlers who brought their own 'La Tène' culture. This included the first wheel-turned pottery known in Britain, the new technique facilitating horizontal decoration. British Museum, London.

49

50

51

52

53

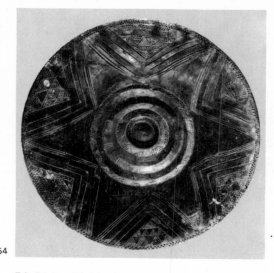

54

52. Jar of smooth-surfaced buff clay with small ring-handles and pushed-out bosses, from Spreewald (East Germany). Lusatian Culture, Bronze Age (1400–1100 BC). Diam. 7½ in. (19 cm.). This remarkable jar demonstrates what striking effects the primitive European potter could obtain with the simple means at his disposal. British Museum, London.

53. Bowl of red-surfaced pottery with incised decoration, from Württemberg. Halstatt culture (7th–6th century BC). Ht. 4⅝ in. (13·5 cm.). The peoples of the Halstatt culture of Central Europe, the creators of the Iron Age in Europe, had direct contacts with Aegean civilisation, and this may be reflected not only in the colour-scheme of much of their pottery, but also in individual motifs of decoration, such as the fret-design which forms the border on this beautifully shaped bowl. Its affinity with the Greek key-fret is striking. British Museum, London.

54. Dish with black and red surface, the designs further incised with a point, from Württemberg. Halstatt culture (about 8th–7th century BC). Diam. 16½ in. (41·9 cm.). Here the primitive potter has contrived to make a dish of noble proportions, the back of which is formed in a series of concentric steps. The basic contrast of black and red triangles in his ornamental design has been emphasised by internal patterning drawn with a point. British Museum, London.

55

56

57

55. Urn of reddish ware painted with brown pigment, from Prunay, France. Late La Tène culture (4th century BC). Ht. 12¼ in. (31·1 cm.). The affinity in shape of this pot with the 'pedestal urns' of Belgic Britain is obvious (cf. fig. 61), but on this urn the potter has resorted to painting in some earth-pigment, rendering his magnificent design in broad lobed leaf-forms and scrolls, which are unmistakably reminiscent of Celtic metalwork. British Museum, London.

56. Jar of black-surfaced pottery with incised decoration, from Marson (Marne). Early period of La Tène culture (4th–3rd century BC). Ht. 6⅞ in. (17·5 cm.). The pottery of this period was much influenced by metalwork, and the jar illustrated shows this clearly in the sharp profile of its neck and shoulder. The smooth surface of these black pots was probably inspired by the black boccaro pottery of Etruria. The jar is decorated with incised lines and panels enclosing cross-motifs, the lines being filled in with red pigment. British Museum, London.

57. Tall urn of black pottery with burnished design, from Saint Rémy-sur-Bussy (Marne). Late La Tène culture (probably 1st century BC). Ht. 11 in. (28 cm.). This tall urn with its high pedestal foot and its glossy surface is characteristic of the pottery made by the Belgae, the tribe which conquered southern England in the 1st century BC. In addition to his horizontal lines tying, as it were, the two sharp profiles together, the potter has traced zig-zag lines with a blunt burnishing tool on the surface before firing. British Museum, London.

Greece

58

58. Krater (made as a monument for a man's grave). Attic Geometric. About 750 BC. From Athens. Ht. 4 ft. (1·23 m.). Above, the corpse on a bier, with mourners; below, the chariots which escorted the funeral to the grave. National Archaeological Museum, Athens.

Greek pottery is famous for its figured decoration, executed in glossy black on fired clay, and for its ceramic qualities. This reputation is justified by what can be seen in the main galleries of museums, but the picture is incomplete. To begin with, on sites of all periods throughout the Greek world figured vases are actually in the minority and most of the finds are either plain or enlivened with bands, wavy lines or stylised ornament. Furthermore, the accumulated experience of centuries was needed to develop a black so durable, impervious and attractive that it became the dominant medium. Finally, although such areas as Attica, Corinth and Apulia had beds of particularly malleable clay, from which skilled hands could shape on the fast wheel thin-walled pots, carefully proportioned, often imaginative, sometimes fantastic, with mouths and feet turned as if on a lathe, many other centres with inferior clay and potters had to content themselves with less ambitious results. Almost all places and periods produced some good pieces, but the proportion of good to bad varies widely, above all in the decoration.

Greek pots were primarily for use, and their shape reflects their function, whether domestic or ritual. Some forms, such as the jug, met universal needs; others, like the 'hydria' (or water-jar), reveal the state of civilisation as well as their purpose. Water was brought in the hydria from the communal well or fountain. When the jar was full, it was lifted on to the head by the two horizontal handles; the vertical one was used when pouring or for carrying the pot when it was empty. The Greek custom of drinking watered wine is responsible for the krater, or mixing bowl. Function and size are also related; wine and oil were stored by the pint or gallon in amphorae; a hydria had to hold what a woman could carry, yet not be so small that two journeys were needed instead of one; cups were obviously in the pint range; olive oil was needed in smaller quantities for food, or instead of soap; expensive perfume came in tiny flasks. Sometimes we know the ancient name (hydria); a Greek word may be used, or misused, in a more restricted sense (lekythos; skyphos); a term may be a combination of ancient and modern (volute-krater) or purely modern (cup). Both the shape and size of these vessels, dictated by their utilitarian purpose, determined the limits within which the vase-painter had to work.

The basic techniques used in making and decorating Greek pottery

59. Krater. Mycenaean. 1300–1200 BC. From Enkomi in Cyprus. Ht. 9⅝ in. (24·5 cm.). Two griffins, one harnessed to a chariot with a driver. On the other side of the krater, two sphinxes. British Museum, London.

60. Octopus vase. Palaikastro, eastern Crete; about 1550 BC. Ht. 11¼ in. (28 cm.). A fine example of the marine style of Cretan pot-painting. The surface of this vessel is covered by a lively and decorative representation of an octopus swimming amid seaweed, coral and shells. Heraklion Museum, Crete.

61a

62

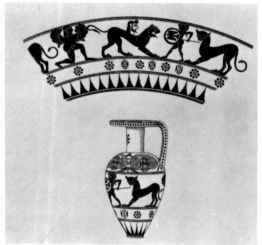

61b

61a), b). Aryballos. 'Proto-Corinthian'. Black-figure, with outline. About 680 BC. From Corinth. Ht. 2⅝ in. (6·8 cm.). A warrior fighting a lion with a man's head growing out of its back, flanked by a winged man and a panther. The subject may be a variant of Bellerophon and the Chimaera, or a story otherwise unknown. Museum of Fine Arts, Boston. Perkins Collection.

62. Column-krater (on either side the rim is expanded to form handle-plates which are joined to the body by columns of clay). Corinthian black-figure. 580–570 BC. From Cervetri. Ht. 16¾ in. (42·5 cm.). Above, a wedding-procession, which may represent the marriage of Peleus and Thetis, the parents of Achilles; below, animals. Museo Gregoriano Etrusco, Vatican, Rome.

were discovered in the prehistoric period. Neolithic Greece already knew pottery with decoration which fired a different colour from the pot. The Bronze Age saw improvements in the preparation of clay, the introduction of the fast wheel, and above all the realisation of the properties of ultra-fine particles of clay in suspension in water. When applied to a pot, this liquid was at its best transmuted by skilful use of oxydising and reducing conditions in the kiln to a deep shiny black with an underlying body which varied from cream through pink and orange-buff to brown, according to the nature of the clay and the temperature to which it was fired.

Up to the Middle Bronze Age (2000–1550 BC) the designs are mostly abstract and sometimes polychrome. In Crete this period saw the advent of forms derived from nature, at first stylised but succeeded in the Late Bronze Age (about 1550–1100 BC) by more naturalistic plant and marine life, such as octopuses and nautiluses surrounded by seaweed, or clusters of lilies, which may spread over the whole vase; human beings and land creatures are absent. Mainland Greece first followed Crete; later Mycenaean artists introduced bulls and birds, a few sphinxes and griffins (copied from the Near East) and human figures, especially in chariots; these subjects are particularly common on kraters. In Crete and Greece the drawing combines broad, bold outline and silhouette; Mycenaean also uses white as an embellishment.

When the Bronze Age communities collapsed, pottery also declined and its decoration dwindled to a few ill-drawn patterns, though the essential techniques were never forgotten. Toward 1000 BC, a new spirit is suddenly apparent; many shapes and motifs

are the same, but the potting is transformed and the designs, now executed with ruler and compasses, are shrewdly placed at strategic points on the pot and organised in zones and panels according to principles which influenced subsequent generations. The maeander is introduced as the principal motif in the succeeding period, while minor bands of ornament become increasingly common and cover more and more of the surface. The new style, aptly termed Geometric, was created by Athens, and apart from its eclipse by Corinth in the 7th century Attic pottery set the pace until the 4th century. Somewhere before 750 BC, an Athenian of genius reintroduced figured scenes as the main theme in vase-painting. This artist, whose name is unknown, came to be referred to as 'the Dipylon Master', after the big double gate (Dipylon) which leads through the city wall to the large cemetery where many of the finest Geometric vases have been found. Because of these finds, older works used 'Dipylon' to mean middle and late Attic Geometric, but with the subsequent addition of 'Black Dipylon' for the preceding phase, its original aptness was lost, the term becoming virtually synonymous with Geometric and therefore superfluous. The earliest figured representations occur on large amphorae and kraters made as grave monuments, and show funerals or battles by land and sea, perhaps legendary, perhaps the achievements of the dead. The figures are conceived in Geometric terms as silhouettes with triangular chests and match-stick limbs; the subordinate zones retain their abstract motifs, with the addition of rows of goats or deer. After about a generation monumental pots went out of fashion, but figured scenes spread to a great variety of shapes and

63

65

66

64

63. Krater. 'Proto-Attic' 690–680 BC. Ht. 15⅜ in. (39 cm.). Above, a procession of chariots; below, lions. Museum Antiker Kleinkunst, Munich.

65. Neck-amphora. Attic black-figure. About 620 BC. From Athens. Ht. 4 ft. (1·22 m.). On the neck, Herakles killing the centaur, Nessos, who had attacked his bride, Deianeira; the names are inscribed. On the body the Gorgon, Medusa, collapses after being beheaded by Perseus, while her two sisters pursue him. The dolphins below may indicate that they are flying over the sea. National Archaeological Museum, Athens.

64. Panathenaic amphora. Attic black-figure. 570–560 BC. From Athens. Ht. 2 ft. (61·3 cm.). The earliest surviving example of the vases which were filled with oil and given to victors at the Panathenaic games, part of the four-yearly festival in honour of Athena. The decoration follows a fixed scheme, with the goddess herself on one side and on the other the event for which the prize was given. Inscribed, 'I am one of the prizes from Athens'. Panathenaic amphorae continued to be made in Hellenistic and Roman times, long after figured work had been abandoned on all other kinds of pottery. British Museum, London.

66. Volute-krater (the handles curl like the volutes of an Ionic capital). Attic black-figure. About 570 BC. Found near Chiusi. Ht. 3 ft. 2 in. (66 cm.). From top to bottom the hunting of the Calydonian Boar, the games at the funeral of Pelias, the gods coming to greet Peleus and Thetis after their wedding, Achilles about to kill Troilos, animals, and warfare between pygmies and cranes. Inscriptions give the names of many of the characters and some of the objects. Signed by Kleitias as painter and Ergotimos as potter. Museo Archeologico Etrusco, Florence.

included incidents from the everyday world, with a few figures that must come from legend. Toward the end of the century the style became less angular, with a growing use of outline, especially for faces; the appearance of the occasional lion reveals renewed knowledge of and interest in the art of the East; abstract ornament declines in quality and variety. We are on the threshold of a new age.

The lead now passed to Corinth, where Geometric was displaced in the last quarter of the 7th century by a system in which birds, animals, fishes and abstract and vegetable ornament were drawn in sweeping curves with much use of outline. About 700 BC, or very shortly after, came the momentous invention of the black-figure technique, in which the figures are black silhouettes on a clay ground with details rendered by lines incised in the black before firing; white and purple (or purplish-red) may also be added in touches or for larger areas of flesh or clothing. With the new technique the artists quickly evolved a style which translated natural forms into a disciplined calligraphy; most of the work is miniature, even minute, above all on little perfume-pots, though medium sized vases also occur. There is an obsessive interest in real and imaginary creatures, some of them, like the lion, sphinx or griffin, drawn from Eastern art, others, such as the bull, boar and goat, being native to Greece. The floral and other motifs, which in the late 8th century appeared on equal terms with the animals, now retreat to the frame of the picture, where like the maeander they persist for centuries. Alongside animal friezes there is a small but important series of representations of human figures, which include scenes from myth and

legend; interpretation is not always easy, since from the outset gods and heroes are given the dress and equipment of contemporary life, while the subsequent practice of identifying them by such attributes as the thunderbolt for Zeus or the bow or club for Herakles is comparatively rare at this stage. Some incidents are self-evident, as when Herakles attacks the centaurs or Bellerophon the Chimaera; the elongated 'Boeotian' shield with an indentation at either side is often given to heroes in later art and its occasional occurrence in this period doubtless serves to mark its bearers as heroic, but many battle scenes may equally well belong to the artist's own day or to the legendary past; hunters and youths racing on horseback surely come from the real world.

The popularity of the animal-frieze, and many of the creatures in it, the curvilinear drawing, and various of the vegetable and other motifs so clearly reflect Eastern art that the whole period is often characterised as 'Orientalising', but the adjective is inadequate, since the style has a distinctively Greek flavour, even at the outset, and the scenes with human figures which so greatly influenced European representational art, derive none of their essential features from the East.

In the first two thirds of the 7th century most of the vases made at Corinth were decorated with patterns or debased and impoverished Geometric designs (Sub-geometric); figured work is found only on a minority and appears to have been produced by a small group of artists and workshops. Then figured pieces become much more numerous, and include many larger vases; miniature drawing goes out of favour. Animals predominate, but the precision and liveliness of the preceding period are lost, and after about 600 BC the decline is rapid. In contrast, scenes with human figures are increasingly plentiful, with a growing range of mythological and everyday subjects; some of the themes and compositions were to have a long future. The drawing is freer and often more expressive than in the preceding era, though less polished; purple or purplish-red is applied in broad masses, and such things as female flesh are occasionally drawn in outline. Some ambitious vases of the second quarter of the sixth century are covered with an orange-brown slip, and white is used on them to achieve an effect comparable to that of outline drawing on normal Corinthian clay. This colourful new technique was part of the attempt to meet renewed competition from Athens; it was unavailing, and significant production ended by the middle of the century.

The Athenian artists had been slower to move away from the Geometric tradition and create a new, stable style. For most of the seventh century they favoured a mixed technique with much outline, some silhouette, and a limited use of incision; white was applied with growing liberality, but purple (or purplish-red) is absent till after 650 BC, the pots are large and the drawing exuberant. At first the repertoire of subjects is meagre compared to that of Geometric; chariots, dancers, animals, with nothing to indicate a specific occasion; from about 680 BC, myth and legend become increasingly common. The last thirty years of the century saw the adoption of the black-figure technique, learned from Corinth but transposed into a larger format to produce figures of great power and robustness; from this point the stylistic tradition runs without a break till the extinction of figured work.

From the start of the 6th century animal groups in their turn decline in importance, though interest in them is never extinguished, and they survived to supply decorative motifs for Roman Imperial art; henceforth the human figure is the centre of attention, the setting being rarely more than indicated. During two centuries the subject matter is progressively enriched. Gods and heroes never lose their popularity, though the themes may change; the gods may be shown as patrons and protectors of mortals in action, or as active participants; Dionysos with his attendant maenads and satyrs is a favourite from early in the 6th century onward; after 550 BC, a group of two or more gods may be shown to us standing, not in action, and the 5th century also discovered the possibility of the single figure. But the great enlargement is in generalised representations of the human world, contemporary or recent history being

67

68

67. Calyx-krater; the shape spreads out like the cup of a flower. Attic red-figure. 510–500 BC. From Capua. Ht. 23¾ in. (35 cm.). Athletes after exercise. A set of studies of movement blended to form a unified composition. Inscriptions give the names of the figures, who are certainly not legendary, and praise the beauty of a contemporary, Leagros. By Euphronios. Staatliche Museen, Berlin.

68. Amphora. Attic black-figure. 540–530 BC. Ht. of picture 9½ in. (24 cm.). Ajax preparing to kill himself; on the right are his spear, helmet and 'Boeotian' shield, balanced by the palm-tree behind him. By Exekias. Musée des Beaux-Arts et d'Archéologie, Boulogne.

69. Hydria. Attic black-figure. About 510 BC Vulci. Ht. 22⅜ in. (57·5 cm.). Of five hydriae in the drawing, three are of the same type, two of a round shape just coming into fashion. Three of the water spouts are lions' heads, the others are surmounted by youths on horseback. British Museum, London.

70. Neck-amphora. 'Chalcidian' (the names are written in the alphabet peculiar to Chalcis in Euboea—perhaps made in Italy by immigrants from that city). 540–530 BC. From Vulci. Ht. 16 in. (41 cm.). One of the Labours of Herakles; his fight for the cattle of the triple-bodied Geryon, who is here shown as winged. Bibliothèque Nationale, Paris.

69

70

71

very rare. Traditional scenes of arming and warfare persist, though to the artist and his customer many of them may still have represented legendary characters. Alongside them there is an ever-increasing representation of sacrifices and religious ceremonies, athletes, dinner-and-drinking-parties, musicians, erotica, people shopping or making things. The later 5th century also adds such subjects as weddings, women dressing, washing or playing, often with an over-sweet, sentimental flavour in the drawing; these pictures no doubt appealed to women in a way that the old theme of the fountain-house with its reminder of daily drudgery could not, 69 and may reflect a change in their status.

The taste for many-figured groups and diverse action taxed the artists' powers of draftsmanship and composition to the utmost. In the 6th century the scale tends to be smaller, with much miniature work, especially on cups. Kleitias, who also worked on small vases, 66 produced a unique krater whose surface is divided into a number of narrow zones, packed though not crowded with figures drawn in a virile, flexible style; Exekias, far ahead of his time in sensitivity and depth of feeling, had a delicacy and sureness of hand which enabled 68 him to use black-figure with unrivalled subtlety and insight. It is no accident that after him came a technical revolution, the invention of 'red-figure'. In 'black figure' black silhouettes were drawn with a 71 brush on the plain clay ground, linear details then being added by incisions cut through the black before firing and into the underlying clay which was leather-hard and therefore offered a definite resistance; the lines therefore varied little in strength and the artist's self-expression was fettered. In red-figure it was the background which was black, drawn by a brush or more precise tool round the figures, which were thereby reserved and so stood out against the black in the colour of the clay—red-brown in Attic pottery. Within these reserved shapes, details were then added by painting them in black, thus allowing the artist far greater fluency; the black lines can be seen to snake across the surface. Moreover, artists were quick to exploit the contrast between the palpable ridge of the relief line, which gives precision to outlines and maps salient features, and the more subtle modulations suggested by the same liquid when diluted to produce a golden brown. With the new colour-scheme, added red and white, so popular in black-figure, are kept for minor details; gilding is occasionally used for jewellery, metal objects and the like. By extension, 'red-figure' is also the name given to the same technique used on wares, whose clay is not red-brown but varies from cream to muddy brown.

72

73

71. Amphora. Attic red-figure. 530–520 BC. From Vulci. Ht. 22¾ in. (58 cm.). A duel between two warriors who are backed by Athena and Hermes. One has a 'Boeotian' shield; the elaborate armour includes a helmet with a crest-holder in the form of a dog. By the Andokides Painter, possibly the inventor of red-figure, named after the potter, Andokides, who signed this vase and others decorated by him. Louvre, Paris.

72. Neck-amphora; a refined version of coarse wine-jars with a pointed base to dig into earth floors of cellars. Attic red-figure. 500–490 BC. Vulci. Ht. 22 in. (56 cm.). On the body, Dionysos with satyrs and maenads; on the neck, athletes. By the Kleophrades Painter, whose works include a cup signed by Kleophrades as potter. From one vase we know he was called Epiktetos, but another artist, who signed freely, has pre-empted the name. Museum Antiker Kleinkunst, Munich.

73. Amphora of Panathenaic shape. Attic red-figure. About 490 BC. From Vulci. Ht. 20⅜ in. (51·8 cm.). Herakles carrying off the oracular tripod from Delphi. The other side shows Apollo pursuing him to recover his property. By the Berlin Painter, who exploited the possibilities of placing a single figure on each side of a pot; he is named after a fine amphora in Berlin. Martin von Wagner Museum, Würzburg.

72–3,
76–7

The red-figure technique enabled two generations of major artists to keep pace with progress in painting on walls or panels and the exploration of anatomy and drapery and the study of the different aspects of the human body as it moves in space. Then the situation changed. Ancient descriptions indicate that from about 480 BC, the interest of painters shifted from externals such as form, incident, or action for its own sake, to character and feeling, shown by nuances of pose, gesture and expression, and to the emotional and spatial relationship between figures. The innovations included the use of different levels instead of the traditional single ground-line, and the representation of the background. From later in the century

80

shading was increasingly employed to convey volume. Bold experiments served only to show that vase-painting could no longer keep pace; the black background was too positive, the line too definite, the reserved clay of the figures too uniform. More and

74

more, vases became vehicles for decoration, with much fine drafts-

78

manship, but diminishing power and feeling, and multi-level compositions were retained merely as a device to produce a well-distributed pattern. One technique, which used outline drawing on a white ground with much colour, came nearest to contemporary free painting, but the medium was not sufficiently durable for

5 (p.20)

everyday use and was soon confined to lekythoi made as offerings to the dead; with a change in custom they too disappeared.

In the 4th century Attic red-figure declines in quantity, variety and quality. Tame groups of Dionysos and his retinue abound; the

journey of Herakles to Olympus enjoyed a brief popularity, Amazons and griffins had a considerable vogue. A few artists

75

attempted to preserve the old standards and at times, as with the nude girl fleeing from us with the receding contour of the pot, we catch the distant echo of a larger art, but the collapse of figured decoration came before the end of the 4th century.

Athens and Corinth dominate the history of Greek pottery, but there were powerful side-currents. In the 7th and 6th centuries many local, short-lived schools flowered and died. In the 5th century the Greek colonies in Southern Italy saw the rise of two small groups of artists whose earliest pieces reveal their Athenian training. They

81
82

fathered a number of local styles, above all Apulian, with its spate of slick trivialities only partly redeemed by learned compositions which foreshadow the Hellenistic correlation between visual art and literature.

Throughout the history of Greek pottery much undecorated ware was made, both coarse and fine. From the 6th century plain black pots became increasingly numerous and well finished, reaching their zenith in Athens in the second half of the 5th century; their quality shared the decline of figured pottery, but less catas-

79

trophically. Plain black ware used some of the shapes of the figured ware, but on the whole it had its own repertory and development, inspired by, and in turn inspiring, contemporary metalsmiths. It flourished into the Hellenistic period until a shift in taste favoured a red finish, the forerunner of the finer varieties of Roman pottery.

74. Volute-krater. Attic red-figure. 440–430 BC. From Grave 57c, Valle Pega, Spina. Ht. 2 ft. 6 in. (77 cm.). Above, a procession coming to sacrifice to Apollo, who is seated in his temple. The omphalos, the central point of the Greek world, shows that the scene is Delphi; the procession includes a girl with a ritual basket, two youths with an incense-burner and oxen as victims. By the Kleophon Painter, one of whose works has an

inscription praising the beauty of Kleophon. Museo Archeologico Nazionale di Spina, Ferrara.

75. Pelike; a jar for oil or wine; the name, though ancient, may not have been applied to this shape. Attic red-figure. About 350 BC. From Camirus in Rhodes. Ht. 16¾ in. (42·5 cm.). Peleus seizing Thetis for his bride, while she was bathing with her sister-

nymphs; one of them screens herself with her clothes, another runs off undressed, while Aphrodite looks on approvingly. The pantomime dragon which bites Peleus in the leg symbolises Thetis's power to change herself into any shape she wished. By the Marsyas Painter; a well-known picture by him shows the musical contest between Marsyas and Apollo. British Museum, London.

74

75

76

77

78

79. Cup. Attic black. 350–330 BC. Ht. 3½ in. (8·9 cm.). Inside, four impressed palmettes. British Museum, London.

80. Calyx-krater. Attic red-figure. About 460 BC. From Orvieto. Ht. 21¼ in. (54 cm.). Apollo and Artemis killing the children of Niobe. The name-piece of the Niobid Painter. Louvre, Paris.

81. Bell-krater. Early South Italian red-figure. 440–430 BC. From Ruvo. Ht. 11½ in. (29·4 cm.). Revellers. The drawing is very close to Attic. Museum of Fine Arts, Boston. Pierce Fund.

82. Volute-krater. Apulian red-figure. About 330 BC. From near Canosa. Ht. 3 ft. 10 in. (1·17 m.). Medea's revenge. After helping Jason to win the Golden Fleece, and having borne his children, Medea found herself cast off in favour of the daughter of Kreon, the king of Corinth. She killed the interloper by poisoned gifts, taken by her children, and then, after killing them, escaped in a magic chariot. Above, Kreon, his dying daughter, and their household ; on either side, divinities ; below, Medea killing one of her sons, while Jason tries in vain to intervene ; in the middle, a snake-drawn chariot stands waiting, manned by Frenzy personified ; on the right is the ghost of Medea's father, Aëtes. Many of the names are inscribed. The picture must be inspired by a lost tragedy. On the neck, Greeks and Amazons. Museum Antiker Kleinkunst, Munich.

76. Cup. Attic red-figure. About 490 BC. From Vulci. Diam. (of picture with border) 7¾ in. (19·8 cm.). Inside, a girl fastening her belt, while an old man protests. By Onesimos. British Museum, London.

77. Skyphos (deep cup). Attic red-figure. 490–480 BC. From Cervetri. Ht. 9⅞ in. (25 cm.). Priam coming to Achilles to ransom the body of Hektor. In its general lines the situation is based on the *Iliad*, where Priam enters when Achilles has just finished his meal, but many of the details are different ; the body of Hektor lies under the couch, and is not still tied to the chariot ; Priam is a proud figure, not a humble suppliant. The artist has re-shaped the scene in his own terms. By the Brygos Painter ; several of the vases decorated by him are signed by Brygos as potter. Kunsthistorisches Museum, Vienna.

78. Hydria. Attic red-figure. About 410 BC. From Populonia. A detail ; Adonis reclining in the lap of Aphrodite ; above, Desire spins a wheel on a cord as a love-charm. The names are inscribed. By the Meidias Painter ; one of his works is signed by Meidias as potter. Museo Archeologico Etrusco, Florence.

79

80

81

82

Rome

Greek pottery had its origins in Greece and was unmistakably Greek in character; but Rome itself had no ceramic tradition and within the political entity of the Roman Empire many and diverse ceramic strains co-existed. In this sense, to speak of 'Roman' pottery at all is perhaps a misnomer. Nevertheless, as with 'Roman' glass, a common feeling for form gave to the pottery of many different regions under Roman rule an authentic and unmistakable 'Roman' flavour.

The type of pottery most widespread in the Roman Empire is that characterised by a red 'gloss' surface obtained by dipping the pot in a suspension of fine particles of a type of siliceous clay known as illite clay and then firing in a bright oxydising fire. The technique was closely akin to that used in Greek pottery (see p. 30), and originally the 'red-gloss' pottery was probably only thought of as a less desirable alternative to the 'black-gloss' wares which formed in the 3rd century BC the most acceptable ceramic substitute for metalwork. The evolution of the 'red-gloss' technique probably took place in the Hellenistic Near East in the course of the 1st century BC, and a second technical feature characteristic of the Roman red-gloss pottery probably also had its origin in the eastern Mediterranean. This involved the production of decoration in relief by the use of moulds which had in their turn been impressed with stamps and roulettes, the latter producing repeating border-motifs in the manner of a pastry-wheel. Bowls made in this way, commonly but erroneously called 'Megarian' bowls (after the town of Megara), were made at a number of centres in the Aegaean and elsewhere in the Greek lands already by the 3rd century BC. Similar bowls, and other 'black-gloss' pottery with relief-decoration were being made in Italy during the early 1st century BC, but an abrupt change in the

industry seems to have come at about the time of the battle of Actium, which marked the final domination by Rome of the Hellenised Near East.

A certain Marcus Perennius Tigranus now emerges as an important manufacturer of 'red-gloss' pottery with figural relief decoration in the old pottery centre of Arretium (the modern Arezzo, not far from Florence). Tigranus is an Oriental name and some of Tigranus' work-people bore Greek names; it seems probable, therefore, that he was an industrial promoter, who brought his team of Oriental Greeks to Italy when it was evident that the commercial centre of balance had shifted from East to West. The early Arretine pottery of the Perennius workshop set a standard for artistic quality which was never surpassed in this type of ware. It had a strict 'classical' arrangement of figures in pairs and a repertory of subordinate decorative motifs which share this simple dignity, often combining with it a fresh naturalism characteristic of Augustan art. The influence of *repoussé* metalwork on the shape and decoration of these wares is immediately apparent and often extends to the forms of the handles, which are not such as would naturally suggest themselves to a potter. One or two instances of close correspondence with actual existing silver bowls have indeed been traced. Alongside the relief-decorated pottery (sometimes called 'sigillata') went wares which depended for their quality entirely on the thrower and the turner, although they too often echoed the shapes of more sought-after silver prototypes. Their clean lines and superlative finish give them a quality which calls to mind the characteristic efficiency of Roman civil engineering.

Other Italian centres than Arretium made pottery of a similar

83

84

83. Mould for bowl, smooth-grained pinkish-buff clay with impressed design. Italian (Arretium); signed 'Perenni Pilades' for the slave Pilades working for Marcus Perennius Tigranus; about 25–10 BC. Diam. 7¾ in. (19·5 cm.). Moulds such as these were made by impressing with pattern-stamps, the same stamp often being used several times, and 'rouletting' the horizontal borders with an

instrument like a pastry-wheel. Details were sometimes incised by hand. In these moulds the clay was pressed and then turned on the wheel, the lip being drawn up beyond the level of the decorated zone. If required, a foot was then thrown and 'luted' on. It displays admirably the restrained classical style of the early Arrentine wares. Victoria and Albert Museum, London.

84. Cup, 'red gloss' pottery with incised 'cut-glass' decoration, found at Araines, France. Gaulish (probably Lezoux); middle of 2nd century AD. Ht. 3¾ in. (9·5 cm.). Wares such as this were incised while the clay was still soft, in imitation of engraved glass vessels. The shape, however, is essentially a ceramic one. Ashmolean Museum, Oxford.

85

type, but seldom equalled it in quality. In the course of the early 1st century AD, the economic centre of the 'red-gloss' pottery industry began to shift westward into Southern Gaul, concentrating in the general area of Toulouse, particularly at La Graufesenque. The Southern Gaulish pottery surpassed its Italian forerunners in the brilliant quality of its gloss, and at least the relief-decorated wares probably robbed the Italian potteries of their overseas markets, although Arretine and other plain wares are discovered in most parts of the Mediterranean, and as far afield as India. With the technical superiority of the Southern Gaulish ware, however, was linked a declining artistic sense. The figural elements of Arretine pottery were discarded, and its naturalistic plant and other ornaments were progressively constrained within horizontal friezes and then vertical panels, the individual elements gradually losing their graceful naturalism and evolving into stylised symbols for use in abstract patterns. In the reign of Claudius (AD 41–54), the emphasis in the industry began to shift from South to Central Gaul, where Lezoux, near Vichy, was the main centre; and then, during the first half of the 2nd century, on again to a series of scattered potteries in the area lying between the upper reaches of the Marne and the stretch of the Rhine below Mainz. These movements were no doubt caused by the onward march of the legions, who, with the progressively Romanised inhabitants of Gaul and Britain, were probably the main customers for the Gaulish tablewares. As the potters moved further in space and time from their Italian origins, the style of the relief-wares became progressively debased, the nadir being reached with the so-called 'free style', in which the earlier stringent arrangement of ornaments in horizontal zones was abandoned, and human figures and animals in progressively inept renderings are strewn meaninglessly round the typical hemispherical bowl. The debasement of the figural wares was even more marked in the potteries of the more marginal provinces—such as, for instance, Colchester in Britain.

By a parallel development, the Mediterranean markets for fine pottery were progressively dominated from the late 1st century onwards by 'red-gloss' wares made in centres other than those in

4 (p. 20)
86

4 (p. 20)

88

86

87

88

89

85. Beaker, 'red gloss' pottery with slip decoration, from the Rhineland. Rhenish (probably Rheinzabern); 3rd century AD. Ht. 6¼ in. (16 cm.). The potter here has shown his skill with the slip-can, trailing on a design of a type which would perhaps have been more at home in white on a dark-surfaced pot of the native tradition. The similarity of these ornamental forms to those of Celtic metalwork is striking. British Museum, London.

86. Cup, 'red gloss' pottery, found in London. Gaulish (La Graufesenque); third quarter of the 1st century AD. Diam. 4⅜ in. (11 cm.). This little cup well exemplifies the clean lines and high finish of the plain shapes found in Roman Gaulish pottery. The same shape is to be seen in opaque-glass cups of the 1st century AD. British Museum, London.

87. Dish, 'red gloss' pottery with stamped and incised designs, from Tunis. North African; probably 4th century AD. Diam. 12¾ in. (32·5 cm.). Gaulish pottery, inspired by Italian pottery, was in due course copied in countries bordering the Mediterranean. Dishes of this form with simple stamped motifs in the centre, although of such late date, hark back to some of the earliest Near Eastern 'red gloss' fabrics, Rijksmuseum van Oudheden, Leiden.

88. Bowl, 'red gloss' pottery with moulded relief decoration in the 'free style', from Wingham, Kent. Gaulish (Lezoux, Paternus pottery); middle of 2nd century AD. Ht. 5¾ in. (14·5 cm.). In the 'free style' figures covered the decorative field, without any sense of a common base-line. Although individual figures might be admirably animated, the compositions are usually crowded and confusing. British Museum, London.

89. 'Poppy-head' beaker, the glossy black surface embellished with rows of dots. British; middle of 2nd century AD. Ht. 6½ in. (16·5 cm.). These beakers, commonly found in England, are quite attractive and were undoubtedly made there. Their general family resemblance to the Belgic pottery of pre-Roman times is obvious (cf. fig. 51). Victoria and Albert Museum, London.

90. Cup, dark-coated light-bodied pottery with trailed slip decoration, from Colchester. Probably British ('Castor ware'); late 2nd century AD. Ht. 3¾ in. (9·5 cm.). Potters in the neighbourhood of Castor, near Peterborough, in Northamptonshire, rose to prominence in the 2nd century, and probably specialised in the slip-decorated dark-surfaced pottery usually called 'Castor ware'. The potter's facility with the slip-can is astonishing, his beast imbued with a sense of bounding energy and urgency. Colchester and Essex Museum, Colchester.

91. Jar, sheeny brown-surfaced ware with applied scales, from Cologne. Gaulish; 50–100 AD. Ht. 4⅜ in. (11 cm.). Not all Roman potters achieved the brilliant 'red gloss' of the central tradition and this brown surface has an indifferent sheen. Its effective thumbed-on scales are matched on 'red gloss' wares. Victoria and Albert Museum, London.

92. Flagon of yellow-coated pink earthenware painted in red and purple, from Faras. Nubian; 1st or 2nd century AD. Ht. 7¼ in. (18·5 cm.). The peripheral peoples of the Roman Empire tended to borrow from its more central products those features which they were able to assimilate and give their own interpretation. The general shape of this flagon is a common one in the Roman world, but the Nubian artist with his network of rhythmically painted overlapping scales, has adeptly emphasised its full swelling form, while at the same time creating a decorative scheme beautiful in itself. Ashmolean Museum, Oxford.

Italy. Most appear to have been made in North Africa ('Late A' and 'Late B' ware) but with the occupation of that area by the Vandals for a century from about AD 430, a fresh centre, probably in western Asia Minor, appears to have taken up the running and continued until as late as the 7th century ('Late C' ware). These different late 'red-gloss' wares are often hard to distinguish from each other. Their surface qualities are usually inferior to those of the Italian and Gaulish pottery, but striking pieces were made in the form of large bowls and dishes with impressed central designs combined with concentric formal borders.

The methods of decoration already described were by no means the only ones used by the Roman makers of fine tablewares. Just as relief-decoration drew on metalwork, so a method of incising formal ornaments in the soft clay was inspired by the facetting of contemporary cut glass. Perhaps more suited to the plastic nature of clay, however, was the use of applied ornament, whether made from small pads of clay or trailed on in the slip technique. Stylised plant-forms had been used on 'red-gloss' dishes as early as the second half of the 1st century AD, and the manner survived to be used with great effect on less sophisticated types of pottery (see below).

The pottery so far described, with its fine surface-finish, was tableware, probably ranking only below silver plate, bronze and glass. In the provinces of the Empire, efforts were made, often with some success, to imitate the red-gloss, and the shining black surface of an earlier style was also perpetuated with a greater or lesser degree of technical perfection. In the northern provinces of Gaul and Britain black-surfaced pottery had been in use before the Roman conquest, and although the shapes of some of these wares were influenced by imported Arretine and Gaulish pottery, some retain a sharp and classical profile of their own, of great distinction, and are often effectively decorated with incised or burnished lines. One well-known class is decorated with rows of applied dots. Much of this pottery was made in the northern parts of Gaul and probably exported thence to Britain, but some was certainly made in England, one centre being at Upchurch, in Kent. Further north, a dark-surfaced ware of unique quality was made in the second half of the 1st century. Its most characteristic decoration was apparently produced by pulling out the surface clay with the finger-tips whilst still wet, to produce irregular protrusions ('rustic ware'). In the 2nd century favourable economic conditions led to the rise of a pottery industry near the modern Castor, not far from Peterborough. Here dark-grey or black-coated ware was made and given slip-decoration. Apart from the plant-scroll motifs derived from the 'red-gloss' pottery (see earlier, p. 38), but here transmuted to resemble the curving forms of Celtic metalwork, the British potters delighted in the rendering of hunting themes, a subject-matter wholly natural to them. Both here and on the Continent of Europe the ornament was often trailed on in white pipe-clay, whilst in the New Forest a pottery industry dating from the late 3rd or 4th centuries produced not only dark-surfaced pottery (often inclining to tones of red or purple) in the shapes used at Castor, but wares—often bottles—decorated with abstract designs in a white pigment which is more a paint than a slip.

Comparable techniques were also used in Rome's southern and eastern provinces for wares which probably ranked in status somewhere between the imported 'red-gloss' pottery and the common indigenous wares. In the 1st century AD, fine painted pottery was produced in Nabataea (the territory of the caravan-city of Petra), and in Nubia (on the southern confines of Egypt). In Egypt itself a pink-bodied ware is found which is slip-decorated with plant-scroll and other simple designs in the contrasting tones of a white pipe-clay and the self-coloured clay of the body.

The decorated wares so far described, often possessing at least an approximation to a 'gloss' surface, must be regarded as relatively sophisticated products. The coarser pottery destined for kitchen or even humbler domestic use was often left with no surface treatment. Its lowly status at the time of its manufacture, however, is no criterion for judging its aesthetic merits. Often these simple pots, made just for use in cooking, or for the storage of food or wine, are thrown in forms of great nobility. In other instances, a cult purpose has produced idiosyncratic shapes of a rare and curious appeal.

All the types of pottery so far described have been merely low-fired earthenwares, with or without a surface treatment to give a measure of impermeability to liquids. In the Near East, however, at least since the early 2nd millennium BC, potters had been able to give their products a coating of glass, or glaze, and so make them water-tight. By Roman times, at least three families of true glazed wares had come into existence.

One of the easiest and therefore most widespread methods of producing a glaze on pottery is by means of lead-compounds, which not only fuse at a low temperature but readily receive colouring by means of metallic-oxides, notably copper, producing a brilliant leaf-green. A large family of pottery with moulded decoration, formed in the same way as that on Arretine ware, is found in Asia Minor dating from the end of the 1st century BC, and the 1st century AD. Its style of decoration and the form of the ring handles on the cups (scyphi), which constitute one of the commonest vessel shapes, equally betray its metalwork inspiration. Fragmentary moulds for the cups have been found at Tarsus, and there are traces of manufacture at sites near Ephesus and Pergamum. Apart from the cups, vases, inkwells, bowls on a foot, flared conical cups (modiolus), and small bag-shaped jugs (askoi) occur. The glaze is usually green, but with open shapes the interior is often yellow. Occasionally slip was used for decoration, and a class of vessels found in South Russia often bears grotesque subjects rendered in this technique, sometimes with additional chromatic effects produced by the use of white or coloured slips under the glaze. Like the 'red-gloss' technique itself, lead-glazing appears soon to have spread to Italy, and thence to Gaul, where by the middle of the 1st century St Rémy-en-Rollat, Vichy and Gannat appear to have become the main centres of manufacture. Lezoux too (compare p. 37 above) at a later date appears to have made green lead-glazed pottery, and the technique was taken up in the Rhineland from about AD 200 onwards. There was even a centre of manufacture in remote Britain at Holt, in Denbighshire, in the 2nd century.

A way of producing a brilliant turquoise-blue glaze was known in Egypt at a very early date. It was achieved by exploiting the fluxing properties of natron (a soda compound found naturally in Egypt) combined with copper-compounds as colorants, on a

93

94   95

93. Beaker, dark-coated light-bodied pottery with trailed white slip decoration, from Duston, Northants. British ('Castor ware'); first half of 3rd century AD. Ht. 4½ in. (11·5 cm.). This little globular beaker was given a slight 'rouletted' horizontal border while still soft, but its real decoration consists of the magnificent bold plant-scroll trailed on in white slip, the terminal scrolls having more than a faint reminiscence of Celtic metalwork. British Museum, London.

94. 'Incense-bowl', of buff earthenware, from Colchester, Essex. British or Gaulish; probably late 1st or 2nd century AD. Ht. 3¼ in. (8·3 cm.). It is not certain what these frilled bowls were used for, but their somewhat unpractical character suggests a cult purpose. Their interesting shape and entirely concordant waved decoration show a great feeling in the potter for an appropriate handling of his material. Colchester and Essex Museum, Colchester.

95. Wine-amphora, of greyish pottery inscribed in red, from Firka, Nubia. Probably 5th century AD. Ht. 19¾ in. (50·8 cm.). Some potters did nothing but throw commercial containers by the thousand. Work under such circumstances demands speed in the operator and practicality in the pot. The rhythm of such work comes out well in this full-bodied amphora from Nubia. No attempt has been made to smooth away the diminishing throwing-spirals, which create their own bold rhythm, culminating in the casual twist of the neck; while the handles are all roughness and strength. An inscription in beautiful rustic capitals probably gives the name of the contents. Ashmolean Museum, Oxford.

quartz body. The technique, in various adaptations and using a number of different colorants, survived the post-dynastic and hellenistic phases of Egyptian culture, to emerge in Roman times with an even glassier and more brilliant glaze and an even richer tone of copper turquoise-blue. This 'glazed quartz fritware' is essentially a body of powdered quartz made reasonably plastic by the addition of salt and water, or natron and water, and glazed by a powder formed by fusing and then grinding up a similar compound. The virtue of this type of pottery lies in its brilliant glass-like glaze and its intense colours; its disadvantage is the lack of plasticity in the body. This difficulty the Roman potter seems to have overcome reasonably well by the use of moulds and by careful carving and piercing. A decorative technique which exploited to advantage the brilliant glaze-colouring consisted of incising designs which then appeared as darker lines where the glaze flowed into them. Shreds of the body material were also applied in overlapping scale-designs, usually in green on a dark-blue or purple ground; and the Roman potter had such a control of his material that he could paint under-glaze designs of considerable delicacy and in several colours on the inside of flat dishes. Most of the glazed quartz fritwares appear to date from the first three centuries AD, but it seems likely that the technique of producing a brilliant turquoise-blue in an alkaline glaze survived into the Islamic era. A comparable technique was practised in Syria and the western provinces of the Parthian kingdom. Here, however, a far more plastic body was used which permitted of fine throwing on the wheel. To ensure the adherence of the alkaline glaze it was necessary to include a high proportion of quartz sand in the body. This 'Parthian' pottery was modest in character, unpretentious in shape and not as brilliant in its blue and green tones as the Egyptian ware. It was simply decorated with incised lines or applied bosses, which perhaps betray its metalwork derivation. Despite its simple character, the Parthian pottery is important as the forerunner of the alkaline-glazed pottery of the Near East in Islamic times.

7 (p. 20)

99

96

97

97. Silver cup with *repoussé* design showing scenes from the history of Troy. Roman; 1st century AD. Found in a burial-deposit at Hoby, Denmark. A fragment of 'red gloss' pottery is known which shows the same subject, actually derived from this cup or one exactly like it. The shape of this cup is also found in pottery (fig. 98). National-museum, Copenhagen.

99

96. Jug, greenish-yellow lead-glazed earthenware with moulded relief decoration, from Colchester. Gaulish (St Rémy-en-Rollat); middle of 1st century AD. Ht. 7¼ in. (18·5 cm.). Lead-glazed pottery was relatively rare in the Western provinces of the Roman Empire, but St Rémy-en-Rollat and Gannat, in the Allier district of present-day France, appear to have been quite prolific centres of production, their wares being found not infrequently in Britain. The present jug appears to have been moulded in its upper section, which has then been 'luted' to a separately thrown base and neck. Colchester and Essex Museum, Colchester.

98. Cup, lead-glazed earthenware with moulded relief-decoration. Asia Minor; 1st century BC or AD. Ht. 2¾ in. (7 cm.). Cups such as this *scyphus* reflect in their handles and style of decoration the contemporary *repoussé* silver cups. Like many of this class of lead-glazed ware, this example is green on the outside and yellow inside. Although not uncommon, these wares must have formed one of the most luxurious types of pottery in the sophisticated Eastern Mediterranean centres of hellenised Roman culture. Victoria and Albert Museum, London.

99. Covered vase, turquoise-glazed 'quartz fritware' with incised decoration. Egyptian (perhaps Memphis); probably 1st century AD. Ht. 6¾ in. (17·2 cm.). The quartz fritware, although offering glaze-colours of unparalleled brilliance, was a difficult body to shape and handle. Here the potter has contented himself with incising a design under the glaze, the depth of which in the incisions effectively strengthens the colour of the decoration. Museum für Kunst und Gewerbe, Hamburg.

98

II The Far East

Introduction

Not surprisingly, the history of Far Eastern ceramics is to a large extent dominated by events in China. For China, exceptional in the continuity and range of her achievement and enfolding movements in arts and religion from all parts of Asia, has over the centuries provided a source of cultural dynamism for the entire region. It was natural, therefore, that potters in such neighbouring lands as Korea, Indo-China and Japan should be profoundly influenced by China's advanced standards, both in technique and in design. The interaction has in effect been a most fruitful one, and in all these countries it has brought a new richness and variety to the indigenous practices and styles.

Clarity and refinement are the classic virtues of the Chinese style in pottery, to which should be added a further elusive quality, more consciously sought after in Far Eastern than in Western art generally, the nature of which is perhaps most readily conveyed by the word 'vitality'. In their endeavour to enliven their materials with the spirit of these ideals, potters in China developed from an early date a technology notably in advance of that practised elsewhere. No particular pre-eminence in technique is to be noted in the wares of China's archaic periods: and it is in the centuries immediately preceding the Christian era that the new momentum becomes apparent. Now, by acquiring a mastery of high-temperature kiln-firing procedures, Chinese potters learnt to make vitrified stonewares and to coat them with highly durable glazes—an essential step towards the later manufacture of porcelain. Gradual improvements in potting, glazing and firing skills during the ensuing centuries fitted their wares increasingly for refined usages; so that by the time of the T'ang dynasty (7th to 10th centuries) they began to compete with the precious metals. This advancing refinement reached an impressive climax in the diversified production of the Sung dynasty (10th to 13th centuries), which in the opinion of many critics touches the summit of the art. The Sung achievement is exemplified in glazes which are superb both in texture and in the restrained subtlety of their colouring, expressing a mood at once vital and contemplative, and it contrives a harmony between materials, form and ornament which for a time remained uniquely balanced and satisfying.

China's greatest single contribution to the advancement of the craft is nevertheless a more purely technical feat—the invention of white, translucent porcelain. Such a ware was already being made by the 9th century; although it was not until the 14th century, when techniques of painting in colours were evolved, that porcelain began to assume its modern role: one from which other forms of pottery were increasingly excluded. For all their richness and variety in form and design, the wares of the Ming and Ch'ing dynasties (14th–17th, 17th–20th centuries) are substantially based on this relatively standardised material.

Porcelains of this kind aroused much curiosity when they began to reach the West. From late Ming times onwards European potters were inspired first to imitate the designs, and finally to create their own art of porcelain. By the 18th century also, trade had attained a level which rendered the imported Chinese porcelains, which were often now shaped and decorated to European specifications, almost a domestic commonplace. Yet these represent only a late phase of China's impact on the world's ceramic art, which had been fostered by exports growing steadily in volume from the 9th or 10th century onwards. Recurrent waves of influence thus came to leave their imprint on the pottery of the Islamic Near East—perhaps her nearest rival in artistry and range of output. Medieval fragments found littering the shores of Asia bear witness to the vast sea-trade which extended to Japan, Indo-China and the entire south-east Asian archipelago, then westward to India and the Arab lands, even down the east coast of Africa to Zanzibar.

The scale of this Chinese achievement should not be allowed to obscure the unusual merit and individuality of much pottery made in other Far Eastern lands. There also, glazed stoneware and porcelain techniques were widely adopted, bringing their essentially practical virtues within reach of city, hamlet or jungle village. Korean wares, even when unpolished, have a charm and serenity that are rare, and under the Koryó kings (10th to 13th centuries), in

100. (*previous page*). Detail of fig. 187.

101. Earthenware funerary jar painted with spirals in black and red earth pigments. Late Neolithic period, about 2000 BC. Ht. 13 in. (33 cm.). A product of the so-called 'painted pottery' culture, this boldly decorated piece is typical of many recovered from cemeteries at Pan-shan, in the north-westerly province of Kansu. Haags Gemeentemuseum, The Hague.

102. Black earthenware jar with burnished surface. Late Neolithic period: about 2000 BC. Diam. 9½ in. (23·9 cm.). Excavated at Yang-shao-ts'un in Honan province. Notable for its finely potted, wheel-turned form, this jar indicates the spread westward to the central plain of the 'black pottery' culture which originated in the north-east of China. Museum of Far Eastern Antiquities, Stockholm.

103. Jar of hard white pottery, with carved ornament and handles in the form of water-buffalos. Shang dynasty, about 14th–11th century BC. Ht. 13 in. (33·2 cm.). The few vessels of this ware so far discovered come chiefly from princely tombs of the Shang at An-yang. The designs echo the style of the superbly cast bronzes of this time. Freer Gallery of Art, Washington.

101

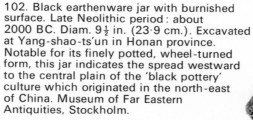

102

103

particular, they reached a high level of refinement. In both Annam (North Vietnam) and Siam (Thailand) also, wares were shaped with an individual elegance. The more remote islands of Japan harboured from early times vigorous rural traditions that ceded only with reluctance to metropolitan taste. The earthy individuality marking many of these wares is quickened by an instinctive feeling for the humblest materials and these qualities were both prized and perpetuated in much later pottery by the unique philosophy of the Tea Ceremony. From the 17th century—when porcelain began to be made—the taste of the great Japanese artist-decorators introduces a note of unconventional brilliance in design which contrasts refreshingly with the more uniform output of the Chinese factories. In their several ways, all these bring distinction to a ceramic tradition which, enriching the fabric of Far Eastern life, has also contributed much to the perfection of the craft elsewhere.

104. Model of a five-storeyed house, painted earthenware. Han dynasty (206 BC–AD 220). Ht. 52 in. (132 cm.). Farm buildings and watch-towers are among the models found in the Han tombs. This outstanding specimen, however, conveys an exceptionally vivid and faithful impression of Han domestic architecture, while the depiction of trees and birds on the lower storey casts an illuminating light on Han styles of painting. W. R. Nelson Gallery of Art, Kansas City.

105. Figure of a spearman, grey earthenware formerly painted in coloured pigments. About 3rd century AD. Ht. 13⅛ in. (33·3 cm.). Human figures, and models of a variety of worldly goods, were in Han times placed in tombs to accompany the dead. Warrior figures such as this were perhaps intended to combat demons; in the following centuries, however, whole troops of soldiers appear in important burials. Arts Council of Great Britain. Seligman Collection.

106. Jar of grey earthenware painted in coloured pigments with a design of volutes and abstract motifs. Han dynasty (206 BC–AD 220). Ht. 21 in. (53·4 cm.). Typical Han tomb pottery: the wine jar (*hu*) is one of the vessels prescribed for the ritual offerings buried with the dead. The design is exceptionally well preserved. Museum of Fine Arts, Boston.

107. So-called 'hill jar' with cover, of red earthenware with brownish-green lead-glaze covering designs moulded in relief. Han dynasty (206 BC–AD 220). Ht. 9½ in. (24 cm.). The lead-glaze was introduced in Han times, probably from Western Asia. The sides of this tomb vessel depict tigers and other animals bounding over a hilly landscape; the mountain-like cover is believed to represent the Taoist paradise, the 'Isles of the Blest'. Victoria and Albert Museum, London.

108. Stoneware jar partly covered with felspathic green glaze; incised and combed decoration. Han dynasty (206 BC–AD 220). Ht. 12¾ in. (32·2 cm.). Well-vitrified stoneware marks a turning-point in the development of Chinese ceramics, and its glaze is the forerunner of the later celadon glazes. The incised bird-headed scrolls, combed patterns on the neck, and the neat side handles vitiate the strength of the form. Victoria and Albert Museum, London.

104

105

106

107

108

China:
Archaic periods

Although early pottery-making in China may seem to belong chiefly to cultural prehistory, it is by no means lacking in aesthetic interest or relevance to later technical developments. By late Neolithic times (about 2000 BC), in an area of north China broadly flanking the Yellow River from Kansu in the far west to coastal Shantung in the east, we can single out among a mass of excavated wares the products of two markedly distinct and individual traditions. Those of the 'painted pottery' culture, centred more to the west, have an apparent affinity with certain types of ware produced also in Western Asia. The funerary jar illustrated, of smooth burnished buff earthenware, hand-shaped and painted with swirling motifs in red and black earth pigments, is typical in its full-bellied form and primarily geometric style of decoration. In comparison, the plainer and rarer 'black pottery culture' wares, found at their finest in the north-east, are of surprising technical sophistication, being often wheel-turned to a remarkable fineness: their varied, almost metallic-seeming shapes include a number, such as the *li* tripod cooking-vessel, which are enduring archetypes.

The first historical era, that of the Shang (from about 1550 to 1025 BC) introduces a powerful civilisation distinguished by brilliant achievements in the art of bronze-casting, which inevitably threw a shadow over the more humble sister craft. Grey-bodied earthenwares—on which the simple Neolithic decorative techniques of incising, cord-impressions, and minor applied features were contrived without marked originality—appear in shapes which also seem largely derivative; and the same tendency characterises even more the common grey wares found in burials of the lengthy Chou dynasty (10th–3rd century BC), on which painted decoration of bronze-style designs eventually reappears. Two rare types, however, lend distinction to the Shang production: the first being a fine-grained white pottery fired to a considerable hardness, and impressively carved in the style of the great bronzes, which may well have been restricted to princely use. The other is a coarse but thinly made stoneware, on which the first primitive felspathic glaze makes its debut. Thereafter the white ware vanishes virtually without trace; but recent finds indicate that glazed stoneware continued to be made at least intermittently under the Chou. By the end of this period, certainly, developments along these lines were taking place in south-east China which gave the craft as a whole a new and significant orientation.

109

109. Part of a tomb retinue, Six Dynasties period, with ox-cart and mounted guards. Painted grey earthenware. About 6th century AD. Max. Ht. 9½ in. (24 cm.). The practice of burying figure models with the dead was further extended in north China during this period of internal strife and barbarian invasion, reflected in the warlike character of many of the retinues. They were coloured in brilliant pigments, of which only part remains. Oriental Fine Arts Inc. Exhibition, New York, 1948.

110. Covered earthenware jar decorated in coloured lead-glazes. T'ang dynasty, 7th–8th century. Ht. 10⅞ in. (27·7 cm.). Near-Eastern influence is probable in the 'chevron-and-rosette' design of this typical T'ang jar, which is executed in the characteristic colours of amber-yellow, green and blue. British Museum, London.

111. Ewer, stoneware with olive-green celadon glaze. *Yüeh* ware, from Chekiang province; probably 6th century. Ht. 13 in. (33 cm.). The spout is in the form of a cock's head, and the shoulder is carved with overlapping lotus petals: a motif signifying the strong Buddhist influence in the arts of this time. The *Yüeh* kilns produced this type of celadon ware over the best part of a millennium. Musée Guimet, Paris.

110

111

114

112

113

112. Tomb figure of a Lady, grey earthenware with incised details; formerly with painting. Northern Wei period (5th–6th century AD). Ht. 22⅛ in. (58·1 cm.). The high-waisted, 'Empire' style robe and high head-dress are typical of this period. The treatment of the features, less severe than earlier, shows the influence of contemporary Buddhist stone sculpture. Arts Council of Great Britain. Seligman Collection.

113. Model of a tomb dignitary, painted earthenware. T'ang dynasty, 7th–8th century. Ht. 41 in. (104·2 cm.). Occurring in the tombs in pairs, such figures are believed to symbolise mythological persons concerned with the future well-being of the deceased. The unusually well preserved painting of the patterned fabrics is in various colours and gilt. Victoria and Albert Museum, London.

114. Ewer, lead-glazed earthenware in cream streaked with green. T'ang dynasty, probably 7th century. Ht. 9¾ in. (24·5 cm.). The form is of Western Asiatic inspiration; and the Hellenistic origin of the applied relief ornament, comprising a dancing boy, acanthus scrolls and other motifs, is unusually clear. Royal Ontario Museum, University of Toronto.

115. Laden camel with drover, earthenware with cream-white glaze. T'ang dynasty, early 7th century. Ht. 8¾ in. (22 cm.). The camels which traversed the Central Asian trade routes are often represented in the tomb pottery. This well-composed group underlines the fruitful interchange which resulted; it dates from the beginning of the dynasty, when lead-glazes were re-introduced. Museum Rietberg, Zürich.

The Han (206 BC–AD 220) and Six Dynasties (AD 265–589) periods

Most early Chinese pottery that survives intact was found buried in tombs—providentially: although it would be unwise to assume that such finds always exemplify the best that was made in their time. Among the first Han dynasty wares to be recognised were earthenwares covered with a soft lead-silicate glaze, tinted green or brown, of a type later familiar enough in Europe and which was in all probability introduced from the Hellenistic world. They take the form of vessels for funerary offerings, simple figurines and a wide range of models that includes buildings, domestic equipment and animals. Finds of these are particularly numerous from tombs in the northern provinces where the capital cities, Ch'ang-an (Sian) and Loyang were situated. They are matched by a class of unglazed grey earthenwares in the older style, often primed with white 'slip' for painting in unfired pigments, which gave scope for a somewhat greater boldness of modelling.

107

106

04–5

115

116. Group of musicians and dancers, painted earthenware. T'ang dynasty, probably 7th century. Troupes of musicians and dancers from many parts of Asia were maintained at the T'ang court. In addition to popularising unfamiliar forms of music and the dance, they were responsible also for introducing new fashions in dress. Royal Ontario Museum, University of Toronto.

119. An Armenian feeding a bird, painted earthenware. T'ang dynasty, 7th–8th century. Ht. 7⅛ in. (18·1 cm.). Westerners, Central Asiatics and peoples from the south-east are represented in the tomb retinues. They served the Chinese in many capacities, but especially as mercenaries and grooms for camels and horses. Arts Council of Great Britain. Seligman Collection.

117. Bottle of black-glazed stoneware with splashes of bluish-grey. T'ang dynasty, about 8th–9th century. Ht. 8 in. (20·3 cm.). T'ang kilns making wares of this type were discovered recently at Chia-hsien in Honan province; the bluish splashes were perhaps the inspiration of the blue glazed *Chün* wares

made there in the following Sung dynasty. The production of stonewares was diversified in late T'ang times. Mrs. Alfred Clark Collection.

118. Dish, porcellanous grey stoneware with incised design of two phoenixes under a celadon glaze. *Yüeh* ware, from Chekiang province; 10th century. Diam. 6⅞ in. (17·4 cm.). The ancient Yüeh kilns reached their peak of excellence in the Five Dynasties period (907–59), when the grey-green celadon ware, with its refined ornament incised with a fine point, was in part reserved for the Court. It exercised a strong formative influence on the following styles of the Sung. Percival David Foundation, London University.

117   118   119

This lavish tomb furniture pointedly reflects the increasing economic power of China under the Han rule: a period of territorial unification at home, and active colonisation in Central Asia, that invites ready comparison with the contemporary role of Rome. At this time was set up the centralised, Confucianist form of bureaucracy which provided the model for later administrations in China. In form, the Han pottery vessels remain largely metal-inspired while their decoration tends to repeat the styles of inlaid bronze or painted lacquer ware—a fantastic arabesque of coiled geometric or animal motifs. Sometimes the animal or spirit figures emerge in more naturalistic form, however, underlining the prevailing interest in superstitions and magic. This absorption is felt more intensely still in the burial models cast in the round, which may be sculpted with real observation and power.

More evidence of regional styles in Han pottery is now gradually coming to light from such provincial centres as Hunan, Szechuan in the west, and Canton in the far south, where a coarse glazed stoneware was made. But most significant of all is the glazed stoneware manufacture carried on in the east or south-east, at centres not yet clearly identified. The typical jar illustrated is of a kind sometimes rather loosely called 'protoporcelain' on account of the felspathic content of its body and glaze. Made of a well-vitrified grey ware with a closely adhering olive-green glaze covering its upper parts, it

is shaped with a plastic freedom notable for its time, achieving an elegance that is echoed in the bands of running bird-headed scroll-work, lightly incised round the shoulder as ornament. During the Six Dynasties period (265–589) that followed the break-up of the Han Empire—bringing a succession of warring principalities, divided also between north and south—it was in the further improvement of such wares that the course of progress lay. Their manufacture became localised around Hangchow, and at other sites further south in the province of Chekiang. In these 'Yüeh wares', various forms of jar, ewer, dish and bowl were evolved, in shapes of relative refinement, well-suited to their substance and use, and clothed in practical olive to grey-green glazes. Apart from occasional moulded or incised features, they tend to be bare of further ornament.

By the 6th century at latest, glazed stonewares in comparable style were being made at other centres and, significantly, now in the north also. In general, however, the northern potters' work is known to us mainly through tomb furnishings that follow the Han tradition. Figures of warriors and cavalry horses in unglazed grey earthenware, vivid both in conception and in their pigmentation, testify to the troubled state of these times: although a more genial spirit is reflected in some large guardian figures, which radiate the sweet serenity of great Buddhist stone sculpture of the period.

120

121

123

122

124

120. Stem cup of white porcellanous ware. T'ang dynasty (perhaps 7th century). Ht. 3 in. (7·6 cm.). Potted so thinly as to be translucent, and of a hard, pure white ware with a clear felspathic glaze, this early wine cup verges on the discovery of a true porcelain. The form is one imitated from silverware. Victoria and Albert Museum, London.

121. Trefoil dish of white porcelain. About 10th century. Diam. 5¼ in. (13·3 cm.). Translucent white porcelain, hard and resonant in material was being made by the 9th century. The elegant, flower-like form here represents a transitional stage between the T'ang and Sung styles. Percival David Foundation, London University.

122. Ewer, porcelain with incised decoration and greenish-tinged glaze. Made in Kiangsi province, about 10th century. Ht. 15 in. (39 cm.). The spout is in the form of a finely-carved phoenix head; it was filled from the top. A fine point was used to incise the bands of floral scrolls and leaves. This ware is the forerunner of the Sung *ch'ing-pai* porcelains, and of the vast later porcelain industry of Ching-tê-chên. British Museum. London.

123. *Ting* ware basin; porcelain with incised peony design and ivory-white glaze. Sung dynasty, 11th–12th century. Diam. 10 in. (25·1 cm.). The most celebrated of Sung porcelain wares, refined in both potting and design. Ting ware bowls and dishes were commonly fired in an inverted position and the rims, being bare of glaze, were often fitted with bands of metal. Percival David Foundation, London University.

124. 'A Literary Gathering': detail from a hanging scroll painted in colours on silk. With cipher and inscribed poem by the Emperor Hui Tsung (r.1101–25), but possibly by an artist of his Court. This painting epitomises the cultivated life of the official 'scholar' class in the Northern Sung period, and its patronage by the Emperor Hui Tsung, founder of the Painting Academy and himself an artist of recognised talent. In the elaborate table setting many shapes of pottery, silver and lacquer vessels of the time can be identified. National Palace Museum, Taiwan.

The T'ang period (AD 618–906)

The period of the T'ang dynasty presents a marked transformation in many fields: and in effect no episode in Chinese art evokes a more potent sense of splendour. The confident might and prosperity of these times was matched by high achievement in the arts and literature alike; and during the 7th and 8th centuries the northerly capital, Ch'ang-an, was in a sense the focus of Asia if not of the civilised world. At no time, also, has China been more receptive of foreign influences. The brief Sui dynasty (AD 581–617) had re-established the Imperial power, and as Chinese armies re-opened the old Silk Roads westward to Central and Western Asia, trade and tribute brought visitors from many lands and with them their arts and customs.

A corresponding surge forward in ceramic art is reflected in the tomb wares, which are of a richness and abundance without precedent. By Sui times they already included a fine whitish earthenware, covered with a pale-coloured lead-glaze in revival of the Han practice; and this was soon appearing in the green and amber-yellow tints (more rarely also with blue and purple) which comprise the so-called 'T'ang three-colour' style. The surfaces were often patterned with mottles, drips, or painted chevrons of glaze to form a kaleidoscopic glow of colour. Typical of the T'ang sense of form is the jar shown: crisp and expansive in contour, with a simple accented flare of the lip and foot. Styles borrowed from abroad are everywhere apparent. Many characteristic shapes clearly owe their inspiration to metal; and the moulded reliefs of a dancing boy and a vine scroll applied in moulded relief on a ewer here reproduced clearly derive from Hellenistic work.

All these are tomb wares, and substitutes probably for the silver and gold plate which was so much in vogue. With them it was still customary to bury sets of figures, varying in size and number with the magnificence of the departed, and which reflect varied aspects of the T'ang scene with remarkable realism. Not all the models are glazed; and some were naturalistically painted in pigments applied over a white 'slip'. Guardians of the tombs are pairs of heavenly warriors of fierce aspect, or the sharp-maned, lion-like 'earth spirits' who ward off demons. More human are dignified officials with

8 (p. 53)

110

114

113

107

113

patterned robes once extensively painted and gilt. Important large tombs contained the celebrated large horses and camels, in pairs together with their grooms: groups of elegant women musicians and dancers reflect the new styles in these arts and in dress introduced from Central Asia. Besides these are servants and retainers of all kinds, often of outlandish race, and recorded with amused but sympathetic observation not without an element of caricature.

Essentially the product of metropolitan taste, the vogue for such wares reached its height early in the 8th century, then gradually declined. A pottery site making 'three-colour' wares was discovered recently in Honan province: but how far these resembled the tomb wares known to us is not yet clear. Kilns making stonewares, however, were also at work, and their greater durability must undoubtedly have commended them for most daily uses: they are found with white, yellow and brown or black glazes, in smaller quantities in the tombs. The 'white' glazed wares are usually light-bodied, but the transparent glaze is applied over a white slip to improve their colour: their shapes often parallel those of the earthenwares. The brown-black varieties favour buff or grey bodies: one attractive type showing decorative splashes of creamy- or bluish-grey is represented by the vase illustrated.

This diversification of production seems to have become more marked in the latter part of the period, as provincial forces reasserted themselves. In much of south China, the grey-green glazed stone-wares of the Yüeh tradition, now flourishing afresh, provided the model to emulate. These developed in late T'ang times an extremely elegant style with moulded and finely incised ornament, chiefly of plants, birds and animals, which was to reach its peak under the succeeding 'Five Dynasties' (AD 906–959). Early texts describe the *pi-se* ('secret colour') ware of this time as restricted to princely use. The Yüeh decorative style represents an important addition to the Chinese potter's repertoire.

The increasing refinement with which the T'ang pottery materials were prepared, shaped and fired, also the skill with which a limited, if expanding range of glazes was handled represent an accomplishment of no mean order. Yet it still remains to discuss the T'ang potter's most influential achievement: the invention of porcelain. This extremely hard, brilliant white material owes its

vitrification and translucency to the combination at high temperature of white kaolin clay and felspar—a crystal-like substance mined in rock form, but present also in clay deposits; felspar being a principal constituent also of its highly brilliant glaze. Glazes approaching the porcelain type appear on some white wares seemingly of early T'ang date, the delicate, thinly potted stem cup providing an example of this; but it remains uncertain whether a true porcelain ware emerged much before the 9th century. (The Chinese language, strangely enough, has no distinguishing word for porcelain: and the term *tz'ŭ* which they employ covers equally all forms of hard and resonant ware). To this date are ascribed some fragments of exported porcelain which were unearthed at Samarra in Mesopotamia. Similar porcelains, translucent and almost colourless, and consisting chiefly of bowls and ewers showing T'ang characteristics of form and potting, have since emerged from Chinese soil. It has been suggested that these are the 'Hsing ware' mentioned in Chinese records, and made in north-easterly Hopei province: but the site remains undiscovered. It would seem that the type continued into the early part of the Sung dynasty, when it was superseded by the celebrated 'Ting ware' of this province.

An equal mystery surrounds the beginnings of porcelain manufacture in south China. There can be little doubt however that kilns in the Ching-tê-chên region of Kiangsi province—destined for a prominent role in the future—were active by the 10th century if not earlier. A famous ewer in the British Museum, topped by the head of a phoenix and made of greyish-white porcelain with a glaze showing a somewhat greenish-grey cast, is believed to have been made at Chi-chou in this province at about this date.

125. *Ju* ware bowl-stand, buff stoneware with crackled, light greyish-blue glaze. Sung dynasty, early 12th century. Diam. 6½ in. (16·4 cm.). The rarest of Sung wares, made for a few years only to the order of the Northern Court; barely thirty specimens exist outside China today. The saucer-like flange is carved in the form of overlapping petals; and the flowerlike elegance of the whole in many ways typifies the Sung potter's ideal. Sir Harry Garner Collection.

126. *Chün* ware bowl with foliated rim, grey porcellanous stoneware with a light blue glaze. Sung dynasty, 12th–13th century. Diam. 9 in. (22·9 cm.). The sumptuous Chün ware is technically akin to the Northern celadons, deriving its luminous blue tints from opalescence in the thick, bubbly glaze. Chinese Nationalist Government, Taiwan.

127. *Chün* ware bottle, with lavender-grey glaze splashed with purple. Sung dynasty, about 12th–13th century. Ht. 11½ in. (29·3 cm.). Percival David Foundation, London University.

125

126

127

The Sung period (AD 960–1279)

Sung pottery is at once more varied, and more polished in style than that of the T'ang. The industry enjoyed a new quality of patronage, at a time when the values of a cultivated scholar class guided taste as never before. The spiritual and intellectual ferment of recent centuries had given rise to movements in art, philosophy and literature whose influence pervaded the Court itself. The Emperor Hui Tsung, for example, was celebrated not only for the brilliance of his circle and for his unrivalled collection of antiquities, but also as a painter of talent, highly accomplished in the genre of 'birds and flowers'. The minute observation of nature found in such works had as its counterpart the majestic sweep of Northern Sung landscape painting. In this culturally enlightened milieu, certain wares were now ordered to be made specifically for the Court. But the Sung was at the same time a period of grave political weakness, beset also

128

128. Contrasting North Chinese wares of the Sung period: a stoneware bottle with lustrous black glaze and leafy designs painted in rust-brown. Ht. 10½ in. (26·7 cm.); and a jar of *Ting* porcelain ware, ht. 6¼ in. (15·8 cm.). Right: a bowl of Yüeh celadon ware. Victoria and Albert Museum, London.

129. Ewer, stoneware with brown-black glaze showing silvery 'oilspot' markings. Sung dynasty, about 12th century. Ht. 5 in. (12·6 cm.). The Sung black-glazed wares make use of iron oxides in oxidising firing conditions; and through skilful control a variety of patternings were induced in them. This rare 'oilspot' ewer is of a type filled through a hole in the bottom. Reproduced by gracious permission of H.M. the King of Sweden.

129

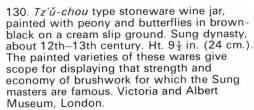

130

130. *Tz'ŭ-chou* type stoneware wine jar, painted with peony and butterflies in brown-black on a cream slip ground. Sung dynasty, about 12th–13th century. Ht. 9½ in. (24 cm.). The painted varieties of these wares give scope for displaying that strength and economy of brushwork for which the Sung masters are famous. Victoria and Albert Museum, London.

131. Massive figure of a Lohan, hard buff-white ware with green and amber glazes. Sung or Liao dynasty, about 10th–11th century. Ht. 47¼ in. (120 cm.), with stand. The Lohans, originally sixteen in number, are the apostles of Buddha. One of a group of figures found in a remote cave-sanctuary near I-chou (Hopei): they are perhaps the supreme surviving examples of Chinese ceramic sculpture. The coloured glazes represent a continuation of T'ang practice, probably in the Liao kingdom of Manchuria. British Museum, London.

132. *Tz'ŭ-chou* type stoneware wine jar with design incised and stamped through a cream-white slip to the underlying body. Sung dynasty, about 11th century. Ht. 14¾ in. (37·5 cm.). The characters read *ch'ing ch'ing jen* ('purity, clarity, endurance'): a maxim for life and perhaps also a commendation of the contents. A large class of stonewares decorated in this and similar techniques were made at a number of centres in north China. Arts Council of Great Britain. Seligman Collection.

131

132

49

133

134

135

136

137

138

133. *Lung-ch'üan* celadon ware wine jar and cover, with light bluish-green glaze. Sung dynasty: 12th century (?). Ht. 10 in. (25·3 cm.). *Lung-ch'üan* kilns produced celadon wares for both domestic and foreign consumption. Some pieces have particularly refined glazes in the bluish tint called '*kinuta*' by the Japanese. The term 'celadon' may derive from a character so named in the 17th-century French novel *L'Astrée* (Honoré d'Urfé) who wore grey-green clothing. Victoria and Albert Museum, London.

134. Trumpet-necked vase, porcelain with peony scroll designs in relief under a grey-green celadon glaze. Yüan dynasty: with an incised inscription dated 1327. Ht. 28 in. (71·1 cm.). The inscription records manufacture of a pair of flower-vases dedicated for use in a temple. The somewhat ponderous form and emphatic decoration reflect changing taste during this period of Mongol occupation. Percival David Foundation, London University.

135. *Chien* ware bowl, stoneware with thick, lustrous black glaze flecked with silvery spots. Sung dynasty. Diam. 7¾ in. (19·2 cm.). Made in a major tea-producing region Fukien, *Chien* ware consists almost entirely of tea bowls. The silvery 'oilspot' effect is rare, and so-called 'hare's-fur' streakings of rust-brown are more common. In Japan, where they were much prized for tea-ceremony use, black-glazed wares in general became known as *temmoku* perhaps after *T'ien-mu*, a sacred mountain in China. Freer Gallery of Art, Washington.

136. *Kuan* ware incense-jar, of dark grey porcellanous stoneware with a thick, creamy-grey glaze, broadly crackled. Sung dynasty: 12th–13th century. Ht. 4 in. (10·1 cm.). The Imperial *Kuan* ('official') ware of the Southern Sung was first made within the grounds of the Palace at Hangchow, although soon imitated elsewhere. The glaze is uniquely sumptuous; and its crackle, and the frequent borrowing of ancient bronze forms, were designed to evoke an impression of archaic dignity and splendour. Victoria and Albert Museum, London.

137. Dish, porcelain painted in underglaze blue with design of a *ch'i-lin* (auspicious mythical beast), plants and rocks. Mid-14th century. Diam. 18 in. (45·7 cm.). The technique of painting in underglaze cobalt-oxide blue, developed during the 14th century, revolutionised Chinese taste in ceramics; and the crowded, vigorously painted designs of this time paved the way for the new styles of Ming porcelain. Ashmolean Museum, Oxford.

138. Dish, porcelain painted in underglaze blue, with a landscape of rocks, trees and flowers. Ming dynasty: early 15th century. Diam. 25¼ in. (64 cm.). An exceptionally large specimen, showing the quality of painting found even on blue-and-white porcelains exported abroad. Topkapi Sarayi Museum, Istanbul.

with recurrent threats of barbarian invasion from the north. In the disaster of 1127 the Chin Tartars seized the capital, Kaifeng, and Hui Tsung himself was taken captive. Thereafter a much diminished Empire of the 'southern Sung' was ruled from the Court at Hangchow: although this city in its turn became a thriving centre of cultural activity, bringing fresh life to the pottery centres of the south.

The excellence of the Sung wares owes much to the sound developments in stoneware techniques which had been made in the preceding period. Particularly with regard to glazes, however, potters now found more sophisticated use for the materials at their disposal, acquiring exceptional skill in the regulation of kiln

temperature and atmosphere. Thus whereas T'ang potters had been aware, for example, that an iron content in glazes could be made to yield yellows, browns, or black in oxidising conditions, while in a 'reduced' (ill-ventilated) firing it might produce green or bluish tints, under the Sung such properties were more systematically explored, and with such other factors as depth and viscosity, they were deliberately calculated as expressions of taste. Restrained monochrome effects were preferred which imitated or harmonised with those of nature: for example, the evanescent shades of foliage, water, or sky. At the same time the well-proportioned forms of the T'ang also underwent a subtle transformation, acquiring a new fluency of line that softened away all traces of metallic origin; and

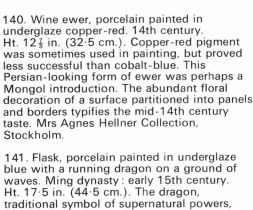

139

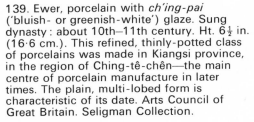

140

139. Ewer, porcelain with *ch'ing-pai* ('bluish- or greenish-white') glaze. Sung dynasty: about 10th–11th century. Ht. 6½ in. (16·6 cm.). This refined, thinly-potted class of porcelains was made in Kiangsi province, in the region of Ching-tê-chên—the main centre of porcelain manufacture in later times. The plain, multi-lobed form is characteristic of its date. Arts Council of Great Britain. Seligman Collection.

140. Wine ewer, porcelain painted in underglaze copper-red. 14th century. Ht. 12⅞ in. (32·5 cm.). Copper-red pigment was sometimes used in painting, but proved less successful than cobalt-blue. This Persian-looking form of ewer was perhaps a Mongol introduction. The abundant floral decoration of a surface partitioned into panels and borders typifies the mid-14th century taste. Mrs Agnes Hellner Collection, Stockholm.

141. Flask, porcelain painted in underglaze blue with a running dragon on a ground of waves. Ming dynasty: early 15th century. Ht. 17·5 in. (44·5 cm.). The dragon, traditional symbol of supernatural powers, and of the authority of the Emperor, was extensively depicted on Chinese porcelain, especially in his natural habitat of water and cloud. Percival David Foundation, London University.

142. Bottle, porcelain with 'pearl-beaded' panels and applied floral reliefs under a *ch'ing-pai* glaze. Yüan dynasty: early 14th century. Ht. 10⅞ in. (27·5 cm.). Typically Yüan in its decorative treatment, this piece represents a phase of experiment in the Ching-tê-chên industry at this time. The bottle has German silver-gilt mounts of the early 18th century; like a similar specimen mounted for the King of Hungary late in the 14th century, however, it no doubt reached Europe in medieval times. Victoria and Albert Museum, London.

143. Jar, and cover, porcelain painted in underglaze blue with a floral scroll design. Mark and reign of Hsüan Tê (1426–35). Diam. 8·6 in. (21·7 cm.). The Hsüan Tê porcelains came to be recognised as classic both for the refinement of their material and glaze, and for the studied perfection of their forms and painted designs, which were undoubtedly affected by the large orders placed for the Court. Percival David Foundation, London University.

141   142   143

with this new plasticity, involving much lobing of sides and foliation of rims, many vessels acquired a distinctly flower-like elegance.

Many new kilns were set up; and the broad pattern of Sung production is one of major centres, at which certain well-defined types of ware were evolved, reinforced by lesser kilns at which these were either reproduced or adapted with local variations. Among the earliest and foremost wares of the 'Northern Sung' period was a porcelain, the so-called 'Ting ware', made in the Ting-chou region of Hopei province; it has a smooth ivory-tinted glaze that distinguishes it plainly from the colder white porcelains of the T'ang. A plain glazed 'black Ting', also a 'red (reddish-brown) Ting' are rare varieties of this ware. Although favoured by the Court, Ting ware

was destined chiefly for everyday uses, with a preponderance of bowls, dishes, jars and other simple forms. It is nevertheless of a marked refinement, heightened further by the delicately carved or moulded designs—consisting of such popular Sung motifs as lotus or peony, or of dragons or fish—which were added as ornament.

Such carved or incised decoration was a legacy from the grey-green Yüeh 'celadon' wares of the south previously described; and it was probably their success that gave rise to another notable Sung type, the so-called 'Northern celadon wares'. Lustrous and olive-green in colour, their glazes cover a well-vitrified, resonant grey body of a kind customarily classified as 'porcellanous stoneware', which is not untypical of the Sung wares in general. The Sung

123

123

118

144

145

146

144. Typical Chinese reign mark, as used from Ming times onwards. Reading down in columns from the right *Ta Ming Hsuan Tê nien chich* 'Great Ming (dynasty) Hsüan Tê period made' (i.e. 1426–35). From the 18th century, marks were often written in the conventionalised 'seal character' script. Other marks found on Chinese porcelains convey good wishes, or name the 'hall' or 'studio'. Victoria and Albert Museum, London.

145. Stem cup, porcelain with brilliant copper-red glaze. Ming dynasty: early 15th century. Ht. 4⅛ in. (10·4 cm.). Fine monochrome-glazed porcelains in white, blue or red were made at this time. The copper-red glaze, which on account of the difficulties of the technique was not much used, must nevertheless have inspired the celebrated *sang-de-boeuf* wares of the following dynasty. Victoria and Albert Museum, London.

146. Wine cup, porcelain decorated in *tou-ts'ai* style enamels with a design of hens and chicks. Mark and reign of Ch'êng Hua (1465–87). Diam. 3¼ in. (8·2 cm.). The introduction of overglaze enamels in the mid-15th century opened up new possibilities of polychrome design. The rare Ch'êng Hua porcelains, which are of exceptional delicacy, favoured the *tou-ts'ai* style in which the outlines are drawn in underglaze blue. Victoria and Albert Museum, London.

9(p. 54)

treatment of form, and its harmonious blending with glaze and decoration, are well exemplified in the vase of this ware shown, with its fluent lines and fine proportions, on which a rhythmical scroll of peony was cut with sparing, oblique strokes before the glaze was applied. Other specimens have mould-impressed decoration. The major centres of Northern celadon manufacture were at Yao-chou in Shensi, and at Lin-ju in central Honan.

126–7

Equally celebrated products of the northern kilns are the Chün wares, characterised by blue glazes ranging widely in tint from pale 'moonlight' through lavender to near-purple: the colour being technically an effect of opalescence. Thickly applied, these glazes often accumulate in heavy drops and rolls near the base of the vessel; they are frequently enlivened also with contrasting splashes of purple or crimson, contrived by the addition of copper. Dishes, bowls, jars and tripod incense-burners are the commonest shapes of this colourful ware, which was made widely in north China down to the end of the dynasty and beyond. Probably the rarest of all Sung ceramics and certainly among the most fastidious is Ju ware, which

125

was made by Court command for a few years only, early in the 12th century. Its parentage lies between Chün and Northern celadon: but its carefully prepared, buff stoneware body and highly refined, light bluish-green glaze, intentionally marked with a light 'crackle' of 'broken ice' fissures, have no precise parallel.

All these were somewhat specialised manufactures: at the same time there were more versatile kilns in north China which produced

plain white, brown or black glazed stonewares as they had done in T'ang times; and often alongside these, wares boldly decorated by the new techniques of painting or 'sgraffiato' work. The plainer glazes themselves were susceptible of decorative variation: and the illustrated lustrous, black glazed bottle, with effectively simple leaf patterns in rust-brown, shows one way in which the varying reactions of iron oxides during firing were exploited. Several other types streaked and patterned by such techniques were made, among them the so-called 'oil-spot' wares, with small markings of metallic silvery-grey, as shown on a rare ewer from the collection of H.M. the King of Sweden.

128

129

The more elaborately decorated types referred to above take their name by convention from the region of Tz'ǔ-chou, on the Honan-Hopei border, although their manufacture is now known to have been widespread. The generally greyish stoneware was primed as appropriate with white or brownish slips, providing a suitable ground for the *sgraffiato* ('scratched') or carved designs that could be executed in many effective permutations of light and dark, and fine or broad treatment. Plant or animal subjects were the most popular, framed in a variety of ornamental borders or grounds, although human figures are occasionally found. Sometimes the covering glazes were tinted brown or green; or the T'ang polychrome style might be followed, as in the case of the superbly modelled large figure of a Lohan or Buddhist disciple—one of a series no doubt made for a temple. According to some students this may emanate

132

131

147. Octagonal flower pot, porcelain incised with arabesques under turquoise, yellow, green and aubergine glazes. Mark and reign of Chêng Tê (1506–21). Ht. 5⅝ in. (13·5 cm.). British Museum, London.

147

148

148. Tiled roofs. Summer Palace, Peking. 18th century. Important buildings were often roofed with pottery tiles glazed in brilliant colours. Both the tile ends and also the ridges and corners of the roofs were frequently ornamented with mythological figures or animals.

8. Dish, earthenware with impressed design and coloured lead glazes. T'ang dynasty, about 7th–8th century. Diam. 12 in. (30·5 cm.). The sumptuous T'ang burials included much glazed earthenware in this striking 'three-colour' style. The design of a flying crane is typical in its symmetry; the impressed technique suggests imitation of stamped and chased metalwork. Bristol City Art Gallery.

9

10

11

12

from the Liao kingdom (907–1125) in Manchuria, where elements of the T'ang style lingered on well into the Sung period. The other main class of Tz'ŭ-chou type wares consists of those with painted designs, executed generally in brown-black, with swift, firm strokes of the brush which are wonderfully expressive. In its later years, painting in overglaze coloured enamels was also introduced. The Tz'ŭ-chou wares in general include a large proportion of heavier pieces—wine vases, storage jars, basins and the like—often potted with splendid vigour; and admirable pots were made to the end of the period and beyond.

Kilns in south China also acquired a certain renown for their brown or black glazes. The Chien ware tea bowls of Fukien province, conical in shape, and coarse-grained in body, are remarkable for their thick, sluggish glazes marked with fine 'hare's-fur' streaks or spots of golden-brown: they were much to the taste of the tea masters of Japan (see p. 66). Those of Chi-chou in Kiangsi province (sometimes known as 'Kian wares') favoured broader mottled effects, and distinctive designs of phoenixes or blossoms reserved in black. These appear to have been achieved through the use of paper 'cut-outs' dipped in wax, or some other glaze-resistant material.

The noblest and most characteristic productions of the Southern Sung period, however, are its celadon wares. Among these, it is the products of the Lung-ch'üan kilns, in Chekiang province, which, for lovers of Chinese ceramics, will always spring most readily to mind. The Sung Lung-ch'üan ware body approaches a white porcelain in character; but its chief glory resides in the luminous, light bluish-green glaze, veiled in its depths, and lustrous and smooth

to the touch, which clothes the strong, clean contours of the ware like an exquisite garment. For the Court at Hangchow an even more luxurious ware was devised: the *Kuan* ('official') ware, which preserves some memory of the Ju ware made previously in the North. A thin, dark grey material was employed, covered with successive layers of celadon-like glaze in tints of greyish-blue or green, or ash- to lavender-grey, and often displaying a fine multiple 'crackle'. It was designed for a variety of uses in palace hall or study; and sometimes adopts the venerable forms of ancient bronzes.

In positive contrast to these are the so-called *ch'ing-pai* wares, made in the adjacent province of Kiangsi in the Ching-tê-chên region; to our eyes these are often both refined and elegant, and yet like the Tz'ŭ-chou wares they were largely disregarded by Chinese connoisseurs of the past, as being of common usage. Of pure white porcelain with a faintly bluish-green glaze, they are most delicately and translucently potted in shapes of impeccable merit.

The new onslaught which the Chinese Empire was to suffer at the hands of the Mongols in the middle years of the 13th century dealt a severe blow to Sung culture, and in the potteries a lower standard soon prevailed. The last Sung Emperor was deposed in 1279 and for almost a century China remained in uneasy subjection, under the Yüan dynasty set up by Kublai Khan. Nevertheless, China was once more opened to foreign influences, and pottery exports were further expanded. Foreign demand had increased greatly since the T'ang period and vast quantities of celadon and *ch'ing-pai* ware in particular were despatched throughout south-east Asia, and to Japan. Much of it came not from major centres but from lesser kilns that sprang up in the coastal provinces of Fukien and Kuangtung,

149

149. Dish, porcelain painted with dragon designs in *wu-ts'ai* style (coloured enamels with underglaze blue). Mark and reign of Wan Li (1573–1619). Diam. 15 in. (38 cm.). Formerly Mrs. A. Clark Collection.

150. Gourd-shaped vase, porcelain painted in underglaze blue. Mark and reign of Chia Ching (1522–66). Ht. 17½ in. (44·4 cm.). The ebullient form is characteristic of Ming taste. The animal, tree and plant motifs are drawn from Taoist mythology and convey wishes for a long and full life. British Museum, London.

151. Figure of a Judge of Hell, hard-fired pottery with coloured glazes. Late 16th–early 17th century. Ht. 54 in. (137 cm.). Colour-glazed statuary of this kind for use in temples was often made in tile-works potteries, and can be of fine sculptural quality. British Museum, London.

9. 'Northern celadon ware' vase with incised peony design. Sung dynasty, 11th–12th century. Ht. 9½ in. (24·1 cm.). A clear, unobtrusive design in porcellanous stoneware. Victoria and Albert Museum, London.

10. Jar, porcelain with coloured glazes and designs outlined in applied 'cloisons' of clay. Ming dynasty, late 15th century. Ht. 15 in. (38·1 cm.). Medium-temperature glazes are applied to a pre-fired body in this colourful ware, decorated with lotus plants and waterfowl. Victoria and Albert Museum, London.

11. Vase in 'pilgrim-flask' form, porcelain, painted in famille rose enamels. Mark and reign of Yung Cheng (1723–35). Ht. 11⅞ in. (30 cm.). A new rose-pink and opaque white give softness and charm to the palette. Percival David Foundation, London University.

12. Food box and cover, for tea use. Oribe ware: stoneware with green glaze and painting in iron-brown, 17th century, named after the celebrated tea-master, Furata Oribe. Such new tasteful wares were used for the spreading cult of the Tea Ceremony. Suntory Gallery, Tokyo.

150

151

where somewhat rougher, but equally serviceable wares were made in these styles: they included such things as small cosmetic pots and boxes for betel-nut, or the large, brown-glazed storage jars which the Dyaks of Borneo still treasure today.

Under the Yüan (1279–1368), much Lung-ch'üan celadon in the form of large dishes, wine jars and so on was made for India and the Near East, as attested for example by the vast collection assembled in the Topkapu Sarayi Palace in Istanbul, much of it no doubt brought back by the Ottoman Sultans from their campaigns in Persia. Occasionally a piece would find its way thence to Europe, like the celebrated 'Archbishop Warham' bowl which was presented to New College, Oxford in 1530. Wares are more heavily potted than the former productions, and show a more prominent use of moulded and carved decoration. A similar coarsening of taste is noticeable also in the *ch'ing-pai* wares of the time, as in the rare, early 14th-century bottle illustrated, which is decorated in a rather fussy, tentative style with applied flowers and other ornament. The so-called *shu fu* ware is another Yüan development of *ch'ing-pai* in which moulded relief ornament was used. Before the mid-14th century, however, a more significant class of wares had appeared on the scene: these were white porcelains comparable in character to those just described, but now lavishly decorated with painting in underglaze cobalt blue: or to a lesser extent, in a somewhat unreliable underglaze copper red.

152. Wine ewer, porcelain with aubergine purple glaze overpainted with gilt designs. Probably reign of Wan Li (1573–1619). Ht. 12⅞ in. (32·5 cm.). Extensive use was made of coloured glazes in the 16th century. Wares with gilt decoration were much prized in Japan, where the style is known by the term *kinrande*. Fondation Baur-Duret, Geneva.

153. Square bottle, porcelain painted in underglaze blue with the Symbols of the Passion. About 1620. 15⅝ in. (38·8 cm.). In the Ming period much pottery continued to be exported throughout Asia, especially in the form of blue-and-white porcelain. Trade with Europeans began when Portuguese ships appeared at Canton early in the 16th century; and occasionally pieces were made and decorated to order. This piece, in the form of a ship's bottle, was perhaps ordered by the Jesuits. British Museum, London.

154. 'Transitional' blue-and-white jar, painted with a gathering of sages. About 1630–40. Diam. 10·5 in. (26·6 cm.). The 'transitional period' between the Ming decline and the Ch'ing revival produced much fine blue-and-white painted in an individual style, which the Dutch East India Company brought to Europe along with more standardised wares. Soame Jenyns Collection.

The Ming period (1368–1644)

The success of these painted wares and consequent decline in popularity of celadon implied the abandonment of the Sung ideal in ceramic art; and as tastes and habits changed, a fundamental shift took place in the pattern of the industry. From this time forward production became increasingly concentrated in the porcelain factories of Ching-tê-chên, which grew steadily in size and number, while the old stoneware manufactures gradually expired or sank to provincial status. The cobalt oxide pigment that initiated this revolution was apparently brought from Persia in Mongol times. In the 'underglaze' painting technique, this was painted on the fine white porcelain surface before it was glazed, and then fired with it at the full heat of the kiln, providing an agreeably permanent—and economical—result that has appealed widely to potters ever since. The decorative repertoire of the mid-14th-century porcelains comprises a remarkable range of plant, flower and animal designs interspersed with other symbolic and auspicious motifs, executed with a freedom and vigour of the brush that matches the originality of this new-found style. Endlessly varied, they are disposed in zones and compartmented areas that frequently cover the entire surface of the vessel.

The restoration of native Chinese rule under the Ming dynasty in 1368 brought no sudden change in taste. Early in the 15th century, however, Court patronage began to inspire wares of the greatest refinement, imposing at the same time a stricter regulation of form and design. The energetic Yung Lo Emperor (1403–24)—who has been called both founder and architect of the city of Peking—spread a mood of constructive vigour which soon found expression in the decorative arts: Ming forms are buoyant with life, as instanced by the very typical jar shown, with its almost baroque generosity of potting, the contours spreading boldly outward at both mouth and foot; while Ming ornament is characterised equally by its restless, rhythmical movement and by the glowing harmonies of its colour.

The glazes of Ming porcelains tend to be somewhat thick and uneven. Those of the much-admired blue-and-white of the early 15th century are fine and lustrous, clouded with tiny bubbles so that the painting, executed in a vibrant, deep violet-blue, seems to float

within them. Splendid, if massive pieces such as the 'moon' flask with lively dragon design, or the huge landscape dish at Istanbul still found their way to the Near East. More delicately potted wares were made for the Court, such as the covered jar bearing the famous reign-mark of Hsüan Tê (1426–35). It was at this time that the practice of adding such marks to porcelain first became regular; so that thereafter we can trace the development of style from reign to reign. But marks can be a hazardous guide: and both the Hsüan Tê style and its mark were much imitated—not necessarily fraudulently—in the following centuries. Immense in scale, and serving a variety of state purposes, the Imperial commissions were responsible for many new types of vessel and patterns of design. Among them

143
144

155

156

155. Pair of beaker-shaped vases, porcelain painted in underglaze blue. K'ang Hsi period. Ht. 19 in. (48·2 cm.). Probably part of a five-piece chimney garniture. K'ang Hsi blue-and-white porcelain is noted for refinement of material and form and for the rich quality of the cobalt used. Much was exported to Europe. Victoria and Albert Museum, London.

156. Vase, porcelain enamelled in *famille noire* style. K'ang Hsi period (1662–1772). Ht. 24½ in. (31·7 cm.). The masterly painting in *famille verte* enamels on the biscuit is enhanced by the rich black ground. There is poetic symbolism in the aged plum-tree, breaking once more into spring blossom. Victoria and Albert Museum, London.

157. Dish, porcelain painted in *famille verte* enamels. K'ang Hsi period (1662–1722). Diam. 24 in. (61 cm.). Six Court ladies are depicted on a terrace, casting arrows in the game known as 'pitch-pot'. National Trust. Ascott Collection.

158. Bowl, porcelain with deep *sang-de-boeuf* ('ox-blood red') glaze. K'ang Hsi period (1662 –1772). Diam. 9½ in. (24 cm.). The K'ang Hsi copper-reds are of a particularly deep and sonorous tone, and rank high among the various high-temperature glazes of this period. Percival David Foundation, London University.

157

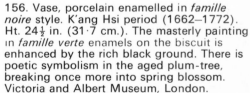

158

are monochrome glazed wares of unusual refinement, notably in
blue, a well-controlled copper-red, or plain white, often with
'secret' (an-hua) designs in moulded relief applied under the glaze
which reveal themselves only under careful scrutiny.

Despite the continuing vogue for blue-and-white porcelains, the
reign of Ch'êng Hua (1465–87) owes its chief fame to a different
technique: that of overglaze enamels. The development of these
glassy pigments, which were fused to the glaze in a separate, low-
temperature firing, opened up new possibilities of polychrome
painting. Ch'êng Hua practice favoured the so-called tou-ts'ai
('contrasted colour') style, with its jewel-like touches of red, green,
and yellow added to designs first pencilled in underglaze blue. The
wares are of an almost effeminate delicacy: yet the tiny cup with a
scene of foraging hens and chicks, must be counted the last word in
porcelain refinement.

A bolder Ming polychrome technique is that employing colours
in the form of medium-temperature glazes, applied direct to a
pre-fired, but unglazed (or 'biscuit') porcelain; to keep them from
running the designs were often outlined in ribbed 'cloisons' of clay.
Superb large jars, vases and barrel-shaped seats were made in this
way, producing an effect of peculiar richness. Double-walled jars
also had designs executed in carved openwork. Alternatively the
motifs might be incised, as on the flower pot bearing the reign-mark
of Chêng Tê (1506–21). Comparable wares with coloured glazes

were made also in the stoneware potteries: many of these existed to
meet the need for roof-tiles, which even today provide one of the
most striking features of the Chinese urban scene. Alongside the
proliferation of symbolic and decorative figure work which this
entailed may be counted the demand for architectural tiling of all
kinds, culminating in the so-called 'porcelain pagoda' built at
Nanking under the Yung Lo Emperor, and no doubt stimulated
further by the construction of the 'Forbidden City' in Peking. Yet
another use for colour-glazed stoneware was in the production of
figures of Buddhist or Taoist deities for use in temples, which are
sometimes of a truly impressive sculptural quality.

Although the 16th century wares hardly live up to the 15th-
century standards of refinement, they nevertheless retain our
interest through their continuing vitality, harmony of colour, and
increasingly unconventional charm in design. The longish reigns of
Chia Ching (1522–66) and Wan Li (1573–1619) produced much
painted porcelain in which Taoist symbolism abounds, depicting for
example such auspicious animals as the deer and crane, familiars of
Shou Lao, the Long-Life God; the long-lived pine and the spring-
flowering prunus; and landscapes in which the peaks of Paradise are
distantly revealed. The Wan Li so-called 'wu-ts'ai' or 'five-colour'
style—represented by the basin decorated with dragons—associates
enamels with underglaze blue painting, in a broader manner than
that of the tou-ts'ai style. Coloured glazes too were much used, both

159. Teapot, porcelain with openwork panels
of bamboo design, and turquoise-blue glaze.
The silver chain attaching the lid was added
in Europe at an early date. Reign of K'ang
Hsi (1662–1722). Ht. 5¾ in. (14·5 cm.).
Victoria and Albert Museum, London.

160. Ewer, porcelain painted in underglaze
blue. Mark and reign of Yung Chêng (1723–
35). Ht . 12¼ in. (31·1 cm.). A significant
aspect of 18th-century porcelain development
is the revival of Sung and Ming styles. The
painting of this ewer imitates that of early
15th-century blue-and-white (cf. fig. 143),
copying even the dark spotting occurring in
the cobalt. The unusual form, however, is
suggestive of early 18th-century French
influence. Chinese Nationalist Government
Collections, Taiwan.

161. Vase and waterpot, porcelain with
clair-de-lune glaze, and a vase with
'peachbloom' glaze. All with mark of K'ang
Hsi (1662–1722), and of the period.
Greatest ht. 8¼ in . (20·8 cm.). Elegantly
shaped for the scholar's table, these vessels
bear two of the rarer glazes of their time. The

pale clair-de-lune ware is also found with the
mark of the following reign. Fondation
Baur-Duret, Geneva.

162. Part of a tea service, porcelain enamelled
in violet-purple and yellow with a 'plume of
feathers' design. About 1730–50. Diam. of

plate: 8 in. (17·2 cm.). More and more
porcelain was shaped and decorated to meet
European requirements after the adoption of
the famille rose enamelling style. This rare
service was no doubt made for a particular
patron. Metropolitan Museum of Art, New
York. Winifield Foundation Gift, 1961.

159 160

161

162

singly and in every feasible combination. The elegant wine ewer,
152 with a rare aubergine-purple glaze, has designs overpainted in gold,
with most sumptuous effect.

Under the Ming, foreign trade remained at a very high level, with
blue-and-white replacing the earlier styles in demand. 'Swatow·
ware'—painted in blue or in red, green and turquoise enamels in a
vigorous pastiche of the leading styles—was produced in Fukien
province for these markets. Direct trading with Europe began with
the arrival of Portuguese carracks in Chinese waters; and by 1557
they had won their still-existing off-shore concession at Macao.
During the 17th century Jesuit missions, which had first been
established in Japan, achieved a growing foothold on the mainland;
153 and the crudely-painted blue-and-white flask depicting the Symbols
of the Passion, and dating from about 1620, is a curious relic of this
time of uneasy, tentative contact. By now, however, the Dutch
were already exercising their superior sea-power and extending their
carrying trade from bases in the Indies. In the declining years of the
Ming much blue-and-white was brought home to be sold in the
auctions at Amsterdam. By the standards of cultivated Chinese taste,
these wares are somewhat crowded and repetitious in design;
nevertheless, particularly during the 'transitional' period before the
next dynasty became settled, there began to appear porcelains of an
154 exceptionally fine glaze and finish, painted with an individuality of
touch which is rare in any period.

163

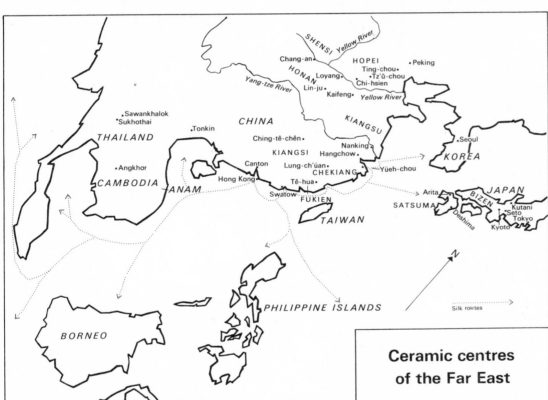

**Ceramic centres
of the Far East**

163. Three fluted vases, porcelain with
celadon green glaze. About 1730–40. French
ormolu mounts in rococo style, bearing the
crowned 'C' mark; about 1745–49.
Ht. 21¼ in. (54 cm.). The rarity of Chinese
porcelains that reached Europe in medieval
and Renaissance times often led to their
being mounted in precious metal and
treasured in 'cabinets of curiosities'. In the
18th century, and particularly in France,
monochrome wares were expensively
mounted in ormolu and used as adjuncts to
interior design. Wallace Collection, London.

164. A pair of ducks, porcelain painted in
famille rose enamels. Middle of 18th century.
Ht. 10 in. (25·5 cm.). Models of hawks,
cranes, ducks and geese, as well as of tigers,
monkeys, horses, dogs and numerous other
animals formed part of the 18th-century
production, which also included figures in
both European and Chinese costume. To a
large extent these would seem to have been
made for the Western trade. Fitzwilliam
Museum, Cambridge.

Ch'ing Dynasty (1644–1912)

The collapse of the Ming dynasty repeats a familiar pattern of
Chinese history: that of a powerful neighbouring race—this time,
Tartars from Manchuria—assuming control at a moment of internal
weakness and revolution. Already habituated to Chinese customs,
the Manchus established the rule of their Ch'ing dynasty on
traditional lines and gave the arts their studious encouragement. The
Ching-tê-chên porcelain factories, however, had suffered much in
the upheaval and for a time the Dutch, who were barred from trade,
were obliged to seek an alternative source in Japan. Their revival
dates largely from 1682, when a new commissioner was sent to

164

167. Chestnut dish with openwork cover, porcelain with enamelled cameos of *putti* and classical swags in sepia, after a Bartolozzi engraving. About 1785. Ht. 10⅜ in. (27 cm.). Chinese porcelain copy of English creamware. Museum of Fine Arts, Boston.

165. Figure of Kuan-yin, 'Goddess of Mercy'; *blanc-de-Chine* porcelain. Tê-hua (Fukien province); early 18th century. Ht. 15⅛ in. (38·4 cm.). This beautiful porcelain, cream or cold white in colour and seldom decorated, was exported as figure models and tea wares, elegant models being apparently reserved for Chinese patrons. Victoria and Albert Museum, London.

166. Vase, porcelain painted in *famille rose* style, after the manner of *cloisonné* work. Mark and reign of Ch'ien Lung (1736–95). Ht. 9⅝ in. (24·6 cm.). An increasing elaboration of style characterises the wares of this reign, when much technical virtuosity was expended on the imitation of objects in other materials and in antiquarian conceits. Victoria and Albert Museum, London.

168. Teapot of unglazed red stoneware. Yi-hsing (Kiangsu province): probably early 18th century. Ht. 3¼ in. (8·2 cm.). Yi-hsing teapots, of red, buff or brown stoneware, were sometimes of elaborate and curious design. Exported along with tea from the second quarter of the 17th century, they were imitated by Dutch, English and German potters. Victoria and Albert Museum, London.

control the Imperial factory. Thereafter the reign of K'ang Hsi (1662–1722) became one of brilliant achievement, which was ably maintained under his successors, Yung Chêng (1723–35) and Ch'ien Lung (1736–95); production in the town was totally reorganised and rose to an unprecedented scale, while in sheer quality of workmanship and technical invention the wares of this period can scarcely be matched.

The Jesuit Père d'Entrecolles, who lived and worked at Ching-tê-chên early in the 18th century, sent home invaluable accounts of how the porcelains were made, describing in detail the processes of production which involved much division of labour, not only in the preparation and shaping of the materials but even in the painting of the wares. The porcelain became whiter and more smoothly glazed than any Ming product and was potted with a new care and precision, so that even the foot-ring of a K'ang Hsi vessel—always a tell-tale indicator of style—may almost alone suffice to establish its date. The reign-mark is seldom found on wares of this period, but their innumerable shapes are all stamped in some degree with its virile character. A firm base, strong, spare contours and a masculine shoulder are typical features to be noted in vases, which are often of new design and unusual size.

In such conditions of mass manufacture the Ch'ing porcelains inevitably lack something of that breadth and individuality of expression which we admire in the Ming; also, they reflect a changing taste that came increasingly to favour refinement at the expense of more robust qualities. In painted design, generous rhythms are replaced by a sprightly elegance of style which, however, descends seldom to banality, while it can rise on occasion to masterly virtuosity. Under K'ang Hsi much blue-and-white was made, painted in a reverberating cobalt that was characteristically

applied to the delineated areas in thin, overlapping strokes of wash. A 'soufflé' or 'powdered blue' glaze was also used, chiefly as a ground colour for decoration in panels. The principal enamelling style is that of the so-called *famille verte* or 'green family': presenting a palette comparable to that of the Ming but clearer in tone and used in a more diffuse orchestration, in which a strong green and a thinner red are dominant, supported by a sharper yellow, violet-purple, black, and newly introduced, a translucent blue. A distinctive and popular variant is that in which the *famille verte* enamels were applied as glazes 'on the biscuit', in colours restricted chiefly to green, yellow and aubergine-purple, with drawing in black. In this category fall the unusually sumptuous *famille noire* wares with glowing black ground, also the yellow-ground specimens known as *famille jaune*: both found especially in the form of large, finely painted ornamental vases. The style was also much favoured for figures of deities and animals.

The subject matter of 18th-century painted decoration is extremely varied and eludes any brief description, much of it embodying symbolic overtones which inevitably escape the Westerner. Plant designs are ubiquitous, and the 'flowers of the four seasons'—prunus, peony, lotus and chrysanthemum—are repeatedly found. Extensive use was made of panelling, with ornamental borders and grounds; there are landscapes, mythological beasts, and figure scenes which derive from prints, often illustrating episodes from history or legend and set in courtly surroundings. Much admirable ware was made for export and porcelain which was made for the 'Chinese taste', although generally more sparing in design, is not too readily distinguishable from it: court taste, however, is clearly revealed in pieces which revive stock 'dragon' and other patterns established in the classic Ming reigns.

155

157

13(p

156

156

156

159

157

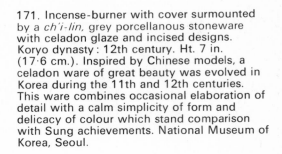

171. Incense-burner with cover surmounted by a *ch'i-lin*, grey porcellanous stoneware with celadon glaze and incised designs. Koryo dynasty : 12th century. Ht. 7 in. (17·6 cm.). Inspired by Chinese models, a celadon ware of great beauty was evolved in Korea during the 11th and 12th centuries. This ware combines occasional elaboration of detail with a calm simplicity of form and delicacy of colour which stand comparison with Sung achievements. National Museum of Korea, Seoul.

169. Engraving of a design for a porcelain closet by Daniel Marot. About 1690. The furnishing of porcelain 'cabinets' or 'closets' for the display of oriental porcelain collections became a princely fashion towards the end of the 17th century. It was brought to England by Mary II, wife of William III of Orange, for whom Marot may well have designed the porcelain rooms in the now vanished Water Gallery at Hampton Court.

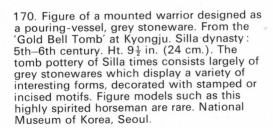

170. Figure of a mounted warrior designed as a pouring-vessel, grey stoneware. From the 'Gold Bell Tomb' at Kyongju. Silla dynasty : 5th–6th century. Ht. 9½ in. (24 cm.). The tomb pottery of Silla times consists largely of grey stonewares which display a variety of interesting forms, decorated with stamped or incised motifs. Figure models such as this highly spirited horseman are rare. National Museum of Korea, Seoul.

170

171

More purely for domestic consumption also were the monochrome glazed wares—a class to which great technical ingenuity and artistry were devoted from K'ang Hsi times onwards. They ranged increasingly over the spectrum of colour, and are set off to great ornamental effect by the elegant, precisely finished forms of the period. Glazes fired at high temperature include the deep and glowing copper-based *sang-de-boeuf* or 'ox-blood' reds—a much prized effect revived from early Ming times, which in later reigns is often found with kiln transmutations of blue and purple which the French call *flambé*; also several shades of cobalt blue, and the lustrous 'mirror-black'—these were often overpainted with gilt designs. Celadon glazes were revived in a variety of tones, often in combination with carved designs. In the medium temperature range are a startling turquoise, yellows, and a deep aubergine purple. In limited quantities all these found their way to Europe and particularly to France where, mounted at great expense in the most finely worked ormolu, they lent their piquant, exotic note to the rich furnishings of the day.

Late K'ang Hsi Court taste introduced further refinements such as the spotted, pinkish-red 'peachbloom' glaze, found in eight forms only which were designed for writing-table use; and the very pale and pure *clair-de-lune* blue. In their delicacy of form and tint these rare pieces foreshadow the style of Yung Chêng's short reign (1723–35), one in which elegant invention reached a new peak. A sensitive revival of the classic Sung glazes—*Ting, Ju, Kuan* and many others—is a feature of this time. Other departures inspired by these experiments are the mottled greenish and brownish glazes descriptively named 'tea-dust' and 'iron-rust', and the speckled 'robin's-egg' blue, while the range of single-coloured glazes was further swelled by the colours of the enamelling palette.

Yung Chêng's reign produced particularly fine reproductions of Ming wares, notably the Hsüan Tê style blue-and-white, and the Ch'êng Hua *tou-ts'ai* enamels: these are sometimes brilliantly deceptive, but more often merely pay tribute through an elegant paraphrase of these celebrated styles. The most influential change of this period was however the superseding of the *famille verte* style of enamelling by that of the *famille rose*. This is named after its dominant rose-pink enamel, newly introduced from Europe; but its character owes much also to the use of opaque white, which enabled all the colours to be mixed for use in shaded tones. The charm and delicacy of the earlier *famille rose* style is seen at its best in the shapely ornamental vase shown, which bears the Yung Chêng mark. The combination of soft pinks, greens, yellows and blues lent itself particularly well to refined painting of 'bird and flower' subjects, and interior scenes with Court ladies and playing children. There is often more than a hint of European influence in the handling of the pigments and also in the minute, crowded painting of grounds and borders, found increasingly in the wares of Ch'ien Lung's reign (1736–95). His curious and antiquarian bent found reflection in the imitation of all kinds of materials in porcelain: objects of wood, ivory or stone, of lacquer and of various metals, including patinated replicas of ancient bronzes. At the same time much care was still lavished on reproducing the classic ceramic wares, while the range of other monochrome and polychrome wares developed under Yung Chêng was extended still further.

These efforts of remarkable, and at times misplaced, virtuosity signal the end of creativity in Chinese porcelain. From the reign of Chia Ching (1796–1820) onwards, the industry was given over increasingly to insensitive repetition of existing models, marked by a corresponding decline in the quality of materials and workmanship.

172

173

174

172. Vase of *mei-p'ing* shape, porcellanous stoneware with designs inlaid in white and black clay under a celadon glaze. Koryō dynasty: late 12th century. Ht. 13½ in. (34·2 cm.). The serene charm of Koryo period design is exemplified in this decoration of willows, lotus and cranes, which is executed in the peculiarly Korean technique of coloured inlays. G. St G. M. Gompertz Collection.

173. Jar, porcelain painted in underglaze blue. 15th–16th century. Ht. 17¼ in. (43·3 cm.). Blue-and-white wares emanating from Annam show a characteristic style of design that derives largely from the earlier Ming wares. They include small cosmetic jars and boxes widely exported in south-east Asia. In late Ming times coloured enamels were also used. Sir David Home Collection.

174. Covered jar, greyish stoneware with incised decoration under a celadon glaze. Sawankhalok: 14th–early 15th century. Ht. 9¾ in. (24·8 cm.). The varied celadon wares made at Sawankhalok and other, lesser kilns at this time display in their forms a typically Siamese combination of strength and elegance. A variety with dark brown glaze is known as 'Kaliang ware'. British Museum, London.

176. Jar, stoneware with 'wood-ash' celadon glaze covering incised plant designs. Late Heian—early Kamakura period, about 12th–13th century. Ht. 15¾ in. (40 cm.). Stoneware techniques and primitive celadon glazes developed slowly in Japan from the 5th century onwards. Both in its form, and in the relaxed, sensitive sketching of the plant designs this jar represents a reaction from the Chinese-dominated art of the preceding Nara period. Keio University, Tokyo.

175

176

178. Urn, coarse buff-red earthenware of rope-and-basketwork design. Middle Jomon period: perhaps 2nd millenium BC. Ht. 14¾ in. (37·5 cm.). The Neolithic pottery of Japan, known as 'Jomon' ware, shows at times an unusual elaboration and refinement in both form and design. In this remarkable piece the later Japanese attachment to textured surfaces, and to curious and ingenious formations, may both be discerned. Tokyo University.

175. Jar, porcelain painted in underglaze copper-red. Yi dynasty: perhaps 17th–18th century. Ht. 11⅜ in. (29 cm.). The noble form of this jar overrides its imperfections of technique, and is reinforced by the economical strength of the painting. Victoria and Albert Museum, London.

177. Bowl, greyish stoneware with pale greenish glaze applied over a light-coloured slip. About 12th–13th century. Diam. 9½ in. (23·1 cm.). Although technically inspired by Chinese celadon or *ch'ing-pai* porcelain wares, this type of Annamese pottery reveals a distinctively native style in its forms. Other varieties of the period include wares with brown glazes, or simple painted designs. Victoria and Albert Museum, London.

179. Water-dropper, in the form of two monsters side by side. Greyish stoneware, painted in brown under a frosted glaze. Sawankhalok ware; probably 15th century. L. 4½ in. (11·4 cm.). Both useful wares and votive objects in animal or human form were made at the Thai kilns. In lands where writing is done with a brush, the water-dropper is a customary part of the scholar's equipment. Victoria and Albert Museum, London.

177

178

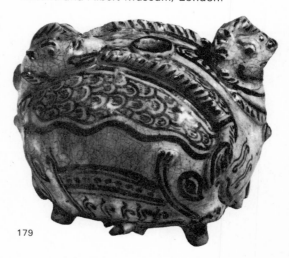

179

Two influential classes of ware not made at Ching-tê-chên, which were imported into Europe in some quantities, call for mention here. The so-called 'blanc-de-chine' porcelain of Tê-hua, in Fukien province, is of an especially fine, milky-white quality, and was for the most part left undecorated. Apart from vessels it includes many models, not only of Chinese animals and deities, but occasionally also of European figures. Secondly, at Yi-hsing in Kiangsu province a form of unglazed red or brown stonewares was made which found particular favour for teapots, often of curious and elaborate design. Both types exercised considerable influence on the contemporary wares of late 17th- and early 18th-century Europe.

By this date there was already in Europe a vogue for collecting Chinese porcelain and for its use in interior decoration, which led to the building of 'porcelain rooms' in many princely houses. The most fervent of such collectors was Augustus the Strong of Saxony and Poland (1699–1733), patron of the Meissen factory, who conceived the project of ornamenting a complete palace in Dresden with oriental and western china. A more widespread fashion developed with the rapid growth of the East India trade which followed upon the re-opening of the port of Canton in 1699. Great quantities of blue-and-white and *famille verte* porcelain were imported, followed in the 1720s by *famille rose* wares and others. Many families ordered table services decorated with their own coats-of-arms: and perhaps the most interesting feature of this trade is the promptitude with which it met every whim of its diverse European patronage, whether as regards form or decoration. A surprising variety of complex shapes in 18th-century ceramics and silverware were laboriously reproduced; and unfamiliar designs of every description, including religious or classical scenes, and much else of a more mundane kind, were faithfully painted after the prints and sketches despatched to Canton. It was only towards the end of the century, as European factories moved towards mass production, that the flow of Chinese wares seriously declined. Western interest in Chinese ceramics revived, however, in the great age of collecting that followed, and received fresh impetus as the earlier, buried wares began to come to light at the beginning of this century.

180. 'Haniwa' figure of a warrior, reddish earthenware. Late 5th–6th century AD. Excavated at Ohta City, Gumma Prefecture. Ht. 4ft. 5¼ in. (1·35 m.). The 'Haniwa' sculptural figures developed from pottery cylinders which were erected above the large burial tumuli customary at this period. They represent men and women in various stations of life, and also include models of animals and buildings. Swiftly worked in the soft clay, their impressionistic features have a strangely arresting quality. Seattle Art Museum, Eugene Fuller Memorial Collection.

180

Korea

Geographically, the kingdom of Korea resembles an appendage of Manchuria extending from the north of China towards the islands of Japan: and it has always come under strong Chinese influence, if not actual subjection to her rule. Yet despite this, its artistic life shows a distinctive independence and much individuality of expression. The Silla kingdom (about 57 BC–AD 935), which originated in the south, was eventually to unify the whole peninsula: its pottery is known to us through burial wares of a hard, grey stoneware typical of which are vessels with a tall, openwork foot, but which also include some highly original and naturalistic figurines. Under the Koryō kings (918–1392), however, the example of Sung China became paramount and its advanced techniques were adopted with notable success: Yüeh, Northern celadon and Ju exercised successive influence on the production of celadon wares which, for all their resemblance to these in style, nevertheless demonstrate a subtly different character.

These wares attained by the 12th century a refinement which impressed even visitors from the Sung Court, who remarked on the originality of many of the designs. The 'kingfisher-coloured' glaze, applied to a grey body, is of a soft brilliance more serene than those of its Chinese counterparts, and there is a special air of repose in the Korean handling of forms, even when drawn from the mainland repertoire. Ingenious pierced and moulded work figures in some elaborate specimens; but more peculiarly Korean is a technique of decoration first incised, then inlaid in white and black slips under the celadon glaze, which displays great charm in such wares as the vase depicting cranes under willow trees. Other Koryō wares were painted in brown under a celadon glaze, or have brown glazes; in addition, a limited quantity of white porcelains was made.

The Yi dynasty (1392–1910) brought impoverishment, and its wares are generally more plebeian in character: their apparent artlessness, however, masks a rugged dignity, which made them much prized for the Tea Ceremony in Japan. Apart from coarser wares, both white and blue-and-white porcelains were made in native shapes whose boldness more than compensates for their frequent lack of technical refinement. Painting in iron brown was transferred to porcelain; and admirable use was made also of copper red. While the history of these wares is still obscure, the inspired, carefree vigour of their brushwork earns them a place in the art that is virtually unique.

Indo-China

Ignorance still prevails concerning much of the older pottery found in that part of south-east Asia known as Indo-China. In Annam and Tonking (now in North Vietnam), buried wares dating from Han times onwards bear witness to early Chinese colonisation; but in Sung times (10th–13th centuries) wares of a light grey stoneware appear which are seemingly of local manufacture. These are found with rather brittle, pale celadon glazes applied over a white slip, or with a dark brown glaze; some brown-painted ware was also made. Common Annamese forms are bowls, often with shallow, in-curving sides decorated at times with fluting, small jars, and covered boxes. Various experimental wares followed; but by Ming times a somewhat coarse, near-porcellanous ware, painted in a distinctive style with strong, blackish blue, dominates the scene.

Even less is known from the remarkable Khmer kingdom in Cambodia: although some medieval stoneware jars of striking form, covered with a good, yellowish-brown glaze, are documented by excavations at the Royal Palace at Angkhor. More extensive evidence is, however, becoming available concerning the potteries of Siam (Thailand), where the Thai people, filtering slowly south from the Chinese border region, first became a political force in the 13th century, with their major capital at Sukhothai. In the 14th century a substantial manufacture of pottery developed at Sawankhalok further to the north, much of which was exported throughout south-east Asia. The ware is a hard, coarse-grained, light grey stoneware, most commonly covered with celadon glazes of a pale grassy or sea-green tint, which bear witness to strong Chinese influence. Its forms, which are simple and strong, yet elegant, are however stamped with the character of the region and show much variety: especially characteristic are globular jars or slender jarlets with ear loops for storing liquids, and open-mouthed jars with covers, often with simple incised decorations. Another type made here, known by custom as 'Kaliang ware', has a dark brown glaze: it includes many small pieces among which are votive figures of animals and humans. Other wares are neatly-potted covered boxes, etc., painted in iron-brown under a transparent, almost bluish glaze or, rarer specimens, under greyish-white glaze. A painted ware was made also at Sukothai itself; and after the abandonment of Sawankhalok in the mid-15th century, the tradition continued for a century or so at other kilns in the north.

181

182

183

184

185

181. Flower vase for the tea ceremony, stoneware with impressed designs and splashed celadon-type glaze. Iga ware. 17th century. Ht. 10½ in. (26·6 cm.). This Iga ware vase illustrates well the deliberate cultivation of 'rusticities' practised at the older country potteries in the 17th century under instruction from the Tea Masters. In less skilled hands, this aestheticism led later to the production of much tasteless work. Victoria and Albert Museum, London.

182. Setting for the Tea Ceremony: a Japanese Tea-house and garden. The essence of the Tea Ceremony is an atmosphere conducive to contemplation, and the interior of the room set apart for this purpose is furnished with the utmost simplicity: decorated only, perhaps, with the hanging scroll and flower vase placed in the recess known as *tokonoma*. This frugality is reflected also in the vessels traditionally used in the ceremony, for which an austere refinement has often been the rule.

183. Bowl, hard-baked ware with soft black glaze. Raku type. By Honami Kōetsu (1556–1637). Raku ware is peculiarly Japanese, devised for tea ceremony purposes. Essentially simple in form, often very low-fired, and covered with soft lead-glazes in sober colours, it provided an ideal medium for amateur potters. Kōetsu, to whom this bowl is attributed, practised various crafts and was perhaps the most influential scholar-artist of his day. Freer Gallery of Art, Washington.

184. Water jar, heavily-potted stoneware with uneven brown glaze. Bizen ware. About 17th century. Ht. 6⅞ in. (17 cm.). Bizen province contained one of the 'Six Old Kiln-centres' at which glazed stoneware manufacture developed in medieval times. Its massively-shaped pots of red-burnt clay, often left unglazed, have an honest, rustic vigour that conforms well with the early ideals of the Tea Ceremony. Victoria and Albert Museum, London.

185. Shallow rectangular bowl, stoneware with design cut through a grey slip under a semi-opaque white glaze. 'Grey Shino ware'. Momoyama period (1573–1614). L. 9⅛ in. (23·1 cm.). The plain white-glazed, brown-painted, and grey or red-slipped varieties of Shino were developed in the Mino region adjoining Seto, a major pottery centre of medieval times. Many of these wares were designed for Tea Ceremony use. Seattle Art Museum, Gift of Mrs John C. Atwood, Jr.

Japan

The vogue for Japanese pottery which grew up in the West in the last century fostered an enthusiasm which was often excessive, considering the frequent mediocrity of what was available. Disillusionment followed, bringing a reaction of neglect which is equally undeserved: for nowhere, perhaps, has the pursuit of aesthetic sensibility become more generally ingrained in a nation than in Japan; and as perceptive critics of that time had realised, their pottery-making offers much of unique interest and value.

The somewhat remote Japanese islands (see map, p. 59) harbour a population of mixed ethnic origins, combining mainland races with immigrants from more southerly, Pacific areas who may well have enriched the more sensuous strain apparent in her culture. Her prehistory is still imperfectly understood; over a period of three thousand years or more, however, much earthenware pottery is found, of a kind which is known collectively as 'Jomon' ware. It was made by the 'coiling' technique, in which strips of clay are progressively built up and then beaten into shape. The vessels are

186

187

186. Octagonal bowl, porcelain painted in enamel colours, in Kakiemon style. Arita ware. About 1700. Diam. 7⅞ in. (19·6 cm.). The development of the soft, astringent harmonies of the Kakiemon enamel palette during the second half of the century was matched by notable innovations in design. The bold asymmetry with which rocks and plants, landscapes and figure scenes were set on the fine porcelain surprised European eyes fed on Renaissance tradition. Many factories from Meissen onwards made careful copies. Victoria and Albert Museum, London.

187. *Arrival of the Southern Barbarians*: a Portuguese or Dutch ship docking in Japan. Detail from a six-fold screen, painted in colour and gold on paper. Japanese; about 1610–14. The Portuguese were foremost in trading with the Japanese during the 16th century, when the Jesuit mission also was highly active there. Thereafter they were displaced by the Dutch, who carried on an extensive entrepot trade round the southern shores of Asia, and who enjoyed a monopoly concession on Deshima Island from 1641.

Their patronage gave great encouragement to the nascent Japanese porcelain industry during the second half of the century. Painted for Japanese patrons, screens of this type convey a vivid sense of the amused curiosity that visiting Europeans aroused there at the time. Cleveland Museum of Art, Purchase, Leonard C. Hanna Jr. Bequest.

188. Three tea jars, stoneware with variegated brown glazes. *Centre*: from Satsuma province. *left*: Zeze (Omi province); *right*: perhaps Seto (Owari). 17th–18th centuries. Maximum ht. 3⅛ in. (8·1 cm.). Overlapping glazes in lustrous blacks and browns were much favoured. Victoria and Albert Museum, London.

188

189

190

191

189. Bottle, porcelain painted in underglaze blue with a design of doves on a maple branch. Arita ware: about 1675. Ht. 13⅛ in. (35 cm.). Porcelain manufacture began at Arita in the early 17th century, and was further encouraged from about 1650 by trade with the Dutch. Much blue-and-white came thus to Europe, decorated mostly in a somewhat heavier rendering of late Ming styles but displaying on occasion, as here, the original composition and spirited humour of native decorative design. Museum für Kunst und Gewerbe, Hamburg.

190. Dish, porcelain painted in red, blue and green enamels with figures in a landscape. Mark: *fuku* ('happiness') in underglaze blue. Kutani ware. Late 17th century. Diam. 13¾ in. (34·9 cm.). Porcelain was made at Kutani for the lords of Kaga during the second half of the 17th century. It is noted for its unconventional boldness in design, and the strength and brilliance of its enamelling palette. The design here of a scholar admiring pine, prunus and bamboo growing together (the *Three Friends*) is borrowed from China. British Museum, London.

191. Dish, porcelain painted in polychrome enamels and underglaze blue with a textile design. Nabeshima ware, made at Okawachi near Arita. About 1730. Diam. 7¾ in. (20 cm.). At this time the princely kilns of Nabeshima made a 'reserved' ware of exceptional refinement. Floral subjects, and textile patterns both abstract and representational, were drawn in blue and enriched with glowing washes of translucent enamel. Fondation Baur-Duret, Geneva.

192. Pair of bottles, porcelain painted in underglaze blue, enamels and gilt, in 'Imari' style. Arita ware: about 1700. Ht. 9¼ in. (23·4 cm.). The undeniable pomp of the Imari red, gold and blue style was plainly emphasised for Western taste, and is in contrast to the simplicity of the Kakiemon style. Japanese exports diminished after the re-expansion of the Chinese trade from 1700 onwards. Victoria and Albert Museum, London.

178 highly distinctive and a much-favoured type of form is an urn with tapering foot: they are decorated with elaborate patterns of ropework or with cord or mat impressions or incised work. The artistry expended on these aspects contrasts strangely with the use of an unrefined, lumpy clay, which appears deliberate: and it is worth noting here that such a fondness for 'naturalness' in materials persists throughout Japanese ceramic history.

Corresponding to the period of a new influx from the Continent which introduced bronze- and iron-working techniques is the so-called 'Yayoi' pottery of about 300 BC to AD 300. Reflecting these changes, and also the introduction of wheel-turning, it is in general less imaginative in style; bag-shaped jars and narrow-necked bottles are among the new forms, which are smoother in finish and bear simple incised geometric patterns. Pottery in continuation of this tradition is found in the extensive burials dating from the Tomb Mound Age (about AD 300–600). Most striking are the red clay 180 *haniwa*—originally hollow, pierced cylinders, numbers of which were erected on top of the burial tumuli, but which subsequently assumed a sculptural form. These swiftly executed studies of men, women and animals, in which the mood of the subject is unerringly caught in look and gesture are expressive works of no mean order.

Of a new type, reflecting advanced mainland techniques introduced via Korea late in the 5th century, are the Sue wares: hard-baked, grey stonewares on which splashes of grey-green celadon glaze sometimes developed when wood-ash from the fires fell on them. Buddhism now reached Japan and soon became the dominant religion, supported by a Court which in the Nara period (710–84) maintained close relations with T'ang China and absorbed much of its cultural influence. The Shōsōin storehouse at Nara—that unique

treasury of T'ang art and of Japanese artifacts, in which many precious objects deposited at that time have been preserved almost untouched—includes a number of ritual earthenware bowls, etc., that were lead-glazed in the dappled T'ang polychrome style.

When these relations ceased in the middle of the Heian period (794–1185) the Chinese influence on the arts declined, and a more relaxed style reappeared: the elegant jar of ash-glazed stoneware 176 with its sensitive, freely-incised plant designs, reflects this trend. In general, however, the ultra-refined aestheticism of the period is inadequately mirrored in the craft of pottery, which for some centuries more was to remain little regarded. It was during the late Kamakura (1185–1333) and early Muromachi (1333–1573) periods that glazed stoneware production began to develop new features in certain centres, which are known as the 'Six Old Kilns': the most interesting being those of Seto, Shigaraki, and Bizen. With coarser materials and inferior techniques the Seto potters in particular now strove to imitate the celadon and brown-glazed wares of late Sung and Yüan China, making handsome *mei-p'ing* vases, bottles and jars with pleasing streaky yellowish-green or caramel-brown glazes covering incised or stamped floral motifs.

It was from Sung China also that the practice of tea-drinking and with it the important cult of the 'Tea Ceremony' (*chanoyu*) came to Japan in these times. Always closely associated with the Zen sect of Buddhism, the ritual was at first conceived as an aid to meditation: but as the vogue spread the 'tea masters' came increasingly to act as influential arbiters of taste in general. In Momoyama times (1573–1614) it acquired a more definitive form under the influence of such masters as Sen no Rikyū, who enjoined a quiet and austere refinement alike in the conduct of the Ceremony, its utensils, the tea house

192

182 itself and its surroundings. The extension of the cult from the aristocracy to the growing middle class brought a new demand for the necessary vessels—tea jars and tea bowls, food dishes, water jars, flower vases and incense-boxes—which the potteries sought to meet in a suitable spirit.

184 Such wares as those of Bizen, heavy and rough-hewn, with their attractive, red-burning surface and partial brownish glazing, or the
181 splendidly battered wares of Iga and coarse-grained Shigaraki, embodied well this ideal of primitive dignity and austerity, as did the simple rice-bowls of the Korean countryside; and under aesthetic guidance their chance defects were painstakingly cultivated as virtues. A less demanding sophistication was developed in the varied wares of Seto, in Owari province, and of kilns in the adjoining
185 province of Mino. The several varieties of their 'Shino' wares: with thick, uneven, and crackled bubbly-white glazes or greyish-white glaze applied over a reddish slip, exploit refinements of form and texture in this vein with great skill. To patternings of slip and glaze were also added simple, bold designs painted in iron brown. The tea master, Furuta Oribe (died 1615), who inspired much of this
. 54) movement, gives his name to a most colourful class with rich green glaze, often allied with painted design in a strikingly original combination, as in the covered dish illustrated.

Among the most celebrated of the tea bowls themselves are those
183 made of the ware known as 'Raku': usually a very low-fired, coarse-grained pottery of seemingly rough, but ingeniously considered form, and with a soft, plain glaze generally in black, red or yellow. Fourteen generations of Raku potters trace their professional descent from the austere Chōjiro (1516–92): among them, Honami Kōetsu (1556–1637)—the celebrated lacquer-maker, calligrapher,

and sword-master, who is credited with the nobly shaped, black-glazed bowl shown. Other tea wares treasured by Japanese families 183 188 include the shapely little tea jars: stonewares of this kind with glassy black, brown or yellowish glazes, often juxtaposed or laid one upon another, were made in profusion at kilns in the Satsuma region of the southernmost island, Kyūshū. Here also, proximity to the mainland brought an influx of Korean potters whose Karatsu wares, coarse-grained and with sober glazes in more opaque cream, grey and brown tints, are of a pleasing simplicity, heightened sometimes by slight, plant-like brushwork in brown which recalls their native style.

It was in this same region that porcelain manufacture began early in the 17th century, following on the discovery of kaolin clay at Arita. Korean potters may have been involved, and certainly the earliest Arita painted blue-and-white bears a strong Korean stamp in form and decoration, although the influence of imported late Ming porcelains soon came to the fore. By fortunate chance the Dutch East India Company's trading post at Deshima, not far away, was 187 established in 1641, on the very eve of the Ming downfall; and for half a century or so their demand for porcelain gave further impetus to the industry. For this trade, such shapes as tankards and jugs were produced after European models, decorated in Chinese styles which, 189 however, were increasingly modified by the native genius for decorative invention. The introduction about this time of overglaze enamels, in a distinctive palette harmonising a soft red with turquoise green, yellow, and blue, is ascribed to the Kakiemon family. The Kakiemon designs are of great originality, displaying a 186 characteristic asymmetry which often leaves much of the surface entirely plain, so that the fine, milky-white porcelain and its clean-

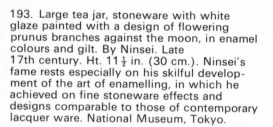

193

194

195

193. Large tea jar, stoneware with white glaze painted with a design of flowering prunus branches against the moon, in enamel colours and gilt. By Ninsei. Late 17th century. Ht. 11½ in. (30 cm.). Ninsei's fame rests especially on his skilful development of the art of enamelling, in which he achieved on fine stoneware effects and designs comparable to those of contemporary lacquer ware. National Museum, Tokyo.

194. Square dish, hard earthenware painted in dark brown under a greyish-cream glaze with a design of a bridge over an iris pool. Signed: Kenzan; the painting signed Kōrin. Early 18th century. W. 8⅜ in. (21 cm.). More of a ceramic artist than a potter *per se*, Kenzan preferred a somewhat low-fired ware for his painting, in subdued colours and a masterly style of broad, economical brushwork. This style is close to that of his brother, the famous painter, Kōrin, who in fact decorated this dish made by him. Freer Gallery of Art, Washington.

195. Incense jar, porcelain painted in under-glaze blue with landscapes and inscriptions in 'Shonsui' style. By Aoki Mokubei. Early 19th century. Ht. 3⅜ in. (8·3 cm.). Mokubei was one of a group of scholar-amateurs who turned to pottery at this time, producing a variety of wares with an antique flavour of revival. This jar reproduces the style of a special class of 17th-century Chinese blue-and-white known as 'Shonsui ware', which was itself designed to meet Japanese taste. Private Collection, Japan.

cut forms are shown to unusual advantage. They were much admired in Europe in the 18th century, where reproduction of 'the best Old Japan' seems to have been almost a mandatory test for nascent porcelain factories (see pp. 211–58). Less distinguished and in heavier taste are the so-called 'Imari wares' made for the Western trade, with a predominance of red and gilding supplementing the somewhat imperfect, purplish-toned underglaze blue; although these, too, still provide handsome enough decoration in many a country house or palace.

Porcelain was made also during the 17th century at Kutani, near Kanazawa in central Honshū. Much prized in Japan, it features deep green, yellow, purple and blue enamels, thickly applied to bold designs which include textile patterns, as well as birds and plants, and landscapes with figures; a brownish red and underglaze blue were also used. Much Kutani-style ware, however, is now thought to be Arita-made. The 18th-century Arita wares are less well-known in Europe. Among them are pieces depicting Dutch merchants and their ships, probably also some with the brocaded 'Japan' patterns copied at Derby and Worcester. The greatest refinement is seen in the Nabeshima wares, reserved for the lord of the region, which in the period from about 1716 to 1735 rivalled those of contemporary China in their perfection of material and design. The typical shallow dishes on which glowing enamels are matched with skilful under-glaze blue drawing, show off the startling originality of Japanese decorative design at this time. Hirado blue-and-white, also famed for its quality, is hardly identifiable before 19th-century pieces with designs of playing boys, painted in a fine, purplish blue.

These porcelains reflect the increasingly widespread and luxurious taste which developed in the decorative arts from the late 17th century, as prosperity spread outwards from such centres as Kyoto

and Edo (modern Tokyo). Many older potteries, however, remained active throughout the Tokugawa, or 'Edo' period (1603–1869); or alternatively their styles were revived and extended by later generations of descendants or imitators. Linked with Kyoto in particular, also, are the various elaborately enamelled wares often described as 'Old Kiyomizu'. Their origin is traditionally traced to the famous late 17th-century potter, Nonomura Ninsei. Ninsei's work shows great versatility; but in design it evidently owes much to the sumptuously ornate lacquerwork of his time, as shown by the large tea jar, with its combination of a smooth, cream-white glaze with neatly outlined, jewel-like enamelling and gilding. The equally celebrated Ogata Kenzan (1664–1743) was influenced at the outset by Ninsei, but turned away from the more showy aspects of his style. His painting in soft browns, blacks, blues and other pigments shows masterly brushwork in a bold, near-abstract manner, often accompanied by calligraphic inscriptions, which owes much to Zen Buddhist painting traditions, as well as to that of the decorative school to which his brother, the painter and lacquerer, Kōrin, belonged.

Such individual artist-potters were peculiar to Japan at this time; and they represent a new and important phenomenon. Among those who followed are Aoki Mokubei (1767–1833) and Ninami Dōhachi (1783–1855): both versatile experimenters who encouraged a revival of Chinese-style wares, including celadon, Ming blue-and-white and polychrome wares, and various others. Cheap industrialisation, however, was on the way, and from the mid-19th century led to the production of much tasteless, over-enamelled ware, particularly for export. As in Europe, it is the work of artist-potters, such as Hamada, Kawai and Tomimoto, that has preserved individuality of handling in the pottery of our century.

III The Lands of Islam

Introduction

The year AD 622, when the Prophet Muhammad fled from Mecca to Medina, is the beginning of the Muslim era. It marked a new phase not only in the political history of the Near East, but also in the cultures and arts of Asia, North Africa and even of Europe. Before Islam the Arabian peninsula was inhabited by heathen nomadic Arab tribes, constantly at war with each other. It was only the personal ability of Muhammad and his attractive ideology, Islam, which united these tribes and made them one of the most powerful and driving forces of history.

Soon after Muhammad's death in AD 632, the Arabs turned to the North and subdued the territories of Syria and Egypt, which were then provinces of the Byzantine Empire. They occupied Iraq and defeated the Sasanians, thus becoming rulers of Iran. In the West they conquered North Africa as far as the Atlantic and later crossed over to Spain.

The Arabs were victorious, but they had to adopt the civilisation and arts of subdued populations, since at that time they themselves had only a low level of culture. It was the skill and ingenuity of craftsmen from Syria, Coptic Egypt and Sasanian Iran, which were responsible for the building and decoration of the mosques and palaces of the Umayyad dynasty in Syria (661–750). Byzantine, Sasanian and also Coptic elements appear side by side in the colourful mosaics of the Dome of the Rock in Jerusalem and in the Great Mosque of Damascus. The hands of Christian painters and sculptors, and of Sasanian stucco workers are clearly recognisable in the wall frescoes of Quseyr Amra, some forty miles south-east of Amman, or in the stucco and stone carvings of Khirbat al-Mafjar in Jericho. There was no sign then of a new Islamic style.

In pottery, Islam first readily accepted and followed the ancient techniques and traditions of Near Eastern potters. The production of glazed quartz fritwares, known from Roman Egypt, continued. In Iran, Mesopotamia and Syria alkaline-glazed pottery had been used since Achaemenian times. Lead-glazed wares with relief decoration were also in use in the eastern provinces of the Roman Empire. The great change in the pottery of Islam did not take place until about AD 800. The new impetus was given by cultural contacts with T'ang China. In fact, the three main periods of Islamic pottery were all initiated by recurring waves of Chinese influence.

There were other circumstances which cannot be overlooked when evaluating the development and achievements of Islamic pottery. These factors were religious ones. It is a commonly accepted notion that Islam has never allowed the representation of living beings. Such a representation by an artist would be an imitation of God's creative power, the greatest of all sins in the eyes of Muslim orthodoxy.

But was there ever such a prohibition? One is unable to find any reference to it in the *Koran*, which is the most sacred book for the Muslims. It is only in the *Hadith* (The Traditions), a work recording the sayings and practices of the Prophet, that the representation of the images of human beings or animals is forbidden. Surviving monuments prove that the Umayyad caliphs disregarded any such prohibition. Iconoclastic doctrines appeared only from the 9th century onwards in Islam, and even then they were not strictly followed. Theologians certainly fully accepted them, but were unable to curb the creative abilities and imaginations of Muslim artists. It was particularly disregarded in Iran, where traditions of painting and sculpture go back to pre-Islamic times. Thus human and animal figures appeared in frescoes, metalwork and miniature painting throughout the Islamic period, but as a rule they were absent from religious buildings.

The potter's art was hardly affected by this prohibition, Islamic pottery being used only for secular purposes until the 13th and 14th centuries. It was then that tiles came to be used for the decoration of prayer niches. On these the designs were restricted to geometrical and floral patterns, with or without inscriptions, the Arabic script being widely used and appearing in two main forms: the angular *Kufic* and the cursive *Naskhi*.

Another Islamic prohibition forbade the use of vessels made of precious metals so that gold and silver should not have been used. Muslims, therefore, used instead clay vessels decorated with metallic pigments, thus further promoting the potter's art.

The history of Islamic pottery can be divided into three main periods: the early period from the 9th–11th centuries which was inspired by the imported T'ang white porcelains and stonewares; the medieval period from the 12th–14th centuries which was influenced by Sung white wares; and the later period from the 15th–19th centuries, a phase initiated by the blue-and-white wares of Ming China.

196 (*previous page*). Court scene from the manuscript *Diwan of Khwajn Kirmani*. Baghdad, 1396. Walls and floor are richly decorated with tile work, in which the Timurid and Safavid periods excelled. On the table are Chinese-style blue-and-white bottles. British Museum, London.

197

198

197. Bowl, lead-glazed and mottled. Mesopotamia, 9th century. Diam. 9¾ in. (24·8 cm.). Inside it is decorated with seven radiating lines in green, manganese-purple and yellow and is mottled in brown between the lines. Ashmolean Museum, Oxford.

198. Large water jar of unglazed lightly fired white clay. Mesopotamia, 8th century or earlier. Ht. 30 in. (76·2 cm.). This jar has an *appliqué* decoration showing birds, cable patterns and dots, typical of a large group of Mesopotamian unglazed wares. British Museum, London.

13. Dog of Fo (Buddhist lion), porcelain decorated in famille verte *enamels are especially rich in effect when applied to unglazed ('biscuit') porcelain, in the form of glazes. This technique was much used for writing table accessories, large ornamental vases, and figures of animals and deities. Fitzwilliam Museum, Cambridge.*

14

15

16

17

The Early Period (9th–11th centuries)
Mesopotamian pottery (9th–10th centuries)

As far as is known today, it was not until the 9th century AD that Arabs began to appreciate the aesthetic possibilities of pottery wares. Earlier wares were rather inferior unglazed vessels, or alkaline-glazed pottery, glazed quartz fritwares and lead-glazed wares, a direct continuation of pre-Islamic pottery traditions. Their decoration was restricted to simple designs, incised or in relief. Vessels were produced strictly for household requirements. This utilitarian attitude, however, gave way to a new artistic awareness, which was due mainly to Chinese influence.

In AD 750, when the Umayyads were overthrown by the Persian Abbasids, a great danger was mounting along the Eastern frontiers of the Empire. The Chinese, exploiting the internal troubles of the Arab Empire, tried to assert their authority in Transoxiana and occupied it. The Abbasids sent a big army against them and defeated the Chinese in AD 751. According to historical sources, some fifty thousand Chinese were killed and some twenty thousand taken prisoner. A Chinese prisoner, called Tu Huan, who was captured and later released, described how Chinese prisoners introduced the making of textiles, gold wares, painting and fine ceramics into Mesopotamia.

Chinese ceramics and textiles had reached the Near and Middle East even earlier, but from this time onwards Far Eastern influences became stronger and more apparent. This was the first cultural contact of the Islamic world with T'ang China (618–906). It was in

199

200

201

199. Large dish, covered with green lead-glaze and gold lustre over a relief decoration. Mesopotamia, 9th century. Diam. 8½ in. (21·6 cm.). The relief decoration presents part of a poem by Muhammad ibn Bakir, a poet of the Umayyad period, written in Kufic characters. British Museum, London.

14. Mina'i ware bowl, painted in polychrome over the glaze. Rayy or Kashan. 1218. Diam. 6¾ in. (17·1 cm.). The subject of this decoration is an unusual one since elephants are rarely depicted on mina'i ware. Edmund de Unger Collection, London.

15. 'Sari ware' bowl with straight flaring sides, painted in manganese purple, brown, yellow and green. Persian. Late 10th or early 11th century. Diam. 11½ in. (29·2 cm.). A walking bird is a characteristic theme on this type of pottery. Edmund de Unger Collection, London.

16. Large dish painted in polychrome lustre. Mesopotamia. 9th century. Diam, 13½ in. (34·3 cm.). Polychrome lustre ware was produced for only a short period. The decoration is confined to geometrical designs and simple floral patterns. Victoria and Albert Museum, London.

17. Large dish, painted in brownish lustre. Kashan, dated: AD 1210, and signed by Sayyid Shams al-Din al-Hasani. The decoration shows a human figure and fishes in a pool in the foreground, a man sleeping on the beach and facing him, his horse and five standing women. Freer Gallery of Art, Washington.

200. Bowl, tin-glazed and cobalt-blue painted. Mesopotamia, 9th century. Diam. 8⅖ in. (21·4 cm.). The cobalt-blue decoration on an opaque white ground shows a Sasanian fire-altar, one of the indications that Persian craftsmen were working in Mesopotamia. British Museum, London.

201. Large dish, tin-glazed and cobalt-blue painted. Mesopotamia, 9th century. Diam. 11¾ in. (29·8 cm.). The shape is unusual for this category of Mesopotamian wares; it has an interesting design; a stylised fish or perhaps a vase with leafy sprays. Ashmolean Museum, Oxford.

202

203

202. Bowl, painted in polychrome lustre. Mesopotamia, 9th century. Diam. 9½ in. (24·1 cm.). The decoration inside shows a peacock painted in two shades of brown and greenish gold lustre. Dots and chevron patterns decorate the plumage of the bird; the background is dotted. Ashmolean Museum, Oxford.

203. Small bowl painted in polychrome lustre. Mesopotamia, 9th century, Diam. 5½ in. (14 cm.). The Sasanian wing motif is represented here in ruby, brown and yellow lustre. Edmund de Unger collection, London.

204 205 206

207 208 209

204. Bowl painted in greenish-yellow lustre. Mesopotamia, late 9th or early 10th century. Diam. 8⅞ in. (22·5 cm.). The lustre decoration depicts a human figure in cross-legged position. The representation of the figure and details of the design reveal a strong Central Asian influence. An inscription in Kufic appears behind the head: 'amala' ('made by' or 'the work of' someone, but the name is not given). Ashmolean Museum, Oxford.

207. Large dish, splashed and *sgraffiato* ware. Nishapur or Samarqand, late 9th or early 10th century. Diam. 16 in. (40·6 cm.). An extensive scroll design appears in *sgraffiato* under the green stripes and splashes of orange. Ashmolean Museum, Oxford.

205. Bowl, slip-painted ware; probably Samarqand, late 9th or early 10th century. Diam. 10½ in. (26·7 cm.). A Kufic inscription appears in manganese-purple on white ground slip with contour panels outlined in tomato-red; there are half-palmettes in the centre. Victoria and Albert Museum, London.

208. Bowl, slip-painted ware; probably Nishapur, late 9th or early 10th century. Diam. 10½ in. (26·7 cm.). Inside there is a Kufic inscription in white on a manganese-purple background. Victoria and Albert Museum, London.

206. Large dish, slip-painted. Samarqand, late 9th or early 10th century. Diam. 13⅞ in. (35·2 cm.). The decoration comprises three palmettes in the middle in tomato-red veined in white, scroll designs on the rim and Kufic inscription in manganese-purple. The inscription is the repetition of the word *al-yumn* 'happiness'. Victoria and Albert Museum, London.

209. Large dish, slip-painted. Nishapur, 10th century. Diam. 10⅝ in. (27 cm.). A comparatively rare design appears on this dish: a bottle with a long neck and an S-shaped handle in the middle, flowers and palmettes above and on either side and a Kufic inscription below. British Museum, London.

Mesopotamia, at Samarra, the capital of the Abbasids between 836 and 883, that the earliest Chinese import wares and their local imitations were excavated.

Though Chinese import wares came both by the sea route and overland, on the 'Silk Route', they could hardly be expected to satisfy the growing demand for them at the luxurious Caliphal court and from the ruling classes of the Arab Empire. Moreover, they were very expensive. It was greatly to the credit of the Abbasid caliphs and princes that they became interested in fine ceramics, gave their support to local craftsmen and set up workshops in different parts of Mesopotamia, so that soon the imitation of Chinese import wares was widespread.

Excavations at Samarra have unearthed Chinese stoneware, white porcelain and splashed or mottled ware, all products of the T'ang dynasty. At Samarra, Susa and Kish Chinese wares were found side by side with local imitations. But the local products soon ceased to be simple imitations. Though the craftsmen of Mesopotamia were unable to find the ingredients of true porcelain, they did eventually arrive at fine glazes which gave the surface of their vessels the appearance of Chinese stoneware or even of porcelain. They also developed the technique of lustre-painting, a momentous discovery, which was to remain a monopoly of Near Eastern potters for centuries, (see pp. 75–6).

Mesopotamian wares may be classified into two main groups: unglazed and glazed wares. The first and numerically largest group appeared in a great variety of vessels: bowls, vases and huge jars made of buff or whitish clay. The decoration which included animal and bird motifs, dots and cable patterning, was moulded, incised or stamped on the body, or in applied relief. Water jars were lightly fired and very porous in order to help evaporation, thus cooling the liquid within. These unglazed wares were produced continuously and appeared in every part of the Islamic world. There is hardly any

198

variation in their form, paste and decoration, which makes identification and dating difficult.

Among the more luxurious glazed wares three types can be established, two of which appear as imitations of Chinese porcelains and stonewares. The first comprises the lead-glazed splashed or mottled wares. The fine red body of such wares was covered with white slip over which the colourless or yellowish, transparent lead-glaze was applied. The range of ornament was limited and was applied under the glaze in green, yellow or manganese-purple. Since lead-glaze becomes fluid in the kiln, pigments were apt to run together. They had, therefore, to be used either in thick wide lines or in large areas. These wares are quite frequently very close to Chinese originals, though they can easily be distinguished from them by their material.

Muslim potters, however, were not satisfied by mere imitation. Frequently incised *sgraffiato* design appears under the glaze. On some pieces eagles or other birds appear in *sgraffiato*. Mottled wares similar to the Mesopotamian, with or without *sgraffiato*, have been found in several sites elsewhere. They were first discovered during excavation at Susa and at Nishapur in Iran. They have also been found among the ruins of Fustat in Egypt.

In this same group of lead-glazed pottery, some vessels had relief decoration. This type was known in Egypt long before Islamic times. The technique did not only survive there, but was further developed by Muslim potters. On Mesopotamian wares found in the palaces of Samarra, the decoration consists of geometrical patterns, birds or Kufic inscriptions. What is probably more significant is that on some of these examples lustre-painting is already present.

The second type of Mesopotamian glazed wares is the opaque white tin-glazed painted pottery, which can be dated to the 9th or early 10th century. These wares were painted under the glaze with cobalt-blue, antimony-yellow or copper-green. The decoration is usually confined to floral patterns or to Kufic inscriptions. The Kufic inscription most commonly found is the repetition of the word *baraka* (blessing). T'ang influence may also be observed in these vessels, the commonest shape of which is the convex-sided bowl, placed on a shallow foot-ring. Some Hellenistic flavour can be discovered in their shapes, but other foreign influences, particularly Sasanian, are also apparent. Possibly Persian craftsmen were present and active in Mesopotamia among whom Zoroastrian traditions were still very much alive. Tin-glazed painted pottery has, in fact, been found in several parts of Iran, but it seems that the decoration on Persian pieces was restricted to green. Similar types were also excavated at Fustat in Egypt. In Mesopotamia, apart from convex-sided bowls, vases and ewers are also known, painted in cobalt-blue and green. The ewers appear to be copies of Sasanian metal vases.

The third and probably the most interesting group of glazed Mesopotamian pottery is that with lustre-painting. The technique probably has its origin in pre-Islamic Egypt, where it appears on glass. In the lustre technique, metallic pigments are painted over a white opaque tin-glaze, covering the closely grained greyish-white or buff earthenware. This technique results in a surface which produces glittering reflections. The lustrous pigment was fixed on the glaze by a second firing under reducing conditions, after which a thin metallic film appeared evenly over the surface. It was used on white grounds in silhouette and was usually surrounded by a narrow white margin.

The colour range of lustre was very wide in the earlier period, varying from vivid ruby through shades of brown to chartreuse and lemon. As time went on the colour range became more and more restricted until, by the beginning of the 10th century, it was reduced to brown or yellow monochrome.

The technique was applied on wall-tiles, as well as on bowls, dishes and ewers. Polychrome lustre tiles were excavated at the Jausaq al-Khaqani and al-Ashiq palaces in Samarra. Similar tiles decorate the wall surfaces around the prayer niche in the Great Mosque of Qairawan (Kairouan) in Tunisia. These tiles, according to historical sources, were exported from Baghdad in the second half

210. Bowl, 'Sari type'; Persian, late 10th or early 11th century. Diam. 7½ in. (19·1 cm.). A bird and flowers on long stalks are depicted in green, tomato-red and manganese-purple on white ground slip under transparent lead-glaze. Victoria and Albert Museum, London.

211. Small bowl, painted in gold lustre. Egypt, Fatimid period, 11th century. Diam. 3½ in. (8·9 cm.). The design depicts an eagle and a heron, the appearance of which is so classical that they give the impression of having originated a few centuries earlier. In fact, Byzantine influence is clearly apparent in Egyptian lustre-ware painting at this time. The two birds are painted in the masterly way characteristic of late Fatimid lustre decoration. Edmund de Unger Collection, London.

210

211

212

213

214

212. Large bowl, painted in brownish lustre.
Egypt, Fatimid period, 11th century. Diam.
15 in. (38·1 cm.). A bull is shown here
against a foliage background, and there are
Kufic inscriptions round the rim. Edmund de
Unger Collection, London.

213. Bowl, lustre-painted; Egypt, Fatimid
period, first half of the 12th century. Diam.
8¾ in. (22·2 cm.). A Coptic priest is painted in
gold lustre against an opaque white background, holding a lamp on chains in his right
hand. The vessel is signed at the base by
Sa'ad, a famous artist of the period. Victoria
and Albert Museum, London.

214. Dish, lustre-painted. Egypt, Fatimid
period, late 11th or early 12th century. Diam.
9½ in. (24·1 cm.). The decoration—representing a cock fight—is reserved in white against
a gold lustre background. Edmund de Unger
Collection, London.

of the 9th century. The decoration of polychrome lustre tiles
consists of geometric ornaments, chevron patterns, cross-hatching,
dots, half-palmettes and what is known as the 'Sasanian wing motif'.
Human and animal figures are notably absent from polychrome
lustre tiles and vessels, though the excavators of Samarra came upon
a few wall-tiles representing cocks and eagles, drawn in a naturalistic
way. One polychrome lustre bowl with a peacock painted on it is
the only known example in existence.

So far no pottery kiln has been discovered in Samarra. It is
believed that Baghdad and Basra, on the Persian Gulf, were the main
pottery-making centres in Mesopotamia. According to historical
sources, there were serious uprisings and revolutions in Basra
between 870 and 880. These political uncertainties and the rise of the
Tulunid dynasty (868–905) in Egypt attracted some of the potters to
emigrate there. They seem to have settled down in Fustat and at
Behnasa. Others appear to have emigrated to Iran, particularly to
Susa, where a great number of lustre wasters have been excavated by
French archaeologists. Excavations at the above-mentioned two
places in Egypt also revealed polychrome lustre wasters. Hardly any
complete vessels in the polychrome technique, however, survive
from Egypt and Iran. During the last few years three intact polychrome bowls have turned up in Iran. Two of these, however, show
close affinities with Behnasa wares. The third example, a conical
bowl in the British Museum, closely resembles Mesopotamian
bowls, particularly the illustrated example of a small bowl with the

Sasanian wing motif, bearing out this interchange of influences.

Later 9th- and 10th-century Mesopotamian lustre wares were
simpler in their colour scheme, although the designs had grown
more complicated. Human and animal figures appear on them in a
rather primitive form, painted in silhouette against a dotted background. A bowl in the British Museum depicts a standing figure, but
more interesting is the design inside another bowl in the Ashmolean
Museum. The centrally seated human figure in a cross-legged
position has long hair and a peaked cap and is holding a curious
object resembling a vase with flowers in its right hand. There is a
hammer-like object in the left hand and the legs are decorated with
scroll patterns. The representation of this type of figure and the
minute detail convey a strong Central Asian flavour. Paintings in
Central Asia depict Boddhisattvas in a similar manner. The background is dotted and, following the usual treatment of monochrome
lustre wares of the period, the rim is edged with a scalloped pattern.
This bowl is considered to belong to the early 10th century, and is
most likely of Mesopotamian origin. It was during the early years of
the 10th century that the Turks, arriving in ever-increasing numbers
in Mesopotamia, introduced Central Asian taste and patterns into
Islamic art as a whole.

By the middle of the 10th century the production of lustre wares
was declining in Mesopotamia. They were, however, made in Egypt
and reappeared in a much more refined and sophisticated form and
design during the Fatimid period, as will be discussed below.

203
16 (p. 72)

202

203

204

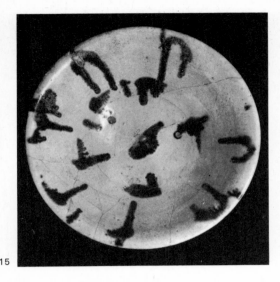

215

216

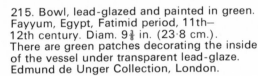

217

215. Bowl, lead-glazed and painted in green.
Fayyum, Egypt, Fatimid period, 11th–
12th century. Diam. 9⅜ in. (23·8 cm.).
There are green patches decorating the inside
of the vessel under transparent lead-glaze.
Edmund de Unger Collection, London.

216. Large dish, *sgraffiato*; Amol region,
Persian late 10th or early 11th century.
Diam. 11⅛ in. (28·3 cm.). Red fine clay
covered with white slip and colourless glaze;
the decoration is in simple *sgraffiato*
depicting a reptile-like animal in the centre
and doves in six panels. The rim is painted in
green. Ashmolean Museum, Oxford.

217. Large dish, *champlevé* ware; Garrus
district, Persia, probably 11th century. Diam.
1 ft. 1 9/10 in. (35·4 cm.). The *champlevé*
decoration depicts a horseman against a
scroll background. The clumsy figure and the
way the face is rendered reflect some
influence from 10th-century Mesopotamian
lustre wares. British Museum, London.

Slip-painted pottery of Iran and Afghanistan (9th–11th centuries)

At about the same time that early Mesopotamian pottery was
flourishing, another important class of pottery emerged in Iran and
Afghanistan. At one time these wares were known as 'East Persian
wares' or 'slip-painted wares of Nishapur and Samarqand', and they
were closely associated with the reign of the Samanid dynasty
(847–999), which ruled over Turkestan and Eastern Iran.

Recent archaeological work in Iran and Afghanistan has revealed
that this type of pottery was present not only in Eastern Iran and
Turkestan, but also in the southern provinces of Iran and in the
North-West. Excavations by the French Archaeological Mission
also uncovered great quantities of the slip-painted pottery at various
sites in Afghanistan.

Excavations in the 1930s by Soviet archaeologists in Afrasiyab (a
suburb of Samarqand) and in other places of Soviet Central Asia,
and those sponsored by the Metropolitan Museum at Nishapur,
revealed different types of the slip-painted wares. These discoveries
enable us to distinguish between products of Afrasiyab and
Nishapur, while the slip-painted wares of Afghanistan and southern
Iran come closer to Nishapur types.

The clay of Samarqand pottery is generally red, while Nishapur
and South Persian vessels are made of buff, sandy earthenware.

Both types are fine-grained. There are not so many kinds of
utilitarian wares among them as is the case with Mesopotamian
pottery. They are mainly bowls, with a projecting base, large dishes
with a flat rim, and sometimes large plates with vertical rims.

While Mesopotamian pottery developed under strong Chinese
influence, such influence is hardly perceptible in slip-painted wares.
Only one group reveals Chinese features—the splashed and mottled 207
pottery which has already been discussed in connection with the
Mesopotamian wares. The type was found in abundance both in
Samarqand and in Nishapur. Most of them carry incised (*sgraffiato*)
decoration under the glaze, showing scroll designs or eagles with 207
spread wings.

The most charming products among the slip-painted wares are
those covered with white slip under transparent colourless glaze, 205, 206,
decorated usually in brown, manganese-purple or tomato-red. The 208
main decorative element is the Kufic script. The inscriptions are
mainly benedictory, wishing peace, prosperity and long life to their
owners. No historical inscription appears yet in Islamic pottery. In
Nishapur, it seems, they employed large bold lettering and ran the
inscription round the rim, sometimes with a bird in the centre, as on
vessels produced at Samarqand.

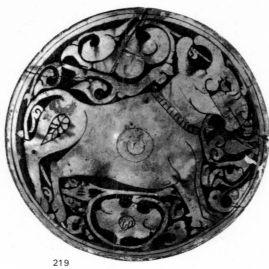

218. Large dish, *sgraffiato* painted in green and brown. Amol region, Persia, late 12th or early 13th century, Diam. 10 in. (25·4 cm.). This vessel is an interesting example of the late Amol *sgraffiato* ware. The incised decoration represents either a stylised plant motif or a Zoroastrian fire-altar (see fig. 200), but here it appears in an abstract style. Victoria and Albert Museum, London.

219. Bowl, *champlevé* ware; Garrus district, Persia, 11th century. Diam. 7 in. (17·8 cm.). Another example of *champlevé* ware, representing an animal; such animals are frequent and favourite subjects of *champlevé* vessels. Usually there is a floral or geometrical design on the body of the animals shown in brown or tomato-red, which gives a very pleasing effect. Edmund de Unger Collection, London.

220. Large dish, 'Aghkand ware', Persia, 12th or early 13th century. Diam. 10 in. (25·4 cm.). It is decorated with incised lines through a white slip depicting an eagle painted in brown and yellow. Victoria and Albert Museum, London.

205, 206, 209

Other dominant decorative elements, characteristic of both areas, are half-palmettes or palmettes arranged into a central medallion and scroll patterns. A comparatively rare design comprising flowers, palmettes, a Kufic inscription and a central representation of a bottle appears on a 10th-century dish from Nishapur, now in the British Museum. Fragments of similarly decorated vessels were found at Nishapur during the Metropolitan Museum's excavations in the mid-thirties. They also date probably from the 10th century. Later on inscriptions became more and more illegible. Having been used exclusively for decorative purposes, the lettering is submerged in the general decorative scheme.

There must have been some attempt to reproduce lustre-painting, since there are some rare examples of lustre imitation including a bowl from Samarqand in the Victoria and Albert Museum. These pieces, however, show that they were never able to reach the high quality of the Mesopotamian and Egyptian lustre technique.

An interesting, though rather primitive type of slip-painted pottery is known exclusively from the Nishapur region. Human figures, birds and animals are represented in yellow, brown and

green colours outlined in manganese-purple under a transparent lead-glaze. The clumsily drawn figures point to some connection with Abbasid monochrome lustre wares of the early 10th century in Mesopotamia.

Another group of slip-painted wares are also related to the Nishapur pottery. These are known as 'Sari wares'. The small town of Sari is in Mazanderan near to the south-east corner of the Caspian sea. Sari wares appear mostly in the form of conical bowls on which are depicted walking birds, flowers on long stalks and pseudo-Kufic inscriptions. The outside of these vessels is usually unglazed and free from any slip.

210
15

Sari wares also appear in the form of large dishes. The designs are simple, but a pleasing effect is achieved through their simplicity and harmony of colours. This type of pottery was apparently made at a number of places in Mazanderan, among them in Amol and Gurgan. Recent excavations by the author at the site of Tammisha, twenty-five miles west of Gurgan, produced a number of slip-painted sherds of the Nishapur and Sari types. These can be stratigraphically dated to the 10th and 11th centuries.

221. Bowl, white very thin composite material covered with white glaze, Persia, 12th century, found in Gurgan. Diam. 6 in. (15·2 cm.). The translucency of the body is enhanced by the openwork of small holes which are filled by the glaze. Potters of

the Seljuq period of Iran were very much impressed by Chinese Sung porcelain and by this method tried to imitate it and achieve its translucency. Raymond Ades Collection, Surrey.

222. Bowl, Seljuq white ware; probably Rayy, Persia, 12th century. Ht. 4½ in. (11·4 cm.). The vessel is decorated with Naskhi inscription and a bird surrounded by pierced holes filled with the ivory-white glaze. Edmund de Unger Collection, London.

223. Bowl, Seljuq white ware; probably Rayy, Persia, 12th century. Diam. 6½ in. (16·5 cm.). The vessel is incised and pierced; three blue lines were added under the transparent white glaze to enhance the decoration. Victoria and Albert Museum, London.

224. Large dish with monochrome blue glaze. Probably Rayy, 12th century. Diam. 15⅒ in. (38·3 cm.). The incised decoration underneath the glaze shows an eagle outlined in red against coiling foliage. British Museum, London.

225. Ewer, covered with turquoise-blue glaze. Probably Rayy, 12th century. Ht. 9 in. (22·9 cm.). Pear-shaped with an openwork outer body, displaying Naskhi inscription and scrollwork. Ashmolean Museum, Oxford.

223

224

The Fatimid pottery of Egypt (969–1171)

It has already been mentioned (see page 76) that the rise of the independent Tulunid dynasty in Egypt attracted a great number of artists from Mesopotamia, who settled down in Fustat (Old Cairo) and at Behnasa in Upper Egypt. The Tulunid rule came to an end in 905, but soon a new dynasty, the Fatimids, emerged. The Fatimid dynasty was actually founded in Tunisia. They occupied Egypt in 969 and remained in power until 1171.

Islamic pottery made great progress under the Fatimids. Lustre wares in particular were favoured and produced. At the beginning their style was very similar to that of Mesopotamia—simple, rather naive human figures and animals appearing in silhouette. It is only by their material that one can distinguish them from Mesopotamian wares. The clay is buff or reddish, sandy and coarse, as against the much finer whitish body of the Mesopotamian vessels.

Fantastic birds, animals, human figures are the most popular subjects on Fatimid lustre ware. Towards the end of the period these were painted in a very accomplished and refined style. The lustre is yellowish-greenish-gold. At the end of the 11th century colours became increasingly sombre, tending more and more to brown. Byzantine art, particularly painting, is reflected in their decoration. A famous artist was Sa'ad, whose name is signed on a great number of vessels. Sa'ad, it seems, was active during the second half of the 11th and early 12th century. He painted in dark yellow or brownish lustre.

Christian subjects are not uncommon on Fatimid pottery. The figure of Christ appears on a lustre sherd which is in the Museum of Islamic Art in Cairo. Some other lustre vessels depict scenes from the life of contemporary Egypt as for example a cock fight, in which the figures show how far Islamic art had advanced in a matter of three centuries.

A different type of pottery was produced in the Fayyum area. At first these wares greatly resembled Mesopotamian splashed and mottled wares. Later on, during the 11th and early 12th centuries, the decoration underwent a considerable change. The designs during this period consisted mainly of radiating lines in green, yellow or brown under a clear lead-glaze.

In 1171, the Fatimids were overthrown by the Ayyubids, who in turn ruled over Egypt and Syria until 1250, when they were succeeded by the Mamluks.

11–2
213

214

215

225

The Medieval Period (12th–14th centuries)

Sgraffiato wares of North and North-West Iran (11th–13th centuries)

At the beginning of the 11th century, or perhaps even towards the end of the 10th century, new pottery centres sprang up in the northern and north-western mountainous parts of Iran, in the Caspian borderland, in Azerbaijan and Kurdistan. Wares which have been found in these regions are of special interest since they are unlike any other Islamic pottery. This is due mainly to their decorative patterns, which differ from those on the wares so far discussed. They reveal a strong Sasanian influence, which is hardly surprising. Though the Arabs conquered the Sasanian Persian Empire in the 7th century and in consequence the majority of the Persians were converted to Islam, Sasanian traditions nevertheless lingered on sometimes taking the form of Zoroastrianism, particularly in the remoter areas of the country, where they survived for centuries. One of the strongholds of Zoroastrian tradition was centred in Mazanderan, which was long ruled by native princes and where owing to the difficult terrain Islam had failed to penetrate.

It was in this part of Iran that pottery-making was taken up as soon as the craft began to decline in Samarqand and Nishapur. The wide distribution of the early slip-painted ware had failed to touch the *sgraffiato* technique, uninfluenced either by the painted ware or by the earlier colour-splashed *sgraffiato* wares such as are known from 9th–10th century Mesopotamia or eastern Iran. Evidently their first inspiration drew upon engraved metalwork. This *sgraffiato* tradition, referred to by the late Arthur Lane as 'rustic *sgraffiato*', bridged the gap between the early Mesopotamian and slip-painted ware on the one hand, and the 'fine Seljuq' ware on the other, chronologically overlapping both.

Three main types of *sgraffiato* ware can be distinguished: the simple *sgraffiato*, also known as 'Amol ware'; '*champlevé*' ware of the Garrus district; and that known as 'Aghkand ware'.

The first type, the simple *sgraffiato*, displays a style of decoration that is simply incised in the white slip and then glazed. It is attributed to Amol in Mazanderan, hence sometimes called 'Amol ware', although the name 'Amol' covers the products of several kilns in many other parts of Mazanderan. The earlier pieces seem to have been inspired by Sasanian and post-Sasanian metalwork. They may be dated to the turn of the 10th century by the similarity of their design to the above-mentioned metal vessels. A great number of

dishes, conical bowls, plates and ewers are known to have been made in this technique. Decoration on these wares generally comprised fantastic animals or birds incised in a white ground slip under colourless glazes while the rims were painted in green. Later Amol products, which can be dated to the 12th or early 13th century, show the incised lines painted in green or brown, and there is change in the decorative design, which became more stylised.

Sherds with simple *sgraffiato* designs were recently unearthed during the excavation of Tammisha near present-day Gurgan. These specimens were almost identical to Amol pieces and represent both the earlier and later types. The same simple *sgraffiato* has been found in southern Iran in the Kirman region. Here the body always seems to be covered with transparent yellowish or brownish glaze.

The second type of *sgraffiato*, the so-called '*champlevé*' ware, was long known as *gabri* ware, as it was believed that it had some connection with Zoroastrian fire-worshippers, who were called Gabri. On *champlevé* ware large areas of the slip are cut away to form the design, thus revealing the usually darker clay of the body. The glaze itself is coloured in green or brown. Animals or human figures, naively drawn against a scroll background, decorate these vessels. On some pieces Kufic inscriptions also appear. The production of *champlevé* ware is known to have been in the Garrus district of Kurdistan (western Iran) or in Zenjan. Excavations in a 13th to 14th-century *caravanserai* in Bisitun brought to light *champlevé* sherds which had green glazes and were decorated with Kufic inscriptions. At the Tammisha excavations again a great number of *champlevé* fragments turned up with scrolls and Kufic characters.

The third type of *sgraffiato* is the 'Aghkand ware', the name 'Aghkand' again denoting more than one kiln. Here the designs are similarly incised in lines into the slip, just as in simple *sgraffiato*, but they serve the sole purpose of preventing the pigment from running over the pattern, a technique derived from metal-working. This is, once more, borrowed from metal techniques as practised in *cloisonné*. The colours on the Aghkand pieces are green, brown and yellow. The usual theme is a centrally placed animal surrounded by birds, hares or floral designs. The type probably dates to the 12th or 13th century. Wares of similar character were also produced in Egypt, Syria and Byzantine territories in subsequent centuries.

226

227

226. Albarello, *laqabi* ware. Rayy or Kashan, Persia, 12th century. Ht. 7¾ in. (19·7 cm.). The body is decorated by scrollwork forming round medallions, alternately filled by lions and birds. Victoria and Albert Museum, London.

227. Vase, black silhouette-painted ware. Rayy, Persia, second half of the 12th century. Ht. 13⅜ in. (34·6 cm.). The finely carved animals on the shoulder are characteristic of the styles of the decoration on Seljuq silhouette wares. Edmund de Unger Collection, London.

Seljuq fine wares of Iran (12th–13th centuries)

The Seljuq Turks from Central Asia overran Iran, Iraq, Syria and Asia Minor and thus built up a great empire in the middle of the 11th century. Iran enjoyed material prosperity under the Seljuqs and as a consequence the arts and literature flourished. In fact, for architecture and the decorative arts it was a Golden Age. The coming of the Seljuqs brought about great changes in Persian pottery-making. First of all, under the influence of Chinese import wares of the Sung

dynasty (960–1279) a new white composite material was introduced. There was a gradual evolution in the methods of decorating this white material—by carving, staining the glaze, painting under the glaze, painting in lustre over the glaze, and as a final step painting in polychrome over the glaze.

Finally, it must be stressed that the interruption caused by the successive Mongol invasions during the early twenties of the

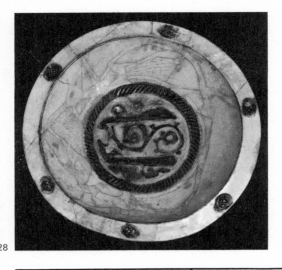

228. Large dish, carved and polychrome painted, known as laqabi ware; Rayy or Kashan, Persia, 12th century. Diam. 13½ in. (34·3 cm.). The decoration of this vessel is rather unusual for this type of pottery: it presents a pseudo-Kufic inscription among scrolls. Edmund de Unger Collection, London.

229. Tankard, black silhouette-painted ware. Rayy, Persia, second half of the 12th century. Diam. 5⅞ in. (14·9 cm.). A Kufic inscription is carved out of the black slip under clear turquoise-green glaze. The inscription reads: *baraka li-sahibihi* 'blessing to the owner'. Victoria and Albert Museum, London.

228   229

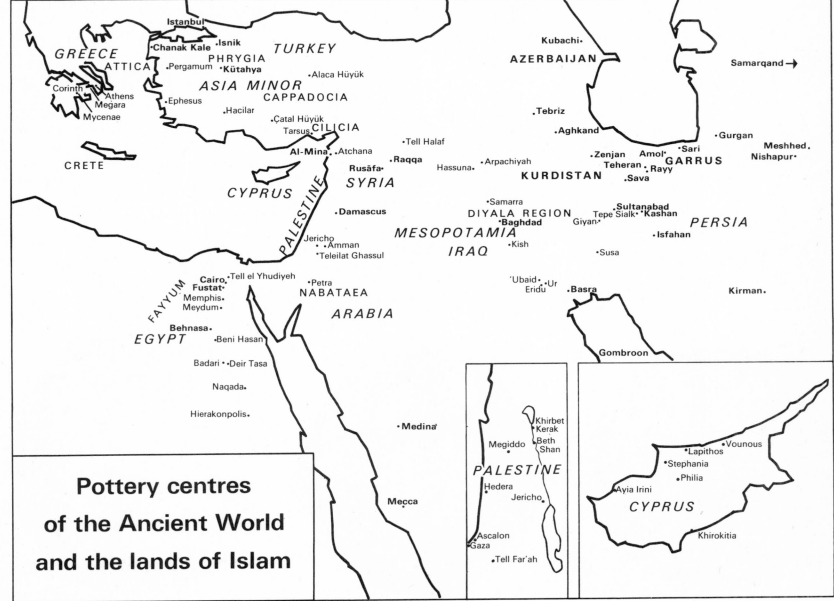

Pottery centres of the Ancient World and the lands of Islam

13th century did not prevent a partial survival of the Seljuq tradition, particularly in the Kashan lustre and underglaze-painted ware, late into the 14th century.

Seljuq fine wares can be classified into seven groups: white ware; ware with coloured monochrome glazes; ware with carved decoration and polychrome glazes, known as *laqabi* ware; silhouette-painted ware; underglaze-painted ware; lustre-painted ware; and overglaze-painted ware of the so-called *mina'i* and *lajvardina* types.

The most striking Sung pottery to earn admiration in the Near East was the white porcelain known as *Ting* ware. The Persian craftsmen began to imitate it during the 12th century with their 'white ware', producing varieties of finely executed bowls, jugs, ewers, vases and tankards, all of which have a white, very hard, thin body. This was an attempt to imitate the qualities of true porcelain, the secret of which was unknown to the Persian potters. They did not have recourse to simple clay, but used a new composite paste of powdered quartz and alkaline frit. The glaze was also made of a similar alkaline frit, thus ensuring that it would adhere. Occasionally these vessels are so thin that they seem nearly translucent, an impression which is further heightened by perforating them. Small holes in the body were filled by the glaze, producing tiny windows, giving the impression of glass. The fine and thin material and the ivory white glaze is so perfect that the overall effect is that of porcelain.

The decorations employed on these white wares consisted mainly of incised floral designs; sometimes blue spots or lines were added. Occasionally, finely-drawn Naskhi inscriptions were added, carved or incised into the body before glazing. In several instances the ornament was moulded, a much cheaper and quicker way of accomplishing fine specimens. The Seljuq white wares with their minutely executed drawings, their fine transparent glazes and elegant shapes are the pre-eminent achievement of Persian pottery. The production of white wares is attributed to Rayy and Kashan, the two great Persian pottery centres, and can be dated to the middle and second half of the 12th century.

The most numerous group of Seljuq pottery is that with coloured monochrome glazes. The colour scheme is fairly wide, ranging from turquoise-blue through different shades of blue and green to aubergine, purple and dark brown. The glaze appears on a variety of vessels from masterpieces to simple domestic utensils. There are large dishes with carved, low-relief decoration displaying carefully drawn birds against coiling foliage. The patterns are similar to those already encountered on Seljuq white wares; these are carved, incised or moulded under the glaze. In this group, however, piercing is not general, occurring only on finer specimens. Here the openwork is used in a masterly way.

There is a special, very charming group of these monochrome glazed wares, made in figural forms. Human and animal figures, including men on horseback, are coated with cobalt-blue, green or turquoise-blue glazes. Coloured monochrome-glazed wares were common all over the Near East and were produced at a number of places. Better pieces are, however, attributed to Rayy and Kashan, and can be dated to the period from the middle of the 12th to the second half of the 13th century.

Persian potters made another bold experiment with their *laqabi* wares when they attempted to paint carved surfaces with polychrome glazes, separating the different glazes either by raised or incised lines. The glaze is applied directly on to the white ground. This technique must be regarded as a variant of the method encountered on 'Aghkand' wares (see page 80) and was used on large dishes. The decoration frequently displays heavily drawn birds, usually peacocks surrounded by plant designs or cable pattern. Less familiar designs comprise pseudo-Kufic inscriptions against a scroll background. The name Persian dealers gave to this type of ware, '*laqabi*', means 'painted'. They are attributed to Rayy and Kashan and dated to the 12th century.

The use of thick coloured slip, out of which the decoration is carved right down to the body, cannot be considered a new method. As has already been seen, it was used by the potters of north and north-western Iran. By the end of the 12th century, however, Rayy and Kashan potters re-introduced the method on their 'silhouette-painted' wares. After carving out the designs from the thick black slip, they covered the whole surface with either a turquoise, or a crackled ivory glaze, thereby succeeding in imparting a rather pleasing effect. The decoration comprises plant designs, Kufic or Naskhi characters or, on finer specimens, human and animal figures. These wares are attributed to Rayy and their date is considered to be the second half of the 12th century.

As a further step in the development of wares that had earlier been painted under the glaze with slip, a new type of underglaze painted wares emerged in Seljuq Iran. Black, blue and turquoise pigment now came to be applied with a brush under a turquoise-blue or deep blue transparent glaze. Finer examples closely resemble Rayy and Kashan lustre-painted wares which are discussed next.

230. Dish, black silhouette-painted ware. Rayy, Persia, second half of the 12th century. Diam. 5 in. (12·7 cm.). The vessel is decorated with a plant design under crackled ivory glaze. Edmund de Unger Collection, London.

231. Bowl painted in blue and black under clear glaze. Kashan, Persia, early 13th century. Diam. 11⅝ in. (29·5 cm.). Three seated human figures are shown here, one of them holding a trumpet-like vessel; the costumes are diapered with coiled foliage and dotted circles; the background is filled with arabesque scrolls in black reserved on blue ground; a Naskhi inscription round the rim is reserved in white. Victoria and Albert Museum, London.

232. Bowl, underglaze-painted ware. Kashan, Persia, early 13th century. Diam. 8 in. (20·3 cm.). The figure of an elephant is painted in blue and black under a clear colourless glaze. The rim on either side has a Naskhi inscription. Victoria and Albert Museum, London.

230

231

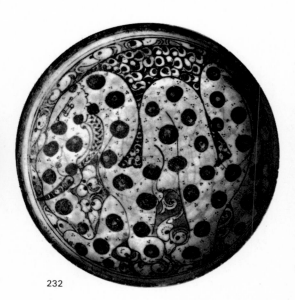

232

233. Tankard, painted in black under transparent turquoise-blue glaze. Kashan, Persia, early 13th century. Ht. 4⅝ in. (11·3 cm.). Plant design on the lip, arabesque on the shoulder and a Naskhi inscription on the body complete the decoration on this vessel. Victoria and Albert Museum, London.

234. Bottle, lustre-painted. Rayy, Persia, AD 1179. Ht. 5½ in. (14 cm.). This bottle is the earliest piece of lustre-painted ware from Persia so far known. The field above the inscription is decorated by seated human figures; these are painted in brownish lustre, while the background is reserved in white; the narrow panel below, however, depicts animals in white on a lustre background. British Museum, London.

233
234

232
231
233
Varied figurative themes appear in the decoration of the underglaze wares, combined with arabesques, scrolls and plant motifs. Inscriptions round the rim are very characteristic of Kashan underglaze-painted and lustre-painted wares, sometimes giving the date of the vessel or bearing the signature of the artist. With the help of dated pieces the bulk of the finer underglaze-painted wares can be attributed to the end of the 12th or more probably to the first half of the 13th century.

After the fall of the Fatimid dynasty of Egypt in AD 1171 the potters of Fustat and Behnasa seem to have left Egypt and settled down in Mesopotamia and Iran, bringing with them the secret of the lustre-painting technique. The greatest difference between these medieval lustre wares and those of the early period is that while on the earlier examples the decoration was painted in lustre, on the later wares the background was lustred, usually but not always with dark brown or yellow, thus leaving the space open for the decoration in reserve. This was a tendency which had already begun on the later Fatimid specimens. At present five important pottery centres are known to have produced lustre ware from the second half of the 12th and during the 13th century: Rayy, Kashan, Sava, Raqqa and the Sultanabad area. Another important place, Gurgan, where a great number of specimens have been found, should be also considered.

The earliest specimens of Rayy lustre ware with their large human and animal figures, arabesques and a scalloped design on the rim, still betray Egyptian Fatimid taste. The earliest dated piece of Persian lustre ware known to-day is a bottle from Rayy in the British Museum. The inscription on the body gives the date as AD 1179.

235

234

The production of lustre ware was discontinued at Rayy after the Mongols had destroyed the city in AD 1224, and it seems that some of the potters emigrated to Kashan, Sava or other pottery centres.

The lustre wares of Kashan are definitely superior to those of Rayy. Delicately drawn and crowded scenes, round faces and long eyes, minutely executed textile patterns, dense arabesque backgrounds, flying pigeons and a pool in the foreground, are the most conspicuous characteristics of the Kashan school. It seems that the Mongol invasion did not do much harm to Kashan and the production of fine lustre wares continued there until nearly the end of the 14th century.

236–7

17 (p. 72)

239

Along with lustre vessels, wall-tiles were also made in Kashan, particularly after the Mongol invasion. Most of these wall-tiles decorated prayer-niches (*mihrabs*) in mosques. Two such complete *mihrabs*, made up of a number of lustre tiles, are preserved, one in the Museum of East Berlin and the other in the Archaeological Museum of Teheran. The Victoria and Albert Museum has several

235. Large dish, lustre-painted. Rayy, Persia, late 12th or early 13th century. Diam. 18½ in. (47 cm.). The decoration shows a centrally placed seated figure, probably a Sasanian king, with four attendants; the background is filled with arabesques and above this there is a half-sun with a human face. Ashmolean Museum, Oxford.

236. Large dish, painted in lustre. Kashan, Persia, dated: AD 1207. Diam. 13¾ in. (34·9 cm.). The decoration shows a man on horseback against a background of scrolls, coiling foliage and doves; the vessel is signed by the artist, Abu Rufaza. Victoria and Albert Museum, London.

237. Bowl, painted in brownish lustre and turquoise. Kashan, Persia, dated: AD 1218. Diam. 7 in. (17·8 cm.). Floral and plant designs decorate this vessel in the best Kashani tradition; as an addition to the dense decoration, certain patterns are painted in turquoise. Edmund de Unger Collection, London.

235
236
237

238

239

240

238. Ewer, painted in brownish lustre. Sava, Persia, second half of the 13th century. Ht. 12 in. (30·5 cm.). The decorative features here, most noticeably the chequer-work on the cypress trees, are characteristic of Sava wares. Edmund de Unger Collection, London.

239. Jug, painted in brownish lustre on a deep blue glaze. Kashan, second half of the 13th century. Ht. 13⅝ in. (34·6 cm.). The vessel is decorated with floral patterns; it is not dated, yet certain features point to a somewhat later date than the previous Kashani piece shown in fig. 237. Edmund de Unger Collection, London.

241 *mihrab* tiles; among them the central panel of a Kashan lustre *mihrab*.

238, 240   Another lustre-producing centre was Sava, which used elements from both Rayy and Kashan. The most striking characteristics of these wares are cypress trees with chequer-work and, sometimes, vertical stripes on the garments of the figures.

During the Second World War some huge unglazed jars were accidentally uncovered at the site of the medieval town of Gurgan (present-day Awdan-Tepe, near Gunbad-i Qabus). These jars contained in sand complete and perfect lustre-painted, underglaze-painted and monochrome-glazed vessels. It seems very probable that they were hidden away from the Mongols when they approached the city in AD 1221. Gurgan was completely destroyed by the Mongols, its inhabitants exterminated and the site abandoned.

An important question thus arises. Were these vessels made in Gurgan, or were they imported from Kashan or other pottery

centres of contemporary Iran? The problem is very complex, since these wares are very fine specimens and display characteristic features of Rayy, Kashan or even of Sava. The ewer, for example, 242- comes very close to the finest specimens of Kashan. The veined and dotted leaves, the arrangement of the inscriptions, the animals in the chase on the shoulder, are all essential elements of Kashan vessels. There is, however, an unusual plant design on the lower part of the body which is unfamiliar in Kashan and might be taken to be an indication of a Gurgan style and origin. An aquamanile from 244 Gurgan on the other hand bears close resemblance to aquamaniles which are known to have been made at Rayy during the second half of the 12th or early 13th century.

It is not possible at present to give a satisfactory answer to the origin of Gurgan wares. Fine underglaze-painted, lustre and monochrome-glazed wares still turn up, however, in large quantities 20 (

241

242

241. Wall-tile from the middle of a prayer-niche (*mihrab*). Kashan, second half of the 13th century. Ht. 24 in. (61 cm.). The decoration is moulded in low relief and painted in dark blue, turquoise and brownish lustre; the inscriptions, which are in Naskhi characters, are quotations from the Koran. Victoria and Albert Museum, London.

242. Seated human figure painted in brownish lustre and pale cobalt blue. Kashan or Gurgan (?), Persia, 13th century. Ht. 7½ in. (19·1 cm.). This figure and the details of his face and decoration of his garment again remind us of Kashani examples; yet, it was found among the treasures of Gurgan. Raymond Ades Collection, Surrey.

240 (*opposite page*). Jug, painted in brownish lustre, with a pseudo-Kufic inscription. Probably Sava, Persia, second half of the 13th century. Ht. 5 in. (12·7 cm.). The vessel was actually found in Gurgan but its decoration points to a Sava origin. The central panel bears a striking resemblance to that on the bottle in fig. 238. Raymond Ades Collection, Surrey.

243. Ewer, painted in brownish lustre. Kashan or Gurgan (?), Persia, 13th century, Ht. 8 in. (20·3 cm.). This ewer comes very close to the finest specimens of Kashan; the veined and dotted leaves, the arrangement of the inscriptions, the animals in the chase on the shoulder, are all essential elements of Kashani vessels. There is, however, an unusual plant design on the lower part of the body which is unfamiliar in Kashan, and might be an indication of a Gurgan origin. Raymond Ades Collection, Surrey.

244. Aquamanile in the form of a bull. Gurgan or Rayy (?). Persia, 13th century. Ht. 4⅛ in. (10·5 cm.). The aquamanile is painted in lustre on a deep blue glaze. Such aquamaniles are known to have been made at Rayy during the second half of the 12th or early 13th century. This piece, however, was again found in Gurgan. Edmund de Unger Collection, London.

243

244

at this site and are put up for sale on the Teheran antique market.

Finally, there are two other kinds of fine pottery made in Seljuk Iran during this period. These are two types of overglaze-painted wares, known as '*mina'i*' and '*lajvardina*' pottery.

'*Mina'i*', meaning 'enamel', denotes a technique in which the colours, usually blue, green, brown, black, dull red, white and gold, are painted over the glaze (opaque white or sometimes turquoise) and fixed by a second firing at low temperature. This kind of pottery is closely related to miniature painting and it is very likely that the best examples were painted by the same artists who illuminated manuscripts. Some pieces display court-scenes with enthroned rulers and attendants, scenes from Persian legends and hunting scenes. Others have only arabesques or geometrical designs. Piercing was also used where the body was thin and gilded reliefs further enrich the charms of these *mina'i* wares.

The best pieces were undoubtedly produced at Rayy before the Mongols devastated the city in AD 1224. Kashan and Sava also contributed a great deal to the *mina'i* technique, though their products are inferior to those from Rayy.

The second overglaze-painted technique, that of *lajvardina*, derives its name from the cobalt-blue glaze which is applied as the ground. It is not so pleasing as the *mina'i*, the range of colours being limited to black, red and white, with the addition of leaf-gilding, and the decorative scheme restricted to scrollwork, geometrical patterns and leaves. Inscriptions and human figures are absent and animal figures are very seldom used.

The production of *lajvardina* wares was connected with the Sultanabad region, although literary sources mention that such pottery was also produced at Kashan. They can be attributed to the end of the 13th or the beginning of the 14th century.

245. Bowl, overglaze-painted, known as the *mina'i* technique. Probably Kashan, dated: AD 1187. Diam. 7⅜ in. (18·7 cm.). The decoration shows seven figures sitting or standing at a pool; the figures and the decoration of their garments present some features of Kashani, but also of Sava wares. British Museum, London.

246. Bowl, overglaze-painted. Rayy, late 12th or early 13th century. Diam. 6⅛ in. (15·6 cm.). The decoration shows two figures meeting at a tree, a rather common design on Rayy *mina'i* bowls. Victoria and Albert Museum, London.

247. Bowl *lajvardina type*. Probably Kashan or Sultanabad region, Persia, about AD 1300. Diam. 8¾ in. (22·2 cm.). The vessel has a cobalt-blue (*lajvardi*) ground and the decoration is painted in opaque white and red; leaf gilding has also been used. Victoria and Albert Museum, London.

245

246

247

Seljuq pottery of Mesopotamia (Raqqa and Rusāfa)

It has already been mentioned that after the fall of the Fatimid dynasty in Egypt some of the potters emigrated to Iran and Mesopotamia. Those who left for Mesopotamia apparently set up their workshops at Raqqa and Rusāfa in the North. The earliest pieces, which might from their appearance have dated from the previous century, were simple monochrome glazed green or turquoise vessels. The production of finer Raqqa and Rusāfa pottery must date from the period between 1171 (the fall of the Fatimids) and 1259 when the Mongols sacked Raqqa.

Two main types were produced: lustre and underglaze-painted wares. In both cases the body is of a white very soft quartz material. The glaze is greenish and is apt to decay. The very dark brown lustre immediately distinguishes them from other contemporary lustre wares. Cobalt-blue was often added. The decorative motifs, which include arabesques, scrolls, birds and Kufic characters, sometimes occur in low relief.

More interesting is the second group which is painted under clear glazes. The earliest specimens of the late 12th and early 13th century were painted exclusively in black under a transparent turquoise glaze; the decoration comprises heavily drawn scrolls, arabesques and inscriptions in Kufic and Naskhi. Later, polychrome wares displayed a finer, more accomplished style of painting. These polychrome painted pieces are akin to contemporary *mina'i* wares. While *mina'i* wares were painted over the glaze, these wares of Raqqa and Rusāfa were painted under a clear glaze—in black, blue, green and dull red. Arabesques, scrolls, human and animal figures are the favourite themes.

Rusāfa is only some thirty miles from Raqqa and the wares of the two centres are clearly related in material, technique and decorative style. Raqqa and Rusāfa wares have also been found in Asia Minor at Konya and a number of other places. Similar pottery was later on made in Damascus and in Egypt during the Mamluk period.

248. Bowl, painted in polychrome under clear glaze. Raqqa, Mesopotamia, 13th century. Diam. 10¾ in. (27·3 cm.). A female figure is shown here sitting sideways on a camel. This may be the Persian legendary figure of Azada. Pseudo-Kufic characters decorate the rim. The whole composition and the colour scheme recall the influence of Rayy overglaze-painted wares. Victoria and Albert Museum, London.

249. Bowl, painted in black under turquoise-blue glaze. Raqqa, Mesopotamia, 13th century. Diam. 5¼ in. (13·3 cm.). The vessel is decorated inside with heavy Naskhi characters and scrolls in black; both features are characteristic of the earlier Raqqa under-glaze painted wares. The shallow bowl with a flat rim is a favourite shape in Raqqa, also seen in the later polychrome type in fig. 248. Victoria and Albert Museum, London.

248

249

250

251

252

250. Albarello, painted in black under turquoise glaze. Raqqa, Mesopotamia, late 12th or early 13th century. Ht. 9 in. (22·9 cm.). It is decorated with arabesques, leaves and pseudo-Naskhi inscription in black. Victoria and Albert Museum, London.

251. Ceramic tiled *mihrab*. Konya, Asia Minor, Sahib Ata mosque, dated 1258. These Turkish tiled *mihrabs* were erected in Asia Minor from the beginning of the 13th century; all together some fifteen such *mihrabs* are known today.

252. Bowl, painted in polychrome under clear glaze. Rusāfa, Mesopotamia, late 12th or early 13th century. Diam. 8½ in. (21·6 cm.). A human figure, birds, flowers and mock Kufic characters decorate this vessel. The design and technique clearly point to a close relationship between Raqqa and Rusāfa, British Museum, London.

Seljuq pottery in Asia Minor

Examples of the same types of techniques, shapes and styles of decoration as have already been described in reference to Iran and Mesopotamia appear also in Asia Minor. Coloured monochrome-glazed wares with moulded, carved and incised designs; simple *sgraffiato* under greenish or yellowish glazes; underglaze-painting of the Kashan and Raqqa types are present also in Asia Minor. Lustre-painted pottery has been found at Isnik, Konya, Diyarbakir and Kubadabad near Kayseri. Hardly any complete vessels, however, have survived and pottery kilns have been discovered only in Isnik.

The greatest contribution of the Seljuq potters of Asia Minor was to architectural decoration. A number of mosques and madrasahs (schools) were faced with ceramic tiles. The earliest monuments on which large wall-surfaces were covered with Seljuq tiles are the 12th-century mausolea in Maraghe in Western Iran, which greatly influenced the tiles of Asia Minor. Seljuq tiles were made in a variety of forms: star-shaped, octagonal, cross-shaped etc. The designs include arabesques, geometrical patterns, inscriptions in Kufic and Naskhi. The colours range from turquoise-blue through shades of green and white to black.

Some fifteen tiled prayer niches (*mihrabs*) still survive in Turkey today, the earliest of which is in the Alaeddin Mosque at Konya, dating from AD 1221. We may presume that some of these Seljuk tiled *mihrabs* were executed by Persian craftsmen who fled to Asia Minor and Syria at the time of the Mongol invasion in the early 1220s. One of the finest of them is in the Arslanhane Cami in Ankara which dates from AD 1290. This excellent tradition of ceramic tile and tile mosaic making was taken up and further developed by the potters of Isnik from the 16th century onwards.

Persian pottery (13th–14th centuries)

The production of fine wares in Kashan, as has already been mentioned, continued without a real break after the Mongol invasion. Traditional lustre ware and underglaze-painted pottery was made well into the middle or probably until the end of the 14th century. Some of the late 13th-century lustre vessels have also been referred to. There is hardly any noticeable difference in the technique or quality of the material and glaze in early 14th-century wares. There is, however, a striking difference in the subjects and style of the decoration. Animals or human figures are painted in blue, black and turquoise on the underglaze-painted wares.

The green glaze of some vessels reveals the latest Chinese influence from imported celadon porcelain. This pottery is thought to have been made also in Kashan during the first half of the 14th century. The decoration is in moulded relief.

The production of wall-tiles, painted in lustre, cobalt-blue, turquoise or even in overglaze-painted (*mina'i*) technique, also continued in Kashan. These tiles appear in a great variety of forms.

251

253-4

255

253

254

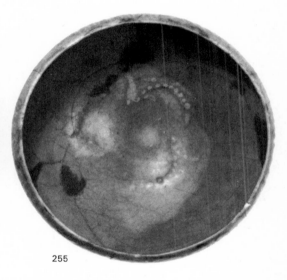

255

256

253. Large bowl painted in black, blue and turquoise under a clear glaze. Probably Kashan, 14th century. Diam. 11in. (27·9 cm.). The heavy lines and simpler design betray already the decline of Kashan pottery-making which came to a halt in the 15th century. Edmund de Unger Collection, London.

254. Large dish, painted in brownish lustre and blue. Kashan, 14th century. Diam. 9 in. (22·9 cm.). The arrangement of the design, the fishes in the centre, the elimination of human figures, fine veined leaves and doves betray a late date. Edmund de Unger Collection, London.

255. Bowl, imitation of Chinese celadon. Kashan, first half of the 14th century. Diam. 7⅜ in. (18·7 cm.). The decoration is moulded in relief: there are fishes inside and inscriptions on the outside of the rim. Ashmolean Museum, Oxford.

256. Wall-tile, lustre and turquoise-green painted. Kashan, early 14th century. 12½ in. square (31·8 cm.). The tiles come from a castle in Mazanderan, northern Persia; it represents the Persian king, Bahram Gur, and his mistress, Azada. Victoria and Albert Museum, London.

256 The designs were not confined to arabesques, geometrical designs and inscriptions, but human and animal figures are also present, often recalling scenes from Persian legends. The most important patterns are accentuated in relief and painted in cobalt-blue or turquoise. Such tiles most probably decorated palaces or even private houses.

The new rulers of Iran, the Il-Khanids, who were themselves Mongols, brought with them a new taste nurtured on Far Eastern styles, clearly manifest on vessels coming from the Sultanabad region.

260 The Sultanabad wares, mostly hemispherical bowls, are usually painted over a brownish- or greenish-grey ground slip. On earlier examples the designs are painted in white and outlined in brownish-black, with flying phoenixes and gazelles appearing in the centre,

rarely also human figures; plant motifs or flowers arranged in compartments on the inner sides; and relief inscriptions on the rim. Later examples have a more complex geometrical design incorporating arabesques and palmettes, and the colour is enriched with blue, turquoise and greenish-black. On the outside of the vessels there are vertical panels with rounded tops.

Then, at the end of the 14th century, many great changes took place in Persian pottery-making. Traditional techniques, such as lustre-painting, disappeared, and were re-introduced only in the 17th century. The mina'i techniques ceased to be practised a century earlier. The new style and techniques of the 15th century were largely influenced by the Chinese Ming blue-and-white porcelain.

Mamluk wares of Egypt and Syria (13th–15th centuries)

The Fatimids were succeeded in AD 1171 by the Ayyubids, who became the rulers of Syria and Egypt until AD 1250. They, in turn, were overthrown by the Mamluks, who reigned over these two countries until the beginning of the 16th century, when the Ottoman Turks occupied both Syria and Egypt. It is one of the greatest merits of the Mamluks that they checked and defeated the Mongols and gave refuge to artists from Iran and Mesopotamia. These refugee potters apparently set up their workshops in Damascus, Cairo and many other places and introduced into these two countries some of the pottery techniques and traditions of their homelands.

The most common ware in Syria and Egypt during the second half of the 13th and 14th centuries was that painted in underglaze blue and black. Large and heavy bowls, albarelli and jars were decorated in this way. These were exported in great quantities to Europe and used for storing Oriental spices and medicine. The

ornaments appear mostly in panels, and in Egypt, following Mamluk tradition, circular medallions enclosed heraldic devices.

Another type of Mamluk pottery in Egypt was a modification of the simple sgraffiato technique. The decoration has an incised outline and often appears in low relief. Inscriptions and blazons are the commonest ornament, under a yellowish-brown lead-glaze.

Underglaze polychrome painting of the Raqqa and Rusāfa style also seems to have been produced in Egypt. Very few complete vessels of this type survive, but a great number of fragments have been found in Egypt, some of which show a perfect Islamisation of style in the rendering of birds. Here is no sign of any Classical or foreign influence, while others, with human figures, remind us of a remote Kashan influence. The production of polychrome underglaze-painted pottery was discontinued some time in the 14th century.

257

258

259

257. Lid of a jar, painted in blue and black under clear glaze. Sultanabad region, 14th century. Diam. 7 in. (17·8 cm.). There is a simple scroll design on the top and a knob in the form of a bird. Edmund de Unger Collection, London.

258. Bowl, lead-glazed *sgraffiato* ware. Egypt, Mamluk period 13th–14th century. Diam. 9 in. (22·9 cm.). Large Naskhi inscription decorates the sides of the bowl inside against a scroll background. Victoria and Albert Museum, London.

259. Fragment of a vessel, polychrome painted under a clear glaze. Egypt, Mamluk period, 13th or early 14th century. The two birds are painted in black, dull-red and yellow. Edmund de Unger Collection, London.

260

260. Large dish, painted in black, blue, turquoise and brownish-grey under clear glaze. Sultanabad region, 14th century. A gazelle is shown in the centre against a foliage background, which continues on the sides interrupted only by the dividing lines and the heart-shaped floral motifs. Edmund de Unger Collection, London.

18. Jug painted in green and red on a white background under a clear glaze. Isnik, about 1570–80. A fine Isnik vessel, decorated with stylised scrolls and floral designs. Victoria and Albert Museum, London.

19

20

The Later Period (15th–19th centuries)
15th-century pottery of Iran

In Iran the slow recovery from the Mongol devastation was briefly interrupted by the ruthless conquests of Timur at the end of the 14th century. He sacked and plundered a number of cities in both North and South. Nevertheless, he had a great respect for beautiful and sacred buildings. Moreover, Timur systematically collected artists in his capital at Samarqand in order to beautify it. Timur's work in the patronage of art continued under his sons and successors, who moved the capital to Herat. Accordingly, the centre of gravity of Persian art and culture was shifted to the East.

The 15th century was not favourable for the potter's art. Timur's and his successors' interest was concentrated rather on architecture and, later, on miniature painting. However, the interest in architecture provided, in a way, an encouragement for the makers of decorative ceramics. Ceramic tiles and mosaics adorned the mosques, madrasahs, mausolea and palaces of Samarqand, Herat and Meshhed. These were painted in cobalt-blue, manganese-purple, yellow and green. The decorations, particularly inscriptions and arabesques, were often made in openwork. Arabesque and scroll backgrounds became so dense that inscriptions were hardly legible.

Pottery-making in Iran itself greatly declined and a number of ceramic types became extinct. Two main types are characteristic of the period. The first type is known from large dishes and plates painted in black on a white slip. The design was incised into the black, presenting scroll and plant motifs in white under transparent turquoise-blue glaze.

The second and more common type is a peasant pottery, denoted as 'cross-hatched ware'. These objects were most probably produced in North or North-West Iran during the 15th century. The body material is red, the decorations which are confined to heavy lines and cross-hatchings, are painted in black, blue and green, on a white ground slip under a clear glaze. It is believed that this type of pottery influenced the development of the Orvieto pottery of Italy.

Our knowledge of later Islamic pottery is very limited. Information concerning it is partly supplied by contemporary European travellers and partly by unreliable antique dealers. There have been practically no scientific excavations in Iran to supply evidence about 15th-century pottery, and very few complete vessels have survived from that period. It seems clear, however, that, under the influence of Chinese Ming porcelain, imitation of blue-and-white started in Iran, probably as early as the late 14th century.

261

261. Section of tilework, carved and painted in turquoise-blue, white and manganese-purple. It comes from the mausoleum of Bayram Kuli Khan at Fathabad, near Bukhara, Uzbekistan, late 14th or early 15th century. L. 5 ft. (1·52 m.). Victoria and Albert Museum, London.

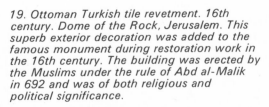

19. Ottoman Turkish tile revetment. 16th century. Dome of the Rock, Jerusalem. This superb exterior decoration was added to the famous monument during restoration work in the 16th century. The building was erected by the Muslims under the rule of Abd al-Malik in 692 and was of both religious and political significance.

20. Lion, with monochrome turquoise-blue glaze. Probably Rayy, 12th or early 13th century. This fine piece was found in Gurgan, but similar monochrome pottery is thought to have been produced at Rayy during this period. Raymond Ades Collection, Surrey.

262

262. Large dish, painted in black on a white slip under clear turquoise-blue glaze. Veramin (?), Persia, 15th century. Diam. 14¼ in. (36·2 cm.). The decoration, which comprises scrollwork and plant design, is incised into the black slip and carved right down to the white background. Victoria and Albert Museum, London.

263

263. Dish, painted in blue and black under clear glaze. Northern Persia, early 15th century. Diam. 9¼ in. (23·5 cm.). The design is based on heavily-drawn cross-hatching, which is so characteristic of 15th-century Persian pottery. Ashmolean Museum, Oxford.

Blue-and-white wares of Iran and Syria (15th–18th centuries)

It is a general misconception to attribute the origin of blue-and-white wares to Yüan China. Recent research has clearly established that the origin of this pottery should be sought in the Near East. In fact, the tin-glazed, cobalt-blue painted pottery of 9th-century Mesopotamia might be considered as the earliest blue-and-white pottery. The type was then forgotten for a few centuries in the Near East, but re-appeared again in the 14th century. It has been mentioned in historical sources that the cobalt ore for the Chinese Ming blue-and-white was imported from Iran.

Whether it was actual Persian blue-painted pottery that gave the initial impetus for making blue-painted Chinese porcelain, or the influence was the other way round, cannot yet be firmly established. Blue-and-white vessels with forms unknown in Chinese porcelain appear on Persian miniature painting in the late 14th century. The earliest of such vessels are shown in a miniature painting in the British Museum dated to AD 1396.

The earliest existing Persian blue-and-white vessels are all small bowls, dating from the 15th century. There is a flying bird on one of these vessels in the Ashmolean Museum, which the late Arthur Lane attributed to the early 15th century. Other vessels are decorated with flowers and plant motifs drawn in a naturalistic way. These can be attributed to the middle or second half of the 15th century. According to the accounts of European travellers Persian blue-and-white was made in Meshhed and Kirman.

Similar vessels were excavated recently in a 15th-century building in East Africa. Persian and Arab colonies existed along the coast of East Africa and Islamic (but mainly Persian) pottery was exported there from the 9th-century onwards.

The presence of Far Eastern influence under the Safavids, who came to power in Iran at the beginning of the 16th century becomes increasingly evident. Later in the century Chinese subjects like dragons, peonies and cloud patterns appear and landscapes are treated in the Far Eastern style. Designs are outlined in black from the 17th century onwards.

There were some political reasons for presenting Persian blue-and-white wares in Chinese style. Europeans had been exporting Chinese porcelain to Europe and the Near East since the 16th century. Because of internal troubles in China during the 17th century the supply of these wares was interrupted. The Dutch, therefore, placed orders with Persian potters to produce blue-and-white in the Chinese style. These Persian wares were then shipped from Gombroon (modern Bender Abbas) in the Persian Gulf.

The production of blue-and-white continued in Iran right up to the 19th century, when the Meshhed and Kirman kilns were still active. Black outlines which had been introduced in the 16th century were favoured in Meshhed and were used to depict elaborate landscapes or still-lifes. The Kirman potters adhered to the use of blue alone and their designs were also closer to the Chinese in presenting dragons and flowers without an elaborate background. Black outline did not appear there until the 17th century.

That blue-and-white—similar in material and decoration to the Persian—appeared somewhat earlier in Syria than in Iran, is suggested by the finds of a Danish excavation at Hama. A number of blue-and-white sherds, fragments of jars, albarelli and bowls were found there which can be dated to the end of the 14th century. More numerous are the blue and black underglaze-painted wares (some already mentioned above). Wall-tiles, painted in black and blue, or sometimes green, under clear glaze—found in mosques, palaces and private houses—were also made at that time in Syria.

The body of the later Syrian blue-and-white painted wares is coarser and heavier than that of the Persian pottery. Designs on these later wares of the 17th–18th centuries are carelessly drawn and the pigments are apt to run under the glaze. Subjects of decoration are entirely different from the earlier wares and are confined to plant motifs and inscriptions. Figural representations are almost completely absent. By the 16th century, pottery-making in Syria was overshadowed by the emergence of the Ottoman pottery of Isnik and by the so-called 'Kubachi wares' of northern Iran.

264. Large jar, painted in blue and black under a clear glaze. Syria, late 14th or early 15th century. Ht. 16 in. (40·6 cm.). Heavily drawn plant motifs and scrolls decorate this large jar which was probably used for storing oil. Victoria and Albert Museum, London.

265. Bowl, blue-and-white. Probably Kirman, Persia, middle or second half of the 15th century. Diam. 6¼ in. (15·9 cm.). Finely-drawn scrollwork decorates the base of the vessel inside and stylised wing motifs appear on the rim. The transparent and almost colourless and crackled glaze can be seen to have a greenish tinge where it is applied more thickly. Private collection, London.

266. Large dish, blue-and-white. Persian, early 16th century. Diam. 16 in. (43·2 cm.). There is a flying heron amidst coiling foliage and flowers, all rendered in the Chinese manner. British Museum, London.

268

269

267

271

267. Panel of wall-tiles, painted in blue and olive-green under clear glaze. Damascus, Syria, about AD 1425. Ht. 5 ft. 3 in. (1·6 m.). Similar wall-tile panels are still preserved in mosques in Damascus. The decoration is confined to floral and plant motifs. Victoria and Albert Museum, London.

268. Large dish, black and blue-and-white. Persian, dated: AD 1697–98. Diam. 17½ in. (43·7 cm.). The decoration of the vessel presents flowers and plant motifs on what seem to be rocks. It is rendered in the strictest Chinese manner, apart from the tassel-like black border with inscriptions on the rim. The vessel may be attributed to Kirman. British Museum, London.

269. Large dish, painted in blue and black under a clear glaze. Persian, about 1700. Diam. 18³⁄₁₀ in. (46·6 cm.). An elephant decorates this dish, which probably comes from Meshhed. There is hardly any Chinese influence here, but the way in which the animal and the dense background, probably a jungle, is shown, is nevertheless alien to Iran. It comes much closer to the Indian style, to Moghul miniature painting particularly. British Museum, London.

270. Wall-tile, painted in black, blue, red, green and yellow under clear glaze. Isnik, about 1666. Ht. 24 in. (61 cm.). It presents a very interesting design: the plan of the Ka'aba in Mecca, with inscriptions above. Victoria and Albert Museum, London.

271. Jug and cover, painted in greenish-blue. Kütahya, Turkey, 18th century. Ht. 8⅞ in. (22·5 cm.). It was probably used as a coffee-pot and could be a replica of a piece of European porcelain. Victoria and Albert Museum, London.

272   273   274

275   276   277

272. Bowl, grey earthenware, painted in dark blue and green on white slip under clear glaze. 'Miletus ware', excavated at Istanbul; Isnik, early 15th century. Diam. 7 in. (17·8 cm.). A six-pointed star decorates the centre of the vessel, surrounded by stylised Chinese cloud patterns. Victoria and Albert Museum, London.

275. Large dish, painted in red, blue and green on white ground under clear glaze. Isnik, second half of the 16th century. Diam. 11 in. (27·9 cm.). The dish is decorated with roses and tulips, while conventionalised scrolls appear on the rim. Victoria and Albert Museum, London.

273. Bowl, fragment of 'Miletus ware'; red earthenware, painted in dark blue and green on white slip under clear glaze. Excavated at the post office in Istanbul; Isnik, early 15th century. Diam. 9¼ in. (23·5 cm.). Victoria and Albert Museum, London.

276. Large dish, painted in red, blue and green. Isnik, second half of 16th century. Diam. 12 in. (30·5 cm.). A sailing boat on waves, probably representing a European ship, shown here with the conventionalised scrolls on the rim. It is very finely drawn and must belong to the best period of Isnik. Victoria and Albert Museum, London.

274. Large dish, painted in blue on a white background under a very thin clear glaze. Isnik, second quarter of the 16th century. 15½ in. (39·4 cm.). Three bunches of grapes, leaves and tendrils are surrounded by floral designs; overlapping scales on the rim. Victoria and Albert Museum, London.

277. Small dish, painted in blue, green, brown and yellow on white background under clear glaze. Kütahya, Turkey, dated: 1719. Diam. 8⅜ in. (21·9 cm.). The Archangel St Michael accepts dead man's soul. Made for Wartabed Abraham, bishop of Tekirdag. Victoria and Albert Museum, London.

Ottoman-Turkish pottery (15th–19th centuries)
Isnik wares

Turkish Ottoman pottery was identified until not long ago as 'Rhodian' or 'Damascus' ware, and accordingly attributed to the island of Rhodes and Syria. Research during the last thirty to thirty-five years has clarified the history of these wares and attributed them entirely to the workshops of Isnik (ancient Nicaea), in Western Anatolia.

Excavations at Isnik have established three main types of wares made there. A first type consisted of slip-painted wares of the pre-Ottoman period (mainly 14th century) which are almost identical to those slip-painted wares known from Iran and Afghanistan (see pp. 77–8).

The second Isnik type used to be known as 'Miletus ware' and dates from the second half of the 14th century up to the end of the 15th. The name is taken from the town, Miletus, where the first of

278

279

280

278. Panel of six tiles, painted in red, blue and olive-green. Isnik, second half of the 16th century. Ht. 23¼ in. (59·1 cm.). The decoration consists of a lunette filled with conventional flowers and arabesques. Victoria and Albert Museum, London.

279. Jar, painted in cobalt-blue under very fine and thin clear glaze. Isnik, end of 15th or early 16th century. Ht. 9⅝ in. (24·4 cm.). The arabesques and peonies may betray some Chinese influence here, but this was never strong in Isnik. Victoria and Albert Museum, London.

280. Standing bowl, painted in blue and turquoise-green on a white ground under a clear glaze. Known as 'Golden Horn' ware; Isnik, second quarter of the 16th century. Diam. 16¾ in. (42·5 cm.). The bowl is decorated with a fine scroll design inside and out, interrupted by rosettes in places. Victoria and Albert Museum, London.

such pieces were found, but without any kiln-wasters or kilns. The 'Miletus wares' are of red clay, painted in blue, black, and green on a white ground slip under a clear glaze. Their decoration consists of geometrical patterns, plant motifs and radiating heavy lines. Recent excavations show that they were made at Isnik. They betray hardly any trace of foreign influence though some of the plant motifs may have been inspired by the effect of Chinese blue-and-white porcelain.

Contemporary with these are blue-and-white painted tiles, apparently also made at Isnik, as such tiles survived in the Muradiye Mosque of Edirne dating from AD 1433.

The third type, first to be designated as 'Isnik ware', may be subdivided into three types. Previously they were divided into four groups: 'Abraham of Kütahya'-type; 'Damascus' group; 'Golden Horn' and 'Rhodian'. The late Arthur Lane divided them into three groups only: Isnik I, including the Abraham of Kütahya type, dating from 1490 until 1525; Isnik II, consisting of 'Damascus' and 'Golden Horn', dated between 1525 and 1555; and Isnik III, comprising 'Rhodian', dating from 1555 until about 1700.

The material used for the wares of all three periods is a rather thick loose-grained white siliceous composition. The decorations are painted under a very fine and thin transparent glaze.

In Isnik I the designs are painted in cobalt-blue on a white ground: flowers, arabesques and inscriptions. The shapes are nearly the same in all three groups: large dishes, standing-bowls, jars, ewers, mosque-lamps, pen-boxes, and wall-tiles. The earliest example of this group can be seen in the mausoleum of Mustafa in Bursa (1474–75) and the latest examples are in the Valide Mosque of Manisa (1522–23). The attribution 'Abraham of Kütahya' comes from an inscription in Armenian on one of the spouted ewers. It is, however, quite clear now that all these were manufactured at Isnik.

Isnik II is considered to date from the period between 1525 and 1555. Here turquoise-green and sometimes purple was added to the

cobalt-blue. The decoration of the second group is based mainly on naturalistic motifs like bunches of grapes, tulips and carnations.

The type previously known as 'Golden Horn' may be dated to the same period. It was believed that they were produced in Istanbul in a district at the Golden Horn. The decoration of these vessels, mainly large dishes and standing bowls, is restricted to finely drawn scroll patterns including tiny flowers. They are painted in mono-chrome blue, sometimes also in green.

Isnik III is dated between 1555 and 1700. The great change in this group is marked by the appearance of a lively red colour in the colour scheme. Beautiful wall-tiles were manufactured in ever-increasing quantities for the decoration of mosques and palaces. The earliest such wall-tiles, painted in red, blue and green, are known from the mosque built by the great Turkish architect, Sinan, for Suleyman the Magnificent in Istanbul between 1550–57. The favourite themes on these 'Rhodian' wall-tiles and vessels are floral designs, sometimes drawn in a semi-naturalistic way. Carnations, roses, tulips and hyacinths appear in the centre, while the rims are filled with the scroll design in blue or in black. The most colourful and finest vessels date from the third quarter of the 16th century. On occasion figures also appear on these Isnik vessels, but whenever they are represented, they betray the hands of Christian, probably Armenian, craftsmen. Sailing boats are shown on some dishes.

The decline started in Isnik during the first half of the 17th century, probably thanks to a falling demand for tiles and vessels. Evlia Chelebi, the great Turkish traveller, reports only nine workshops in Isnik in the middle of the 17th century. Quality now never reached the same height as before; colours are apt to run under the glaze, designs are carelessly drawn.

A number of Ka'aba tiles are known to have been made at Isnik during the second half of the 17th century.

By the end of the 17th century, pottery-making came to a halt in Isnik and the centre of Turkish pottery shifted to Kütahya.

2–3

279

274

280

278
19 (p. 90)

275
18 (p. 89)

276

270

Kütahya and Chanak Kale pottery

Literary sources mention pottery production in Kütahya as early as the 17th century. Evlia Chelebi also writes of Kütahya potters that they were disbelievers, obviously referring to Armenians, as becomes evident from the many inscribed vessels and tiles. Though production must really have started in the 17th century, Kütahya pottery is known only from the 18th and 19th century. Kütahya kilns were working mainly for Armenian and other Christian communities in the Ottoman Empire. Later they produced tiles for mosques and palaces in Istanbul, but these were inferior to Isnik tiles. Examples survive in the cathedral of St James in Jerusalem.

Kütahya pottery is made of fine white earthenware, and patterns are painted in blue, greyish-blue, green, yellow and red on a white ground under a very fine clear glaze. The vessels made are mainly utensils like coffee-pots, and saucers, small dishes etc., often very attractive. The influence of European porcelain is quite evident on them. A number of vessels and tiles bear inscriptions and their date

in Armenian. From the middle of the 19th century Kütahya potters tried to imitate Rhodian Isnik wares, without much success.

Another pottery centre of less importance was flourishing in Chanak Kale in the Dardanelles during the 18th and 19th centuries. Bowls, jars, large dishes and water containers in the form of animals were made in greyish-white or buff earthenware. The decoration, mainly flowers and plant motifs, was painted in blue, red, and white, either on a white ground slip or direct on the greyish body under a transparent, somewhat yellowish glaze. The decoration of large dishes and jars show them to be a type of peasant pottery rather than refined vessels for the use of the upper classes. Production of Chanak Kale pottery came to an end sometime in the 19th century.

There were two attempts in Turkey, in Istanbul, during the 19th century to produce porcelain. On both occasions, however, the enterprises soon went out of business since they could not compete with the cheap European imported porcelains.

281. Small water container in the form of a horse, Chanak Kale, Turkey, 19th century. Ht. 8¾ in. (22·2 cm.). The figure is mottled in brown and green. Victoria and Albert Museum, London.

282. Jar, buff earthenware, painted in blue under clear glaze. Chanak Kale, Turkey, 18th century. Ht. 9 in. (22·9 cm.). Finely drawn scrolls and cross-hatching below the lip decorate this vessel, which has two handles attached to it on the upper part. Victoria and Albert Museum, London.

283. Large dish, greyish-white earthenware, painted in red, blue and white on a greyish background under clear glaze. Chanak Kale, Turkey, 18th century. Diam. 12½ in. (31·8 cm.). Flowers are emerging from a pot in the centre, scrolls and leaves decorate the rim. Victoria and Albert Museum, London.

284. Large dish, painted in blue and brown under clear glaze. Known as 'Kubachi' ware, North Persian, early 17th century. Diam. 15½ in. (39·4 cm.). In the centre is the portrait of a man with floral and scroll design around. British Museum, London.

285. Dish, mottled in black under a clear blue glaze, Persian. 17th century (?). 8½ in. (21·6 cm.). Compare with fig. 287. Ashmolean Museum, Oxford.

281

282

283

284

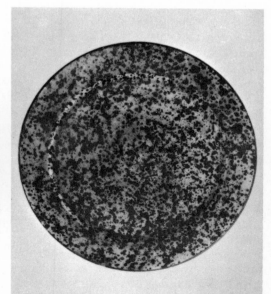

285

Pottery of the Safavid and Kajar periods of Iran (16th–19th centuries)

There was stagnation in the production of fine wares in Iran, apart from blue-and-white pottery, for about two hundred years. Renewed interest in fine ceramics and their support came only with the rise of a nationalist dynasty, the Safavids, at the beginning of the 16th century. Then there was a genuine renaissance, not only in the field of ceramics but in all the visual arts of Iran.

Several new pottery types appeared, and old techniques, such as lustre-painting, were revived. Frequently, however, it is hardly possible to determine the provenance of these later wares. The interest of scholars and archaeologists has been drawn to earlier pottery rather than to the problems of Safavid and Kajar pottery.

Among these later wares we may distinguish the following five main types: the so-called 'Kubachi wares'; 'Gombroon wares'; late lustre-painted pottery; polychrome-painted wares; and monochrome and miscellaneous wares.

The name 'Kubachi' is derived from the name of a small town in

these wares were transported to Europe and to the Far East. Their actual origin is not known. Gombroon wares have a very hard, white and thin, almost translucent body. Jars, ewers, bowls and plates were produced. Decorations were incised under the glaze and frequently, just as was done in the case of Seljuq white wares, small holes were pierced in the body and became filled with glaze. Sometimes blue and black painting was added. They are dated to the 16th and 17th centuries.

The employment of the lustre technique ceased sometime at the end of the 14th century, and it was not until the second half of the 17th century that it was re-introduced. On these later lustre wares, in contrast to medieval examples, the designs are painted in lustre, reserving the ground in white (as on the earliest lustre pottery of the 9th–10th centuries). The glaze is either colourless or stained in deep blue. The lustre is ruby-brown or greenish-brown, giving a coppery reflection. The decoration on these wares—the only later Persian

286

286. Ewer, known as 'Gombroon ware'. Persia, 16th or early 17th century. Ht. 8½ in. (21·6 cm.). It has a very thin and hard white body and is covered with a fine white glaze; the decoration is incised under the glaze. Ashmolean Museum, Oxford.

287. Ewer, mottled with black dots under transparent turquoise-blue glaze. Persian, probably 17th century. Ht. 8½ in. (21·6 cm.). The body is thin and very hard. Victoria and Albert Museum, London.

288. Bowl, known as 'Gombroon ware'; Persia, 16th or early 17th century. Diam. 7⅝ in. (19·4 cm.). Victoria and Albert Museum, London.

287

288

Daghestan in the Caucasus, where most of this pottery was discovered. It is evident that these wares were not produced locally, since Kubachi had no pottery tradition. The inhabitants were excellent metalworkers, and produced particularly fine weapons. The plausible explanation is that they may have exchanged their weapons for pottery. The actual provenance of this pottery is not yet known, but some evidence points to north-west Iran— to the Tebriz region. Some influence of Turkish Isnik wares, contemporary with Kubachi, seems apparent.

In Kubachi vessels, mostly large dishes and plates, the polychrome colours—dull red, brown, green, white, yellow and black—are painted under a clear colourless crackled glaze. Earlier specimens display human or animal figures, portraits with floral or scroll design. On later wares the decorations become more and more simple, being restricted to plant motifs, painted in black under a turquoise blue glaze. The attempt by potters to paint in polychrome under clear glazes was indeed very successful, but unfortunately came to an abrupt end sometime in the later 17th century.

The designation 'Gombroon wares' is derived from the port of Gombroon (modern Bender Abbas) in the Persian Gulf, whence

wares to show no foreign, Chinese or Anatolian influence—is restricted to floral or plant design. Late lustre wares have the same hard, white and thin almost translucent body as the Gombroon wares. The place of production has not yet been identified.

There is also a late class of polychrome-painted pottery; accounts of European travellers and merchants unanimously refer to it as a product of Kirman. The body of this polychrome-painted pottery is fine and white but somewhat softer than those of Gombroon or late lustre wares. Colours range from dull red through shades of blue to dark green and brown. The designs reflect the influence of Chinese Ming wares, though the subjects are Persian, as for example on a *narghile* (water-pipe) representing the legendary figures of Khusraw and Shirin. Some of the polychrome wares are dated, and these dated specimens show that they are to be considered 17th-century products.

A great variety of monochrome-glazed vessels were manufactured from the 16th to 18th centuries. They owe their origin to Chinese celadon, though the glazes have many different colours. The main centre of production seems once again to have been Kirman. A great variety of monochrome vessels are preserved in museums and private collections. Their colour ranges from celadon through yellow and brown to vermilion and deep blue. Often decorations were added in relief, or flowers and plant motifs appear painted in white, or are cut through the coloured glaze down to the white body.

One very rare type of late Persian ware has a very hard, metallic body covered with blue or turquoise glaze and speckled in black underneath. The place of manufacture is not known and its date is considered to be 17th or early 18th century.

Over the last century Isfahan and Teheran have been producing polychrome vessels and tiles presenting human and animal figures in relief. Their quality is very much inferior to those of earlier centuries. This was, however, a period when mass-produced and cheap European porcelain and faience made local products uncompetitive and eventually caused the complete decline of Islamic pottery-making.

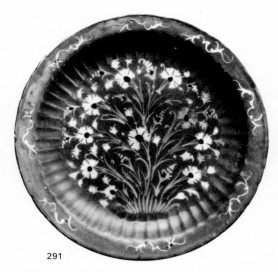

289

290

291

289. Large dish, painted in red, yellow, blue and green and outlined in olive-green. 'Kubachi ware', North Persian, early 17th century. Diam. 13½ in. (34·3 cm.). The figure of a gazelle is shown here amidst flowers and plants. The design is so well drawn that one is tempted to believe that it was copied from a miniature painting. Victoria and Albert Museum, London.

290. Plate, lustre-painted. Persian, late 17th century. Diam. 8½ in. (21·6 cm.). The vessel has a very thin hard white body, the decoration is painted in greenish-brown lustre, presenting a cypress tree, flowers and two animals in the centre. Ashmolean Museum, Oxford.

291. Large dish, covered with brown glaze and painted in white. Probably Kirman, Persia, 17th century. Diam. 10¼ in. (26 cm.). The decoration presents flowers in the centre and scrolls on the rim. Victoria and Albert Museum, London.

292. Flask, lustre-painted. Persian, 17th century. Ht. 6 in. (15·2 cm.). The body is very thin, hard and white and the design appears in brownish lustre. Victoria and Albert Museum, London.

293. *Narghile* (water-pipe), painted in polychrome colours on a white ground under a clear glaze. Kirman, Persia, about 1700. Ht. 11⁷⁄₁₀ in. (30·3 cm.). The decoration on the globular body represents the legendary figures of Khusaw and Shirin. British Museum, London.

292

293

IV Europe: Lead-Glaze and Salt-Glazed Stoneware

ICI FIST DEL EVE VIN:

Introduction

The use of a lead-oxide, sprinkled in powder form on the surface of the clay, is one of the simplest ways of obtaining a glaze on pottery, the lead requiring only a relatively low temperature (about 800° Centigrade) to bring about the fusion of glaze with pot. A lead-glaze may be brilliant and luscious in quality, and may readily be coloured with other metallic oxides, usually copper to produce leaf-green or iron to give tones of yellow or brown. The ease with which lead-glazed ware could be produced and its many potentialities as a ceramic medium made it one of the main types of pottery to be used in Europe over a period of almost fifteen hundred years. With the development of more technically sophisticated and practically advantageous ceramic bodies and glazes in the 18th century,

however, lead-glazed wares tended to be relegated increasingly to the status of peasant pottery, whilst the discovery of the nature of lead-poisoning towards the end of the same century further militated against its widespread use for other than decorative purposes in modern society.

The technique of making lead-glazed pottery had been known in many parts of the Roman Empire (see pp. 36–40), and even with the break-down of the Empire the art was never wholly lost. Even if it was extinguished in the western and northern provinces, it was certainly conserved in the eastern provinces which formed the traditional heartlands of the Byzantine Empire, the great successor to the power of Rome in the east.

294 *(previous page)*. 13th-century representation of medieval jugs. There are jugs stored on shelves in a cupboard *(left)*; water is being drawn from a well *(right)*, while jugs of water are being carried to an upper floor *(centre)*. MS. British Museum, London.

295 a)

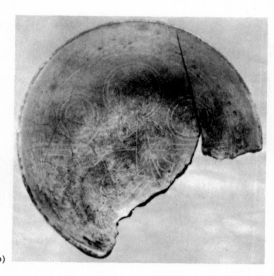

b)

c)

295 a). The Constantine bowl. Thin buff body with incised interior decoration (see 295 b), covered by a uniform pinkish-white lead-glaze, underfired, full of bubbles and consequently opaque and rather thick. Rome (?); about AD 330. Diam. 5⅛ in. (13 cm.). On the exterior, radial and

concentric lines of the same glaze form small panels which are filled alternately with white and blue glaze. Within the foot, a central disc is reserved in the pinkish-white glaze; also radial lines, which are filled with yellow glaze. Formerly Collection of Count Tyszkiewicz. British Museum, London.

295 b) and c). Interior incised design of the Constantine bowl: seated three-quarter length figure of Christ in frontal view. In the field two medallions with profile heads of Constantine the Great (left) and the Empress Fausta, identified by the Latin inscription below the rim.

Byzantine Pottery (4th–14th century)

Beside the products of court patronage in the Near and Far East, Byzantine pottery occupies a lower rank in the ceramic scale. In Constantinople, the New Rome, initially at least, the potter's was a modest craft, as it had been when Rome itself was the capital of the Empire. Vessels of refined quality, like the Constantine bowl, doubtless found their way there, but at court the demand was for gold and silver. For humbler functions, production of traditional utility earthenware continued, probably in many centres, and descendants of the Roman red-gloss tablewares were long made in the East.

At Constantinople glazing was neglected in the age of Justinian, but not unknown. Pottery from an early 6th-century level at Sta Sophia includes a glazed bowl-centre with a cross in relief impressed in the whitish clay, the counterpart of stamped red-gloss contemporaries. This is a poor relation of a green-glazed bowl from Rome in the Metropolitan Museum, New York, which has inside an impressed relief medallion with seated figures of St Peter and St Paul. Other early glazed fragments were found in the Great Palace and a whole bowl in a Byzantine wreck off the Carian coast, in both cases with 7th-century coins.

Glazed earthenware became more general as adversity put vessels of precious metal increasingly out of reach. There is evidence of active experimentation, in clay, glaze and firing, during the 8th and early 9th century, coinciding with the rapid development of Islamic glazed pottery. A whitish body without slip was preferred to the Roman red, and it was commonly covered with a canary-yellow, more rarely a green glaze. But moulded interior decoration in relief in the *sigillata* tradition was retained and, among external treatments, the application of 'petals' of different clays recalls a relief decoration found on Italian slip-decorated lead-glaze ware of the 1st century and on the glazed cups of Roman Asia Minor. To the same period belong the first essays in decoration drawn with a stylus or a toothed tool in the whitish body, including a group with liturgical inscriptions. Similar techniques were used over a long period on red-bodied vessels also, likewise without slip and sometimes enhanced with applied plastic ornament.

The developing industry was not confined to Constantinople. At Corinth local potters were active from the revival of the city around AD 850, initially making chafing-dishes and other kitchen wares with transparent yellow glaze showing brown over the red body. Further afield, a Byzantine parentage is suggested for a glazed ware made in Rome from the late 8th century and the re-appearance of glazing in Anglo-Saxon England is also attributable to the communication of Byzantine techniques.

The Byzantine recovery under the Macedonian dynasty (AD 867–1057) saw a wide distribution of the white-bodied pottery, both the moulded relief ware in its developed form and a superior white fabric with painted decoration. The moulded designs range from elementary crosses and rosettes to birds and creatures of the bestiary art which the iconoclasts had popularised. Scenes with human figures also occur, in the 'Hellenistic' style characteristic of the Macedonian renaissance. Much of this relief ware reached South Russia in the 9th and 10th centuries; in Greece its importation continued into the 11th century.

The contemporary painted pottery, known as 'polychrome ware', was the most ambitious of all Byzantine fabrics. A superior quality of the white clay was used, on which the decoration was added in vitreous colours. That done, the whole surface was sometimes covered by a thin transparent glaze, but often the white ground appears matt and bare. Occasionally an opaque white was also used. Crosses and rosettes within foliate borders, as well as animals, birds and figure-subjects, were outlined in black against the white ground, and enriched with yellow, green, blue and other colours. Red, apparently the clay known as Armenian bole, was more sparingly used, often to stipple the ground, and occasionally a pigment made from powdered gold. A variant more in keeping with 11th-century style employed a thick lustrous black in tightly-knit designs, while another later variety favoured a green or blue ground for its animal and figure subjects. Although this is a fragile luxury ware and far from common, it has been found in Russia, Bulgaria, Greece and Sicily, as well as in Istanbul. Its repute in the West won it a chapter in the craftsman's compendium, compiled by the monk Theophilus, and it may well have been the progenitor of the earliest Italian maiolica.

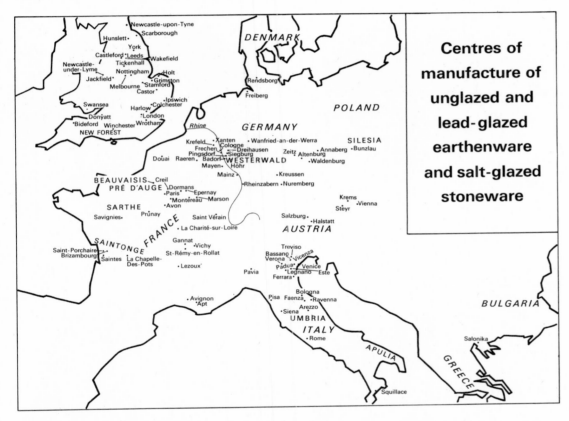

296

296. Unglazed amphora; buff body with horizontal ribbing. Byzantine, 6th–7th century. Ht. 20 in. (51 cm.). Found in a well in Athens. Ribbing, continuing a late Roman tradition, was long used on Byzantine plain wares. Similar amphoras, shipwrecked off Turkey, were datable by coins. Agora Museum, Athens.

297 a) and b). Bowl of green lead-glazed earthenware with impressed decoration. Probably Constantinople, 4th–6th century AD Diam. 5½ in. (14 cm.). This bowl, found in the catacombs on the Via Appia at Rome, bears, inside in the centre, an impressed medallion with the seated figures of St Peter and St Paul with a Chi-Rho monogram

within a wreath between them. This motif is repeated in four impressed medallions on the outside of the bowl. The use of impressed decoration is perhaps a continuation of an earlier Roman tradition. Metropolitan Museum of Art, New York. Fletcher Fund Purchase, 1952.

298. Centre of bowl of moulded relief ware; white body with deep yellow lead-glaze. In central medallion, a huntsman or warrior stripped to the waist, wearing crested helmet and armed with a spear, follows his hound. Exterior unglazed. Byzantine; 10th century. From Istanbul (Post-Office site). Private collection.

297 a)   b)

298

The white body was perhaps inspired by the creamy-white T'ang porcelain, which 9th-century Mesopotamian potters also emulated. This Byzantine pottery shares other features of Near-Eastern ceramics: its decoration (but not its technique) has been compared with the 10th-century slip-decorated ware of Samarqand and is sometimes akin to that of the Baghdad lustre wares, although there was no close imitation. Even the appearance on the Byzantine wares of motifs based on the Kufic script does not necessarily imply direct copying from Islamic vessels, for, as a result of the general cultural interchanges between Islam and Byzantium, these motifs had become part and parcel of the Byzantine repertory.

Likewise, when the Byzantines adopted ceramic tiles for architectural decoration it is not certain that they were borrowing from Islam. The earliest dated Baghdad tiles, those of about AD 860 in the Great Mosque at Kairouan, are indeed somewhat earlier than the polychrome 'plaques of glass' with floral designs employed by

Basil I (AD 867–886) in the Great Palace. But the oldest surviving Byzantine tiles, including those made in Bulgaria for the new capital built by the Tsar Symeon (AD 893–927), represent a mature industry. In contrast to their Islamic counterparts, they were purpose-made for their particular functions as colonnettes and cornices: they are also much thinner, sometimes as little as 3 mm. Some of the designs do have oriental connections, but usually through use of Sasanian motifs, long previously adopted by Byzantium.

Most of the Byzantine tiles come from churches, where they evidently served to embellish the screens, icon-frames and other focal points. Figure-subjects of a sacred character are not uncommon. They include small medallions with busts of saints recalling contemporary enamels; while among a series of larger tiles is one with a bust of the Virgin and Child. The technique is that of the polychrome pottery, and analysis has shown a high lead content in the vitreous colours.

299

300

301

302 a)

b)

c)

299. Green-glazed jar; dark red body with bands of ornament impressed with triangular stamps of diminishing size, and circles at the rim; covered by a green lead-glaze. Byzantine; 9th–10th century. From Istanbul. Ht. 7½ in. (19 cm.). Comparable plain glazed kitchen wares include chafing-dishes which incorporate a hollow stand with perforations and a larger opening for the insertion of live coals. Victoria and Albert Museum, London.

300. Fragmentary dish of moulded relief ware; white body with pale green glaze. Spread eagle in central medallion. Byzantine; 10th century. From Istanbul. Max. width 6½ in. (16·5 cm.). This type of decoration, made by impressing a carved stamp into the soft clay, was commonly applied to vessels of fruit-dish form, some of them of substantial size. David Talbot Rice, Edinburgh.

301. Plate of 'polychrome ware'; white body. Byzantine; 10th century. Diam. 8¼ in. (21 cm.). Ht. 1⅞ in. (4·7 cm.). In the central medallion two parrots flank a tree on a white ground; they are blue with yellow wings, green and yellow tails and red beaks. The panels of the inner border are alternately purple and green, edged with yellow. The half rosettes of the outer border are white with red centres on alternately green and blue grounds. The rim is blue. From Taman. Hermitage Museum, Leningrad.

302. Fragments of Byzantine white-bodied 'Polychrome ware' 10th–11th century.
a) Dish centre: a youth in green tunic with staff and shield; surrounding panels alternately purple and green, edged with yellow. Max. width 5½ in. (14 cm.). Collection of Hüseyin Kocabasi, Istanbul.
b) Rim fragment probably from a goblet. On the exterior, below a blue edging, a pseudo-Kufic border reserved in the white ground and outlined in lustrous black. In the interior, yellow glaze. Max. width 2¾ in. (7 cm.). Arkeoloji Müzeleri, Istanbul.
c) Dish centre: between foliate sprays, four radial tongues with spots of green; four larger tongues in the outer zone, enriched with green and blue. On the exterior, splashes of red within the foot and on the side. Max. width 8⅛ in. (13 cm.). Arkeoloji Müzeleri, Istanbul.

303

304

305

306

307

308

306. 'Polychrome ware' tile colonnette; white body with decoration in yellow, pale green and blue on white within black outlines. Byzantine; 10th–11th century. From the excavation to the south of St Irene. Ht. 16½ in. (42 cm.). Fragments of similar colonnettes with the addition of gilt decoration have been found at Bodrum Camii in Istanbul, identifiable as the church erected about 920 by the Emperor Romanus I Lecapenus to shelter his tomb. Ayasofya Müzesi, Istanbul.

303. 'Polychrome ware' tile; white body, painted in brown-black on white ground with yellow-brown and green. Byzantine, 10th–11th century. From Uskube, Istanbul. 11¾ in. (30 cm.) square. Essentially an image of the Incarnation, this composition echoes that of the famous icon, *Nicopoios* (Our Lady of Victory), through whom divine intervention in support of Byzantine arms was sought. This was held in particular esteem from the time of Emperor John I (964–76), whose coins were the first showing the Mother of God in this form. Louvre, Paris.

304. Dish roughly painted in underglaze-purple and green on a white body: a goat with head turned back. Byzantine, late 12th century. From the Great Palace excavations in a late Comnenian context. Diam. 7⅞ in. (20 cm.). Some dishes of this type are painted in blue alone. Despite their somewhat crude decoration, many of these dishes were exported to the Crimea, and fragments have been found in Corinth also. Arkeoloji Müzeleri, Istanbul.

305. Fragmentary bowl painted in underglaze-green and -brown on white slip covering red body. Byzantine; late 11th century. Excavated in Athens with a coin of Nicephorus III (1078–81). Diam. 10½ in. (26·7 cm.). Although comparatively few specimens of this type of decoration have been found so far in Istanbul, it is unlikely that it was used exclusively in Aegean factories. It recurs in conjunction with another technique on the bowl from Istanbul illustrated in fig. 310. Agora Museum, Athens.

307. Slip-trailed jug (handle missing); red clay, decorated with white slip under light green glaze. Byzantine; late 11th century. Excavated at Corinth and probably manufactured there. Ht. 11 in. (28 cm.). This type of decoration is also often applied to bowls and some particoloured examples are known in which half the vessel is glazed green and half yellow. Simple slip-trailed designs also figured on the exteriors of bowls decorated in the *sgraffiato* technique, particularly in the 13th century. Old Corinth Museum. From a water-colour drawing by Piet de Jong.

308. Detail of an entablature revetment of 'Polychrome ware' tiles; white body with decoration in purple, yellow and green on white within black outlines. Byzantine; 10th century. Combined ht. of all the tiles: 14½ in. (37 cm.); about 3/16 in. (5 mm.) thick. Excavated in Imrahor Camii (Church of the Studion monastery) Istanbul, probably from the sanctuary screen. Byzantine tiles were often used with effect for decorative detailwork in churches. Arkeoloji Müzeleri, Istanbul.

309

310

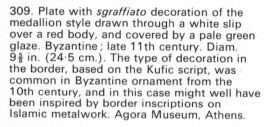

311

309. Plate with *sgraffiato* decoration of the medallion style drawn through a white slip over a red body, and covered by a pale green glaze. Byzantine; late 11th century. Diam. 9⅝ in. (24·5 cm.). The type of decoration in the border, based on the Kufic script, was common in Byzantine ornament from the 10th century, and in this case might well have been inspired by border inscriptions on Islamic metalwork. Agora Museum, Athens.

310. Deep bowl, red body with white slip; *sgraffiato* decoration combined with painting in matt green and brown. Byzantine (Constantinople); early 12th century. In the central medallion, a pigeon is depicted between foliage sprays. In the surrounding border the triangular motifs are brown, the spandrels between them green. Formerly Collection of Theodore Macridy. Benaki Museum, Athens.

311. Plate with *sgraffiato* decoration in the free style, drawn through white slip over a red body, and covered with a pale yellow glaze. Byzantine, 12th century. From Miletus, Diam. 9 in. (23 cm.). A lively rendering of a griffin pouncing on a gazelle. The 'free style' initiated a phase of bolder animal and figure subjects showing scenes of action from wild life and popular mythology. Staatliche Museen, Berlin.

The original home of the polychrome vessels and tiles is sought in the hinterland of Nicomedia (Ismid), for 'Nicomedian' pottery is known to have adorned the interior of a church on the Golden Horn. It seems probable that it was situated in the territory overrun by the Seljuqs after the disastrous battle at Mantzikert (AD 1071). This would explain the disappearance of the ware about the time the Seljuqs established their capital at Nicaea (Isnik, later the home of Turkish ceramics) as well as the inferior quality of the later Byzantine painted pottery. The latter included white-bodied dishes with animals roughly outlined in manganese-purple which tended to run in the glaze, often touched up with green or blue under a clear lead-glaze.

Meanwhile, a red-bodied slip ware, painted under a clear lead-glaze in matt green and brown, had come into its own. Wasters of this ware have been found in Corinth, where the source of its inspiration is suggested by the presence of fragments of an analogous Persian fabric. In the late 11th century, the Corinthian potters perhaps also sought to reproduce the effect of the Islamic lustre-wares, when painting on the white slip in a red clay below a transparent glaze. A simple slip-painted pottery was already being made, probably at several centres, and it was to enjoy a long vogue: both rectilinear and cursive patterns were trailed in white slip direct

on to the buff to red body under a yellow or green-tinted glaze.

Parallel with this range of painted decoration, the *sgraffiato* technique was developed, initially, in the 10th century, enriched with green and yellow by dabs of metallic oxides in the glaze covering the white body, in the manner of the T'ang prototypes. But in the 11th century, Byzantine potters, like their Persian contemporaries, preferred a plain glaze, usually of yellowish tint, and the more effective method of incising through a white slip to expose a darker body. Plates and bowls with central medallions and elaborate borders drawn in minute detail were evidently made in Constantinople well before AD 1100, by which time provincial factories were already copying them. Occasionally this *sgraffiato* technique and the painted green and brown decoration appear side by side. A little later the *sgraffiato* technique was applied to figure and animal subjects in a free style filling the whole interior, but still drawn with a fine point. A bowl of this type in the campanile of Santi Giovanni e Paolo in Rome (about 1181) illustrates the arrival of Byzantine wares in the West, by way of the Empire's dwindling foothold in South Italy and in the baggage of returning Crusaders. In a local variety made at Corinth the designs were stippled with dots of red slip before glazing.

In the course of the 12th century the use of the gouge was

304

305

307

309
310

310

311

312

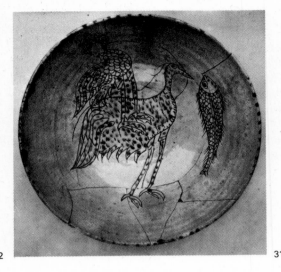

312

313

312. Bowl of slipped red ware with free style *sgraffiato* decoration stippled with dots of red slip, under pale yellow-green glaze (exterior green) : a fish, and a harpy on a stork. Byzantine (Corinth) ; 12th century. Diam. 8¼ in. (20·8 cm.). Old Corinth Museum.

314

315

316

313. Yellow-glazed plate of red ware covered with white slip, cut away to form a medallion with a figure scene in relief, representing, it has been suggested, the rape of the daughter of the Emire Haplorrabdes, as told in the Byzantine epic of Digenes Akritas. Byzantine ; late 12th century. Diam. 9⅞ in. (25·2 cm.). Excavated with coins of Manuel I (1143–80) and Alexius III (1195–1203) at Corinth, but probably an import. Old Corinth Museum.

314. Yellow-glazed plate, with white slip over the red body, partially cut away so as to form an animal medallion showing a lioness bringing down a deer. Byzantine, late 12th century. Diam. 10¼ in. (26 cm.). This technique remained popular in the 13th century, especially on bowls with hares in small medallions. Excavated at Corinth, but probably an import. Old Corinth Museum.

315. Plate with free style decoration incised with the gouge through a white slip over a red body, and covered with yellow glaze. Byzantine, late 12th century. Diam. 15½ in. (39·5 cm.). The warrior here is probably the frontier hero, Digenes Akritas, who has been identified on other plates decorated in the same technique. The poem and the ballads which recount his exploits could have inspired such representations ; they give a vivid picture of conditions in the borderlands between Byzantium and Islam. Similar plates found at Corinth are regarded as imports. Norman Colville Collection, London.

316. Large *sgraffiato* plate with hero slaying a monster, drawn through a white slip over a red body, and covered by a yellow glaze. Sparse touches of brown on the border. Byzantine (Cherson) ; late 12th century. Diam. 13¾ in. (35 cm.). The border treatment links this plate and a dish found with it (decorated with a highly stylised beast in a central medallion) to bowls found in Istanbul. Hermitage Museum, Leningrad.

developed, initially to emphasise the elements of fine *sgraffiato* decoration by exposing more of the body. Later it was employed alone to incise the design on a class of plates with bold over-all subjects including heroes of the Asiatic frontier immortalised in Byzantine ballads. In a final development, the gouge was used for the reverse technique, in which the background of the design was cut away often removing part of the body as well as the slip and leaving the design in slight relief. This technique, also found on the contemporary slip ware of Persian Kurdistan and the Caucasus, was applied to characteristic Byzantine medallion treatments, among which animal subjects predominate.

The colouring of *sgraffiato* designs with fugitive yellow-brown and green tints, which tended to spread in the glaze, was widespread under the Palaeologue emperors (AD 1261–1453). The practice was foreshadowed on some early 12th-century plates where painted decoration in stable brown and green appears side by side with *sgraffiato* patterns. The tentative use of colour to pick out the latter appears on a ware which was apparently already current before the Latin seizure of Constantinople (AD 1204). This ware is also the first of Byzantine style to employ tripod stilts to separate the pots during firing. It is a thinly potted, well-fired red fabric, commonly represented by small bowls with minimal fine-point and gouge decoration

reinforced with sparse strokes of yellow-brown; the more ambitious plate from Cherson with the slaying of a lion may well be related to it. This ware is widely distributed, from Black Sea sites and Istanbul to Greece and Cyprus, where it had a local derivative. At Al Mina in Syria it antedates the regional 13th-century ware of this class. If this early coloured *sgraffiato* was made in Constantinople, as its distribution suggests, it is noteworthy that, after the recovery of the city by Michael Palaeologus in 1261, incised decoration without added colour also seems to have remained in favour. Indeed, the most elaborate examples of the incised technique, both bowls and jugs, are best assigned to the early Palaeologue period; while derivatives with rudimentary stars, plaits and monograms appear to have been made right up to the Turkish Conquest in 1453. The presence of these Palaeologan incised wares on Black Sea sites is probably attributable to Genoese trade based on the Golden Horn. But there were other centres of production, and Salonika was one of them, to judge by local finds of distinctive bowls, on which the gouge was used to darken the breasts of the much favoured birds.

The development of coloured *sgraffiato* pottery at Byzantium and elsewhere was doubtless stimulated by Crusader distribution of the superior variety made in Syria in the 13th century. Decorated in a mixed style for both Saracen and Crusader markets, this ware

105

reached the Aegean and even Italy. Features of the Syrian bowls and dishes are repeated on Palaeologan pieces found in Istanbul, such as the flat rim and the use of purple in addition to the usual green and yellow-brown. Some of the Palaeologan ware is of fine quality, understandable since now pottery was used even at the emperor's table; but though the colours could be neatly applied they have often run in the glaze. It was by the arrival of such vessels as these and their counterparts from other centres that the technique was communicated to Italy.

The potteries of Salonika also adopted the coloured *sgraffiato* manner and among other centres of manufacture one of the most active was Cyprus. There, under the Lusignan dynasty (AD 1191–1489), an initially Byzantine style, making some use of the gouge in sparse decoration with little or no added colour, gave way to fully-coloured designs in the Syrian manner. The 14th-century Cypriot bowls have distinctive vertical rims and increasingly high feet; as an alternative to rosettes and knots of Byzantine character,

they frequently bear a loving couple or a festive female figure. Goblets, jugs and jars are less common, but the bowls were exported to neighbouring countries and even to Italy.

More specifically Byzantine pottery had for a long time been finding its way to the West. It is true that already in the 13th-century Italian monopoly of the Levant trade had carried the proto-maiolica ware in the reverse direction, to the Aegean and to Syria; but it should not be overlooked that this evidently South Italian fabric, owed much to Byzantine antecedents. Likewise, after the Fall of Constantinople, when the humble Levantine descendants of Byzantine wares were eclipsed by more sumptuous competitors, the *sgraffiato* and carved fabrics imported from North Italy were returning, in a sense, to the place of their birth. The interest of the parent Byzantine wares lies less in their quality than in their variety, in their tenuous thread of continuity from the ancient world and in their intermediary but vital role in the revival of glazed pottery in Western Europe.

317

318

319

320

317. Jug with rich decoration incised through white slip over red body, and covered with yellow glaze. Byzantine (probably Constantinople); late 13th century. Ht. 9½ in. (24 cm.). The gouge is freely used, notably to cut away the ground of the split-palmette motifs. From the excavations to the south of St Irene. Ayasofya Müzesi, Istanbul.

318. Jar with *sgraffiato* decoration drawn through white slip over red body and coloured with green and yellow-brown, which have run in the clear covering glaze. Cyprus; 14th century. Ht. 12 in. (30·5 cm.). Found in Nicosia. Cyprus Museum, Nicosia.

319. Deep bowl with *sgraffiato* decoration drawn through white slip over red body and coloured purple, green and yellow-brown under a clear lead-glaze. Byzantine (Constantinople); 14th century. Diam. 10⅜ in. (26·3 cm.). The use of purple, in addition to the usual green and yellow-brown, is not common, though it occurs in the 13th-century Syrian ware. Benaki Museum, Athens.

320. Bowl with up-turned rim and *sgraffiato* figure drawn through white slip over red body and sparsely coloured with green and yellow-brown under a clear lead-glaze. Cyprus; 14th century. Diam. 6¼ in. (16 cm.). The serving maid or courtesan (note the long

head-scarf and elegant robe) carries a wine jug and beaker. Collection of Christakis Loizides, Morphou (Cyprus).

21. The Peasant Dance by Pieter Breugel the Elder. About 1567. All the jugs depicted in this painting and shown in the details 21a) and b) above are Rhenish salt-glazed stoneware. Large quantities of stoneware were made in the Rhineland and widely exported. A three-handled jug, very similar to the one represented here, appears on a wing in the Nikolaikirche, Kalkar (Lower Rhine, Germany, not far from the Dutch border), in part of a painting by Jan Joost of 1508–12. The Breugel painting is in the Kunsthistorisches Museum, Vienna.

a

b

21

Medieval Pottery

Italy

Following directly on from the late Roman tradition, the type of pottery found in Italy in the early Middle Ages was purely utilitarian. Side by side with receptacles of poorer workmanship—like the vats for storing water, wine or oil which were directly descended from the coarser Roman wares—there was a finer type of pottery, used for tableware and also in the kitchen and for pharmacy, in which the plain earthenware body was often coated with a coloured lead-glaze to make it non-porous. These were small vessels of various shapes, amphoras, jugs, small pots, bowls etc. Some pitchers, reminiscent of the elegant shapes of classical art, with a footless ovoid body, short neck and small tubular or flattened spout, have been recovered from the spring of the nymph, Juturna, in the Roman Forum, and at Ostia. In these the refined decoration of figurative modelling in relief of the Imperial Age has been abandoned, and where there is any ornamentation at all it is limited to a reproduction of the very simple motif of a pine cone, with the scales spaced out in a few vertical lines, or clustered together haphazardly. Flasks with spherical bodies and tall necks, found as often in the North as in the South, have no decoration at all other than a coating of a tawny or yellowish glaze. Vases with a dark green glaze, like those in Rome, have been discovered at Tharros in Sardinia. In the Ravenna-Romagna region, at Faenza, handled jugs with spouts (formed by folding the lip resulting from the drawing in of the roughly cylindrical body) appear side by side with small short-necked spherical pots, also with handles, and covered with a more or less luminous green glaze. An elaborately formed pitcher, in the shape of two opposed truncated cones, with a tubular spout and a handle decorated with pine scales on the shoulder, the whole entirely coated with an amber glaze, was recently brought to light in excavations in the old parish of Sta Maria in Padovetere in the Spina district of the Comacchio valleys. Together with the bowls and plates from the monasteries of the low-lying land round Ferrara, Comacchio, Ravenna (Pomposa, Valle de Mezzano) and in the city of Ravenna itself (S. Vitale), this pitcher shows the persistence of styles which stemmed from those examples of technical achievement which were originally brought to Rome from the Near East. Their influence was consolidated by Byzantine wares in the areas of Italy which kept the closest contacts with the Eastern Empire. The warm-toned glaze, coloured with iron oxide, was used until Renaissance times and even later.

321

322

22. Relief-decorated polychrome lead-glazed stove-tiles, with tin-glaze for the white only. Nuremberg; mid-16th century. In the late Middle Ages in Germany the tiles decorating domestic room-heating stoves became increasingly ornate and their manufacture a widespread industry. Particularly fine tiles were made at Nuremberg; the costume of the royal couple on the tiles illustrated mirrors Nuremberg fashion of the mid-16th century. The growing influence of maiolica, a medium ultimately preferred for tile-production, is here clearly apparent in the polychrome palette. Germanisches Nationalmuseum, Nuremberg.

321. Vase of ovoid form with narrow foot and long neck in the shape of a truncated cone. The lead-glaze is dark green on the outside, thinner and amber-coloured inside. Paleo-Italian ceramic period. Italy, Sardinia, 7th century. Ht. 6⅞ in. (17·5 cm.). This example, like most vases of this period, is without any decoration, but the shape reveals a noble tradition, shown also in the technique of the two colours (of the outside and inside), common to vessels of the Imperial age. The vase was found at Tharros in Sardinia, together with coins of the Emperors Justinian and Heraclius. British Museum, London.

322. Jug of ovoid form (spout missing), coated with dark green glassy glaze; decorated with flattened bosses scattered apparently at random over the surface, with a short cylindrical neck with horizontal reeding. Paleo-Italian ceramic period, 8th–9th centuries. Ht. 10¼ in. (26 cm.). This jug shows the continuation of the technique of vitreous glaze known to Roman potters of the Imperial age throughout all the lands of the Empire. The ornamentation in relief is reminiscent of the refined decorative style of the Golden Age. From excavations in the Roman Forum (Fountain of Juturna). Antiquarium of the Roman Forum.

By the year AD 1000, through contacts with the Byzantine and Islamic worlds, the whole of the Mediterranean basin, including Italy, knew and had been influenced by their pottery. The plain green- and amber-coloured glazes, which had been the only ones used for the last thousand years, now began to give way to a new, if timid, sense of colour. This was revealed in painted or incised (*sgraffiato*) decoration. The lead-glaze often lost its colouring matter to show a white background underneath, which was first achieved with a light coating of white slip, applied directly on to the coloured body of the vase or plate beneath the glaze, and later with a layer of

glaze rendered opaque white by the addition of tin-oxide to the transparent silico-alkaline mixture ('enamel'). This glaze provided both a non-porous surface and a white ground for decoration.

These were the first uncertain steps in the making of tin-glazed earthenware ('*maiolica*') and of the slipped lead-glazed wares ('*mezza-maiolica*') with incised ('*sgraffiato*') designs, which were to develop side by side during the next few centuries, each of the two groups having its own particular manifestations. Maiolica is dealt with in the chapter on tin-glazed pottery and the later developments of Italian *sgraffiato* ware further on in the present chapter.

323

324

323. Jug, yellow-glazed earthenware, with relief decoration, French; 14th century. Ht. 9¼ in. (23·5 cm.). The protruding points and lines in relief protect as well as embellish the body of the vessel. The patterns were applied before firing by means of slip trailed through the open tip of a bull's horn. Examples of these primitive implements have come down to us. Louvre, Paris.

324. Set of four tiles (made-up group) in lead-glazed pottery with white decoration inlaid on red clay. French (originating from the church at Haulzy, Marne); 14th century. Each tile 5⅛ in. (13 cm.) square. This 'wheel' or dial-shaped composition over four juxtaposed tiles is of a type common to French medieval pavements. It comes with a concentric inscription which, in this instance, gives the name 'Henault', no doubt the donor, since other tiles of the same group bear the words 'Colins me fist' ('Colins made me'). Louvre, Paris.

France

On the territory of Roman Gaul the technique of lead-glazing was known in at least one centre in Roman times (see p. 39). After the Roman period it seems for a while to have been forgotten. A group of vessels from cemeteries in Paris, which can only be roughly dated to between the 10th and 13th centuries, are mostly decorated with parallel lines of red pigment but spots or drips of lead glaze (perhaps accidental) are also found on them. Some yellow or green glazed fragments may go as far back as the 9th century. It is, however, only in the 14th century that the art of making glazed pottery was truly established in France, from when the traditional processes have survived unchanged to the present day.

A large number of small objects of coloured lead-glazed earthenware, such as money-boxes, water whistles, children's toys and various decoys, as well as anthropomorphic vessels, come from the moats which in 1356 were dug along the old city wall of Paris (Left Bank), built by Philippe-Auguste. The Paris sewers and the bed of the Seine have also yielded examples which display interesting types of relief and polychrome decoration. Other rather similar examples, found in the south of England, from the bed of the Thames at London, or in the Low Countries, are products of the same technique and give medieval glazed pottery a somewhat international character. Attribution to a locality or to a precise date remains virtually impossible. These decorated jugs, with their lines in relief and raised spots which were probably intended to protect the body of the vessel, continued in use for a long time. They are all the same capacity and may have been used as liquid-measures.

More certain information can be obtained about tiles, an important branch of medieval pottery, by studying the architecture

of the buildings where they have often remained *in situ*. Several tiles covered with a thick green glaze, for example, from Sainte-Colombe-lès-Sens (Yonne), could date to as far back as the 9th century. The tile pavements of the 12th-century Cistercian abbeys were incised with simple geometric designs in the lines of which green or brown glaze collected.

The first important tile floors known to us are those which Viollet-le-Duc discovered in the Basilica of St Denis. They probably belong to the time of Abbé Suger, in the middle of the 12th century. They are made in the same way as hard-stone mosaics, by the juxtaposition of small monochrome tiles of different shapes and sizes according to the needs of the design. The end result is highly decorative and has a precision of style extremely architectural in nature, but the difficulties of assembling the tiles must have caused this sort of work to be abandoned. In the well-known floor rosette of the church of Saint-Pierre-sur-Dives (Calvados), which dates from the beginning of the 13th century, the square tiles all have their own individual decoration; they provide an early example of the use of slip, that is to say of a surface layer of fine clay into which designs of a contrasting colour are inlaid.

This process produced most of the fine tile-pavements of the 13th, 14th and 15th centuries, which are very common in France, particularly in the northern and eastern regions, as is borne out by the rich collection of the Baron de Baye, acquired by Sèvres Museum. The same types of decoration are to be found everywhere because the tilemakers were itinerant craftsmen who travelled from one place to another with their moulds. Towards the 13th century a new style developed, the elements of which are borrowed directly from French heraldry. Each tile has a ground design of heraldic character, such as hatching, chequers, chevrons, lozenges, etc. or is charged with heraldic motifs such as fleurs-de-lis, trefoils, quatrefoils or cinquefoils, quadrupeds, fishes or birds. There are endless permutations. In general the motifs are merely ornamental which the tilemaker arranges at will with a skill and intelligence that are astonishing, exploiting the contrast of light clay on dark and vice versa. The human figure, employed from the 13th century onwards, became more and more common in the 14th and 15th centuries, when it appears in scenes taken from contemporary life—from

hunting and falconry, raised in the Middle Ages to the status of a true art, or showing jugglers, fools, and tumblers and so on who were the favourite entertainment of the time.

Decorated tiles grouped in fours or multiples of four sometimes also make up magnificent floral rosettes, wheels or clock-dials, surrounded by inscriptions from which we learn the names of tilemakers no doubt renowned in their day.

Subsequently the tile-pavements of glazed earthenware gradually lost ground to those of painted faience; but for generations the tilemakers continued to use the old moulds.

324

325

326

325 a)–d). Drawings of costrels and cressets (with inset cross sections).
a) Medieval barrel costrel, 13th century. W. 5⅝ in. (14·3 cm.). From Winchester.
b) Late Saxon globular costrel, 10th century. Ht. 9¼ in. (23 cm.). From the Saxon town of Thetford. Norwich Castle Museum. Both these types of water container or 'pilgrim's bottle' were in use in Late Saxon and Medieval times and could be suspended from the waist.
c) Spiked and d) footed cresset lamps, 10th and 11th century, from the Saxon town of Thetford. Norwich Castle Museum. Ht. 3·4 in. (8·6 cm.) and 3·2 in. (8·1 cm.). These oil lamps were lit by means of a floating wick.

326. Two-handled Cistercian ware cup from Kirkstall Abbey, Yorkshire. Hard dark red ware with black glaze. Applied decoration in yellow stamped strips. Late 15th or early 16th century. Ht. 6 in. (15·2 cm.). Cistercian ware was made at kilns near Wakefield and Leeds and is common on monastic sites in Yorkshire. Leeds City Museums, Kirkstall, Leeds.

England to 1550
The Saxon Period

After the departure of the Romans in the early 5th century, there was a complete breakdown in the highly organised and industrialised pottery industry in England. The Anglo-Saxon settlers came from parts of northern Europe where well made wheel-thrown pottery fired in developed kilns was unknown. Over large parts of England rough hand-made pottery fired in simple clamp or bonfire kilns in the tradition of the Pre-Roman Iron Age continued in use with very little change for many hundreds of years. Urns decorated with stamped and incised designs were used for burying the ashes of the dead in those parts of the country, mainly the Midlands and Eastern England, where cremation was practised. Early urns have simple linear incised patterns between pushed-out bosses but in the 6th century stamped designs appear and gradually the bosses disappear, leaving stamped patterns defined by incised lines. These designs often form pendant triangles. Pottery used in the home was usually coarser, as might be expected, and was largely undecorated.

Over most of Southern and Midland England these rough hand-made types of pottery continued in use for nearly six hundred years until just before the Norman Conquest. In East Anglia, however, after the end of the Pagan period and during the conversion to Christianity in the early 7th century, there was increasing trade contact with North-West Europe. In the Rhineland the Roman pottery tradition had survived unbroken and during the second quarter of the 7th century pottery made on a slow wheel and fired in proper kilns was introduced from there into East Anglia. Large-scale manufacture begun at Ipswich (Suffolk), one of the first important trade towns to be established in Saxon England and which was to

327. Hand-made pagan Saxon cinerary urn with typical decoration of pushed-out bosses and incised and stamped patterns. Ht. 7½ in. (19 cm.). From the Anglian cremation cemetery at Lackford, Suffolk. Late 6th or early 7th century AD. University Museum of Archaeology and Ethnology, Cambridge.

325

327

328

329

remain a centre of the pottery industry for five hundred years. This pottery (Ipswich ware) comprised small unglazed cooking pots, bowls and spouted pitchers showing influence from the Rhineland and Frisia, thereby providing archaeological evidence for the activities of Frisian traders who, according to documentary sources, were in control of most of the trade routes across the North Sea at this time.

Ipswich ware persisted for two hundred years, during which time it spread over most of East Anglia but no further, although some of the pitchers were traded as far away as Canterbury and York. During the second quarter of the 9th century there were further influences from the Continent, where a flourishing pottery industry was now established at Badorf and at Pingsdorf, near Bonn, resulting in a better quality pottery made on a fast wheel with a considerable degree of precision. This Late Saxon improvement first went into manufacture at Ipswich, where it is found together with imports of Badorf and Pingsdorf wares confirming contacts with the Rhineland. The main forms were, as in the Middle Saxon period, small cooking pots, bowls and spouted pitchers, but other forms were now developed, such as storage jars, cresset lamps and costrels.

By the early 10th century, wheel-thrown pottery was widespread over eastern England and nine groups of Late Saxon pottery have

now been identified between Suffolk and Northumberland. This distribution covers the area of the Danelaw, and it is thought that the increased trade throughout this area as a result of the Danish settlement was responsible for the quick spread of pottery produced on an industrial scale. Most of these pots were in unglazed hard sandy fabrics usually reduced to a grey colour in the kiln, but at Stamford (Lincolnshire) a much finer pottery was made. 'Stamford ware' was made from special estuarine clays with very little iron content so that in an oxidising atmosphere they fired to a fine off-white colour. The spouted pitchers, and some of the bowls, were glazed with a thick even pale yellow, orange or green lead-glaze. This was the first time since the Roman period that glaze was used in England. The technical tradition no doubt derived from Byzantium or the Islamic world, probably by way of intermediaries as yet unidentified. From the 8th century onwards, however, lead-glazed pottery was made at various scattered centres in Italy, France and southern Germany, and these may have provided the link with the Mediterranean. Stamford glazed wares were traded all over England and at Winchester in the same period a second centre of lead-glazed pottery was set up, possibly in the 10th century. 'Winchester ware' was much coarser than Stamford ware but was more highly decorated with incised and applied motifs.

328
326

328. Late Saxon cooking pot, bowl and spouted pitcher. Hard grey sandy ware. 'Thetford ware', from the Saxon town. 10th or 11th century. Typically small cooking pot. Ht. 6⅖ in. (16·3 cm.). Typical pitcher with tubular spout and three handles. Contrast with medieval shapes (fig. 339). Castle Museum, Norwich.

329 a)–d). Medieval jugs and cooking pots. Oxford; 13th century. Cooking pots are wide and squat, quite different from Saxon ones. b), c). Ht. 8 3/10 in. (21 cm.); 3 7/10 in. (9·5 cm.). Globular jugs with vertical applied strips or horizontal grooves replace Saxon pitchers. a), d). Ht. 9 1/10 in. (23 cm.); 11 1/10 in. (28 cm.). Ashmolean Museum, Oxford.

330. Grimston ware face jug. Hard grey sandy ware with green glaze and applied patterns in brown. Ht. 12 in. (30·5 cm.). Late 13th or early 14th century. A kiln site near King's Lynn, Norfolk, supplied Norfolk and Cambridgeshire and even Bergen, Norway. University Museum of Archaeology and Ethnology, Cambridge.

331. Midlands type of hard buff ware jug with green glaze and applied brown scrolls. Coventry; late 13th or early 14th century. Ht. 14 9/10 in. (37·7 cm.). Coarse copies of Midlands scroll jugs were made near Bristol, in Lincolnshire and elsewhere. Herbert Art Gallery and Museum, Coventry.

330

331

332

The change to medieval forms

Late Saxon good quality wheel-thrown pottery continued for three hundred years until the middle of the 12th century with very little change. The term 'Saxo-Norman' is used for this overlap period. During the first half of the 11th century there was a resurgence of the rough hand-made types of Saxon pottery which had been made in Wessex and other parts of England not affected by the Saxo-Norman wheel-thrown types. New shapes were introduced: the cooking pots became larger and the Saxon small tall narrow cooking pot was replaced by the wide squat medieval shape. This must be due to a change in methods of cooking food but the reason for the change is not fully understood. At the same time the spouted pitcher with its applied spout and small strap handles was gradually replaced by the medieval type of jug with a single large handle and a small pinched-out lip. These developments also took place in eastern England and the two groups seem to have existed side by side for over a hundred years with very little interchange of form between them. The new medieval types were clearly based on

Saxon traditions and at first the cooking pots were largely built up by hand. This period, however, seems also to have seen the introduction of the slow wheel, on which the rim of the pot could be brought into true and properly finished.

By the 12th century the pottery was of better quality and was made on a fast wheel though the lack of kiln sites found for this period suggests that primitive types of kiln were still in use. During the medieval period there was a tremendous variation in pottery fabrics and shapes in different parts of the country. The kilns producing coarse wares seem to have had a range of less than twenty miles for the distribution of their goods, resulting in intense regional variation. Jugs during this period were usually very simple and poorly glazed. Decoration was almost unknown, being confined to simple incised or applied patterns. As in the earlier period the main shapes were cooking pots, jugs and bowls. Other forms were rare but included cressets, crucibles, storage jars and firecovers.

The finely decorated Saxo-Norman Winchester ware seems to have died out in the early 12th century to be replaced by simple decorated tripod pitchers which spread over most of Wessex and the south Midlands. Stamford ware, however, became more highly decorated during the 12th century and a group of vessels, datable to the 12th or early 13th century, included not only applied strips and incised patterns but also applied decoration in full relief, the direct ancestors of the highly decorated 13th and 14th century jugs which were the peak of the medieval potter's art. In the Midlands this development started in the middle of the 13th century when the simple decorations used previously suddenly became alive and, from the hands of the individual craftsmen potters, a remarkable series of highly decorated jugs was produced. It is not known where this started but there must have been influence from the decorated Stamford ware as nowhere else was there a background for this change. The fashion soon spread and regional styles of decoration grew up with complicated spiral patterns of applied strips instead of simple vertical or horizontal patterns. Jugs were made with faces on the neck in various regional styles and at several centres fine jugs were produced with figures in relief and fully modelled hunting scenes. Most of this decoration was in one colour, usually the green lead-glaze so common in the medieval period. This was most commonly produced by reduction firing, but oxidised vessels were usually given a green colouring by the addition of copper to the lead. In some areas two-colour designs were made with the use of different coloured slips. In London three-colour decoration was

333

334

332. Aquamanile from Castle Road, Scarborough, Yorkshire, made in the form of a ram with curled horns and applied scales. Buff ware with green glaze. Late 13th or early 14th century. Length 14½ in. (36·9 cm.). Aquamaniles were used at the table for washing hands with water after eating before the general introduction of forks. The Scarborough Museum.

333. Knight jug from the Moot Hall, Nottingham. Hard sandy brown ware with dark green glaze. Tubular spout with human mask. Applied decoration in relief of knights on horseback hunting stags with hounds. Late 13th or early 14th century AD. Ht. 14 in. (35·6 cm.). Only a few of those highly decorated jugs are known. They were made in various centres besides Nottingham, e.g. Bristol and Scarborough. Castle Museum, Nottingham.

334. Jug from Whitefriars Street, London. Buff ware with yellow-green glaze. Late 14th or 15th century. Ht. 8⅗ in. (21·8 cm.). The regular shape of the body with its incised lines, the waisted foot and the projecting animal head spout are all copied from metallic forms, a common feature of late medieval jugs. The London Museum.

copied from the north French imports of the late 13th century.

During this period of the highly decorated and glazed jugs, which lasted roughly one hundred years from 1250–1350, many other forms of pot were made, though unglazed cooking pots remained the most common. There were never any medieval pottery plates or cups. These were made in wood or other materials and examples have been found on water-logged sites where they have been preserved. During this period there occur the remarkable and individual pottery aquamaniles modelled in zoomorphic forms. Types in daily use included storage jars, costrels, bottles and urinals; also mortars copying stone forms.

During the 14th and 15th century there was a marked change in medieval pottery. The individual creations of the potters of the highly decorated period were replaced by stereotyped forms which were hardly ever decorated. Jugs were produced in graded sizes of similar shape and the earlier tendency for every pot to be different was suppressed, though there was still intense regional variation. This change was clearly due to the greater industrialisation of the processes and the general effects of mass-production. Many of the forms copied metal prototypes. In certain areas such as East Anglia jugs continued to be decorated in the *sgraffiato* technique while in south-eastern England they were painted with a brushed slip.

Post-medieval pottery

The improved methods of pottery manufacture, especially the ability to control kiln temperature, led to many changes in the late medieval period. It was no longer necessary to use so much sand and grit tempering with the clays (previously necessary in order to open up the clay and prevent the uneven drying out and cracking caused by the inability of early potters to produce an even fixed temperature in their kilns) and by the early 16th century smooth red 'flower-pot' type wares came into use in south-east England. These were usually oxidised and had a brown glaze. There was a very great increase in the different types of vessels made and these included chafing dishes, candlesticks, perfume pots and many other forms. Cups were now

made for the first time and various types of plate and shallow dish. In northern England black-glazed wares were made including 'Cistercian' ware decorated with trailed white slip patterns foreshowing the 'tygs' and slipwares of the 17th century (see p. 122). In Surrey 'Tudor green' wares—with a green glaze over an off-white body—were produced, following on from the earlier tradition of rougher green-glazed buff wares and copying continental forms such as the lobed cup. With these changes the comparatively restricted series of medieval wares and shapes was replaced by an ever widening variety of form and decoration which led to the important developments of the 17th century.

335

336 a)

b)

335. Jug from Fen Ditton, Cambridgeshire. Hard red ware with painted decoration in white under a clear glaze. 14th century. Ht. 10 in. (25·3 cm.). This type of decoration is typical of many areas of south-east England in the 14th and 15th centuries. Cambridge University Museum of Archaeology and Ethnology.

336. Two jugs with a grey body akin to stoneware. Lower Rhine, Germany. (Left) about 1200; (right) about 1300. Ht. 7½ in. (19 cm.); 11 in. (28 cm.). These two jugs show the development from the squat to the slender form. The earlier jug is decorated with bands of rouletted decoration on neck and rim, and the impressions produced by the potter's

fingers on the wheel take on an ornamental character, becoming *Gurtfurchen* ('girth-grooves'). On the later examples the grooves are closer together and more regular and appear only on the neck and shoulders of the pot, gradually becoming shallower as they descend. Kunstmuseum, Düsseldorf.

Germany and Northern Europe

In the 8th century a new type of unglazed pottery supersedes the post-Roman wares of Western Central Europe with their characteristic shapes, this new ware being typified by vessels of more or less rounded form. Even if the birthplace of the new range of shapes has not yet been precisely identified, it is at least certain that the preference for rounded vessels was most marked in Lower Saxony and Friesland. It was here that the true '*Kugeltopf*' ('rounded pot') was developed, the base of which sat comfortably in the ashes of the open hearth. With the gradual sinking of the shoulders a pot of depressed pear shape ('*Bombentopf*') emerged and with the pinching-out of rudimentary feet or the addition of three legs, the skillet ('*Grapen*') was born which later became the standard product of the bronze-founders.

In the Rhineland, too, a less marked though appreciable tendency towards squatter, almost spherical shapes made itself felt. Here were produced three groups of vessels which overlap chronologically. Pottery made at Mayen ('*Mayener Ware*'), decorated with grooves and wavy lines, is made of a clay fired to a stoneware hardness and of a red tone shading to violet. The continuation of a local decorative style based on Roman models is to be seen in the rouletting of the raised bands with which the capacious storage-jars of 'Badorf' type are decorated. A resurgence of the provincial Roman tradition is also shown from the 9th century onwards by the fine pottery made of pale clay and decorated with red strokes, circles, wavy lines and dots, which is to be found in the Rhineland, in parts of northern, central and southern Germany, in Holland, northern France and southern England. The most important ware of this type from the economic point of view was the so-called 'Pingsdorf ware' which was made in the same workshops as the 'Badorf' pottery and imitated over a wide area, continuing in use until the 13th century.

Already in this early period Rhenish pottery and pottery made in the North Sea area and on the Baltic coast (then Slav territory) had reached Sweden. These wares have been excavated in the region of Lake Mälaren, side by side with local wares which have little pretension to artistic quality. Dorestad, in Friesland, achieved a position of importance as a trading-centre for the western wares which were transported from there *via* Hollingstedt on the River Treene along the 'Danewerk' an earthwork across the isthmus of Jutland to Haithabu (Hedeby) on the River Schlei, and from there to Birka, the chief trading town of central Sweden.

The use of lead-glaze spread from Byzantium, in the south and south-west *via* Italy and France, in the north *via* the sea-routes. Pots with glazed outsides appear in Hamburg as early as about 900, at the same time as in southern England (Stamford) and in the Netherlands. It seems, however, as if the German and Netherlandish potters put less glaze on their wares in the following period. The outsides of the vessels made in the 11th and 12th centuries were still only partially glazed. Lead-glaze was mostly used to seal the inside of the pot and to protect the mouth, which was subjected to especially heavy wear. From the 12th century onwards it was used for artistic effect but only on wall-tiles and floor-tiles. Nevertheless, unglazed tiles with moulded decoration were preferred. From the 13th century onwards coloured lead-glazes appear in the ornamental brickwork on the façades of North German buildings.

The relative insignificance of lead-glaze in Germany and German-influenced areas during the early and High Middle Ages may be explained at least in part by the growing diffusion of the proto-stoneware which began in the 12th century to replace Pingsdorf ware in the Rhineland. This usually blue-grey (but sometimes also reddish-brown or ochre-yellow) ware with incised grooves and

337

338

337

338

337. Tripod cooking pot ('*Grapen*') made of grey clay. North Germany, 13th–14th centuries. Ht. 7⅝ in. (19·5 cm.). These pots were made all along the North German seaboard from the 12th century onwards. They usually have a projecting handle on one side but are occasionally found with a loop handle. This northern type of vessel was copied in Hesse and Thuringia. Museum für Kunst- und Kulturgeschichte, Lübeck.

338. Bellied pot, made of bright yellow earthenware, partly glazed. Holland, about 1200. Ht. 8⅝ in. (22 cm.). Recovered from the Wieringermeer and probably made before the flooding of the village of Wieringen at the beginning of the 13th century. This type of bellied vessel with the handle set on the upper edge of the collar was used everywhere in Holland and Germany in the High Middle Ages, probably as a container for hot water. Rijksmuseum van Oudheden, Leiden.

336 rouletted decoration, from which the true stoneware evolved in the 14th century (cf. p. 129), was from a ceramic point of view superior to lead-glazed pottery. Even in the unglazed state it possessed a stronger and more compact body. If a glassy finish was desired, a wash of a vitrifiable clay was used instead of a lead-glaze, the latter being unable to withstand the high temperatures employed. A distribution map showing the spread of this ware would show that it was made in the Rhineland, in nearby Belgium and Holland, and in parts of northern central and southern Germany. In the eastern regions it appears as 'Colonial ware,' occasionally showing the influence of Slav cultures, and other variants are found in the south-east, in Moravia. Numerous finds prove that it was prized in

Scandinavia as well. From the 13th century onwards its distribution fell into the hands of the Hanseatic towns.

Where there were no suitable clays or where an older tradition lingered on, as happened in the Danube basin, in Vienna and in Hafnerzell, near Passau, the potters tried to give hardness to their pots by means of graphite, either mixed with the clay or laid on the surface. The makers of this so-called 'Eisentonware' ('iron-clay pottery') were called 'Schwarzhafner' ('black potters'). There also appeared in Swabia remarkably elegant 'smoked vessels'. These, too, testify to an older tradition, which in folk art has maintained 339 itself up to the present day.

339a)   b)   c)

339. Three black 'smoked' vessels. South Germany, 13th–14th centuries. Ht. 6¾ in. (17 cm.), 7¾ in. (19·6 cm.) and 8¾ in. (21·5 cm.). By throwing green twigs into the kiln during the firing and at the same time blocking up the air-vent, a thick, smoky atmosphere was created which produced a greyish black or black colour with a metallic sheen on the surface of the pot. Maximilian-Museum, Augsburg.

Renaissance Pottery
Italy

340–44 The characteristic lead-glazed ware of the Italian Renaissance is the slipped pottery with incised decoration sometimes called 'mezza-maiolica'. This ware, which is closer to the early Italian tradition in the way in which it is made, answered the need for colour with a red-white contrast obtained by scratching with a sharp point through the film of white slip which covered the rich red of the clay 26 beneath. This elementary colour scheme, sometimes found under a (p. 126) plain transparent green or orange glaze, might also be embellished 340–1 with a variety of flecks, streaks, marbling and cross-hatching in the same orange and green, occasionally with the addition of dark blue and purple.

The distribution of the workshops seems to have been very widespread from the 14th century onwards, especially in the 15th and 16th centuries: Northern Italy with Venetia, Emilia and Lombardy, central Italy with Tuscany and Umbria, and Apulia and Calabria in the south. In other areas the evidence which has been accumulated is still limited; we do not know if this is because insufficient attention has been given to excavations or because the work really was less extensive. However, in the southern districts the production of household wares was flourishing, both those with

a white slip surface and a transparent glaze, and others with green or tawny glazes where the underlying decoration was sometimes drawn with a brush dipped in the slip.

In Venetia, besides the two more famous centres of Venice and Padua, during the course of the 15th and 16th centuries a number of 343 other workshops were set up at Verona, Legnano, Vicenza, Bassano, Treviso, Lendinara, Este and Pordenone.

The sustained maritime contacts that Venice, the principal centre in Venetia, had with the East, and the possibility of obtaining the raw material, white clay, from the nearby clay-pits of Vicenza encouraged this method of finishing ceramic wares. The stylised foliage patterns were supplemented by heraldic motifs and inscriptions and eventually with animals and human figures intended to represent stock types, or occasionally characters from a tale or from history. Incised decoration was bold and decisive in the 15th century, and at the beginning of the 16th, but the drawing became lighter and more sketchy as the 16th century progressed, owing to developments in the maiolica potteries. Sometimes the decoration was achieved in the same way as on champlevé enamel, that is by removing large areas of white slip with a spatula so that the

343 pattern appeared in light shallow relief against the darker red background of the clay. Sometimes this basic colouring was left on its own; often it would be added to by touches of green, orange, pale yellow, dark blue and purple, seldom with much respect for the contours of the design.

In Lombardy the production of simple wares, decorated mainly with geometricised plant-motifs, was followed late in the 17th century by more refined products from the workshops of the Cuzio 342 family at Pavia, where the priest Antonio Maria left a series of plates decorated with foliage, coats-of-arms, and figures, all drawn in minute detail, under an amber or sometimes a green glaze, taking

care to perpetuate the memory of the artist with beautiful inscriptions in humanistic lettering.

Emilia's importance is derived mainly from the workshops of Ferrara and Bologna, although Ravenna, Faenza and other centres of 341 Romagna and Emilia can also boast of activity in this particular field of ceramics.

The 15th- and 16th-century pots from Ferrara and Bologna— bowls, jugs, footed basins, plates and floor tiles—were of solid and 340 compact shape with well-defined, sometimes moulded decoration which included plant motifs. These characteristics are especially apparent in the later period, the 17th and 18th centuries, in the large

340

341

342

343

340. Bowl on tall foot, white slip with *sgraffiato* decoration under the glaze. Diam. 13½ in. (34·5 cm.). Italy, Ferrara or Bologna, second half 15th century. The bowl is enriched with modelling on the upper and lower rims, and three supporting lions. The contrast between the white slip and the iron-rich red clay beneath, revealed by the *sgraffiato* bands of foliage, is softened by the green and amber yellow dappling. The interior decoration shows a mandoline player between two women, in a typical border of scrolled leaves. Louvre, Paris.

341. Round basin with narrow rim, coated with slip, with incised decoration under the glaze. Diam. 10¼ in. (26 cm.). Faenza, Italy. 14th century. The design, traced with a fine point on the pale slip, reveals the colour of the clay below, which is dark brown, not red, being poor in iron content, not presenting, therefore, the striking contrast offered by the red clay used in the following century. The colouring consists of scattered thread-like specks and patches in copper green and amber yellow. Museo Internazionale delle Ceramiche, Faenza.

342. Plate with deep well, coated with slip; incised decoration beneath amber-yellow glaze. Foliage and braid design cut out of the white slip. Pavia, last quarter of 17th century. Diam. 14¾ in. (37·5 cm.). Around the central floral design a Latin inscription states that the plate was made by the priest Antonio Maria Cuzio, Papal Apostolic protontary. That Cuzio, like other dignitaries of the Church, amused himself by making ceramics, is proved by other plates known to have been made by him, some of them dated 1676 and 1694. Malaspina Collection Museo Civico, Pavia.

343. Decorative mural plaque coated with white slip with incised (*sgraffiato*) decoration under the glaze, using *cavata di fondo* for the figurative design (left in white slip against the exposed red clay). Diam. 20½ in. (52 cm.). Padua, Italy, second half of 15th century. The image of the Virgin and Child, seated on a rich throne between St Roche and St Lucy, with little angels at their feet, framed in a border of conventionalised foliage, is taken from a print by Nicoletto Rosex of Modena, and reflects contemporary Ferrarese and Paduan painting. Museo Civico, Padua.

vases used for the preparation of 'treacle' or *theriac*, the universal remedy of the ancient Pharmacopoeia, which was prepared in all pomp and ceremony with the participation of religious and civil as well as scientific authorities. Heart-shaped leaves with serrated edges grafted on to a trailing vine, especially the 'bean' motif (*baccellature*), furled leaves reminiscent of the great cusps which decorate the spires and pinnacles of Gothic structures, and ribbons, braids and checkers frame the main subject-matter. This might consist of a bust of a man or woman, a coat-of-arms, a dog or rabbit, a heart etc.—often set in a 'garden of love', bordered by a hedge and orchard, inspired by early wood-engravings. Here, too, the speckling and cross-hatching with iron-brown and copper-green heighten the contrasting tones, for there was very rarely any additional colour.

26
(p. 126)

Tuscany—Pisa, Siena and the Florentine region—seems to have preferred the '*sgraffiato*' decoration where the simple red and white contrast of the incised design is allowed to stand on its own under a faintly ivory glaze. A beautiful long, scrolled leaf with serrated edges attached to a trailing vine, is particularly prominent, but there are also geometrical patterns and motifs.

344

Umbria presents the same picture. But in the South, especially in Apulia, the play of colours became predominant, enlivening jugs and great ceremonial plates and platters with symbolic animals or foliage patterns. A minutely decorated plate from a 17th-century workshop at Squillace associates Calabria, too, with this style.

344

344

France

Towards the end of the 15th century the technique of glazed pottery improved rapidly, reaching perfection in the 16th century. At the height of the Renaissance, in spite of the popularity of 'maiolica', this traditional pottery remained in favour and was often used for princely gifts. It flourished in a number of French provinces, such as Normandy, Poitou, Saintonge and Beauvaisis, where the existence of potters since the Middle Ages is confirmed by documentary evidence.

Any distinction between the various centres of production is difficult, for they all made pottery decorated in white or coloured slips, or with bas-reliefs, obtained by stamping pads of soft clay; the whole was then covered with a fine glaze speckled with green, yellow and brown.

It is customary to attribute to La-Chapelle-des-Pots, in Saintonge, a group of vessels with double walls, the outer one pierced, jugs and pilgrim bottles bearing emblems, monograms or princely coats-of-arms, as on the pilgrim bottle in the Musée du Louvre which bears the arms of the High Constable de Montmorency. The Constable made several visits to Saintes and the inventory of his possessions in 1568 mentions ewers and flagons of Saintes earthenware. Brizambourg was one of the places where, in 1574, according to the historian, Jacques de Thou, Henri III ordered potteries to be built.

345

Recent discoveries relating to the continual references, from the end of the 14th century onwards, to Beauvais earthenware or to the style of Savignies, confirm the importance given to the region of Beauvaisis by the old historians—as do the objects themselves, which have been identified by comparison with innumerable fragments found in the course of rebuilding in Beauvais. Besides luxury objects, all sorts of practical objects were made in Beauvaisis, for pottery once fulfilled all the requirements of everyday life. Many items of tableware have come down to us, such as plates, bowls, and

345

344. Shallow bowl, with *sgraffiato* decoration on white slip under the glaze. Diam. 14⅛ in. (36 cm.). Italy, Tuscany or Umbria, beginning of 16th century. The very limited range of colour—greyish blue and tawny brown—is restricted to the two central intersecting squares which form the star-shaped panel enclosing a long necked bird, coloured greyish blue. The sprays, leaves and ribbon work, and the ornamental bands in

the background and around the borders, which all belong to the familiar repertory, present the usual contrasting tones of ivory white slip and underlying red clay, without the addition of any other colour. Victoria and Albert Museum, London.

345. Flattened earthenware flask with four loops, of the so-called 'pilgrim's flask' type. Decoration in low-relief, green-glazed.

French (Saintonge, attr. to La Chapelle-des-Pots) ; middle of the 16th century. Ht. 11¾ in. (30 cm.). The coat-of-arms and the motto 'A PLANOS', are those of the High Constable, Anne de Montmorency, who is known to have owned some 'Saintes earthenware.' Owing to their similarities, a whole series of green-glazed pieces decorated with emblems and coats-of-arms is attributed to Saintonge. Louvre, Paris.

346

347

348

346. Salt-cellar, lead-glazed earthenware with decoration in two tones of brown clay. French (Saint-Porchaire); about 1540. Ht. 4⅛ in. (10·5 cm.). Salt-cellars played an important part on the table in the medieval and Renaissance periods, and it is not surprising to see a wealth of ornament lavished on the present example, both applied reliefs in the form of masks, and elaborate arabesques and other designs in contrasting tones of brown clay. Victoria and Albert Museum, London.

347. Dish, green-glazed earthenware with low-relief decoration, French (Beauvais); 1511. Diam. 14¾ in. (37·5 cm.). Round the Sacred Monogram set in a nimbus, two concentric zones bear royal coats-of-arms, the fleur-de-lis of France, the ermine of Anne of Brittany and 'K' for Charles VIII, with the words AVE MARIA, and, beneath croketed arches, the emblems of the Passion of Christ. A number of famous 'Passion dishes', glazed in green or yellow, survive. Musée National de Céramique, Sèvres.

348. Dish in lead-glazed earthenware incised through a slip to reveal the red clay underneath. The glaze is cream, touched with green. French (Beauvais); 16th century. Diam. 16 in. (40·5 cm.). In the centre of this dish is a tree, whilst on the rim, in Gothic lettering formed by very characteristic wide strokes made up of parallel scratches, is the proverb: 'Je suis planté pour reverdir. Vive Truppet.' ('I am planted to turn green again. Long live Truppet.'). Musée National de Céramique, Sèvres.

drinking vessels, as well as containers for storing liquids and food such as bottles, flagons, jars for oil and pickling-jars etc., and even domestic utensils such as lamps or stands for chafing-dishes. Examples of a religious character also exist, such as the plates decorated with the emblems of the Passion, which were doubtless meant to be hung on the wall as *ex voto* offerings or to mark the stations of the Cross; others, which were deeper and smaller, were used for the collection during services.

All these examples of Beauvaisis pottery are of a fine and rather hard clay which is light and slightly greyish in colour. They are decorated with the common methods of relief under a green or yellow glaze or engraving in the slip. In the latter case the ornament —which may consist of geometric or floral motifs, or occasionally of human or animal figures—is usually accompanied by inscriptions in Gothic letters composed of serrated bands which must have been produced with a comb-like tool. As well as the items of Beauvaisis pottery mentioned, there are also some remarkable statues of horsemen and musicians, modelled in the round, and to be found capping the finials on roofs.

The quality of glazed pottery (and of stoneware—see p. 134) attests to the skill acquired by the 16th century in French workshops and to the advanced state of their technique, which explains the appearance of exceptional work such as that by unknown potters of Poitou and that of Bernard Palissy. The fine ivory-coloured pottery of Poitou, originally just called '*Henri Deux*' ('Henri II') ware, has, over the last century, stimulated the interest and research of historians and given rise to various hypotheses. Benjamin Fillon in 1863 attributed it to Oiron on the Gouffier family's estate, and then Edmond Bonaffé, in 1888, to Saint-Porchaire. The last name has prevailed. These are in any case neighbouring localities, both in Poitou in the department of Deux-Sèvres.

The attribution to Saint-Porchaire is based on references to 'Saint-Porchayre earthenware' in the inventories of 1542 and 1577 of the Château de Thouars which belonged to François de la Trémoille, governor of Poitou, and in the 1556 inventory of the belongings of Pierre Laval de Montmorency, lord of Saint-Porchaire. Some of the descriptions in it, although summary, correspond to known objects which often bear the arms of the Laval and Montmorency families. But the name of the potter is, in fact, still unknown and it is surprising that none of the names mentioned

in these old documents has been passed down to posterity, for the author of these works of art was a great master.

Pieces of Saint-Porchaire earthenware are listed in the inventories among the precious objects. This luxurious manufacture was of short duration, lasting from approximately 1530 to 1570, and limited in output. The analysis of a fragment taken from under the foot of the cup in the Musée de Sèvres has shown that the clay is fine-grained and with a high silica content; it stays white on firing and is merely covered with a transparent, colourless lead-glaze. The decoration is not inlaid, as has been claimed, but, according to M. Fourest and some specialists, is applied on to the surface; Benjamin Fillon suggests the possible collaboration of a printer.

A first group of pieces, of rather heavy shapes, is decorated with small, repeating ornaments in monochrome brown or black, arranged in zones one above the other. Others, in the second group, are of an architectonic and three-dimensional character, decorated with intricate traceries in Renaissance style, like those on contemporary bindings, and heightened by a few touches of colour. Finally, on some very rare examples, there appear reptiles in high relief which are not unlike those on the 'rustic' wares of Bernard Palissy.

The life of Bernard Palissy, like the pottery which he created, is not very well known to us, for it has taken on a legendary character given credence by the writings of the master himself and by an abundant literature on the subject. He was born near Agen about 1510 and at first worked as an artist in stained glass, in which profession he undoubtedly became familiar with the techniques of enamelling and firing. It is not known exactly what he could have discovered in about 1540 when a cup 'made of clay thrown on the wheel and glazed' inspired in him his vocation and eager research. By 1542 he was established at Saintes, where his experiments came to a successful conclusion. He gained such a reputation that the High Constable de Montmorency became his patron, and in 1555 commissioned from him one of the rustic grottos then very much in fashion for gardens in the Italian manner; it was intended for the Château d'Ecouen, but was never installed. Thus it was that Catherine de Médici saw it in the workshop when she passed through Saintes in 1564, and wanted it for the garden in the Tuileries. She made the potter come to Paris, where he set himself up in 1566.

349

350

349. Oval dish in earthenware with green, yellow and brown lead-glazes, decorated in high relief. French (Bernard Palissy); second half of the 16th century. L. 20¾ in. (53 cm.). A snake, lobster, lizards against rockwork, shells, foliage, and fishes—a decorative arrangement typical of Bernard Palissy's rustic ware, possibly inspired by fashionable descriptions of rustic grottos in the Italian *Dream of Polyphilus,* in 1546. Louvre, Paris.

350. Oval dish in earthenware with vivid, mottled green, blue, yellow and purplish brown lead-glazes, decorated in low-relief with an allegory of *Fecundity*. French (studio of Bernard Palissy); second half of the 16th century. L. 19¾ in. (50 cm.). The elongated, elegant figure is in the style of the School of Fontainebleau. The white flesh-tone is faintly tinged with mauve. Louvre, Paris.

351. Spouted vessel in the form of a figure, in cream-coloured earthenware with a mottled green and brown glaze. French (Saintonge, La Chapelle-des-Pots); beginning of the 17th century. Ht. 12 in. (31 cm.). A small female figure, not unlike the one which surmounts this vessel, has been excavated at La Chapelle-des-Pots. Louvre, Paris.

351

During excavations of the site, remains of kilns and important fragments from the former grotto were found. These fragments, authentic works by the master, are of prime interest for the study of the processes used by him. The fine body, which is light in colour apart from some use of red slip, resembles the pottery from Saintonge and Poitou. Bernard Palissy had in fact made his début as a potter at La Chapelle-des-Pots, and speaks highly of the earthenwares of Savignies and Poitou. His extraordinary skill in handling polychrome glazes considerably enriched the potter's palette for producing bright marbled grounds. He was undoubtedly familiar with glaze rendered opaque by the addition of a little tin, and was thereby enabled on occasion, to obtain a fairly pure white. Casts, taken from life and naturally reproduced, of snakes, lizards, frogs, fishes, shells and foliage, won him fame and in 1562 earned for him the title of 'inventor of the king's rustic pottery'. The well-known dishes of this type, in which the ardent scholar, the man of science and the technician take priority over the artist, are nearest to the fragments from the grotto. For designs which incorporated the human figure, for scenes with people, Bernard Palissy had to turn to contemporary sculptors of the school of Jean Goujon. Casts from silver or pewter dishes were also made in Bernard Palissy's workshop, notably one by François Briot decorated with an allegory of *Moderation*.

The master-potter, who had suffered as a Protestant in the Wars of Religion and had been imprisoned for heresy, died in about 1590. But his work lived on after him; not only did his moulds continue to be used long after his death, but he also had countless imitators right into the 19th century.

In the course of the 17th and 18th centuries in France the kilns of the Saintonge and Beauvaisis regions continued to function, and it is thus probable that a number of earthenware vessels, in the Renaissance style and with green or speckled glazes, were made at this time with the aid of old moulds, as were imitations of Bernard Palissy's work. Large ceremonial dishes, decorated with washes of white clay or with *sgraffiato* on slip, bear moral maxims, the names of their intended recipients, inscriptions mentioning Savignies or other places in Beauvaisis, and dates which place them in the 17th and 18th centuries.

349

350

351

352

352. Dish in brown-glazed earthenware with decoration engraved through slip. French (Beauvaisis, Savignies), 1748. Diam. 24 in.

352

(61 cm.). This large ceremonial plate shows the traditional technique of the Renaissance potters persisting right into the 18th century. Around the cavetto and on the rim, inscriptions indicate that the dish was made by Nicolas Fosse at Savignies and intended for François Rétré, Gamekeeper to the Duke Fleuris, lord of Envoille. Musée National de Céramique, Sèvres.

353

354

355

353. Statuette, *Child with dogs*, earthenware with polychrome lead-glazes. French (Avon, Seine et Marne); beginning of the 17th century. Ht. 10¼ in. (26 cm.). Here we have a typical example of the Avon figurines, modelled with charming spontaneity. The child's flesh-tones are of a distinct ivory shade, while his garments and the markings on the dog are of a fine manganese-purple peculiar to Avon. The same model may be found in several sizes with variations in colouring. Louvre, Paris.

354. Ewer of double ogee profile, with a high scrolled handle, in lead-glazed earthenware of a reddish-brown shade. Southern France; 17th century. Ht. 11 in. (28 cm.). It is customary to attribute to Avignon this family of brown or russet-red wares with elaborate shapes. Inspired by metal-work, they lean strongly towards the Italian style. Louvre, Paris.

355. Roof-finial in earthenware with coloured lead-glazes. It is made up of nine superimposed components threaded on a central shaft, with a crown of flowers and a dove above. French (Normandy, Le Pré d'Auge); beginning of the 17th century. Ht. 4 ft. 7⅛ in. (1·40 m.). The lingering Renaissance style and the influence of the Della Robbias' work are very pronounced here. This roof-finial may be related to those kept in the Museum of Bernay (Eure). Musée National Adrien-Dubouché, Limoges.

356. Terrine for pâté in earthenware, shaped like a saddle of hare, decorated in low relief under a light brown glaze. French (Champagne, Dormans), 1712. L. 16⅜ in. (42 cm.). The lid of this pâté-pot features, among its ornaments, the date 1712 and the word 'Dormans', the name of a place near Epernay. Pieces of this kind were manufactured in various provinces of France in the course of the 18th and 19th centuries. Although functional items, they are not devoid of a certain artistic quality. Musée National de Céramique, Sèvres.

357. Fountain with accompanying basin, of lead-glazed red and yellow earthenware with incised and relief decoration and a figure modelled in the round on top. French (Ligron, Sarthe), 1786. Ht. of fountain 18½ in. (47 cm.), width of bowl 13½ in. (34·3 cm.). The branches, figures and animals (a camel, an elephant etc.) on the body of the fountain are applied in white clay. It is possible that the picturesque figure in wig and bands sitting on the top of the cover is a portrait of 'Guemonneau de la Forterie, surgeon at Courcelles near Ligron' for whom—according to the incised inscription—this remarkable piece was made in 1786. At the bottom of the shell-shaped bowl, three frogs, three crayfish and a fish are all modelled in high-relief, in the tradition of Bernard Palissy. Musée National de Céramique, Sèvres.

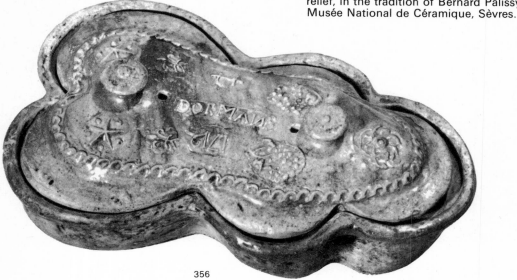

356

357

The influence of Bernard Palissy is found again at Avon, near Fontainebleau, where a factory was directed by Barthélemy de Blénod, to whom no doubt the mark 'B' should be ascribed. Jean Héroard, physician to the future Louis XIII, relates in his diary how he bought the little prince 'quaint little pottery figures' in Avon. In 1620 an inventory of the Avon workshop lists 'small children', 'dogs', and a number of other figurines modelled with charming spontaneity.

In Normandy, Manerbe made dishes similar to those by Bernard Palissy, and the Pré d'Auge region made roof-finials its speciality. The signature of Jean Guincestre of Armentières-sur-Avre has been found on quite a few pieces of brown earthenware bearing dates in

the region of 1750–77. Englefontaine (North) was also a centre of production. The names of places in Champagne, 'Dormans' and 'Epernay', are to be found on terrines in the shape of a hare, for containing pâté, and on long fish dishes. Finally, the factories at Ligron and Courcelles (Sarthe), are in a category on their own on account of their unusual earthenwares glazed brown, russet and yellow, and covered with figures in high relief of human grotesques or animals, which continue the fine traditions of the potter's art.

Attributed to the Midi of France, and in particular to Avignon, is the brown and russet glazed pottery in elaborate shapes, derived from silversmiths' work, which is directly related to North Italian art and is rarely earlier than the 17th century.

England to about 1730

In the sphere of lead-glazed pottery the direct effects of the Renaissance only made themselves felt on the so-called 'Tudor green' wares (see p. 114)—cisterns, wall-sconces, dishes and stove-tiles decorated with stamped relief motifs, often including the initials of the reigning monarch, accompanied by decorative Renaissance elements which reflect developments in the major arts. This trend was not sustained beyond the reign of Queen Elizabeth I and the art of the lead-glaze potter sank back to a more mundane plane, with green-, yellow- and brown-glazed wares of varying types, the last-named sometimes embellished with simple motifs in white slip under the slightly straw-coloured lead-glaze. In the 17th century this technique was developed to a high pitch, the resultant wares often making up in boldness and spontaneity what they lacked in subtlety or refinement.

The slipwares of the 17th century were evidently in the normal way a by-product of potters producing as their staple plain brown or red-bodied pots for daily use. They are frequently commemorative in character, celebrating a marriage or a birth, and were evidently special commissions. This appears to hold good of the earliest

considerable family of these slipwares known to us—those of Wrotham, in Kent, where there was a brickworks in production already in the 16th century. A number of site-wasters have been found of a hard brown-glazed earthenware which in a 16th-century context would be called 'Cistercian' ware. The earliest of the Wrotham slipwares are cups with three or more handles usually known as 'tygs', the earliest recorded example bearing the date 1612. These early pieces are decorated with sparsely applied pads of white slip bearing impressed devices such as rosettes, plant-sprays, rampant lions, fleurs-de-lis, etc., and their double loop-handles are frequently decorated with a cable of red and white clay and surmounted by a cottage-loaf finial in white. Towards the mid-century the decoration was elaborated by the use of the slip-can to trail on white slip in dots and dashes, the latter often used in conjunction with the applied motifs to give the impression of their being stitched to the body of the pot. Simple decorative designs and inscriptions were also slip-trailed. The clay used at Wrotham was of two colours—a lighter showing up as reddish-brown and a darker showing as a dark brown under the glaze. The ornamental pads of white slip

358. Lead-glazed earthenware 'tyg' with slip-trailed decoration and stamped pads of white clay. English (Wrotham), dated 1649. Ht. 6¼ in. (15·9 cm.). This four-handled cup has the initials 'IL' (sic) stamped on one of the applied pads, for John Livermore, one of the earliest slipware potters working at Wrotham

(died 1658). His signed works date from 1612 to 1649. This 'tyg' also bears the initials 'WSC' of the couple for whom it was made. Victoria and Albert Museum, London.

359. Lead-glazed earthenware 'tyg' with slip-trailed decoration in white. English

(probably Harlow), middle of 17th century. Ht. 7¾ in. (19·7 cm.). This example of 'Metropolitan slipware' was found in the City of London. It perpetuates a two-handled form already well-established in the dark-bodied pottery of the 16th century. Guildhall Museum, London.

358

359

360

361

360. Dish, lead-glazed earthenware with decoration in slips of different colours. English (probably Staffordshire); early 18th century. Diam. 13¾ in. (34·9 cm.). Slip-trailing demands great dexterity, and even so, its effects can only be rapidly drawn and impressionistic. In consequence, the best slipwares show rhythmical designs of great freedom, enhanced by the warm tones of the red and brown clays used. Victoria and Albert Museum, London.

361. Lead-glazed earthenware honey-pot with slip-decoration. English (Staffordshire), about 1700. Ht. 5⅜ in. (13·7 cm.). This honey-pot, with trailed white slip trefoils on a dark brown ground, exemplifies the fine simple shapes and masterly stylised ornament characteristic of the best Staffordshire slipwares of the late 17th and early 18th centuries. Victoria and Albert Museum.

were frequently impressed with the initials of potters recorded as working at Wrotham and one or two of the latest wares (the dates run until at least 1739) have white slip inscriptions on the reddish-brown clay recording explicitly the place of their manufacture. Apart from the tygs, the Wrotham forms included globular cups with one double-looped handle, elaborate four-nozzled candlesticks, jugs, puzzle-jugs and, rarely, large dishes decorated in the *sgraffiato* technique.

Overlapping the Wrotham wares in date is a series of slipwares of far simpler character, usually dubbed 'Metropolitan slipwares' because most have been found in London. It was long thought that they were probably made, as well as found, in the London area, but recent archaeological discoveries suggest that they may have been made in the vicinity of Harlow, in Essex. The inscriptions which form the greater part of the decoration are usually of a Puritan character ('For Earth I am', or 'Remember God') consonant with the spirit of mid-17th-century London, and the remaining decoration is restricted to dashes, wavy lines and sketchy foliage. The shapes made were usually tankards, mugs, jugs and dishes.

Of far greater moment both artistically and in their portent for the future were the slipwares of North Staffordshire, where a happy conjunction of abundant clay, good coal-measures and reasonable accessibility provided the ideal conditions for the rise of the pottery-industry. Here all the resources of the slipware potter were exploited to the utmost. The craft perhaps reached its peak in the reign of Charles II, with the great slip-trailed dishes associated with the name of Toft. These were some 17 to 22 inches (43 to 56 cm.) in diameter and 3 inches (7·6 cm.) deep, flat-based and with a broad, flat rim. The body was of red clay covered with a white slip on which the design was drawn with a darkish-brown slip, areas of solid colour being normally rendered in a slip of a lighter and redder tone. The design was then emphasised with dots of white slip which give life and sparkle to the whole effect, the rim usually being ornamented with a lattice formed of diagonally placed lines of the two contrasting red slip-colours. The ornamental themes of these dishes are mainly confined to Royal 'portraits' (e.g., Charles II and Catherine of Braganza), coats-of-arms, or emblematic representations such as the Pelican in her Piety, or a mermaid combing her hair. Signed

360–1

23 (p. 125)

362

362. Lead-glazed earthenware posset-pot
with applied decoration. English (South
Wiltshire), dated 1697. Ht. 8¾ in. (22·2 cm.).
Simple lead-glazed earthenwares of this
general type were made in many English
country potteries in the 17th–18th centuries.
This spouted posset-pot is inscribed with the
owners' names 'William and Mary
Goldsmith'. A posset was a drink of milk
curdled with wine or ale and was sucked
through the spout of the posset-pot.
Fitzwilliam Museum, Cambridge.

Toft pieces where datable belong mainly to the 1670s, but other potters with well-known Staffordshire names, such as Simpson and Meir, produced slipwares of a comparable character during the last quarter of the 17th century. The elaboration of the Toft dishes, however, tended to be modified, the slip being simply trailed in white on dark or *vice versa*, dexterity with the slip-can being the prime virtue. A new technique was 'combing', whereby lines of slip, usually dark on a light ground, were drawn into feather- and arcade-patterns: occasionally lines of slip were shaken and jogged into marbled patterns. These new techniques were used on many-handled posset-pots (often with applied crinkled strips of clay as additional ornament), small cups and jugs, dishes and small models of cradles made to commemorate a birth or christening.

Staffordshire, however, was by no means the only Midlands centre making slipwares in the late 17th century. At Tickenhall, in Derbyshire, had been made the earlier dark-bodied 'Cistercian' ware, and some of the earliest dark-brown wares with slip decoration have been attributed to that centre. It is extremely likely that dark wares with white trailed slip-decoration continued to be made there in the 17th century. A somewhat similar ware with a dark-brown glaze

shading off into tones of purple and green was made at various centres. In Wiltshire was produced a red-bodied pottery, usually with a dark purplish-brown glaze, decorated with leafy sprays, inscriptions, interlaced ornament and so on, either incised or applied. Comparable wares were made at Buckland, in Buckinghamshire; and at Gestingthorpe, in Essex, during the 18th century there was produced a red-bodied pottery with a brown-flecked yellow glaze, decorated with roughly incised flower-sprays and inscriptions. A true *sgraffiato* ware with floral motifs and scrollwork scratched through a white slip to an underlying red body, the whole under a yellow glaze, was made in North Devon, mainly at Bideford and Barnstaple, and much exported to the American colonies during the 17th century. At Donyatt, in Somerset, this type of ornament was enhanced by mottling the yellowish glaze in green produced by copper. Many of the posset-pots, tygs and dishes so decorated bear dates in the second half of the 17th century. Fareham, in Hampshire, is accredited with a type of posset-pot of light-red clay decorated with inscriptions and simple motifs formed of notched strips of light clay often stained purple with manganese or green with copper. These mostly bear early 18th-century dates.

363. Lead-glazed earthenware dish with
sgraffiato decoration. English (North Devon),
second half of the 17th century. Diam. 12 in.
(30·5 cm.). Dishes of this type were much
exported to the English colonies in North
America in the 17th century. The present
example was excavated at Jamestown,
Virginia. The simple design of tulips and
carnations is comparable with those of the
contemporary delftware 'tulip chargers', and
is obtained by cutting through the white slip
to the underlying red body, the whole being
covered by a yellow-toned lead-glaze.
Colonial National Historical Park, Jamestown,
Virginia, U.S.A.

363

23. Lead-glazed earthenware dish with slip-
trailed decoration in white and two tones of
brown, by Thomas Toft. English
(Staffordshire), about 1675. Diam. 17¼ in.
(43·8 cm.). This dish displays a well-known
17th-century theme of a mermaid combing
her hair. It was no doubt intended for
display on a dresser. Victoria and Albert
Museum, London.

23

24

25

26

27

Germany and Northern Europe

About the turn of the 15th–16th century, lead-glazing assumed a growing importance in the German lands. In the recent study of ceramics it has become customary to group together under the name 'Hafner ware' the different families of German lead-glazed pottery which had their artistic heyday from about 1530 until the early 17th century. This term, which originated in the South German linguistic region, is used in antithesis to common red earthenware and stoneware, although originally it embraced all types of pottery. German lead-glazed earthenware was decisively influenced by the stove-maker's craft.

It is not difficult to explain the artistic interaction of stove- and pottery-making when one considers the close connexion between potter and stove-maker in former times. The tiled domestic stove which in the High Middle Ages gradually ousted the open fire-place in Germany, originated in all probability in the workshops of potters. Basically it represents nothing more than a system of joined clay bowls. This is also borne out by the term 'Kachel' (tile); for the Old High German 'cachala' means 'bowl'. The 'basin-' or 'bowl-tile', thrown on the potter's wheel, is the original form of the German stove-tile and evolved from the earthen cooking pot, which, for the conservation of warmth and enlargement of the heated surface, was initially just pressed into the clay sides of the stove. It was immaterial whether the aperture of the vessel was placed pointing inwards or outwards—the effect of warmth achieved was the same. Both methods occur in the oldest types of tiled stove. In the late Middle Ages they began to coat the visible surfaces of the tiles with lead-glaze, so as to convert a part of the radiated heat into an even and more economical heat. In this way the most important ornamental feature of the tiled stove evolved.

The tiled stove, which in the course of its development has assumed the most varied forms, probably originated in the inhospitable climate of the Alps. Its representation on a fresco in Constance at the turn of the 13th–14th century, and on a Zürich armorial register of only slightly later date, permits us to assume that by this time it had already been in use for some time. In Alpine districts, particularly Tyrol, even the oldest forms remained unchanged, thanks to the remoteness of the mountain villages. In north Germany the word 'Kachelenoven' ('tiled stove') first appears in 1405, in a Hildesheim document.

The essential precondition for the development of an autonomous stove-making art was provided when, in the 15th century, the lead-glazed stove-tile merged with the relief-decorated wall- and floor-tile, and adopted its three-dimensional embellishments. This process was consummated especially in the Gothic cylindrical tile. These tiles formed the wall of the tower-like structure which rose 364

24. *Figure of a musician, earthenware with yellow, brown and green lead-glazes. French (Beauvais); first half 16th century. Ht. 24¼ in. (61·5 cm.). This animated figure which crowned a roof-finial bears witness to the technical skill of Beauvais potters. The costume conforms to early 16th-century fashion. Musée National de Céramique, Sèvres.*

25. *Face jug, buff ware with polychrome applied decoration. Bishopsgate, London. 14th century. Ht. 10-3/16 in. (26 cm.). This jug shows several influences: polychrome colours from the Mediterranean, copied from imports from SW France and yellow pellets on a brown ground from the Rouen area and SE England. Guildhall Museum, London.*

26. *Interior of dish with sgraffiato decoration under the glaze. Diam. 15½ in. (39·5 cm.). Italy (Bologna or Ferrara); last quarter 15th century. The deeply incised design offers a marked contrast between red clay and white slip and is enriched by marbling with flecks of green and amber-yellow. Victoria and Albert Museum, London.*

27. *Bowl with vertical rim above incurved shoulder; sgraffiato decoration inside and out, drawn through white slip over red body; coloured with green and yellow-brown which have run in the clear covering glaze. Byzantine (Constantinople); 14th century. Diam. 8¼ in. (21 cm.). Dumbarton Oaks Collection, Washington.*

364. Deep recessed tile depicting St Christopher, deep green glaze. Upper Austria; end of the 15th century. Ht. 13¼ in. (33·5 cm.). The rectangular moulding with arched top and holly-leaf spandrels, which forms an additional frame to the panel, shows the transition from the sculptural style with the figure in a niche of tracery to the more pictorial style of the Renaissance. Österreichisches Museum für angewandte Kunst, Vienna.

365

366

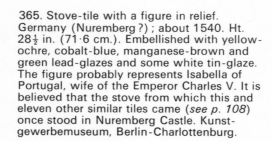

367

365. Stove-tile with a figure in relief. Germany (Nuremberg?); about 1540. Ht. 28½ in. (71·6 cm.). Embellished with yellow-ochre, cobalt-blue, manganese-brown and green lead-glazes and some white tin-glaze. The figure probably represents Isabella of Portugal, wife of the Emperor Charles V. It is believed that the stove from which this and eleven other similar tiles came (*see p. 108*) once stood in Nuremberg Castle. Kunstgewerbemuseum, Berlin-Charlottenburg.

366. Stove-tile with an Allegory of Autumn; black-glazed. Germany (Nuremberg); dated 1611. Ht. 30½ in. (78·5 cm.). The mould for this tile was made by Georg Vest the Younger, who was born in Kreussen in 1586 and then worked in Nuremberg, at first for Wolfgang Leupold and later for his

successor, Georg Leupold. Georg Vest is the most important member of a famous family of Kreussen potters, whose name is closely connected with Kreussen stoneware. Victoria and Albert Museum, London.

367. Handled jug, with blue, yellow, green, manganese-brown and white glazes. Germany (Nuremberg workshop of Paul Preuning); about 1550. Ht. 21⅛ in. (53·5 cm.). The Adoration of the Magi in the upper part is also found on a tile in the Sigmaringen Collection. On the lower part of the jug is depicted *The Massacre of the Innocents*. Victoria and Albert Museum, London.

364
365
22
(p. 108)
366
367
371
370

above the fire-box in a series of open niches which, following an architectural pattern, were each closed off in the upper part by a sort of canopy and occupied by a figure. Even when, in about 1500, under the influence of Italian maiolica, the potters substituted for the rich green they had used before, a polychrome palette previously unknown in the North, they still preferred relief decoration. Gothic designs were replaced by Renaissance designs which from the second quarter of the 16th century onwards show the influence of Mannerism. The best and most refined modelled decoration of all 17th-century stove-tiles is to be found on those made by the Leupold family in Nuremberg. Here, instead of a green or coloured glaze, a black glaze was used, sometimes effectively heightened by a sparing use of gold.

Among the countless places where the manufacture of useful wares was influenced by the art of the stove-maker, Nuremberg was undoubtedly the most important. Here the members of the Preuning family maintained a continuous tradition from the second quarter of the 16th century until the beginning of the 17th century. The jugs of Paul Preuning and of his followers were for many years considered to be the work of the versatile writer and artist Augustin Hirschvogel (see p. 160), thanks to an inexact statement by Johann Neudörffer, a kind of Nuremberg 'Vasari.' They are distinguished by their variety of colours set against a bright blue ground. An ornamental pattern of raised lines prevents the green, brown, manganese-purple, yellow

and white glazes from running into each other, and in the free spaces are set figures in relief, occasionally with the Crucifixion modelled in the round and set in a niche, clearly following the example of the stove-tiles. Biblical and mythological themes are most commonly found. The allegories of the Virtues are reminiscent of Peter Flötner's series of plaquettes, and the dancing peasants are derived from engravings by Hans Sebald Beham. Well-known figures in contemporary life appear, occasionally confronting each other, and they give a vivid picture of the religious and political controversies of the day. The value attached to these jugs, which were bought as presents rather than as objects to use, led to their being imitated in other places. The jugs made in the valley of Krems in Austria are strongly reminiscent of those made by the Preuning family, while at Annaberg, in Saxony, a certain Merten Koller was influenced by the Nuremberg decorative technique. Another Nuremberg speciality were the jugs sprinkled with sand to roughen the surface and covered with a coloured lead-glaze and fired. These may well have been made by Oskar Reinhard, who signed a lidded tankard made for the reformer Zwingli. It has not yet been established whether the jugs found in Cologne were made there or whether they were imported from Nuremberg. A notable series of elaborate dishes was made in Silesia in a technique which is doubtless derived from the *sgraffiato* wares of Italy; but, whereas in Italy the lines were scratched through a slip, in Silesia they were incised directly in the still soft body. The

368

369

370

371

368. Peasant dish with angels. Germany (Wanfried-an-der-Werra), dated 1615. Ht. 12¾ in. (32·5 cm.). The brick-red body is decorated with white slip-trailed designs: the figures have incised details and the draperies are shaded with patches of green in the glaze. The front is covered with a transparent greenish glaze, the back being left unglazed. The Wanfried wares found a market in East, West and North Friesland, and also in England, the main entrepôt being Bremen. Victoria and Albert Museum, London.

369. Peasant dish with an equestrian figure. Germany (Rayen), dated 1774 and signed by Albert Mures the Younger. Diam. 16⅜ in. (44 cm.). Slip-painted with incised drawing in reddish-brown, yellow, green and dark manganese-brown on a yellowish ground. The inscription probably refers to Duke Ferdinand of Brunswick, the victor at the Battle of Krefeld in 1758: it reads 'Long live the Prussian commander, a brave hero who does not allow himself to be worried by any other lord or potentate.' Kaiser Wilhelm Museum, Krefeld.

370. Costrel ('Beutelflasche' or 'Krause') sand-sprinkled ware. Germany (Cologne or Nuremberg). About 1531. Ht. 7⅛ in. (18 cm.). The figure shows the Emperor Charles V in a dark green cloak, yellow jacket with pale pink collar and a green cap, all on a blue ground. The hair is coloured brown, the face rendered with white tin-glaze. The vine-tendrils surrounding the medallion are yellow, the pointed leaves rising from the base green. On the reverse side are bust-portraits of Ferdinand, King of the Romans, and his wife Anna of Hungary. Perhaps the bottle was made to commemorate the Coronation of Ferdinand in Cologne on January 5th, 1531. Formerly in Figdor Collection, Vienna.

371. Handled jug. Germany (Annaberg, in Saxony); dated 1569. Ht. 21¼ in. (54 cm.). As on the jugs made by Preuning at Nuremberg, the relief decoration is picked out with yellow, green, manganese-brown and white glazes against a blue ground. Between bands of leafy scrollwork is depicted the Creation of Eve. On both sides of the jug are reliefs showing Christ crucified between the Virgin Mary and St John. Museum für Kunsthandwerk, Dresden.

ridges on either side of the lines which resulted from this process, had the same function as the raised lines used elsewhere. The effect is a kind of broad mosaic pattern which suits the rather summary drawing. This technique was used in Austria as well, in the district of Traun, particularly in Steyr, but also in Salzburg. The Austrian stove-makers, however, in contrast to the Silesians, preferred abstract designs.

In the course of the 17th century the development of faience reduced Hafner ware to the level of peasant art, and so it has remained almost to the present day. At the end of the 16th century the *sgraffiato* process became the favourite technique of the peasant potters. Wanfried-an-der-Werra, in Hesse, produced the earliest examples, but peasant potteries soon sprang up all over Germany, Austria and Switzerland. The most important were those on the Lower Rhine, clustered on the range of hills between Krefeld and Xanten. Biblical scenes, figures in contemporary dress, potters at work and soldiers and officers of the Prussian army are some of the subjects which appear frequently on the colourful Rhenish dishes, both the subjects and the execution bearing witness to the lively narrative sense of their makers.

368

369

Stoneware
Germany

The most important contribution made by Germany to the ceramic art, apart from the discovery of hard-paste porcelain, is undoubtedly the development of salt-glazed stoneware from the hard-fired ware of the High Middle Ages (see p. 115–6). This development took place towards the end of the 14th century, whether in the Eifel region or at Siegburg is not certain. Stoneware has in common with porcelain a hard, resonant and non-porous body which is resistant to acids (except hydro-fluoric acid) and which strikes a spark from a steel. The clay used has a rich content of silicic acid and vitrifies at a high temperature. Since lead-glazes cannot withstand such a heat, a salt-glaze was used. This glaze is produced by throwing a certain amount of common salt into the kiln, whereupon the soda combines with the silica and alumina in the body, leaving a thin, colourless, glassy film on the surface of the pot. The colouring of the glaze was achieved by a wash of vitrifiable brown clay.

Although the Rhineland may claim precedence in the discovery of stoneware, it may well be that the earliest types of stoneware with artistic pretensions were in fact made in Hessen. It is believed

372

373

374

372. Baluster jug, the 'Daun Cup of Welcome' grey stoneware with brown wash. Germany (Dreihausen?), early 15th century. Ht. 14¼ in. (36·3 cm.). The jug shows the typical chequer and zig-zag patterns. No attempt is made to give a naturalistic appearance to the masks by means of painting. This cup belonged in 1517 to Count Daun. Staatliche Kunstsammlungen, Kassel.

373. Bellarmine, stoneware with a light brown salt-glaze. Germany (Cologne, Maximinenstrasse workshop); about 1530. Ht. 8¼ in. (21 cm.). The East Germans were decorating their wares with human faces as early as 800 to 900 BC, but the Cologne tradition probably derives from Roman pottery *via* the local medieval types. Kunstmuseum, Düsseldorf.

374. Jug, brown salt-glazed stoneware. German (Dreihausen); 16th century. Ht. 11⅛ in. (28·5 cm.). The iron-oxide in a clay imparts a brownish colour to the fired pot, and this jug has a lustrous brown surface. The small handles once held rings of the same stoneware material, no doubt to create a cheerful noise as the jug was passed about the table. Victoria and Albert Museum, London.

that a group of silver-mounted cups with a decoration of masks in high relief were made in Dreihausen, a centre of pottery-making to the south-east of Marburg. To judge from an engraved inscription on one of the mounts, these were used to welcome guests and so were called a '*Willkomm*' ('welcome'). Six examples have survived —a cylindrical beaker (Limburg Cathedral); a cup with 'hedgehog' decoration on the bowl, a spreading foot of Gothic silver-shape and, round the knop, projecting figures of mountain-goats and a man's head (National Museum, Copenhagen); and four other vessels of slender baluster shape (two formerly in the Figdor Collection at Vienna, one at Frankfurt-am-Main and one at Kassel). A brown clay wash, shading to reddish-purple, covers the grey body. All except the Copenhagen example are decorated with an impressed chequer pattern divided by horizontal bands or zig-zags. On the shoulders of most of these vessels are two bearded male heads in high relief, the beard and hair-style being in the fashion of the early 15th century. On the Frankfurt cup these masks are painted in flesh tones and have gilt hair, while one of the cups in the Figdor collection had two full-length figures of saints instead of the masks. The stoneware which is proved by sherds to have been made at Dreihausen in the 16th century has a similar glaze and colouring. The typical vessels

here are the beakers with flaring mouths ('*Trichterbecher*') and loose ring-handles, handled jugs and jugs with beak-like spouts ('*Schnabelkannen*'). The older tradition must by then have been long since forgotten, for the 16th-century inscription on the mount of the Limburg beaker claims that it was made 'from the earth of St Paul's in the island of Malta.'

The rich deposits of clay on the slopes of the Westerwald near Höhr and Grenzhausen, and at Siegburg and Frechen, further downstream, and, to the South of Aachen, at Raeren, made the Rhineland the most important centre of stoneware manufacture. Moreover the busy commercial river and the trading facilities at Cologne assured for the stoneware potters not only a profitable German market but also a thriving export trade to the Netherlands, England, Scandinavia and France. Potters are mentioned in the records of Siegburg as early as the 14th century. The early Siegburg wares most usually have a grey body, partly or completely covered with a yellow salt-glaze shading to reddish-brown. The sides are decorated with the horizontal grooves which go back to the 12th century. The pinched-in, waved foot too is a continuation of an older tradition. In the course of the 15th century, stamped decorative reliefs, applied to the surface in a manner recalling the techniques of pewterers,

374

21
(p. 1

372

375. Spouted jug ('*Schnabelkanne*') of white stoneware. Germany (Siegburg, workshop of Christian Knütgen); dated 1590. Ht. 10¾ in. (27·5 cm.). The jug has an English silver mount, which shows that this was one of the very many pieces of Rhenish stoneware exported to the British Isles. Victoria and Albert Museum, London.

376. '*Jakobakanne*' type of jug, made of brownish-yellow stoneware. Germany, (Siegburg); 15th century. Ht. 10⅜ in. (26·5 cm.). From about 1400, Siegburg jugs are of marked slenderness, appearing as wine jugs next to the drinking vessels in contemporary altar paintings of the Last Supper and also used at baptisms. Victoria and Albert Museum, London.

377. Tankard ('*Schnelle*'), white stoneware, with relief decorations. Germany (Siegburg); dated 1559 marked 'FT' for F. Trac, one of the leading decorators of Siegburg stoneware, working mainly for Anno Knütgen. Ht. 15⅛ in. (38·5 cm.). The medallions have scenes from the life of Christ. The ornamental motif is from an engraving by Heinrich Aldegrever. Museum Roseliushaus, Bremen.

bell-founders and skillet-makers, came to be used more and more, the designs being obtained from seals, coins, medals and ornamental plaques. Animals, scrolls, Gothic letters and pairs of lovers are also found, while a decorative motif peculiar to Siegburg are the scrolls of holly-leaves incised with the modelling-tool. From about 1400 onwards, a new shape appears—the tall and slender '*Jakobakanne*' with ring-handle. The '*Ratskanne*' with its high conical foot is derived from a metalwork shape. Beakers with flaring mouths, bowls and puzzle-jugs were also made in large quantities.

The change from the Gothic to the Renaissance style took place in Cologne during the first half of the 16th century and heralded the finest and most artistic period of Rhenish stoneware. It was the immigrant potters from Frechen who, in spite of the unremitting hostility of the native Cologne potters, created in the short time they were there (from about 1520 until towards the end of the century) the shapes and designs which subsequently became standard. Freely applied oak-leaves on curling stems, like those in the pattern-books of Peter Quentel, are the usual decoration of the bellied jugs and beakers with flaring mouths made in the workshops in the Maximinenstrasse. In the Komödiengasse Herman Wolters produced narrow-necked jugs, the swelling sides of which were decorated with applied rosettes and bosses. The 'Bellarmine' ('*Bartmannskrug*'), which is of Roman-Germanic ancestry, is also characteristic of Cologne. A speciality of the Eigelstein workshop was the tall tankard of tapering shape called a '*Schnelle*'. The decorative bands round the mouth and the foot recall the iron hoops with which coopers bind the staves of their casks.

Whereas the dull, grey clay of the Cologne and Frechen wares had to be given its colouring, ranging from golden yellow to dark brown, by means of a wash which often had a mottled appearance, the effect of the Siegburg wares depends on the natural brightness of the white-firing body. The *Schnellen* made at Siegburg, in five sizes corresponding with the standard Cologne measures, are so slender that they give an impression of almost exaggerated elegance. The ancestry of the richly decorated spouted jugs ('*Schnabelkannen*'), whose neck and middle section are cylindrical in form like the other Siegburg handled jugs, is to be found in the medieval spouted pots. According to the documents four families in Siegburg must have exerted a decisive influence on the manufacture of stoneware there— the Knütgens, Vlachs, Zeimanns and Omians. Among the workmen responsible for the artistic relief decoration the most important was F. Trac. Yet such a wealth of figural and ornamental motifs could

131

378

379 a)

378. Jug with a frieze of Centaurs, stoneware with a brown salt-glaze. Germany (Raeren); dated 1576, marked 'I.E.' (*sic*) for Jan Emens Mennicken. Ht. 21¼ in. (54 cm.). The upper frieze depicts the procession of the Wise Men of the East visiting the Queen of Sheba; the lower frieze depicts the battle of the Centaurs and Lapiths referred to in the inscription round the neck. Kunstmuseum, Düsseldorf.

379 a). Tankard with an allegory of the Four Seasons ('*Jahreszeitenkanne*'), grey stoneware with a blue glaze. Germany (Höhr or Grenzhausen, in the Westerwald); dated 1589, marked 'I.E.' (*sic*) for Jan Emens Mennicken. Ht. 14½ in. (36 cm.). The date refers only to the mould for the main frieze with the procession of the Seasons. The frieze round the neck is from a mould by Hans Hilger, which shows that moulds of

different origin were often used on one piece. Kunstmuseum, Düsseldorf.

379 b). A later development of the Westerwald style, with a regular diaper of stamped motifs, picked out in manganese-purple, is seen in the accompanying still-life by Herbert von Ravensteyn of Dordrecht. The picture is dated 1664. Rijksmuseum, Amsterdam.

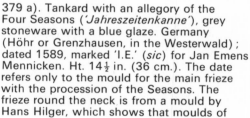

b)

hardly have been produced without the influence of the work of Nuremberg graphic artists. Countless engravers, among them Peter Flötner, Heinrich Aldegrever, Virgil Solis, Hans Sebald Beham and Théodore de Bry, provided models for the potters to copy, and much use was made of all kinds of hollow moulds, such as those used for making gingerbread and marzipan. About 1570 an individual style emerged at Raeren, seen at its best in the workshop of Jan Emens Mennicken. A dark brown tone distinguishes the Raeren jugs from the related wares made at Siegburg and Cologne. The somewhat diminished precision of the figural and ornamental reliefs is compensated for by the subordination of the applied decoration to the overall design. In 1587 Jan Emens Mennicken was the first to apply to his stoneware the cobalt-blue glaze which was later to become so typical of the Westerwald potteries.

Even before the pottery workshops at Siegburg and Raeren were either destroyed or paralysed in the 1630s as a result of the Thirty Years War, some of the owners had already migrated to other places. Anno Knütgen, for example, moved to Höhr in 1590, taking his sons with him, and, at the turn of the century, the Mennicken and Kalb families from Raeren settled first in Grenzau and then soon after in Grenzhausen, near Höhr. There was at first some rivalry among the potters of the Westerwald, but in time they formed a guild among themselves. The Westerwald jugs at first were made by using the Siegburg and Raeren moulds and then, in about 1630, the characteristic Westerwald type emerges, having an ovoid body rising directly from the foot-ring and ending in a narrow neck.

377

378

379 a

379 a

379 b

380

381

380. Tankard ('*Humpen*') decorated with the Planets (so-called '*Planetenkrug*'); brown stoneware with polychrome enamelling. Germany (Kreussen); dated 1627. Ht. 7 in. (18 cm.). Both the manner of painting and certain details of the decoration show clearly that the painter of this tankard had been trained as a glass-painter. This is easily explained by the proximity of the Fichtelgebirge and the Böhmerwald, which were famous for their enamelled glass. Victoria and Albert Museum, London.

381. Jug, grey stoneware painted in black and white enamels. Germany (Freiberg, in Saxony, probably made in the workshop of Samuel Günther). Ht. 7 in. (18 cm.). The carved patterns, also found on Kreussen wares, are derived from Rhenish stoneware. Victoria and Albert Museum, London.

Instead of the rich figural decoration these jugs have a regular diaper of stamped floral and leaf motifs joined by incised lines which effectively separate the cobalt-blue and manganese-purple glazes. The 'blue decoration' ('*Blauwerk*') carried out in this traditional technique has been continuously practised as a peasant art in the Westerwald up to the present day, and was copied in Hesse.

The manufacture of stoneware was not confined to the Rhineland. At Kreussen, in Franconia, members of the Vest family, who had come from Austria in 1512, made stoneware as well as the traditional Hafner ware (see p. 127–9) in their workshops. The finest examples date from the 17th century, although production carried on until 1731. A dark brown salt-glaze covers the brownish body of these wares. One group of tankards has a profusion of applied reliefs rather like the Rhenish wares, although the shapes and decorative motifs are different. Another group, decorated with applied reliefs, is painted in opaque enamel colours—blue, yellow, red, white, green and even gold—the same colours being used on the plain surfaces of a group of pieces decorated with figure-painting having obvious affinities with that of the contemporary glass-enamellers. The great majority of Kreussen wares can be divided up into families according to the recurring themes of their decoration; thus there are tankards showing the Apostles, the Electors of the Empire, the Planets, and scenes from the chase, as well as those commemorating families or marriages. Related to these are the pear-shaped jugs made at Freiberg in Saxony decorated with carved designs—palmettes and bands of leaves and rosettes—painted over in colours, often restricted to black and white. As early as 1490 Penig, also in Saxony, was famous for its stoneware. A group of jugs, which may have been made there or possibly in Zeitz, depict a potter, a certain Hans Glier, named in an inscription, who sometimes appears as a youth, sometimes as a grey-beard. The jugs made at nearby Waldenburg, decorated among other things with allegorical reliefs and coats-of-arms, have, just below the mouth and round the foot, a series of fine parallel grooves between which a zig-zag pattern is incised. The same kind of decoration appears on a group of wares with a pale brown glaze possibly made in Altenburg. The pear-shaped jugs of the Voigtland with coloured reliefs on the brown ground are influenced by the Kreussen types, while the so-called 'beaded jugs' ('*Perlkrüge*'), on which scrolling foliage, flowers, figures and coats-of-arms are formed out of little dots of clay, are pure peasant art.

Stoneware was also made in Silesia from the 17th century onwards. The jugs made at Bunzlau were at first rather clumsy and provincial in their imitation of the Renaissance shapes, but in the 18th century, under the influence of porcelain and creamware, they became more elegant. The only decoration found on these jugs—of which the grey-brown body was covered with a shiny glaze ranging in colour from coffee to rust-brown—consisted of coats-of-arms, figures and flowers in relief. Similar wares were made at Naumburg on the River Queis, and also in nearby. Lusatia where Muskau and Triebel became centres of a long continuing tradition.

France (Beauvais)

It has now been established beyond any doubt that towards the end of the Middle Ages, thanks to the nature of their local clay and to their methods of firing, Beauvais potters were the first in France to make the hard non-porous pottery known as stoneware. Stoneware fragments with a bluish glaze have recently been excavated in the area and Monsieur Chami has rediscovered the well-known text of 1545, attributed to Rabelais, which refers to 'our fine Beauvais flagons which are coloured and wonderfully good'. The fine quality of Beauvais stoneware, was widely acknowledged, since it was exported to places as far afield as the Low Countries and England, and was particularly valued for use as drug-jars.

From the 16th century onwards stoneware was also made in the Puysaie area. Decorated with Renaissance motifs in relief, this stoneware—said to have come from Saint-Vérain (Nièvre)—can be distinguished by its colour, which is always a rather dark shade of blue. It was used up to the 18th century, especially for tiles.

Another early pottery centre, which is still active today, is situated in the Berry region. In the 16th century a hard, grey, salt-glazed ware was produced there which ranks as a stoneware. Most of the known examples of Berry stoneware, however, belong to the end of the 18th and to the 19th century, a period when the craftsmen of the Talbot dynasty at La Borne (Cher) won great fame for their stonewares and their ordinary pottery.

382

383

382. Stoneware dish with blue-tinted glaze, decorated in low-relief with an escutcheon quartered, surrounded by fleurs-de-lis. French (Beauvais); beginning of the 16th century. Diam. 17 in. (43 cm.). This dish, of prime importance for the history of French stoneware, is authenticated and dated by the coat-of-arms, which is that of Louis Villiers de L'Isle Adam, Bishop of Beauvais from 1497 until 1521. It is also one of the finest known specimens of these 'grès azurés de Beauvais' ('blue stonewares of Beauvais'), mentioned in an apocryphal text of a follower of Rabelais, dated 1545. The same coat-of-arms is featured on a fragment from a flask of identical material which was excavated at Beauvais (now in the Musée de Sèvres). Louvre, Paris.

383. Hexagonal salt-cellar in blue-glazed stoneware, the sides decorated in low relief alternately with an escutcheon of fleurs-de-lis and busts in profile. French (Saint Vérain, Nièvre); second half of the 16th century. Ht. 3 in. (7.5 cm.). The architectural shape of this small object has parallels in certain salt-cellars by Bernard Palissy and others made at Saint-Porchaire. Its decoration is still in typical Renaissance style, and the glaze is of a more even blue than that of Beauvais stoneware. Musée National de Céramique, Sèvres.

England

Stonewares, whether unglazed or salt-glazed, had been reaching England from Germany in some quantity since, at latest, the end of the 15th century, and it was natural that efforts should be made in England to replace this importation by a native industry. Already in the reign of Queen Elizabeth I a certain William Simpson, whilst seeking the monopoly for the import of the German stonewares, at the same time undertook to 'draur to the making of such like pottes into some decayed town within the realm, wherebie manie a hundred poor men may be sett at work.' No English-made 16th-century stoneware, however, has ever been identified. The same may be said of isolated ventures in the 17th century, such as that of Thomas Rous and Abraham Cullen, to whom a patent was granted in 1626 to 'put in use the arte and feate of frameing, workeing, and makeing of all and all manner of potte, jugge, and bottelle, commonly called or knowne by the name or names of stone potte, stone jugge, and stone bottelle . . .'; or of another consortium which in 1635 obtained a patent for 'Makeinge . . . all sortes of Panne Tyles, Stone Juggs, Bottles of all sizes . . .'

The majority of the imported stonewares took the form of jugs or bottles having a bearded mask at the base of the neck, usually called 'Bellarmines' after the Cardinal of that name who had earned the hatred of the Protestants of northern Europe. The 'jug faced with a beard' was a commonplace in English 17th-century literature, and innumerable fragments of such bottles have been found in excavations in England. It is not surprising, therefore, that when finally salt-glazed stoneware came to be made in England, a special effort was made to replace these masked bottles from Germany by English products.

In 1671 a certain John Dwight, previously an ecclesiastical lawyer, was granted a patent for 'The Mistery of Transparent Earthenware, Comonly knowne by the Names of Porcelain or China and Persian Ware, as alsoe the Misterie of the Stone Ware vulgarly called Cologne Ware'. In 1676 and 1677 Dwight contracted to supply the

Glass Sellers' Company (who traded in bottles generally) with stoneware bottles of his making, and on the site of his pottery at Fulham two of his 'Bellarmines' were discovered in the 19th century. They closely resemble the German bottles, except for differing medallions decorating their fronts and slight differences in the method of manufacture.

Much more important, however, were Dwight's fine stonewares, which probably represent his nearest approach to the porcelain named in his patent, some of the thinnest specimens being in fact at least partially translucent. These fine stonewares were greyish, and some instances almost white. Sometimes white and black clays were mingled to form marbled embellishments on the brown stoneware bottles, which were also decorated with small applied reliefs. From the greyish body were made finely potted small mugs, but far more important were Dwight's figures, which range from small

384

385

384. Handled bottle, brown salt-glazed stoneware with marbled black and white clay patterning, and applied moulded reliefs. English (probably Fulham, pottery of John Dwight); about 1690. Ht. 7½ in. (19·1 cm.). John Dwight is known to have supplied the Glass Sellers' Company with salt-glazed stoneware bottles, but the piece illustrated is probably much more elaborate in character than these commercial bottles. The reliefs correspond roughly with some stamps found in a walled-up chamber at Fulham, but the

correspondence is not exact, and this bottle may have been made by one of Dwight's rivals. Victoria and Albert Museum, London.

385. Figure of *Lydia Dwight*, in grey salt-glazed stoneware. English (Fulham, pottery of John Dwight), about 1673–74. Ht. 11¼ in. (28·6 cm.). John Dwight was probably the first English potter to undertake figure work in his pottery. Dr Plot, a fellow member with Dwight of the Royal Society, said of him

that he had "so far advanced the *Art Plastick* that 'tis dubious whether any man since Prometheus have excelled *him*, not excepting the famous *Damophilus* and *Gorgasus* of Pliny". It is not known who the modeller was, but he had a fine feeling for the stoneware material, the salt-glaze of which does little to obscure the fineness and detail of the modelling. The figure shows the potter's little dead daughter, Lydia, rising from her shroud to meet the Resurrection. Victoria and Albert Museum, London.

A Decantor

A Carved Teapot

A Flower-Pot

A Capuchine

A Mogg

A Carved Jug

Such as have Occation for these Sorts of Pots commonly called Stone-Ware, or for such as are of any other Shape not here Represented may be furnished w.th them by the Maker James Morley at y Pot-House in Nottingham

386

387

386. Advertisement of the Nottingham stoneware potter, James Morley. About 1700. This advertisement shows three of the commonest shapes of drinking-vessel current at the end of the 17th century, and found in earthenware, stoneware and delftware alike. It also shows clearly the style of decoration, by means of piercing through an outer wall, characteristic of the Nottingham stonewares of this period. Bodleian Library, Oxford.

387. Mug of unglazed red stoneware with applied moulded decoration. English (probably Staffordshire, the Bradwell Wood pottery of John and David Elers), end of 17th century. Ht. 4 in. (10·2 cm.). It is difficult to distinguish between the work of John Dwight and that of his rivals, the brothers Elers. The fine quality of the workmanship in such pieces probably served as an inspiration to the indigenous Staffordshire potters, and the decorative technique of applying moulded motifs to a piece of pottery was continued by them until well into the 18th century. Victoria and Albert Museum, London.

mythological personages to portrait busts of almost life-size, most striking of all being two small figures showing his little dead daughter, Lydia. In all of these the fine modelling shows up to great effect under the tightly fitting, scarcely perceptible salt-glaze.

In 1693–4 Dwight took legal action against a number of potters who, he alleged, had infringed his patent of 1684 which confirmed and expanded that of 1671. Amongst them were members of the Wedgwood family from Burslem in Staffordshire, and James Morley of Nottingham—the former for making 'brown mugs', examples of which, obviously dating from the period, have been excavated in Staffordshire. James Morley too made brown stonewares, and the range of his products is shown by a trade-card which is still preserved. Existing examples of late 17th-century Nottingham stonewares reveal high standards of potting and a predilection for pierced ornament which is evident from the list on the trade-card.

Of greater significance for the future of the English ceramic industry, however, were John and David Elers, also of Fulham, who were included in Dwight's indictment. They were accused of infringing the patent not only with regard to 'brown muggs', but also 'red theapotts' which corresponded to the 'Opacous, Redd, and Dark coloured Porcellane . . .' of Dwight's patent. These wares themselves imitated the unglazed red stonewares of Yi-hsing commonly imported from China at this period. Probably as a result of Dwight's lawsuit, the Elers moved up to Staffordshire, and at Bradwell Wood continued their manufacture of unglazed red stonewares in the form of teapots, beakers, cups and saucers, teabottles, and small mugs with bulbous bodies and cylindrical reeded necks like those made by Dwight. They are normally decorated with finely moulded sprigs of flowers and leaves and other motifs applied in relief, and very occasionally are gilt or even enamelled— a precocious instance of enamelling on a ceramic body, perhaps inspired by the Elers' experience of metalworking, for they had been silversmiths before they became potters. Wares attributable to the Elers are notable for delicacy of potting and fineness of finish and may well have acted as a catalyst in the Staffordshire pottery industry at the turn of the century (see p. 260).

385

386

387

V Europe: Tin-Glaze

389

390

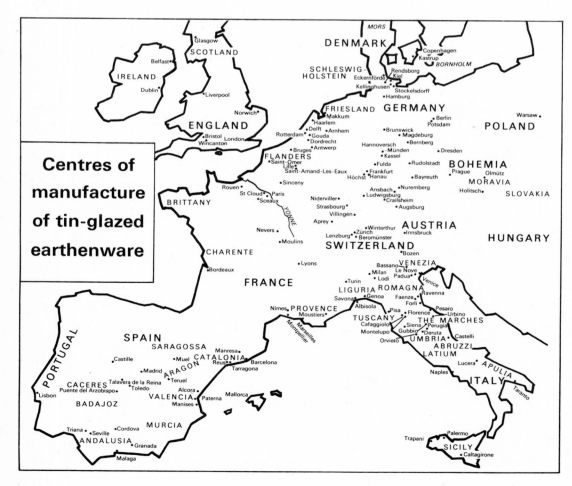

**Centres of
manufacture
of tin-glazed
earthenware**

388. Drawing from *Li Tre Libri dell'Arte del Vasaio* (*The Three Books of the Potter's Art*) by Cipriano Piccolpasso, Casteldurante, 1556–9. Two potters work at their kick-wheels, one throwing a dish, the other drawing up a large vase. Victoria and Albert Museum, London.

389. Alhambra Palace, Granada. *Sala de las Camas*. The floor of this ante-room and the walls, below the carved plaster decorations, are covered with tesserae, called *aliceres*, cut from glazed tiles of many colours and fitted together like the pieces of a puzzle. Although the ceramic dados in this room are mostly a restoration, the Moorish patterns are good replicas of 14th-century work.

390. Wing-handled vase. Málaga. Late 13th–early 14th century. Ht. 46⅛ in. (117 cm.). Encircling bands and roundels of large Kufic letters, floriated at the tips, are painted in gold on white in the elongated and angular style of the 12th century. The words may be translated as a series of salutations meaning 'pardon', 'blessing', 'felicity', 'prosperity' and the like. Magical power against the evil eye was attributed to the conventionalised hand, or *khams*, which appears on the wing-shaped handles of this vase. Hermitage Museum, Leningrad.

Introduction

Tin-glazed pottery is characterised by the use of a glassy lead-glaze, opacified by the addition of oxide (ashes) of tin. This when fired produces a dense white glaze which masks any colour in the underlying clay, and furnishes an ideal background for painted decoration. Tin-glazed pottery is confusingly known by different names in different countries—*maiolica* in Italy, *faience* in France, *Fayence* in Germany, and *delftware* in England—but is essentially the same everywhere. It is made by dipping the once-fired clay (formed in any of the ways available to the potter) into a slurry composed of the ground glaze-material mixed with water. The 'biscuited' body soaks up the water, leaving an even deposit of the glaze-material on the surface of the clay. This is now ready for the painter, who traces his designs on it in a variety of metallic pigments, limited in number to those which will stand the relatively high temperature of the glaze-firing ('high-temperature colours')—cobalt for blue, manganese for purple, copper for green, antimony for yellow, and iron for a brick-red. The wares so painted are then carefully packed in 'saggars' (safeguards) to protect them against smoke and fumes, and fired in the 'glost' (or glazing) kiln—usually with wood, although coal began to be used in England after the middle of the 18th century. The firing both fused the glaze and developed the colours of the painted decoration. In the 13th–17th centuries in Spain, and in the 16th century in Italy, 'lustre' decoration was painted over the once-fired glaze and fixed in a second firing under 'reducing' (smoky) kiln-conditions. In the 18th century, under the influence of porcelain, tin-glazed wares began to be decorated over the once-fired glaze with enamel-colours. These again are pigments based on metallic oxides, but the lower temperature of the subsequent firing in a 'muffle' kiln enabled a far wider range of colours to be used than was possible in a 'high-temperature' firing. In France such enamels were characterised as '*petit feu*' colours, in contrast with the '*grand feu*' pigments of the high-temperature technique. Gold could similarly be used as a further embellishment.

The use of tin-glaze (sometimes confusingly referred to as 'tin-enamel') was known in the ancient Near East, and was firmly established in Mesopotamia by the 9th century. From there, thanks to the Islamic conquests in North Africa, it spread ultimately to the Omayyad kingdom of Spain, and thence to the rest of Europe.

Spain (14th–15th centuries)

The golden age of Spanish ceramics began in the mid-13th century with the production at Málaga of lustre pottery. Reported by Muslim writers as peerless in beauty, this 'golden' ware was admired in the Moorish kingdom of Granada, as well as shipped to Sicily, Egypt, and outlying regions of the Hispanic peninsula. England imported Málaga lustre as early as 1303, and by the time another century had passed, Muslim potters had carried the art of lustre-painting to Murcia and Valencia.

How the potters of Málaga first learned the well-guarded methods for producing lustre on the surface of tin-glaze can be explained by a probable migration of artisans from Iran or countries of the eastern Mediterranean to southern Spain. Bearing out this supposition, the patterns on Spanish lustreware show a close relationship with the designs on the pottery of Rayy, Kashan and Raqqa. Combined with distinctly Eastern motifs are others in the traditionally Andalusian style that had evolved in the Iberian peninsula under

391. Drug-pot with heraldic decoration. Teruel (Aragon). 15th century. Ht. 15⅛ in. (38·5 cm.). Three heraldic shields are placed equidistantly against a background of green and black foliage; one bears a triple-towered castle, another the Gothic letters 'AT' and the third a green basket. A broad scroll of white palmettes reversed on black and another band of black scrolls on white completes the Moresque-Gothic decoration. The Hispanic Society of America, New York.

392. Dish with painting in green and brown on a white ground. Paterna, Valencia. 14th century. Diam. 12⅜ in. (31·5 cm.). The decoration here consists of a pattern of interlaced bands and heraldic shields. The Metropolitan Museum of Art, New York.

391

392

393 a)

b)

394

395

393 a), b). Bowl with painted decoration in brown-gold lustre and a blue stripe encircling the brim. Manises, Valencia. Early 15th century. Diam. 20 in. (50·8 cm.). The decoration shows a Portuguese sailing ship and four dolphins. The tree-of-life designs on the exterior are based on earlier Andalusian motifs; also the shape, with its straight, sloping surface, is related to prototypes made at Málaga. Victoria and Albert Museum, London.

394. Dish painted in green, outlined in black, on a white ground. Paterna, Valencia. Early 14th century. Diam. 14⅝ in. (37 cm.). The design is of a crowned dancer holding little cymbals. Round her are four encircling fishes. The Cleveland Museum of Art, Cleveland, Ohio.

395. Drug-jar, or *albarello*. Paterna, Valencia. 14th century. Ht. 8½ in. (21·5 cm.). Horizontal bands, coarsely painted in green and purplish-black on white, display palmettes, stylised Kufic letters and wheels. The Cleveland Museum of Art, Cleveland, Ohio.

the rule of the North African Moors, the Almohades (1174–1212).

Although small vessels, such as bowls, dishes, and pitchers, were usual products of the kilns at Málaga, the most astonishing pieces of lustre are great wing-handled vases, standing between three and four feet high, found nowhere else in the Islamic world. In the Alhambra at Granada, where several of them were unearthed, the vases served as ornaments in rooms opening on the palace gardens and patios. Of the nine or so wing-handled vases known at present, certainly the one called the 'Alhambra vase', since it never left the confines of the palace, is the most famous. Perhaps a century later in time than a well-known vase at Leningrad, it is taller and slimmer in shape, with a more gracefully curved line to the collar. Among Hispano-Moresque motifs painted on it in blue and a dull, brownish gold are pairs of confronted gazelles, represented in a schematic manner.

To build the large and complex shapes of these vases in clay required skill, since the potter had to form them in separate parts, later fitting the sections together. The entire piece was then fired, after which the white tin-glaze was applied to the surfaces. If blue designs were to be a part of the decorative scheme, the colour was brushed directly on the crude white and the vessel then fired in the glost kiln. The lustre, a thin film of metal which formed when the oxides or sulphides of copper and silver were reduced in a low-temperature kiln, was applied in liquid form directly on the already fired tin-glaze. The designs were painted with brushes and quills.

Pottery decorated with lustre, however, is not the most prevalent type of ceramics to be found in the Moorish kingdoms of southern Spain. More often one sees multicoloured mosaics of tile, fitted together in complicated geometrical, star, and interlace patterns that cover the walls and pavements of all important buildings. The

ceramic tesserae might be cut from either glazed or unglazed tiles. In the latter case, the small bits had to be glazed separately. A variety of tin- and lead-glazes supplied the colours—white, blue, turquoise, green, black, honey-yellow and brown. Well-heads and storage jars —carved, moulded, or stamped with relief designs in Almohade style—continued a technique that had been familiar to potters in the Western Caliphate at Córdoba (756–1031). These vessels, while sometimes glazed in part with a tin-glaze, were usually covered with green or honey-yellow lead-glazes.

Traditions of their Muslim forefathers were retained also by the potters of Aragón, Valencia, and Catalonia. What they knew of Hispano-Moresque decoration they mingled with Romanesque, Gothic, or whatever European style was then current. From the 13th century, Teruel in Aragón and Paterna in the Valencian region produced almost identical wares, both of them related to an 11th-century Cordovan pottery painted in green and blackish-purple on opaque white. Decorations of heraldry and figures of dancing girls and jousting knights bring European fashions and customs to an Islamic type of ceramics. But the geometric designs, Kufic calligraphy and creatures of Near-Eastern origin remind one of the potters' Muslim ancestry. Ceramic wares of comparable decoration, colours, and glaze technique have been excavated from sites at Manresa in Catalonia and in south-eastern France.

From the Muslim kingdoms of Murcia and Granada potters went in the 14th century to reconquered Valencia and associated themselves with native craftsmen to make 'golden pottery', the so-called 'Málaga work'. An important industry developed at Manises, where fine examples of lustreware imitated exactly the Málagan in shape and decoration. Several potters travelled from Manises to France to make lustreware for a cardinal at Avignon and for the Duke of

390

389

391

392

396. Drug-jar, or *albarello*, decorated with bands of blue and gold vine leaves, gold acacia leaves and flowerlets. Manises, Valencia. About 1435. Ht. 12⅜ in. (32 cm.). The decorative pattern on this jar was standard in the potteries of Manises and came into use as early as 1427, lasting until the end of the 15th century. The Hispanic Society of America, New York.

397. Drinking vessel, or *biberón*, with multiple spouts. Manises, Valencia. Mid-15th century. Ht. 13¼ in. (33·7 cm.). Seemingly a forerunner of the modern Spanish *cántaro*, it is painted in blue and gold lustre with a tangle of plant forms identifiable as bryony or parsley, another favourite background pattern. An Italian escutcheon bears a lion rampant, possibly the arms of Gentili of Florence. British Museum, London.

398. Detail from a *Nativity* (*The Portinari Altarpiece*) by Hugo van der Goes. About 1475. Hugo van der Goes painted this picture for an Italian patron, but it reveals its Netherlands character in the meticulously painted details of irises and a lily in an *albarello* (or pottery drug-jar), and of aquilegia and pinks in a glass beaker. The *albarello* with its design of ivy-like leaves probably represents an imported Spanish jar with painting in blue and copper ('gold') lustre (cf. fig. 396). Galleria degli Uffizi, Florence.

396

397

398

Berry at Bourges and Poitiers. The work of Manises was commissioned also by Martin I and Alphonse V, Kings of Aragón, who ordered it to be sent to their dominions of Naples and Sicily. From documents, the names of master potters are known, but no piece bears an identifiable mark or signature. A group of bowls, produced about 1400 and close copies of vessels found at Granada and Málaga, are painted in a red-gold lustre with iridescent effects in tones of blue, red and pale gold. Combined with the lustre is painting in deep cobalt blue.

While at first they were faithful copyists of Moresque decoration, the potters of Manises occasionally brought to their lustre-painting representational designs, like that of a Portuguese sailing ship painted on a bowl. Contemporary potters at Málaga also were depicting scenes, some including human figures clad in European dress. So similar is the work done at Málaga and Manises during the 15th century that it is sometimes impossible to distinguish between the products of the two centres. Heraldic shields of famous families and individuals help to tell the story of its spread to every country of Europe. We learn that, about 1428, dishes of Manises lustreware belonged to Philip the Good of Burgundy, to the Queens, Blanca of Navarre and María of Castile, and to John II of Castile. These shields relied on designs that were purely Hispano-Moresque in character, such as trees-of-life, scrolls, palmettes, and bands of stylised Arabic script, painted entirely in lustre or essentially in blue with the secondary motifs in lustre.

About 1450, Manises ware became very popular in Italy. It was then that the Italians first gave the name 'maiolica' to Valencian lustreware. An impressive number of table pieces from Manises, indentifiable by their coats-of-arms, belonged to the illustrious families of the Medici, Gondi, Gentili, Morelli, and many others.

393 a), b)

397

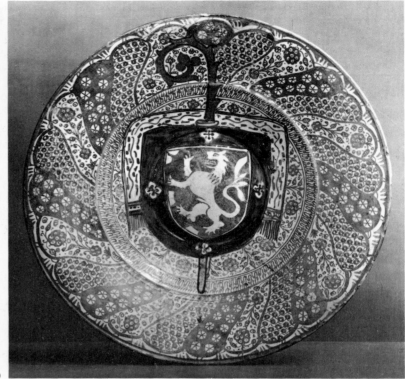

399

400

399. Plate in heraldic style with the lion passant painted in golden-orange and pale grey-blue on a flecked white ground. Probably Puente del Arzobispo, Toledo. 16th century. Diam. 14¼ in. (36 cm.). The influence of Mudéjar designs done by the potters of Manises in Valencia province is strong, even though an orange-yellow glaze is substituted

400. Plate painted in blue and gold, bearing the arms of Joan Payo Coello, Abbot of Poblet Monastery. Possibly Catalonia, in imitation of Manises. About 1475. Diam. 18⅛ in. (46 cm.). The heraldic shield bears a

for lustre. The Hispanic Society of America, New York.

lion rampant on a gold ground, surrounded by a blue bordure with four gold crosses. An abbot's crosier and stole, supporting and mantling the shield, are outlined in blue. Payo Coello was abbot from 1480 to 1499, proving that ornamentation like that on the brim dates back to the 15th century. The Hispanic Society of America, New York.

401
396–8

400

402
399

Background patterns for these heraldic shields were limited principally to blue-and-gold vine leaves, to the flowers and foliage of bryony and parsley, to the fern-like leaf of the acacia, and to a palmette-type foliage. Another background frequently used was a gadroon pattern, filled in with a patchwork of minute motifs and painted on flat or convex surfaces. While it was most popular in the first quarter of the 16th century, the gadroon has been traced back to the 1480s or '90s. The repetitious and limited motifs painted so meticulously on the face of dishes should not deceive one into thinking that Valencian potters could not draw bold designs of remarkable beauty and verve. Sometimes an obverse exemplifies this virtuosity in an animal pattern which is interesting to compare with contemporary work in the region of Castile. More often the splendid creatures done at Manises decorate the reverses of plates and basins made from about 1430 to 1475.

At first, based on the same Muslim shapes as those from Málaga, Valencia lustre pottery was simple in form. The cylindrical drug-jar of Near-Eastern origin continued in use, and about 1470 certain newer and more complicated shapes began to emerge from the wheel or from moulds with which the potter attempted to imitate the shapes of silverware.

Beyond Valencia, in the old provinces of Aragón and Catalonia, lustre pottery began to be made towards the end of the 15th century, or early in the 16th, in imitation of Manises ware. Although similar in a way to Valencian lustre, the slightly different designs, the quality and colour of the glazes and body-materials, as well as differences in craftsmanship, help to identify these wares as from Barcelona, Reus, and Tarragona, or from Teruel and Muel.

Simultaneously, from the workshops of both Christians and Moriscos (Spanish Muslims converted to Christianity after the

395-
397
403

403,
406

401

402

401. Plate with painted lustre decoration, outlined in heavy blue. Manises, Valencia. About 1450. Diam. 16¾ in. (41·5 cm.). A knight bearing both shield and spear strides forth against a background of boldly-painted leaves. His costume indicates a 15th-century date. Instituto de Valencia de Don Juan, Madrid.

402. Plate with painted lustre decoration. Manises, Valencia. Early 16th century. Diam. 18¾ in. (47·5 cm.). Drawn in blue outline, the gold-lustre lion rampant fills the circular space in regal style. A pattern of lustre foliage covers the white ground. The Hispanic Society of America, New York.

28. Circular relief (tondo) of terracotta from the workshop of Andrea Della Robbia, late 15th or early 16th century. Diam. 3 ft. 3 in. (1 m.). Museo Nazionale, Palazzo Bargello, Florence.

28

29

30

31

403. Ewer with painted lustre decoration. Aragón province. 16th century. Ht. 6⅞ in. (17·5 cm.). Geometric and stylised floral designs are painted in coppery lustre; the form is that of a helmet-shaped vessel, used so much for silverware in the 16th century. The style of decoration indicates that this piece was made in the province of Aragón, perhaps at Muel. Instituto de Valencia de Don Juan, Madrid.

405. High altar of the Convent Church of San Juan de la Penitencia, Toledo. The altar frontal, steps, and floor are paved with glazed tiles combined with others of unglazed terracotta. Geometric patterns of interlace, based on earlier Hispano-Moresque motifs, are glazed in the so-called *cuenca* technique in green, white, blue, transparent yellow and black. The convent was founded in 1514, and it is probable that the tiles date from about the same year.

404. Baptismal font from Toledo. 15th century. Diam. 34 in. (86·5 cm.). The octagonal basin is glazed in opaque white, brightened with green-glazed motifs in relief, most of them Christian, principally a floriated cross and the monogram 'IHS' in Gothic letters. Border patterns of interlace and impressions of the *khams* and magic eye reveal Mudéjar work. The Hispanic Society of America, New York.

403

404

405

Reconquest of 1212) in Toledo and Seville, came sturdier types of ceramic ware. These inclined towards the architectural—finials, tiles and other details—or heavy pieces for practical purposes—storage jars for grain, oil and water, also well-heads and baptismal fonts. The decoration on these large objects was generally a combination of Moorish and Christian-Gothic designs, known in Spain as 'Mudéjar' (derived from the word 'Mudéjares', the name for unconverted Muslims living in Christian Spain after the Reconquest). Following the Moorish techniques of earlier centuries, these potters were skilled in cutting, moulding, and stamping designs on their work, and lead-glazing it in emerald-green and honey-yellow, or covering it with a white tin-glaze.

405
404

The tableware made in the potters' quarter of Triana, at Seville, was thick and cumbersome, glazed in the '*cuerda seca*' ('dry cord') technique. This process, familiar to the potters of Andalusia since the 11th century at Córdoba, came to the peninsula from the Near East. At Seville, the outlines of the Mudéjar designs, usually a portrait-head, animal, or chimeric beast, were drawn with a mixture of manganese and grease, and the spaces filled in with white and coloured glazes. After the glaze-firing, the design appeared as enamel-like patches of colour, separated by dark, unglazed outlines. Innumerable tiles glazed by this method were made at Seville and Toledo in imitation of earlier tile-mosaics.

407

29. Rectangular panel, maiolica painted in rich and delicate polychrome. 'Beautiful' style. Italy (Faenza, signed 'B T', an artist known as the 'Master of the Resurrection Panel'); about 1515. 9¾×8 in. (25×20·5 cm.). Details recall Dürer's 'Large Woodcut Passion' of 1510. Victoria and Albert Museum, London.

30. Ewer with rope handle, in faience with high-temperature decoration of white and two shades of yellow on the blue-tinted tin-glaze. French (Nevers); middle of the 17th century. Ht. 8¼ in. (21 cm.). This perfect example of the 'bleu de Nevers' displays the typical decoration of stylised bouquets with birds and insects known as 'Persian decoration' ('décor persan'). The rope handle is also typical of Nevers faience. Musée National de Céramique, Sèvres.

31. Dish (London) depicting Alexander and the family of Darius; about 1640. Painted with lead-glazed back. The design must be derived from an engraving, but the drawing on the dish lacks assurance. The combination of the Urbino 'grotesques' and the panels of Chinese (late Ming) inspiration is unusual. Victoria and Albert Museum, London.

406

406. Plate in the style of Manises, Valencia. Shown in the centre are the arms of Domingo Porta, abbot of Poblet from 1502 until his death in 1526. The shield is supported by an abbot's stole and crosier outlined in blue. Museo Nazionale, Palazzo Bargello, Florence.

407

407. Plate with 'dry cord' glazing. Seville. 15th century. Diam. 15¼ in. (39·5 cm.). A harpy. This method of glazing, known as *cuerda seca* or dry cord, was brought to Spain from the Near East in the 11th century. The Hispanic Society of America, New York.

The Development of Maiolica

Italy and Sicily

The first Italian pottery with painting on a tin-glaze appears as early as the 11th–12th centuries. The decoration, timid at first, was drawn in brown to stand out against grounds which were not always made white but sometimes left biscuit-coloured, and also in green, on bright yellow tin-glaze. In Apulia, at Taranto, and Canne, the brown, yellow and green of the Arabo-Norman tradition in Sicily, were replaced by brown and red on a thick white slip background.

At Gela in Sicily, too, as at Lucera in Apulia, there have been discoveries of plates and cups decorated with braids, animals and human figures drawn in brown and dark blue on a white tin-glaze. These are like others found in excavations in places which had once been Crusader strongholds in the eastern basin of the Mediterranean. In spirit and decorative style these finds are close to the archaic group of maiolica most richly represented by the 13th- and 14th-century finds in central North Italy. Here the predominant colouring was the combination of manganese-brown and copper-green, or else occasionally, brown and cobalt-blue, on a white tin-glaze which covered only the areas to be decorated, while the rest of the pot—the foot and the inside of the hollow vessels, the outside and reverse of bowls and plates—was at most rendered impermeable by means of a lead-glaze. The brown-green colouring was widespread in the Mediterranean, in Italy until the early 15th century.

The centres of greatest achievement in the central and northern regions of Italy have been identified as Orvieto and Viterbo in the Umbria-Latium region; Montalcino near Siena, S. Gimignano, Pisa and Florence in Tuscany, and Faenza, but also Forli, Cesena, Rimini, Fano, Ravenna and elsewhere, even as far as Padua, in the regions of the Romagna and the Adriatic.

Careful collocation of excavated wares shows that the industry flourished in many places in the areas mentioned; but usually this evidence refers us back, through stylistic affinities, to the products of the main centres which are also richer in archival documentation concerning the 13th, 14th and 15th centuries.

Decoration was introduced either as a dominant feature against the white tin-glaze background or reserved against a ground of minute and precise brown cross-hatching. The design was always firmly drawn with a thick brown unbroken outline filled in with green except for the strapwork often painted round the borders of jugs and bowls, in which green alone was used. The repertory of design reveals contacts with the art of miniature, wall-paintings, textiles and occasionally with architectural ornament, which not only inspired stylistic features but also artistic conceptions. This repertory was composed of geometrical elements, foliage, animals, coats-of-arms and inscriptions.

It is not always easy to tell the difference between the styles of one area and those of another; at Orvieto and sometimes in Tuscany the decoration may be enriched with details modelled in low relief—trailing vines bearing bunches of grapes, busts, coats-of-arms—which does not seem to have been the custom at Faenza and in the Romagna. The jug with a trilobate mouth common to all three areas, is frequently more slender in form, with a strongly splayed foot in the Tyrrhenian, Tuscan and Umbria-Latium areas, while the Adriatic region seems to have preferred a rather more cylindrical shape narrowing slightly at the base and neck, and in some cases, the development of a severe biconical shape.

The cylindrical or flattened spout, shaped like a nose, inserted into the shoulder of the pot is more frequently found in the centres of Umbria and Latium than in the Romagna. In the same way the

408

409

410

408. Small maiolica bowls, painted in brown and green. Archaic period. Orvieto; end of 14th century. Diam. 4½ in. (11·5 cm.); 4⅞ in. (12·5 cm.); 4⅝ in. (12 cm.). The decoration consists of geometrical, animal and plant motifs, from various sources, which were part of the common repertoire of all Italian potters in the workshops of the archaic period. Victoria and Albert Museum, London.

410. Large maiolica basin, painted in green and brown, green predominant. 'Severe style'. Florence; 1425–50. The severe shape suggests metal prototypes. The sophisticated design, a heraldic lion with a standard bearing the Florentine lily, on a background richly scattered with sprays of leaves and flowers of Gothic inspiration, reveals a new and more mature decorative spirit, although still in the green and brown of the archaic period. Louvre, Paris.

409. Small maiolica plate painted in brown and cobalt-blue on white enamel. Diam. 9 in. (23 cm.). Archaic period of maiolica. Apulia, end 13th century. The warrior amid palms has a triangular shield bearing the lily of Anjou. Representation of the human figure is rare in this period. Blue is used to fill in the brown outlines; this is unusual, the fill-in being generally green. This dish, excavated near Lucera, is an excellent example of the part played by potters in southern Italy in the formation of taste in maiolica ware, and in its technical evolution, now including a final coating of tin-glaze. Museo Civico, Lucera.

411

412

413

411. Large maiolica jug painted in brown and green. Archaic period. Siena; 14th century. Ht. 12⅜ in. (31·5 cm.). The design of confronted birds and two griffins supporting a coat-of-arms is influenced by the Bestiaries of Oriental inspiration which were much used in Romanesque art, especially in cathedral ornament. In Tuscany this fashion was given wider currency by ornamental bowls, usually from the East, which were hung on the outer walls of churches and other public buildings. Museo Nazionale, Palazzo Bargello, Florence.

412. Drug-jar for liquids or ointments, painted in brown and thickly applied cobalt-blue. 'Severe style', 'relief-blue' family. Florence; 1430–60. Characteristic ovoid form. The decoration is in raised cobalt-blue. The animals, paired back to back, are similar to those on archaic vessels, but here the background of oak leaves provides a name for a whole series of these jars—'Oak leaf jars'. The technique, common to Faenza and Umbrian workshops seems of Oriental, probably Byzantine inspiration. Museo Nazionale, Palazzo Bargello, Florence.

413. Biconical maiolica jug, painted in brown and blue on white tin-glaze. Archaic period. Faenza; 14th century. Ht. 8¼ in. (21 cm.). The small-scale decoration is of the kind used for textiles and miniatures. The potter, now expert in tin-glazing—with its double function of preventing porosity and offering a light background for pictorial decoration—here restricts it to the part to be decorated. The foot and the inside of the jug are simply coated with a thinner, less costly transparent glaze without tin oxide. Museo Internazionale delle Ceramiche, Faenza.

bowl with upright sides which calls to mind classical prototypes is more often found in Latium than elsewhere, with lobed or plain bowls made in imitation of wooden and metal models.

The 15th century saw the fusion of the greatest stylistic achievements with perfected techniques and a richer palette. Austerity of form and decoration, with strict subordination of the ornamentation to the shape of the pot, and the use of a range of primary colours, have all led to this phase being called 'severe'. It was, in fact, an extremely active phase in the work of Italian maiolica artists. To facilitate study the gradual increase of the repertory of designs has been indicated in a series of groups or 'families' which extend from the second quarter of the century to its close, or a little beyond. The first of them is the 'green family' (la famiglia verde), a group of products characterised by the predominance of copper-green used to fill in shapes outlined in manganese-brown—the same elements as used in the 'archaic' style from which the green family is derived.

But they are applied here to more complicated motifs which suggest a more sophisticated conception of figurative expression, with outlines vibrant with life and strength, and a feeling for the correct presentation of the main theme, be it page boy, noblewoman, animal or coat-of-arms, which stands out against a background of foliage. This transition from the 'archaic' to the 'severe' in the second quarter of the 15th century appears to have been the work primarily of the Tuscan potters and, I would say, particularly of the Florentines who must have been sensible to the stimulus provided by daily life among painters, miniaturists, textile designers and engravers in an atmosphere of great artistic activity.

The next development was marked by the almost contemporary family of wares in 'relief blue' (zaffera in rilievo) which is of the same inspiration as the green family but with the decorative subject treated in a dark blue colour thickly applied, so that it stood out in shallow relief against the background. The most characteristic

414

415

416

414. Ovoid maiolica vase, painted in cobalt-blue, manganese-purple, orange and green. 'Gothic-floral' family, in the 'Severe style'. Possibly Tuscany, about 1460. Ht. 12½ in. (32 cm.). These portrait-busts are typical of the decorative style in Tuscany and other Italian centres. The 'peacock-feather' motif, characteristic of another group, also occurs here. Victoria and Albert Museum, London.

415. Drug-jar (*albarello*) with sacred monogram ('IHS'), maiolica painted in cobalt-blue, manganese-purple, orange and green. Italo-Moresque family; 'Severe style'. Tuscany; 1450–80. Ht. 10 in. (25·5 cm.). The background consists of the typical 'bryony leaf' design of the Valencian Hispano-Moresque ware. The lustre technique of the original ware being unknown, the potter used manganese-purple. Victoria and Albert Museum, London.

416. Ovoid maiolica vase painted in cobalt-blue, green and orange. 'Severe style', 'Persian palmette' group. Faenza; end 15th century. The Persian palmette motif, although somewhat similar to 14th-century Persian models, is closer to Turkish versions of the later 15th century. The neck is decorated with the 'wavy rays' motif, and the two-colour circular forms near the foot are found in the 'Gothic-floral' family. Kunstgewerbe-museum, Berlin-Charlottenburg.

product of this family is found in Tuscany in the little two-handled jars with their typical oak leaf decoration (the 'oak-leaf jars' of Wallis), which used to adorn the pharmacies of the Florentine hospitals. It is a family common to workshops in the Romagna as well as to the Umbria-Latium area, sometimes with additional touches of green in relief. It may be that the initial inspiration for this family came from contacts with the East, and particularly with the Byzantine world.

More certainly derived from the East—the Islamic East which had spread to Spain—was the third group called 'Italo-Moresque' because of the prevalence of elements which had been faithfully copied from prototypes that wool and silk merchants and bankers had imported from Valencia *via* the island of Majorca. These were imitated as much by the Tuscan manufacturers of maiolica ('*maiolicari*') as by those in the Romagna, both in the monochrome ware—blue on white—and in the polychrome ware which, with its high-temperature blue, green, yellow, orange and purple, had the same attractiveness as the blue and lustre ware of the Hispano-Moresque originals. By the middle of the century, or a little later, the maiolica-artists had claimed all the primary colours for their palette. The rich contribution from Spain which was interpreted in a more colourful key in Tuscany but more austerely in monochrome in the Romagna, was adopted magnificently by the Italian potters, who from this Italo-Moresque style developed the unrivalled richness and variety of the 'Gothic-floral' style. It is to this group that the most creative and imaginative wares belong, in which decoration reaches the highest possible level offered by this material.

The flowering of Gothic linear stylisation is the most mature expression of that feeling for decoration which within a few years was to pave the way for the achievements of the Renaissance. The colours of the palette were clear and striking, and the subject-matter mainly composed of highly stylised foliage patterns. A beautiful, elegantly scrolled leaf was particularly predominant, derived from the prototypes in miniatures, or inspired by architectural motifs, and

417

417. Maiolica plate, painted in cobalt-blue, orange, green, and manganese-purple. 'Peacock-feather' family; 'Severe style'. Faenza; 1470–80. Diam. 9⅞ in. (25·5 cm.). This popular design, in breaking up the surface, harmoniously distributed the basic colours of the palette, creating the illusion of greater richness. The reverse is painted in concentric rings of cobalt-blue and orange. Victoria and Albert Museum, London.

418

418. Detail of pavement with regular hexagonal maiolica tiles, painted in cobalt-blue, yellow, orange, green and purple. 'Severe style' Faenza; 1487. W. of tiles 3½ in. (9 cm.). This is probably the richest Italian maiolica 15th-century pavement still *in situ*. More than 1,000 tiles, the work of a certain Petrus Andrea of Faenza and his collaborators, contain a fantastic decorative

repertoire, each tile having an independent design and a border with ornamentation of the contemporary 'Gothic-floral' type, the peacock-feather and Persian palmette motifs and, above all, characteristic Renaissance designs. Church of S. Petronio, Bologna.

419. Square pavement tiles, maiolica painted in cobalt-blue, orange, green and purple.

'Severe style'. Possibly Pesaro; about 1494. W. 9¼ in. (23·5 cm.). The decoration on the tiles, which are of considerable thickness, shows the heraldic arms and devices of the Gonzaga family, the Lords of Mantua. The pavement, fragments of which are now dispersed, was originally in the old Castle of Mantua. Victoria and Albert Museum, London.

419

there were bands of spur ornament, braids or chains, or the device of S. Bernadino of Siena—rays encircling the sacred monogram 'I.H.S.'. There were lobed and pointed, oval and circular panels enclosing the main subject—a bust, animal, figure or initial, which in its turn was framed by a 'contour panel' roughly following its outline, a device of eastern origin. Apart from the pots themselves this style is well illustrated in the small square and hexagonal tiles of the floors of some Neapolitan churches, particularly in the Caracciolo chapel in the church of S. Giovanni at Carbonara.

On to this rich and varied style—the Gothic-floral—was grafted first a peacock-feather eye motif and then a 'Persian palmette', which persist to the end of the century. The range of colours characteristic of the Gothic-floral style reached the most refined

expression in these two groups, as it did in the Renaissance motifs which were to herald the '*stile bello*' ('beautiful style').   418

The so-called 'peacock-feather eye' motif, with the minute breaking up of the coloured surface—mainly orange with cobalt-blue, green and purple—the rhythm consisting in the subject being repeated in a semi-circular, diaper or branching pattern—was originally derived from remotest antiquity, but found its happiest expression in the Italian ceramic art of the last quarter of the 15th century. At Faenza this motif was connected with political events which made of it an expression of the popular spirit in so far as it represented a verbal allusion to the name of Cassandra Pavoni ('*pavone*' meaning 'peacock'), mistress of Galeotto Manfredo, Lord of Faenza (d. 1488), to whom the maiolica-artists intended it as a mark of homage.   417

The motif of the Persian palmette, in the form most closely linked with contemporary Anatolian prototypes at Isnik (Nicaea) and the art of Abraham of Kütahya, with markedly full-bodied 'cones' and rounded petals, as seen in Faenza, and in a less exaggerated form in later Tuscan examples, was most richly applied in the bands bordering the entire floor of the chapel of S. Sebastian in the Church of S. Petronio in Bologna. This floor, laid at the expense of Canon Donato Vaselli in 1487, with a wealth of subjects and motifs in the separate compartments formed by individual hexagons, offers a vast and most effective pattern book of designs from a Faenza studio—in this case from the workshop of a certain Petrus Andrea, who is plainly portrayed on one of the tiles. The tiles not only display the traditional designs of the Gothic-floral group, the Persian palmette and the peacock-feather eye, but are further enriched with a whole repertory derived from designs from classical and Renaissance architecture, which we see here for the first time. Beadings, bezants, ovolos, masks, grotesques, arms trophies, braids or cable designs and broken bands, are combined with a free and fanciful collection of elements from everyday life—bowls and plates, working tools, eyeglasses, fetters, animals and townscapes to   416 418 419

420

421

420. Young girl carrying a basket, tin-glazed earthenware. Della Robbia workshop, Florence; end of 15th century. The modelled works of the Della Robbia family belong to the world of sculpture, interpreted in glazed terracotta. But their workshops also produced wall-panels, pavement tiles, and vases, and there is always a strong colour-sense in the

wreaths of fruit and flowers framing the profoundly religious figurative compositions, which stand out in white relief on a sky-blue background. Galleria Buonarroti, Florence.

421. Inkstand (?) with polychrome figures representing *The Nativity*. Faenza; about 1509. Ht. 9½ in. (24·5 cm.). This is one of the fairly

common three-dimensional productions of the Faenza potters, made towards the end of the 15th and at the beginning of the 16th century. It is reminiscent of the Gothic style and is not without popular appeal. This model was reproduced several times and there are various copies. Victoria and Albert Museum, London.

mention only a few—and all introduced harmoniously into the context. This was the narrative freedom of the Humanist Renaissance, the forerunner of the style about to burst into being— the *istoriato*.

It was also at the end of the century that contacts with the Near and Far East made their contribution, especially with the revelation of Chinese porcelain. By way of Venice perhaps, this light, fine, exotic product had as much influence on shapes, which became more delicate, subtle and varied, as it had in increasing the repertory of ornament. This was the beginning of the motifs called 'alla porcellana' ('in the style of porcelain') painted in cobalt-blue on a white background and inspired by the styles of the Ming dynasty potters. They echoed the floral motifs of the chrysanthemum and peony, of sprays, tiny leaves and vines, either trailing or hanging in minute festoons from the border—and at first framing subjects often connected with the life of those distant lands—junks, pagodas, silkworms, etc. This 'family' was already found in the workshops of Faenza by the end of the 15th century and continued there for several decades of the 16th. But fashions spread, and the whole of the Adriatic region was soon familiar with the style, and at Cafaggiolo and Montelupo in Tuscany it appeared with variations

of one kind or another throughout the 16th century.

One manifestation which, because of the concept which inspired it, has been considered as a separate phenomenon of artistic activity, but which must be included in the mainstream of maiolica because of the medium employed and certain of its techniques, is the work of the Della Robbia family. Luca (1399–1482), Andrea (1435–1525) and Giovanni (1469–1529) were the most important, but there were also Giovanni's brothers, one of whom, Girolamo, went to France, and several followers and imitators.

It would be wrong to think that in the workshops of ceramic craftsmen, before and after the Della Robbias, there was no place, beside all the variety of shape and pictorial decoration, for sculptural expression—whether it was only complementary— handles, spouts, braiding, etc.—or a completely freestanding figurative art, of a greater or lesser simplicity, often inspired by wooden or metal prototypes. It would be surprising if the contrary were true, this form of expression having been widely used in ceramics in every age and every country. Thus three-dimensional work is found as much in the 'archaic' phase as in the 'severe style', and as often in the 'beautiful style' as in the successive phases of maiolica, right up to the present day.

The Della Robbia phenomenon, however, stands on its own, because here the sculptural element is completely dominant, manifested first in the imperious temperament of Luca, the creator of works in marble and bronze who turned to ceramics primarily for practical reasons, and later in Andrea and Giovanni. In fact, the last of the three minimised the play of light and shade in his sculpture with a rich overlay of colours which is not found in the figurative compositions of Luca and Andrea, who kept to white tinglaze against a sky-blue background. From this point of view he was more of a maiolica-artist than either his father or his uncle, and was more attracted by the threefold nature of the ceramic art—material, shape, colour. With Luca and Andrea this was limited to the garlands framing roundels and lunettes, like those with which Luca, in his early days, surrounded some pieces of marble sculpture—the tabernacle of Peretola, the Federighi tomb in Santa Trinità in Florence, and so on. Later on these devices were used for floors and for adorning walls, as in the chapel of the Cardinal of Portugal in Santa Croce, Florence, where the great sculptor set his hand to a project typical of a craftsman's workshop.

The Della Robbia workshop is unique, and not only because it has a completely different character from that of traditional maiolica workshops. Their work is distinctive, first because of the nature of the glaze, which is generally dry and not very vitreous, secondly in the opaque and thickly applied colours, and finally and especially in the decoration, which never drew on the usual repertory of the maiolica-artists, and never developed in their style. It was, in fact, an isolated phenomenon which surprised the second half of the 15th century and the early 16th century with outstanding works, among which are the memorable *putti* of the Ospedale degli Innocenti in Florence, by Andrea, and the frieze depicting the works of charity at the Ospedale del Ceppo at Pistoia, on which Giovanni and his followers worked, and which shows how genius finds expression in any medium, and can ennoble any material with its own essential qualities.

The humanistic culture which had for some time been making itself felt—without ever completely penetrating the maiolica workshops—was very much in evidence in the '*stile bello*' phase almost throughout the first half of the 16th century. The elements borrowed from classical architecture, mentioned above, were followed by stories, legends, and descriptions of historical events past and present, mythological fantasies and edifying religious subjects. This was the *istoriato* style which, assisted by the printer's art—wood- and copper-engravings—came with all its trappings to take the place of the more or less abstract decorative concepts which had formed the basis of the 'severe style'.

Anonymous artists from Faenza were the first tentatively to break the new ground. An artist with the monogram 'B T' was the creator of a series of works executed between the first and second decades of the 16th century. Among these were the two panels, the *Martyrdom of St Sebastian* (in the Bargello, Florence) and the *Resurrection of Christ* (in the Victoria and Albert Museum, London), which was inspired by a Dürer print. Because of this panel, the artist came to be known as the 'Master of the Resurrection Panel'. Both works are painted in detail, confidently drawn and in delicate colours—in which shading plays an important part. By the same artist, there is a plate showing the subject, *Jesus among the Doctors* (also in the Victoria and Albert Museum), executed in blue and white on a grey-blue or lavender-grey (*berettino*) background and made in the workshop of a Master Jeronimo da Forli, together with a figural fragment (in the Hermitage in Leningrad) signed with the monogram 'I.C.'; to this same artist can be attributed other works painted with a light touch. The 'Master of the Death of the Virgin' was so named after a plate (now in the British Museum, London), on which the scene was taken from an engraving by Martin Schongauer. The 'Master P.F.' is also known as the 'Painter from the workshop of Francesco Torelli', who in 1522 signed a plate painted in dark blue with the *Incredulity of St Thomas*, now in an English private collection. Among others were the 'Painter of the Assumption', so named after a panel now in the Victoria and Albert Museum; the 'Painter of Lucretia' from a plate depicting the *Death of Lucretia* (Museo Civico, Bologna) and the 'Master of the Triumph of Selene' after a dish in the Bargello, Florence.

The dispersal of works such as those by these artists, and sometimes of the craftsmen themselves, carried the new genre further afield and led to its adoption in other centres. At Siena we find a Master Benedetto di Giorgio da Faenza, who from 1503 onwards had an important studio in the quarter of Porta San Marco. Among various other pieces, he signed a plate depicting St Jerome, in dark

29
(p. 144)

424

420

423

422

423

424

422. Small maiolica dish painted in cobalt-blue on white. 'Severe style'; *alla porcellana* group. Faenza; end 15th century—beginning 16th century. Diam. 7⅞ in. (20 cm.). This refined and delicate decoration imitates that of Chinese porcelain of the Ming dynasty, acquired probably by way of Venice, reaching the West along the silk trade routes. The reverse is decorated with a rayed border of alternating long oval and star-shaped motifs. Museo Internazionale delle Ceramiche, Faenza.

423. Maiolica dish, painted in polychrome. 'Beautiful style'. Faenza; 1507. Diam. 10¾ in. (27·4 cm.). Heraldic shield of the Gambara family. The decoration with grotesques on the brim—cranes, eagles, dolphins, cornucopias, clasped hands, books, ribbons and scrolls had not yet become stereotyped in the rigid forms which it was to assume in subsequent decades. The reverse is decorated with the 'daisy petal' motif, with drawing of details in cobalt-blue and orange. Galleria Estense, Modena.

424. Plaque painted in cobalt-blue with frugal use of pale complementary tones. 'Beautiful style'. Faenza; 'Master of the Death of the Virgin'; about 1510. Diam. 10½ in. (26·7 cm.). This composition, derived from Martin Schongauer's engraving, *Death of the Virgin*, has given its name to the artist of a whole series of works by an anonymous early *istoriato* Master. On the back is a decorative pattern of finely drawn scale-designs. Also characteristic are the sharply pleated folds of drapery, facial expressions and restrained palette. British Museum, London.

425

426

427

425. Large 'show dish' or ceremonial maiolica plate, painted in cobalt-blue and golden lustre. 'Beautiful' style. Deruta; early 16th century. Diam. 16 in. (40·5 cm.). Very characteristic of this type of dish is the division of the rim into compartments enclosing floral and classical motifs. The central figure is St Jerome. The painting in cobalt-blue is careful and vigorous, further enlivened with lustre. Museo Internazionale delle Ceramiche, Faenza.

426. Maiolica plate, painted in cobalt-blue, green, yellow, orange, blackish purple and red. 'Beautiful' style. Cafaggiolo; Master Jacopo; about 1510. Diam. 9¼ in. (23·5 cm.). A maiolica-artist is decorating the rim of a plate in front of two patrons whose portraits are to be painted in the well. The decoration extends over the whole surface, with a background of dark blue brush strokes, frequently seen in the workshops of Faenza and its circle. Victoria and Albert Museum, London.

427. Maiolica bowl with grotesques, painted in polychrome on a dark-blue background. 'Beautiful' style. Casteldurante; Zoan Maria Vasaro; 1508. Diam. 11⅝ in. (29·5 cm.). This is the only work which carries the name of this Master. The complicated decoration of grotesques, heraldic arms, religious texts and symbols, garlanded angels and fauns, is in the style of a whole series of works which helped to introduce Faenza styles to Urbino. Lehman Collection, New York.

blue on white, and with a border of arabesques (Victoria and Albert Museum). In Siena there was a remarkable development of designs for pavements, which ranged, in the first decade of the century, from the austere elegance of the Piccolomini Library in the Cathedral to the wealth of grotesques in the Palazzo del Magnifico Pandolfo Petrucci.

At Deruta, near Perugia and not very far from Siena, there was a flourishing production of polychrome ware with a Renaissance-type decoration of geometrical patterns or foliage which is often confused with Sienese products. There is a series of large 'show dishes' decor-
425   ated with male and female busts of Peruginesque origin, or with religious scenes and figures where polychrome is often replaced by a combination of cobalt-blue with a greenish gold lustre. Characteristic of these plates is the border round the wide brim, divided into panels, enclosing a repeating sequence of motifs of leaves and over-lapping scales in combination with other design elements. It seems that by the beginning of the 16th century the use of lustre had spread to many more centres in Italy than was originally believed, and that it produced a number of minor masterpieces, with or without relief, which will be discussed later on in connexion with the workshops of Gubbio.

In the early 16th century a workshop was set up in the castle of Cafaggiolo, built by Michelozzo in the Mugello under the patronage of a younger branch of the Medici family. It profited from the collaboration of two artists from Montelupo, Stefano and Piero di Filippo. From the brushes of these masters came a series of 'istoriato' works of high quality, intimately connected with the styles of Faenza, but influenced by the Florentine figurative style. The roundel of *Judith and her Maidservant*, signed by one 'Jacopo in Chaffaguolo', and the plate initialled 'S.P.' with a flourish on the back, portraying
426   a betrothed couple about to have their portraits painted by a maiolica artist (both in the Victoria and Albert Museum, London), are examples of the blue backgrounds and vigorous brush-work typical of late 15th-century wares in Faenza. The plate with *St George* after Donatello (also in the Victoria and Albert) and that with *Diana and Endymion* from the Damiron Collection show how the painter was influenced by Florentine culture and in the latter especially by the painting of Botticelli. They are framed in superb borders of grotesques which recur in other works, sometimes dominating them 428

429

428. Pilgrim flask, maiolica painted in polychrome. 'Beautiful' style. Urbino; Francesco Xanto Avelli; 1531. Ht. 11 in. (28 cm.). The scenes on this bottle (a *guastada* or *mesciroba*) represent the *Dance of the Gods at Psyche's Banquet* and the *Death of Psyche*, are freely composed of individual figures derived from engravings—a usual practice of Avelli, a strange and prolific artist, considered the greatest of Pellipario's followers. Museo Civico Correr, Venice.

429. Oval maiolica dish, with moulded rims and painted with Raphaellesque decorations in polychrome. 'Decorative' style. Urbino; workshop of Orazio Fontana; 1565–71. L. 26⅛ in. (66·5 cm.). Part of the table service made by Fontana for the Duke of Urbino. These Raphaellesque designs, sophisticated and gay, lightly and swiftly executed, inspired by the designs by followers of Raphael in the Loggie of the Vatican, are widespread in the second half of the 16th century. Museo Nazionale, Palazzo Bargello, Florence.

entirely. Other painters, like the one known as 'the Vulcan Painter', can be identified in work from Cafaggiolo, which after this peak of activity was to drag on for the best part of the century with no particular characteristics of its own.

The colouring, the styles and the fantasies of Faenza were brought to Casteldurante in the Duchy of Urbino by Zoan Maria Vasaro, who in 1508 painted a bowl with the coat-of-arms of Pope Julius II against a curious dark blue background filled with grotesques (Lehman Collection, Metropolitan Museum, New York). The characteristics found in this bowl by Zoan Maria have been identified in a number of other significant works—decorated with grotesques or narrative subjects—in Italian or foreign museums. From these it has been possible to reconstruct his artistic personality, which is one of the most important in the early period of *istoriato*.

The *istoriato* style, and the decoration inspired by humanist taste characteristic of the '*stile bello*', matured and developed during the first half of the century, not only at Faenza and in the Duchy of Urbino but in Venice and other less important places.

The seeds that Zoan Maria had sown in the duchy were cultivated there by Nicola Pellipario, a native of Casteldurante, but a wanderer at heart. His first known works, seventeen plates of a service for Piero Ridolfi (now often known as 'the Correr service' as they are kept in the Correr Museum in Venice) show remarkable affinities with the style of the artist 'B.T.'—the 'Master of the Resurrection Panel' mentioned above—particularly in his taste for pale colours.

The plates from the dinner service made some years later in 1519, for Isabella d'Este Gonzaga, are painted in much brighter colours and already have certain formal and landscape details which were to be a constant feature of work to come. These plates are now scattered in museum collections in Italy, France, Germany and America. There is a bowl dated 1521, with an enthroned king, in the Hermitage, which has his mark, 'Nicolo' in monogram. Two plates made in 1527 at Fabriano are an indication of his confirmed wander-lust, as a large dish, decorated with the *Martyrdom of St Cecilia* (after a Raphael print), bears the following inscriptions in full, together with Nicola's monogram: *Historia de Sancta Cicilia la qualle e fata in botega di Guido da Castello durante in Urbino 1528* ('Story of St Cecilia which was done in the workshop of Guido of Casteldurante in Urbino 1528'). Guido was Nicola's son.

The 1528 plate marks a new trend in Pellipario's work, towards a much richer, warmer palette, and a tendency to use *grisaille* which we find he still retains in his next period, together with trophy designs and various elaborate grotesques, found earlier in 1519 in the workshop of Sebastiano di Maforio, and dishes with beautiful women, on which, following a classical practice from 5th-century vases depicting Athene, the adjective '*bella*' meaning 'beautiful' (the Greek word was '*Kalos*') accompanied their name.

Working alongside Nicola in the Urbino workshops from about 1530 was a native of Rovigo, Francesco Xanto Avelli. Trained in Ferrara and Faenza, his most famous activity was at Urbino in the fourth and fifth decades of the century.

A cultured man, a courtier and writer of verses, Avelli adopted the custom of signing his works with his name written in full— 'Francesco Xanto Avelli da Rovigo in Urbino'—or sometimes abbreviated, with some indication of the scene represented and a precise reference to the author and the passage of the work which had inspired it.

His vivid colours, the dark, heavy outline of the design, the same figure repeated in different attitudes and functions in different compositions, and signs of the use of 'sponses' or pricked papers ('*spolveri*'), make of Avelli a master with a recognisable character, even if he lacks the refinement of his great contemporary.

His education led him to choose subjects from classical works and modern poems as well as from the living history of his own day. In the same way his compositions, like those of Pellipario and other '*stile bello*' artists, were often inspired by engravings, especially of the school of Raphael. Sometimes he would take single figures from a print and rearrange them in new compositions, always imbuing them with his sense of style and colour.

Although Avelli does not appear to have left any descendants it is said that Pellipario's son, Guido (in whose workshop a dinner service was made for the High Constable, Anne de Montmorency, in 1535, and another for Cardinal Duprat) was himself the father of three sons. The eldest, Orazio, who had already developed a distinct personality between 1540 and 1550, was later to make in his own workshop for Duke Guidobaldo II the splendid service famous for its moulded shapes, delicate Raphaellesque themes and *istoriato* scenes. Later it passed from the Grand Duchess Vittoria Della Rovere

430

431

432

433

430. Dish, maiolica painted in rich and luminous colours. 'Beautiful style'. Casteldurante, Nicola Pellipario; about 1519. Diam. 13 in. (33 cm.). The heraldic shield, in a *bianco-sopra-bianco* border of palmettes, identifies this service made for Isabella d'Este, with her favourite devices, by N. Pellipario, the greatest Urbino Master of *istoriato* style. The scenes of the birth of Adonis are after woodcuts illustrating Ovid's *Metamorphoses,* published Venice, 1497. Museo Civico Archeologico, Bologna.

431. Dish from a maiolica table service, with *istoriato* decoration in polychrome. 'Decorative style'. Urbino; workshop of Orazio Fontana; 1565–70. Diam. 15⅜ in. (39.5 cm.). A scene from Roman history and the arms of Urbino. The crowded figures and landscapes, in bright polychrome, are typical of Orazio and the 'decorative style'. Victoria and Albert Museum, London.

432. Dish, maiolica painted in dark blue, yellow, orange, green and white on a lavender-grey enamel. 'Beautiful style'. Faenza; Casa Pirota; 1525–30. Diam. 9⅞ in. (25.5 cm.). Around Cupid with animals a border of groups of knots and arabesques. Round the rim 'embellishments and refinements' (*vaghezze e gentilezze*) afford a delicate play of colour on the lavender-grey (*berettino*) glaze. Victoria and Albert Museum, London.

433. Large maiolica show dish, painted in cobalt-blue and white on lavender-grey glaze. 'Beautiful style'. Venice; workshop of Maestro Giacomo da Pesaro; 1543. Diam. 18½ in. (47.5 cm.). The 'candelabrum' motif (*candeline*), with leaves and fruits, and three medallions, with portrait-busts of war-like heroines of classical antiquity around a fourth central medallion against a background of arabesques. Victoria and Albert Museum, London.

to the Medici family and part of it now is in the Bargello Museum in Florence. There was also all the equipment for the ducal pharmacy, which was later on presented by the Duke Francesco Maria to the Santa Casa at Loreto.

Faenza did not exhaust all her creative energy with the early *istoriato*. This vital upsurge gave rise to a remarkable number of workshops. Outstanding for the quantity and quality of their products are those of the Pirotti brothers—the well-known Casa Pirota whence came the plate showing the coronation of Charles V (Civic Museum, Bologna)—and the workshop of the Bergantini brothers, which produced the 1529 goblet with lavender-grey ('*berettino*') glaze and the scene *Curtius casting himself into the abyss* (Private Collection, Paris). There was the workshop of the Manara family, too, where in 1536, or thereabouts, the painter, Baldassare, probably worked; he is the artist of several pieces—now in French and English museums—which reveal a knowledge of Pellipario's styles. There was also the workshop of Francesco Risino, called Mezzarisa, which carried on a considerable trade with Sicily and in which was made the panel with the *Crucifixion* signed by Brame, which is now in the Palermo Museum; and there was the Gulmanelli workshop, and many others.

A painter of considerable merit, active about 1525–30, was the Master 'F.R.', who left a superb set of plates of white and lavender-grey glaze, painted with very lively, forcefully drawn *istoriato* scenes. Keeping alive their decorative tradition the artists of Faenza, side by side with the *istoriato*, painted stylised designs of grotesques, trophies, fruit and flowers, all pretexts for coloristic effects, against the *berettino* or lavender-grey glaze. These were extremely elegant and were described in the old documents as the 'embellishments' ('*vaghezze*') and 'refinements' ('*gentilezze*') of Faenza.

Pesaro was among those centres that were active in the first half of the 16th century. As the ducal seat of Urbino, it had absorbed the

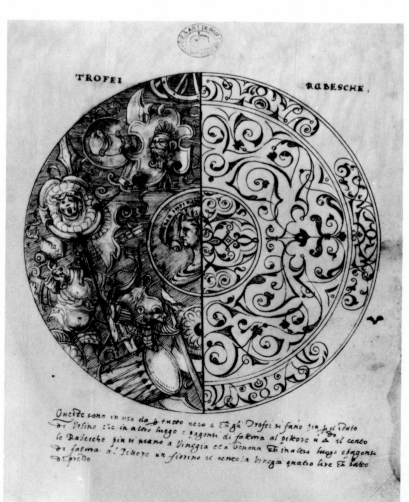

TROFEI · RABESCHE.

434

432

154

435

436

434. Drawing from *Li Tre Libri dell'Arte del Vasaio* (*The Three Books of the Potter's Art*) by Cipriano Piccolpasso of Casteldurante, a manuscript compiled probably between 1556 and 1559. Two different styles of maiolica decoration—one with trophies of arms (*Trofei*), the other with arabesques (*Rabesche*). Trophies were made more throughout Urbino; arabesques mostly in Venice and Genoa. Elements of both styles may be seen in fig. 433. Victoria and Albert Museum, London.

435. Dish, maiolica with raised bosses, painted in cobalt-blue and green, with ruby-red lustre. 'Beautiful style'. Gubbio; workshop of Maestro Giorgio; about 1535. Diam. 9½ in. (24·5 cm.). The decoration modelled in relief is intended to enhance the play of light and so intensify the effect of the lustre. In the centre is St John the Baptist, as a child. Around this figure is a wide border with raised bosses in the shape of pine cones. Victoria and Albert Museum, London.

436. Small footed bowl painted in cobalt-blue, yellow and orange on milky-white tin-glaze. *Compendiario* style. Faenza; second half 16th century. Diam. 10 in. (25·5 cm.). Renewed emphasis on form, increased purity of the glaze, the scant ornamentation, restricted palette and impressionistic style in which figures are drawn, mark the appearance of the famous *bianchi* of Faenza, which revolutionised taste in maiolica. Museo Internazionale delle Ceramiche, Faenza.

istoriato tradition, at latest during the decade 1540–50; but before this Pesaro had had a life of its own, like Rimini, which was affected by the stylised designs both of Faenza and Urbino, and like Ravenna and Forli. Above all, Venice should be remembered for the workshops of Maestro Giacomo da Pesaro and of Maestro Lodovico, with their predilection for the delicate colouring of deep blue and white on a lavender-grey glaze; and for Maestro Domenico's workshop, in which are found some of the brightest examples of polychrome painting, with medallions enclosing busts, rendered in warm colours which stand out against a field of flowers and foliage accentuated by a dark blue background.

Gubbio stands by itself because of the iridescent lustres peculiar to its ceramic art. Introduced by Maestro Giorgio Andreoli in the second decade of the 16th century, these lustres differed from those of Deruta in their range of characteristic colours—gold, ruby-red and silver. They were used not only on pieces prepared expressly to receive the pigment which produced the lustre—with details in relief enlivening the planes of the surface so that the play of light accentuated the sheen of the metallic film—but also on finished works, sometimes by great masters, which the purchaser liked to have embellished with this much prized addition. A typical example is the plate with the *Presentation of the Virgin at the Temple* in the Civic Museum in Bologna, painted by Nicola Pellipario and heavily lustred by Maestro Giorgio who states on the back, '*1532 M(aestro) G(iorgio) fini de maiolica*', that is, finished with an application of '*maiolica*' (lustre). The term 'maiolica' in the sense of an iridescent metallic lustre is confirmed in the 16th-century treatise *Li Tre Libri dell' Arte del Vasaio*, written about the middle of the century by Cavaliere Cipriano Piccolpasso, of Casteldurante.

Vivid, multicoloured, narrative decoration was by now the main aim of all maiolica craftsmen, forgetful of the functional aspect of their products. Towards the middle of the 16th century this style

began to show signs of decay, partly because of the mutual influences of painting and sculpture, which were turning to the conceits of Mannerism in a search for forms full of movement to heighten the contrast of light and shade.

The art of Parmigianino made its influences felt in the field of maiolica too. Although enhanced by the strict accuracy of the drawing, narrative painting had gradually been losing any feeling of life. Now with the adoption of a new criterion, it was freshness of touch, designs left unfinished and sketchy, and a limited range of colour—only cobalt-blue, yellow and orange, which characterised the style which we call *compendiario*. As a result the tin-glaze, spread over the whole surface, became thicker, more milky and of an intense whiteness. Its new role was to enhance the shape of the piece, no longer interrupted by painted decoration, which once again becomes a supplementary feature, when it does not disappear altogether.

This new style of maiolica made its appearance in the workshops of Faenza towards 1540, and with the enormous quantity produced spread abroad not only the fame of the town (*Faenza—faience*), and of its white wares (*bianchi*), but the taste and fashion for them. The Faenza white wares gave rise to similar products in many regions of Italy: in Tuscany, where professional soldiers were depicted at Montelupo; in Umbria, where a green was added; in the Marches and in Abruzzo, where the drawing became more calligraphic, at Turin, and in France, Switzerland, Holland and England. It spread as far as the countries of Central Europe—to Austria, Hungary and Bohemia, where potters of heretical religions from Faenza took refuge with their Anabaptist co-religionists. They took their ceramic art with them, and it became a permanent feature of the pottery of those groups, and when they disappeared it was passed on to the various indigenous peoples, whether or not they had reverted to Catholicism.

434

433

435

436

France

The technique and distant Oriental origins of the ceramic material known to historians as 'faience' have already been explained in the previous sections. All European faience has its roots in Moorish Spain and Italy. In France the Duc de Berry, at the end of the Middle Ages, called in a certain Jehan of Valencia, who worked on the decoration of the châteaux of Bourges and Poitiers between 1332 and 1338. Muslim potters, moreover, expelled from Catholic Spain, settled in the Narbonne region; but their work is difficult to identify.

The first examples of faience found in the coastal departments of southern France may date back to the end of the 14th century. They are related to the standard Mediterranean faience, with painted decoration in copper-green and manganese-purple, to be found in Paterna as well as in Orviete, Faenza or Siena. Faience only began to be produced regularly in France in the Renaissance, and at first it was really Italian maiolica, made mostly by Italians. The famous tile-pavement in the church of Brou, made in about 1525 on the orders of Marguerite of Flanders, is probably their work. The presence of Italian potters in Lyons in about 1512 is confirmed by documentary evidence. They eventually won the support of Cardinal de Tournon, a devotee of maiolica, who was elected Archbishop of Lyons in 1551, and were granted privileges allowing them to follow their calling in the town.

Their work was for a time confused with that of the Urbino workshops, but since the end of the last century scholars have demonstrated the French origins of a whole series of *istoriati*, with vignettes reproduced from Salomon Bernard's illustrations to books edited by the Lyons printers, Jean de Tournes and Guillaume de Rouille. A plate in the British Museum inscribed 'Lyon 1582' confirms this.

The Italians soon taught their art to French potters; Masséot Abaquesne, the first great French master of faience, had probably worked with Girolamo Della Robbia when the latter went to France. First heard of in Rouen in 1526, Abaquesne was director of an important enterprise there, and responsible for grand schemes of 437

architectural décor in the style of the Fontainebleau school, such as those of the Château d'Ecouen executed in 1542 and the chapel of the Château de La Bâtie d'Urfé in 1557. A contract of 1545 with the apothecary, Pierre Dubosc, for an important delivery of drug-jars makes it possible to attribute to Abaquesne a group of *albarelli* and spouted drug-jars, decorated with figures or busts in the Faenza manner, but in a style that is nevertheless very French. 438

437. Dish, faience with high-temperature ('*grand feu*') decoration; Lyons; 1582. Diam. 16⅜ in. (41·5 cm.). Mark: 'Lyon 1582. CT.VE'. Because of its unique mark this dish is the historical document on which tentative attributions to Italian potters at Lyons are based. The reference to the subject depicted, Aaron's rod changed into a snake, is in Italian on the back. The style and range of colours are exactly those of the last *istoriato* Urbino maiolica, but the subject is taken from a French engraving by Salomon Bernard. British Museum, London.

438. Spouted drug-jar, in faience with polychrome high-temperature decoration, by Masséot Abaquesne; Rouen, about 1545–50. Ht. 9½ in. (24 cm.). The decoration with a bust, much favoured by the potters of Faenza, is here treated in a realistic manner that is truly French; the wreath of leaves and the floreated scrolls have assumed a new, naturalistic character. The simple colour-range is restricted to blue, green, yellow and brown. Musée National de Céramique, Sèvres.

439. Flat flask in faience with high-temperature polychrome decoration by Antoine Syjalon. Nîmes, 1581. Ht. 15 in. (38 cm.). This famous piece, of remarkable quality, is marked: 'Nismes' and dated. On a blue ground, it bears the arms of the Elector Palatine of Saxony, surrounded by grotesques, the Huguenot potter thereby giving them a satirical character. The memory of Italian models '*a candelieri*', notably those of Cafaggiolo, is strongly felt here. Metropolitan Museum of Art, New York. Samuel D. Lee Fund, 1941.

438

439

Antoine Syjalon, a Huguenot potter working in Nîmes from the middle of the 16th century, is responsible for some fine pieces of faience painted with satirical subjects directed against the Catholic League; a pilgrim's bottle with the arms of the Elector Palatine is inscribed 'Nismes 1581'. But some of the drug-pots formerly attributed to the Nîmes potter ought, according to M. J. Thuile,

to be re-attributed to the workshops of Montpellier, where Pierre Estève was master of his craft in 1570, and where the Faviers and the Olliviers began their careers at the beginning of the 17th century. Montpellier was the seat of a powerful faculty of medicine, and the equipment needed for the numerous hospital pharmacies of the area must have provided the faience makers with their outlet.

The Netherlands

It is permissible to conjecture, on the evidence of Flemish paintings and illuminations, that pottery of maiolica type was produced in Bruges in the 15th century, but no extant piece can be proved to have been made there. In the 1480s Bruges lost its predominance in Flanders to Antwerp, where we tread on firmer ground, and the long story of Netherlands maiolica and 'Delft' may be said to have begun. Moreover, it was from Antwerp that the seed which was blown across from Italy was disseminated throughout Europe, spreading the craft of tin-glazed earthenware to almost every country.

In 1512 Guido Andriesz, a potter from Casteldurante, set up a pottery in Antwerp, which was carried on by his sons, who died in the 1570s. One son founded the first recorded pottery in Holland, at Middelburg in 1564. Another son or grandson moved to Norwich in the late 1560s and then on to Lambeth, launching English delft on its distinguished career. The rival Antwerp pottery family of Floris also worked in Spain later in the century. When we consider these colonisations and realise how the most celebrated of them, grown to independence at Delft, was to carry the craft to Frankfurt and Hanau, whose descendants multiplied into the innumerable faience factories of Germany and Scandinavia, we realise that Antwerp played the supreme part in transforming Italian maiolica into the 'delft ware' which was to be produced in such enormous quantities, and in forms varying from show pieces to the most humble kitchen articles, all over Europe until the beginning of the 19th century.

Among the first productions of Andriesz's pottery were probably

tiles, as in a famous pavement to be seen at The Vyne in Hampshire, where the tiles show, among other things, busts of heroic or royal personages, sometimes surrounded by lettered scrolls. Their dark blue, rich green, orange and yellow is again found on drug-jars, which also occur in blue monochrome. The decoration is still Italianate, mainly Venetian in its inspiration. A more idiomatic style was evolved by the rival factory of Floris. It was based on the scrolls and coils of strapwork, imitating cut leather and wrought iron, deriving ultimately from the *cartouches* on Roman sarcophagi and more immediately from the engraved pattern books of such men as

440

440. Dish, tin-glazed earthenware painted in blue, yellow and manganese-purple. Dutch; early 17th century. Diam. 15¼ in. (39 cm.). This dish, in Urbino style, shows clearly the 'grotesques' deriving ultimately from Raphael's decorations for the *Loggie* of the Vatican. Victoria and Albert Museum, London.

441. Drug-pot, tin-glazed earthenware painted in polychrome. South Netherlands (Antwerp); about 1570. Ht. 8½ in. (21·5 cm.). Drug-pots of this form were intended for the storage and dispensing of syrups and other fluid medicaments, while the unspouted *albarello* was used for ointments and dry medicines. The strong lemon-yellow used on this pot suggests an Antwerp origin. Victoria and Albert Museum, London.

442. Miniature, *The Adoration of the Magi*, from a *Book of Hours*, illuminated by the 'Master of Mary of Burgundy'. Netherlands; late 15th century. Of the wares shown in this detailed miniature, the vase at the top left may be of Italian maiolica and the bowls of 'Hispano-Moresque' pottery, but the vase shown bottom left is virtually certainly of Netherlands origin. A considerable number of these 'altar vases' have been excavated in England, where much Netherlands maiolica of the late 15th and early 16th centuries has been found. Bodleian Library, Oxford.

441

442

Coecke and Vredeman de Vries. Very carefully and boldly designed in blue outline, with much of the strapwork left white and the background filled in with a brownish orange, the whole enlivened with touches of green and a peculiarly clear lemon-yellow, these important pieces are peculiar to Antwerp, and their type did not long survive the decay of the potteries which resulted from the Spanish wars in the late 16th century, though the strapwork motif was eagerly accepted by the architects of Jacobean England and played a big part in the development of Netherlandish engraving.

Another Antwerp introduction from Italy is that of the *grotesques*, those elegant whirls of stylised foliage and fantastical animals, drawn in blue or orange and yellow on a white ground, which Urbino had copied in the latter half of the 16th century from the decorations done in the Vatican by Raphael, who, in his turn, had derived them from decorations found in the 'grottos', that is, the ruins of Imperial Rome. In its heyday the Antwerp plates of this type are almost entirely covered with grotesque scrolls, centred round a small cherub or a figure of St John, but gradually the centre-piece became more and more important and the *putti* and fantastical creatures retreated to a stylised border. The design was certainly adopted in the North Netherlands, but never as copiously as some enthusiasts would claim. As we have seen, the Antwerp potteries declined towards the end of the century, but had already sent out their missionaries to Spain, England and Holland. As we must now consider the tin-glazed wares of the latter country, it is worth noting that Antwerp potters are known to have settled in Middelburg (1564), in Dordrecht (1586) and in Haarlem (1573), which in turn colonised Delft in 1584 and Rotterdam in 1612. Though the North Netherlandish, that is, the Dutch tin-enamel factories, especially those at Delft, were to become the most famous and the most productive in the whole history of ceramic art, it is to Antwerp that they owe their inception.

443   444

443. Plate, tin-glazed earthenware painted in strong dark blue, ochrous yellow and bright opaque green. Dutch (probably Rotterdam); about 1630. Diam. 9¾ in. (24·8 cm.). Such plates as these, inscribed with pious admonitions ('Honour the Lord above all') are still Netherlandish in palette. Though made in Holland, probably Rotterdam, they reach back through Antwerp to Italian and Spanish prototypes. Victoria and Albert Museum, London.

444. Dish, tin-glazed earthenware painted in white and polychrome on a dark blue glaze. Dutch (probably Rotterdam); about 1620. Diam. 13½ in. (34·3 cm.). On the evidence of fragments, plates like this seem mostly to have been made in Rotterdam. Design and colour hark back to Italian maiolica. Victoria and Albert Museum, London.

445. Dish (probably Lambeth) depicting Charles II, dated 1661; Diam. 12¾ in. (32·4 cm.). Painted mainly in pale blue with a blue-dash border, but with a strong yellow on the pillars and the King's cloak and some brown and orange shading; the King has a bluish purple wig. Two other dishes with this design and date are known; they may be the 17th-century equivalent of the 'Coronation Souvenir'. On loan to Birmingham City Gallery, A. C. J. Wall Loan.

England

In 1567 Jasper Andries and Jacob Jansen came to Norwich from Antwerp, and in 1571 they applied for permission to establish a maiolica factory in London. There had already been attempts to set up the industry in England. A group of jugs covered with a coloured or speckled tin-glaze in imitation of Rhenish stoneware appears to be of English manufacture and of 16th-century date, and these jugs may have been made by Flemish potters known to be working in England at the time. These potters were banished in the reign of Queen Mary but allowed back under Queen Elizabeth, and presumably Jasper Andries and Jacob Jansen were among the first to avail themselves of the privilege.

While Jasper Andries appears to have remained in East Anglia, Jacob Jansen came to London soon after 1571 and, together with other Flemish potters, is recorded in the Parish of Aldgate. It is possible that the small dish dated 1600, depicting the Tower of London, was made in Jansen's factory; it is the earliest in a long series of dated specimens of English tin-glazed pottery. The combination of an English motif with an Italian border seen here was to recur on many other pieces of 'English maiolica' made in the first sixty years of the 17th century. Apart from the Urbino 'grotesques', the parti-coloured leaves and pomegranates typical of Venetian 16th-century maiolica also appear, either as a main decoration or as a border framing a central design which may be a scene from the Bible, derived as was usually the case, from contemporary engravings, a ship, a vase of flowers of Dutch inspiration, or the

445

royal family. An unusual subject in 'English maiolica' is the *Family of Darius before Alexander*. The design is presumably derived from an Italian engraving. Especially interesting is the panelled border of birds in blue derived, incongruously enough, from Chinese porcelain. Other dishes of the middle of the 17th century were moulded in imitation of the French 'Palissy Ware', the commonest design being that known as 'La Fécondité.'

Towards the middle of the century a particular type of dish became an important part of the potter's output. This was a shallow dish made for decorating a dresser or a wall, hence the broad flange round which a string could be tied. Such dishes were painted with a bold design, usually having a narrow border of hatched lines in blue round the edge. Most of the earlier examples, until about 1690, have a lead-glazed back, but after that the dishes were normally tin-glazed on both sides. The designs are, in the main, variations on

particular themes. The Kings and Queens of England appear as 'effigies' rather than as portraits, and there are many stylised figures of men in armour and on horseback. One very large group, usually rather crudely drawn, shows Adam and Eve with the Tree of Knowledge while another is decorated with boldly painted tulips or fritillaries, either in a vase or growing from a mound. In the brilliance of the colours and the vigour of the brush-strokes some of these floral dishes are ceramic masterpieces comparable to, and possibly inspired by, contemporary Isnik wares. The dishes depicting royal personages, generals and Adam and Eve continued to be made until well into the 18th century with little variation in the colours or designs. For this reason they are included in this survey of 'English maiolica', though English potters had long been producing a different type of ware intended to offer an acceptable imitation of the very popular and fashionable Chinese porcelain and Dutch Delftware.

446

447

446. Inscribed plate, London, perhaps Aldgate, dated 1600. Diam. 10 in. (25·5 cm.). Painted mainly in blue, but with orange on the buildings and border and touches of manganese-green and yellow: thin blue-dash border. The building depicted is perhaps the Tower of London, which is near Aldgate. The border 'grotesques', derived from Urbino wares, show the influence of 16th-century Netherlandish potters. It has indeed been suggested that this plate was made in the Aldgate factory of Jacob Jansen, the Flemish immigrant potter. London Museum.

447. Dish depicting Adam and Eve. London, about 1660–75. Diam. 16 in. (40·6 cm.). Painted in yellow, manganese, grey, green and blue; blue-dash border. Lead-glaze back. There are nearly 200 dishes known with this subject, dating from 1635 until the early 18th century. This specimen is less clumsy than many. A curious feature is the double outline of the figures in yellow and manganese. Ashmolean Museum, Oxford.

448. Faience dish, depicting Samson and Delilah; painted in blue, malachite-green, yellow ochre and manganese-purple. Bozen, Austria; dated 1526, and signed 'P.R.', for Peter Rieder. Diam. 10 in. (25·5 cm.). The figures are freely adapted from a woodcut by Hans Burgkmair. Germanisches Nationalmuseum, Nuremberg.

Germany and Northern Europe

At the beginning of the 16th century, a few German stove-makers (*Hafner*) in the South Tyrol and Nuremberg began to produce tin-glazed earthenware. This was no new technical innovation, for tin-glaze had long been used together with various lead-glazes to decorate the earlier coloured wares with designs in relief. The most notable products of these South Tyrolese 'white-potters' are the stoves, wall-tiles and floor-tiles painted with a profusion of figure-subjects, and we have the name of one such painter and designer of stoves—Bartholomäus Dill, who worked in Bozen from 1526 onwards. Dill, the youngest son of the Würzburg sculptor, Tillmann Riemenschneider, had been a pupil of Dürer and painted easel-pictures and wall-paintings as well as stoves. A stove in Burg Kreuzenstein, near Vienna (destroyed in 1945), decorated with scenes from the lives of Hercules and Samson, bore his signature, and in the Victoria and Albert Museum, London, there is a signed series of tiles from Tramin which illustrate the legend of Jason. Round these can be grouped a number of other tiles. If the monogram on a dish dated 1526 and depicting Samson and Delilah is correctly interpreted as that of Dill's father-in-law, Peter Rieder, who worked in Innsbruck and Bozen, then this must be considered the earliest documentary piece of useful ware made in the South Tyrolese maiolica workshops. The fact that the figures of Samson and Delilah are derived from a woodcut by Hans Burgkmair shows that though the maiolica-painters were following an Italian fashion they preferred to draw their subjects from artists working at Nuremberg and

448

Augsburg. Other designs are derived from the same source.

The name of Augustin Hirschvogel is repeatedly mentioned in connection with the manufacture of maiolica at Nuremberg, although its early history is still uncertain. Hirschvogel was born in Nuremberg in 1503, lived for a time in Laibach and later enjoyed court patronage at Vienna (see p. 128). The fact that this versatile artist, who was at once glass-painter, medallist, engraver, mathematician, cartographer and potter, formed a brief partnership in 1531 with the Hafner-potters, Oskar Reinhard (see p. 128) and Hanns Nickel in order to produce 'stoves, jugs and pictures in the "Antique" manner', as his compatriot Johann Neudörffer states, has given rise to considerable speculation, but the character of Hirschvogel's ceramic work has never been convincingly established. The earliest pieces claimed for Nuremberg—a few dishes, an *albarello* and two ring-

flasks, with dates between 1530 and 1555—are linked together by the use of finely drawn plant-scrolls which are occasionally reminiscent of Venetian maiolica. Other pieces have half-length Renaissance-style portraits of men and women, while the survival of the late Gothic tradition is exemplified by a dish depicting the 'Madonna in Glory'. Some dishes of the late 16th century show a combination of scrollwork and portraits. At the beginning of the 17th century, dishes with a wavy rim appear, in the centre of which are representations of biblical and profane subjects, sometimes within a wreath-border of stylised leaves, in the manner of the Faenza wares made in the workshop of Virgiliotto.

Lidded jugs in the shape of an owl, painted in high-temperature blue, often with traces of unfired painting and gilding, seem to have been a speciality of the German maiolica workshops. Several of

450

449

449. Faience 'owl-jug', painted in high-temperature blue, with traces of unfired colour. Switzerland, mid-16th century. Ht. 13¾ in. (35 cm.). The vessel was thrown on the wheel, the moulded details being added later. Kunstgewerbemuseum, Berlin-Charlottenburg.

450. Faience dish, depicting the Madonna in Glory, painted in blue. Germany (Nuremberg), dated 1530. Diam. 16⅛ in. (41 cm.). The figure of the Madonna is probably derived from a contemporary engraving. The row of dots surrounding the centre of the dish probably represents a rosary. Germanisches Nationalmuseum, Nuremberg.

32. Bottle (Liverpool); about 1760. Ht. 8⅝ in. (21·9 cms.). Painted in yellow and green and touches of black, with exotic birds and a butterfly. This decoration, in similar colouring, is also found on bowls, such as the 'Monmouth' ship-bowl of 1760 (now destroyed) and on the 'Speed the Plow' bowl of 1762 (Liverpool Museum). It represents Liverpool colouring at its most delicate and harmonious. Bristol City Art Gallery.

33. Pot-pourri vase and cover, decorated with applied branches, flowers and leaves painted in enamel colours. Marieberg (Sweden); about 1760–65. Ht. with cover 12½ in. (31·5 cm.). Mark, three crowns over MB in monogram, and E (for Ehrenreich, the Director of the factory); also SF and MB repeated in blue. Inside the rim is the monogram of the painter Per Akermark, in black enamel. Victoria and Albert Museum, London.

34. Dish, tin-glazed earthenware painted in polychrome. Dutch (Delft); about 1730. Diam. 13½ in. (34·5 cm.). This dish copies the colours of the Chinese famille verte porcelain as closely as the Dutch potter was able with the different materials at his disposal. Victoria and Albert Museum, London.

32

33

34

35

36

these 'owl-jugs' bear Austrian coats-of-arms, or the arms of the Holy Roman Empire and of its Electors. A jug of this type in Berlin is more likely to have been made in Switzerland than in the Tyrol, since the reverse shows William Tell shooting at the apple, which also suggests that the vessel may have been offered as a prize in a shooting contest. The relief design on the front, depicting a pair of lovers and a jester, is also found on stove-tiles, which confirms the supposition that the owl-jugs were produced in the workshops of the stove-makers.

Towards the end of the 16th century, the stove-makers in Winterthur (Switzerland) also began to follow the new fashion, above all Ludwig Pfau the Elder and his son, Ludwig Pfau the Younger, whose signatures are found on pieces of early date. The Winterthur productions include richly painted stoves, bellied jugs decorated with plant-scrolls, dishes with figures, landscapes or coats-of-arms and borders of scrollwork or naturalistic fruit. A series of finely painted stove-tiles comes from the workshop of Hans

Weckerly in Zug. The stoves made by Hans Kraut at Villingen in the Black Forest are related to those made at Winterthur.

In Slovakia, Upper Hungary and Moravia the '*Habaner*' potters were producing a type of pottery which was also made in Alvinc in the Siebenbürgen and in Zittau. The '*Habaner*' were an ethnically separate, German-speaking sect of Anabaptists, their name deriving from the Hebrew *ha-banim* ('the true children of God'). It was forbidden for them to depict human beings or animals, so that their pottery was at first decorated exclusively with flowers and leaves. It was only towards the end of the 17th century that birds and architectural motifs were added to the decorator's repertoire, when the Brotherhood was already breaking up. In the 18th century, Habaner ware was absorbed into Slovakian and Moravian folk pottery. Instead of plant patterns, animated figurative scenes were encountered, such as were characteristic of the factories at Olmütz and Sternberg. There was also a change in decoration at Holitsch with the influence of elegant rococo motifs.

451

452

451

452

451. Faience lidded bowl on a high foot, painted with scrolling foliage, Winterthur, Switzerland, 1599–1605. Signed 'L.W.P.' standing for Ludwig Winterthur Pfau. One of the three coats-of-arms on the bowl can be identified by the inscription as that of the Master Butcher Heinrich Bürkli, a member of the Council of Twelve of the Order of the Golden Fleece, and from 1599 to 1605 Steward of the erstwhile properties of the Augustinian monastery. Kunstgewerbemuseum, Berlin-Köpenick.

452. Screw-topped faience flask. Moravia; dated 1614. Ht. 6¼ in. (16 cm.). This example of Habaner ware is decorated with floral scrolls in blue, green and yellow, outlined in manganese-purple. Museum für Kunst und Gewerbe, Hamburg.

Spain

At Toledo and Seville, the *cuenca* method of managing the glaze, comparable to enamelling in *champlevé* technique, rapidly supplanted the *cuerda seca* during the early 16th century. Before firing, slabs of clay were impressed with moulds that produced hollows defined sharply by outlines in sharp relief. The depressions, like little bowls, held the glazes, while the arrises barred the several colours from intermingling.

The individual patterns used on *cuenca* tiles were confined to the limits of one, two or four tiles, but the numbers of these patterns

seem endless, some based on Moresque geometric forms, interwoven bands and stars, others on Gothic tracery, flowers and animals, and even more on the motifs of the early Spanish Renaissance. *Cuenca* tiles served as high wainscots in religious and civil buildings and in salons, patios, and balconies of palaces like the Casa de Pilatos, Seville. For pavements, small *cuenca*-glazed squares were combined often with tiles of red terracotta. Frequently, rectangular tiles, paired to form a large square, were set between the wooden beams of ceilings.

405
453

35. Kitchen of the Amalienburg pavilion at Nymphenburg, near Munich, built 1734-39. The Amalienburg was designed by the French-born architect François Cuvilliés as a pleasure-pavilion, and this highly decorative kitchen was made more for the entertainment of the ladies than for serious catering. The walls are lined with Dutch tiles, including three upright panels in polychrome showing flowers in vases, with birds and insects, probably made at the Flowerpot factory of the Aelmis family in Rotterdam.

36. Deep dish, or brasero. Manises, Valencia. About 1430. Diam. 19 in. (48·2 cm.). Bands and medallions of mock Arabic inscriptions in blue and gold lustre encircling a shield that bears a coat-of-arms perhaps those of the Despujol family of Catalonia. The reverse side of the dish shows a large heraldic eagle painted in gold lustre with free, sweeping strokes. The Hispanic Society of America, New York.

453

454

453. *St John the Evangelist,* inset tile panel. Seville. About 1535, The three rectangular tiles depicting the Saint were painted probably by Francisco Niculoso's son, Juan Bautista. The panel is set among *cuenca*-glazed tiles in a wall of La Cartuja, the former Carthusian Monastery of Nuestra Señora de la Cuevas, now a pottery factory at Triana, Seville.

454. *The Visitation,* tile panel by Francisco Niculoso. Found in a demolished building in Lisbon in 1882. 20½ × 15⅜ in. (52 × 39 cm.). An inscription at the base, on the centre tile, reads NICVLOSO ITALIANO ME FECIT, but there is no date. The pictorial panel of twelve tiles was painted within the first quarter of the 16th century at Seville. Rijksmuseum, Amsterdam.

455. *The Adoration of the Magi* (detail) in the Chapel of the Epiphany, Córdoba Cathedral. About 1565. The altar frontal of tiles has been attributed to a Sevillian, Roque Hernández, the pupil of an Italo-Flemish tile-decorator. The scene, stretching across eighty tiles, depicts the procession of the Three Kings leaving their distant cities on camel-back to follow the star.

At the time of their greatest popularity, *cuenca* tiles were exported to Portugal, the West Indies and Italy. Myriads of them were made for buildings in regions where a Muslim influence in decoration remained strong. As restorations for dados and pavements in the Alhambra, they replaced damaged tile mosaics, their pattern imitating geometrical forms in Moresque style.

The art and methods of Italian maiolica-painters reached Seville with the arrival of one Francisco Niculoso. This man, who signed himself 'the Italian', or again, 'the Pisan', left Italy for Spain before the year 1500, predating the emigrations of Italian potters to Antwerp and Lyons. Although he may have been a Pisan, as he claimed, Niculoso probably studied at Faenza, since he followed the Faventine manner of painting with strong dark blue and black outlines on a white or yellow surface, filling in areas with a maze of cross-hatching, graining, and stipple. The colours, too, were Italian— deep orange, lemon-yellow, purple that could be paled to mauve, tawny brown, and brilliant greens. His religious compositions were based on engravings or prayer-book illustrations, and his ornamental designs in Renaissance style on the decorative prints of the Italian artists, Nicoletto Rosex da Modena, Zoan Andrea and Giovanni Antonio da Brescia.

Niculoso's picture-tiles, bearing dates between 1503 and 1520, cover the vertical surfaces of altar-pieces, altar frontals, wall-tombs, and doorways. Although accustomed in Italy to wall-plaques painted with religious and mythological subjects, he probably knew nothing of the vast wainscots of tile and tile-mosaics that had decorated Andalusian buildings for centuries. Upon his arrival at Seville, then,

455

456

he must have conceived the idea of adapting maiolica-painting to architectural surfaces faced with tiles.

An important work of great beauty is his altar of *The Visitation* made in 1504 for the royal oratory in the Alcázar, Seville, and there is also a small, twelve-tile panel of the same subject signed by him. The church portal of Santa Paula is perhaps his most elaborate composition, yet the tremendous altar-piece done in 1518 for the Monastery of Santa María de Tentudía (Badajoz) is a masterpiece, depicting in seven scenes the life of the Virgin, a miracle performed by her at Tentudía, and the vicar's portrait. Except for a son, Juan Bautista, Niculoso left no pupils to carry on his style of tile decoration at Seville. Attributed to the younger Niculoso are five panels portraying saints, of which *St John* is one.

For a period of about thirty years after Francisco Niculoso's death in 1529, Spanish potters reverted completely to the *cuenca* tradition. In mid-century, however, a new stimulus brought back to the Hispanic peninsula the Italian style of maiolica-painting. This time, the efforts of Italo-Flemish potters from Antwerp were combined with those of Italians emigrating directly from Genoa and Albisola to revive a pictorial type of decoration similar to Niculoso's.

The appearance of Antwerp tile-masters who planned to work in Spain began in the early 1560s, when Juan Flores (Jan Floris) settled at Plasencia and Frans Andries went southward to Seville (1561) under contract to work for a year and a half in a factory at Triana. From Andries, the Sevillian potters learned the art of maiolica-painting and how to mix Italian glaze-colours. His methods influenced greatly the work of many tile-makers at Triana, among them Roque Hernández and his brother-in-law, Cristóbal de Augusta, whose tile wainscots in the Alcázar, signed and dated 1577–78, were designed to imitate Flemish tapestries. Instead of painting picture-panels like the Italo-Flemish masters, many of the native potters held to their tradition of purely decorative motifs. Designs differ from one panel to another, each being separated by

borders of Italian Renaissance patterns mixed with Flemish strapwork and masks.

Genoese potters, Tommaso Pesaro and his company of workmen, brought with them the particular styles of Genoa and Albisola in maiolica-painting. They settled in Seville about 1570, to be followed somewhat later by several more Ligurians, who were said to have worked in the 'Venetian manner'. Two of these men, Antonio and Bartolommeo Zambarino, whose father had come from Albisola, supplied painted tiles between 1584 and 1593 for the Alcázar and the cathedral at Seville.

In Castile, the Fleming, Juan Flores, did well, since he was given the important commission by Philip II to design tiles for the Madrid Alcázar and for the palaces of El Pardo and Segovia. As his pupils, or at least imitators, a group of tile-painters developed in the 1560s and '70s at Talavera and Toledo, where they produced panels beautifully drawn and painted, splendid enough to rival the best work of their Italian contemporaries. Juan Fernández was one of these masters. His blue-and-white tiles, ordered in 1570–72 for the Monastery of San Lorenzo del Escorial, may still be seen in the apartments of Philip II. A Flemish-style wainscot of *The Crucifixion* at Plasencia may be attributed to him, as well as drug-jars and pots displaying the arms of El Escorial Monastery.

Because working in another locale might be simpler than shipping their wares, certain Castillian potters went forth to Mallorca, Valencia, or Barcelona. One of these men was Lorenzo de Madrid, who worked at Burjasot on tiles for a church in Valencia and again, in 1596, at Manresa for the Palacio de la Generalidad in Barcelona. Superb tile-panels in Italo-Flemish style are those forming a wainscot in the Diputación at Valencia. Signed as having been made in Toledo by a master known simply as Oliva, they are a series of panels containing medallions. Framed with strapwork, masks and fruit, these pictures represent the Virgin and Child, St George, and the heraldic arms of Valencia.

456. Tile border, attributed to the tile master, Alonso Garcia (detail). Chapel of the Convent of Santa Clara, Seville. Dated 1575. The Renaissance designs are painted in green, blue, orange and brown on a golden-yellow background.

457. Portal of the Convent of Santa Paula, Seville (detail). Completed 1504. Francisco

Niculoso designed the great portal, painted the tiles with Italian Renaissance decoration and glazed the sculptural work, which was done by the Sevillian artist, Pedro Millán. Represented in the medallions, which are framed with wreaths of fruit in the Della Robbia manner, are pairs of saints and a Nativity scene.

458. *The Crucifixion with the Virgin and St John,* a portion of a tile wainscot. Talavera de la Reina. About 1570. This is one of a series of panels decorated with representations of Dominican saints. The tiles are painted in polychrome in an Italo-Flemish style possibly by the master tile-decorator, Juan Fernandez. Sacristy, Convent of Santo Domingo, Plasencia.

459. Drug-jar, painted in Flemish style in yellow and several shades of blue on white. Talavera de la Reina, or Plasencia. About 1565. Ht. 17 in. (43 cm.). This jar was made for the pharmacy of the Monastery of San Lorenzo del Escorial. The arms of the abbot appear in a frame of ironwork with grotesque terms. Museo Arqueológico Nacionale, Madrid.

457   458

459

The Dominance of Delft (about 1630 – 1700)

Although the style of maiolica had been affected during the 16th century by the blue-and-white colour-scheme and the decorative styles of Chinese porcelain, a further and stronger wave of influence from China swept over Europe in the first half of the 17th century. Although its effects were felt in Italy (p. 176-7), this influence was most marked in northern Europe generally and at Delft in particular.

Holland

The golden age of Delft itself stretches roughly over the hundred years from 1650–1750. In its beginnings North Netherlands maiolica was much like its Antwerp prototype, without achieving the bravura of its finest 'strap-work' pieces. It is indeed often difficult to state categorically that an object was made in the South or the North. Tiles and drug-pots were made in the old palette of dark blue, orange and green. If anything the colours were even stronger and tended to be less smoothly absorbed in the glaze. Boldly painted dishes with a border of blue dashes—a type later adopted in the English 'blue-dash chargers'—for many years had only the front painted in tin-glaze, while the back was covered in transparent lead-glaze. This practice was in fact continued until late in the 18th century by Frisian potteries. Specifically Dutch are the smaller plates with a border of raised knobs and the centre decorated with pious inscriptions, milkmaids carrying pails on a yoke (these were a great favourite) and spurious coats-of-arms, possibly an echo of Italian heraldic dishes but more likely expressing the genteel hankerings of an emergent middle class. All these pieces are unsophisticated but robust, a homely folk-art. The blue is very dark and rich, the orange ochreous rather than red, the green opaque and yellowish rather than transparent and coppery. In these early days the Dutch potters were learning their craft, with Haarlem and Rotterdam leading the way. Rotterdam produced, and continued to produce, huge quantities of tiles and also, to judge by the large number of fragments excavated there, a new departure in the plates covered in dark blue glaze and decorated with birds or animals. But there were still some years to wait before the newly independent nation, in the full surge of its rising confidence and prosperity, found its own idiom and spoke a ceramic language which was to be adopted and translated all over Europe.

443

444

460

460. Bottle, tin-glazed earthenware painted in blue. Delft; the *Greek 'A'* factory of the Kocks family; about 1710. Ht. 10½ in. (26·7 cm.). Mark, monogram 'AK', in blue. This bottle with the polyhedral body and Chinese-style decoration, is a fine example of the sophisticated work produced by the *Greek 'A'* factory. Private collection.

461. Dish, tin-glazed earthenware painted in blue. Delft; the *Greek 'A'* factory of Samuel van Eenhoorn; about 1690. Diam. 19¼ in. (50 cm.). Mark 'SVE' in blue. This large dish is characteristic of one type of decoration painted during Van Eenhoorn's directorship of the *Greek 'A'* factory, which also produced large vases with this pattern. Victoria and Albert Museum, London.

462. Wig-stand, tin-glazed earthenware painted in mauvish blue and manganese-purple. Delft; the *Greek 'A'* factory of Samuel van Eenhoorn; about 1675. Ht. 7¼ in. (18·5 cm.). Mark, monogram 'SVE' in blue. The decoration of this wig-stand still strives to reproduce as closely as possible a Chinese original. Victoria and Albert Museum, London.

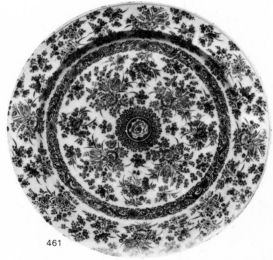

461

462

The determinant proved to be the arrival in Amsterdam, at the very beginning of the 17th century, of two shiploads of Chinese porcelain. Occasional pieces of Ming blue-and-white had reached Europe overland during the last hundred years and had been accorded the awe and reverence generally associated with rare and precious stones. Now that it could be seen and handled in quantity, some of the mystery evaporated and familiarity bred a desire to imitate. A major artistic revolution had taken place. At first some of the elements of design were naively incorporated with the old Netherlandish patterns, in the old polychrome. But soon the Dutch potters were striving to reproduce as closely as possible the large blue-and-white dishes of Wan Li type, and very successful they were. In the process they learnt three things: their potting became much finer, to recapture the thin texture of the porcelain: their drawing became more delicate: the backs as well as the fronts of the dishes were covered with tin-glaze, and decorated with the noughts and crosses of the originals. For over a century Chinese designs were more popular than any other on Dutch tin-glazed earthenware and on its progeny in England and Germany. Though one may marvel at how closely they could imitate—a skill they maintained even in the 18th century, when required to make good a Chinese set of which one piece had been broken—soon a more personal and national character appeared. The most remarkable pieces produced during the purely imitative period, that is to say during the first quarter of the 17th century, were reproductions of late Ming dishes, decorated with the familiar geese, deer, or baskets of peonies, the border showing buddhist emblems in reserves, surrounded by fretwork and scrolls. Some of these dishes measure as much as thirty inches across. The blue is sober, almost greyish at its lightest, inky when dark. The glaze itself is of a pale greenish blue tinge. At first they were probably made at Haarlem but soon the centre of the national industry shifted to Delft, where it remained.

It is always difficult to say why a light industry should settle in a particular place. Yet Delft enjoyed many advantages. It was situated with easy access to the great waterways, important both for the export of the finished wares and for the steadily increasing import of finer clays from abroad. Delft's staple industry, brewing, was declining rapidly, mainly owing to English competition, and the disused breweries offered easily adaptable premises. The rebuilding of a large part of the town after the explosion of the arsenal in 1654 (in which the painter Fabritius lost his life) also provided an outlet for the investment of capital. It is significant that the breweries dwindled from nearly two hundred to a bare fifteen by the 1670s and that many potteries took over the name of the brewery whose premises they occupied, such as the *Drie Klokken* (*The Three Bells*), *De Roos* (*The Rose*), *De Paauw* (*The Peacock*) and *De Grieksche 'A'* (*The Greek 'A'*).

In discussing the wares produced at Delft, some mention must be made of marks, and that must be prefaced by a word of caution. The marks, either pictorial, as three bells, or a stylised rose or, more frequently, initials or monograms, refer in the vast majority of cases to the name of the factory or its proprietor, and not to individual artists. Many of the marks cannot be definitively attributed, the patient searching of archives for the names of potters with corresponding initials yielding only a surmise. Finally, marks were often pirated, and even recur on Chinese porcelain. Though many marks are a safe guide, a collector should first consider such matters as glaze, quality and style before claiming a piece for any one factory.

Blue-and-white wares were the first truly Dutch tin-glazed pottery to be made after the break-away from the old maiolica in the Antwerp tradition, and remained, in the eyes of the world, the characteristic production of Delft. Two innovations were soon added to those mentioned above. Outlines were drawn in manganese-purple, direct on to the fired but unglazed clay, before the blue was applied. This 'trek', as it was known, imparted a livelier and firmer sense of drawing and is only rarely found elsewhere. Secondly, a final coat of lead-glaze called 'kwaart' was applied, to the front surface only, in order to recapture the high polish of the Chinese porcelain imitated.

Earliest among the classic pieces produced at Delft are those marked 'SVE', the initials of Samuel van Eenhoorn, who ran the

463. Tulip-vase, tin-glazed earthenware painted in blue, with manganese-purple outlines. Delft, the *Greek 'A'* factory of Adrianus Kocks; about 1700. Ht. 10⅜ in. (26·5 cm.). Mark, monogram 'AK' in blue. Many-spouted flower-holders of this kind were made in innumerable shapes. In this case the lid is a self-contained vase, and the lower half could have been used for sweetmeats, etc. Haags Gemeentemuseum, The Hague.

464. Candlestick, tin-glazed earthenware painted in blue. Delft; the *Greek 'A'* factory of the Kocks family; about 1710. Ht. 11¾ in. (27·5 cm.). Mark, monogram 'AK', in blue. This candlestick, although clearly modelled on a European metalwork original, is nevertheless painted with Chinese motifs, including Chinese written characters. Private collection.

465. Wall-tile, tin-glazed earthenware painted in blue. Delft; the *Greek 'A'* factory of Adrianus Kocks; about 1694. 24¼ in. (62 cm.) square. William III commissioned these large tiles for Queen Mary's dairy at Hampton Court, "in which Her Majesty took great delight". They are the most sumptuous tiles ever made in Delft. This one displays medallion portraits of William and Mary. Victoria and Albert Museum, London.

463

464

465

466

467

466. Cream-pan, tin-glazed earthenware painted in blue. Delft; the *Greek 'A'* factory of Adrianus Kocks; about 1694. Mark, monogram 'AK', in blue. Diam. 19 in. (48 cm.). The ornamental motifs on this cream-pan (made, as was the tile of fig. 478, for Queen Mary's dairy at Hampton Court) are as usual, based on designs of Daniel Marot, while the

miniature landscapes are 'pounced' from engravings by Merian after Bloemaert. Victoria and Albert Museum, London.

467. Tulip-vase, tin-glazed earthenware painted in blue. Delft; the *Greek 'A'* factory of Adrianus Kocks; about 1694. Ht. 12 in. (30·5 cm.). This ornamental vase, of bold

baroque design, was made for Hampton Court Palace just before 1695. Like all such pieces made for the Palace, it derives in design from the work of the Dutch Court architect, the Frenchman Daniel Marot. The bills for all these pieces still exist and are dated 1695. Victoria and Albert Museum, London.

Greek 'A' factory from 1675–86. It is illustrative of the complexity of Delft manufacture, and of attribution, that that particular factory had a long subsequent history under a number of different directors or, possibly, just proprietors. The 'SVE' pieces are mostly elaborate but accurate versions of Chinese scenes and ornamentation. The blue has a violet tinge and the manganese trek varies from pale mauve to black. With added touches of palely transparent violet, on the pale Cambridge blue glaze, the total colour scheme is of great aqueous delicacy.

The factory was taken over by Adrianus Kocks, whose 'AK', generally in monogram, became one of the most famous and most often pirated of all Delft marks. His vases and other wares come very close to the purest and deepest K'ang Hsi blue and the earliest pieces stick closely to the Chinese designs. Yet soon conventional baroque ingredients appear. By the 1690s very large and important pieces were made, in uncompromisingly European shapes. Notable among these are vases and cisterns, many of them more than three feet high, made for William and Mary's palace at Hampton Court, where they may still be seen. The designs on these and on the specially large tiles made for the same palace at the same time, were based on those of the official Dutch court architect, Daniel Marot. The quality of the workmanship suggests, here as elsewhere, that for special commissions outside artists were called in to do the decoration. The same would apply to many of the plaques, made to hang as pictures in a room; landscapes, portraits, commemorative emblems, executed with a confidence and original artistry that one would not find in a pottery craftsman. These were the work of artists in their own right, working for the occasion in the tin-glaze medium, just as Sir James Thornhill decorated a series of plates with

468

460
464
463

467
466

465

469

470

468. Vase, tin-glazed earthenware painted in
high-temperature polychrome. Delft; *The
Young Moor's Head* factory of Rochus
Hoppesteyn; about 1690. Ht. 10⅜ in.
(26·5 cm.). Mark, monogram 'IW', in blue,
designates an unknown outside decorator.
The design is after an engraving by H. Goltzius.
Victoria and Albert Museum, London.

469. Plate, tin-glazed earthenware painted in
bright blue. Delft, perhaps *The Metal Pot*
factory of Lambertus Cleffius; about 1670.
Diam. 8¼ in. (21 cm.). Plates such as this are
traditionally ascribed to Frederik van Frytom.
They may, however, be the work of an
independent Haarlem artist. Victoria and
Albert Museum, London.

470. Jug, tin-glazed earthenware painted in
polychrome, including a fine carnelian red,
and gold. Delft; *The Young Moor's Head*
factory of Rochus Hoppesteyn; about 1690.
Ht. 9½ in. (24·5 cm.). Mark, a moor's head in
blue (ribbon in red), and 'RHS' in monogram.
Musées Royaux d'Art et d'Histoire. Evenepoel
Collection, Brussels.

471 the signs of the Zodiac when he visited 'Delph' in 1711. From the
end of the 17th century date the highly remarkable landscapes
469 plaques, either circular or rectangular, of F. van Frytom, who is also
known to have painted in oils, very much in the manner of Wynants.
Beautifully executed, slightly overcrowded in composition, they are
closely related in style to the countless landscape etchings which had
poured forth from Haarlem and Amsterdam since early in the
century. Even more distinguished is a series of landscape plates with
the border left white. Delicately drawn in subtly receding shades of
very bright blue, these are perhaps the most accomplished landscape
drawings in all ceramic art. Traditionally they are ascribed to
Frytom, but on grounds of style would seem more probably the
work of some other independent artist. Kocks' son, Pieter, took over
from his father in 1701, but soon died, his widow carrying on and
using his 'PAK' monogram, probably conjointly with the 'AK',
which continues to appear on pieces which, on stylistic grounds,
must be later.

470 The jugs and plates produced by Rochus Hoppesteyn at *The
Young Moor's Head*, in the late 17th century, are among the great
rarities of Delft, and extremely beautiful. There is a contemporary
cousinship with the 'SVE' pieces, but the wares marked 'RHS' are
more brilliant in glaze, the drawing is bolder, the composition more
economical and often the whole effect is heightened by gold and by
the addition of a uniquely clear, warm, garnet red. Very similar in
tone, only more individual in drawing, is a number of vases and
468 chargers marked 'IW' in monogram. These used to be attributed to
Hoppesteyn's father, but that can be ruled out on evidence of style
and date. They are the work of an independent decorator, who
added an opaque green to Hoppesteyn's palette, and a new border

motif of palm trees. His masterpieces are among the first Dutch
pieces to derive their decoration direct from engravings. The
splendid service made for the Elector of Brunswick is based on 472
engravings by Giovanni-Battista Galestruzzi, P. Bartoli and others,
sometimes reproducing Raphael's cartoons, the originals of which
now hang in the Victoria and Albert Museum. From now on the
dependence on engravings becomes ever more marked. Elaborate
and highly finished decoration is either unique and unrepeated, the
work of an outside artist, or reproduced, seldom free-hand, but by
'pricking' a drawing or engraving and rubbing powdered pumice
through the master copy. A similar technique was used for the
mass-production of tiles in both Holland and England and many of
the original 'pounces' have survived, as in the Friesch Museum at
Leeuwaarden.

Amongst these classics of Delft, one must mention the *De Roos*
factory, all the productions of which are distinguished for their
accomplishment. Famous among them is a series of blue-and-white
plates, illustrating scenes from the New Testament, surrounded by a 473
border of clouds and cherubs, a last echo of the Italianate *grotesques*,
though the painting within is unequivocally Dutch. A great set of
five vases, now in the Victoria and Albert Museum, is enlivened by 474
touches of red and green, and closely follows the Ming-Ch'ing
Transitional style. Such sets of vases, three of baluster shape and two
of beaker, became a stock production at Delft. Known as a *Kast-stel*,
or cupboard set, they were intended for the five ledges on the cornice
of the large baroque cupboards found in every well-to-do household.

A word must be said at this point about what was, in sheer
quantity, the most widespread and typical of all the productions of
Dutch tin-enamel factories: the tiles.

471

472

473

471. Plate, tin-glazed earthenware painted in blue by Sir James Thornhill. Delft; 1711. Diam. 8½ in. (22·5 cm.). Signed 'J. Thornhill fecit. Delph Aug. 1711'. This plate is one of a set decorated with signs of the Zodiac, by Sir James Thornhill, the father-in-law of William Hogarth. British Museum, London.

472. Dish, tin-glazed earthenware painted in high-temerature polychrome, the centre in cobalt-blue. Delft; *The Old Moor's Head*; about 1670. Mark, monogram 'IW', in blue (compare fig. 468). Diam. 15⅞ in. (40·5 cm.). The design is after an engraving by Galestruzzi. Victoria and Albert Museum, London.

473. Plate, tin-glazed earthenware painted in a rich blue. Delft; factory of *The Rose*; about 1710. Diam. 8⅞ in. (22·5 cm.). Mark, 'Roos' in blue. This plate, one of a set made at this factory, shows Christ with Zacchaeus; its high quality is typical of the factory. Victoria and Albert Museum, London.

Tin-glazed tiles were never used on floors, but for the wall-surfaces of kitchens and dairies and as a skirting in living-rooms, as may be seen in countless contemporary paintings. They were also used for large decorative effects and to form small pictures. The earliest tiles elaborated the designs and continued the palette of the Antwerp potteries. The patterns aimed to produce a bold overall effect of lozenges, stars and elongated hexagons. Early in the 17th century, bright central designs were introduced, showing fruit, flowers and foliage, patently returning for their inspiration to Venice and Faenza. The corner motifs, in strong blue, dominated the surface covered, and the effect was not unlike that of the hangings of Spanish leather in favour with the wealthy. Soon Chinese influence could be observed in the scalloped surround of the central design, and in the fret pattern of the corners, though it is curious that actual Chinese scenes figure but rarely on Dutch tiles of any period. As time went on the corner pieces became ever less important until, by the second half of the 18th century, they vanished altogether. Meanwhile more and more attention was paid to the central figures. Men-at-arms, often copied from the engravings of Hendrik Goltzius, horsemen, marine monsters, ships of every size, feature increasingly, as do everyday scenes of all kinds. In the 18th century simple landscapes became popular. From about 1680 onwards the most numerous of all were illustrations of the Old and New Testaments and from the turn of the century these began to be executed in manganese-purple as well as in blue. Later still, tiles were drawn in blue on a reserve of powdered manganese. Many single pictures of six or eight tiles, showing cats, dogs, horses, windmills and the like, were made by all factories. Sometimes major artists' designs were used to produce important decorations, as in the huge allegorical composition to be seen at the Victoria and Albert Museum, consisting of over three hundred and fifty tiles and based on a cartoon for a stained glass window at Gouda, where it was almost certainly made. Cornelis Boumeester of Rotterdam painted many fine seascapes, with characteristically streaky waves, in the first quarter of the 18th century. Most famous of all are the tall vases of flowers painted in brilliant polychrome, such as one finds still in the kitchens of French *châteaux* and the Amalienburg pavilion near Munich.

Tile-makers in the main worked independently of the main potteries and seem not to have been so strongly centred on Delft. The greatest manufactures were at Rotterdam, Gouda, Haarlem and later at Harlingen and Makkum in Friesland, whence enormous quantities were exported to North Germany. But the export trade was wide. France, England, Flanders and Portugal were also generous customers, and Dutch tiles were more widely known, and more widely imitated, than any other single form of Dutch tin-glazed ware. The closest copies were made in north-eastern France, at Lambeth, Bristol (where even the huge flower pieces were imitated) and Liverpool.

In dating tiles it should be remembered that the earlier specimens are of a reddish body and as much as three-quarters of an inch thick. By 1650 the body has become a pale buff, and the tiles themselves— almost always 5 inches (about 13 centimetres) square—became thinner and thinner. The designs (see above) were repeated over and over again. Yet their variety, and the variety of their setting, seems inexhaustible.

35
(p. 16)

474

474. Set of vases for the top of a cupboard, tin-glazed earthenware painted in high-temperature polychrome. Delft; *The Rose* factory; about 1710. Ht. of covered vases 15½ in. (39·5 cm.). Mark, 'Roos', in blue. Vases such as these were made in sets, usually of five, to go on the tops of cupboards. The present set follows closely both in shape and colour the 'Transitional' style between the Ming and the Ch'ing dynasties. Victoria and Albert Museum, London.

475 476

475. Dish, painted in a strong blue of dark tone. Southwark, London, about 1635–40. Diam. 19½ in. (49·5 cm.). The style of decoration and the border, both derived from late Ming export porcelain, are also found on contemporary Dutch maiolica. The dish is one of a group of pieces which were probably made in the factory of Christian Wilhelm. Victoria and Albert Museum, London.

476. Bowl, painted in blue on the faintly green ground typical of late 17th-century Lambeth wares. Lambeth, inscribed 'RPI 1681'. Diam. 11¾ in. (29·9 cm.). The 'Oriental' figures are derived from Chinese 'Transitional' porcelains perhaps via Dutch imitations, and are found on contemporary Hanau and Frankfurt faience. The interior bears the arms of the Cooper's Company. Victoria and Albert Museum, London.

477. Jar, with a design of peacocks and rockwork outlined in blue-black and painted in a darkish blue, red-brown and orange-yellow. Probably Lambeth, about 1700–10. Ht. 6½ in. (16·5 cm.). Pieces of this kind were made both in Bristol and Lambeth. The design, apart from the peacocks, is of Chinese inspiration, as are the borders. Ashmolean Museum, Oxford. Warren Collection.

England

In England the manufacture of tin-glazed earthenware was concentrated in three main centres—London, Bristol and Liverpool—though mention must also be made of the factory at Wincanton which operated for a few years in the middle of the 18th century. The ware was made continuously in London from about 1575 to 1800, at first in the parishes of Aldgate and Southwark, but in the 18th century mainly in Lambeth. It was two potters from Southwark who, in the middle of the 17th century, set up a factory at Brislington, near Bristol, which lasted until about 1750. In 1683 Edward Ward, a Brislington potter, set up the first delftware pottery in Bristol itself, two other potteries being started there a little later. By 1770, the production of delftware in Bristol had virtually ceased. In 1712 some London potters started a delftware factory in Liverpool where by 1750 at least seven other factories at work were producing enormous quantities of delftware, until they too were put out of business by the popularity of creamware in the 1770s. There were one or two delftware factories in Ireland, the most important one being in Dublin, operating from about 1730 till around 1771. In Scotland in the second half of the century, there was a very active factory in Glasgow, known as 'Delftfield', but little is known about its products.

Until about 1740, the decoration of English tin-glazed earthenware, apart from the wares classed as 'maiolica' (p. 158), closely followed Dutch styles—hence the term 'English delftware'. But in the matter of potting and glaze there are considerable differences between Dutch Delft and English 'delftware'. The finest Delft has a neatness of finish and a purity of body which was rare for the contemporary English wares. Moreover the potters at Delft invariably gave a high shine to their wares by sprinkling an additional lead-glaze ('kwaart') over the tin-glaze. This extra glaze was also used in England, about 1690–1740, though never with such brilliant effect: English delftware, though sometimes shiny, is nevertheless duller in finish. It may be supposed that this technique was brought to England by immigrant Dutch potters, some of whose names have been found in the Lambeth parish registers, and there is good reason to suppose that there were Dutch journeymen-potters at work in Bristol as well as in London, using not only Dutch techniques but also Dutch designs. It is often impossible to say if a piece of English delftware was made by an English potter copying a Dutch design, or if it was made by a Dutch potter working in England.

The vogue for 'Chinese' decoration lasted as long as the fashion for delftware. In the first half of the 17th century the immigrant potter, Christian Wilhelm, produced at his factory in Southwark a large number of pieces decorated in blue after Wan-Li originals, the

boldness of the decoration more than compensating for its derivative nature and the relative coarseness of body and glaze. Later in the century, the Lambeth potters, possibly in imitation of the Dutch, were copying the style of late Ming and 'Transitional' porcelain with its typical motifs, such as tall plants, sketchy landscapes and stylised figures. In Holland such pieces of Dutch manufacture are known as 'Hollands Porceleyn' and some are indeed deceptively like the porcelain originals, but no English piece in this style is of such high quality; most are laboured and many extremely clumsy. In the early 18th century 'Chinese' designs appear in polychrome sometimes blending 'Chinese' motifs with 'European' subjects, or repeating figures from the Chinese romances as depicted on K 'ang

476
31
(p. 144)

477

478

475

477

478

479

Hsi porcelain, again possibly by way of the Dutch copies. However, from about 1740 onwards there was a much greater effort to copy Chinese motifs, or at least to give a greater refinement to the *chinoiserie* designs, at a time when Chinese porcelain was flooding into Europe through the East India Companies. Thus a plate depicting the 'Horses of Mu-Wang' is very close to the Chinese design while a Lambeth dish with its pavilions and trees, is pure *chinoiserie*. This dish has also been embellished with '*bianco-sopra-bianco*' ('white on white'), a technique used at Lambeth, 1747 to about 1755 and at Bristol after 1755, probably being introduced to both by the Swede, Magnus Lundberg, who brought it with him from the Rörstrand factory. This form of embellishment is also seen on a tea-caddy from Bristol: here it sets off admirably the fantastic 'Chinese' figure which may well have been copied from one of the many collections of 'Chinese Ornament' published at the time.

In the early 18th century the Dutch style of landscape decoration was imitated, though in a rather rough form and never with the subtlety of an artist such as Frederik van Frytom. There is a group of pieces, mostly with dates between 1700 and 1710, decorated with rustic figures in a landscape with rather stiffly drawn trees, but the best piece in this style is the bowl (Ashmolean Museum, Warren Collection) depicting a militia company marching out to exercise. Other pieces made use of Dutch engravings, such as a large punch bowl, dated 1697, decorated on both sides with tavern scenes in the manner of Teniers or Ostade. In the 1740s a more English style of landscape drawing appears, such as the scene of the stag-hunt depicted on the bowl signed by Lawrence Harrison in 1748 which also follows an engraved original. Such hunting scenes are fairly common on punch bowls of the period. At the same time the influence of the French artist, Hubert Gravelot, was felt at Bristol, where Joseph Flower, a young pottery decorator, used the designs of Gravelot and Bickham engraved for the *Musical Entertainer* to decorate two punch-bowls in 1743. Gravelot, who spent a number of years in England, was at one time Gainsborough's master and perhaps this is why the small basin of the period with its tall figures and park landscape recalls both Watteau and the rococo landscapes of Gainsborough. Many pieces in this style, including tiles, were made in Bristol in the 1760s, and some of these represent English pottery decoration at its finest.

480

481

483

484

479

485

478. Bowl, painted in deep blue, brown-red, olive-green and canary-yellow. Bristol, about 1730–35. Diam. 11½ in. (29·2 cm.). A dish of this type in the Bristol City Gallery is dated 1733. The colouring and design are typical of a group of Bristol wares of the 1730s. The same figures occur on various pieces and are sometimes repeated on the same piece, which suggests that they were part of a decorator's 'repertoire'. Bristol City Art Gallery.

479. Bowl, depicting a stag-hunt. Liverpool, dated 1748. Diam. 15⅝ in. (40·3 cm.). Painted in blue except for the stag which is in pale manganese. The illustration shows the outside of this well-known bowl signed on the base by Lawrence Harrison, a Liverpool pot-painter. The inside depicts a drinking scene copied faithfully from Hogarth's engraving *A Midnight Modern Conversation* of 1734. Indeed it is likely that the hunting scene and the landscape are also derived from prints. Manchester City Gallery.

480. Plate, painted in pale blue. Liverpool, about 1750–60. Diam. 10½ in. (26·7 cm.). This plate is a good example of a design copied more or less directly from a Chinese original known as the *Horses of Mu-Wang* and recapturing something of the verve of the original, although the trees are somewhat stiff. Ashmolean Museum, Oxford.

481. Dish, painted in a greyish blue. Lambeth, about 1747–55. Diam. 13¾ in. (35 cm.). The border embellished with a *bianco-sopra-bianco* design typical of Lambeth, as is proved by excavated sherds. The central design, showing a fanciful version of the 'bamboo, plum and pine' is a piece of pure *chinoiserie*. Ashmolean Museum, Oxford.

482. Jug, painted in brilliant polychrome. Liverpool, dated 1763. Ht. 9⅝ in. (24·5 cm.). French blue, pale yellow, violet, olive-green and clear red—here comprise the so-called 'Fazackerley' colours after the mugs traditionally made for Thomas and Catherine Fazackerley, 1757–8. Flowers in similar colours are found on bowls, tea-ware, plates and tiles. Bristol City Art Gallery.

480

481

482

Although many maiolica dishes are found with bold floral designs, it was not until the second half of the 18th century that floral decoration again came into fashion, perhaps under the influence of porcelain. 'Botanical' flowers are rarely found on English delftware, and the greater part of the floral decoration consists of brightly-coloured, stylised flowers, rather neatly drawn. This style of decoration seems to have originated at Liverpool but may also have been copied in Bristol.

The British love of the sea is shown by the 'ship-bowls' which were commissioned by the captains of trading ships, so that they are usually inscribed with his name as well as that of the ship, and usually wish success to them both. Many such bowls were made at Liverpool from about 1750–75, but Bristol potters also made them, both for English captains and for the captains of foreign ships visiting Bristol. A notable bowl in the Manchester City Gallery depicts the Swedish ship 'Wigilantia' and has an inscription in Swedish giving the date of its visit to Bristol Docks. This bowl is decorated outside with a landscape not unlike that seen on the basin. The outsides of Liverpool 'ship-bowls' are painted with a variety of designs—*chinoiseries*, flowers or exotic birds. This bottle also shows the influence of porcelain decoration, the exotic birds often being found on contemporary Worcester, and other porcelain.

Naturally there is an enormous variety of decoration on English delftware; it must suffice here to mention the large number of pieces with sketchy 'portraits' of Kings and Queens, the pieces commemorating historical events and personages, the armorial pieces, and the sets of plates with rhyming inscriptions. In the 18th century, however, pieces decorated with religious subjects of any kind are extremely rare.

English delftware is not a sophisticated product; yet it has an undeniable charm, above all because the decoration is rarely mechanical. There is nearly always a personal touch in the design. But it has its triumphs—the 'Chinese' pieces of Christian Wilhelm are bold and powerful in their effect, as are the 'tulip-dishes' of the late 17th century, and then, in the second half of the 18th century there is the late flowering of delftware at a time when creamware was already driving delftware off the market. Pieces like the basin are fine pottery by any standards and the bottle with the exotic birds can hold its own in any company.

483. Octagonal tea-caddy. Bristol, dated 1763 and inscribed 'ANN SCOTT'. Ht. 4⅞ in. (12·4 cm.). Painted in a strong blue and embellished at each corner with *bianco-sopra-bianco* designs typical of Bristol. The other side of the tea-caddy shows a similar *chinoiserie* figure holding a parasol. The top has four diaper patterns in blue alternating with four panels of *bianco-sopra-bianco*. Bristol City Art Gallery.

484. Punch-bowl. Brislington or Bristol, dated 1697. Ht. 14¼ in. (36·2 cm.). This elaborate piece probably had once had a cup which fitted on the top, possibly shaped like a crown. The designs of tavern scenes painted in a clear blue with blackish outlines ('*trek*'), are presumably derived from Dutch or Flemish engravings. The diaper-work and the various borders are inspired by Chinese porcelain. British Museum, London.

485. Basin, painted in a warm blue. Bristol, about 1750–60. Diam. 10½ in. (26·7 cm.). This is one of the finest specimens of a typical Bristol style of landscape painting attributed, without good reason, to the hand of John Bowen. The rococo motifs and the Gainsborough-like figures are notable features of this basin which, accompanied by a bottle, was probably used for rose-water. Bristol City Art Gallery.

483

484

485

486

487

486. Bowl, inscribed: 'Success to the Prescott—James Bennett Master'. Liverpool, about 1750–60. Diam. 10¼ in. (26 cm.). Painted mainly in rich blue, with the flag and pennant picked out in red, the coat-of-arms in green. The outside has a running design in blue of birds and stylised flower-sprays of Chinese inspiration. This is a typical specimen of a ship-bowl made for the captain. The contrast between the Chinese border and the European grape-vine is worthy of note. Liverpool City Museum.

487. Large maiolica plate painted in cobalt-blue, yellow, orange, green and manganese-brown. Montelupo; early 17th century. Diam. 13 in. (33 cm.). Horses painted in the effective concise *compendiario* style, but with a full palette over the entire surface. The Montelupo region was probably the most productive in Tuscany continuing to make maiolica the longest, from the 15th century on. Though lacking originality, it had individuality due to the material used and to the artistic interpretation, and was marked (end 16th–17th century) by strongly drawn figures painted in striking colours. Museo Nazionale, Palazzo Bargello, Florence.

Italy

The fashionable Faenza 'white wares' (p. 155), with all their variations in style in the different centres—in colour, design and shape—but retaining their coating of white tin-glaze more or less unchanged, continued throughout the 17th century, and in some places, through being adopted by popular art, survived until the 19th century. All in all, white wares were one of the most vital forms of maiolica.

As well as the later types of white wares, the 17th century in Italy saw the development of new styles. Regions which had not previously been so much in evidence began to establish themselves. Besides the Romagna, Venetia, Tuscany, Umbria and the Marches there were now the Abruzzi, Apulia, the Campagna, Sicily and, above all, Liguria.

In the Romagna, at Faenza, the white wares tended towards elaborate baroque shapes where painting had no proper role, or turned to an over abundance of figurative, geometric and floral decoration which kept faithfully to the colouring and techniques of the *compendiario* style.

Characteristic types in Tuscany were plates and jugs with figures of ladies, soldiers, bravos, and their mounts, etc., treated with swift strokes reminiscent of the *compendiario* style but richer in colouring. Cobalt-blue, orange, green and manganese-purple often contrast with grounds of a resonant pale yellow. This luxuriant output is peculiar to the Montelupo workshops, and includes jugs finished with jesting inscriptions which have the flavour of popular speech. Other regions of Tuscany and Umbria reflect these styles.

In Umbria, alongside the outworn 16th-century formulae of busts and scenes framed by polychrome panelled borders, there evolved at Deruta a *compendiario* style enriched by a palette dominated by tones of orange. The votive panels in the oratory dedicated to the Madonna dei Bagni at Casilina, a few kilometres from Deruta, are good examples. There are several hundred *ex voto* images painted in polychrome on maiolica with the swift strokes of the *compendiario* style—in which besides being the image of the Virgin of the miracles, the scene of the miracle is naively depicted. This type of ware continued in production into the 18th and 19th centuries.

With the return of the Duchy of Urbino to the Holy See, and the consequent loss of patronage, the Marches seem to have lost their maiolica manufacture. But we have very effective proof of its vitality in the 17th century in the great vases made for the luxurious residences of the Barberini in Rome, and for other wealthy houses. They were the work of Rombaldotti of Urbania (the new name adopted by Casteldurante in 1638 in honour of Pope Urban VIII) and of other artists who with their plates, cups and vases, restored the glories of the previous century. In true Italian tradition they used the designs of great artists, and maiolica found a new lease of life as a pictorial medium and so won a place for itself in great baroque painting.

During the course of the 16th century, Sicily had received considerable supplies from Venice, Faenza and Casteldurante, and through its contacts with Liguria too, had absorbed the Renaissance and post-Renaissance spirit. Its activity can be seen in the workshops of Palermo, Trapani, Collesano, Sciacca and Caltagirone, now so far removed from their Moorish past that they show no trace of its influence.

In the Campagna the prevalence of extensive maiolica tiled floors still found *in situ* in churches in Naples, Anacapri and other smaller places, reveals a manufacture of masterly technical achievement and exuberant imagination. At Benevento, or to be precise, at Cerreto Sannita (home of the Giustiniani, who worked in Naples in the next century) there were flourishing workshops where the traditions of the Campagna, Apulia and the Abruzzi were combined.

Apulia has recently revealed a concentration of activity in factories at Grottaglie, Laterza, Nardo, Novoli, and S. Pietro in Lama, which moved from the field of purely utilitarian and popular ceramics to undertake pictorial and decorative works. A group of artists from Laterza created a body of work which, although affected by influences from the nearby Abruzzi, has definite characteristics and personality of its own. Outstanding among these artists seems to have been Leonardo Antonio Andriuzzo, creator of little panels and vessels (now in the Museo Internazionale delle Ceramiche in Faenza), painted with a restricted palette. In the same way, artists were active at Grottaglie, though, here it should be noticed, they were working on a more functional level and using a richer palette.

489

488. Baluster-shaped pharmacy vase, maiolica painted in polychrome. Palermo; early 17th century. Ht. 13 in. (35 cm.). Decorated with superimposed parallel borders of trophies, braids, strapwork, etc., and with a scroll enclosing the figure of a saint. Freely inspired by mainland models, which Sicily imported in large quantities in the 16th century. Musée National de Céramique, Sèvres.

489. Large maiolica dish painted in greyish-blue. Apulia; workshop of Leonardo Antonio Andriuzzo, Laterza; 1680–90. Diam. 12¼ in. (31 cm.). This scene of a man eating macaroni, with two *putti* holding a spoon and fork, is probably derived from an engraving. Apulia, which is shown by such pieces to have had excellent painters, especially in the workshops of Laterza, readily accepted

influences from the neighbouring centre of Castelli in the Abruzzi. Museo Internazionale delle Ceramiche, Faenza.

488

At Angarano in the Veneto, the Manardi brothers made beautiful ware with landscapes, or flowers and geometrical patterns on pearly white (*latesino*) enamel, and at Bassano the Roman, Bartolomeo Terchi, whom we also find at Siena, was a successful painter of scenes, landscapes and figures in which yellow and purple create a special chromatic effect. But the areas which, one might say, burst into prominence in the 17th century were the Abruzzi and Liguria.

In the Abruzzi, the basic forms and colours—cobalt-blue, green, orange and yellow—of the Romagna workshops, were exemplified in the panel with the Virgin, dated 1551, and signed by Orazio Pompei, or perhaps even more in the tiles with the saucy portrait-busts of women dating from the early 16th century, which now adorn the floor of San Donato, but which may formerly have been on the ceiling. About a century later these were followed, at Castelli, and afterwards at Atri and elsewhere, by the development of the Faenza white wares. The most extensive use of the style is found in the little tiles with Saints in the abbey church, and in the ceiling of the little church of San Donato, executed in 1515, 1516 and 1517 by members of the Pompei family. There was also a rich crop of vases and dishes with the characteristic *compendiario* forms, perhaps a little stylised, but full of vitality.

Besides these types, which later declined into a peasant art, the evolution of the late *istoriato* of the Marches, in the hands of Francesco Grue, whose signature and initials we find on panels and dishes of the fourth and fifth decades of the 17th century, led to the typical Castelli style, shown in the works of Grue's son Carlantonio, and of other members of the family—Dr Francesco Antonio, Saverio etc. There was a feeling for rural landscape, figurative compositions inspired by the great baroque decorators of the Bolognese, Roman and Neapolitan schools, delicate shades of colour, especially in Carlantonio's work, and an appropriate use of gilding.

490

491

492

493

490. Oval maiolica dish with border of foliage in relief, painted in delicate colours on pearly white tin-glaze (*latesino*). Angarano; late 17th century. L. 13¼ in. (34 cm.). The shape is inspired by an original model in silver. A classical landscape often decorates dishes such as this, variously attributed to workshops in Venice, or the Venetian province and called *latesino*, because of the pearly tones of the glaze. Victoria and Albert Museum, London.

491. Small maiolica plate, the design outlined in manganese-brown and filled in with pale colours. Francesco Grue (1648–73). Castelli d'Abruzzo; mid-17th century. The hunting scene, framed in a border of flowering sprays with Cupids, animals and grotesques, is characteristic of the Master who created the Castelli style, using some features of the late *istoriato* of Urbino and of the *bianchi di Faenza*. The Grue family, of which Francesco was the head, and the Gentile family contained the greatest Castelli maiolica during the 17th and 18th centuries. Museo Internazionale delle Ceramiche, Faenza.

492. Baluster-shaped maiolica vase, painted in polychrome by Carlantonio Grue (1655–1723). Castelli d'Abruzzo; early 18th century. Ht. 21⅝ in. (55 cm.). *Flight into Egypt*, after a painting by Federico Barocci, set in a sylvan landscape and surrounded by Cupids, is one of the Master's most poetic works, with both delicacy of touch and fine shading of colours. Carlantonio's painting, inspired by baroque taste, eliminates his father's rigidity and depends mainly on colour. Museo Nazionale, Naples.

493. Wall panel, maiolica painted in polychrome. Genoa; about 1524. The figure of St George, (counterpart of St John the Baptist the other side of the chapel), is framed in tiles (*laggioni*) decorated with cable-patterns, rosettes, etc. in clear flowing lines, side by side with Spanish *a cuenca* tiles with rigid geometrical designs. The painting, both in form and range of colour, ties in with the best schools of maiolica painting of the Romagna and the Marches, which took Masters to Genoa from the early 16th century. Botto Chapel, Church of Santa Maria di Castello, Genoa.

An important contribution to the Castelli school was made by members of the Gentile family and later by the Capelletti and the Fuina, as well as by the Grue family. This school attracted much attention and during the 17th and 18th centuries spread not only in the southern regions but also to the North—in the persons of Ferdinando Maria Campani and members of the Terchi family—and beyond the borders of Italy.

The other great 17th-century region for ceramics, with the inevitable subsequent developments in the 18th century, is Liguria. We know of an industry in Genoa, dating from the 16th century at least, and probably even earlier, especially famous for the execution of *laggioni*—tiles for facing walls—in the style and technique of Mediterranean Spain, and of figurative panels like those in the Botto Chapel in Santa Maria di Castello. We know that artists from parts of central Italy—the Romagna and the Marches—who wished to cross into France, to Lyons and other towns, would stop at Genoa, and these short visits nourished the ceramic art of Liguria, as can be seen by works still *in situ*. Liguria is a land of navigators and merchants, and it was here that the early imports of Chinese porcelain had some influence and introduced a taste for blues; the fusion of this taste

493

494

495

494. 'Show dish', maiolica painted in monochrome cobalt-blue. Savona; third quarter of 17th century. Diam. 17½ in. (44·6 cm.). A central figural design, derived from drawings by G. B. Castello, is framed in a border of radiating panels enclosing landscapes, flowers, etc. The shape of the moulded plate is evidently inspired by baroque models in silver, frequently imitated by the Ligurian potters. Direzione Belle Arti del Comune di Genova, Genoa.

495. Plate with plain surfaces, maiolica painted in cobalt-blue, green, yellow and dark purple. Savona, workshop of G. Valente; early 18th century. Diam. 17⅞ in. (45·3 cm.). Peasants dancing, with the characteristic arcade at the side, and a suggestion of broken branches, reminiscent of the style of the Levantino family of Albisola. On the back the mark of the workshop 'V'. Musei Civici, Genoa.

with elements of the *compendiario* style gave rise to several genres which brought success to this region.

There were, for instance, fantasies of animals in luxuriant vegetation, inspired by the porcelain of the period intermediate, between the end of the Ming and the beginning of the Ch'ing dynasties,—in what was called the 'calligraphic' style. In addition there were children at play, conversation pieces dominated by buxom ladies, and sketchy landscapes etc., obviously of baroque inspiration and drawn in blue on a pearly tin-glaze. They were designed in the concise *compendiario* style, by G.A. and Bartolomeo Guidobono and their followers and imitators in Savona, on various

shapes of amphorae, drug-pots, pharmacy jugs and show dishes with moulded rims which recall prototypes in precious metal from the workshops of gold- and silversmiths. 494

Later on, polychrome was to triumph in the works of Agostino Ratti, and Luigi and Andrea Levantino in Albisola; these last two were the authors of animated little figures in sketchy landscapes with arcades, flowers etc. 495

During the 17th and 18th centuries factories followed one after the other, and with the exchange of craftsmen and easy imitation of styles, the various types were commingled in the centres of Savona and Albisola.

France

It was again under the aegis of Italy that manufacture began in Nevers. Luigi dei Gonzaga, Duke of Nivernais through his marriage to Henrietta of Cleves in 1565, attracted many Italian potters to the region, among them the Conrade brothers from Albisola, who are considered to have been the founders of the Nevers faience industry. Their partnership was accorded recognition in 1603 by the king, Henri IV, who granted them a privilege for the succeeding thirty years.

The early work of the Conrades is not easy to distinguish from that of the Italian potters of Lyons. Julio Gambin had in fact left Lyons to join the Conrades in Nevers; he was established there by 1588, and introduced patterns for *istoriato* maiolica. The Conrade brothers were also responsible for beautiful sculptural work in the Della Robbia tradition.

496

From about 1630, when the Conrades' privilege expired, other factories were opened in Nevers—by Berthélemy Bourcier, and later by Nicolas Estienne at the sign of the *Ecce Homo* and by Pierre Custode at *The Ostrich*. The Italian tradition survived until the end of the century, but the Nevers style evolved as French engravings and the works of the ornamental designers of the time of Louis XIII and Louis XIV were increasingly taken as models. The large decorative dishes surrounded by rich borders, and the vases of elaborate form inspired by the work produced by the Royal goldsmiths were made at this period. After 1660 a family of faience in a typically French style (*franco-nivernais*) reveals a more informal manner: country scenes and pastorals reflect the spirit of fashionable novels such as *Astrée* by Honoré d'Urfé.

497

The faience with solid coloured grounds, the so-called '*bleus de Nevers*' ('Nevers blues'), were popular for a long time after about 1630. They were decorated in the main with birds and sprays of flowers drawn in yellow and opaque-white, or inversely, on a few rare specimens, in blue and white on a yellow ground; because of certain associations with the East, this has wrongly been called 'Persian decoration' ('*décor persan*'). Monochrome green was also used, on a white glaze.

When the porcelain imported in large quantities from the Far East by the East India Companies became so immensely popular, the Nevers potters, like those of Delft, took steps to imitate the 'blue-and-white ware of China'. 498

In Rouen, faience went through a new phase of brilliance and prosperity after the middle of the 17th century. On August 27th, 1644, Nicolas Poirel, Lord of Granval, obtained a special licence to make faience in the province of Normandy; in the following year the licence was confirmed and its duration extended from thirty years to fifty. When the Rouen Parlement registered the authorisation on February 29th, 1648, Nicolas Poirel had already let out his licence on contract to Edme Poterat. A few rare pieces of faience, still resembling the 'white ware' of Faenza ('*bianchi*', see p. 155) bear witness to Edme Poterat's first factory and carry the inscription '*faict a Rouen 1647*'.

In 1656 Edme Poterat set up his kilns in the suburb of Saint-Sever-lès-Rouen, beside the road from Elbeuf. Of his two sons, the second, 496

496. Statue of the Virgin giving the Christ-Child an apple; white faience with touches of yellow and blue for the hair and for the stripes on the garments; the facial features are painted in purple. Nevers; workshop of the Conrade family; 1636. Ht. 3 ft. 7¾ in. (1·11 m.). A monogram 'DLF', incised, is interpreted as the signature of Denis Lefebvre, who worked in the Conrade atelier 1629–49. This fine figure, displaying great nobility and serenity, is directly linked with the Della Robbia tradition. Musée Frédéric-Blandin, Nevers.

497

Michel, succeeded him on his death in 1687; the elder, Louis, who had in 1673 applied for a new authorisation, set up his own factory on the cross-roads of La Croix-Bonne-Nouvelle.

In the last quarter of the 17th century with the 'Dutch-Chinese' style the influence of Italy was replaced by that of Delft and of Nevers. Rouen's period of originality came only shortly before 1700. It was then that the decorative scheme known as the '*style rayonnant*' developed, a style that is typically Louis XIV. Its main characteristic is the constant use of triangular motifs pointing towards the centre of the dish, which are comparable to the festoons of drapery, or 'lambrequins', on the borders of the bed canopies and the window-recesses of contemporary interiors (see p. 185).

In the south all faience was dominated by two great centres, Moustiers and Marseilles, which developed side by side from about 1675 onwards under the direction of the two sons of Antoine Clérissy: Pierre, who took over his father's factory in Moustiers, and Joseph, who settled in Marseilles in the suburb of Saint-Jean-du Désert. The Clérissy brothers produced faience of fine quality, decorated in monochrome blue, in the direct classical tradition introduced from Italy by way of Nevers. Large dishes are painted with central medallions with radiating borders, and enclosing animated pictures taken from engravings. These are mostly hunting scenes from the sets of prints by the Florentine, Antonio Tempesta. Some of these pieces bear the signature of a member of the Viry family, the great dynasty of southern painters. François Viry had accompanied Joseph Clérissy to Marseilles and, on the latter's death, married his widow. The work of Moustiers and Marseilles in this initial period was thus very similar.

497. Dish in faience with high-temperature polychrome decoration. Nevers; about 1675. Diam. 14½ in. (37 cm.). The central picture, *The Rape of Europa*, is taken from the engraving by François Chaveau, which M. Charles Meyer identified as an illustration to a 1674 edition of Ovid's *Metamorphoses*, rendered into verse by Isaac de Benserade. The Italian tradition is also preserved in the border of a blue wave-pattern decorated with swans and sea-deities. Louvre, Paris.

498. Ewer in faience with high-temperature decoration, in blue camaieu touched with strokes of purple on a slightly blued tin-glaze. Nevers; about 1660. Ht. 21¼ in. (54 cm.). The decoration of Chinese scenes is derived from that on the Chinese blue-and-white

porcelain of the so-called 'Transitional period' between Wan-Li and Kang-Hsi, but the French Nevers potters were able to avoid pastiche and to keep the original character of faience in their work. Musée des Arts Décoratifs, Saumur.

499. Helmet-jug, faience decorated in blue with touches of yellow. Rouen; about 1710–20. Ht. 10⅝ in. (27 cm.). Arms of the Moncel family. The shape of this ewer copies that of the silverware which faience was to replace. This decoration of elaborate 'lambrequins', set alternately on a ground and in reserve, is derived from the compositions of the ornamental engravers from the end of Louis XIV's reign. This is the Rouen decoration *par excellence*. Louvre, Paris.

500

498   499

500. Oval dish, faience with decoration in high-temperature blue camaieu. Clérissy factory, Moustiers; about 1700. L. 22⅞ in. (58 cm.). The signature in full, 'G. Viry f. à Moustiers chez Clérissy', lends this beautiful dish value as an historical document. The picture in the middle, a bear-hunting scene, is derived from an engraving by the Florentine, Antonio Tempesta. This rich decorative border of chimeras, plant-scrolls and lion-masks is typical of the early period of Moustiers. Musée National de Céramique, Sèvres.

37. *Lustre-painted bowl. Manises (Valencia). About 1400. Diam. 18 in. (45·7 cm.). The decoration, a close copy of designs found on 14th-century lustreware made at Málaga, shows how successful the Valencian Muslims were in copying Andalusian models. Painted in golden lustre with accents of blue, petal-shaped segments radiate from a blue star-rosette. Among the motifs filling these petals may be recognised the tree-of-life, the calligraphic scrolls, palmettes, and the curled white leaf so familiar in Almohade ornamentation. The blue scrolls filling wedge-shaped spaces around the rim are the debased letters of a Nasrid script. The Hispanic Society of America, New York.*

38

39

40

501

502

503

501. Screw-topped flask, painted in blue. Kreussen; workshop of Leonhard Schmidt?, dated 1618 and marked 'L.S.' in blue. Ht. 9 in. (23 cm.). The shape and the relief decoration are derived from stoneware proto-types produced in the Vest workshop. The row of letters below the arms of Saxony and the monogram may be interpreted 'Johann Georg Herzog von Sachsen, Herzog und Curfürst zu Sachsen'. The other side has an inscription. Museum für Kunst und Gewerbe, Hamburg.

502. Jug with the arms of Hamburg, the monogram 'P.L.' and a *Hausmarke* (owner's device) painted in blue. Hamburg, dated 1643. Ht. 13¼ in. (25·5 cm.). The feathery leaves are derived from Portuguese faience. The ovoid body with the lower part flaring out from the base, and the narrow neck are typical of Hamburg. Victoria and Albert Museum, London.

503. Vase of double-gourd shape, painted in blue. Hanau, about 1680. Ht. 16¾ in. (42·5 cm.). The shape of the vase with the diagonal ribbing clearly shows the influence of the nearby Frankfurt factory, but the pale, rather dull blue is typical of Hanau. European flowers are grouped in the manner of the Chinese flowering shrubs, thus providing an excellent example of the mingling of European and Oriental motifs. Staatliche Kunstsammlungen, Kassel.

Germany

The faience tradition of the Renaissance in Germany continued at the beginning of the 17th century with a group of drug-jars and dishes, together with cups in the shape of birds, all painted in blue and marked 'L.S.' A recurrent motif on these pieces is a tulip or lily on a long stalk with scrolling leaves, at first finely drawn but later on rather broadly and summarily treated: the flowers are occasionally accompanied by inscriptions, Roman capitals and dates. A group of screw-top flasks made in 1618 for the Court Pharmacy at Dresden shows obvious affinities with the stoneware vessels made at Kreussen. These are usually considered to be the work of Lorenz Speckner, who married the widow of Georg Vest the Younger, a stoneware-potter at Kreussen, and continued to run his business. However, the moulds and models which Speckner used for his stoneware are not

marked 'L.S.' but 'L.S.P.', and occasionally 'H.L.S.P.', and in 1618, when the pharmacy jars were commissioned for the Dresden court, he was only twenty years old and had not become a master-potter. For this reason the potter who made the faience wares marked 'L.S.' is more likely to be Leonhard Schmidt who also had a work-shop in Kreussen, where he became a freeman in 1612, and where he died in 1665. In point of time this workshop, which existed for some fifty years, overlaps a second workshop established probably in Hamburg. The 'Hamburg' wares often show the arms of Hamburg or of its citizens. The striking dependence of the designs on Portuguese models is explained by the close commercial ties which existed between the Hanse-town and Portugal. As on the Portuguese wares, many decorative elements derived from Persian pottery and

501

513

38. *Pair of small pharmacy jars, maiolica painted in enamel colours. Italy (Venice, factory of Geminiano Cozzi); second half of 18th century. Ht. 7½ in. (19 cm.). Inscriptions: Ogl(io) di Camom(illa) (Oil of Camomile) and Oglio rosato (Oil of roses). Above, festoons of flowers and on the handle a small medallion with a landscape. On the base, conventionalised leaves. The petit feu decoration was peculiar to the Italian workshops in the later 18th century. Museo Internazionale delle Ceramiche, Faenza.*

39. *Double-gourd vase, painted in over-glaze enamel colours. Germany (Fulda), 1741–4. Signed 'F.v.L.', for Adam Friedrich von Löwenfinck, accompanied by the shield of Fulda, in black. Ht. 13¾ in. (35 cm.). While the lower part is painted with rhythmically-drawn scroll work, rushes and flowers, alternating with iron-red diaper-work, the neck and shoulders are decorated with Chinese borders of purple pendant flowers on a black ground, gourd-shaped vases and scrolls. Museum für Kunst und Gewerbe, Hamburg.*

40. *Dish showing the Emperor Rudolf II. Germany (Silesia, perhaps Neisse), about 1600. Diam. 14¾ in. (38 cm.). The Emperor wears lavender-blue armour, striped with yellow, and manganese-purple breeches. His face and hands are painted white and heightened with purple. The yellow ornaments on the Imperial Orb have dots of turquoise. The inscription reads 'RUDOLPHUS SECUNDUS ROMANORUM IMPERATOR'. The figure of the Emperor is freely adapted from an engraving of 1596 by Giacomo Franco. Victoria and Albert Museum, London.*

504

505

504. Dish, painted in blue. Frankfurt-am-Main, about 1680. Diam. 18⅝ in. (47·5 cm.). The 'Master of the Tall Vases' to whom this dish is attributed, owes his name to a series of large decorative vases. He was the most talented of the Frankfurt decorators, and on this dish he shows great skill and freedom in the way in which he incorporates the rim of the dish into his design, whereas other painters

divided up the rim after the fashion of Wan-li porcelain. The central boss is the focal point of this design of finely painted *chinoiseries*. Museum für Kunst und Gewerbe, Hamburg.

505. Detail from Joachim von Sandrart's painting *Abraham and the Angels* of about 1680. A simple earthenware dish occupies the centre of the table. The salt and pepper

pots are of silver; the two plates of pewter. Whereas the fruit-dish on the left may be of Chinese origin, the dish on the right is clearly a Frankfurt 'nine-lobed dish' ('*Neunbuckelschüssel*'). The shape and decoration of the jug from which the angel pours the wine are characteristic of Frankfurt faience. Hessisches Landesmuseum, Darmstadt.

Chinese porcelain are found, together with European figures, coats-of-arms and emblems, painted mainly in cobalt-blue, usually with touches of intense yellow. Green, manganese-brown and an iron-red are more rarely used. Large numbers of Hamburg jugs have survived, together with a few dishes, jars and bowls.

Whereas the existence of these two factories forms an interlude, neither of them having any influence on the later development of faience manufacture in Germany, the founding, in 1661, of a factory in Hanau by Dutch religious refugees marks the beginning of the golden age of German faience which lasted until the end of the 18th century. The influence of Dutch Delft decorated in Chinese style was at first paramount, but early on European designs began to be used alongside the Oriental decoration. A kind of *leitmotiv* in the Hanau style of decoration is the so-called *Vögelesdekor*, a pattern of scattered flowers interspersed with small exotic birds and groups of dots. This pattern is often used to decorate the typical Hanau tall-necked jugs with plaited or rope-twist handles, whose shape developed in accordance with local taste from the more rounded Dutch type to a shape which emphasised the contraction between neck and shoulder and between body and foot. About 1750, under the directorship of Hieronymus von Alphen, the factory followed the prevailing fashion and made polychrome wares painted both in high-temperature colours and in overglaze enamels.

German faience of the 17th century reached its artistic zenith at Frankfurt where a factory was started in 1666 by Jean Simonet, a Parisian who had until then been active at Lille, Brussels, Hanau and Heusenstamm. In 1667 the factory passed into the sole possession of Johann Christoph Fehr, one of Simonet's financial backers. The connections of the new owner, who was a member of a distinguished Frankfurt family, assured him a wealthy clientele eager for self-advertisement. For this reason far more decorative vases and show-pieces were made at Frankfurt than at Hanau, where the clientele consisted mainly of the lower middle classes. Most of the Frankfurt pieces are painted in blue, with a notable use of '*kwaart*', an additional lead-glaze which gives greater brilliance to the various

502

503
506

506

506

182

tones of blue and allows them to stand out against the snowy white glaze. Together with dishes and plates with smooth, ribbed or nine-lobed rims of Dutch type (which were also made at Hanau), the Frankfurt potters made monumental vases, jugs, dishes, basins, stoves for drying baby's clothes and other vessels, decorated with the typical Frankfurt Chinamen in a stylised landscape with rocks, shrubs, birds, butterflies and insects. Other high-temperature colours were also used, occasionally with unfired colours added over the glaze. As well as the Chinese patterns derived from Wan-Li porcelain, European designs are also found. These consist of large baroque flowers of a type also found on Hanau faience, a pattern of scattered flowers, finely drawn, coats-of-arms, and occasionally portraits, all of which were as popular as the religious and mythological scenes on the so-called 'history-plates' (*Historyteller*). On the other hand the jugs painted in purple monochrome, mainly of the 18th century, with flower-sprays tied with a ribbon, are quite independent of Delft influence. The high quality of Frankfurt faience gradually drove Dutch Delftware from the German market, and indeed it was appreciated in Holland itself, as may be seen from the fact that pieces are occasionally included in Dutch paintings. In German painting it appears for the first time in 1680, in Joachim von Sandrart's *Abraham and the Angels*, where a Frankfurt dish and jug may be seen next to vessels of other materials, including Chinese porcelain.

In view of the close connection between Brandenburg and Holland it is not surprising that the Delft tradition lingered on for a long time in Berlin and Potsdam. This is shown by the products of the two Berlin factories, that of Gerhard Wolbeer, founded in 1678 at first under the direct patronage of the Elector, and that of the Dutchman, Cornelius Funcke. These wares and those made at Potsdam in the factory founded by Christian Friedrich Rewend in 1739, are not easy to tell apart; they all have the same thin glaze through which the pinkish tone of the body can be seen, and on all of them can be found the motif of a peacock on a rock between flowering shrubs, which was also used by other German factories. Funcke's wares are the most individualistic: he liked baroque swag-patterns and coloured grounds, and occasionally imitated the Turkish wares made at Isnik.

The factory at Kassel, founded in 1680, also long imitated Dutch Delft; although, in the 1690s, the baroque flowers borrowed from Hanau are also found. There is a clear relationship here with the neighbouring factories in Lower Saxony, at Wrisbergholzen and Brunswick. From Strasbourg the Kassel decorators took over a pale blue swag-pattern of Rouen type. Yet the Kassel style is distinctive, among other things because of the neatness of the drawing.

The '*Hausmaler*' (outside decorators) at Nuremberg and Augsburg played a special role in the decoration of faience, using the style they had evolved for painting on window- and vinil-glass, an individual style which was German rather than Dutch. This was some time before the founding of the Buremberg faience factory (1712), so that their work is to be seen mainly on Hanau and Frankfurt faience. Johann Schaper (1621–70) painted tiny landscapes in black and red monochrome enamels, and his style was copied by Johann Ludwig Faber (who is mentioned in documents between 1687 and 1693). Wolfgang Rössler (c. 1650–1715) favoured large roses in bright colours as a framework for landscape panels which he then washed over with a colourless glaze. Abraham Helmhack (1654–1724) also began by painting in black monochrome but later painted in polychrome. Also worthy of mention are Johann Heel (1657–1709) and Mathias Schmidt (1684–1712). In Augsburg, Bartholomäus Seuter (1678–1737) decorated faience in a polychrome style reminiscent of Helmhack's.

507   508

506. Narrow-necked jug with blue painted decoration on a grey ground. Hanau, about 1689, painted Johannes Polts(?). Ht. 12 in. (30·5 cm.). Marked 'J.P.' in blue. The jug shows the fully developed Hanau shape with the characteristic *Vögelesdekor* consisting of scattered flowers and various birds. Staatliche Kunstsammlungen, Kassel.

507. Double-gourd vase, painted in polychrome. Berlin; Cornelius Funcke's factory, about 1730. Ht. 15 in. (38 cm.). Though imitated from the Turkish faience of Isnik, the ships with lateen-sails have been altered to correspond more closely with European craft. The ground of this vase is yellowish-green but others have a turquoise ground. The stylised waves and rocks are painted in iron-brown. Kestner Museum, Hanover.

508. Beaker vase ('*Stangenvase*'), painted in blue. Kassel, about 1720. Ht. 15½ in. (39·2 cm.). Marked 'HL' in blue. The motif of an elegant Chinese lady with an attendant bearing a fan appears also on a Bernburg garniture and on Berlin faience made in the factory of Gerhard Wolbeer. It is derived from a series of engraved Chinese scenes published in 1710–15 by Johann Christoph Weigel of Nuremberg. Staatliche Kunstsammlungen, Kassel.

Spain

The period when Talavera pottery reached the peak of its development, when it excelled and earned world-wide recognition, was the 17th century. During these years Castilians surpassed all other Spanish potters, and even the masters of Triana admittedly imitated Talavera pottery. Indeed, a collaboration had existed between Seville and Talavera since 1566, when Jerónimo Montero travelled northward on orders of the King to test glaze ingredients and to show the Talaveran potters how to improve the quality of their products.

Circumstances played a part in the meteoric rise of this pottery. A silver shortage in Spain helped to promote it from lowly households to the tables of royalty, nobility and clergy. In 1601, a decree of Philip III ordered silver table-services and church plate to be inventoried, restricted, or even confiscated. Patriots complied proudly, and by mid-century Talavera ware was regarded as entirely acceptable for the tables of noblemen. Poets of the century referred frequently to it, comparing its beauty to that of their sweethearts, although Lope de Vega's Casilda, a labourer's wife, setting her table with Talavera plates of carnation pattern, longed for a silver service.

Quantities of pottery were in use in the convents and monasteries of religious Orders, for the refectory or the pharmacy, where stood rows of drug-jars marked with the heraldic arms of an Order and often, too, with the names of antidotes, ointments, herbs, syrups, and powders. Spanish nobles, finding Talavera pottery attractive for the beauty of its painted decorations, the wide variety of designs, and the clear, bright colours, collected handsome table services and ornamental vases. The shapes of these vessels were manifold, ranging from simple forms thrown on the wheel to more complicated objects built up of numerous parts, or moulded to imitate silverware. Since many of the pieces bear heraldic shields, the original owners can be identified.

No matter how noteworthy a vase, a jar, or a dish might have been, potters of Talavera did not sign or mark their hollow ware. When names appeared, they were those of the owners, as on dishes bearing the names of friars and priests of the Escorial Monastery. Tiles were inscribed rarely with the decorator's name, but quite often with a date.

The basic material from which the potters formed their wares was a clay of fine texture, well levigated and worked, which fired to a light tan. An opaque tin-glaze, thick and milky white, formed a ground of eggshell texture for the painted decorations in blues, emerald-green, golden yellow and orange. All colours were painted on the basic white while it was dry but unfired. With black, purple, or dark brown the decorator drew the outlines and details. For sky and distant spaces of landscape, the general tonality of the best Talavera pottery is blue over opaque white. Green, streaked with blue, tints the foliage. This blending of colours on leaves is further brightened by yellow. Later in the century, a white background predominated, contrasting either with blue patterns, after Ming porcelains and Delftware, or with Italianate decorations in polychrome.

From this flourishing period of development the variety of pictorial designs painted on Talavera pottery is infinite. Many of them are architectural, based on prints of buildings, some in 'plateresque' style—an early Renaissance Spanish architectural style, so named for its resemblance to the work done by silversmiths

509

510

509. Pharmacy of the Monastery of Santo Domingo de Silos, Burgos. Talavera drug-jars, painted in blue with the arms of the abbot and names of the drugs, line the shelves; below them are drawers labelled for other drugs. While the pharmacy dates back to the 17th century, the decorations on the jars and the woodwork indicate an 18th-century date.

510. Detail of a jar, showing the technique in painting with glaze colours. Talavera de la Reina. About 1580. Ht. (whole jar) 21 in. (53·5 cm.). The hunting scene is based on an engraving (Antwerp, 1578) of a drawing by Johannes Stradanus. The Hispanic Society of America, New York.

(*plateros*)—some in early Herreran style, so named after Juan de Herrera (1530–97), an architect for the Escorial Monastery of San Lorenzo. A large number copy more or less faithfully the hunting scenes engraved in 1578 after Johannes Stradanus, depicting deer and wolf hunts, the slaying of pythons, falconry, fishing and the snaring of partridges. Towards the end of the century, instead of copying the Stradanus engravings completely, the decorators used figures isolated from the landscape backgrounds. The hunting prints of Antonio Tempesta, a pupil of Stradanus, also furnished models for decoration.

Next to hunting, the favourite amusement depicted on Talavera pottery is the bullfight. Mounted on spirited horses and armed with lances, young men gallantly attack the bulls, only resorting to the sword when dismounted. The *toreros* wear the costumes, feathered hats, and short capes in fashion about 1670. Dances and theatrical scenes are represented, one of them being from the tragedy of Lucretia, depicted at the moment when she plunges a dagger into her breast.

Tile-panels, notably those in the City Hall of Toledo (1696), display vigorous battle scenes painted in a masterly style comparable to the work of Italian maiolica-decorators. Other panels of a religious nature, illustrating the genealogy and Mysteries of the Virgin and representing numerous saints, ornament the Church of Our Lady of El Prado at Talavera.

511

512

513

511. Covered jar from Talavera de la Reina. About 1700 Ht. with cover 26¼ in. (66·8 cm.). Two Italianate scenes painted in multi-coloured glazes decorate this jar: on the side illustrated, hunters standing with dogs and a white horse, and on the other side, Lucretia plunging a dagger into her breast as two men and a maidservant look on. The Hispanic Society of America, New York.

512. Bowl, painted in coloured glazes on white. Talavera de la Reina. About 1670. Diam. 18¼ in. (46·4 cm.). The scene represents a bullfight taking place in the country. The gentleman *rejoneador* wears a costume in fashion about 1670. Victoria and Albert Museum, London.

513. Dish, tin-glazed earthenware painted in blue. Portuguese (probably Lisbon); mid-17th century. Diam. 13¾ in. (35 cm.). The real development of Portuguese tin-glazed wares began in the early 17th century. Portugal was the first Western country to be in direct contact with the Far East; it was therefore natural that the Portuguese tin-glaze potters (in Lisbon or possibly Braga) should turn early to imitations of Oriental blue-and-white. The dish illustrated clearly shows Chinese influence in its border and the central motif of a bird on rocks. Victoria and Albert Museum, London.

The 18th Century

France

In the 18th century the extent and range of French faience increased considerably. Under the impact of the Chinese porcelain styles and Dutch Delftware, Italian influence had now been left behind and new styles emerged. Centres of production multiplied and the wares of Rouen and Moustiers were to provide a widespread source of inspiration.

The ruinous cost of wars to France had caused the issue of edicts in 1689 and 1709 ordering all vessels of gold and silver to be melted down. Subsequent orders for banqueting services, therefore, many with armorial bearings for princely tables, gave the faience industry a marked impetus. According to Saint-Simon's famous comment (*Mémoires*, 1709): 'Every man of any status or consequence turned within a week to faience.' New factories were thus opened; according to the reports published by André Pottier, there were eight in 1720 and thirteen by 1722, so that it became necessary to limit their ever-increasing number for fear of a fuel shortage.

Shortly before 1700, under the influence of contemporary interior design, the Rouen factory developed its *style rayonnant* with its characteristic 'lambrequins' (see p. 178). These appeared as a rich embroidery of lines in blue on a white ground, or inversely, reserved against a blue ground, often patiently traced out by women. The *style rayonnant* was soon enriched by a discreet use of polychrome, with touches of red; exceptional in high-temperature faience, this red was responsible for the success of Rouen. Some very fine specimens of about 1720 are decorated with naked children dancing with linked hands, delicately modelled in blue and standing out on a painted ground of yellow ochre, with black niello-like arabesques which are reminiscent of jewellers' work. On other specimens, tracery like that found in contemporary wrought iron work stands out on the white glaze. The great round Rouen dishes may be as much as sixty centimetres in diameter, for they were piled high with food; 'eighteen to twenty partridges in one dish, twelve or fifteen chickens in another', as the Duc de Luynes informs us. Plates and

514

514

515

514. Gadrooned oval basin, faience painted in blue camaieu with touches of red. Rouen; about 1710–20. Diam. 17¾ in. (45 cm.). The decoration of radiating lambrequins is combined here with an exotic scene in the style known as 'Sino-Dutch', themselves free adaptations of the K'ang Hsi models. Musée National de Céramique, Sèvres.

515. Rectangular table-tray, faience painted in high-temperature polychrome with touches of red. Rouen; about 1740. L. 20¼ in. (51·5 cm.). This considerable size implies great technical skill. A classical bear-hunting

scene has a rich rococo framework of shells, palms, scrolls curved and counter-curved from which spring garlands and flowering stems. On the left, the decorative rendering of the spiral shell is known as a 'vignot' (periwinkle), often found in the local clay used by Rouen potters. Louvre, Paris.

516. Heavenly globe in faience with high-temperature polychrome decoration. Rouen, Pierre Chapelle factory; 1725. Ht. 59 in. (1·50 m.). This huge sphere bears the words: 'Rouen 1725, painted by Pierre Chapelle' plus an inscription indicating that

it was made according to the method of the Rouen scientist, Hacquet, who had just published his system of astronomy. It is known that at this date Pierre Chapelle was working at the Lecocq de Villeray factory. The celestial globe and its counterpart the terrestrial sphere rest on a high pedestal formed of four brackets supported by recumbent lions. Between them are allegorical figures representing the Four Elements and the Four Seasons, painted in a subtle colour-range dominated by blue. Musée des Beaux-Arts et de la Céramique, Rouen.

dishes were accompanied by innumerable accessories for the table:
519 ice-pails were much in favour, salt-cellars, dredgers for powdered sugar, then the only sort known, boxes for the spices which were considered a precious commodity, and so on. Faience was used for a variety of objects, such as tobacco-graters for the considerable quantities of snuff taken in the 18th century, boxes for soap, and cisterns which were intended to be hung above their basins on the
515 wall. There were also table-trays, and monumental ornaments such
516 as the well-known globes, signed by Pierre Chapelle, in the Rouen Museum, the busts of the *Seasons* in the Louvre, or that of *Apollo* in the Victoria and Albert Museum.

The apogee of 'Chinese' Rouen faience comes between 1720 and
517 1750, when the name of Guillibaud spelt out or else the monogram 'GB' is often found underneath skilful versions of Chinese *famille verte* porcelain of the K'ang Hsi period. About 1740, Rouen adopted the rococo style, and shells and garlands of naturalistic flowers framed pictures with amorous or pastoral subjects, which reflect contemporary painting and the work of Watteau and Boucher. Chinese motifs were Europeanised in the popular decoration 'with
518 cornucopias and carnations' ('à la corne et aux œillets'). Towards 1775, when Rouen faience was going out of fashion, some skilful manufacturers by the name of Levavasseur were to adopt the new methods of enamel decoration, and to rival porcelain and the faience of Marseilles and Strasbourg.

The influence of Rouen spread throughout France, and is to be found from the Paris area (Paris and Saint-Cloud) and Brittany (Rennes, Quimper), to the Charente (La Rochelle, Saintes, Angoulême) and the centre of the country (Moulins). It is particularly noticeable in the north of France: Dominique Pellevé, from Rouen, is mentioned in 1737 as director of the factory that the lord of Sinceny (Aisne) had set up in his castle, and the Rouen
519 decorators of Sinceny excelled in painting Chinese scenes. The
520 founders of the first factory in Lille, Féburier and Bossut, had come from Tournai in 1696; their faience was of a high quality and, with the fineness of its body and the purity of its glaze, is related to the tin-glazed wares of Delft; but it is in the main decorated with the 516

radiating lambrequins of Rouen. Lille, like Rouen, turned to polychrome and to the Chinese taste, and produced picturesque statuettes in the manner of those in soft-paste porcelain, and later, charming rococo models. Saint-Omer must also be mentioned, for Lévesque of Rouen was director of a factory there from 1751; the skilled faience-makers of the Fauquez family came from Belgium to Saint-Amand-les-Eaux, where their art was handed down from father to son between 1718 and 1793; they specialised in making delicate faience decorated with floral and lace patterns in white on a pearl-grey glaze of a characteristically northern charm.

About 1710 there came into general use a completely different style of decoration, inspired by the ornamental engravers, in particular by Jean Bérain, both father and son, who were also, as 'dessinateurs du Cabinet du Roi', the official Court designers providing designs for theatrical costume and décor for Louis XIV. The décor Bérain, which revived the grotesques of the Renaissance and with its light fantasy made them truly French, was extremely popular.

A new era in the history of the Moustiers factory opened in 1738, when Joseph Olerys took his brother-in-law, Jean-Baptiste Laugier,

technique. From the factory of Madeleine Héraud and her son, Louis Leroy, situated since 1709 in the Bourgade Saint-Lazare, come the very beautiful pieces of faience, in which the rayonnant style of Rouen and Chinese grotesques are treated with great originality in a harmonious range of high-temperature colours, heightened with red.

Joseph Fauchier, who had been in charge of production in Madeleine Héraud's factory from 1711 to 1725, set up in business on his own account and later built a large factory in the Place du Pentagone, a vast estate in which his noisy troop of young apprentices, aged between twelve and sixteen years, were lodged, supervised, fed at the master's table, and even clothed. Among the earliest works by Joseph Fauchier himself are the large sculptures, signed and dated 1725, which he made for the church of his native village, Peyruis, and which are now in the Sèvres Museum. He died in 1751, leaving all his possessions to his nephew, Joseph, who was to prove himself worthy of the task of continuing his work. The Fauchiers are generally accepted as creators of naturalistic flowers painted in high-temperature colours, with roses in manganese-

517. Dish in faience with high-temperature polychrome decoration, touched with red. Rouen, Guillibaud factory; about 1728. Diam. 13¾ in. (35 cm.). The dish is signed in full: 'Guillibeaux'. On it are the arms of the duke of Montmorency-Luxemburg, and it belongs to a service which he was no doubt given by the town of Rouen on the occasion of his nomination as governor of Normandy in 1728. The 'Chinese style' has here supplanted the style rayonnant; the wide chequer-work border dotted with flowers is a simplified version of those on Chinese famille verte porcelain. Louvre, Paris.

518. Dish, faience painted in high-temperature polychrome with touches of red. Rouen; about 1750. Diam. 15 in. (38 cm.). The 'décor à la corne' or cornucopia theme of decoration (here a double cornucopia) is one of the most popular of those used at Rouen. From the horn of plenty with its curling tip issue brown branches covered with red and blue carnations, still faintly reminiscent of the East. A frieze of small arches emphasises the moulded rim. Musée des Arts Décoratifs, Paris.

519. Ice-pail in faience with high-temperature polychrome decoration. Sinceny; about 1750. Ht. 7½ in. (19 cm.). This is a good example of the Chinese decorations of Sinceny, which show water-scenes with fishing or hunting in the foreground. This type is called 'à la jonque' ('junk-style'), after the Chinese flat-bottomed boats—'junks'. Notice the tuft of tall reeds and the water-lilies with their broad leaves. The rather pale colour-range includes a lemon-yellow peculiar to Sinceny. Musée des Arts Décoratifs, Paris.

517

518

519

into partnership. The monogram mark 'OL' is attributed to them. Joseph Olerys had come back from Spain, where he had been in charge of the factory of Alcora, bringing with him the fashion for polychrome decoration. Since table-services of faience were beginning to be used by all classes of society, designs for them were created—garlands, medallions, little figures, grotesques said to be inspired by the engravings of Callot, 'potato flowers', flags, and so on. The range of high-temperature colours, is dominated by a more or less orange-toned yellow and the decoration is sometimes entirely in monochrome yellow or green, or more rarely mauve. Part of this output, and some of the large plaques, may be attributed to the factory set up in 1749 by Olerys' former workmen, Fouque and Pelloquin. Another faience-maker, Gaspard Féraud, between 1779 and 1792 attempted to resuscitate the high-temperature style of decoration, whereas the Ferrat brothers owed their success, on the contrary, to the adoption of new methods of firing (p. 188).

In Marseilles master faience-makers adhered to the traditional

purple (for lack of red) on a white or yellow glaze; this decoration is typical of French faience in the second half of the 18th century.

The faience of Montpellier is related to that of Moustiers and Marseilles. Archives and some rare signed pieces reveal the existence, scattered along the valleys of the Rhône and the Garonne, and in Provence, of small factories whose output must have been considerable: Lyons, where Joseph Comue from Moustiers settled in 1733; Varage, Aubagne, Taverne, La Tour d'Aigues; Bordeaux, where Hustin enlisted the aid of some faience-makers from Montpellier in 1712; Samadet, which was known for its monochrome-green wares; Toulouse and many others, for faience in France was an essentially provincial art.

In the 18th century the numerous factories in Nevers (see p. 177) only survived by making enormous quantities of faience for everyday use. The items of 'talking faience' (faiences parlantes), bearing long satirical or humorous inscriptions, were ornaments for middle-class sideboards; items of 'patronymic faience' (faiences patronymiques),

520

522

521

523

524

520. Plate of faience with high-temperature polychrome decoration with touches of red. Lille; 1767. Diam. 9⅞ in. (25 cm.). Mark, an escutcheon bearing the word, 'Lille', with the date above. Several specimens of these plates are known which display a ribbon supported by two Cupids, with the name of Maître Daligne, no doubt the recipient of the service. It is the prototype of a delicately floreated rococo style, painted in a soft palette. Musée National de Céramique, Sèvres.

521. Fountain in the form of a dolphin, in faience with high-temperature decoration of *bianco-sopra-bianco* and blue on a pearl-grey ground. Saint-Amand-les-Eaux, Fauquez factory, about 1760. Ht. 21⅜ in. (55 cm.). Mark, interlacing double 'f's. The decoration of opaque white on a ground of tinted tin-glaze, reminiscent of the Italian *bianco-sopra-bianco* of the Renaissance, met with great success throughout northern Europe. The Fauquez wares reveal a remarkable feeling for plasticity. Musée National de Céramique, Sèvres.

522. Large dish, faience painted in blue. Moustiers, Clérissy factory; about 1710. Diam. 23 in. (58·5 cm.). The mythological panel in the centre of this dish is set in an extensive framework of wiry scrollwork inhabited by terms and figures, the whole in the style associated with the Court designer Jean Bérain. The border of diaper panels and scrollwork, although faintly resembling those used at Rouen, is nevertheless very characteristic of the southern factory. British Museum, London.

523. Bowl in faience with high-temperature polychrome decoration. Moustiers, Olerys and Laugier factory; about 1740. Diam 10¼ in. (25·7 cm.). Mark, 'OL' in monogram, and 'P'. One of the finest examples of garland and medallion decoration. The pictorial designs or miniatures are painted with great delicacy in a subtle and harmonious palette of colours dominated by a shade of orange-yellow. Victoria and Albert Museum, London.

524. Scalloped oblong dish in faience with high-temperature polychrome decoration. Moustiers, Olerys and Laugier factory; about 1750–60. L. 14¼ in. (36 cm.). Mark, monogram 'OL'. Decoration of grotesques, painted in green and orange touched with purple. The small fantasy figures are set on terraces framed by tufts of flowers which have been erroneously identified as potato-flowers. This decoration was copied by all the factories in the south of France. Louvre, Paris.

with the picture of the patron saint of the recipient, commemorated events of family life such as births and weddings. Later there appeared faience of a revolutionary character, summarily decorated with emblems and mottos that mirror the political fluctuations of the day. It was imitated in all the little factories of the Auxerrois and Yonne valley until well on into the 19th century.

Strasbourg played the initial role in the technical transformation which took place in the French faience industry towards the middle of the 18th century. This involved a change from decoration painted directly on the raw glaze and then fired at a high temperature (*grand feu*), to enamel decoration on a glaze previously fired, the colours then being fired on to the glaze at a lower temperature (*petit feu*). The new method, borrowed from porcelain manufacture, came from Germany.

The history of Strasbourg faience is linked to the history of the Hannongs, whose factory, the only one in the town, was handed down from father to son for three generations. Charles-François Hannong was from 1710 director of a factory producing clay pipes, and in 1721 he began to make faience with a German potter, Carl Heinrich Wackenfeld. In 1724 he set up a second factory in

Haguenau, the district where he obtained his clay.

At first the Hannongs adopted the *style rayonnant* decoration of Rouen, painted in blue, and later with the four high-temperature colours. It was Paul Hannong who about 1740 introduced polychrome; and who from this date began research into decoration on the fired glaze. The fashion for *chinoiserie* followed, together with the fanciful 'India flowers' (*fleurs des Indes*). 529

The great period of Strasbourg faience opens in 1748 and 1749 with the arrival of German porcelain painters of the famous Löwenfinck family, who perfected muffle-firing and the use of bright reds derived from gold ('purple of Cassius'). They introduced the style of painting naturalistic 'German' flowers (the '*deutsche Blume*') which were soon to become the '*fleurs de Strasbourg*'. A 533 team of skilled modellers, among them Jean-Guillaume Lanz and Jean Louis, provided the models for large ornamental objects in 530 Baroque style, for figures which display a vivid realism, and for 534 those strange tureens in the shape of an animal or a vegetable which 531 were so much favoured for the decoration of sideboards or banqueting tables. About 1753 Paul Hannong introduced the use of the monogram 'P.H.' as a mark. By his death in 1760 the Strasbourg

525

526

527

528

529

525. Fountain, faience decorated in high-temperature polychrome with touches of red. Marseilles, Leroy factory; about 1750. Ht. 13⅜ in. (34 cm.). Leroy's Chinese grotesque design is original, by virtue both of its animated figures and of its strangely exotic vegetation, in which star-shaped flowers hatched in red constantly appear. Leroy's red contrasts with a subtle blue which melts into the shiny tin-glaze, with touches of yellow. Musée Cantini, Marseilles.

526. Dish, faience painted in yellow monochrome. Marseilles, probably Fauchier factory; about 1750. L. 14⅛ in. (36 cm.). This dish, although exhibiting a typical baroque silver-shape, is painted wholly in the rococo taste, with its borders of asymmetrical curves and panels of diaper, and the central design with its reminiscences of Lancret or other such designers of *galanteries*. Louvre, Paris.

527. Statue of St Roche as a pilgrim, accompanied by his dog; white faience with touches of blue. Marseilles, Joseph Fauchier factory; 1725. Ht. 16½ in. (42 cm.). The back of this figure bears the explicit inscription: *'donnée par moi Joseph Fauchier Jan 1725.'*. It originates from the village church of Peyruis, Fauchier's birthplace; broadly modelled beneath the fine white tin-glaze, it is a truly sculptural work. Musée National de Céramique, Sèvres.

528. Salad-bowl with scalloped rim, faience with high-temperature polychrome decoration. Nevers; 1751. Diam. 13 in. (33 cm.). This bowl reproduces the satirical subject, *The Tree of Love*, popularised by the Epinal pictures. Three women attempt to saw through the trunk of the tree where their lovers have taken refuge, while three others, with a ladder, a rope, or by offering gifts are urging them down. Pieces of this type are referred to as *faiences parlantes* because of the long explanatory inscriptions. Musée National de Céramique, Sèvres.

529. Octagonal tray of faience painted in high-temperature colours. Strasbourg; Paul Hannong factory; 1744–48. L. 17¼ in. (43·7 cm.). Ht. 12¾ in. (32·3 cm.). The scene of Chinese smokers and drinkers gathered on a terrace is painted in the usual range of high-temperature colours; some, however, have been applied in a second firing at a lower temperature. Thus this fine and exceptional piece shows in its heterogenous technique the first partial attempts at *petit feu* firing. Musée des Arts Décoratifs, Strasbourg.

faience works had reached their artistic apogee.

After two years of disastrous administration by his younger brother, Joseph Hannong took over the management of the Strasbourg and Haguenau factories, which now entered a new and brilliant phase. Joseph Hannong, who was a great industrial leader and social light, greatly enlarged the factory and organised its output systematically. It was to some extent codified in the *Prix Marchand*, a descriptive catalogue printed in 1771, in which the numbers correspond to those which appear on the objects themselves, together with the new monogram 'J.H.'. Taste in form and decoration improved under French influence, which henceforward predominated, and the delicate and naturalistic flower-painting was given a new richness and freedom. Simpler bouquets continued to be painted, however, in flat tones surrounded by an outline (*chatironné*), as the *fleurs des Indes* had been hitherto, and an original 'Chinese' model was created.

The landscapes painted by the Anstett brothers of Strasbourg, who had worked there since Paul Hannong's time, must also be mentioned, as must the plain white faience heightened with gold which was also produced.

However, in spite of the enormous success of his faience, Joseph Hannong was ruined by his attempts to make porcelain. In 1779 the death of his patron, the old Cardinal de Rohan-Guéménée, was a fatal blow for the great faience-manufacturer, who was imprisoned for debt and declared bankrupt in 1781. He took refuge in Germany, where he died in poverty at the beginning of the 19th century.

Under Strasbourg's influence other factories had been opened in Alsace and in Lorraine. In Niderviller, near Sarrebourg, the faience works were the extravagant diversion of those cultured aristocrats the Baron de Beyerlé and his wife, herself a painter and poet, who had acquired the estate in 1748. They had enticed workers away from Hannong, among them François-Antoine Anstett, who was director of their factory from 1754 onwards. Beyerlé's faience, which is marked 'NB', is known for the elegance of its forms, inspired by silversmith's work, and for its decoration of flowers or landscapes painted in a range of delicate shades. Under the Comte de Custine, who purchased the estate in 1770, the mark was changed to a double 'C'; landscapes in pink monochrome, and a curious *trompe-l'œil* decoration of an engraving pinned on a ground of grained wood, were very popular. Niderviller, moreover, produced a range of the

532

535 most perfect little figures in faience which rival those in Meissen porcelain. Most of the moulds for them were made by Paul-Louis Cyfflé, sculptor to Stanislas Leczinsky, and by his pupil from Lunéville, Lemire.

The three Lorraine factories of Niderviller, Lunéville and Saint Clément (which from 1772 onwards had as its director Mique, Marie-Antoinette's architect) adopted the Louis XVI style, and by using the fine Lorraine clay (*terre de Lorraine*) produced a hybrid ceramic material resembling the hard English creamware, known in France as '*faience fine*' (see p. 280), which was just beginning its period of great popularity. The small factory of Les Islettes, near Verdun, on the other hand, continued to make the traditional popular faience until well into the 19th century.

In the second half of the 18th century the faience-manufacturers of Marseilles produced both high-temperature and enamelled wares with equal mastery. The first experiments with enamelled decoration
536 were probably made shortly after the middle of the century in the factory of Pierrette Caudelot, the famous Veuve Perrin (mark: 'VP') whose business associate was Honoré Savy. The latter, who set up business on his own account in 1764, managed to find commercial outlets by exporting to places as far away as the countries of the
537 Orient. In 1759 Gaspard Robert founded a well-known factory, his

delicate faience being influenced by the porcelain which he was also making at the time. One of his apprentices, Antoine Bonnefoy, in his turn rented a faience works in 1777, and several other craftsmen worked in Marseilles, all producing the wares currently in fashion. They treated the most varied subjects all with the same southern verve—fanciful *chinoiseries*; flowers in loose sprays painted with a fresh naturalism on the white or yellow glaze of exuberant rococo tureens; picturesque trophies with fish, shells and all the fruits of the 536 sea, mingled with fishing tackle and evocative of Marseilles, the sea port. On some plates and tureens is to be found a reflection of contemporary painting: an amorous scene from Watteau, Boucher, 537 or Lancret, a sea-port from Joseph Vernet, or ruins in a park inspired by the compositions of Hubert Robert.·

The influence of Marseilles spread across France to overlap with that of Strasbourg. Some products, as for example those of the factories of Aprey (Haute Marne) and of Meillonas (Ain), can claim kinship with both centres; enamel-painting was introduced in both by a painter of Swiss origin, Protais Pidoux, in 1760 and 1763 respectively. The Aprey factory is known above all for its decorations of birds and of flowers, and for its grounds with striped 538 pink ribbons imitating Louis XVI silks.

A separate paragraph must be reserved for the factory of Sceaux,

530

531

532

533

530. Hanging wall-clock with applied decoration in faience with polychrome enamel *petit feu* decoration. Strasbourg, Paul Hannong factory; about 1750–55. Ht. 44 in. (1·12 m.). The model for this wall-clock, exuberantly rococo in style and surmounted by an allegorical figure of Father Time armed with his scythe, is by Jean-Guillaume Lanz. Strasbourg faience is here competing with Meissen porcelain in its use of brilliant *petit feu* reds and greens. Louvre, Paris.

531. Tureen in the shape of a boar's head on a dish of vine leaves, in faience with polychrome enamel painting. Strasbourg, Paul Hannong factory; about 1755. Ht. 7⅞ in. (20 cm.). L. 11⅜ in. (29 cm.). Mark, monogram 'PH'. One of the favourite Strasbourg models, by the sculptor J.-Guillaume Lanz. This boar's head with its naturalistic painting, is represented with a strange fidelity, even down to the details of the fur and the eyes. Musée des Arts Décoratifs, Strasbourg.

532. 'Silver-shape' plate in faience with polychrome enamel decoration. Strasbourg, Joseph Hannong factory; about 1770. Diam. 9½ in. (24 cm.). Mark, monogram 'JH'. The usual type of 'Chinese decoration' henceforth loses any Oriental feeling. A Chinese fisherman is sitting on a bank of rocks and shrubbery, which are painted rather coarsely in green and brown. Musée National de Céramique, Sèvres.

533. Oblong dish in faience with polychrome manual decoration. Strasbourg, Joseph Hannong factory; about 1770. L. 21⅜ in. (55 cm.). Mark, monogram 'JH'. This dish displays a magnificent decoration of '*fleurs fines*' or '*fleurs de Strasbourg*'. The effect of the bouquet, cleverly arranged around two full-blown roses and a tulip, is lightened by flowers in clusters. The petals are delicately modelled by fine, graded brush-strokes, and the green leaves are shaded in black. All trace of outlining or of contours has vanished. Musée des Arts Décoratifs, Strasbourg.

534

534. Hunting-group, with figures of a huntsman blowing his horn, a boar and a hound, in faience with polychrome enamel *petit feu* decoration. Strasbourg, Paul Hannong factory; about 1750–55. Ht. (of huntsman) 8¼ in. (21 cm.); (of boar) 7⅛ in. (18 cm.). These popular figures, endowed with a lively realism, made up complete groups for use as table-centres at hunt banquets. The models for them were almost all supplied by J.-Guillaume Lanz. Musée des Arts Décoratifs, Strasbourg.

535. Figure group *Gardener and Companion*, in faience with polychrome enamel decoration. Niderviller; Custine factory; about 1770–75.

Ht. 8½ in.; 8¾ in. (21·6 cm.; 22·2 cm.). Each figure is shown standing on a little patch of earth sown with flowers, together with the tools of his trade. Notice the mannered postures and the striped costumes. The dainty Niderviller figures were sometimes produced in '*terre de Lorraine*' or in porcelain. Victoria and Albert Museum, London.

535 a)

b)

situated in the Paris region on the estate of the Duchesse du Maine, by virtue of its precocious technical skill. The able chemist, Jacques Chapelle, appointed in 1748, had discovered a formula for soft-paste porcelain; but, frustrated by the Sèvres privilege, he had to be content with making faience of an exceptionally good quality, known as *'faience japonnée'* ('Japanned faience'), which closely imitated Sèvres. In 1763 he rented his factory to two of his fellow-workers, Jacques Jullien and Symphorien Jacques, who concentrated on the manufacture of porcelain (see p. 236) Richard Glot, who acquired the factory in 1772, obtained the patronage of the Duc de Penthièvre, the nephew of the Duchesse du Maine, who ordered table-services for all his châteaux. Sceaux, which enticed artists away from Sèvres, had in its service fine painters of flowers, fruits, landscapes, as well as specialists in the painting of animals and birds. Its wares, which are of an extraordinary technical virtuosity, were the last flowering of the art of faience in France. At the end of the 18th century, faience passed out of fashion and was reduced to the status of everyday ware, forced from its position of eminence by the hard wares, by porcelain for luxurious use on the one hand and on the other by the practical and economic English creamware, of which the importation was considerably encouraged by a commercial treaty in 1786.

536. Dish with reeded rim painted in *petit feu* enamel colours. Marseilles, Veuve Perrin factory; about 1760. Diam. 18¼ in. (46·5 cm.). The decoration of piled up fish, crustaceans, shells and fishing tackle is naturalistically rendered in a wide range of colours. It is so realistic that specialists claim to be able to identify the various species of Mediterranean fish. Local fruits—pears and blackcurrants—are often, as here, found with the Marseilles 'sea trophy'. Musée des Arts Décoratifs, Paris.

537. Plate, faience painted in *petit feu* enamel colours. Marseilles, attributed to Gaspard Robert; about 1775. Diam. 9⅝ in. (24·5 cm.). The seascape, painted like a subtle watercolour and framed by two slender green sprays, takes up the entire base of the plate, whilst blossoming branches intertwine with graceful emblems, sprays and bullrushes, embellish the rim. Musée National de Céramique, Sèvres.

538. Plate in faience with polychrome enamel decoration. Aprey, Haute Marne; about 1775. Diam. 9½ in. (24 cm.). This charming decoration of perched birds painted in soft shades of blue and pink with a few touches of yellow, rivals the painting on Sèvres and Sceaux porcelain, but the bands of pink ribbons with picot edging which adorn the rim of the plate, are an original motif created by Aprey. It is inspired by the fashionable Louis XVI silks. Musée des Arts Décoratifs, Paris.

539. Dish in faience with polychrome enamel decoration. Sceaux, Jacques Chapelle factory; 1753. Diam. 16½ in. (42 cm.). On the back, an escutcheon displaying three fleurs-de-lis is accompanied by the inscription '*à Sceaux 1753*'. The small bouquets of this early period are still a bit stiff, and the colour-range of Sceaux is not so bright as that of Strasbourg, the red verging on brown. The odd border of naturalistic cabbage leaves was often employed by the Sceaux factory. Musée des Arts Décoratifs, Paris.

540. Tureen and stand in faience with polychrome enamel decoration. Sceaux, Richard Glot factory; about 1780. Ht. 9⅞ in. (25 cm.). L. 18⅛ in. (46 cm.). Mark, 'OP'. The fantastic birds, like long-feathered waders, are featured here grouped in a landscape of a composition common to Sceaux, which employed notable animal painters. Louvre, Paris.

541. Vase with cover, maiolica painted in cobalt-blue monochrome. Lodi, factory of A. M. Capelletti; about 1730. Ht. 33½ in. (85 cm.). The elaborately moulded shape seems to have been inspired by an original in metal. In each ornamental zone are conventionalised branches and leaves inspired by the French '*à broderie*' or '*rayonnant*' style of the Rouen factories. Museo Civico, Lodi.

Italy

In the 18th century, developments in maiolica in the various regions of Italy were influenced by the advent of the Rococo style and by the adoption of new materials, such as porcelain, and later on, cream-coloured earthenware, all of which contributed to the evolution of shapes and ornaments during this period.

The first half of the century was characterised by decoration in the traditional *grand feu* technique, and the second half by the diffusion of the *petit feu* technique (see p. 188) special to porcelain, which found its way into almost all the Italian workshops.

At Faenza the acquisition in 1693 by Count Annibale Carlo Ferniani of the factory which had once belonged to Francesco Vicchi and later to the Cavina Grossi Tonducci families, gave renewed vigour to the work there. The traditional white wares were given new life by graceful motifs in blue, which later developed into floral and geometrical themes of Dutch, French and German inspiration. Side by side with the monochrome repertory was another in polychrome, with a basic floral decoration and *rocaille* cartouches enclosing little figurative scenes. The potato-flower motif, which had conquered France and the rest of Europe, is used here both in monochrome blue or yellow, and in full polychrome. The same is true of the *castelletto* ('little castle') theme, the '*rovine*' ('ruins') and later on in the second half of the century in the two *chinoiseries*

designs called 'the carnation' or '*porcellana nuova*' ('new porcelain'), and the 'little house' or '*alla chinese*' (*sic*) ('Chinese-style') motif. Exchanges of craftsmen with other ceramic centres, such as Milan and Bassano, facilitated the absorption and exchange of styles, while the intake of French and German artists enriched their repertory.

Among the French craftsmen a certain Nicola Letourneau of Nevers is recorded in 1739. In 1740 after a stay in Faenza he moved to Doccia, to work with the Ginori. Here in a factory best known for its porcelain, he established the decorative style of the maiolica department, which had a much more considerable and continuous development in the 18th and 19th centuries than is usually believed.

Still in the *grand feu* technique were the developments in Lodi and Milan, Pesaro and Urbino, which were linked to some extent by the transfer and exchange of craftsmen and renewed their vitality by establishing connections with centres in the Veneto with their refinements of glaze-quality and decorative themes; and with those of Liguria and the Abruzzi, already established in the previous century, and of the Campagna and Sicily.

The *petit feu* came into Italy from France, Holland and Germany in the second half of the century. Many workshops adopted this technique which aimed at protecting maiolica from the threat of the new product, porcelain, and so far they have not all been identified.

541

542

543

542. Table-centre, maiolica painted in cobalt-blue, green, yellow and purple. Faenza, Ferniani factory; first half 18th century. L. 18⅞ in. (48 cm.). Tiny buildings (*a paesino*) and potato-flowers are typical of this factory in cobalt-blue or yellow, and sometimes in polychrome. The potato-flower had become a fashionable motif in Europe due to the increasing importation of the precious tuber from South America. Museo Internazionale delle Ceramiche, Faenza.

543. Plate, with waved rim, maiolica painted in cobalt-blue, yellow, green and brown. Turin, Rossetti factory; 1750–60. Diam. 16⅞ in. (43 cm.). In the centre, a landscape within a *rocaille* panel; around the rim naturalistic flowers and cartouches with lattice-work. The Rossetti had a workshop at Lodi too, which explains some affinities with products of that centre, especially those painted in blue monochrome. Museo Civico, Turin.

544

544. Ribbed cover for dish, maiolica painted in cobalt-blue, yellow, green and brown. Nove di Bassano, Antonibon factory; about 1750. Diam. 13 in. (33 cm.). *Chinoiserie* designs of a seated figure with a dove on his right hand, the usual 'little bridge' and flowers, probably dating from the time when Pasquale Antonibon was directing the factory. Museo Internazionale delle Ceramiche, Faenza.

545

546

545. Round plate, maiolica painted in cobalt-blue and red. Milan, factory of (?)F. Clerici; about 1770. Diam. 8⅞ in. (22·5 cm.). Decoration inspired by Far-Eastern models, with pagodas, trees and tiny figures, called in Milan '*Carabiniere*'. Museo Poldi Pezzoli, Milan.

546. Interior of an Apothecary's shop (*La Bottega dello Speziale*), by Pietro Longhi (1702–86). Venetian; about 1750–60. The drug-jars shown on the shelves in Longhi's apothecary's shop closely resemble surviving examples which have been reasonably attributed to Nove, near Bassano, in Venetian territory. The spouted jars were for 'syrups', the handleless jars (*albarelli*) for dry medicaments. Gallerie dell' Accademia, Venice.

In the North the Venetian factory of Geminiano Cozzi, like that of the Ginori, manufactured maiolica as well as porcelain. This, and the workshop at Nove di Bassano of the Antonibon, who were also drawn to porcelain, were contemporary with the Lodi-Milan group, with the Ferretti family engaged in the former centres and the Clerici, Rubati and Confalonieri in the latter. A floral decoration based on the rose was the main element of *petit feu* decoration at nearly all the European factories, and was therefore adopted in Italy too. It was used in Milan together with figure subjects and imitations of patterns in German porcelain, just as French porcelain was imitated at Nove—and above all there were *chinoiseries*, which even sometimes succeeded in being faithful copies of Chinese and Japanese originals.

From Lodi the maiolica-artists, Callegari and Casali, left to go to Pesaro; they not only executed *grand feu* decorations on a miniature scale, but also a vast amount of finely executed *petit feu* work in a variety of patterns and qualities.

At Faenza *petit feu* production flourished—mainly the work of members of the Benini family, who ran the Ferniani factory with the collaboration of Filippo Comerio, and of Piani and Pani. The Faenza wares were decorated with monochrome and polychrome

flowers, *chinoiseries*, little figures and ruins in black and green (in which Comerio excelled), and scattered roses.

With the Ginori, at Doccia, *petit feu* decoration on maiolica was produced side by side with *grand feu* ware, as at Bologna in the workshop of the Viennese Finck; at Savona in the workshop of Boselli, who often signed himself Boselly in the French style; at Castelli in that of Gesualdo Fuina; at Naples in that of the Giustiniani; and at Palermo. All Italy had its outburst of *petit feu*, an outburst which seemed to die, as in France, with the end of the century, and as a result of the upheavals following the French revolution.

Together with cream-coloured earthenware—the latest product from England (see p. 228)—the 19th century brought *grand feu* decoration back into favour. It was used on shapes which were inspired in the first place by classical models unearthed in excavations and then by the Renaissance and post-Renaissance forms which gave new values to *istoriato* and Raphaellesque styles. In the second half of the century expertise reached its height, in the imitation of easel paintings, portraits, landscapes and scenes of great pictorial effect, especially in the work of artists from Faenza, with Achille Farina at their head.

547

548

549

550

547. Holy water stoup for bedroom, maiolica with decoration in relief, painted in green, cobalt-blue and yellow. Caltagirone; 18th century. Ht. 15¾ in. (39 cm.). A modelled piece which illustrates the elaboration of the holy water stoups throughout southern Italy. Museo Internazionale delle Ceramiche, Faenza.

548. Vase and cover, maiolica painted in polychrome on one side only. Naples, Lorenzo Sallandra; 1748. Ht. 18⅞ in. (48 cm.). Biblical scene of the Angel appearing to Abraham. The foreground inscription reads: 'Laurentius Sallandra Pinxit An(n)o D(omi)ni 1748'. Sallandra, working with Donato Massa and P. Criscuolo, is the artist of the maiolica decorations of the convent of S. Chiara at Naples. Museo Internazionale delle Ceramiche, Faenza.

549. Stand for holding ink, pounce and pens, maiolica decorated in enamel-colours. Pesaro, factory of Callegari and Casali; about 1763. Max. diam. 10⅝ in. (27 cm.). Sprays of roses frequently appeared with *petit feu* decoration in factories in Italy as in France, Germany and elsewhere. Filippo Callegari and Antonio Casali came to Pesaro from Lodi in 1763 bringing with them this special technique learnt in the Ferretti factory. Musei Civici, Pesaro.

550. Large moulded maiolica plate, painted in black and green enamels. Faenza, Ferniani factory; 1775–80. Diam. 12¾ in. (32·5 cm.). The figure of a man is seen beside rocks and shrubs. On the rim are tiny leaves picked out in purplish red. The decoration is typical of the Milanese painter, Filippo Comerio, who from 1775–80 worked in Faenza also on maiolica, in the factory of the Counts Ferniani and in that which his brothers-in-law, the Benini brothers, directed for a year, 1777–78, in partnership with Tomaso Ragazzini. Museo Internazionale delle Ceramiche, Faenza.

Holland

Throughout the first half of the 18th century production flourished. Chinese designs were as popular as ever. Some very fine replicas were made of K'ang Hsi plates, illustrating scenes from Chinese romances. But the first impetus was soon lost and much of the work became repetitive. One can trace the gradual estrangement as each successive 'edition' becomes clumsier, the painters less and less aware of what they are copying, until in the latter half of the century, and in the Lambeth versions, a vase will have become a blob and a flight of steps a series of meaningless lines. Much more lively were the native scenes of trades or fisheries, gallant company or emblems of the months. Baroque patterns of lambrequins replaced Chinese borders. Gradually the Rococo made itself felt. Shepherds and shepherdesses, lacking French elegance, flirted against an unmistakably Dutch landscape background. Yet the best, including many biblical illustrations, remained of high quality in colour and in potting. To the established factories were added *De Starre* (*The Star*), *De Klaeuw* (*The Claw*), *Het Bijltje* (*The Axe*) whose pictorial marks

are obvious—*De Lampetkan* (*The Ewer*), with its initials 'LPK', and many others.

In the 1770s came frequent loyal tributes to the House of Orange. Yet by then the main production was of bold plates with trees (laden with patriotic oranges) or decorated with a fan of peacock's feathers or a goddess of plenty. All factories made these plates, which from 1760 onwards often had a bright yellow edge, simulating the gold of Meissen and Ch'ien Lung. The heyday was passed in mid-century. By the end of it, Delft had succumbed to the ever-increasing competition from German porcelain and English creamware. Only two Delft factories survived into the 19th century.

The polychrome wares of Delft soon developed away from the maiolica of their beginnings. To the basic blue and manganese were added a dull green, a bright but not translucent yellow and an iron red, quite distinct from that used by Hoppesteyn. This red was an innovation in European pottery and made its appearance around 1710 simultaneously in Delft and Rouen. The cross-fertilisation between these two towns was always strong, most of all in matters of decoration. At first, production was confined to very close reproductions of oriental wares, especially those known in Europe as 'Imari', copying the Japanese dishes made at Arita. The grandest

551

553

551

552

553

554

551. One of a pair of fruit-dishes, tin-glazed earthenware painted in blue. Delft, the *Greek 'A'* factory of Jan Theunis Dextra; about 1760. W. 12⅛ in. (31 cm.). Mark 'A/D 12', in blue. The decoration of this dish shows how late the traditional Ming blue-and-white designs survived at Delft. Rijksmuseum, Amsterdam.

552. Teapot, tin-glazed earthenware painted in yellow on a black ground. Delft, probably, the *Metal Pot* factory of Lambertus van Eenhoorn; about 1720. Ht. 5¼ in. (13·3 cm.). Mark: '5' in yellow' The black-ground Delft pottery was probably made in imitation of Oriental lacquer, and the Van Eenhoorn factory was one of the first to undertake its manufacture. Fitzwilliam Museum, Cambridge.

553. Covered vase, tin-glazed earthenware painted in blue. Delft; the *Axe* factory; about 1760. Ht. 13½ in. (34·5 cm.). Mark, an axe, in blue. This vase, one of a set, although of a traditional Delft shape, betrays the rococo influence in its finial and in the scrolled cartouches which frame the main theme of the decoration. Fitzwilliam Museum, Cambridge.

554. Figure of a cock, tin-glazed earthenware painted in polychrome enamels, the base painted black. Delft, the *Greek 'A'* factory of the Kocks family; about 1720. Ht. 7¾ in. (20 cm.). Monogram 'APK' in red enamel. The *Greek 'A'* factory was especially prolific in enamelled wares. The black enamel on this figure is characteristic of the second phase, when the colour was applied over the white glaze and not direct on to the 'biscuit'. Musées Royaux d'Art et d'Histoire, Brussels.

objects of all were tall reeded vases covered with an embroidery of small leaves and flowers, in which a rusty brown predominates. The type was known as '*cachemire*' and was made from the late 17th century by all the factories mentioned above, except 'SVE'. These high-temperature colours were used throughout the 18th century at Delft, more often to enliven the border and scrollwork on a plate or vase mainly decorated in blue. But soon after 1750, in emulation of the brilliance of German porcelain, more ambitious colours were added in a second firing in the mufflekiln. Gold was added to the oriental designs, producing the 'brocaded Imari' style. Delicate table wares and sets of small vases were produced as well as plates and soon an attempt was made to reproduce the colouring of the *famille verte*. A light blue, a warm red, clear yellow and a transparent coppery green were enhanced by the brilliant white of the underlying glaze. After 1760 appear the toys and trinkets, sleighs and butter dishes decorated with *fêtes galantes* or the oriental harbour scenes in the style of the Meissen artist, Herold (see p. 220). Charming though these are, one feels that the native strength of Delft is becoming exhausted.

Marginal to all this polychrome ware are the important coloured grounds, of which the most sought after is the black. The earlier black-ground pieces are glazed all over on a red clay body and then painted with olive-green and yellow, to which are added minute touches of bright blue, red and green. The intention seems to have been to reproduce lacquer, at that time highly fashionable in

furniture, the yellow and green being meant to suggest gold. A few of these early pieces are marked 'SVE'.

The second and slightly commoner type of black ground is painted over the white tin-glaze, leaving white reserves to be decorated in enamel colours. These mostly bear the mark of the 'APK' factory, which also produced most polychrome enamelled wares.

Many other coloured grounds were made during the 18th century. Though not all are marked, the evidence suggests that each shade was the speciality of one particular factory. Chocolate grounds are mostly marked 'CK', olive-green 'LVD'. Later comes the brilliant turquoise—decorated in manganese and yellow, marked 'IHL'. The *Peacock* (*Paauw*) factory produced convincing imitations of the *bleu persan* of Nevers, also imitated at Lambeth, with white drawing on an opaque, chalky and very thick dark blue enamel. Yet closely though these colours followed Nevers, the shapes were uncompromisingly Dutch.

In the middle years of the 18th century polychrome was also applied to figures, again in emulation of Meissen. When one considers the manual skills required to produce the elaborate and many-spouted tulip vases which were such a feature of earlier years at Delft, one is surprised at how clumsy and provincial the more ambitious of these later figures are. It is only in the simpler butter-boxes etc., with lids fashioned as fruit, sitting plovers or grebes, coiled pike and the like, that Delft figure work attains to any

552

554

555

artistic vigour. These were made at most of the later factories such as *The Axe* and *The Ewer* ('LPK').

Of the other towns in Holland where tin-glazed wares were made, Haarlem was one of the earliest. The decoration was well drawn in a peculiarly brilliant light cobalt, very like that of Frankfurt. But the industry was soon eclipsed by that of Delft. Of the potteries in Friesland that at Makkum was the most productive. Here as at Harlingen and Bolsward, innumerable tiles were made and also heavy chargers adorned with fruit or clumsy biblical scenes and tin-glazed only on the front, the back being covered with a lead glaze. Makkum itself produced more competently drawn Bible stories, marriage and alphabet plates. The body is coarser than that

of Delft, the potting heavier and the blue inkier. The factory at Arnhem produced, in the third quarter of the century, rococo wares of the highest quality. They can compete with the *faience fine* of France or Scandinavia or anywhere in Europe, but stand apart from the tin-glazed wares for which Holland—and above all Delft—had become famous. Those wares, made in every shape from bird cages to violins, and for every purpose, from wall-covering and pompous ornament to the humblest household article, were imitated throughout Europe, though seldom equalled and never surpassed. They form, collectively, an imposing landmark, not only in the history of ceramic art, but in that of the European taste in the age of the Baroque.

555. Three butter-dishes, tin-glazed earthenware painted in polychrome. Delft; mid-18th century. Ht. (of left-hand piece) 5½ in. (14·5 cm.). These butter-dishes exemplify the rococo taste for utilitarian vessels in the disguise of natural phenomena: (left) a

crested grebe, marked *'De Bijl'* for the factory, *The Axe;* (centre) a cover formed of pears and plums, marked 'LPK' for the *Ewer* factory (*De Lampetkan*); (right) a cock, marked *'Ipkan'*, also the *Ewer* factory.
Fitzwilliam Museum, Cambridge.

556. Dish, tin-glazed earthenware painted in blue. Dutch (Makkum); late 18th century. Diam. 14 in. (35·5 cm.). The broad painting and coarse blue are typical of Makkum, the most productive of all the Friesian factories. Victoria and Albert Museum, London.

557. Bird-cage, tin-glazed earthenware painted in blue. Delft; the *Greek 'A'* factory of P. van Marksveld; 1785–1811. Ht. 13½ in. (34·4 cm.). Mark, 'A.PVMV'. This is an unusually attractive example of the more fanciful objects made after the golden age of Delft was over. The front and back are curtained like the proscenium of a private theatre, and all four sides are decorated with rococo landscapes of French inspiration. Haags Gemeentemuseum, The Hague.

555

556

557

Germany and Central Europe

From the early 18th century onwards, faience factories were established all over Germany in ever-increasing numbers, thanks to the splitting-up of the Empire into major and minor principalities whose rulers, following the ideas of Colbert or else their own love of pomp, strove to be self-supporting. The earlier types of vessel continued to be made, but there was now a demand for tea, coffee and chocolate services, since the fashion for these beverages, which dates back to the second half of the 17th century, quickly became wide-spread. The cylindrical mug ('*Walzenkrug*') became the drinking-vessel of the people, and beer-mugs have been of this shape ever since. The repertory of shapes was enriched by tureens, basins and boxes in the shape of vegetables, fruit, tortoises, game-birds and domestic fowl. The discovery of porcelain by Johann Friedrich Böttger at Meissen (during the year 1708–9), forced the owners of faience factories in the 1740s to reproduce on their wares the fashionable porcelain designs, and they were in fact well able to hold their own against the more expensive ware, however much finer it may have been from the ceramic point of view. It was only the introduction of cheap creamware from England, and the continental imitations of it, which drove faience from the market towards the end of the century.

Nevertheless, the influence of Delft lasted until well into the first half of the century. In some factories—Hanau, Ansbach, Künersberg, Fulda and Cassel—a simplified Rouen design was introduced as a novelty. As in all the various applied arts in Europe, ornamental engravings played an important part in ceramic decoration. Numerous engravers, of whom the most versatile was Paul Decker, had been 'translating' Bérain's designs into a German idiom, the result being the 'leaf- and strapwork' (*Laub- und Bandelwerk*) style, which was succeeded towards the end of the century by the '*rocaille*' ornament after designs by Nilson, Habermann, Wachsmuth, Baumgartner, Stockmann and others. From about 1737 the adaptation of the 'India flowers' (*Indianische Blumen*) of the Meissen factory by the painters at Bayreuth, Ansbach, Fulda and Höchst produced masterpieces of faience decoration. The activities of Adam Friedrich von Löwenfinck who had fled from Meissen in 1736 had much to do with this trend. Soon afterwards he brought to the faience manufactory at Strasbourg-Hagenau the 'German flowers' of Meissen porcelain. There these were subtly adapted to the requirements of tin-glazed earthenware and, as 'Strasbourg flowers', influenced the German factories in their turn, and those of the nearby regions. There was also some influence from the Du Paquier porcelain

558

558. Dish, painted in blue. Nuremberg, about 1755. Marked 'GK' with three blue dots, for Georg Friedrich Kordenbusch. Diam. 13⅜ in. (34 cm.). Kordenbusch, the most skilled of the Nuremberg factory-decorators, derived the central motif from an engraving by J. E. Nilson, of Augsburg, called *L'Invention d'une cascade*. A repetition of this design by Kordenbusch himself and a Brunswick wall-sconce testify to the popularity of the design. Museum für Kunst und Gewerbe, Hamburg.

559. Plate, painted in blue. Bayreuth, 1734? Marked 'BK/C' in blue, for Johann Clarner. Diam. 8⅝ in. (22 cm.). The arms of East Friesland and Brandenburg allude to the wedding in 1734 of Karl Edzard, the last Count of East Friesland, and Sophie Wilhelmine, daughter of the Margrave Georg Friedrich of Brandenburg-Culmbach, their monograms appearing below the arms. The plate is part of a service, pieces of which are preserved in various museums. Museum für Kunst und Gewerbe, Hamburg.

560. Covered vase, painted in two shades of green, yellow, blue, manganese-purple and dark iron-red. Ansbach, about 1730. Ht. 11 in. (28 cm.). This vase, which together with five others forms a *garniture*, is decorated with the so-called 'Carp pattern', with peonies, fish and birds in reserved panels, separated by broad vertical areas filled with flower-sprays on a green ground. The green of the Ansbach *'famille verte'* was never rivalled at any other factory and was kept a close secret. Kunstindustrimuseet, Copenhagen.

560

559

561

562 b)

factory at Vienna, the designs of which were tastefully adapted by Joseph Philipp Dannhöfer. A common pattern about the middle of the century was a floral decoration akin to the 'Strasbourg flowers' but painted in the four high-temperature colours rather than in overglaze enamels; these bouquets of large flowers are to be seen at their finest on the Flörsheim wares. If these were the main decorative trends—to be discussed further below—there were original creations and individual fancies in abundance, so that 18th-century German faience gives an impression of extraordinary diversity.

At the beginning of the century the centre of production shifted from the Lower Main region to Franconia, where three important factories were established—Nuremberg (1712), Ansbach (1708–10) and Bayreuth (1714). The influence of Delft is to be seen in the early products of the Nuremberg factory, particularly in a series of large portrait plaques depicting the owners of the factory, Christof Marx, Johann Conrad Romedi and Johann Jacob Mayer. A Nuremberg style soon evolved, with painting in blue against a white, bluish or grey ground. A typical motif is a curling flower-stem with finely

560

559

561. Tea-tray, painted in overglaze enamel-colours. Abtsbessingen, Germany; 1744–47. W. 24¼ in. (61·5 cm.). This tray, painted by J. Ph. Dannhöfer, exemplifies three current decorative trends. That he had earlier worked in the Du Paquier porcelain factory at Vienna, is shown by the 'leaf- and strapwork' ('*Laub- und Bandelwerk*') border round the rim. The finely painted landscape with ruins is reminiscent of the Nuremberg outside

decorators (*Hausmaler*). 'German flowers' fill the remaining spaces. Museum für Kunsthandwerk, Frankfurt.

562 a). Covered tureen, painted in overglaze enamels—purple, iron-red, green, yellow, blue and brown. Proskau, Germany; period of Count Leopold, 1763–69. W. 8¼ in. (21 cm.). The knob of the cover is in the form of a pear on a stalk. The fluted sides are decorated with flower-sprays and scattered flowers. Karl Schafft Collection, Darmstadt.

562 b). Tureen, painted in overglaze enamel-colours. Flörsheim, Germany; 1765–70. L. 13 in. (33 cm.). The 'Strasbourg flowers', perhaps most beautifully painted at Flörsheim, had become a recurrent theme in German factories. Here they are in purple, blue, green, yellow, iron-red and black. Staatliche Kunstsammlungen, Kassel.

561

562 a)

b)

563

564

563. Cylindrical tankard ('*Walzenkrug*'), painted in overglaze enamel colours. Künersberg, Germany; about 1750. Ht. 7⅛ in. (18 cm.). The palette includes green, purple, iron-red, blue, yellow and black. The Künersberg hunting scenes were taken over by Marcus Hünerwadel's factory in Lenzburg (Switzerland). Similar scenes are also found occasionally on the faience made at Holitsch (Hungary). Bayerisches Nationalmuseum, Munich.

564. Madonna and child. Schrezheim, Germany; 1771. From the doorway of a house in the main street, Wolframeschenbach. Incised mark 'JMM' (sculptor and modeller, Johann Martinus Mutschele). Ht. (without base) 45¼ in. (115 cm.). The figure is unpainted, but the hem of the dress, the plastic decoration of the globe and the edges of the *rocaille* on the base were once gilt; the yellow ground for this gilding still survives. A far more elaborate work by this Bamberg sculptor is a faience altar in St Anthony's Chapel, Schrezheim. Leo Levi Collection, Lucerne.

drawn feathery leaves and stylised flowers which, combined in various ways with acanthus leaves and other decorative elements, cover the surface of jugs, dishes, tureens and plates. The same pattern is found at Bayreuth and a derivation of it at Ansbach. Often the centre of the dishes is decorated with a basket of fruit and birds. Religious and mythological scenes are distinguishable from the Frankfurt 'story-plates' (*Historyteller*) of the 17th century by the hatched drawing in the manner of an engraving. The palette consists of a thin green, a warm yellow and pale manganese-purple. The landscapes are reminiscent of the outside decorators (*Hausmaler*), while the boldly drawn monograms recall the Nuremberg writing-masters. A more 'rococo' style was introduced in about 1750 with finely painted hunting scenes and scenes of social life.

In Ansbach the Hanau *Vögelesdekor* appears more frequently than at Nuremberg (see p. 182). A speciality of this factory were the vases in Imari style, the red being added over the glaze in unfired pigment, as is the case with a series of figures of the goddess, Kuan-Yin. The most notable Ansbach products are the plates and vases in the Chinese *famille verte* style (*die grüne Familie*). From 1737 to 1740 Adam Friedrich von Löwenfinck was at work in Ansbach following a brief stay in Bayreuth after leaving Meissen. At both factories he left traces of his decorative style on the jugs and services painted in the 'India' taste. Peculiar to the Bayreuth factory are the tea and coffee services, jugs and plates imitating Böttger's Meissen stoneware. This is a substitute ware painted with Chinese figures in gold or silver on the yellow, pale brown or dark brown ground. At the same time J. P. Dannhöfer was producing his delightful landscapes in overglaze enamels framed with 'leaf- and strapwork' ('*Laub- und Bandelwerk*') in the manner evolved by Du Paquier at Vienna. The same sort of strapwork combined with coats-of-arms is also found on blue-painted wares. In the Thuringian factories—Dorotheenthal (1707), Rudolstadt (1720), Bernburg (1725) and Abtsbessingen, (1739)—this style of decoration was especially popular. At

Abtsbessingen, between 1744 and 1747, Dannhöfer produced some of his finest works.

In the 1740s a decisive influence was exerted by Fulda (founded in 1741) and Höchst (founded in 1746), both places lying on the borders of what is today Hessen. In 1741 Adam Friedrich von Löwenfinck arrived in Fulda, and it is to him that the factory owes its superb vases with Chinese decoration. At Höchst, where he was technical director from 1746 until his departure to Strasbourg-Hagenau in 1749, Löwenfinck produced further works, some of them in collaboration with his talented wife, Maria Seraphia (*née* Schick). Whereas the majority of useful wares made at Fulda are painted in a blue which sometimes has the violet tone of copying-ink, at Höchst a polychrome palette was preferred and the decorative motifs include 'grotesques' as well as 'India' and 'German' flowers. At both factories Ignaz Hess, like Dannhöfer (who also worked at Höchst), decorated vases with attractive landscape panels, and at both factories remarkable figures were produced. At Fulda the Bohemian, Wenzel Neu, modelled the *Four Seasons*, which may be considered the finest of German faience figures. At Höchst, Gottfried Becker made a large number of faience animals, either as vessels or simply as figures. Flörsheim, also in Hesse, is another factory worthy of mention, above all for its attractive interpretation of the 'Strasbourg flowers'; this manner of painting also appears in high-temperature colours, with manganese and yellow predominating, but with some blue and green, and drawing in black. A similar decoration is found at Hanau, Hannoversch-Münden, Magdeburg and other factories.

Among the faience factories of Bavarian Schwabia and Württemberg, Crailsheim, then linked politically with Ansbach, was outstanding for its glowing high-temperature palette. One particular group of wares exhibits a favourite use of yellow. Besides influence from Ansbach, Strasbourg influence is discernible in the Oriental and 'German' flowers also found on Crailsheim faience. A

561

561

558

560

561

559

561

565

562 b)

565. Tureen in the form of a turkey-cock, painted in overglaze enamel-colours. Höchst, Germany; 1748–53. Marked with the six-spoked wheel and the painter's mark 'I.Z.' (sic) for Johann Zeschinger, in black. Ht. 17¼ in. (44 cm.). L. 19⅜ in. (49 cm.). The model is by Gottfried Becker. The feathers are coloured black and grey, the head blue, manganese-purple and yellow-brown. The centre of the stand is decorated with green foliage, the rim with a wreath of downy feathers. The turkey-cock, of which two examples are known, clearly shows the influence of J. J. Kändler's models at Meissen: Becker worked for Kändler before coming to Höchst. Museum für Kunsthandwerk, Frankfurt.

566. Small teapot, painted in high-temperature colours. Durlach, Germany; about 1760. Ht. 4 in. (10 cm.). The lively and amusingly painted Chinese figures of the Durlach factory came into fashion about 1760. Manganese-purple, pale blue and yellow, with drawing in black, are combined with celadon-green on this small teapot. Badisches Landesmuseum, Karlsruhe.

567. Dish, painted in overglaze enamel-colours. Marcus Hünerwadel's factory, Lenzburg, Switzerland; about 1765. Thickly applied colours standing out in relief and a palette of green, blue, yellow and violet are typical of early Hünerwadel pieces. Lenzburg was greatly influenced by foreign factories, but the recurring motif of a single flower may be said to be characteristically Swiss. Private collection, Zürich.

568. Coffee-pot, painted with flowers in purple, green, yellow, blue and orange. Holitsch, Hungary; 1750–60. There are many versions of the service to which this piece belongs, but all have rocaille relief on the sides. The floral decoration is more reminiscent of Höchst than of Strasbourg. In 1754 Johann Buchwald was working in Holitsch as 'repairer and arcanist'. He had worked in Höchst and Fulda, and later contributed much to faience manufacture in North Germany and Sweden. Moravské Museum v Brně, Brno, Czechoslovakia.

preference for high-temperature colours also links the other factories of the region—Ottingen-Schrattenhofen, Donauwörth, Goggingen, Friedberg, Schrezheim and Göppingen, together with Ludwigsburg, where, in the second half of the century, the decorators went over to enamel colours under the influence of Ludwigsburg porcelain. Künersberg, near Memmingen, occupies a place apart. Herr Jacob Küner, Knight of Künersberg, who was a banker in Vienna, encouraged his decorators to paint in the style of Du Paquier porcelain. Hörold's chinoiserie figures also appear on Künersberg faience, together with delicate variations of the Meissen gold lace-work, landscapes, flowers, birds and lively hunting-scenes. At Schrezheim, the Bamberg sculptor, Johann Martinus Mutschele, triumphed over the technical difficulties of the material to produce large and imposing figures.

In nearby Switzerland the wares made by Marcus Hünerwadel's factory in Lenzburg (founded in 1762) occasionally echo those of Künersberg, other patterns being derived from Strasbourg, Niderviller and Marseilles. A decoration of flowers and storks painted in manganese-purple shows some relationship with the factory of the Pidoux brothers at Vuadens (Canton Freiburg). This decoration was taken over by the Zürich factory, whose products in general imitate the porcelain made there. Another later factory was founded in Lenzburg by Jakob Frey, who subsequently went to Beromünster. His most notable productions were stoves in 'rococo' or Louis XVI style which were a continuation of the great Swiss tradition of stove-making. Andreas Dolder, who was active in both Beromünster and Lucerne, was influenced by the Lunéville and St Clement wares.

Among the faience factories in Baden mention may be made of Durlach, near Mosbach, founded in 1723. Its most notable products were those decorated with charming and lively Chinese figures, painted at first in the fashionable celadon-green and manganese, but later in a characteristic palette of celadon-green, cobalt-blue and orange-yellow. At Durlach the painters made skilful use of various shades of black to paint their designs.

There is not much to be said about the Rhenish factories, and even Saxony, which had faience factories in Dresden and Hubertusburg, does not occupy in the history of faience the important place it

563
564

567

566

569

570

569. Covered vase, with painted decoration. Belvedere factory, Warsaw; about 1775. Marked 'W' in green. Ht. 17¾ in. (45 cm.). The rockwork, peonies and birds of paradise are in a clear blue, two shades of rich green, yellow, purple, iron-red, brown and gold: the outlines and details being carefully drawn in brown. Museum für Kunst und Gewerbe, Hamburg.

570. *Pot-pourri* vase, with pierced decoration and painting in high-temperature colours. Hannoversch-Münden, Germany; about 1760. The pierced outer wall is detached from the inner lining except at the top and bottom. The intersections of the lattice are decorated with small forget-me-nots. At Magdeburg similar floral decoration, in high-temperature colours, is found, but also figures and landscapes. Kestner Museum, Hanover.

occupies in the development of stoneware and porcelain. At Proskau, in Silesia, there was a productive factory whose best period was between 1764 and 1769 under Count Leopold. The decoration there was derived mainly from Strasbourg, as was the case at Holitsch in Upper Hungary, where there was a factory founded in 1743 under the patronage of Francis of Lorraine, the consort of the Empress Maria-Theresa. At Holitsch there was also some influence from the local 'Habaner ware' (see p. 163) and from the later Castelli maiolica. Both the Belvedere factory at Warsaw, founded by Stanislas Poniatowski with the help of Baron Schütter, and the factory of Count Michael Oginsky at Telechany favoured '*chinoiserie*' decoration, but the Warsaw factory also shows the direct influence of Meissen porcelain. Some pieces decorated in Imari style and with Turkish inscriptions come from a service made in Warsaw in 1776 for Sultan Abdul Hamid I.

Among the North German factories there are a number which deserve mention. Most of these were in Lower Saxony, Anhalt, Brandenburg, and Pomerania, and in Schleswig-Holstein. At Brunswick the factory of the Chely family showed far more originality and invention than did either the other factory there which, founded in 1707 under the Prince's patronage, had since then had a succession of managers, or the factory at Wrisbergholzen, in the region of Hanover. A speciality of the factory at Hannoversch-Münden, founded in 1737, were the vases, tureens and basins, painted in the four high-temperature colours and having double walls, the outer one being pierced in reticulated patterns. This kind of work was copied at Magdeburg and Anhalt-Zerbst, and at Rheinsberg in Brandenburg. All four factories produced excellent floral decoration. Again at Brunswick, but also at Hannoversch-Münden and at Jever—in East Friesland but at that time part of the Principality of Zerbst—some attractive figures were made, which deserve mention here.

Scandinavia

The concept of 'Scandinavian faience', although not usually admitted by ceramic literature, is a real and defensible one. The faience of Schleswig-Holstein is normally grouped with German faience, with which admittedly it has many strong connexions. In the 18th century, however, Schleswig-Holstein was effectively part of the Danish kingdom, and the faience-factories of the two Duchies enjoyed privileges stemming from this political dependence. Within the Scandinavian area, moreover, there was a constant interchange of work-people between factory and factory, so that, for instance, Johann Buchwald worked successively at the Swedish factories of Stralsund, Rörstrand and Marieberg, then at Eckernförde, Kiel and Stockelsdorff in Schleswig-Holstein; whilst Peter Hoffnagel, the founder of the Norwegian factory of Herrebøe, later went on to make faience at the Copenhagen factory of Østerbro, and the manager at Herrebøe, J. G. Kreibe, had worked at Schleswig and later went on to Mors. These close interconnexions are matched by the similarities between the wares produced in the whole area.

Large-scale trays for fitting into table-tops were made in Swedish, Danish, Norwegian and Schleswig-Holstein factories alike. Tiled stoves were a virtually universal product, a common answer to a common need in an area subject to bitter winters. The distinctive mitre-shaped bowl designed for drinking 'Bishop' (a kind of punch) began in Copenhagen, but spread to Schleswig-Holstein on the one hand and to Norway on the other. These affinities also extend to technical characteristics; the bright cobalt-blue found in so many of the 'Scandinavian' factories, for instance, is probably due to the presence at each of them of Johann Buchwald or his pupils.

Sweden

The making of faience in Northern Europe began with the arrival in Copenhagen in 1721 of a certain Johann Wolff. Wolff was a Holsteiner by birth, and had worked in the faience factory at

571

572

573

571. Jar and cover, tin-glazed earthenware painted in blue and *bianco-sopra-bianco*. Rörstrand; about 1760. Ht. 15¾ in. (40 cm.). Vases of this type in Sweden were called '*oppsatzpotter*' (garniture vases), and were made in sets of three or five. The example illustrated is decorated with a theme similar to J. E. Rehn's design for Rörstrand (cf. fig. 586). Rörstrand was one of the first factories in northern Europe to employ the *bianco-sopra-bianco* technique, and the background design on this jar is one much used at the factory. Nationalmuseum, Stockholm.

572. Tin-glazed tureen and cover, elaborately modelled in the rococo style and painted in high-temperature colours. Rörstrand; dated 1768. Ht. 9⅞ in. (25·1 cm.). The Scandinavian tin-glazed wares in general, and Rörstrand's in particular, were often very fully marked. This tureen bears the mark 'Rörstrand 22.10.68' and the stand which belongs with it is marked 'Rörstrand 3.10.68—LB', the initials being those of the hitherto unidentified painter. Nationalmuseum, Stockholm.

573. Design for a plate, probably by the Swedish artist, J. E. Rehn, for the Rörstrand factory, about 1750, but not known to have been executed. As industrial designer, employed by the Office of Manufactures to assist various branches of industry, particularly the textile industry, Jean Eric Rehn was sent more than once to France to keep in touch with developments. Returning in 1756, he brought with him samples of French faience for copying at Rörstrand. Nationalmuseum, Stockholm.

Nuremberg. He persuaded the Danish king to set up an experimental establishment for the making of 'Delft porcelain', and toward the end of 1722 a Company was formed and privileges granted for the setting up of a proper factory. Wolff, however, was clearly a difficult man and probably also defective in the technical knowledge to which he laid claim. Since only one piece of faience can reasonably certainly be associated with Wolff's stay in Copenhagen, the history of the Store Kongensgade factory will be dealt with below, in the context of the other Danish factories. By September, 1725, he had arrived in Stockholm to set up a faience factory there, taking with him A. N. Ferdinand, one of the best workmen, and the factory's supply of the expensive cobalt pigment.

In 1726 a Company was formed in Stockholm to finance a faience factory at Rörstrand, near Stockholm, and Wolff took up residence there by the end of May, 1727. Foreign work-people were called in, and in August the first firing took place in the presence of the King himself. Wolff soon proved as unsatisfactory as he had done in Copenhagen and was dismissed, to be succeeded briefly by the notorious Christoph Conrad Hunger and A. N. Ferdinand (1733–39). The factory's greatest success, however, was to be achieved under the general managership of Elias Magnus Ingman (later ennobled with the name Nordenstolpe), with Anders Fahlström as technical manager. The factory's production and the numbers of its staff rose steadily. In 1754 there were no fewer than seventeen painters and fifty-three painters' apprentices working at Rörstrand. Fahlström's death in 1760, however, and the foundation

574. Sauce- or creamboat, silver by the Stockholm silversmith Lars Boye (active 1762–84). This sauceboat reveals clearly the origin of the faience design illustrated in fig. 575, a shape often used at Marieberg. Nationalmuseum, Stockholm.

575. Sauceboat in plain white faience, following a silver model. Marieberg; dated 1766. Ht. 4 in. (10·2 cm.). Much of the Marieberg faience was left in the white, to show off the fine quality of the thick unctuous glaze. This shape of sauceboat is

copied faithfully from a silver model apparently peculiar to Sweden. Victoria and Albert Museum, London.

574

575

576

577

578. Tin-glazed butter-box in the form of a
reclining shepherd, painted in enamel-colours.
Marieberg; dated 1770. Ht. 5⅛ in. (13·1 cm.).
Pierre Berthevin, manager of the Marieberg
factory from 1766, is recorded as having
modelled a butter-box with a reclining
shepherd. This model seems to have replaced
a cruder version of Ehrenreich's period. It is
distinctly reminiscent of a type of porcelain
snuff-box made at the Mennecy factory,
where Berthevin had previously worked.
Röhsska Konstslöjdmuseet, Göteborg.

577. Tin-glazed *pot-pourri* vase, partly
printed and partly painted in black. Marieberg;
about 1770. Ht. 10⅜ in. (26·1 cm.).
Vases of this type (the present example lacks
its cover) were made to contain *pot-pourri*, to
combat the smells of a generally malodorous
age. Many other Northern factories also made
vases of this general type, but the peculiar
formation of the base as a staircase is typical
of Marieberg. The animal at the foot of the
stairs is more normally a rabbit.
Victoria and Albert Museum, London.

578. Tin-glazed vase painted in enamel-
colours. Stralsund, Sweden; dated 1768.
Ht. 10⅛ in. (25·7 cm.). Vases of this exact
shape with the same decorative scheme are
commonly found at Marieberg, from which
factory Stralsund derived much of its staff
during its greatest period. The vase has on the
base the usual elaborate Stralsund mark made
up of compartments, the central one
containing the device of the city of Stralsund,
stylised, with 'E' below, for 'Ehrenreich'.
Victoria and Albert Museum, London.

of a rival factory at Marieberg in 1758, were both serious blows to
the Rörstrand concern. Undaunted, Nordenstolpe undertook
extensive rebuilding, and by the mid-1760s both production and
staff stood at their height. In the late 1760s, however, a variety of
factors, culminating in Nordenstolpe's death in 1773, seriously
affected Rörstrand. By 1771, moreover, the factory had begun to
make cream-coloured earthenware, and from this date until about
1797, when it was finally discontinued, faience manufacture
progressively declined in favour of creamware.

The earliest Rörstrand faience was painted in blue only, normally
in an adapted '*style rayonnant*' of a sort found in many contemporary
German factories, but also occasionally with figure subjects. By 1745
a method of painting over a tinted glaze in a white pigment ('*bianco-
sopra-bianco*') had evolved at Rörstrand, and a high-temperature
polychrome painting of soft blue, manganese-purple, yellow and
green, with black for outlines, is equally characteristic of the period.
Enamel-painting was successfully introduced in 1758, and the
Rörstrand palette was remarkable for strong yellows and greens
normally dominating the rose-purple and blue. In another field of
decoration, however, Rörstrand was an innovator, the painter,
Anders Stenman, introducing there before the end of 1767 the
transfer-printing process.

Rörstrand made a wide range of faience shapes, copying at the
beginning Delft and the German factories, but soon extending the

573

571

572

578

repertory to include characteristically Scandinavian forms, such as the large tea-table trays, or sauceboats of a form otherwise peculiar to Swedish silver. Rörstrand is perhaps the most Swedish of the Swedish faience-manufactories, but Marieberg, too, despite its emulation of Strasbourg and its fashionable styles, displays many national characteristics.

The Marieberg factory was founded by Johann Ludwig Eberhard Ehrenreich, a German who had come to Sweden in 1747 as Court Dentist to King Frederick I. In 1758 he approached the Government for support in erecting a factory, but was advised to seek private capital backing. The estate of Marieberg, on Kungsholmen in Stockholm, was acquired in the same year 'for the establishment of a manufacture of true porcelain'. Work began in April, 1759, but a month later the factory building was burnt down. The only piece attributable to this period is one porcelain bowl. When, undeterred, Ehrenreich raised fresh money and rebuilt his factory later that year, the whole emphasis was laid on faience-manufacture. Marieberg was from the outset conceived on a grand scale, and by 1760 it surpassed Rörstrand in the number of its personnel. Financial failure drove Ehrenreich from the factory, but under his directorship much had been achieved. The Marieberg glaze was finer and whiter than Rörstrand's, and was seen to great effect on a range of finely modelled wares left in the white. Marieberg's success in the modelling branch being due to the employment of the best artists available, including some employed at the Royal Palace. Even more noteworthy was a palette of enamel-colours which rivalled that of Strasbourg in range and brilliance; effective use was also made of an intense blue monochrome.

Ehrenreich was succeeded by Pierre Berthevin, a French modeller from Mennecy. Berthevin further improved the factory's enamel-colours, and gradually introduced the quieter and more subdued palette of the neo-classical mode in place of Ehrenreich's rococo style. Transfer-printing in black was also introduced, far surpassing Rörstrand's in quality. Berthevin left the factory in 1769, and under his successor, Henrik Sten, faience was gradually abandoned in favour of cream-coloured earthenware. The factory was sold to the Rörstrand owners in 1782.

Other faience factories of less importance were set up at one time and another in Sweden, but none rivalled Marieberg or Rörstrand, whose styles they copied and from which in fact most of their

work-people came. Gustavsberg-Vänge, not far from Upsale, although founded in 1755, produced very little identifiable faience before the arrival in 1786 of Henrik Sten, previously manager at Marieberg. A few plates display a stencilled version of one of Rörstrand's patterns, but this factory probably soon went over to making creamware. A factory at Sölvesborg, near Kristianstad, founded in 1773 by Baron Gabriel Sparre, produced faience of variable quality, the best of it closely reminiscent of Marieberg, where in fact its chief painter, Peter Åkermark, had learned his craft. In the earliest Sölvesborg wares, however, there are distinct reminiscences of Schleswig-Holstein faience, and this is even truer of a little factory at Pålsjö, north of Helsingborg, founded in 1770 by Michael Anders Cöster with work-people from various factories in Denmark and Schleswig-Holstein. The factory ceased production in 1774. Apart from these modest concerns, there were smaller workshops, many probably in Stockholm, producing tiles for stoves, made after the improved heat-saving design perfected by the architect, Carl Cronstedt, in 1767.

More important was the faience-factory at Stralsund, then a Swedish city. It was in production by 1757 under the technical management of Johann Buchwald, a typical wandering 'arcanist', with experience in the factories of Fulda, Höchst and Holitsch. Buchwald left for Rörstrand within the year and the factory struggled on until in 1766 it was leased to J. L. E. Ehrenreich, coming from Marieberg with some forty work-people from that factory and Rörstrand. The great period of Stralsund's activity now began, with the introduction of sophisticated Marieberg vessel-shapes and high-quality enamel-painting by such Marieberg painters as J. O. Frantzen and P. Åkermark, who were later at Sölvesborg. Notable Stralsund productions were enamel-painted table-trays and gigantic *pot-pourri* vases on elaborate bases formed of figures, inspired by those of Marieberg, but far outdoing them in elaboration and size. In the simpler wares a characteristic high-temperature palette of manganese-purple and green produced an effect of considerable charm.

A factory at Reval, in modern Esthonia, was started about 1775 by K. C. Fick, who came from Stralsund. The rather coarse-glazed wares are characterised by rococo modelling and painting in a strong green and a deep-toned yellow. The factory came to an end in 1792.

580

579. Tin-glazed punch-bowl in the form of a mitre, painted in blue. Store Kongensgade factory, Copenhagen. Ht. 13¾ in. (34·9 cm.). Bowls of this shape were used for drinking a type of punch called 'Bishop'. The pun needs no underlining. The mitre-shaped bowl was probably introduced for the jollifications of a religious society. The present example bears the inscription 'Prosperity to King and Country'. The shape was copied in a number of the Northern factories. Nationalmuseet, Copenhagen.

579

580 a), b). Tea-table with tray or tin-glazed earthenware painted in blue. Store Kongensgade factory, Copenhagen. Large faience trays for tea-tables were a speciality of many of the Northern factories. The form was probably first developed by the Store Kongensgade factory, although somewhat similar trays had been made at Rouen. The present example still retains its blue-painted wooden table. The tray itself is painted with family marriage arms. Kunstindustrimuseet, Copenhagen.

Denmark

That the Store Kongensgade factory in Copenhagen (briefly referred to above), quickly recovered from Johann Wolff's defection, was thanks mainly to the energy of the leading shareholder, Rasmus Aereboe. In 1727 a new manager, Johan Ernst Pfau, began a period of successful activity which lasted for twenty-two years until he came into conflict with the main shareholder, a brewer named Christian Gierløf whose manic temperament drove him not only to dismiss Pfau but to contest in the most extravagant fashion any infringement, imagined or real, of the factory's privilege of 1722. This privilege, renewed in 1752 for twenty years, conferred the monopoly of manufacturing 'Delft porcelain' (that is, faience) and forbade the import of blue-painted wares into Denmark. Gierløf tried to stop faience imports from Schleswig-Holstein, and more important, violently opposed the setting up by Peter Hoffnagel in 1763–64 of a factory at Østerbro, in Copenhagen itself. A series of law-suits terminated in 1769 with a judgement unfavourable to Gierløf, and the already moribund Store Kongensgade concern came to an end.

Throughout its working the Store Kongensgade factory almost exclusively used the blue colouring reserved to it by the 1722 privilege, an occasional variant being afforded by a powdered manganese-purple ground, usually on tankards and tiles. The earlier wares are characterised by simple shapes, circular or oblong with bevelled corners, and the blue decoration is an amalgam of the '*style rayonnant*' with the floral designs and diaper-borders of Chinese porcelain, both filtered through the styles of the Dutch and German factories. Larger objects occasionally display somewhat naively painted figures in a landscape with buildings. In mid-century Gierløf attempted to move with the times, introducing waved contours and rococo decorative styles. Characteristic Store Kongensgade forms, probably invented there, were the mitre-shaped 'Bishop' bowl and the great table-tops, at first deep and with bevelled corners, later shallower with rounded corners. A number of these were decorated with figure subjects after engravings, and with elaborate rococo border designs, by individual artists signing in full, which may perhaps signify that they were not the normal factory painters.

Christian VI of Denmark, as a contribution to his ambitious building-plans, felt the need of a factory which could make architectural accessories in faience and to this end in 1738 established the '*Blaataarn*' ('Blue Tower') factory near the Christiansberg Palace. At first manned by Germans, it was then, from 1740 onwards, effectively managed by A. N. Ferdinand from Rörstrand. At his death in 1749, he was succeeded by Heinrich Wolff from the Store Kongensgade concern. The *Blaataarn* products consisted mainly of white stoves, tiles, vases and plaques for architectural use, often decorated in relief, and covered with a glaze of indifferent quality. Occasionally the reliefs were gilt, less often picked out in colours. The factory was closed in 1754 and its effects and personnel transferred to a factory at Kastrup (Amager Island, Copenhagen) started in 1749 by the Court stone-mason, Jacob Fortling, as part of an industrial complex originally intended to supply the demands of his architectural work.

In 1755 Fortling was granted a privilege to make any sort of faience which did not infringe the Store Kongensgade monopoly, and Kastrup faience has been identified in a series of wares, usually bearing the mark 'F', characterised by the use of plastic decoration and enamel-painting, introduced by artists from Strasbourg. The Kastrup wares included not only large decorative vases and fashionable table-wares, but figures and groups, often of considerable size. Fortling died in 1761 and the Kastrup faience manufacture was replaced, probably in the 1770s, by the more fashionable creamware.

At Peter Hoffnagel's factory at Østerbro, already referred to, were probably made wares painted in the blue of which Gierløf complained, in manganese-purple, and less often in a combination of these colours. Their shapes and decoration reflect the styles current at Herrebøe and Schleswig, and the same may be said of a small factory founded in 1774 by Thomas Lund on the island of Mors and probably managed by J. G. Kreibe of Schleswig and Herrebøe (see p. 208). The Mors factory foundered in 1777 and ends the tale of faience-factories working in the Danish kingdom in the 18th century. Little need be said of the products of the early 19th-century factories at Gudumlund, Antvorskow and Hesbjerg, or those on the islands of Bornholm and Øland, for their output was in a clearly impoverished style marking the degeneration of faience into a peasant craft.

581. Tin-glazed earthenware dish, painted in high-temperature blue. Schleswig, Schleswig-Holstein; about 1755–8. L. 21½ in (54·5 cm.). This dish, the relief-border of which is reminiscent of silverware, is painted in high-temperature blue, unusual for Schleswig. Such a dish would not have been imported into the Danish Kingdom because of the Store Kongensgade monopoly. It bears the early mark 'S' for 'Schleswig' linked with 'O' and an artist's initial 'L' below, perhaps for Johann Leihamer, or a painter named Lohmann. Nationalmuseet, Copenhagen.

582. Basin for a wall-fountain, tin-glazed earthenware painted in enamel colours. Eckernförde, Schleswig-Holstein; dated 1768. W. 16¾ in. (42·5 cm.). The mark O/E/B Director/AL 68 stands for 'Otte/Eckernförde/Buchwald Director/Abraham Leihamer (pinxit) 1768'. This basin shows the wild *rococo* modelling characteristic of the Eckernförde factory. The wall-fountain has a finial of a dolphin with tail in the air, spouting water out of its mouth. Such wall-fountains and basins were used for perfunctory ablutions in the 18th century. Museum für Kunst und Gewerbe, Hamburg.

583. Tin-glazed earthenware dish, painted in enamel colours. Kastrup, Denmark; about 1760. L. 19⅞ in. (50·5 cm.). This dish, as is so often the case with 18th-century faience, clearly betrays its origin in a silver shape. It is decorated with a style of flower-painting which is unmistakably that of the Fortling factory, the 'F' mark of which is painted on the underside of the base. Nationalmuseet, Copenhagen.

581

582

583

Schleswig-Holstein

The Store Kongensgade factory had been established in Copenhagen for thirty-two years before the first application was made for the founding of a factory in the two Duchies—at Schleswig in 1754. This initiative came from J. C. L. von Lücke, a characteristically unscrupulous 'arcanist'. A Royal Privilege was conceded in 1755 granting tax-exemptions, customs-concessions on imports into the Danish kingdom and a prohibition on pottery imported into Schleswig-Holstein. Von Lücke was dismissed in 1756 and succeeded as manager by J. G. Kreibe and then Asbjörn Erichsen, previously of the Store Kongensgade factory. From 1758 until about 1800 the factory was owned and run by Johann Rambusch and his son F. V. Rambusch.

The Schleswig faience is characterised by a good-quality glaze and by a predilection for *rocaille* in both modelled and painted decoration. Although some enamel-painting was practised, the best Schleswig wares show a preference for a brownish manganese-purple high-temperature pigment, often tellingly combined with a greyish-green. Only a few blue-painted wares were made, because of the Store Kongensgade monopoly, and polychrome high-temperature wares are even rarer. The factory employed many good artists, pre-eminently Johann Leihamer, an accomplished figure-painter, who was to play an important part in the Schleswig-Holstein faience-industry.

When in 1758 J. Rambusch bought out the other Schleswig shareholders, one of them, Johann Nicolaus Otte, decided to start his own faience-factory on his estate of Criseby, near Eckernförde. By 1761 a privilege had been obtained, but Otte had already decided on a move to Eckernförde, probably completed by 1765. Financial difficulties, however, caused a decline from 1768 onwards.

The Criseby faience was of a simple character, with dishes and plates (but also tea-caddies, coffee-pots, etc.) of simple shapes painted in high-temperature blue or manganese. With the move to Eckernförde, however, coincided the arrival from Marieberg in 1765 (see p. 201) of Johann Buchwald. In 1767 Buchwald's daughter married Abraham Leihamer, son of Johann Leihamer and already a skilled faience-painter. Henceforth the destinies of this formidable team were linked together in their progression from one Schleswig-Holstein factory to another. With Buchwald's arrival, a marked change occurs in the Eckernförde style, with the introduction of enamel-painting and a strong emphasis on plastic decoration. This was characterised by a kind of barbaric wildness, much emphasised by the strong rose-purple and yellow commonly combined with iron-red, which seem to have been a speciality of Buchwald's. A limited range of figures was even produced. Fine painting was done (particularly on the large table-trays) by the two Leihamers and the flower-painters, G. F. Zopff of Stralsund and Johann August Jahn, who in 1768 succeeded Buchwald as manager. After this date enamel-painting appears to have yielded to decoration in high-temperature blue and manganese-purple only.

Possibly the most distinguished of all the Schleswig-Holstein faience-factories was that set up in the city of Kiel somewhat before 1763 by J. S. F. Tännich, a Saxon who had served in the great factories of Meissen, Strasbourg and Frankenthal, and himself founded small faience-factories in Wittmund and Jever (both in Oldenburg). Before Tännich's enterprise, there had already been three abortive factories in the city, only one of which left behind any trace—a simple marked tureen made at J. T. Kleffel's factory about 1763. Tännich's concern was under the direct patronage of the Duke of Holstein and its wares are initially amongst the most aristocratic produced in Northern Europe. By the aid of two Strasbourg painters, the brothers Rühl, and a fine enamel-palette on an unctuous glaze of uncommon purity, Tännich produced at Kiel wares rivalling those of Strasbourg itself, particularly in the painting of '*fleurs fines*'. Production expanded rapidly, but in 1766 the Grand-Ducal Government sold out to a private company, and by 1768 Tännich and the Rühl brothers had withdrawn, to be replaced by Johann Buchwald and the two Leihamers. The earlier palette was now replaced by Buchwald's more violent tones of rose-purple, blue and brilliant yellow, although the shapes remained virtually unchanged. These included a characteristic *pot-pourri* vase,

584

585

584. *Cachepot* of tin-glazed earthenware, painted in enamel colours. J. S. F. Tännich's factory, Kiel, Schleswig-Holstein; about 1765. Ht. 5½ in. (14 cm.). Flower-holders of this shape were produced in considerable numbers in the fourth Kiel factory. The present example is signed 'C', almost certainly for Christoph Christophersersen, an artist who specialised in 'India flowers' of the type with which this *cachepot* is decorated. Victoria and Albert Museum, London.

585. Tin-glazed earthenware dish, painted in enamel colours. J. S. F. Tännich's factory, Kiel, Schleswig-Holstein; about 1765. Diam. 15¼ in. (38.7 cm.). This large dish with its silver-inspired waved border, well demonstrates the heights which the best Kiel painting of '*fleurs fines*' could attain. It is signed by the painter, J. A. G. Adler, who specialised in this kind of work under both Tännich and Buchwald. Victoria and Albert Museum, London.

586. *Pot-pourri* vase, tin-glazed earthenware painted in enamel-colours. Stockelsdorff factory, Schleswig-Holstein; about 1771–4. Ht. 13 in. (33 cm.). This *pot-pourri* vase is modelled in a shape peculiar to the Stockelsdorff factory, and bears the mark 'Stff/B/AL', indicating that it was made between Buchwald's assumption of the management in 1771 and Abraham Leihamer's death in 1774. Victoria and Albert Museum, London.

586

587
584

588
587

590

table-trays, stoves, 'Bishop' bowls, wall-fountains and square *jardinières* with excellent painting by the Leihamers or by J. A. G. Adler, a flower-painter from Tännich's time. Financial difficulties now forced a decline in production and in 1771 Buchwald and his relations left. Their departure marked the end of Kiel's period of artistic importance, although the factory struggled on until 1787.

When Buchwald and the Leihamers left Kiel, they moved to Stockelsdorff, near Lübeck, where positions were waiting for them at a factory established by N. Lübbers to exploit a high-quality clay found on his estate. In 1776, however, Lübbers clashed with the powerful potters' guild in Lübeck, especially over the sale of stoves, and from this time onwards the factory seems to have been in difficulties. Apparently only one ambitious piece bears a date later than 1778. In 1786, Lübbers was offering the factory for sale, and production probably ceased about this time, Buchwald himself disappearing from the records after 1785.

There is a marked affinity between Stockelsdorff and Eckernförde which no doubt reflects Buchwald's influence. The painting was often of high quality, Abraham Leihamer (d. 1774) being succeeded by an able painter in C. T. F. Creutzfeld, and the flower-painters including J. A. G. Adler from Kiel and the competent D. N. O. Seritz. Stockeldorff's *pot-pourri* vases are strongly reminiscent of Eckernförde's, whilst the wall-fountains, table-centres and *bouquetières* somewhat resemble those of Kiel. The factory's chief glory, however, is its stoves, from the rococo examples with fanciful plastic decoration and figure-painting by A. Leihamer to the neo-classical forms surmounted by pyramids or ovoid vases and decorated by the more subdued painting of Creutzfeld.

With the closure of Stockesldorff the artistic interest of Schleswig-Holstein faience drops sharply. A factory at Rendsborg, founded in 1764, had made faience of a modest and derivative but not unattractive character, decorated mostly in high-temperature blue, but in 1772 it had gone over wholly to making cream-coloured earthenware. More lasting were a number of small factories at Kellinghusen, where faience of an unpretentious 'peasant' character and often considerable charm, continued to be made until well into the 19th century. A small factory also existed from at latest 1771

587

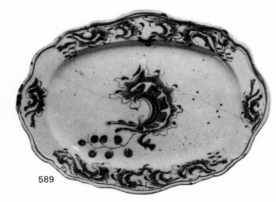

588

589

590

588. Table-tray in tin-glazed earthenware, painted in high-temperature blue. Stockelsdorff factory, Schleswig-Holstein; about 1775. L. 33⅛ in. (86 cm.). This large tray-top from a tea-table now lost is painted in blue by the painter, C. T. F. Creutzfeld, who succeeded Abraham Leihamer as the factory's main figure-painter. The tendrils of leaves and flowers are very characteristic of the Stockelsdorff factory. Schleswig-Holsteinisches Landesmuseum, Schleswig.

590. Dish of tin-glazed earthenware painted in high-temperature colours. Kellinghusen, Schleswig-Holstein; about 1830. Diam. 10¼ in. (26 cm.). In the early 19th century the Kellinghusen factories abandoned all pretensions to make fashionable wares, and the results, with their bold, rhythmical painting and bright colours, display all the virtues of an energetic peasant art. Victoria and Albert Museum, London.

587. Stove, of tin-glazed earthenware painted in enamel-colours. Stockelsdorff factory, Schleswig-Holstein; dated 1775. Ht. 9 ft. 3½ in. (2·83 m.). The characteristic Stockelsdorff stove had a fire-box in cast-iron, with a superstructure in faience. This example betrays the growth of the neo-classical movement in its urn-shaped upper member and in the general symmetry and sobriety of its modelling. On closer examination, however, a host of rococo details meet the eye, such as the opposed C-scrolls, the wanton tendrils of leaves, or the shell motifs on the central axis. The scene-painting is signed by J. A. G. Adler, previously of the Kiel factory. This stove was formerly in the possession of the Aschenburg family. St-Annen Museum, Lübeck.

589. Tin-glazed earthenware dish painted in high-temperature blue. Herrebøe, Norway; about 1765. L. 21 in. (53·3 cm.). The painting on Herrebøe faience displays the ultimate development of the rococo style, with a flickering quality peculiarly its own. It can be readily analysed in the alternating thick and thin strokes which outline the *rocailles* and in the quick nervous brushwork of the parallel strokes which form the centres of the designs. Vestlandske Kunstindustrimuseum, Bergen.

until the early years of the 19th century in the city of Altona, and stove-makers were active in Hamburg itself, Copenhagen and Lübeck throughout most of the 18th century. There were also small factories at Oldesloe, Itzehoe and Plön, but their productions, so far as they have been identified, were of little artistic significance.

Norway

In the 18th century, Norway formed part of the Danish kingdom and its industrial enterprises were to some extent controlled and encouraged from Copenhagen. When, therefore, Peter Hoffnagel (see p. 201 above) found on his estate at Herrebøe (near the modern Halden) a clay suitable for faience, he started a factory there, stated by him to have been in production in 1758 or 1759. A surviving wall-fountain is inscribed: 'Herrebøe Ao 1760'. Hoffnagel in 1762 sold out to a company, which now did its utmost to increase sales. The next ten years were probably the most fruitful in the factory's history, but in 1772 adverse economic circumstances prompted the company also to attempt a sale. However the property was not finally sold until 1778.

The Herrebøe faience was a ware of reasonable technical quality, most often painted in high-temperature blue or manganese. A few polychrome pieces are known, and an occasional example is found with a turquoise-green ground. The shapes are somewhat akin to those used at Schleswig, including the table-trays and the 'Bishop' bowl, no doubt because the first manager, J. G. Kreibe, came from there (see p. 206). The table-wares are noteworthy for the liveliness of their rococo modelling in relief, and the Herrebøe painting illustrates the most extreme aspects of that style, with a wild flickering quality in the handling of *rocaille* which is peculiar to the factory. It is known that the German-Norwegian painter H. C. F. Hosenfeller, worked at Herrebøe, and one or two pieces of unusual quality are marked with the initials 'HF', probably his.

Faience of less interest was made in a small factory at Drammen at the head of the Drammensfjord, between about 1763 and 1780. Its wares were usually painted in high-temperature blue (less often manganese-purple) in a style reminiscent of Herrebøe's, but also occasionally in a manner which recalls English delftware.

589

591

Spain

A revival of activity in the manufacture of ceramics occurred early in the 18th century at Alcora, near Castellón de la Plana. As part of the estates belonging to the counts of Aranda, this little town had been a pottery centre long before 1727, when the ninth Count of Aranda set himself up as patron of a factory, later considered the best in the kingdom. Hoping that his workers would produce *loza fina*, that is, faience of fine quality, Aranda brought artists from France to teach the Spaniards how to decorate their pottery in the accepted mode of the day. From this period at Alcora come decorative pieces and tableware, some moulded in the forms of silverware and most of them painted with the delicate arabesques of Jean Bérain, with *chinoiseries*, pictorial subjects copied from engravings and rococo floral motifs. Edouard Roux from Moustiers and Joseph Olerys from Marseilles painted plates, octagonal plaques, and other subjects decorated with these designs exquisitely drawn in blues or in polychrome. The decorations of Olerys working at Alcora resemble so much those done after 1739, when he established himself at Moustiers, that it is often impossible to distinguish between the pieces of one factory and the other.

Spanish painters proved themselves to be his talented pupils, well able to reproduce the French style of decoration. One of these men, José Causada, was persuaded, about 1743, to break his contract and

591–2

594

592

591–2. Water tank and basin or *aguamanil* of glazed earthenware. Alcora. About 1730. Tank: Ht. 17¾ in. (45 cm.). Basin: W. 18½ in. (47 cm.). The Bérain-style decorations are in blue, yellow, grey-green and purplish black. Musée Nationale de Céramique, Sèvres.

593

594

593. Bowl with painted decoration. Alcora. 1730–40. Diam. 13¾ in. (35 cm.). Small figures of huntsmen, birds, insects and floral sprays are painted in colours on white. Musée Nationale de Céramique, Sèvres.

594. Flowerpot, or *macetero*, with mask handles. Alcora. After 1729. Painted in colours on white, the pot is decorated with swags and clusters of flowers in the style of the faience decorator, Joseph Olerys from Marseilles, who came to Alcora in 1729 and worked for about twenty years. Museo Arqueológico Nacional, Madrid. (Formerly in the Boix Collection.)

595. *St Michael*, plaque of white glazed earthenware painted in blue with brown, pale green and yellow. Alcora. About 1740. 9 × 6 in. (24·3 × 17·2 cm.). The archangel is represented at the moment before striking with his flaming sword the powers of evil, portrayed as a dragon. In the sun's rays above him may be read QUIS SICVT DEVS. On the crownpiece of the frame the name of Cristobal Cros is recorded as the painter. British Museum, London.

596. *Earth*, a rococo plaque of white-glazed earthenware, painted in colours. Alcora. About 1760. 20½ × 19½ in. (52·1 × 49·5 cm.). This autumnal scene is one of a set of allegorical representations of the four

elements. Another in the series is a composition of sea nymphs representing Water, which is signed by Vicente Ferrer. Victoria and Albert Museum, London.

595

596

597

597. Count of Aranda, earthenware
portrait-bust. About 1775. Ht. 27½ in.
(70 cm.). This portrait-bust of the tenth count
of Aranda was probably modelled from a
French original. It is glazed in opaque white,
with colours used for the features and the
costume, which is predominantly golden
yellow, accented with olive green and dark
blue. The Hispanic Society of America,
New York.

598

598. Winter, figurine of porcellanous
cream-white glazed earthenware. Alcora.
About 1780. Ht. 8 in. (20 cm.). The bearded
old man, wrapped in thick robes and warming
his hands over a flaming brasier, is one of a
set, The Four Seasons. Victoria and Albert
Museum, London.

go to a factory in Talavera for a short period. Possibly this man was
responsible for a sudden flourishing there of French faience decoration. Scenes painted and signed by Miguel Soliva at Alcora show
his brilliant skill in reproducing engraved pictures in coloured
glazes, and important examples also bear the names of Cristóbal
595 Cros, Miguel Vilar, Cristóbal Mascarés, and other decorators. These
native Alcorans were masters at glaze mixing, and their formulas for
lustre and enamel-glazes were probably taken back to France by
Roux and Olerys.

A lively period of work came to the Aranda factory after the title
597 descended in 1742 to the famous tenth Count, Pedro Pablo, who
represented his king successively at the courts of Portugal, Poland,
and France. Until his death in 1798, the factory was an experimental
plant for the investigation of new methods of making porcelain,
creamware (see p. 280), jasperware (see p. 274), and in improving
the quality of loza fina.

Although interest in the development of a porcelain paste ran
high, the factory modellers also used faience for table services, vases
596 and the like. Shapes, as well as painted decorations, took on a rococo
appearance, and large portrait-busts, half-figures, statuettes and
figurines of loza fina filled a demand for ceramic sculpture. Some of
these works were tin-glazed, left white or painted in part with
enamel-colours; others were covered with a cream-coloured glaze.

About 1775, the Alcora workers made in faience the almost life-sized
bust of Aranda, several replicas of which still exist.   597

A list of sculptural figures done at the factory in 1777 makes note
of tritons, soldiers, dancers, musicians, exotic and historical
personages, animals, mythological groups and allegories of four
Continents and the Seasons. During the last years of the century, the
Aranda factory added to its products a type of pottery known as
terra de pipa, which imitated English creamware. A figurine of
Winter in creamware was modelled probably by Joaquín Ferrer,   598
then the factory's official sculptor and mould-maker. While it was
usual for master decorators and sculptors to sign their work, there
was no official mark for the Aranda factory until 1784. From this
date pottery was sometimes, but not always, marked by a block-
letter 'A', incised or painted in terracotta red, black, brown or gold.

In Europe as a whole, towards the end of the 18th century, the
growing success of English-style cream-coloured earthenware on the
one hand, and the cheapening of porcelain on the other, gradually
began to exert an economic stranglehold on faience. Creamware
was new and fashionable, and porcelain had an obvious appeal to
those wishing to ape their betters, whereas faience was associated
with the démodé rococo style. It had, however, practical disadvantages
compared with creamware, being soft-bodied, with a glaze which
chipped readily. By 1800 its manufacture had virtually ceased.

VI European Porcelain

Early soft-paste porcelain

Italy

Isolated examples of Chinese porcelain percolated through to Europe in the Sung and Yüan periods, but it was only in the late 15th and 16th centuries that it began to reach Europe, primarily Italy, in any quantity. This porcelain was chiefly 'blue-and-white'. Its effects on the designs of Italian maiolica have already been noted and attempts were also made to imitate its substance, both in opaque white glass and by other means. The first successful experiments were concluded at Florence at the instigation of the Grand Duke Francesco I de' Medici. Most of these pieces were made between about 1575 and his death in 1587, though there is record of production as late as 1613. Two pieces are dated, 1581 and 1585 or 6. Vasari tells us that the person mainly responsible for the invention was the painter, sculptor and architect, Buontalenti. We have records of about sixty pieces surviving till recent times. Most are marked underneath with a depiction of the dome of the Cathedral in Florence, or with the six balls of the Medici arms inscribed with the Grand Duke's initials.

Medici porcelain is of the type known as 'soft-paste', of which the surface, unlike that of the later 'hard-paste' (which more closely resembles eastern porcelain), can be scored with a steel point. It precedes any other successful European porcelain by a century (although there is record of porcelain-making at Pisa in 1619; and two porcelain cups, attributed to a pottery at Padua, are dated 1627 and 1638). No doubt output was limited and the porcelain was never intended for sale; and we can only guess why production stopped. It generally conveys an air of experiment—heavy potting, jugs which sag, a piece marked 'Prova' ('test'), glaze rather cloudy, and colour rather weak. Nevertheless, it is far more than a false dawn. The mere fact that it was made at Florence, in the 16th century and with such exclusiveness, ensure its great artistic and historical importance.

The objects made were few in kind, and apparently ornamental: dishes and basins, jugs, vases and bottles. Their shapes and rhythms are mainly those of decorative earthenware, with sometimes a distant resemblance to bronze objects or designs for them. The painting is in blue, sometimes with purple in outline; only one polychrome example is known. Blue and white was already the colour-scheme which Oriental imports brought into general favour, but its sobriety also reflected the austerity of aristocratic taste at the time. Here it was embodied in grotesques, armorials, and flower and leaf patterns. These designs recall sometimes the work of the maiolica painters at Urbino, sometimes Chinese prototypes, and sometimes the gay designs on contemporary wares made at Isnik in Turkey. One of Buontalenti's assistants is said to have been a Levantine. Three large dishes show figures of Evangelists, copied from prints after the German artist, Pencz. A unique medallion at Florence is modelled with a portrait of Ferdinand.

603

602

600

601

602

599. (*previous page*). Portrait of his first wife painted by J. Heindrich Tischbein. In her right hand is a coffee cup, on the table a teapot and teacup of Meissen porcelain about 1745–50. Gottfreid Keller Foundation (On loan to the Kunstmuseum, Berne).

600. Vase of elongated ovoid shape, soft-paste porcelain decorated in blue camaieu. Rouen, ascribed to Louis Poterat; end of the 17th century. Ht. 6½ in. (16·5 cm.). The 'pot' and the 'rat' which appear in the centre of the decoration have been interpreted as a play on words, representing Poterat's signature in the form of a rebus. The decoration of mantlings and pendants in the Bérain style is very close to that on Rouen faience. Musée National de Céramique, Sèvres.

601. Ice-pail in soft-paste porcelain with polychrome decoration. Saint-Cloud; about 1710–20. Ht. $7\frac{1}{10}$ in. (18 cm.). This is the Far Eastern style of decoration, known in the 18th century as 'Korean', whereas it was, in fact, inspired by the creations of the famous Japanese potter, Sakaïda Kakiemon. The designs of flowers and exotic birds, crossed bamboos and 'hedge' motifs are amongst those most frequently reproduced. The colours are bright and lively and strongly contrasting. Musée National Adrien-Dubouché, Limoges.

602. Ewer, painted in blue. Medici porcelain, Florence, 1575–87. Ht. 8¼ in. (21 cm.). In shape this resembles ewers and vases made at about this time by the maiolica potters of Urbino. The swirling flower-painting resembles that on contemporary Turkish wares. Musée Jacquemart-Andre, Paris.

41. *Porcelain Room made for the Royal Villa at Portici, near Naples. Capodimonte; 1757–59. (See also figs. 659–60). Rooms fitted out with porcelain had been well-known in Europe since the late 17th century, but rooms actually panelled in the material were much rarer.*

42

43

44

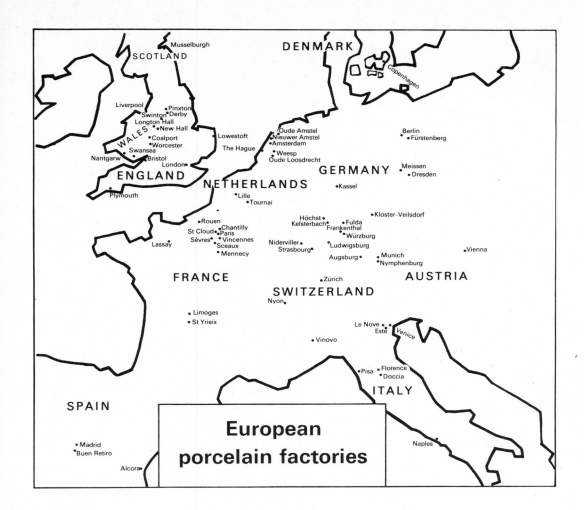

603

604

France

After the Italian experiments, there is a hiatus of almost forty years in the history of European porcelain. During this period there was an influx of Chinese porcelain into Europe, thanks to the activities of the East India Companies and the China mania spread in ever wider circles among the upper classes of European society. The introduction of the exotic drinks, coffee and tea, the latter, brought with the china in the East India Companies' ships, gave a further impetus to the fashion for porcelain and before the end of the 17th century, the first attempts had been made at the faience factories of Rouen and St-Cloud to imitate its delicate translucency. Kaolin for making hard-paste porcelain was still unknown in France but eventually ceramic experiments resulted in an artificial paste from which a 'soft' porcelain of rare aesthetic merit could be made.

In 1673 a special licence was granted to Louis Poterat of Rouen authorising him to make porcelain as well as faience, but since Poterat worked alone and in the greatest secrecy, to the ruin of his health, his output was precarious and ceased with his death in 1696. It is difficult to identify his work today. One can only attribute to him with some hesitation a few rare pieces with the mysterious mark 'A.P.'. These are all decorated in blue camaieu with lambrequins and arabesques, after Bérain, in the style of contemporary Rouen faience. **600**

Pierre Chicaneau, a faience maker of St-Cloud who died sometime before 1678, must also have known a formula for making porcelain, one which was to be turned to profit by his son, Pierre, exploited by his widow, who married Henri Trou, and by their descendants. The factory was on the estate of 'Monsieur', the Duke of Orleans, brother of the King, and owed its rapid rise to his protection. It was in production when the English traveller, Martin Lister, went there in 1698 (and complained of the exorbitant price of the porcelain) and in 1700 it had the honour of a visit from the Duchess of Bourgogne, who, according to the account given in the *Mercure de France*, admired a quantity of very fine porcelain. The Chicaneau family had a shop in Paris, in rue de la Ville-l'Evêque. For marks they used in turn a sun and the letters 'SC', usually accompanied by a 'T'.

St-Cloud porcelain sometimes has a blue decoration similar to that of Rouen, but is remarkable for its precocious taste for gilding and polychrome, which implies a knowledge of slow-fired (*petit feu*) enamels. Its decoration, in the Japanese 'Kakiemon' style is in **601** brilliant colours. St-Cloud also imitated Chinese white Fukien, as did Meissen, but the quality of soft-paste lends them a new charm. **604**

---

42. Vase with purple ground, painted by J. G. Horöldt with polychrome chinoiseries. German (Meissen); about 1725. Mark, 'A R' monogram in underglaze-blue. Collection of Frau Dr A. Torre, Zürich.

43. Soft-paste porcelain vase, from a set. Italian, Capodimonte factory, c. 1745–50. Painted in enamel colours. Ht. 13¼ in. (33·5 cm.). Mark, a fleur-de-lis in blue enamel. Chinoiserie paintings were based on engravings, which were sought by the factory in Paris and Germany. The shape of the vase is of Chinese derivation, but also comes via Germany. Victoria and Albert Museum, London.

44. Table-top in pietra dura depicting a selection of porcelain, some of it clearly Oriental (mainly Japanese) but some of it of Doccia origin (a coffee-pot, a teapot and a covered bowl). Italian, Florentine. About 1770. Museo degli Argenti, Pitti Palace, Florence.

603. Plate, painted in blue. Medici porcelain, Florence, 1575–87. Diam. 9¾ in. (24·8 cm.). Both the detail of the decoration, and its general restraint, with large areas of white unpainted surface, show the influence of Chinese porcelain of the late Ming period. British Museum, London.

604. Cream-pot with lid, in soft-paste porcelain with low-relief decoration. Saint-Cloud, Trou factory; about 1730. Ht. 3⅕ in. (8 cm.). This exquisite, soft, smooth porcelain is in imitation of Fukien *'blanc-de-Chine'*, widely emulated in 18th-century Europe. A whole series of small three-dimensional pieces display the distinctive, naturalistic decoration simulating overlapping leaves like those of an artichoke or fir-cone. Musée National Adrien-Dubouché, Limoges.

German hard-paste porcelain

Meissen

The ceramic experiments at Rouen and St-Cloud to rediscover the formula of Chinese porcelain, which led to the production of the fine cream-coloured soft-paste material, have already been described. The secret was being sought not only in France and Italy but also in Germany where the costly eastern porcelain was put on show in the art collections and lacquered cabinets of every prince, notably Augustus the Strong, King of Poland and Elector of Saxony, through whom, thanks to a curious chain of circumstances, the epoch-making discovery of how to make true, white, translucent porcelain was achieved.

The key figure in this discovery was an alchemist named Johann Friedrich Böttger who, at eighteen, was working for an apothecary in Berlin by name of Zorin. Böttger was one of the adepts of that time, whose ambition was to transmute base metals into gold. His efforts appeared to be successful because of a tincture given to him by a mendicant Greek monk, Lascaris. The king of Prussia, Frederick I, became interested in this valuable young man who escaped his clutches by fleeing to Wittenberg in Saxony where he signed on at the University as a student of medicine.

Augustus the Strong, ruler of Saxony, was no less in need of gold than the king of Prussia and he had the young prodigy arrested and brought to Dresden. Böttger was subsequently transferred to the castle of Albrechsburg near Meissen, where he had to work at producing gold. After three years of failure to transmute lead and mercury into gold, he was in 1704 put under the direction of the celebrated physicist, then of world-wide fame, Ehrenfried Walther, Count von Tschirnhaus. In the hope of producing precious or semi-precious stones, Böttger and Tschirnhaus carried out tests on earths

and minerals from Saxony to find their resistance to heat and their chemical changes at high temperatures. In so doing they discovered the principle of making real hard-paste porcelain—by mixing refractory clay with fusible earths. First of all, from 1707, the imprisoned alchemist made his famous hard, red stoneware of a type that had hitherto been imported from China, England or Delft.

Aided by the court silversmith, Irminger, Böttger modelled some outstanding pieces in this red body, and they were shown with great effect for the first time at the Leipzig fair of 1710, where they brought an onsurge of respect for the new enterprise. Böttger called his red stoneware 'Jasper', the name of a semi-precious stone, as he was convinced that he had created something costly. He treated his invention accordingly and applied a lapidary's technique to his new product, cutting, engraving and polishing it, as one would a precious stone. The glass industry being well developed in Saxony, there was no lack of facilities for such embellishment. Böttger had also developed a dark brown glaze which would take gold and lacquer decoration and the court lacquer artist, Martin Schnell, decorated Böttger's ewers, cups, vases and larger vessels with green, blue, red and yellow lacquers.

In 1708, by substituting for the red clay a fire-resistant white clay from the neighbourhood of Meissen (and, later, from Aue in the Voigtland), Böttger rediscovered Chinese porcelain. 'Meissen' immediately became the envy of an astonished Europe and provided Augustus the Strong with a unique means of parading wealth and power. In 1710 he founded the Meissen manufactory which is still in production today. It is known that Böttger had inscribed over the entrance to his laboratory the words: *Es machte Gott, der Schöpfer, aus*

605. Large covered vase with two applied masks, Böttger stoneware. Meissen; about 1715. These vessels, fired at 1200° C, were then of stone hardness, resonant and water-tight. To produce them, Böttger used a red clay from Okrilla, near Meissen, and as flux an easily fusible red earth from the Plauenscher Grund, near Dresden. Collection of Frau Dr A. Torré, Zürich.

606. Teapot of black-glazed Böttger stoneware, painted in gold. Meissen; about 1715. The fine brown stoneware seen in the previous illustration was lacking in surface-brilliance—that festive means of expression which the Baroque era could not forego. Böttger produced this glaze from lead-oxide

with manganese or cobalt. Nothing quite like this was known in China. The Smithsonian Institution, Washington, D.C.

607. Buddha in *blanc-de-Chine*, a type of Böttger porcelain, moulded from a *blanc-de-Chine* original. Meissen; about 1715. Not all squatting pagoda figures are straight mouldings—many are remodelled or new creations. Since this 'Minfo' was the Chinese god of Voluptuousness, he was especially suitable as a lover's present. Perhaps this explains the often admirable decoration in gold and enamel-colours. These Chinese figures were also used as incense-burners, in which case they have a small round hole in the head. Private collection, Zürich.

605

606

607

608 a). 'Callot' figure in Böttger porcelain, with gilding. Meissen; about 1718. Ht. 3¼ in. (8·3 cm.). This subject was derived from the print shown in fig. 608 b), and demonstrates the taste for the exotic or grotesque at this time. By courtesy of the Metropolitan Museum of Art, New York. Gift of Judge Irwin Untermyer.

608 b). 'Mad Meg' from *Il Calloto resuscitato*, a collection of engravings, published in Amsterdam in 1716 and intended as a pastiche of certain aspects of the work of Jacques Callot (1592–1635), whose more bizarre figures and outlandish subjects were in keeping with current fashion. British Museum, London.

609. Table centre-piece in silver-gilt, by Johann Engelbrecht, of Augsburg. The porcelain is Meissen; about 1730. The porcelain has polychrome painting of *chinoiseries* by Johann Gregor Höroldt, working at Meissen, 1725. Höroldt was the creator of the famous Meissen *chinoiseries*, but modern attributions of almost all of these to this master are unwarranted. True there are characteristics that identify certain paintings as his. Between 1723 and 1735, however, there were artists who knew how to imitate Höroldt's style down to the smallest details. (Recently on one piece a signature, 'P E S', has been assigned to Philipp Emanuel Schindler, whose style differs from Höroldt's only in a certain stiffness.) Rijksmuseum, Amsterdam.

610. Travelling-trunk, with fitted Meissen tea-service of about 1720. The porcelain is painted with gold *chinoiseries* by Johann Aufenwerth of Augsburg, about 1725. Teapot, tea-caddy and sugar-box of Augsburg silver, of about 1725. Antique Porcelain Co., New York—London.

611. Coffee-pot in Böttger porcelain. Meissen; about 1719. The coffee-pot has bronze mounts by Elias Adam of Augsburg, and is decorated with gold *chinoiseries* by J. Aufenwerth of Augsburg, about 1725. The attribution to Augsburg of this form of etched gold *chinoiserie* is nowadays made with greater caution than formerly. There are, however, pieces of Chinese and Meissen porcelain decorated in underglaze-blue with lustre inscriptions (but not numbers), which undoubtedly were not decorated at Meissen. There are also contemporary sources and marks that justify the assigning of this form of decoration to Augsburg. Private collection, Zürich.

608 a)
608 b)

609

611

610

612

einem Goldmacher einen Töpfer (God the Creator has made a potter out of an alchemist).

The earliest vessels and also, in particular, the figures were imitated or derived from the East India Company's imports of original Chinese and Japanese porcelain, among them copies of *blanc-de-Chine* figures. By 1710, however, Böttger was already working in a new and specifically European style based on silver, gold and pewter wares. Irminger, the court silversmith, and the sculptor, Miller, supplied drawings and themselves assisted in the work at Albrechtsburg. Pots were covered with sprays of roses and acanthus leaves, handles were given sweeping curves and spouts were decorated with masks.

607

At the turn of the century, there was a marked taste for foreign, exotic and bizarre things, for strange peoples and grotesque dwarfs, fools and cripples. Curiosity mixed with revulsion was the mood of the time, and it fed on prints by Jacques Callot and 17th-century illustrated tales of travellers and embassies abroad. Small modelled figures of outlandish or ridiculous creatures made ideal subject-matter for porcelain. One of these is a character from *Il Callotto resuscitato*, a book published in Amsterdam in 1716 and based on the idea of a series of etchings like Callot's *Varie Figure Gobbi* (a series of grotesque dwarfs). Figures like these were being reproduced in wood, stone, ivory and other materials—the Boston Museum of Fine Arts even has a Peruvian tapestry depicting figures from Callot's series, *Capitano de Baroni*, showing paupers, cripples and the like.

608 a)
608 b)

Böttger's first attempts at embellishing his porcelain with gold and enamel colours also took place during this period. On May 2nd, 1711, he dispatched a crate of undecorated ware worth 462 florins to the Augsburg goldsmith, Tobias Bauer. There the pieces were to be set in silver, bronze or gold mounts and painted with gold or coloured *chinoiserie* and hunting scenes. Augsburg decoration of

612. Painting by Johann Kupetzky. A typical portrait of the baroque period; in the right hand a Meissen tea-cup of about 1720. In order to lay special stress on the rank and wealth of the subject, he has been portrayed holding a Far Eastern or Meissen cup. The cup shown in the painting has the Japanese brocade pattern, which was reproduced at Meissen at a very early date. Collection of Dr H. Meyer-Werthemann, Zürich.

613. Engraving by Johann Gregor Höroldt, signed and dated, 1726. A further 24 ink drawings by Höroldt are known. This example, on paper with a Saxon watermark, depicts Indian flowers and flowering shrubs on which large birds are perched, such as is frequently found on tableware of the years 1730–35. The paintings based on this and another drawing were executed about 1730. Schultz Collection, Leipzig.

614. Dish, painted with *chinoiseries* by Adam Friedrich von Löwenfinck. Meissen; about 1735. Mark: crossed swords in underglaze-blue. In the Meissen factory journal are six admirable designs, picked out in colour, with fabulous animals, horseman and figures in landscape, such as Löwenfinck painted on faience at Bayreuth. This style is now known as 'Löwenfinck painting'. Collection of R. Wark, St Augustine, Florida.

613

614

611 Meissen wares in the workshops of Johann Aufenwerth and Bartholomäus Seuter really came to flourish only after Böttger's death in 1719, by which time Meissen as the manufacturers were fighting them as serious and damaging competitors. Augsburg goldsmiths were selling decorated Meissen ware to their own customers or pairing it with items in gold as a set for some day-to-day use, selling

609 it together with table settings or small presents. Sometimes they assembled travelling sets of porcelain pieces together with silver jugs

610 in satin-lined coach-boxes.

The limited palette of enamel colours used by Böttger was unspectacular but the splendid effect of his copper lustre more than compensated for it and, combined with gold, produced a distinctive decoration. One of Böttger's lustre-painted cups is held by a man in

612 one of Kupetzky's paintings.

Böttger died in 1719 without having exploited his invention industrially. New energies were needed for this. Augustus the Strong was not satisfied with table services and little figures. He wanted more, on a gigantic almost impossible scale. Two new arrivals proved equal to the Elector's demands: Johann Gregor Höroldt and Johann Joachim Kändler.

Höroldt, born in Jena, joined Meissen in 1720. Nothing is known about his artistic training but judging from his work, he must have been an uncommonly gifted artist. He learnt porcelain painting at

628 Du Paquier's rival factory in Vienna (see p. 200) and so on his arrival at Dresden on April 12th, 1720 (in company with the fugitive kilnmaster from Meissen, Samuel Stölzel), he was able to submit several of his own painted porcelain vessels to the factory's management committee. From the moment of his appointment he began with boundless enthusiasm improving and augmenting the enamel-colours and by 1722 had a varied and vivid palette at his disposal.

Höroldt's first genre scenes were still entirely under the spell of the travellers' tales from China, India and Japan. They must have

615

615. Cylindrical tankard with silver lid, painted by Christian Friedrich Herold. Meissen; about 1735. Mark: crossed swords in underglaze-blue. Herold did not paint only harbour scenes. A signed tankard, with brown glaze, in the Metropolitan Museum of New York, is painted with *chinoiseries* in gold. Signed enamels for Fromery in Berlin, and from Meissen, show typical scenes: two or three merchants standing together in conversation, a

servant kneeling beside bales of wares, in the distance a tall stone tower. Primitive Watteau scenes by him are also known. The Smithsonian Institution, Washington, D.C.

616. Cup and saucer, painted by Johann Georg Heintze, showing Albrechtsburg (seat of the factory) and the town, Görlitz. Meissen (marked); about 1740. Heintze's style can be identified from a signed enamelled plaque at

Stuttgart, painted in purple, with trees and dated milestones. An excellent *genre* painter, his landscapes have Italian Comedy characters making music and pairs of lovers, after Watteau. R. Wark, St Augustine, Florida.

617. Hexagonal vase, painted with polychrome *chinoiseries* by Johann Gregor Höroldt. Meissen (marked); about 1725. Collection of Dr E. Schneider, Düsseldorf.

616

617

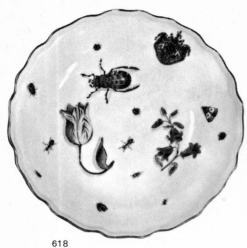

618

619

620

618. Plate, painted by Johann Gottlieb Klinger, with shaded 'German flowers' and beetles, and arms of the Prince Bishop of Ermeland. Meissen; about 1736. Mark: crossed swords in underglaze-blue. Flowers of this kind (after wood-cuts) had been painted since about 1732 at Meissen. This decoration is to be seen in a service made between 1732 and '35 for the Doge Carlo Ruzzini in Venice. There had been patterns in great number for this type of flower-painting ever since the 17th century. Flower pattern-books were published for goldsmiths, cabinet-makers and painters. Collection of Dr Schneider, Düsseldorf.

619. Cup and saucer, porcelain painted in enamel-colours by Bonaventura Gottlieb Häuer, signed Häuer. Meissen; about 1745. Mark: crossed swords in underglaze-blue. Only pieces with scenes of miners survive by this artist. Private collection, Zürich.

620. Pot with mask-spout and snake handle. Würzburg; 1775. Mark: 'C G W' impressed. This unusual form may have been from a silver vessel. A series of Italian Comedy figures from this factory is attributed to the famous monumental sculptor, Ferdinand Tietz. Collection of Mrs T. H. Clarke, London.

621

impressed him deeply for he copied the engravings down to the finest detail on to what remained in stock of Böttger's ware. Very soon, however, he evolved an entirely new painting style of his own in his *chinoiseries*. These were original inventions, although 617 inspired by the designs of the many engravers of the 17th–18th centuries, and they were painted in countless variations on the new Meissen wares. Höroldt drew such designs in a sketchbook, which still exists today, or else he engraved them on copper. Apart from 613 inventing the Meissen *chinoiserie*, Höroldt also started other themes and styles, among them the series of stylised Oriental flowers known as 'India flowers' (*indianische Blumen*); the more natural-looking 'German flowers' (*deutsche Blumen*); mercantile, and harbour scenes; 618, 61 Watteau vignettes; parkland scenes; pictures of miners and heraldic 614, 61 devices. Even the blue flower and onion pattern which is much admired nowadays was one of Höroldt's, although he derived it from China. Tischbein's portrait of his first wife shows her using 599 this type of porcelain.

By 1731, Höroldt had forty painters at his disposal. Some he had trained himself, while others were engaged for him by Eggebrecht's faience factory in Dresden. Noteworthy among Höroldt's artists were Heintze, Häuer, Herold and Klinger.

Johann Georg Heintze was Höroldt's first apprentice. Just three weeks after arriving in Meissen, he had taken him on as general hand and colour grinder, and then later as an apprentice. In the course of a few years, Heintze emerged as a painter of considerable ability, especially as a landscapist. His view of the Albrechtsburg, the site of the manufactory, can be seen on a Meissen saucer and a view of 616 Görlitz runs round the cup. Some of his work was signed but Heintze's work is recognisable from a dated milestone or obelisk, often with the addition of a postillion's horn.

Christian Friedrich Herold arrived in 1725 from Berlin, where he had been in the employ of the goldsmith and enameller, Fromery. He was a versatile artist specialising in *chinoiseries*, landscapes and 615 above all, harbour scenes.

Adam Friedrich von Löwenfinck was a controversial figure about whom there is considerable literature. Signed drawings, recently brought to light in the Meissen archives, demonstrate the great difference between his style of *chinoiseries* and those of Höroldt. 614 In 1736 he left Meissen but continued painting in exactly the same way at a number of other factories.

622

621. *Heron*, modelled by Johann Joachim Kändler in December, 1731, and intended for the Japanese Palace in Dresden. Meissen; almost 1731–35. It was a great achievement for Kändler to have resolved difficult problems of technique during his very earliest period when he had never before worked in the ceramic field. Kändler sketched and modelled for days on end at the *ménagerie* or collection of stuffed animals in Dresden or Moritzburg and his animals are uncommonly animated and true to life. Pflueger Collection, New York.

622. Banqueting table at the wedding of the Emperor Joseph II to Isabella of Parma in 1760. Section of a painting by Martin van Meytens, at Schönbrunn. On the table, mirrors framed in *rocaille* with porcelain groups. Such figures merit the term 'works of art', for they do not differ fundamentally from many porcelain figures of other factories, regarded as small-scale modelling with the character of an applied art, which were no longer intended for table-decoration, but as cabinet pieces to ornament consoles, mantelpieces and chests-of-drawers.

623. Tureen from the 'Swan Service' made for Count Brühl and his wife. Model by Kändler, 1738, with their joint arms of Brühl-Kolowrat. Meissen; 1738. Mark: crossed swords in underglaze-blue. The so-called 'Swan Service' (so named in the 19th century), the most beautiful and magnificent table service ever to have been executed by a porcelain factory (originally 2,200 individual items, Kändler and Eberlein working on it from 1737–41) reveals the pre-eminence of Kändler in his modelling. The sauce-boats in the form of swans, owing to the lavish modelled decoration, carry no arms. Messrs. Sotheby & Co. Ltd., London.

619 Bonaventura Gottlieb Häuer is known at Meissen from 1724 onwards as a painter of mining scenes, which it was not unusual for him to sign in full. This, however, would hardly have been the only sort of painting he did.

Finally, among the outstanding painters, there is Johann Gottlieb Klinger. A tankard, signed and dated by him, displays an entirely new decorative style which must have won Höroldt's approval. This consisted of German flowers from woodcuts with deep 618 shadows, combined with butterflies, caterpillars and other insects. Klinger painted the great dining service for A. S. von Götzendorf-Grabowski, prince-bishop of Ermeland.

After hundreds of experiments, Höroldt succeeded in so improving the difficult underglaze-blue that he was able to make exact copies of the costly K'ang Hsi wares. Until the outbreak of the Seven Years' War in 1756, Meissen was the source of classic porcelain with an exceptional richness and brilliance of coloured decoration which from about 1750 was emulated by every manufactory in Europe.

These wares still did not measure up to Augustus the Strong's ambitious plans even although they might serve to deck out his table and make the court confectionery look more splendid. He longed to set up enormous vases and life-size animal figures in his new Japanese Palace at Dresden, all to be displayed according to a precisely worked out plan. The late 17th- and 18th-century princely rooms where porcelain collections were proudly displayed are known to us from copper engravings; one of these, of 1705, shows a room in the Schloss Charlottenburg, Berlin, where original Chinese *boccaro* ware, in practically every form imitated by Böttger, was arranged round the walls on ornate gilt stands in alcoves and above these on ledges and in niches between stuccowork scrolls.

In 1727 the first chief modeller was placed under contract, Gottlieb Kirchner. He was made responsible for the decoration of the Japanese Palace and also for new designs for the commercial ware. He modelled two large-scale figures of the apostles Peter and Paul for the Palace chapel, as well as St John Nepomuk, St Wenceslas and the Virgin. Only four years later, however, the king summoned to the Meissen manufactory Johann Joachim Kändler, a young pupil of the court sculptor, Benjamin Thomae. Kirchner was dismissed in 1733. Kändler was used to large-scale sculptural work and created an entirely new and individual style in the new medium. He thereby became the creator of porcelain sculpture in Europe.

623

624. Three harlequins by J. J. Kändler: one with beer tankard (1738) one with slapstick (1740), and one with monocle (1740). Meissen; 1738–40. All have the crossed swords mark. Together with others of his

Commedia dell'arte figures, these harlequins are among Kändler's finest creations in the medium of porcelain sculpture to which he contributed so much. Private collection, Zürich.

Kändler's project for a life-size figure of the king, however, was too ambitious for the nature of his raw material, china-clay, was unsuited to it. On the other hand, his figures of the apostles copied from the façade of St John Lateran and large figures of animals and birds for the Japanese Palace are outstanding works of art and were then the most audaciously baroque things yet modelled in porcelain. The life-size heron shown here is one of two versions made by Kändler at the beginning of his Meissen career in the autumn of 1731. The frog making its escape from the bird's beak round the base is a typical example of Kändler's inventive wit. To support the figure during firing, he used stout reeds—a considerable achievement by the inadequate technical standards of the time. His heron holds its own with early Chinese bronzes.

Kändler also designed a wide range of vessels and utensils—ewers, soup tureens, bowls, clock-cases, vases, candelabra and many smaller articles, all modelled with rhythm and an appreciation of the material. Count Brühl, Augustus' minister, ordered the largest of Kändler's table services, consisting of several hundred pieces which he chose to decorate with an aquatic theme of tritons, mermaids, swans, rushes and so on. Other people of high rank placed orders for Meissen porcelain—Clemens August, prince-bishop of Cologne, Frederick the Great of Prussia and Catherine the Great of Russia.

Monumental figures are not the only expression of Kändler's art at its best. He excelled also in small groups and figures for the cabinet, the console, the lady's boudoir and above all for table decorations. It has been the custom in Germany from the Middle Ages to have at banquets a table centrepiece and round it mythological or allegorical figures modelled in wax, confectioner's gum or sugar. Court confectioners had to be real artists. It was in this sphere that porcelain modellers found their new role, but with the growth of porcelain sculpture, this function was taken over by the manufactory. Such pieces are often found to bear the mark KHC or CHK in purple or black on the base signifying *königliche und churfürstliche Hofkonditorei* (the Royal and Electoral Court Confectionery).

Of all Kändler's figures, the most valuable and those most suited to porcelain sculpture are his *Commedia dell'arte* characters and groups of lovers. No other theme had preoccupied 18th-century artists more than this one with its Harlequin, Columbine, Scaramouche, Mezze-

tino, the Capitano, Pantaloon, the Doctor and all the others. Even great painters produced canvases on this theme or dedicated to it whole cycles of pictures with which Kändler would have been familiar. He may even have encountered these actors in person at the court theatre in Dresden. His figures are exceptionally alive, impulsive, inspired, and with it somewhat exaggerated and pathetic. The use of strong black, yellow, green and red sharply heightened their expressiveness. The harlequins reproduced in this book are among Kändler's finest figures and, although they are not recorded with his other models, may be dated to 1738–40. All have strong solid pedestals still adorned with flowers. This gives added weight to the whole figure together with strong baroque sentiment. Kändler remained true to his own style into old age and made few concessions to rococo.

The new porcelain sculpture was highly prized. In Paris, around 1750, figures were set in ormolu and used for clocks and table decorations. The piece with Columbine and Pantaloon, for example, was made by Kändler in 1741 and its mount added in Paris about 1750. Costly exhibition pieces such as these were sold by Lazare Duvaux in Paris for very high sums to customers such as Louis XV, the Queen, the Dauphin, Madame Dubarry, the kings of Prussia and the Kaiser of Russia, the French nobility and ambassadors from all over the world at the French court. In short, everyone of note bought these Kändler figures from Duvaux in Paris.

Kändler produced other figures of an equally high standard: beggars, criers and other hawkers, those poor devils of the common people who pressed through the streets and swarmed in the squares attracting customers by their shrill voices crying their wares; also shepherdesses, dancers, singers, musicians, artisans, miners and, more rarely, allegorical figures. Kändler's loving couples display the same artistic qualities; they lack, however, a touch of discreet frivolity. Each little piece is boldly modelled in Kändler's unmistakable style, with strong treatment of light and shade tending at times to exaggeration. Made for the luxurious trappings of the sumptuous palaces of Augustus the Strong and Augustus III, these works were in complete contrast with the future daintier styles of Bustelli and Melchior. Kändler's principal assistants and disciples were Johann Friedrich Eberlein, Johann Gottlieb Ehder and Friedrich Elias Meyer.

625. Family group in Spanish costume. Model by Anton Grassi. Vienna; about 1780. Private collection, Zürich.

627. Tureen, painted with 'India flowers'; as knob of cover, pair of birds fighting. Ludwigsburg; about 1765. Mark: double 'C' with crown, 'I R 2 V' incised. Ludwigsburg had a skilled chief of the painting department in the person of Gottlieb Friedrich Riedel, who made designs for a number of vessels and produced copper-plate engravings of them. The best-known are his engravings of birds, which were published in 1770 at Augsburg and were intended for use by the factory painters. Collection of Dr Pauls, Riehen, Basle.

628. Coffee-pot, painted with Chinese landscape and Chinese woman, seated. Vienna (Du Paquier period); 1725. The decoration is based on an engraving by Peter Schenk of Amsterdam. There were other engraved models used in Vienna for the *chinoiseries*, deriving from books on travel and descriptive accounts by the Jesuits in the 17th century, copied by engravers in Nuremberg and Augsburg and signed with their own names. All these sheets, by contrast with the originals, were engraved in reverse. The best-known engravers and publishers of *chinoiseries* were Elias Baeck, Jeremias Wolff and Johann Christof Weigel. Collection of Dr Pauls, Riehen, Basle.

629. *Pantaloon and Columbine*, porcelain painted in enamel-colours and gilt, 1741. Meissen; the French ormolu clock, 1750, was added to enhance the already high commercial value. Rijksmuseum, Amsterdam.

625

630. *Corinna*, from the Italian Comedy. Model by Franz Anton Bustelli. Nymphenburg; 1760. Mark: lozenge shield, impressed. Museum of Art, Rhode Island School of Design, Providence, R.I., U.S.A.

626

626. *Door-keeper and girl*, known as *Footman and consort*. Model by Franz Anton Bustelli. Neudeck; 1760. Mark: lozenge shield, impressed. Bustelli created his figures from his own imagination, but the names of his Italian Comedy figures he took from engravings by Martin Engelbrecht. In these, we encounter Corinne, Julia, Lucinde, Lalage, Donna Martina, Don Anselmo, Octavio and Leandro. These, however, were only a starting-point, for the models are new and independent designs. Bäuml Collection, Nymphenburg.

627

628

629

630

631

632

633

631. Large Chinese House, modelled by Karl Gottlieb Lück. Frankenthal; about 1765. Mark: 'C T', in underglaze-blue. The figures by Wilhelm Lanz, who had migrated to Frankenthal from the faïence works of Paul Hannong at Strasbourg, are simple and stiff. It was only with the arrival of the Lück brothers that the style changed. Both previously under Kändler at Meissen as 'repairers' and probably also as modellers, they are typical representatives of the rococo period, their costume figures being superbly

painted. They modelled other Chinese and pagoda figures, although by then the Chinese fashion was long past. Collection of Dr Pauls, Riehen, Basle.

632. *Venus with Cupid*, modelled by Konrad Linck. Frankenthal; 1765. Mark: 'C T' in underglaze-blue. An example of the elegance of Linck's masterly small-scale porcelain sculpture; its flowing lines do not detract from the dignity of the subjects, drawn from classical mythology. Reissmuseum, Mannheim.

633. Group of children with he-goat, by Simon Feilner. Fürstenberg; 1760. Mark: 'F J' incised. There has been speculation as to where Feilner received his first training. Recently archives at Weiden (Upper Rhine) showed that Feilner's grandfather was a widely known pottery artist, and his uncle, Leimberger, worked as a skilled modeller in Fürstenberg porcelain factory. He would have served his apprenticeship with his uncle at Weiden, later going on to Paris to learn stuccowork. Kestnermuseum, Hanover.

With the outbreak of the Seven Years' War in 1756, the Kändler style came to an abrupt end. A new era was dawning with rococo which brought the diminution, prettification and convolution of forms. Kändler died at the age of sixty-nine in 1775. The new artists, Carl Christoph Punkt, Michel-Victor Acier, Johann Carl Schönheit and Christoph Gottlieb Jüchtzer favoured this lighter style. Bases were now pierced and scrolled, the corners voluted; the figures were graceful, elegant, coquettish, the colours clear.

The triumph of neo-classicism towards the end of the 18th century brought with it a preference for the cold marmoreal pallor of 'biscuit' porcelain in imitation of antique marble sculpture. In the early 19th century the Meissen factory was also producing excellent painted ware, such as the 1st Duke of Wellington's 'Saxon' service at Apsley House (1818). Today, the factory is still in production, turning out Kändler's old models painted in a new way to appeal to current taste.

Other German centres

For about forty years the porcelain secret remained in the sole possession of Meissen, with the one exception of Vienna. In 1719, the gilder, Christof Konrad Hunger, and the kiln-master, Samuel Stölzel, deserted Meissen for Vienna, where they helped the court official (the councillor of war), Claudius Innocentius Du Paquier, to start production at a rival manufactory. Although Stölzel returned to Meissen a year later, with the painter Höroldt (after first destroying everything, spoiling the material in protest against arrears of payment), Du Paquier was able to continue producing true white porcelain until 1744, when financial difficulties obliged him to sell his business to the Empress Maria Theresia.

Du Paquier's ware was decorated mainly with *chinoiseries* of a distinct character, though occasionally with copies of Meissen *chinoiseries* by Höroldt. A characteristic and classic Viennese decorative style was leaf and strapwork (*Laub- und Bandelwerk*), which is derived from ornamental prints of the 17th and early 18th centuries, mostly by Paul Decker, Caspar Gottlieb Eisler and Jean Bérain.

The Empress expanded the factory and appointed Johann Josef Niedermeyer, a professor at the Imperial Academy, as chief modeller.

Together with Leopold Dannhauser and Anton Grassi, he produced many new figure types, of which a great number related to Kändler's at Meissen. Grassi, however, was an advocate of classicism and his work was allied with that of Johann Melchior and Wilhelm Beyer, whose pupil he was.

In the final years of the 18th century, after a period of recession, the Vienna factory prospered anew under Konrad von Sorgenthal, with designs on red, yellow, green and blue grounds framed by gilded ornament, a style that had been invented by Sèvres some time before.

During the second half of the 18th century there were twenty-three manufactories in the German states producing true porcelain to the Meissen formula. It was not the Meissen factory, however, which was answerable for this disastrous expansion but Vienna. A kiln-hand there named Johann Josef Ringler had succeeded, through his friendship with the director's daughter in getting possession of the 'arcanum'. In 1750 he left the Empress's porcelain factory and travelled to Höchst (porcelain production 1750–96), to Strasbourg, where he gave the secret to Paul Anton Hannong. From there

625

628

634. *Sleeping boy*, modelled by Peter Melchior. Höchst; 1770. Mark: wheel with Electoral cap. Melchior first executed this recumbent *putto* in alabaster for a Princess of the von Thurn und Taxis family, and later carried it out in porcelain as well. By means of factory records, it is possible to attribute close on 180 different figures and groups to Melchior. Russinger and the figure-modeller, Ruppel, also created original models. Not every piece modelled at Höchst possessing artistic value derives exclusively from Melchior. Altertumssammlung, Mainz.

634

Ringler went to Frankenthal (1755–1800), then to Nymphenburg (1747 till the present day), Memmingen (1757), Ellwangen (1757–59) and finally to Ludwigsburg (1759–1824), where he settled down and held the post of director until his death in 1804. Ringler left behind an interesting notebook about the secret formula, from which it emerges that everywhere he went he constructed a kiln of Viennese type and ordered clay from Passau.

Other factories owed their porcelain production to two of Ringler's assistants at Höchst, Johann Benckgraff and Niklaus Paul the Elder, such as Fürstenberg (1753 till the present), Berlin (1715 till the present), Kassel (1766–88). Only Kelsterbach (1761–68) and Ansbach (1758–1860) were established through deserters from Meissen. The many Thüringen factories, all of them still in existence, were set up without the aid of an 'arcanist' and independently of either Meissen or Vienna. The most important of these were Volkstedt, Kloster-Veilsdorf, Wallendorf and Limbach.

Although all these factories produced porcelain modelled and painted in the Meissen style of the mid-century, some of them turned out some quite impressive original designs. The Ludwigsburg tureen has an unusual handle in the shape of two fighting birds, while the male mask for spout and serpent for handle on the Würzburg ewer are unique for the period. The baroque influence of Kändler might be suspected, were it not for the pearl border and the running dog which date it to between 1770–75. The factory at Würzburg under Caspar Geyer, was short-lived but of considerable interest, though its history has not yet been fully investigated.

Although most of these factories certainly followed Meissen in their choice of shape and decoration, the high standing and prestige of individual master modellers should not be underestimated, for they were producing work of the greatest originality: Simon Feilner at Fürstenberg, Johann Peter Melchior at Höchst, Wilhelm Lanz, Konrad Linck and the Lück brothers at Frankenthal, Bustelli at Nymphenburg and Wilhelm Beyer at Ludwigsburg. These artists were all working intensively at the same time over a very short period and producing porcelain of often superb quality in either the prevailing German rococo manner or in the neo-classical style recently introduced by Winckelmann.

If Kändler was the master of baroque porcelain sculpture, his rococo opposite number was Franz Anton Bustelli at Nymphenburg. Where he was trained is unknown, but that he knew Italian can be concluded from the words that are written on the page of music held by his figure of Corine: '*Voi sarete ricordato delle parolle*

promesse Toutto vostro Leandro'. It is certain only that he was engaged as a figure modeller by the Munich manufactory of the Elector of Bavaria, Maximilian Joseph, on November 3rd, 1754. Bustelli's appointment marks the beginning of a period of supreme fulfilment in the art of porcelain modelling. It seems probable that Bustelli, like Kändler, had previously worked as a sculptor and it has been suggested that he might have been a pupil of the Bavarian rococo master, Ignaz Günther (1725–75).

The bodies of Bustelli's figures are of an exaggerated slenderness, their delicate faces ultra-refined. There is a forceful antithesis in their movement and they are all vitality, rhythm, wit, statement and counterstatement. Many of his figures are designed as pairs engaged in lively interplay. He imparted the same elegance and sense of movement to his tableware. Bustelli died in abject poverty on April 18th, 1763. His successor, Dominikus Auliczek, was a far lesser artist, though widely travelled, having studied in Vienna, Paris and Rome.

Beside those of Bustelli, the figures of the Lück brothers at Frankenthal, in a refined style that was altogether rococo, are more like costly toys. Favourite subjects among these were figures of hawkers, artisans, musicians, huntsmen, social gatherings and *chinoiseries* and, though not great works of art, they are remarkable minor works which are most expensive and engaging. Konrad Linck, who was appointed court sculptor and master figure-modeller at Frankenthal in 1762, was a more considerable artist. He carved the monumental pieces of stone sculpture at Mannheim, Heidelberg and in the gardens of Schloss Schwetzingen. More important, however, is his small-scale work. He took his ideas mainly from classical mythology—muses, gods and graces. His group of *Venus Amor*, with its softly modelled, elongated bodies, is a good example of his lyrical and academic style. Linck was an early follower of French neo-classicism.

A modeller to whom notice has only more recently been given was Simon Feilner at Höchst and, from 1753, at Fürstenberg. He studied in Paris and then worked as a stucco-artist at Schloss Saarbrucken. He arrived at Höchst in 1750 and according to Gölz, the factory's owner, he there learnt how to model in clay. This sounds improbable, however. A mid-18th-century stucco-artist, who was nothing if not a craftsman, would hardly need to learn anything about modelling from a potter. Feilner made nearly a hundred very original figures and groups at Höchst and Fürstenberg. The best known of these are his figures from the Italian Comedy, though

627
620

630
626

631

632

635

636

635. *French horn player*, modelled by Wilhelm Beyer. Ludwigsburg; about 1765. Mark: double 'C', in underglaze-blue. Within the sphere of German modelling, Wilhelm Beyer is the first representative of the neo-classical style. His figures of solo musicians show the *contraposto* and the artificial draping of the costume typical of Beyer. All the same, details such as the stockings falling down and the open shirt, are surviving echoes of the rococo. Collection of Dr Pauls, Riehen, Basle.

636. *Pair of lovers with bird-cage*. Berlin, Wegeli period; about 1755. Mark: 'W' incised, '2 99 23'. By contrast with the academic figures of the *Modellmeister*, Elias Beyer, and his brother, Wilhelm Christian, who both worked in the style of the French school of sculpture, the early modelled pieces of the Wegeli period, by the sculptor, Reichhard, are forceful, fresh and lively and have affinity with the work of Kändler. Collection of Frau Dr A. Torre, Zürich.

640. *The Decked Hat*, modelled by Peter Melchior. Höchst; about 1770. Mark: wheel in underglaze-blue. Melchior worked from Nature; on occasion, however, his inspiration was stimulated by engravings. This may here be the case, the engraving being Nilson's *Maius*. Collection of Dr Pauls, Riehen, Basle.

there can be no comparison with Kändler's. Feilner's groups of children, on the other hand, are good life-studies although they betray the eternal stucco-artist. Heads like these can often be seen in the stuccowork of German baroque churches. Ten years later, Melchior was to interpret his children quite differently.

In his own time, Johann Peter Melchior of Höchst, Frankenthal and Nymphenburg, was a great and celebrated artist. Under the influence of Goethe's *Werther* and the writings of Rousseau, his style was elegaic, even sentimental. In 1767 he was engaged as master-modeller at Höchst and gave the factory its first success. Melchior saw something sublime and exalted in the representation of the human form. In an essay entitled *On the Sublime*, Melchior wrote: 'thus is the Supreme Spirit made visible to the senses in the form of a body, so that even through lifeless marble it inspires our awe'. These were the principles according to which he worked. His interpretation of the *Cries of Paris*, therefore, is quite different from others; for him these are human beings, independently observed and realistically portrayed. His special love was children, at play, in earnest, in distress, with all their little joys and sorrows. Although Melchior's visit to Paris has not been proved beyond doubt, it is nevertheless

certain that he was very well acquainted with the sculpture of Etienne Falconet and François Duquesnoy. The recumbent *putto* which Melchior carved in marble before repeating it in porcelain, is a variation of Duquesnoy's *Infant Hercules*. *The Decked Hat* began Melchior's series of matching pairs. To it belongs *The Decked Lamb*, and together they show his naturalism of treatment. At Frankenthal and Nymphenburg his style was strictly neo-classical and his portrait-busts in a marmoreal 'biscuit' are representative of a new age of feeling. Melchior died at Nymphenburg in 1825.

The last great porcelain artist was Wilhelm Beyer at Ludwigsburg. He was an architect, painter and sculptor with for those days an unaccustomed training in Dresden, Paris and Rome. He entered the service of Duke Carl Eugen of Württemberg at Stuttgart in 1759 and in 1761–67 worked as modeller at the Ludwigsburg factory. Later, he was commissioned to decorate the imperial gardens of Schönbrunn with statuary. According to his biographer, Beyer was responsible for finally 'supplanting the simpering shepherdesses in the Augsburg taste with plain and simple Artemises and Cleopatras and the nobler nymphs'. His porcelain figures are obviously the work of someone used to full-scale sculpture and although their

637. *Boy with dog and cat*. Fulda; about 1775. Mark: a cross. The painting of most Fulda porcelain figures is harmonious and delicate. Many were modelled by the Bohemian, Wenzel Neu, previously *Modellmeister* at Kloster-Veilsdorf. There is a series of figures based on those by the Lück brothers at Frankenthal. There is documentary evidence that Fulda purchased figures from Frankenthal as patterns. These Fulda pieces show similarities with the contemporary Zürich figures. Collection of Dr A. Wiederkehr, Zürich.

638. *Pair of Rustics*. Zürich; about 1770. Zürich nearly always modelled its groups and figures as related pairs. Most of the plaster moulds are still preserved. Sometimes a single figure may consist of twenty or more separate moulded parts, which the skilled 'repairer' then had to put together to form the completed work of the artist. This called for particular skill and patience. There are no pretensions or rococo sophistication in the choice of subject-matter at Zürich, which, as a local enterprise, had a totally different character from many other European porcelain factories. Collection of Dr A. Wiederkehr, Zürich.

637

638

movements are rococo, their correct anatomy reveal Beyer as a fundamentally neo-classical artist. His best known series of figures were *The Soloists* of around 1765.

Besides these great masters, other less gifted artists were at work in porcelain factories elsewhere, as at Berlin, Fulda, Felsterbach. Their works are not widely known but are prized by collectors and museums. The Berlin factory was one of the seven biggest in the German states, but now its pieces are not much sought after except for some rare figures produced during the Wegeli period (1751–57) and the magnificently painted table services from royal castles. Most Fulda figures were based on Höchst and Frankenthal models, but their fastidious modelling and restraint in their decoration gave them, especially in the hands of Wenzel Neu, an enduring artistic value that can command high prices today. In the short time of eight years several groups with striking originality of form and feeling were modelled at Kelsterbach by Jakob and Cornelius Carlstatt, Carl Vogelmann and Peter Antonius Seefried (a pupil of Bustelli).

In connection with the manufacture of German porcelain, two

Swiss manufactories at Zürich and Nyon can appropriately be mentioned here. Zürich was a democratic foundation inaugurated in 1763 by some members of the local scientific society, of whom the pastoral poet, painter and engraver, Salomon Gessner, was the most prominent. Its soft and hard-paste porcelain, its biscuit-ware, as faience and cream-coloured earthenware are highly prized. The tableware was richly painted. A few of the porcelain painters at Zürich are known by name, among them Valentin Sonnenschein from Stuttgart and the young Johann Wilhelm Spengler, who later worked at Derby. Among the Zürich products, there are no grand crinoline groups and fine cavaliers; the people shown are ordinary townsfolk who compensate by their engaging charm. The enterprise at Nyon founded in 1780 in western Switzerland produced fine white ware decorated in the prevailing style with floral swags, scattered blossoms and medallions.

In conclusion, it may be said that European porcelain is inextricably linked with the 18th century as one of the most costly and colourful artistic products of a brilliant age.

639. *Female cembalo player.* Model by Carlstatt. Kelsterbach; about 1765. Formerly in Germanisches Nationalmuseum, Nuremberg.

639

640

Developments in Italy

The resumption of porcelain making in Italy in the 18th century was mainly due to German and Austrian inspiration, artistic as well as technical. The factories which were then established fall into these groups: a cluster mainly in and around Venice in the north; that at Doccia near Florence and those of the Bourbon kings in Naples and Spain. Of these the first two made hard-paste, the secret of which they owed ultimately to the Vienna factory. Capodimonte at Naples as its successors made soft-paste. Capodimonte was a Court factory, like Nymphenburg or Ludwigsburg. Doccia's inception was aristocratic but it and the others were essentially commercial undertakings.

In 1720 Francesco Vezzi founded a factory in Venice with the help of the Meissen arcanist, Christof Konrad Hunger. In 1727 Hunger returned to Meissen and caused the supplies of Saxon kaolin to be cut off, and the factory closed.

At its best Vezzi's porcelain is clear and with a fine and shiny glaze. Hunger and Vezzi were both goldsmiths. Most of the products

were for the tea-table, and their shapes, when moulded are reminiscent of the baroque silver of the time, with much raised ornament. The variations of shape are so numerous that each piece seems a new invention; but the factory showed a fondness for eight-sided teapots with looped or angular handles; and these carry some of the best Vezzi painting, of half-length figures in strong reds, greens and yellows. Other subjects of decoration are sprawling flowers, heraldry, *chinoiseries*, and figure-subjects, the best of these being signed by one Lodovico Ortolani. The use of an inky underglaze-blue shows that Venice could command this colour as early as Meissen. The factory mark was the painted name of Venezia, often abbreviated to Vena. The initial 'V' was sometimes written with an exuberant flourish.

Vezzi's factory did not survive long enough to develop a tradition of its own; but its utilitarian and provincial air also characterises the other north Italian porcelains. Two refugee Saxons, N. F. Hewelke

641

642

and his wife, had a small factory at Udine and then in Venice between 1757 and 1763. Other minor factories existed in the last decades of the century at Vinovo, near Turin; at Este (where some excellent figures were made) and elsewhere. But these were all obscure undertakings and their products are rare or unrecognised.

The large and prosperous factory of Geminiano Cozzi is better documented. It was founded in Venice in 1764 and lasted until 1812. The porcelain it made was a greyish hard-paste fired at a relatively low temperature. The factory exported much of its output, which is still fairly common today.

By the late 18th century, Venice was in decline. Cozzi's porcelain is derivative. He accepted the rococo style from Germany and used it charmingly in moulded scroll and ribbon decoration, but this seldom amounts to original invention. The neo-classical and Empire styles made their way here, too, but in diluted strength.

With this qualification, Cozzi's porcelain is gay and lively enough. The painting was good, as befitted a factory with a cosmopolitan clientele. The subjects included heraldry and formal designs, flowers, figure-compositions, and landscapes. The last provided in particular a pleasant motif of garden-buildings seen in arbitrary perspective and set among over-large flowers, all painted in rich green and purple-grey, a subject referred to as *à bersò* (like a bower) in a factory catalogue of 1783. The factory also made much use of Oriental patterns of stylised flowers and landscapes, like certain English factories. The gilding on these tablewares—using real gold procured from gold coins—is neat and of a soft honey colour.

Most of Cozzi's tablewares were marked with an anchor drawn in red. This anchor is much bigger and bolder than Chelsea's, and its presence is a useful recognition-aid. Cozzi's figures, on the other hand, are seldom marked, and their recognition is harder. They include the usual dwarfs, Chinese 'pagodas', peasants, groups of classical mythology, etc., and are sometimes placed on drum-shaped

pedestals. The colours on the enamelled ones afford a clue to identification, but many of them are left white.

There was a rival factory at Le Nove, near Bassano, an extension of a maiolica factory belonging to Pasquale Antonibon. Porcelain was made here for him from 1765 (after a false start in 1762) to 1773, by a lessee called Francesco Parolin between 1781 and 1801, and by Parolin's successor, Giovanni Baroni, until 1825.

There was some movement of workmen between Antonibon's and Cozzi's factories, and their wares are similar. The pastes of the two factories are virtually indistinguishable, and some schemes of decoration (for example, the landscapes *à bersò*) appear on both. It seems that Cozzi was as a rule the initiator of these; but Le Nove porcelain has its own character, being in general a little more adventurous. The early wares convey their own brand of rococo delicacy, both in shape and in the painting of *chinoiseries*. And Le Nove was more responsive to French and English styles. The maiolica factory began to make Staffordshire-type creamware in the 1780s, and the same smooth and sedentary shapes also appear in the porcelain. The shape of the vase (illustrated) was an old Vincennes invention: its painting by Giovanni Marconi, resembles that of Sèvres in the 1760s. Le Nove figures are in general so like those of Cozzi that it is very hard to distinguish them. The modeller, Domenico Bosello, was in charge of this department from 1786 to 1821, and in 1789 signed an admirable bust-portrait of the parish priest of Le Nove, which is now in the Correr Museum. The factory mark was a painted star, made of three or four crossed lines.

The factory at Doccia, near Florence, was founded by the Marchese Carlo Ginori in 1735, but sales to the public could not begin until 1746. The factory was run on enlightened lines, with provision of houses, schools and a hospital for the workmen. During the experimental years, Ginori was aided by the painter, C. W. Anreiter of Vienna, and his son.

643

644

641. Hard-paste porcelain teapot. Venice, Vezzi's factory; about 1725. Ht. 3 in. (7·7 cm.). The paste is compact and translucent, the glaze rich, the potting assured, but the painting, in pink, pale blue, and green enamels, is naive. National Museum of Wales, Cardiff.

642. Cup and saucer, with applied decoration and gilding. Venice, Vezzi's factory; about 1720. Ht. 5 in. (12·7 cm.). The raised prunus pattern appeared on 17th- and 18th-century Chinese porcelain (Fukien province) which was widely emulated in Europe, particularly at Meissen, St-Cloud, and Bow. Victoria and Albert Museum, London.

643. Hard-paste porcelain jug, painted in enamel and gilt. Venice, Cozzi's factory; 1765. Ht. 6⅜ in. (16·8 cm.). British Museum, London.

644. Group of glazed hard-paste porcelain, of Venus appearing to Aeneas and Achates. Este.; about 1785. Ht. 8 in. (20·4 cm.). This factory was run by Chiarina or Fiorina Fabris, a widow. Models for the rare figures were probably made by her husband, Jean-Pierre Varion, a Frenchman who had worked at Vincennes and Le Nove. Museo Civico, Turin.

645

646

647

648

645. Hard-paste porcelain teapot, painted in underglaze-blue, and mauve and green enamels. Venice, Cozzi's factory; about 1770. Ht. 4½ in. (11·5 cm.). The upward lift of the shape, implying lightness, typifies the rococo style, as does the fanciful spout. National Museum of Wales, Cardiff.

646. Hard-paste porcelain flower-vase. Le Nove factory; about 1800. Painted in enamels by Giovanni Marcon, or Marconi, and gilt. Ht. 8¼ in. (21 cm.). The shape is that of a Sèvres *vase hollondais*. Marcon was the chief painter from the end of the 18th century, under the successive managers, Francesco Parolin and Giovanni Baroni. He is recorded to have been eccentric and to have painted only on Tuesday. Victoria and Albert Museum, London.

647. Group of glazed hard-paste porcelain, of a faun, boy, and goat. Venice, Cozzi's factory; about 1780. Ht. 5⅛ in. (13 cm.). The figures attributed to Cozzi's factory cover a wide range of subjects including most of the favourite themes of 18th-century porcelain sculpture. Museo delle Ceramiche, Faenza.

648. Hard-paste porcelain teapot. Le Nove; about 1765. Ht. 5¼ in. (13·3 cm.). Marked 'NOVE' in relief. This is one of the factory's earliest productions, which displays a rather flamboyant virtuosity and exaggerated rococo fussiness; however, its shapes did not long retain this character, but became simpler, and no doubt easier to make and use. The painting is in enamel colours. Museum für Kunst und Gewerbe, Hamburg.

Local clays were used for most of the 18th century, and these produced a coarse, greyish ware with a smeary glaze. Doubtless because of this, from about 1770 to 1790, the factory used an opaque, tin-oxide glaze. At the end of the century kaolin was imported to give a whiter body. The factory-mark, in use from about 1770, was a star, painted or impressed (its solid centre differentiates it from the mark of Le Nove). The factory remained a family business until 1896, and still survives.

Early and rare productions include vessels of Chinese inspiration with white outer walls moulded with floral designs and fretted to reveal inner walls painted with designs in inky blue; other rare vessels were also decorated with flowers stencilled in the same colour. Both classes date from the factory's earliest years. By the middle 1740s, however, the painters had at their disposal a range of fine strong colours, and these accord well with the baroque shapes of dishes, jugs, and other useful wares, which remained in fashion until 1770–80. Rococo daintiness, indeed, hardly appears at all. The Doccia designers had a persistent liking for sculptural form, which is shown in heavily moulded dish-rims, spouts, lids, and handles. The typical bottle-shaped jugs, with spouts like rearing snakes, may be classed among European porcelain's most memorable creations.

Sculptural in another way are certain teapots and cups and saucers which are moulded with festoons, sometimes coloured, sometimes not. A certain obscurity surrounds the origin of these things. They have been claimed for Capodimonte: many bear the Naples mark of the crowned 'N': but it now seems that they were all made at Doccia, some in the middle of the 18th century, but the marked ones much later.

The painted designs include stylised depictions of fighting-cocks, derived from China, and of flowers; little figure-scenes set in scrolled panels of red and mauve, inspired by Meissen designs of the 1730s; and landscapes well painted in red monochrome.

Gaspare Bruschi was the factory's first figure modeller, and no doubt it was he who established the factory's style, of which typical features were vigorous gesture, small heads, and large limbs. Flesh tints are generally stippled, and drapery-colours are dominated by a purple-crimson, lemon yellow, and pale blue. These figures often stand on bases of tight, wave-like scrolls. Somewhat different are certain relatively large religious and allegorical compositions. These are generally in the white. Some are copies after Michelangelo and other sculptors and others seem to have been original designs by the veteran sculptor Massimiliano Soldani-Benzi; but copies or originals, they demonstrate porcelain's ability, in Italian hands, to assume the grand manner with success.

All the factories so far mentioned produced hard-paste porcelain of varying characteristics, whereas the porcelain of the famous Capodimonte factory was a soft-paste, made of clays from Fuscaldo in Calabria, and the factory's style was distinct. The factory was founded in 1743 by Charles IV, King of Sicily, who married a Saxon princess, and Meissen influence is discernible. A Belgian called Gaetano Schepers was responsible for preparing the paste. The first painter was a Saxon, J. S. Fischer, who had previously worked at Le Nove; others were Giovanni Caselli, Maria Caselli, his niece, who painted flowers, Luigi Restile, and Giuseppe della Torre. The chief modeller was Giuseppe Gricc. The factory produced wares mainly for the court, but public sales were held annually on St Charles' day.

In 1759 the king succeeded to the throne of Spain, and transplanted the entire factory to new buildings at Buen Retiro outside Madrid. Here operations continued under successive members of the Schepers and Gricc families. Production was strictly for the court until 1788, when an unsuccessful attempt was made to put the factory on a commercial footing. A new director called Bartolome Sureda introduced a much-improved, hard-paste body in 1803, and began an extensive production of tablewares; but the factory was destroyed in the Peninsular War, in 1812. Both Capodimonte and Buen Retiro products were marked with the Bourbon fleur-de-lis. It is not always

651
650
652
653
654

649

650

649. Group of hard-paste, glazed porcelain, of a boy with a monkey. Le Nove factory; late 18th century. Ht. 5½ in. (14 cm.). This long-nosed and curly-headed youth with the tilted hat appears repeatedly in Le Nove groups. He may have been modelled by Bosello. Fitzwilliam Museum, Cambridge.

650. Hard-paste porcelain plate, with tin-enamel glaze. Doccia factory; about 1770–90. Diam. 9¼ in. (23·5 cm.). The painting, in enamel colours and gold, is of stylised flowers in a pattern called 'del tulipano'. This seems to be derived from Turkish earthenware. The pattern was a very popular one. National Museum of Wales, Cardiff.

651. Hard-paste porcelain bowl, Doccia factory; about 1740–45. Diam. 5½ in. (14 cm.). The inner wall, painted in inky under-glaze-blue, can be seen through the floral fretwork. This kind of decoration originated at Fukien in China, where it was practised with great virtuosity, possibly a veggino, or hand-warmer. British Museum, London.

652. Hard-paste porcelain teapot, painted in underglaze-blue. Doccia factory; about 1742–45. Ht. 6⅜ in. (16 cm.). The flowers around the lid are stencilled. The heavy simplicity of the shape and the swan-shaped spout are typical of early Doccia wares. Victoria and Albert Museum, London.

45. 'Harlequin and Columbine', the former by J. J. Kändler at Meissen, about 1738, the latter by F. A. Bustelli at Nymphenburg, about 1755–60. Ht. 6½ in. (16½ cm.) and 7¾ in. (19·5 cm.). Mark on Columbine, a shield lozengy, impressed. These figures, by the two greatest 18th-century porcelain modellers, emphasise the contrast between the baroque and the rococo handling of the Italian Comedy theme. Victoria and Albert Museum, London.

46. Crinoline group, 'Sale of heart-shaped boxes', modelled by J. J. Kändler, German, Meissen; 1738. Collection of Dr Pauls, Riehen, Basle.

651

652

45

46

47

48

49

653. Group of hard-paste, glazed porcelain, *The Deposition*. Doccia factory; about 1770. Ht. 11 in. (27·8 cm.). The composition, representative of the more serious subject-matter which was one aspect of Doccia's output, is attributed to Massimiliano Soldani-Benzi 1658–1740, some of whose models were acquired by Ginori. British Museum, London.

654. Spanish soft-paste porcelain cup and saucer painted in enamel colours. Buen Retiro factory; about 1780. Diam. of saucer 5½ in. (14 cm.). The simple squares and circles of the shapes and painted panels bespeak neo-classical severity, though this is tempered by the scrollwork painted in blue and rose. National Museum of Wales, Cardiff.

655. Soft-paste porcelain cup and saucer. Capodimonte factory; about 1750. Diam. of saucer 5 in. (12·7 cm.). Painted in enamel-colours, probably by Maria Caselli. A distinctive Capodimonte painting style was evident at this time in sometimes unusual subject-matter. National Museum of Wales, Cardiff.

653

654

47. Flower-tub and two fan-shaped jardinières *in soft-paste porcelain with polychrome and gold decoration. French (Vincennes, painted by Vieillard), 1754. Ht. 9 in. (22·8 cm.) and 7¼ in. (18·3 cm.). Mark of two 'L's with the letter 'B'. Rich gold arabesques frame and enhance the small pictures. Musée National de Céramique, Sèvres.*

48. Pot-pourri *vase of the design known as* vaisseau à mât, *in soft-paste porcelain with polychrome and gold decoration. French (Sèvres), 1758. The decoration of fantastic birds is set in a lobed panel surrounded by a broad green-chequered band contrasting with the royal-blue ground vermiculated in gold. Very rare luxury pieces, these* vaisseaux à mât *are technical masterpieces, in view of the lack of plasticity of the soft-paste material. Wallace Collection, London.*

49. Hard-paste porcelain figures of Ceres, *representing Summer in a set of the four seasons. Italian (Doccia factory), c. 1770. Painted in enamel colours, with gilding. Ht. 8 in. (20·5 cm.). The figures of this set were copied from ivory carvings by the German sculptor Balthasar Permoser (1651–1732). British Museum, London.*

easy or even possible to separate early Buen Retiro from Capodimonte.

The Capodimonte paste was white and for a soft-paste could be worked very thinly. Small objects like cups and saucers are in consequence highly translucent. Sometimes, however, the body was covered with a dull, parchment-like glaze. The painting, characterised by stippled brush-strokes and strong colours, included battle-scenes and marine views as well as the more usual landscapes, cupids, and flowers. These themes were continued in Spain, but the Spanish clays produced a yellower and coarser body, not unlike that of Staffordshire creamware. Later, huge vases were made, and decorated with copies of Wedgwood plaques or of the mawkish classical pictures of Angelica Kauffman. Early in the 19th century, services were made with pedantic copies of ethnological and botanical illustrations.

Gricc's figures rank with the finest. They are sparingly painted, but sometimes the glaze itself is tinted pale green. The modelling is bold, as befits soft-paste; and though attitudes and gestures are sometimes violent, the pose is never forced. The mood is one of detached amusement. These figures generally have tiny heads, and eyes painted with stripes and dots. Later, in Spain, the figures lose these pleasant

655

658

656

661

658

655

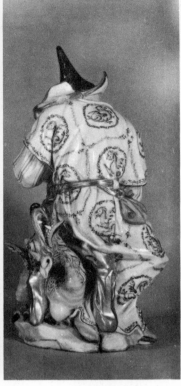

656

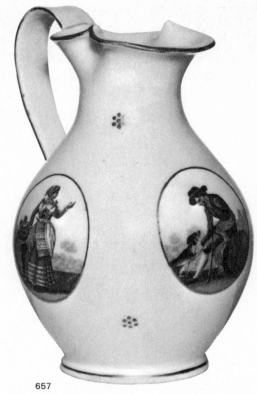

657

656. Soft-paste porcelain figure of a
Chinaman. Capodimonte factory; 1743–59.
Modelled by Giuseppe Gricc and painted in
enamel colours. Gricc reigned supreme as the
foremost modeller of soft-paste porcelain to
which his dextrous style was ideally suited.
Museo e Gallerie Nazionali di Capodimonte,
Naples.

657. Soft-paste porcelain jug. Naples factory;
about 1800–6. Ht. 6¾ in. (17 cm.). The shape
is a copy of the Greek *oenochoe*, a wine-jug
with a trefoil lip. Right at the source of the
neo-classical movement, Naples imitated
antique forms but the enamel painting here
depicts a woman in peasant costume.
Fitzwilliam Museum, Cambridge.

658. Unglazed soft-paste porcelain group,
Venus disarming Cupid. Spanish, Buen Retiro
factory; about 1780. Modelled by Felipe Gricc.
The group is derived from an engraving after
Angelica Kauffmann, *Three nymphs distressing
Cupid*, which was published in 1776 and
which was also utilised by the Derby factory.
National Archaeological Museum, Madrid.

658

characteristics, and tend to be more serious and ambitious.

The most spectacular achievements of these Bourbon factories are
the three complete rooms of porcelain, made for the palaces of
Portici (1757–59, Capodimonte), and Aranjuez (1763–65) and
Madrid (1770–80, Buen Retiro). These still survive, though the
Portici room has been moved to Capodimonte itself and has lost its
porcelain floor and ceiling. The rhythm and detail of the Madrid
room belong to early neo-classicism, and are therefore relatively
sober and static. The earlier rooms have a fairy-book gaiety. Everything—walls, furniture and light-fittings—is of shining white
porcelain painted in gold and flashing colours, and the figures of
exotic birds and Chinamen display rococo fantasy at its most
captivating.

Charles IV left his throne in Naples to his son, Ferdinand, who
re-established a porcelain-factory there in 1771. Neo-classicism had
had its origins at Naples, with the excavations carried out in the
1740s at Pompeii and Herculaneum, so it was fitting that the new
factory should pay scrupulous regard to antiquity. 'Etruscan' vessels
were both closely copied and portrayed on special services. Some of
the first workmen, however, were old Capodimonte men, and the
earliest Naples wares show a belated rococo style. It was only when
Domenico Venuti became director in 1779 that the new style was
adopted (and the wares put on public sale). Figures were produced
under the guidance of Filipo Taglione, director of the 'Academy of
the Nude'. These were as grandiose as the title suggests, but Naples
also made lively and unpretentious little figures and groups of
middle-class citizens dressed in the fashions of the day. One of these
is signed by P. Giordano. The Naples factory-marks were firstly the
monogram 'FRF' under a crown (up to about 1787) and later a
crowned 'N', impressed or painted in underglaze-blue.

The royal factory was closed in 1806. Its later revival under private
ownership, 1807–34, was of no moment.

659

660

659. Part of the room made in soft-paste porcelain for Queen Maria Amalia's palace at Portici. Capodimonte factory. 1757–59. 18×14×14 ft. (5·5×4·3×4·3 m.). About 3000 interlocking porcelain plaques cover the walls. Modelled by Giuseppe and Stefano Gricc; painted by J. S. Fischer and L. Restila. The cost: 70,000 ducats. Museo e Gallerie Nazionali di Capodimonte, Naples.

660. Spanish soft-paste porcelain. Buen Retiro factory; 1763–5. Part of the porcelain room at the palace of Aranjuez; modelled by Giuseppe Gricc. Though so similar to those in the Portici room, the figures are a little more suave, perhaps because Gricc had seen, in Madrid, *chinoiserie* frescoes by G. B. Tiepolo, the famous Venetian painter. The porcelain materials used here were probably brought from Naples. The cost of this room was 571,555 reales.

661. Soft-paste porcelain figure of a china-seller. Capodimonte factory; 1743–59. Ht. 8 in. (20·3 cm.). Street-traders were a popular subject; this one is typical of early models. Ex Messrs. Christie, Manson & Wood.

662. Soft-paste porcelain group. Naples factory; about 1790–1806. Numerous groups of ordinary townsfolk restore an element of realism to porcelain sculpture. Museo e Gallerie Nazionali di Capodimonte, Naples.

661

662

The Dominance of Sèvres

French soft-paste porcelain

The St-Cloud factory (see p. 215) survived until well into the 18th century, only finally closing its gates in 1766. In the meantime, despite efforts made to keep the manufacturing processes secret, they soon became widely known through deserting workers and other factories were opened in the Paris area, always under the patronage of some great nobleman. It was, in fact, difficult to derive any profit from the expensive manufacture of soft-paste porcelain, but to own or support a porcelain factory in 18th-century France was a just title to glory; at the same time, the scientific aspect of research attracted the attention of enquiring collectors and amateurs of the time. Thus it was that Louis Henri de Bourbon, Prince de Condé, in retirement on his estate at Chantilly, had established there towards about 1726 a porcelain factory, directed by Ciquaire Cirou, who received his letters patent in 1735. It was undoubtedly from St-Cloud that he had obtained his formula for the porcelain-body; but for the glaze he occasionally used a tin-glaze which was enamel similar to that used in faience, imparting a special clarity to the painting. The painters of Chantilly found their immediate inspiration in the magnificent collection of about two thousand items of porcelain from China and Japan, which had been assembled in the castle by the Prince; he had even had working drawings made of some of them by his appointed draughtsman, Jean-Antoine Fraisse, to act as models in his porcelain factory.

Chantilly, however, broke away fairly rapidly from the spell of the East and from the influence of Meissen. In fact, from about 1740 onwards, its art takes on a very individual character. French taste prevailed henceforward and flowers appeared on the porcelain: roses, convolvulus, cornflowers were naturalistically painted, or modelled in relief with a delicate charm which at once distinguishes them from the '*deutsche Blumen*' (German flowers). Later, services decorated simply in blue camaieu were made for the various residences of the Condé family. Chantilly, which in many ways antici-

pated Vincennes, also counted the King among its clients; where the famous hunting-horn mark is absent, it is sometimes difficult to distinguish between the two factories, for each enticed artists away from the other. The Dubois brothers, for example, are craftsmen from Chantilly who are found in the first workshop at the Château de Vincennes in its earliest days.

At Mennecy, not far from the château of the Duc de Villeroy, there was already a small faience factory, to which, in 1748, François Barbin transferred his porcelain manufacture, which had probably been started in 1734 in Paris, in the rue de Charonne. He took as his mark the letters 'DV', from the name of his patron. The porcelain of Mennecy is connected with that of Chantilly and evolves in the same way. After an Oriental phase, its taste, very much of the 18th century, is also for a fresh naturalism and for the fashionable rococo. Besides charming and picturesque figures, Mennecy, even more than St-Cloud, seems to have made a speciality of modish trinkets such as snuff-boxes, knobs for canes or handles for knives; of such small articles of coquetry as jars for cosmetics and patch-boxes; and of desk furniture, ink-wells, pounce-pots and so on, which were kept in the compartments and drawers of the many small ladies' tables which were used for hair-dressing as well as for writing.

After Barbin's death in 1768, his successors, Jullien and Jacques, united Mennecy with the neighbouring factory of Sceaux, where as early as 1749 the able chemist, Jacques Chapelle, had discovered a formula for making porcelain. The undertaking later passed to Bourg-la-Reine, under the protection of the Comte d'Eu.

Several other attempts were made in the provinces before mid-century, particularly in the north, in the Dorez factory in Lille, between 1712 and 1730. Finally, under French influence, in 1751, the famous Peterinck factory was set up at Tournai, a town alternately French and Flemish. The Dubois brothers of Chantilly went there, and English work-people were engaged.

663. Chinese *magot* sitting in front of a vase, in soft-paste porcelain with polychrome decoration. Chantilly; about 1730–40. Ht. 6½ in. (16·5 cm.). The *magots* or *'poussahs'* were inspired by the Chinese *Pu-t'ai*, the fat and jolly god of contentment, and were a favourite subject of all the earliest European porcelain. Those of Chantilly, close copies of the originals, are still amusingly comic. Musée National de Céramique, Sèvres.

664. Figures of a chamois buck and doe in soft-paste procelain. Chantilly; about 1740–50. L. of buck 10⅜ in. (27 cm.). The animals, taken from real life, are shown in a natural setting, perfectly observed, their customary postures and expressions, the texture of the pelt faithfully rendered. Chantilly artists found models in the nearby forest or the Prince de Condé's Menagery. Musée National de Céramique, Sèvres.

665. Oval dish in soft-paste porcelain with polychrome and gold decoration. Chantilly; about 1750–60. L. 10⅜ in. (27 cm.). Mark: a hunting-horn in blue. A charming design peculiar to Chantilly, on which bouquets of flowers are painted in reserved panels, on a blue chequered ground with gold dots. Henceforth, the influence of Sèvres made itself felt in the production of table-services. Musée des Arts Décoratifs, Paris.

663

664

666. *Pot-pourri* vase in soft-paste porcelain with polychrome decoration. Mennecy; about 1750. Ht. 8¼ in. (21 cm.). The pot, flanked by a naturalistically rendered spaniel, stands on a broad *rocaille* base. It is decorated with the bouquet of flowers with soft pink as its predominating colour, typical of the Mennecy factory in the middle of the century. Musée National Adrien-Dubouché, Limoges.

667. Group of *Child Musicians*, porcelain. Mennecy; about 1760. Ht. 9½ in. (24·5 cm.). Porcelain figures were frequently used for table decoration, and so required to be seen to advantage from any side. This was particularly difficult to contrive with groups comprising a number of individual figures. An unknown modeller at Mennecy was particularly successful in resolving this problem, as may be seen in this group. Victoria and Albert Museum, London.

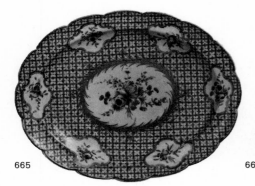

665   666   667

All the early French factories, however, were to be eclipsed by the royal works at Sèvres. Sèvres owed its later foundation with the arrival at Vincennes in 1738 of the Dubois brothers from Chantilly. They obtained subsidies and premises within the castle wall, for in the eyes of the Superintendent of Finances, Orry de Fulvi, the manufacture of a specifically French porcelain had become as much an economic necessity as a question of national prestige. The Dubois brothers were dismissed in 1741 and replaced by François Cravant, their former workman, who possessed a 'recipe' for soft-paste porcelain. A company set up in the name of Charles Adam received official recognition in a decree passed by the Council of State on 24th July, 1745, granting it a special licence for making porcelain; and it seems to be at this period also that Vincennes was authorised to have as its mark the fleur-de-lis or the King's monogram.

However, the losses of the Charles Adam Company were on the mount, and a new decree of the 19th August, 1753, transferred the licence, quite exclusively, to Eloy Brichard. The King became the principal shareholder of the enterprise, which was given the title of

'Royal Manufacture'. From this moment on the Sèvres mark containing two interlaced 'L's was used systematically, with the letter of the alphabet for each year. 'A' thus corresponds to 1753, 'B' to 1754, and so on. From 1778 double letters were used: 'AA', 'BB', etc.

The plan to move the factory to the village of Sèvres also dated from 1753. Sèvres was well situated, being on the road from Paris to Versailles and near the Château de Bellevue built for Madame de Pompadour a few years earlier. There she received the King and surrounded herself with contemporary works of art. The role of patron of the arts played by Louis XV's favourite mistress is well known and it was certainly due to her influence that the porcelain factory received so much royal favour.

Three years passed before the new buildings were ready; they had enormous costs and provoked lively criticism. At the end of 1756 the factory at Sèvres started production, and the King, for whom a luxurious apartment had been prepared, came to visit it in 1757.

This initial phase at Vincennes and the first years at Sèvres, an experimental period with unstable organisation and financial diffi-

669

670

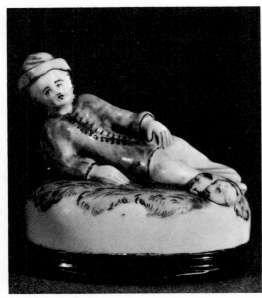

668   669

668. Oval snuff-box in soft-paste porcelain, with polychrome decoration: its lid, in the form of a grassy hillock, bears a young reclining woman with her dog lying curled up beside her. Mennecy; about 1750. L. 2¾ in. (7 cm.). This is an unmarked piece, but the pink bouquets which adorn the sides of the box and the inside of its lid betray its origin. The young woman is wearing a blue jacket, laced over a light yellow skirt, while her pink bonnet has a yellow lining. Musée National Adrien-Dubouché, Limoges.

669. View of the castle of Vincennes where the Dubois brothers obtained premises for starting up the manufacture of soft-paste porcelain in 1738. This early initiative at Vincennes has special significance in the history of French porcelain manufacture since it was from here that stemmed the inception of the great Sèvres factory. Central picture of a bowl in Vincennes soft-paste porcelain dating from about 1745. Musée National de Céramique, Sèvres.

670

671

672

673

culties, was nevertheless the great creative period during which Sèvres wares were developed. It was then that the technical progress was made which was to ensure success and that the technical and artistic personnel was established. Millot, a specialist in body-compositions, began his long career at Vincennes; Jean Hellot, the chemist, member of the Académie des Sciences, who was joined in 1757 by Pierre-Joseph Macquer, supervised the processes of manufacture, while Hultz, the painter, was responsible for the decoration. The letter of 21st September, 1751, which the latter addressed to Boileau, the new inspector of the industry, well expresses his concern to create an original art, all elegance and grace, the expression of French genius: '. . . let us shun what is heavy and trivial, and produce things that are light, delicate, new and varied. . . .' The court purveyor, Lazare Duvaux, who dictated taste in high society, went each week to Sèvres and his day-book informs us about the purchases of opulent clients. Claude Duplessis, the King's goldsmith, provided a large number of forms. Jean-Jacques Bachelier, artistic director from 1751 to 1793 played an outstanding role; and he called in the best artists of the day, Jean-Baptiste Oudry and François Boucher, which resulted in the charming models of children which were either painted or modelled. At first these were glazed figures but after 1751 they were made in 'biscuit' (unglazed porcelain) in order to present every detail of the modelling.

Vincennes devoted itself largely to the manufacture of artificial flowers; from 1745 'forty-five women and girls of all ages' were working there under the supervision of Madame Gravant. These porcelain flowers were mounted on slender metallic stems and placed in vases or used to decorate chandeliers or candelabras and were an immense success. The fashion had come from Meissen when the marriage of the young heir to the throne of France to Marie-Josèphe of Saxony had strengthened the ties between the two countries. The enormous bouquet of four hundred and eighty flowers sent by

the young Dauphiness to her father, Augustus of Saxony, in 1749, was intended to prove that Vincennes was the equal of Meissen. Lazare Duvaux's diary mentions numerous deliveries of flowers to Madame de Pompadour, who, one winter's day, received the King at Bellevue before a bank of flowers—porcelain flowers which had been sprayed with the appropriate scents.

Vases were soon made especially for these flowers, while plates, soup plates, bowls, innumerable goblets, breakfast trays, ice-pails, etc., were naturalistically painted with flowers, at first with a rather heavy touch—doubtless because the many fan-painters employed at the factory were used to gouache—but later with extreme delicacy.

Birds, as well as flowers, were a favourite theme and a triumph of Vincennes-Sèvres. The names of some of the painters who specialised in birds and landscapes are known to us—François Aloncle, Etienne Evans, Jean-Pierre Ledoux, etc.—for these were individual artists with the right to sign their work. The same is true of the painters of gay and amorous subjects or of children's games, Viellard, Dodin and others. The decoration may be in a wide and subtle range of colours, or in monochrome blue, pink, or gold.

Very soon the foundation of Vincennes coloured grounds made their appearance; these were either plain, or interspersed with delicate pebble or meander motifs in gold, later dotted with 'œil de perdrix' ('partridge-eye' motifs). These coloured grounds were to become more and more dominant, until they almost completely covered the fine white glaze, for the artists wanted to exploit to the maximum the special quality possessed by soft-paste porcelain of showing colour to its best advantage. At first it was blue that was in favour; *lapis lazuli*, royal and sky blues were used in turn in the course of 1753. The latter was employed as the ground colour on the great dinner service delivered to Louis XV in 1755. They were followed by the rare and precious daffodil-yellow, the apple-green, and the bright pink always associated with the name of Madame de

670. *Goddess of Friendship*, Madame de Pompadour offering her heart to the King; soft-paste biscuit-ware. Vincennes, 1755. A replica of a marble statue ordered from Falconet for the gardens of her mansion of Bellevue. During the Vincennes period, the patronage of Madame de Pompadour was of considerable importance in maintaining the King's interest and financial support, so that the factory was able to continue, expand and improve and by the time the Royal Manu-factory of Sèvres was opened, French porcelain equalled Meissen in its standards of artistry and technical achievement. Musée National de Céramique, Sèvres.

671. Covered bowl and stand in soft-paste porcelain with polychrome and gold decoration. Vincennes, painted by Capelle; 1754. Diam. of bowl: 6⅜ in. (16·2 cm.); of stand 9½ in. (24 cm.). Mark of two 'L's with the letter 'B'. The decoration of birds, both perched and on the wing, is set in reserved panels that are framed by rich gold sprays of leaves. It stands out against a ground of deep blue, known as '*bleu lapis*' (lapis lazuli) or '*bleu royal*' (royal blue), pebbled with gold ('*caillouté*'). Musée National de Céramique, Sèvres.

672. Flower-vase in the so-called 'Duplessis' form, in soft-paste porcelain with painted decoration relief ornaments heightened with gold. Vincennes; about 1750. Ht. 9½ in. (24 cm.). Mark of two 'L's with a dot. This type of vase with the flared, scalloped rim and upright handles, for which the model was supplied by Duplessis, the celebrated goldsmith to the King, is one of the first ornamental vases created at Sèvres. Here, the decoration of sprays of natural flowers is inserted in a framework of bands of deep blue ('*bleu lapis*') 'pebbled' with gold ('*caillouté*'). Louvre, Paris.

673. Workshop of royal Sèvres manufactory. The painter-decorator is shown at work, brush in hand, a specially privileged artist, he is authorised to carry the sword. Anonymous drawing—18th century. Archives de la Manufacture Nationale de Sèvres.

674. *The Little Girl Gardener*, figure in white soft-paste porcelain with enamelled decoration. Model by François Boucher. Vincennes; 1752. Ht. 7½ in. (19 cm.). From a first series *Boucher's Children* (*Les Enfants de Boucher*). This is an example of models designed especially for the factory by foremost artists of the period. The charming little girl, having thrown down her watering-can at her feet, is holding up with both hands panels of her skirt which is adorned by a large bow of ribbons. This figure was also executed in matt biscuit. Musée National Adrien-Dubouché, Limoges.

675. Bouquet of naturalistic flowers mounted in metal, soft-paste porcelain painted in colours. Vincennes; 1749. This monumental bouquet, a masterpiece of technical skill, consists of no less than 480 flowers of various kinds. It was presented in 1749 by the Dauphine of France to her father Augustus III, Elector of Saxony. The flowers are arranged in a vase of white enamelled porcelain, decorated with relief sprays and framed by two groups symbolising the Arts by Dupierreux. The superb *rocaille* base is by Duplessis. Dresden Museum.

676. *The Grape Eaters*, group in soft-paste biscuit porcelain. Vincennes or Sèvres; after 1752. Ht. 9½ in. (24 cm.). Mark 'B', incised. The original model is ascribed to Boucher and is one of those afterwards most frequently reproduced in later times. A youth is plying his graceful female companion with a bunch of grapes taken from the full baskets in their laps. Musée National de Céramique, Sèvres.

674

675

676

677

678

677. Ice-cream freezer and plate, soft-paste porcelain with polychrome and gold decoration. Sèvres, decoration by Dodin; 1783–92. From the great service, strictly classical in style, ordered by Louis XVI for Versailles in 1783. In 1792, 197 items were completed. Pictures with subjects drawn from mythology are painted in medallions set at the bottom of the plates, or in reserved panels on a royal blue ground covered with leafy garlands and scrollwork in gold. Royal collections, Windsor Castle. Reproduced by gracious permission of H.M. the Queen.

678. Pair of ornamental vases in the form known as ('bouteille à rubans') ('bottle with ribbons') in soft-paste porcelain with deep blue ground and gold. Sèvres; about 1770. Ht. 15 in. (38 cm.). These vases, their lobed forms emphasised by gold fillets, rank, by virtue of their sober elegance and harmonious proportions, among Sèvres' most

perfect creations. These, the only known examples of this model, formerly belonged to Lord Harewood's collection. Louvre, Paris.

679. *The King's Hunts*, plaque in soft-paste porcelain with polychrome decoration. Sèvres, painted by Asselin; 1782. Nine porcelain plaques designed for one of the King's dining-rooms at Versailles were executed from the models with which Oudry had supplied Gobelins between 1735 and 1745, for the famous tapestry. *King Louis XV's Hunts*. The figure of Louis XV was simply replaced by that of Louis XVI. The King is seen in the foreground, mounted on his grey among horsemen and whips blowing their horns, whilst in the background the pursued stag holds the hounds at bay. The scene takes place in the forest of Fontainebleau, by the Franchart rocks that have been drawn from nature. Oudry has depicted himself at work (bottom right). Musée National de Versailles.

680. 'English-style tea in the drawing-room of *The Four Mirrors* at the Temple, with all the Prince de Conty's court listening to the young Mozart in 1766', central group showing la Maréchale de Mirepoix pouring out tea for Mme de Vierville in front of a small table covered with pieces from a porcelain service. Detail from a picture by Olliver which appeared at the 1777 salon. Louvre, Paris.

681. Breakfast-tray with appartenances, in soft-paste porcelain with polychrome and gold decoration. Sèvres, painted by Fontaine; 1770. L. of tray 12⅝ in. (32 cm.). Ht. of teapot 4⅜ in. (11 cm.). On this charming breakfast-tray the laurel-wreathed panels enclose Cupids painted in *grisaille* against a light blue ground, covered with a fine diaper of dotted circles, *œil de perdrix* (partridge-eye pattern). Jacques Fontaine specialised in this kind of decoration. Musée National de Céramique, Sèvres.

679

680

Pompadour, who liked it particularly. Items with pink grounds were delivered to her in 1757 and 1758.

When the factory moved from Vincennes to Sèvres it could be said to have reached its artistic apogee, but the state of its finances continued to be precarious. In order to save it the King had to purchase it in 1759, after the Eloy Brichard Company was dissolved. A new stage in the factory's history begins in that year; as part of the royal estate it was heavily subsidised; and the King took such an interest in it that he went so far as to sell his porcelain himself, in the course of exhibitions which were organised during the December of each year in the drawing-rooms of Versailles, and in which his

courtiers felt obliged to play a lavish part. Madame Victoire and Madame Adelaide, both members of the royal family, placed substantial orders. Sèvres porcelain was used for diplomatic gifts, as we know from the 'register of the King's presents' in the Archives of the Ministry of Foreign Affairs, and from the accounts of the factory itself, in which Monsieur P. Verlet has identified numerous deliveries of large dinner-services to foreign sovereigns: to the Empress Maria Theresa, to the King of Denmark, to the King of Sweden, to the Empress Catherine II of Russia, etc.

After 1760 an evolution of style can be detected more markedly after the death of Madame de Pompadour in 1764. The great

685

681

682

682. Plate and ice-cups, in soft-paste porcelain with polychrome and gold decoration. Sèvres, painted by Taillandier, gilt by Le Guay; 1778. Diam. of plate: 9½ in. (24 cm.). Ht. of cups: 3⅜ in. (8·5 cm.). From the service, delivered to the Empress Catherine II of Russia in June, 1779, one of the most important produced by Sèvres (740 items together with the monumental centre-pieces for the table and coffee-service). The much-favoured 'bleu céleste' ('sky-blue') ground enhances classical subjects painted in grisaille, and the effect is further enriched by inlays of porcelain cameos in gilded silver mounts. The plate's central initial 'E' (standing for Ekaterina, the Russian form of Catherine), made up of a garland of flowers, surmounted by the imperial crown. Musée National de Céramique, Sèvres.

683. Secretaire (Secrétaire à abattant) perhaps by Martin Carlin (d. 1785), various veneers on oak, with gilt bronze mounts and Sèvres

porcelain plaques of various dates. Ht. 47 in. (119·4 cm.). The four corner-pieces were painted by Commelin (1768–1802); the lower central plaque by the flower-painter, Boulanger (working 1754–1800). Wallace Collection, London.

684. Combined work- writing- and reading-table (Table à pupître) by Martin Carlin (d. 1785), veneered on oak with tulip-wood, and fitted with gilt bronze mounts and Sèvres porcelain plaques of 1783. Max. ht. 43 in. (109·2 cm.). Wallace Collection, London.

685. Plate with waved edge in soft-paste porcelain with polychrome and gold decoration, that of the service presented by Louis XV to Empress Maria-Theresa of Austria in 1758. Sèvres; 1757. Diam. 9⅞ in. (25 cm.). Green braids, edged with a gold gimp, (à galon vert festonné) form a wide strapwork design interlaced with garlands of flowers. Louvre, Paris.

683

685

684

service with her cipher which was delivered in 1771 to Madame du Barry—also a faithful client of Sèvres—is decorated with incense-burners 'in the antique manner' as well as with garlands of flowers. The light fantasy of rococo little by little gives way to a grandiloquent style which prefers richness to grace, and which is represented in a series of ornamental vases, items for display as part of the furnishings of an interior. Moreover, the habit of including porcelain plaques in the furniture itself spread to the best cabinet-makers such as Leleu, Martin Carlin, and those signing themselves 'BVRB' or 'RVLC'. It was the merchant, Poirier, 'at the sign of the golden crown' (where he was succeeded by Daguerre), who undertook to

678

683

supply them. Finally, through technical improvements, pictures or delicately rendered portraits were painted on porcelain plaques.

This extensive activity did not, however, win prosperity for the royal factory; on the contrary, the wastage and embezzlement for which the new Director, Parent, was responsible between 1772 and 1778 nearly brought about its ruin. Charles-Claude de Labillarderie, Comte d'Angiviller, Director-General of Factories, to whom the industry was handed over in 1780, re-established order with difficulty, but it could not last long. The great dinner-service for Louis XVI was the last to be made in soft-paste porcelain; ordered in 1783, it was not completed before the fall of the monarchy.

679

677

686

687

686. Figure of a child with goat, in hard-paste porcelain with polychrome and gold decoration. Strasbourg, Paul Hannong; 1751–54. Ht. 7¾ in. (19·5 cm.). Recessed mark 'PH' incised. This sturdy child offering a bunch of grapes to a goat is one of the first examples of hard-paste porcelain made in France with kaolin imported from Passau in Bavaria. The naked body of the child is of a

slightly coarse white, swathed in blue drapery, while its face is lightly touched with pink, and its hair is light auburn.
Musée National de Céramique, Sèvres.

687. Milk-cup and saucer in hard-paste porcelain with polychrome decoration. Sèvres, model attributed to Langrenée; 1788. Ht. of cup 4⅜ in. (11 cm.). Diam. of saucer

7⅛ in. (18 cm.). This goblet, originating from the dairy at Rambouillet which Louis XVI gave to Marie-Antoinette, shows evidence of the new taste in its shape 'with Etruscan handles' as well as in its rustic decoration, of farm animals. The range of colours remains deliberately severe—black, violet, purple and yellow are the only ones used, but no gold.
Musée National de Céramique, Sèvres.

French hard-paste porcelain

Although soft-paste porcelain continued in favour in France right up to the end of the 18th century, research into the methods of making the real hard-paste porcelain was pursued nonetheless. The great Strasbourg faience-maker, Paul Hannong, was the first to succeed in France, between 1751 and 1754; but he used kaolin imported from Germany and was forced by the special licence accorded to Sèvres to move to Frankenthal. Joseph Hannong was only to take up the manufacture again in 1771.

Apart from a few short-lived attempts like that of the Duc de Brancas-Lauraguau in his château at Lassay (Orne), the manufacture of hard-paste porcelain was not possible in France until the discovery of deposits of kaolin at Saint Yrieix in the Limousin. The name of Darnet, knight and physician of Saint Yrieix, continues to be connected with the history of this discovery, which has become something of a legend. According to this, Darnet recognised the value of the precious white clay which his wife, for lack of soap, used to do her washing. However that may be, the Sèvres chemists, Hellot and Macquer, went to the spot in 1768, and had a barrel of four hundred pounds of kaolin sent to the factory. The first pieces of hard-paste porcelain were presented to the Académie des Sciences, and then to the King at Versailles, at the end of 1769. Regular manufacture began in 1772. From this date Sèvres produced hard-paste porcelain known as 'Royal Porcelain', bearing the usual monogram but surmounted by a crown, concurrently with the old soft-paste porcelain, the 'French porcelain'.

Hard-paste porcelain, which withstands high-temperature firing better and is more plastic, made it easier to produce monumental vases and important allegorial groups in biscuit after Louis-Simon Boizot, who succeeded Etienne Maurice Falconet, and in his turn took over in 1773 the supervision of the modelling workshop. The younger Lagrenée, a painter who had begun work in the factory in 1785, introduced the antique style, and graceful Pompeian arabesques and pastoral themes were used on the vessels for the

Trianon and Rambouillet dairies, where Marie-Antoinette played at being a milkmaid with the ladies of her court.

The factory became state property in 1793, and had to replace the royal monogram with the initials of the French Republic, and to adopt revolutionary emblems as decoration. A few large dinner-services of a documentary nature were made in hard-paste porcelain, copying engravings from Buffon's natural history and contemporary books on botany.

Once the revolutionary period, in which Sèvres workers had been reduced to penury, was over, the Consulate and the Empire restored the factory to its former prosperity. In the 19th century, under the firm administration of Alexandre Brongniart, it was completely reorganised and the manufacture of soft-paste porcelain abandoned. A number of undecorated pieces were sold at this time, which gave rise to an insidious form of imitation: over-glaze decoration. Sèvres played a large part in the rehabilitation of craftsmanship. The Emperor revived the tradition of the Ancien Régime by placing large orders for his palaces and for diplomatic gifts. The painters of Sèvres—Christophe-Ferdinand Caron, Nicolas-Antoine Lebel, Jean-Baptiste-Gabriel Langlacée, Jean-Charles Develly etc.—depicted the Napoleonic era on porcelain with astonishing skill. The glory of Austerlitz is recalled on large 'Etruscan' vases or the famous 'Marshals' Table' ordered in 1808 from the architect, Charles Percier, and painted by Jean-Baptiste Isabey with portraits that are as detailed as miniatures. The countries through which the Great Army marched are depicted on plates from the first service, for his own use, ordered, by the Emperor in 1807; the service, which was ordered from his Headquarters at Eylau, was delivered to the Tuileries Palace on 27th March, 1810, just in time to embellish the table at the wedding of Napoleon and Marie-Louise. Memories of the Egyptian campaign, recorded by Vivant Denon in his album of drawings, resulted in the creation of several 'Egyptian' tea-services covered with hieroglyphs. The most important of them, that of

687

690

689

688

688

688. Egyptian coffee-set in hard-paste porcelain with polychrome and gold decoration, from Napoleon I's service at the Tuileries. Sèvres, painted by Robert, Lebel and Béranger; 1810. Ht. of milk-jug 8¼ in. (21 cm.). On a royal blue ground, covered with gold hieroglyphics, are Egyptian landscapes and monuments, taken from sketches drawn on the spot by Vivant Denon. The insides of the moulded pieces are gilded. Louvre, Paris.

689. *Vase d'Austerlitz*, hard-paste porcelain with polychrome and gold decoration by Bergeret. Sèvres; 1806. Ht. 4 ft. 4⅜ in. (1·33 m.). This commemorative 'Etruscan'-style vase depicts in red on a black ground Napoleon as a Roman emperor in a chariot driven by Victory; it adorned his cabinet at Saint-Cloud. Château de Malmaison. Louvre, Paris.

690. Plate, porcelain painted in enamel-colours by Charles Develly and gilt. Sèvres; dated 1823, from the 'Service des Arts Industriels'. The interior of the Enamelling and Gilding workshop at the Sèvres factory. In front, an apprentice grinds colours; behind him painters decorate vases and a showroom assistant holds up a vase for two visiting ladies. Musée National de Céramique, Sèvres.

689

1810, which the Emperor took with him to St Helena, has fortunately been identified by Monsieur S. Grandjean and is now in the Louvre. A large Egyptian service, which included a monumental centrepiece of biscuitware four yards long, was offered in 1812 by Napoleon to the repudiated Josephine, who refused it proudly. Madame Jacquetot, a specialist in the genre, painted on cups portraits of Josephine and Marie-Louise, and of the new nobility.

These were outstanding examples of technical skill which attest the great talent of the artists of the imperial factory, but which opened the way to developments which endangered the future of porcelain.

While the Sèvres factory continued its brilliant career, the discovery of the kaolin of Saint-Yrieix made Limoges the 'porcelain town' that it still is today. A porcelain medallion in the Musée Adrien-Dubouché in Limoges, a precious historical document, bears on the reverse the explicit inscription 'First porcelain of Limousin clay 1771', and on the obverse the arms of Turgot, the Limousin Intendant who gave the manufacture its first impetus.

It was in fact at Turgot's instigation that the manufacture of porcelain began in the old faience works belonging to Massié and his associates, the Grellet brothers, who were money-lenders. From 1773 to 1777 the establishment benefited from the patronage of the Comte d'Artois, then in receipt of an endowment from the Viscounty of Limoges, whence the use of the mark 'CD' which was subsequently retained. In 1784 Massié and Gabriel Grellet persuaded the King to buy their factory, which was in financial straits, and it was then known as a 'Royal Factory' on the same footing as Sèvres, and like it was placed under the control of d'Angiviller. He envisaged close collaboration between Sèvres and Limoges: Limoges was to provide Sèvres not only with the porcelain body but with porcelain for decoration. Unfortunately the relationship between the two royal factories proved difficult, and Limoges did not survive the Revolution.

691

690

691

692

In the 19th century the production of porcelain in Limoges passed to private enterprise, which was able to develop it on broad lines. The great manufacturers of the first third of the 19th century, Alluaud, Baignol and Tharaud families, are responsible for the many technical improvements that led the way to the era of industrial prosperity.

Once kaolin in the desired quantities was supplied by the Limousin deposits, the manufacture of hard-paste porcelain spread rapidly throughout France. Several faience-makers experimented with it, notably the Comte de Custine of Niderviller and Joseph Robert of Marseilles. Numerous factories were opened in the provinces as well as in Paris itself and its outskirts. In order to avoid legal persecution by Sèvres, which did its utmost, but in vain, to safeguard its monopoly, they placed themselves under the protection of members of the Royal family. The King's brothers, the Comte de Provence and the Comte d'Artois, the son of the latter, the Duc d'Angoulême, who was still a child, and the Queen herself, Marie-Antoinette; all had their privileged factories in Paris. Many others could be mentioned, all favoured by the decrees of 1784 and 1787 which checked the interference of Sèvres, and all obliged to use trade marks, which alone make precise attribution possible.

The generic term 'Paris porcelain' of 'Old Paris' refers to all this production of the end of the 18th century and of the first quarter of the 19th. It was of good quality but without much originality and was inspired more or less directly by the models created at Sèvres, which by prolonging the 'Louis XVI' style, was to maintain the fame of French porcelain.

692

691. Tea-service in hard-paste porcelain with polychrome and gold decoration. Limoges, factory of the Comte d'Artois; about 1775–80. Ht. of teapot 4⅞ in. (12.5 cm.); of milk-jug 6¼ in. (16 cm.). Double mark 'CD', incised and painted in red. The bouquet with the Limoges rose, a round rose with a strongly shadowed centre, is painted slightly more heavily than the Mennecy bouquet (from which it was derived), but it has plenty of naturalism about it. Whether in a bouquet or scattered, the rose is the decoration *par excellence* of the Comte d'Artois porcelain. A serrated band of gold emphasises the rim of every object. Musée National Adrien-Dubouché, Limoges.

692. Sugar-bowl with conical lid and accompanying stand in white hard-paste porcelain touched with gold. Limoges, Baignol factory; about 1810–15. Ht. 6¾ in. (17 cm.). Diam. of dish 8⅘ in. (22 cm.). The 'white' is the triumph of Limoges. Here, the purity of the shapes brings out the purity and technical perfection of the substance itself and combines happily with the extreme and classic simplicity of the decoration. These strings of pearls standing out on concentric gold bands are a characteristic feature of Baignol's art. Musée National Adrien-Dubouché, Limoges.

693. *Jardinière* in hard-paste porcelain decorated in gold and polychrome. Paris, Faubourg Saint-Denis, factory of the Comte d'Artois; about 1785. Ht. 5⅞ in. (15 cm.). Mark 'C.P.', crowned. The regular geometrical shape of this half-moon *jardinière* recalls that of the commodes of the purest Louis XVI style. Between the fluted pilasters is a graceful *scène galante*, painted with consummate skill, the rococo charm of the Watteauesque type of subject-matter recommending itself once more as it did so often to porcelain-decorators in all the foremost centres in Europe. Musée National de Céramique, Sèvres.

694. Cylindrical teapot and cup in hard-paste porcelain with polychrome and gold decoration. Paris, rue Clignancourt, factory of Monsieur; about 1780–90. Ht. 6¼ in. (16 cm.) and 2½ in. (6.5 cm.) respectively. Mark: a crowned 'M'. This charmingly simple decoration, known as 'cornflower' ('*au barbeau*'), consisting of a diaper of cornflowers and green leaves, is one of the most widespread in French porcelain of the end of the 18th century, used by all the factories. The gold is employed discreetly to set off the rim, the curve of the handle and the knob of the lid. Musée National Adrien-Dubouché, Limoges.

695. Water-jug and bowl, in hard-paste porcelain with polychrome and gold decoration. Paris, rue Thiroux, the Queen's factory; about 1780. Ht. of jug 7½ in. (19 cm.) L. of wash-basin 12 in. (30.5 cm.). Mark: a crowned 'A'. The Parisian factory, under the protection of the Queen, is here venturing to compete with Sèvres in elegance and richness of decoration and in so doing is continuing the Sèvres tradition, still the dominant inspiration in all the Parisian factories at the end of the century. The bouquets, in subtle polychrome, are accompanied by gold arabesques which reflect the Pompeian taste. Musée National de Céramique, Sèvres.

693

694

695

696

697

696. Group of white porcelains with moulded relief-decoration. Chelsea factory; about 1745–8. Mark on jug and cup, an incised triangle. Ht. of jug 4⅜ in. (10·5 cm.). The earliest Chelsea wares were decorated in moulded relief, and only towards the end of the 'incised triangle' period (about 1745–48) were enamel colours mastered. Much

'blanc-de-Chine', however, was left in the white and decorated with relief-designs. Nicholas Sprimont himself was a practising silversmith and therefore used to thinking in terms of *repoussé* designs, and some Chelsea models indeed directly derived from prototypes in silver by Sprimont himself. Victoria and Albert Museum, London.

697. Part of a porcelain service painted in enamel-colours, with mazarine-blue ground and gilding. Chelsea; about 1762–3. Mark, a gold anchor. Ht. of tureen 10¼ in. (26 cm.). Made as a present for Queen Charlotte's brother and said then to have cost £1200. Reproduced by gracious permission of H.M. Queen Elizabeth the Queen Mother.

Separate developments in England

On the Continent of Europe the foundation of a porcelain factory had normally only been undertaken by a royal or noble patron as a matter of prestige. In England, however, where royal expenditure was more tightly controlled and the nobility was more interested in land-improvement, the manufacture of porcelain was undertaken by middle-class entrepreneurs, often those otherwise engaged in the arts—such as Nicholas Sprimont, goldsmith and manager at Chelsea, or Thomas Frye, painter, mezzotint-engraver and co-founder of Bow.

Of all the English factories, Chelsea came nearest to enjoying high patronage. Sprimont himself was a favourite silversmith of Frederick Prince of Wales (d.1751), and Sir Edward Fawkener, who appears to have been closely connected with the factory, was secretary to the Duke of Cumberland, of whom it was said in 1751 'the Duke is a great encourager of the Chelsea China'. When later Queen Charlotte wished to make a present to her brother, the Duke of Mecklenburg-Strelitz, it was Chelsea which received the commission for a huge combined dinner, tea and coffee service. It is not surprising, therefore, that Chelsea porcelain was the most fashionable, luxurious and desirable of all English wares. In its day, it set the tone for the other English porcelain manufacturers, and consideration of Chelsea may serve as a review of the best in English porcelain up to about 1770.

The earliest wares identified as Chelsea porcelain are small cream-jugs bearing the date 1745 and usually associated with a triangle incised in the paste. Their form readily betrays their metalwork origin and this imitative tendency continues throughout Chelsea's early period, not surprisingly in view of Sprimont's profession. Shell-salts with a crayfish in relief closely resemble still surviving picture of both silver salts made by Sprimont for Frederick Prince of Wales. The earliest Chelsea body is a beautiful glassy porcelain which probably gave trouble in the firing. A more robust body evolved towards 1750. An advertisement of that year shows a great increase in the factory's range: 'A Variety of Services for Tea, Coffee, Chocolate, Porringers, Sauce-Boats, Basons, Ewers, Ice-Pails, Terreens, Dishes and Plates of different Forms and Patterns, and of a great Variety of pieces for Ornament in a Taste entirely new'.

Enamelling had made tentative beginnings in the 'triangle' period, but in the succeeding phase, when the factory mark was a moulded anchor in relief, it became fully established. Painted decoration consisted mainly of flowers, either in the 'Kakiemon' manner ('India plants'), or in the quasi-naturalistic 'European' style developed at Meissen. The Meissen 'Harbour Scenes' were only briefly copied at Chelsea, but the same palette was used in a more original style exploiting the themes of Aesop's *Fables*. Slightly later, classical figures in landscapes with ruins, painted in a soft monochrome purple, formed a very special Chelsea genre.

A few isolated figures had been made in the 'triangle' period, but the 'raised anchor' period witnessed a serious incursion into this field. A fine series of figurines after engravings in George Edwards' *Natural History of Uncommon Birds* (1743) was presumably ultimately inspired by the Meissen bird and animal figures. Some 'raised anchor' pieces appear to have derived directly from sculptural originals, but probably before 1750 Chelsea had installed its own modeller, Joseph Willems. In the following phase (about 1752–58), when the factory mark was a painted red anchor, Willems really created a 'factory style'. Although many of his models were copies from Meissen, others were skilfully adapted from engravings. A sale catalogue of 1755 reveals their range, including sets of allegorical figures, such as *Sciences*, *Seasons*, *Continents*, *Senses*, and *Arts*; types from everyday life, such as *Fishermen*, *Carpenters*, *Cobblers*, etc. Italian Comedy characters; and exotic subjects such as a Chinese mask, or 'two fine figures' a man and a woman in a Turkish dress. These figures were no doubt intended to embellish the desserts which concluded contemporary banquets—a German fashion already well established in England by 1753, when Horace Walpole wrote in *The World*: 'Jellies, biscuits, sugar-plums, and creams have long given way to harlequins, gondoliers, Turks, Chinese, and shepherdesses of Saxon china . . . By degrees, whole meadows of cattle, of the same brittle materials, spread themselves over the whole table; cottages rose in sugar, and temples in barley-sugar; pigmy Neptunes in cars of cockle-shells triumphed over oceans of looking-glass or seas of silver tissue . . .'

697

696

698

701

698. Figures of *Painting* and *Astronomy*, porcelain painted in enamel colours, with slight gilding. Chelsea; about 1755. Ht. 5¼ in. (13·3 cm.); 5⅜ in. (13·7 cm.). These little figures from the series *Liberal Arts*, clearly show the style of Joseph Willems, Chelsea's Anglo-Flemish figure-modeller. Touches of gold herald a more opulent style. Victoria and Albert Museum, London.

699. *Figure of a Girl in a Swing*, white soft-paste porcelain, possibly a flower-holder. Probably Chelsea; about 1749–54. Ht. 6¼ in. (16 cm.). A number of early English porcelain figures show characteristics of modelling different from the usual run. A possible second Chelsea factory is named after the present model, known in two examples. Victoria and Albert Museum, London.

700. Scent-flask, porcelain painted in enamel colours, gilt-mounted. Chelsea, 'Girl-in-a-Swing' factory; about 1749–60. Ht. 3 in. (7·6 cm.). One of the more playful aspects of the English porcelain of the mid-18th century were the 'Chelsea toys' fripperies suitable as gifts from lovers or husbands. This scent-flask is inscribed *'L'Heure du Berger Fidelle'* (*sic*.) Victoria and Albert Museum, London.

The make-believe extended also to table china. Covered dishes appeared as artichokes or bunches of asparagus, and large tureens were formed like a boar's head, a swan, or a hen with her chicks. All these were modelled at Chelsea with a loving care which caught the creature's character and painted with a delicacy that miraculously conjured up fur or feathers. Much was inspired by Meissen; but already by 1756 the Chelsea sale catalogue reveals the Vincennes-Sèvres influence in green and black landscape painting and a deep 'mazarine' blue ground, the Chelsea equivalent of '*gros bleu*'. Rich gilding, too, now came increasingly into use, even for the anchor mark (about ¯1755–69). Along with the coloured grounds (a greenish turquoise and a crimson 'claret' were soon added) went a vogue for painting exotic birds, elaborate mythological or *chinoiserie* figure-subjects after Boucher and other French artists and lush bouquets of flowers. These richer painted decorations were matched by an exuberance of modelling scarcely paralleled elsewhere and certainly completely alien to Sèvres.

The figures which consorted with these elaborate 'gold anchor' wares were still mostly the work of Willems, until he left the factory in 1766. They tended to be large, their elaborate rococo-scrolled bases richly gilt, their costumes flowered and diapered in polychrome enamels and gold. In this period the porcelain figure appears to have moved from the dessert-table to the mantelshelf and the cabinet, and in consequence was given a frontal aspect only, the customary supporting tree-trunk sprouting a luxuriant 'bocage' of leaves and flowers to show the figure as if it were in a leafy bower.

Tablewares and figures by no means exhausted the Chelsea reputation. Perhaps building on the success of another factory established probably in the same vicinity, Chelsea produced a great quantity of small trinkets and objects of luxury—*bonbonnières*, scent-flasks, bodkin-cases, fob-seals—known as 'Chelsea toys'.

Chelsea was sold in 1769 and thereafter run in combination with the Derby factory. The 'Chelsea-Derby' period (1769–84, when Chelsea finally closed) was marked by the gradual introduction of the neo-classical style which began in the 1760s to dominate all the arts. The more sober 'Louis XVI' Sèvres became the admired prototype with its striped and garlanded designs and grisaille painting of classical themes. The old styles, however, were slow to die out and fine flower-painting survived well into the 'Chelsea-Derby' period.

With Chelsea as yard-stick one may take a more measured look at the other 18th-century English porcelain factories. Probably the earliest and certainly the most important was Bow (Stratford-le-Bow in East London). As early as 6th December, 1744, Edward Heylyn and Thomas Frye took out a patent for a material from which porcelain could be made, although actual production was probably delayed for two or three years. In 1749 they obtained a further patent mentioning a material produced partly by 'calcining all animal substances'. This no doubt alluded to the use of bone-ash; the consequent phosphoric acid content has long been recognised as characteristic of the Bow body. The bone-ash produced stability in the kiln, and this desirable property ensured its increasing use. By 1800 almost every English factory employed it and bone-china became England's greatest contribution in the field of porcelain manufacture.

Bow, although it produced some porcelain of superlative quality, probably aimed at a middle-class market. A commentator in 1761 wrote that Bow China 'though not so fine as some made at Chelsea, or as that from Dresden, is much stronger than either and therefore better for common use; and, being much cheaper than any other China, there is a greater Demand for it'. In contrast to Chelsea, Bow had a large output of the cheaper blue-and-white porcelain, often employing a beautiful mauvish-toned blue. Of the enamelled wares, those in 'Kakiemon' style were perhaps the commonest, the painting often being such 'as to equal most of that from Dresden'. Fine 'European' flowers were also painted, in a delectable soft palette including a rose-purple and an opaque light blue virtually peculiar to Bow. The factory was prolific of figure-models, many indeed copied from Meissen, but others taken from engravings and reflecting a strong topical interest—whether theatrical subjects, such as *Kitty Clive* and *Henry Woodward* in Garrick's farce *Lethe* or, celebrating the victories of 1759, *General Wolfe* and the *Marquis of Granby*. Apart from these individual figures, there was the usual rout of ladies and gentlemen, shepherds and shepherdesses, goddesses, Turks and Italian Comedy characters. After about 1760 a decline sets in, the colours growing harsher, the painting more perfunctory, and the modelling more slovenly. All in all, Bow was a factory of uneven performance, but endowed with a strong individuality and an unmistakable English flavour.

A small factory founded at Lowestoft (in Suffolk) about 1757,

697

699
700

705

707

703

701

701

702

701. Figure of *Neptune*, creamy soft-paste. Bow; about 1755–60. Ht. 6¼ in. (16 cm.). This little figure of *Neptune* astride a dolphin is characteristic of the vigorous modelling found at the Bow factory in the 1750's. He forms a companion to a *Jupiter* astride an eagle, and both models perhaps derive from Italian baroque originals in bronze. Victoria and Albert Museum, London.

702. Jug, porcelain painted in enamel colours. Lowestoft; about 1765. Ht. 7 in. (17·8 cm.). The Lowestoft factory catered on the whole for a local market, although much of its porcelain was also exported to Holland. The decoration of the jug illustrated is characteristic of the somewhat naive wares made at the manufacture. It shows a cricket match in progress, probably on the Denes at Lowestoft, and is taken from a print by H. Roberts after L. P. Boitard. Victoria and Albert Museum, London.

703. Porringer and cover, porcelain painted in enamel colours with touches of gold. Bow; about 1755–60. Diam. 6 in. (15·2 cm.). This handled porringer (sometimes miscalled a bleeding-bowl) is painted with design of quails in a landscape which is very commonly found at the Bow factory (so-called 'partridge pattern'). It derives from the Arita porcelain in the Kakiemon style imported from Japan at the end of the 17th and the beginning of the 18th century. Victoria and Albert Museum, London.

704. Picture showing a tea-tray and urn. English School; about 1770–75. This painting well shows the equipage of an English tea-table in the third quarter of the 18th century. The silver accessories are dateable in the period 1740–70. The porcelain is blue-and-white with gilt rims, and may possibly be identified as Worcester. Victoria and Albert Museum, London.

703

705. Toilet-set, porcelain painted in green enamel and gilt. Derby; about 1780. Ht. of central box 3 in. (7·7 cm.). The central box of this set is surmounted by two doves with a quiver between them, while the two cylindrical pomade-pots have knobs in the form of a boy caressing a lamb. The Sale *Catalogues* of the united Chelsea and Derby factories frequently mention 'dressing-boxes' and 'pomatum pots'. Victoria and Albert Museum, London.

704

705

seems to have stood in some relationship to Bow, using a similar bone-ash formula and comparable decorative styles in the blue-and-white wares. The enamelled wares, however, mostly made after 1770, are quite different from those of Bow, and only a few undistinguished figures were produced.

The establishment of a factory at Bristol in 1748 was probably motivated by a parallel search for a robust porcelain body. Here the formula included soaprock, a natural substance found in Cornwall. The relative proximity of Bristol may have recommended it as the seat of manufacture rather than Limehouse (London), where the original experiments apparently took place. The Bristol concern was soon taken over (1752) by the Worcester Porcelain Company and the earliest wares of this 'Bristol-Worcester' concern, which are generally indistinguishable, may be considered together. The greyish soapstone porcelain (green by transmitted light) permitted thin potting and crisp moulded detail. It was moreover tough. The *Annual Register* for 1763 records: 'We have indeed, here, many other manufactories of porcelain ... but, except the Worcester, they all wear brown, and are subject to crack, especially the glazing, by boiling water'. Useful blue-and-white porcelain undoubtedly provided the bread-and-butter of the Worcester trade. Fine enamelled decoration was nonetheless practised, at first in Oriental-inspired patterns, later in 'European' flowers of marked individuality, birds, and European figures in landscapes.

Far more important, however, was the introduction from the enamel industry of transfer-printing. Although some Bow porcelain had been printed, Worcester was the first porcelain factory to use printing on a large scale, Robert Hancock being mainly responsible for the prints used at both. In transfer-printing, a paper pull from an engraved and specially inked copper-plate could be applied to the porcelain, the transferred design being then fixed in a low-temperature firing. From a single plate innumerable objects could be quickly decorated and this discovery was of cardinal importance to the later commercial expansion of the English ceramic industry (see p. 271). At first in over-glaze black (from 1757 at the latest), the transfer-process was subsequently (not later than 1760) extended at Worcester to underglaze-blue, further cheapening blue-and-white.

In the 1760s Worcester began, like Chelsea, to react to French influence, and imbricated ('scale') blue, and crimson grounds became common, the painting, usually of exotic birds and flowers, being carried out in reserved panels outlined with rich gilt scrollwork. An accession of Chelsea painters in 1768 probably greatly strengthened this side of the factory's work, and a number of great vases painted with figures by the miniaturist, John Donaldson, and by J. H. O'Neale with figural and animal subjects, date from this period. Much Worcester porcelain was painted in the London atelier of James Giles, in individual bird-, flower- and figure-styles, often combined with turquoise and imbricated grounds peculiar to the workshop. Very few figures were made at Worcester.

A number of factories took up the basic Worcester formula, notable amongst them being Caughley, in Shropshire. Here, from 1772 onwards, much blue-and-white was made, both painted and printed, much of it closely resembling Worcester.

In Liverpool, too, four factories seem to have sprung up in

706

708

707

706. Sauce-boat, soft-paste porcelain, painted in enamel colours. Bristol; about 1752. L. 6⅜ in. (16 cm.). Mark: BRISTOLL in relief, painted over with a leaf in green enamel. The Bristol concern was bought by the Worcester factory in 1752, and amongst the stock some pieces bore the moulded mark of the older company, sometimes painted out when the piece was decorated, presumably at Worcester. Victoria and Albert Museum, London.

707. Plate, porcelain printed in underglaze-blue. Bow; about 1760. Diam. 7·8 in. (20 cm.). One of England's main technical contributions to ceramic history was the invention of transfer-printing, first overglaze printing, then by about 1760 a printing in cobalt-blue under the glaze, a development which was destined to have great economic significance for the English pottery and porcelain industry from the late 18th century. The same *chinoiserie* print (*La Dame Chinoise*) is also found on porcelains made in other English factories. British Museum, London.

708. Coffee-pot and cover, porcelain, printed in black. Worcester; about 1765. Ht. 8¼ in. (20·7 cm.). Transfer-printing was begun about mid-18th century. One of its pioneers was Robert Hancock—later a partner in the Worcester porcelain factory; his prints were first used about 1755 when he was either working there or supplying engravings from his Birmingham workshop. *The Tea Party* shown here is his best-known composition, a typical *galanterie*. On the other side is a version of Watteau's *La Diseuse d'Avantage*. Victoria and Albert Museum, London.

1754–55, apparently sometimes using bone-ash and sometimes soapstone. Mainly blue-and-white was made, much of it in Worcester shapes and styles. Liverpool was also a centre for transfer-printing, the firm of John Sadler (see p. 272) being particularly well-known, and in one of the factories (William Ball's) soapstone porcelain was decorated by 'polychrome printing'—a system of outline-printing in two or three colours, supplemented by enamel washes.

A factory making a glassy soft-paste porcelain was founded about 1749 at Longton Hall, near Stoke-on-Trent in Staffordshire. It had as manager William Littler, a Staffordshire man, who had probably acquired porcelain-making experience at Limehouse. Longton Hall suffered serious economic vicissitudes, probably due to firing-losses, eventually ceasing production in 1760. At first the factory appears to have made figures more easily than tablewares, the latter being moulded for preference, rather than thrown. A speciality of the factory was a brilliant blue ground like that used on salt-glazed stoneware, also associated with Littler (see p. 268). The tablewares were often in leaf forms enamelled in particularly brilliant yellow and green tones, often supplemented by bird or flower painting of

an easily recognisable character, or by landscape vignettes of great charm. The Longton Hall figures, which at first were often warped in firing and over-thickly glazed, were frequently based on Meissen or Chelsea originals, whilst some of the more original models are amusing puppets of no great artistic pretension. Later, however, a greater technical assurance was achieved and a factory style becomes discernible. The proprietary partnership was dissolved in 1760, Littler retiring to Musselburgh, near Prestonpans in Scotland, where he continued to decorate Longton stock for the Scottish gentry, whose heraldic bearings often appear on such pieces.

Longton Hall had a short life, but another Midlands concern with somewhat similar beginnings survived to be, after Worcester, the longest-lived porcelain manufactory in the country. This was the Derby factory, established by 1750. In 1756, William Duesbury who had run an enamelling establishment in London during the early 1750s, joined the company. A 1757 advertisement speaks of the 'Derby or second Dresden' factory, which now began to produce innumerable versions of Meissen figures. The painted decoration of this period includes readily recognisable flower-sprays on thin thread-like stalks. Comparatively little blue-and-white porcelain

709. Jug, porcelain, printed in underglaze-blue. Caughley; about 1780. Marks, 'S' (for 'Salopian') and a cross, in underglaze-blue. The 'Salopian' factory at Caughley, in Shropshire, was largely inspired by the Worcester concern, and jugs of this shape, with moulded cabbage-leaves as decoration and a mask-spout, were first made at Worcester. Caughley catered for a mass-market, and the blue print decorating this jug is perhaps its most frequent design—characteristic *chinoiserie* with its Chinese fisherwoman, cormorant on the rock, and rocky shoreline and sea receding into the distance. Victoria and Albert Museum, London.

710. Garniture of five vases and ewers, porcelain, painted in colours and gilt, on a dark blue ground. Liverpool, Philip Christian's factory; about 1770. The Liverpool factories tended to look to Worcester for their models, and the elaborately painted panels reserved on the blue ground of these vases no doubt derive their inspiration from the same source. Here, however, the panels deal with religious subject, which was probably without parallel at Worcester. Garnitures such as these, but normally of three baluster vases and two trumpet-shaped 'beakers', were a normal decorative unit for a mantel or the top of a piece of furniture. Liverpool City Museum.

711. Mug and small cup, porcelain, enamel-painted. English (probably Richard Chaffers' factory); about 1756. Ht. of mug 4⅞ in. (12·5 cm.). The secret of using soapstone in a porcelain body was brought illicitly from Worcester to Liverpool by two absconding Worcester workmen, and first used in the factory of Richard Chaffers and Co. which produced not only blue-and-white china, which was the backbone of the trade, but enamel-painted wares of high quality. This Chinese lady feeding a parrot is an amusing example of a decorative style commonly found on Chaffers' polychrome wares. Victoria and Albert Museum, London.

712

713

714

716

715

712. Group, porcelain painted in enamel colours, with traces of gilding. Longton Hall; about 1756–57. Ht. 5⅛ in. (13 cm.). Groups such as this, of *Two Putti feeding a Goat*, were made in pairs at the Longton Hall factory, and were no doubt intended as chimney-piece ornaments. The stock-in-trade of the Longton Hall factory was sold in Salisbury in 1760, and some of its models reappear later in hard-paste porcelain at the Plymouth factory, as does this one. Victoria and Albert Museum, London.

713. Group of *Two Virgins awaking Cupid*, biscuit porcelain. English (Derby); about 1785. Ht. 12 in. (30·5 cm.). This group was inspired by an engraving by W. Wynne Ryland after a painting by Angelica Kauffmann. Published in 1776, the engraving well represents the sentimental view of neo-classicism then popular in England. Biscuit porcelain, with its covert reference to classical marble, no doubt seemed the appropriate material for such a theme, the original model for which was probably made by Pierre Stephan. The incised triangle shows that the group was put together, or 'repaired', by Joseph Hill. Victoria and Albert Museum, London.

714. Set of *Four Seasons*, white porcelain. Derby; about 1750–54. Ht. of *Autumn* 5¼ in. (13·3 cm.). Sets of allegorical abstractions such as these *Seasons* were popular with the English 18th-century porcelain manufacturer, as may be seen in figs. 698 and 722. Here beautiful glassy soft-paste porcelain admirably sets off the quality of the modelling, although it is possible that the figures were originally painted in unfired colours, which have subsequently rubbed off. Victoria and Albert Museum, London.

715. Decorative ewer, porcelain, painted in grey, blue and gold. English (Derby); about 1785. Ht. 10⅞ in. (27·5 cm.). Mark, 'D' under a crown, in gold, and '892' incised. The subject and the delicate *grisaille* painting of this ewer bring out well the flavour of the curiously sentimental neo-classicism which found favour at Derby. The finely controlled shape, and the rich but chaste striped ground give a great elegance to this piece. It has been suggested that the figure was painted by Richard Askew, who had previously worked at Chelsea, and the landscape behind her by Zachariah Boreman, one of the best Derby landscape painters, also previously a Chelsea hand. Victoria and Albert Museum, London.

716. Plate, porcelain, painted in enamel colours and gilt, with a royal-blue border. Longton Hall; about 1755, decorated about 1760–65. Diam. 8¼ in. (21 cm.). One of the hallmarks of Longton Hall was a brilliant royal blue ground colour, called 'Littler's blue' after the manager of the factory. The 'dishevelled birds' here in a style occurring on porcelain from other factories, suggests that the work was done by an outside decorator very probably James Giles who had an atelier in Berwick Street, Soho, in 1763. Victoria and Albert Museum, London.

717. *Jardinière* and cover, porcelain painted in enamel colours and gilt. Worcester, Chamberlain's factory; about 1815. Ht. 8⅛ in. (20·5 cm.). Mark: 'Chamberlains Worcester', in gold. Chamberlain's, the second factory started in Worcester, was fully the equal of the original factory in the quality and elaboration of its painted decoration. The *jardinière* illustrated is painted with the theme of *Orpheus and Eurydice*, probably by Thomas Baxter (1782–1821). It was intended to be filled with flowers, stuck through the holes in its cover. Victoria and Albert Museum, London.

718. Teapot and cover, hard-paste porcelain painted in enamel colours. New Hall factory; dated 1803. Ht. 6 in. (15·3 cm.). Throughout the 18th century the English porcelain-makers tended to copy the shapes of silverware as in this New Hall teapot which reflects the contemporary straight-sided silver teapot of lozenge shape, with vertical fluting. The artless painting of flowers, however, reveals a very unsophisticated art compared with what had gone before. Porcelain was now descending the social scale and being mass-produced for a middle-class clientele. Victoria and Albert Museum, London.

719. Plate, bone-china printed in underglaze-blue. Etruria, Wedgwood factory; about 1815. Diam. 9⅛ in. (23·2 cm.). Mark: 'WEDGWOOD'. The great Josiah Wedgwood professed to scorn porcelain, even though he liked to think of his white jasperware as a kind of porcelain. His successors, however, were tempted into the porcelain field in 1812, and in accordance with the best traditions of the firm, made wares of high technical quality. The close copying of Chinese themes here, however, was perhaps unexpected from a factory hitherto so firmly attached to classical modes. Victoria and Albert Museum, London.

was ever made at Derby. In the 'Chelsea-Derby period' (see p. 247) Derby produced numerous figures and groups, their costumes painted in pale colours, and their rock-work bases picked out in green and salmon-pink. An important innovation was the biscuit porcelain figure inspired by Sèvres (see p. 238), in the manufacture of which Derby was by far the most important English factory.

Chelsea was finally abandoned in 1784 and two years later William Duesbury died, to be succeeded by his son of the same name. This change corresponds roughly with a development of style, small landscape and seascape vignettes or classical figure subjects being painted in plain panels reserved on a ground, tones of green, yellow and salmon-pink now replacing the earlier dark blue and crimson. Flower-painting on a white ground, however, still persisted, and William Billingsley (see p. 254) devised a naturalistic method of painting flowers—particularly roses—by applying the pigment and then wiping out the highlights, a manner which became standard in the English factories. The years before and after 1800 were indeed remarkable for the excellence of the painting at Derby. The Derby styles were reflected in the porcelain of the short-lived Pinxton factory, near Nottingham (1795–1813).

At Worcester, this period was characterised by parallel developments, with bird-, flower-, shell- and landscape-painting in panels on coloured grounds, and elaborately finished figural painting in the classical or romantic vein by painters such as Thomas Baxter or James Pennington. The grounds became far more diverse in colour, sometimes patterned with marbling or *vermiculée* designs, and supplemented by elaborate borders of the rich brassy mercury gilding characteristic of the early 19th century.

In 1811, Robert Bloor took charge of the Derby factory. Financial stringency forced him to decorate existing stock in summary styles, such as the scattered Paris sprig design and the 'Japan' patterns predominantly in underglaze-blue, iron-red and gold—an economical palette used with hideous effect both at Derby and at the numerous contemporary Staffordshire factories.

One episode in the history of English porcelain stands outside the mainstream—the independent discovery of true 'hard-paste'

porcelain by William Cookworthy, a Devon apothecary. As early as 1745 Cookworthy was investigating the 'porcelain-secret', finally identifying in Cornwall the china-clay and china-stone which are the essential ingredients. In 1768, after a period of experiment, he took out a patent. A company of thirteen shareholders was formed to exploit the new discovery in a factory at Plymouth, but the undertaking there was short-lived, and probably by the end of 1770 the factory had been transferred to Bristol. The leading personality then, was Richard Champion, an original Plymouth shareholder, who now mastered the intricacies of porcelain-manufacture. Financial difficulties, however, forced Champion to sell out to a consortium of Staffordshire potters, and Bristol finally closed in 1781. The work recommenced in 1782 at a pottery in Shelton (Staffordshire), known as the New Hall, and here a modified hard-paste porcelain was made until about 1812, mostly in tea-services decorated with simple sprig-designs in 'Cottage' style.

The earliest porcelain made at Plymouth was technically defective, fire-cracked and stained brown, the underglaze-blue being greyish in tone. A number of striking figures, however, include animals and birds, and a set of large *Continents* and smaller *Seasons*. These correspond to Longton Hall models and prompt the thought that the Longton moulds may have been presciently bought in 1760. Under Champion's direction some of the earlier defects were corrected and an increasingly elaborate range of tablewares and vases was produced, many lavishly enamelled and gilt in the most sumptuous style of the period. A number of figures were also added to the repertory, apparently the work of the Derby modeller, Pierre Stephan. The Bristol hard-paste, however, did not lend itself to figure-modelling and the factory's figures lack suppleness or grace. More successful were the biscuit plaques with flower-wreaths elaborately worked in relief, traditionally ascribed to Thomas Briand.

Before 1800 the standard English 'bone-china'—a modified form of the original Bow formula (see p. 247) had evolved in Staffordshire, a development usually credited to the first Josiah Spode. Practical in manufacture and use, and agreeably translucent, it

719

720

720. Dish, soft-paste porcelain, painted in enamel colours and gilt. Welsh; about 1820. L. 20⅝ in. (52·5 cm.). Mark: 'SWANSEA', impressed. William Billingsley at Swansea and Nantgarw made some of the most beautiful white china ever produced in England, much in demand by big china-merchants' decorators in London, where much of the most ambitious decoration was done, including that on this dish from the Burdett-Coutts service. Noteworthy is the fine lacy gilding of the border, and the lush rendering of pink roses in the manner pioneered by Billingsley. Victoria and Albert Museum, London.

721. Group of two mugs and a salt-cellar, hard-paste porcelain painted in underglaze-blue. Plymouth; about 1770. Ht. of salt-cellar 2⅞ in. (7·3 cm.). Hard-paste porcelain, demanding very high temperatures in its manufacture, which always presented difficulties in the early stages of its production often becoming cracked with heat. Plymouth was no excpetion to this rule; the thrown pieces were technically defective, often betraying a spiral 'wreathing', the underglaze-blue being of a greyish colour, and the glaze frequently stained brown by fumes. Victoria and Albert Museum, London.

722. Set of the *Four Continents*, hard-paste porcelain painted in enamel colours and gilt. Plymouth; about 1770. Ht. 12½ to 13⅛ in. (31·8 to 33·5 cm.). The *Four Continents* were favoured abstracts to be made up into sets by the porcelain-maker for table decorations and other purposes. The moulds for these figures were probably bought by William Cookworthy at the sale of Longton Hall stock at Salisbury in 1760. Nevertheless, the production of such large figures in the difficult hard-paste material represents a considerable technical achievement. Victoria and Albert Museum, London.

721

723

722

723. Plaque, porcelain painted in enamel colours and gilt, with a deep blue border. Derby; about 1833–40. Ht. 9⅛ in. (23·2 cm.). Mark: crossed swords in blue. This oval decorative plaque well represents the taste of the early Victorian period, with its sentimentality and romanticism (epitomised in the little coloured boy and the vaguely oriental setting). It was painted by John Haslem, the historian of the Derby factory. The gilt border in the 'revived rococo' taste common after about 1825, in conjunction with the rich blue ground on which it stands, is opulent enough for any taste. Victoria and Albert Museum, London.

offered a fine white surface for decoration in all the current modes. These virtues strongly attracted the practical minds of the Staffordshire potters, and as the 19th century advanced Staffordshire attained a progressively dominant place in the English industry: of the old-established factories, only Derby and Worcester survived outside the Potteries. Between 1800 and 1850, at least twenty Staffordshire firms making porcelain have been identified. Their styles defy analysis, for even the smallest factory might have hundreds of patterns current, and all plagiarised without scruple, stealing patterns indifferently from Derby, Worcester or each other.

Outside Staffordshire in this period a development occurred which in a sense harked back to the 18th century. William Billingsley (see p. 252), after founding the Pinxton factory, had spent five years at Worcester, where he developed a beautiful glassy white porcelain. In 1813, breaking the terms of his contract, he absconded from Worcester and established a small factory for making this porcelain, at Nantgarw, between Cardiff and Pontypridd. Despite initial success, financial difficulties forced him in 1814 to transfer the manufacture to the Cambrian Pottery in Swansea. Three years later Billingsley returned to Nantgarw and resumed production there until in 1819 shortage of money forced him to leave again, this time to take employment with the Coalport factory (see p. 296).

The Nantgarw porcelain was of a whiteness and beauty hardly seen since the 18th century, but it was not economic, and at Swansea the formula was adapted to include first bone-ash and later soap-stone, producing more stable but less attractive bodies. These wares were frequently decorated outside the factory, mainly in London workshops. The factory's own decoration was usually relatively simple—mainly flower-painting either by or in the style of Billingsley. A number of other talented artists worked in the Swansea factory who, after the factory's closure in 1826, helped to spread its fresh naturalistic style of flower-painting.

In 1820, Billingsley joined John Rose at Coalport not far from Caughley (see p. 249) which factory Rose had bought out in 1799. Already by 1816 Coalport had been manufacturing porcelain for the London market, and Billingsley and his son-in-law, Samuel Walker, were hired to reproduce at Coalport the Swansea and Nantgarw bodies. In 1822 the Swansea moulds were bought. The Coalport porcelain of this period, therefore, is a fine white ware comparable with that of Swansea and often decorated in the same general styles. Walker developed a number of ground-colours, but the decoration most characteristic of Coalport evolved in the 'revived rococo' period after about 1820, when the porcelain was ornamented with elaborately modelled stems and flowers. The elaboration of the Coalport wares was rivalled at the 'Rockingham' porcelain factory at Swinton, in South Yorkshire, which began in 1826 to make a bone-porcelain of Staffordshire type.

These styles of the second quarter of the 19th century, however, with their paintings in panels on coloured grounds and their applied ornaments, in a sense only provided a coda to a tradition which was by now almost exhausted. In the 1830s and 1840s more vital developments were taking place which were a prelude to the true Victorian style dealt with in the chapter on modern ceramics.

724

725

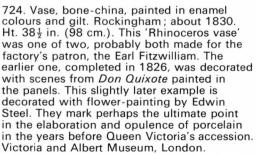

724. Vase, bone-china, painted in enamel colours and gilt. Rockingham; about 1830. Ht. 38½ in. (98 cm.). This 'Rhinoceros vase' was one of two, probably both made for the factory's patron, the Earl Fitzwilliam. The earlier one, completed in 1826, was decorated with scenes from *Don Quixote* painted in the panels. This slightly later example is decorated with flower-painting by Edwin Steel. They mark perhaps the ultimate point in the elaboration and opulence of porcelain in the years before Queen Victoria's accession. Victoria and Albert Museum, London.

725. Teapot and cover, porcelain, painted in enamel colours and gilt. Coalport; about 1820. Ht. 6¼ in. (16 cm.). Of all the factories making high-quality porcelain over the period 1820 50, Coalport probably made most use of 'encrusted' decorations of applied flowers and leaves in the 'revived rococo' style supplemented by quite elaborate painting. This teapot exploits a watery theme, with its rockwork base, lily-pads and swan-finial, and these elements are integrated into the design with uncommon skill. Victoria and Albert Museum, London.

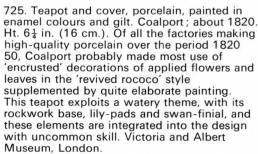

726. Jug of soft-paste porcelain painted in enamel colours. Copenhagen, Louis Fournier's factory; about 1760–65. Ht. 5½ in. (14 cm.). Mark: 'F 5' in blue enamel (for 'Frederick V'). Signs of French influence here are presumably due more or less directly to Fournier. The knob of the cover is strongly reminiscent of Sèvres, while the handle, both in form and colouring, resembles models used at Chantilly. Other examples of this jug have a twiggy handle which perhaps accords better with the applied stems and leaves on the cover. Victoria and Albert Museum, London.

Other European centres

Denmark

Porcelain manufacture in Scandinavia was as bedevilled by false dawns as it had been anywhere else. The notorious C. C. Hunger was in Copenhagen in 1730 (probably in connection with his employment in the Swedish faience factory at Rörstrand) and again in 1737. The equally notorious J. C. L. von Lücke won royal support for various essays in porcelain-making in Copenhagen in 1752–54 before accepting a pension and in 1755 a privilege to found a faience-factory at Schleswig (p. 206). No objects can with any confidence be attributed to either of these undoubted charlatans. A third alchemist, named D. McCarthy, from England this time, after comparable attempts with royal subvention, did at least produce a soft-paste medallion with the head of Frederick V, inscribed on the reverse: 'God Bless your Mayes and I wish you a happy New Yr 17 DMC 54'. Two painters from Meissen, Jürgen Gylding and Johann Gottlieb Mehlhorn, also received subsidies, but no porcelain by them has been identified, although a number of plaques enamelled by Gylding are known.

The first successful production of porcelain in Copenhagen was due to the Frenchman, Louis Fournier, who had been a modeller at Vincennes and subsequently worked at Chantilly. Fournier arrived in Copenhagen in 1759 and was successful in making a creamy soft-paste porcelain of French type, decorated in predominantly French style, although some pieces owe more to Meissen. The pieces made were almost all small, a bust of Frederick V being probably the largest model produced. The tablewares were usually painted with flowers, in a style reminiscent of Mennecy, but on later pieces fruits also appear, and very rarely figure-painting in association with plain or scale, coloured grounds. On these later pieces of fine quality gilding is sparingly used, and the factory mark 'F5' (for 'Fredrik V') is also gilt. A number of medallions with portrait-heads were made, but the main output was of tea-table and dinner-table wares, vases and covered toilet-pots.

Fournier's manufacture proved too costly, and the King ordered it to stop production in 1765, although a single piece marked 'C7' (for 'Christian VII') indicates that some pieces were at least enamelled after his death in 1766. Fournier was found to divulge his secrets to commissioners, of whom one was the Guardian of the Mint, Frantz Heinrich Müller. This man, who was an able chemist, was interested in the porcelain secret and, after a series of experiments, founded in 1775 a company to make porcelain with the kaolin which had been identified twenty years earlier on the island of Bornholm. An accession of artistic staff from Meissen, Berlin and Fürstenberg (including the modeller, A. C. Luplau, who seems also to have been the leading technician) greatly raised the standard of modelling and painting, and imparted an unmistakable German flavour to the factory's products. In 1779 the factory was taken over by the King and received the title of 'The Royal Danish Porcelain Factory'. This financial prop saved the factory, which, unable to fill its stockrooms with perfect wares, had therefore sold almost nothing.

The earliest Copenhagan porcelain of a greyish colour, is decorated in underglaze-blue with adapted versions of Meissen designs, notably the 'immortelle' pattern. The shapes often show Fürstenberg influence, and much use was made of relief-decoration and piercing. The earliest enamelling appears to have been in purple or iron-red, but a palette of colours soon evolved in which flowers and less frequently birds, landscapes and figures were painted with varying degrees of skill. The factory's output was by no means unambitious, including large and elaborate vases and flower-holders, complete tea- and coffee-services, as well as small objects of *galanterie* such as snuff-boxes and needle-cases, usually painted with more than usual care. By far the most important of its productions, however, was the famous *Flora Danica* service originally intended for Catherine II but ultimately taken over by the King. Begun in 1789, it was decorated with named plants from G. C. Oeder's *Flora of the Danish Kingdom*, painted by J. C. Bayer, a Nuremberg artist living in Copenhagen since 1768. When production was countermanded in 1803 the service numbered nearly two thousand pieces.

Figure-modelling began on a modest scale in the period 1776–79, but gathered momentum after 1780, probably under Luplau's direction. The figures are mostly adaptations of German and French prototypes, and are usually not of particularly good quality. Biscuit porcelain was not infrequently used for figure models.

The Copenhagen factory reacted to the changing tastes of the late 18th and early 19th centuries, keeping up with developments in the main European factories, but seldom creating usual styles of its own. The production of figures, however, was given fresh life with the introduction after 1835 of models by the great Danish sculptor, Thorvaldsen.

727
728
729
730

726

727

727. Tureen and cover, hard-paste porcelain, painted in underglaze-blue. Royal Danish Porcelain Factory, Copenhagen; about 1780–90. Ht. 11¾ in. (30 cm.). Mark: three wavy lines. Painting in underglaze-blue was one of the first specialities of the Copenhagen factory, and one of the first patterns adopted has also proved to be of timeless appeal. It was, appropriately enough, taken over from the 'immortelle' design at Meissen. The knob of the cover is made in the shape of an artichoke. Private collection.

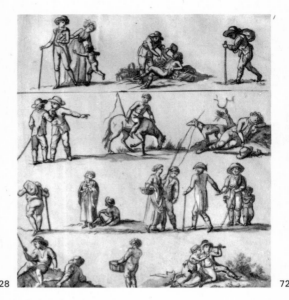

728. Sheet of drawings for porcelain-decoration. Pen and wash, by Elias Meier, for the Royal Danish Porcelain Factory, Copenhagen; about 1780–90. Ht. 9⅞ in. (25 cm.). Graphic work by ceramic artists rarely survives and these sprightly drawings reveal a talent of no mean order. Meier, one of the factory's most versatile decorators, painted polychrome landscapes on breakfast-services, animals, birds, 'Antique heads' after B. Picard's *Pierres antiques gravées*, and 'quodlibets' (haphazard arrangements of familiar objects in a '*trompe l'œil*' style). Library of the Royal Danish Porcelain Manufactory.

729. Covered *pot-pourri*, hard-paste porcelain, painted in enamel colours and gilt. Royal Danish Porcelain Factory, Copenhagen; about 1780–85. Ht. 18¼ in. (46·4 cm.). Mark: three wavy lines and 'K' incised. This *pot-pourri* vase, one of several similar models, is elaborately decorated with applied coloured flowers and leaves, and in front a portrait-medallion of the Crown Prince Frederick (later Frederick VI) in sepia monochrome, probably by F. C. Camradt. *Pot-pourri* vases with their sweet-smelling dried petals and spices were much used in an age plagued by bad smells. Victoria and Albert Museum, London.

730. Ice-pail of hard-paste porcelain, painted in enamel colours and gilt. Royal Danish Porcelain Factory, Copenhagen; about 1790–1800. Ht. 10⅜ in. (26·5 cm.). Ice-pails with a galleried cover, a liner and the pail itself were for cooling food-stuffs as well as drinks. This one is from the great 'Flora Danica' service, painted by Johann Christoph Bayer from 1789–1802. Some Chelsea porcelain plates had as early as about 1755 been decorated by detailed copying of botanical prints, but this service was the first example of the relentless following-through of such a programme continuing until Bayer was 64 and his eyesight ruined. Rosenborg Castle, Copenhagen.

Sweden

Hunger had been in Stockholm as he had been in Copenhagen (p. 255), but seems not to have engaged in porcelain manufacture at the former capital. It was not until 1759 that the first porcelain appears to have been made in Sweden. In 1758 J. L. E. Ehrenreich, a German who had come to Sweden in 1747 as court dentist, approached the Government with a proposal to erect a factory for making porcelain and faience. The estate of Marieberg, on Kungsholmen in Stockholm, was bought and buildings erected 'for the establishment of a manufacture of the true porcelain'. The first full-scale firing took place in May, 1759, but at the end of that month the building burnt down, and although Ehrenreich rebuilt his factory, he thenceforth concentrated entirely on faience. The only piece of porcelain attributed to this period is a leaf-moulded dish in the National Museum, Stockholm. No further porcelain was made at Marieberg until Ehrenreich was replaced in 1766 by the Frenchman, Pierre Berthevin, who had been a modeller at Mennecy. At Marieberg Berthevin made a creamy soft-paste porcelain not unlike that of Mennecy and decorated mainly in the Mennecy style of flower-painting in soft-colours. The shape most favoured was the typical French ice-cream cup with cover, decorated with spiral mouldings, but small vases with dolphin handles and a limited range of small-scale porcelain-figures was also made, mostly copying Meissen and Frankenthal models.

Berthevin left Marieberg in 1769 and was succeeded by Henrik Sten, of the rival Rörstrand factory. By 1772 Sten appears to have succeeded in producing a chalky bastard body, much harder than Berthevin's, but not a true hard-paste. The latter was probably only achieved in 1777–78 when Jacob Dortu, who had been trained at Berlin, was working at Marieberg. Production probably ceased before 1782, when the factory was sold.

The wares made in the improved bodies at Marieberg were a continuation of some of Berthevin's models, particularly the ice-cream cups, but larger and more ambitious pieces, such as small

tureens, teapots, bowls and *tête-à-tête* sets, were successfully made in styles inspired by Berlin, Sèvres and other leading Continental factories. Although often perfunctory, the painting could be, at its best, of high quality, and was sometimes deployed on fine scale-grounds. In the later period the figure-modelling was greatly extended in range, but apart from a few stiff renderings of indigenous Swedish peasant and other types, never attained an original factory style.

731

256

731. Ice-cream cup, soft-paste porcelain, painted in enamel colours. Marieberg (Sweden); about 1766–69. Pierre Berthevin took over the managership of the Marieberg factory in 1766, and succeeded in making soft-paste porcelain there. Berthevin had worked at Mennecy, and the little 'cream-cups' or 'jelly-pots' made for different kinds of sweets at Marieberg at this time reflect Mennecy influence in the paste, shape and enamel-painting. Between 1772 and 1788 about 15,700 of them were made at the factory. Victoria and Albert Museum, London.

732. Teapot and cover of hard-paste porcelain, painted in colours and gilt. Dutch, *Oude Loosdrecht* factory; about 1776. Ht. 4⅝ in. (12 cm.). Mark: 'MOL' in underglaze-blue. Dutch porcelain, although not usually of marked originality, was often of high quality. Scene-painting of the character revealed by this teapot shows a high order of achievement, and was a speciality of the Oude Loosdrecht concern. The acorn-knob on the cover of the teapot is a shape otherwise much used at the Tournai factory. Victoria and Albert Museum, London.

733. Group soft-paste porcelain painted in enamel colours. Marieberg (Sweden); about 1766–69. Ht. 6⅛ in. (15·6 cm.). Mark: 'MB' in monogram, incised. Although Pierre Berthevin's French type of porcelain was a soft-paste, Marieberg frequently copied Meissen's hard-paste models. This group is taken from one by J. J. Kändler of 1755–56. Aeneas is carrying his father, Anchises, from the sack of Troy; his little son, Ascanius, follows behind. Anchises carries the Palladium, the sacred image governing the fortune of Troy. Nordiska Museet, Stockholm.

732

733

Holland

In 1757 the same D. McCarthy who has already been seen experimenting in Copenhagen (p. 255) started a factory at Weesp, not far from Amsterdam. The concern was taken over in 1759 by Count Gronsveld-Diepenbroick-Impel, and hard-paste porcelain was made with the help of German work-people. The most notable of these was the 'arcanist', Nikolaus Paul, who subsequently helped to set up the factory at Fulda (p. 227). In 1771 the Weesp factory was bought by a pastor, named Johannes de Mol, and transferred with its moulds to Oude Loosdrecht, not far away. Here another well-known 'arcanist', L. V. Gerverot, who had been at a variety of German factories, played a leading role. Mol died in 1782 and the factory was sold to a company which in 1784 moved it yet again, this time to Oude Amstel, when it was placed under the direction of the German, F. Däuber. In 1799 it was sold again, being removed in 1809 to Nieuwer Amstel and finally ceasing production before 1820.

These factories successively produced a hard-paste porcelain of good quality decorated in the style current in contemporary Europe, with some peculiarities of their own, including a liking for open-work and moulded decoration, and, at Oude Loosdrecht, a style of painting peasants in landscapes rendered in a tonality dominated by brown. A few figures were made at Weesp and Oude Loosdrecht, mostly the work of the Tournai modeller, N. Gauron.

A porcelain factory at the Hague appears to have grown out of a decorating establishment, a character which was not wholly lost after porcelain began to be manufactured there. The concern was in the hands of the Lyncker family, of German origin, of whom Anton Lyncker is first recorded as a dealer in German porcelain in 1773, but who by 1776 had started to manufacture porcelain. Anton Lyncker died in 1781 and the concern passed to his son, Johann Frantz, who continued it until 1790.

The porcelain made at the Hague showed no great originality of form, but was well-painted in contemporary styles, including excellent flower-painting, land- and sea-scapes, figures in landscape, etc. Much Tournai porcelain (and to a lesser extent Höhst and other German porcelain) was decorated in the same styles at the factory, a light blue ground colour being used to considerable effect in combination with fine gilding and flower-, bird- and fruit-painting of high quality.

Russia

In 1744 C. C. Hunger left Stockholm (p. 256) at the instance of the Empress Elizabeth, to start a porcelain factory in Saint Petersburg. Here, too, Hunger was unsuccessful and, after four years of fruitless experiment, was discharged in favour of Dmitri Vinogradoff, who continued without much success beyond producing some small objects such as snuff-boxes, in a hard-paste porcelain made from china-clay identified at Gjelsk, near Moscow. Regular production only began after Vinogradoff's death (1758) under the Saxon arcanist, J. G. Müller. After the accession of Catherine II in 1762 came the heyday of the factory, first under Alexander Tchepotieff

(d. 1773), assisted by a Viennese arcanist named Joseph Regensburg, then under Prince Viazemski, who remained in charge until 1792.

The earliest Saint Petersburg porcelain revealed no markedly individual style, and under Catherine II the French and Vienna fashions were emulated, with dark ground-colours and rich gilding, or scrollwork and cameo-painting after the Antique. More original were the figures of Russian peasant types taken from the engravings of a Description of all Nations of the Russian Empire published in 1776–7. These were modelled by the Frenchman, Dominique Rachette, who had been engaged in 1779, and who then and later

734. Figure of a Samoyed woman, hard-paste porcelain, painted in enamel colours. Russian, St Petersburg factory; early 19th century. Ht. 8 in. (20·5 cm.). Mark: 'SM', incised. One of the most characteristic types of figure-model made in the Russian porcelain factories—by no means restricted to the Imperial factory—was that showing peasants in the different costumes of the Empire. Those made in St Petersburg, including this one, were usually derived from the Abbé

J. G. Georgi's *Description de toutes les Nations de l'Empire de Russie,* a work dedicated to Catherine II and first published in 1776–7. The simple and direct modelling of this doll-like figure is particularly successful. Victoria and Albert Museum, London.

735. Plate, hard-paste porcelain with mainly silver and gold decoration. Russian, St Petersburg factory; about 1765. Diam. 9¼ in. (23·5 cm.). Mark: black eagle and

'No. 1' in gilding. From one of the most splendid services produced by the Imperial Porcelain Factory, made for Count Grigoryi Orlov, one of the conspirators who placed the Empress Catherine II on the throne, subsequently her closest friend and adviser. The Count's initials decorate the centre of the plate, while the border is decorated with contrasting gold and silver touched with dots of blue enamel giving an effect of great splendour. Private collection.

734

735

modelled the most important biscuit and other figures.

The factory was re-organised in 1803 under the Emperor Alexander I, and ultimately a number of foreign technicians were introduced, notably the painter, J. F. J. Swebach (from 1815 onwards), and others from Sèvres. Not unnaturally, the Empire style as practised at Sèvres flourished at St Petersburg, with huge vases of classical forms, elaborate enamelling closely simulating oil-painting, and profuse brassy gilding. The peasant figures, often in idealised versions, continued to be popular throughout the 19th century.

734

A porcelain factory had been established as early as about 1765 by an Englishman, Francis Gardner, at Verbilki, near Moscow. The Gardner factory made porcelain of a quality rivalling that of the Imperial factory, and in much the same styles, including versions of the peasant figures. The decoration was, if anything, more full-blooded, and included in the early years of the 19th century some bright matt blue and maroon grounds.

A porcelain factory had been established as early as about 1765 by a second factory near Moscow—that at Gorrunovo, the property of A. Popoff. It flourished after the Napoleonic Wars, making wares much in the same manner as Gardner's. A number of other factories also were founded in and near Moscow in the early 19th century, but none of their products was especially remarkable.

Poland at this time formed part of the Russian Empire, and about 1790 Prince Ivan Czartorysky founded a factory at Korzec with the assistance of a foreign technician Michael Mezer. The factory, however, burned down in 1797, to be re-established at Gorodnitza, where it continued in production until 1870. Mezer himself moved on about 1801 to found a factory at Baranovka, near Volhynia in Poland, where porcelain of good quality continued to be made throughout the 19th century. The Polish porcelain followed the lines established in the Russian factories, and achieved no significant national styles.

VII Staffordshire and the Rise of Industrialism

Introduction

A previous chapter has traced the history of English peasant pottery in the 16th–17th centuries (pp. 100–36). In that period Staffordshire was only one district amongst a number of others making primitive lead-glazed slipwares and rudimentary salt-glazed stonewares. The 18th century witnessed its rise to become the predominant centre of the English pottery industry, which provided a precocious illustration of the Industrial Revolution, with its sophisticated mechanical appliances, division of labour, rationalisation of working methods, and standardisation of raw materials.

The outstanding success of English salt-glazed and lead-glazed wares in the 18th century at Staffordshire and other centres ensured that the less practical, and ultimately less fashionable tin-glazed earthenware (both the English and Dutch delftwares and French faience) was effectively driven from the market by 1800.

Early stonewares—Dwight, Elers and Place

Towards the end of the 17th century, John Dwight of Fulham, a lawyer and man of letters (see also pp. 135–6), and John Philip and David Elers (see p. 136), silversmiths from Germany, who first worked under Dwight and later settled at Bradwell Wood in Staffordshire, successfully met the challenge to English pottery from abroad caused by the importation of salt-glaze bottles from Germany and of red stoneware teapots from China when tea-drinking in England became fashionable. It may be said, in fact, that it was the taste for tea which brought about the refinement of the early 18th-century wares that compared more than favourably with those from abroad. As a result English pottery was to be seen for the first time not only in the kitchens but also in the drawing-rooms of the rich. The great changes in styles, technical methods and classes of ware that revolutionised English pottery during the 18th century may be said, therefore, to have had their beginnings at John Dwight's pottery at Fulham.

Dwight's salt-glaze was either a light drab colour, or brown. In the first, apart from his superb portrait busts and figures, we find some charming mugs with a bulbous body, narrower upright reeded neck and grooved loop handle, the lower extremity of which after being pressed into the bowl reappears slightly lower as a little roll quite separate from the upper part. Bottles were usually brown and marbled with lighter and darker coloured clays spiralling upwards. Small reliefs were sometimes used stamped on to the body of the piece itself or on to pads of red or white clay affixed to the body of the ware with slip and then trimmed. Some of the brass moulds from which these were made were found on the site of Dwight's works at Fulham and are now in the British Museum. This process developed into that of 'sprigging', whereby clay was pressed into the moulds and afterwards luted on to the ware with slip.

It is hard to distinguish between the unglazed red stoneware of Dwight and the Elers as undoubtedly both bore small applied reliefs derived from those on the Chinese redware teapots and were made in the forms currently used at the time. The bulk of English red stoneware was made between 1740 and 1780 and the amount that can be attributed with any confidence to Dwight or the Elers, who worked much earlier, is small indeed.

At York, contemporary with Dwight, Francis Place—portrait-painter, engraver and architect—made refined stoneware mugs and

736 *(previous page)*. British painting, about 1720. A well-to-do English family at tea, using Chinese blue-and-white porcelain cups and saucers and a red unglazed stoneware teapot of Elers type. Victoria and Albert Museum, London.

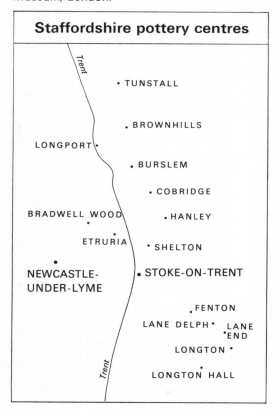

Staffordshire pottery centres

- TUNSTALL
- BROWNHILLS
- LONGPORT
- BURSLEM
- COBRIDGE
- BRADWELL WOOD
- HANLEY
- ETRURIA
- SHELTON
- NEWCASTLE-UNDER-LYME
- STOKE-ON-TRENT
- FENTON
- LANE DELPH
- LANE END
- LONGTON
- LONGTON HALL

Trent

737

737. Brown salt-glazed stoneware bowl with the incised inscription on the outside and tooled ornament. This bowl has the silvery sheen usually associated with Nottingham salt-glaze. Diam. 12 in. (30·5 cm.). Victoria and Albert Museum, London.

738. Press-moulded slipware dish; between the ridges a moulded design of pineapples

and fleurs-de-lis; filled in with dark brown and red-brown slip on the yellow glazed background. Diam. 12 in. (30·5 cm.). Inscribed on the front in slip 'S and W.L. 1715'. Victoria and Albert Museum, London.

739. Dish of marbled or 'combed' slipware on which a fine design is made by mingling a dark brown with a yellow slip by means of a wire brush or comb; early 18th century.

Diam. 13¾ in. (35 cm.). Victoria and Albert Museum, London.

740. Jug, *sgraffiato* decorated, marbled in two tones of brown and coated with cream-coloured slip. The design is made by cutting through the slip to show the brown marbled body underneath. Inscribed 'John & Dorothy Cook 1766'. Ht. 9½ in. (24 cm.). Victoria and Albert Museum, London.

738

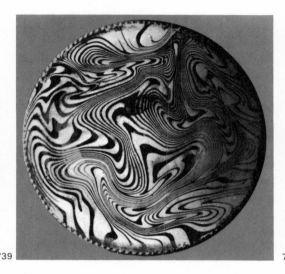

739

740

741

742

743

741. Marbled earthenware posset-pot in two tones of brown with two large and two small handles, and two narrow bands of roulette tooling, glazed with lead. Staffordshire; about 1740. Ht. 6⅜ in. (16·5 cm.). Victoria and Albert Museum, London.

742. Lead-glazed agate ware teapot with depressed globular body, hexagonal spout, double knob and thick loop handle, and formed of blue and brown clay. Probably Whieldon; about 1745. Ht. 4 in. (10 cm.). Victoria and Albert Museum, London.

743. Glazed red earthenware teapot with applied stamped reliefs in cream-colour; hexagonal spout, thick loop handle and acorn knob. Probably Staffordshire; about 1745. Ht. 4⅛ in. (10·25 cm.). Victoria and Albert Museum, London.

jugs, usually in drab-coloured salt-glaze with darker and lighter marbled spiral markings. These were wares of great refinement and raised English potting to a much higher plane than ever before. Potters throughout the country were not slow to follow the lead. They were stimulated to enterprise by a new awareness of the importance of their craft, although this was accompanied by only a very rudimentary scientific knowledge, often the result of accident. Experiment succeeded experiment, but nevertheless the industry was still a craft and each vessel was individually formed. In Staffordshire, particularly, conditions favoured a development of the industry. There was a variety of clays at hand so that experiments could be made with clays of different colours, and also coal nearby so that the costs of transporting fuel were reduced to a minimum.

Staffordshire was not, however, alone in the development of new styles and techniques. Other potting centres were also experimenting and probably the most successful during the early years of the 18th century was Nottingham, where the Morley family took the brown salt-glazed stoneware of Dwight and of Staffordshire, where an imitation of his brown stoneware was being made, and developed it into a ware of great refinement and beauty. The body was coated with a ferruginous wash before glazing which produced a brown surface with a silvery sheen. It was usually decorated with incised

patterning and inscriptions, sometimes combined with openwork decoration made with a knife or punch. The potting was skilful and the proportions well considered. This type of ware became one of the most popular forms of pottery of the first half of the 18th century and was eventually made not only at Nottingham, but in Derbyshire, Yorkshire and elsewhere.

Unglazed red stoneware, like that made by Dwight and the Elers at the end of the 17th century, seems not to have been manufactured during the years 1710–40 since today no known examples survive from this period, after which we find it being made by Whieldon (pp. 269–70) and others in the forms current at the time. Uncoloured stamped reliefs predominate as decoration until the advent of engine-turning in the 1760s. Many pieces, even at this date, were impressed with a square mark, simulating the seal-marks underneath the Chinese redware teapots. Some bear impressed names or initials. A stamped relief of frequent occurrence depicts the marriage of George III in 1761. When engine-turning supplanted reliefs, we find this ware being made not only in Staffordshire but in other factories such as Leeds. A magnificent punch-kettle and stand in the Schreiber Collection (Victoria and Albert Museum) is an example of Leeds red stoneware. The drawing books of this factory make frequent references to this class of ware, sometimes as *terre rouge*.

737

747

744. Glazed red earthenware teapot with straight sides, conical spout, loop handle and fluted knob, decorated with engine-turning on the spout cover and body. Probably Staffordshire; about 1765. Ht. 4½ in. (12 cm.). Engine-turning as decoration superseded the small applied stamped ornaments, on red and black lead-glazed wares, just as it did on unglazed red stoneware at this time. Victoria and Albert Museum, London.

745. Glazed black earthenware teapot with three feet and crabstock handle and spout, and bird knob, decorated with a vine and flower in applied relief. Ht. 4½ in. (11 cm.); about 1750. This type of ware often called 'Jackfield' was made by a number of factories in Staffordshire and elsewhere. Because of the characteristic high gloss of its finish, it is sometimes referred to as 'shining black'. Victoria and Albert Museum, London.

746. Glazed black earthenware teapot with applied cream-coloured reliefs on a vine. Crabstock handle, spout and handle to cover also in cream-colour. Probably Whieldon; about 1750. Ht. 4¾ in. (12 cm.). Vine leaves and tendrils in relief, sometimes coated with cream-coloured slip, as on this example, were a common embellishment on 'Jackfield' ware. Victoria and Albert Museum, London.

Lead-glazed and variegated wares

Meanwhile lead-glaze slipware continued to be made to supply local needs for a coarser type of ware and was in fact still being produced in Yorkshire almost into the 20th century. About 1710 in Staffordshire moulds were introduced which made possible the reproduction of a particular design on a number of dishes. A *biscuit* mould at the Victoria and Albert Museum shows how the main design was incised on it. This would appear in raised ridges on the dish taken from it. Slip was then used to fill in and augment the design.

Other forms of slip decoration followed. A magnificent result could be obtained by combing different coloured slips while they were in a liquid state. By a further technique (*sgraffiato*) a design was formed by cutting through an upper coating of slip so as to reveal the contrasting tone of the body of the pot beneath.

Lists of Staffordshire potters compiled during the first half of the 18th century show that many were then specialising in ware formed from the admixture of different coloured clays. Such a process was not in fact new, as we find 'marbling' being used both by Dwight and Place on their stonewares, but during the 18th century there were developments by which clays were mixed or pressed together in various ways to produce different effects ('solid agate' ware). These processes were used not only in making salt-glazed stoneware but for lead-glazed earthenware as well. Samuel Bell of Newcastle-under-Lyme may be quoted as a maker of marbled earthenwares, usually red in colour with the marbling on jugs and mugs in a contrasting colour. An oblique marbled effect was the inevitable result of throwing on a wheel. Thomas Whieldon (pp. 269–70) brought the solid agate ware to its greatest perfection of design and execution. Tea- and coffee-pots, cups and saucers, knife and fork handles, salad-bowls and many other pieces were made in mixtures of brown, cream, blue or green. Other forms of variegated decora-

tions will be discussed, later in the chapter, in the context of the potteries where they were used.

Further use was made of coloured clays in the production of a charming group of lead-glazed earthenwares, the body of which was in one colour, decorated as a rule by cream-coloured stamped motifs in relief, sometimes with additional touches of blue or green. The range of colours used for the body of the pot includes various shades of ochre from pale buff to orange and brown. The reds varying from light to very dark chestnut formed another range.

These wares have in the past been attributed to John Astbury of Shelton. A quantity of sherds of this type of ware was found on the site of his pottery, but others were found on the site of Joshua Twyford's pottery, also at Shelton, but whoever originated the ware, it was being made from about 1740 or a little earlier by a number of potters, not only in Staffordshire. It was, for instance, being made in quantities in Yorkshire as late as 1770 where it was being advertised in *The Leeds Mercury*. From the late 1760s much of this lead-glazed earthenware was decorated with 'engine-turned' patterns somewhat resembling basket-work. These were turned on a lathe with the axis off-centre which produced an eccentric motion. By the addition of manganese to both the clay and glaze a black ware was produced which today is sometimes styled 'shining black' or more often 'Jackfield', but was in fact being made in Staffordshire long before the Shropshire pottery of Jackfield was established. The black undoubtedly varied in tint according to the factory producing it, some of the ware appearing to be rather brown in colour while other specimens have a silvery sheen. It was often decorated with vine-leaves and tendrils which were sometimes gilded or attractively coated with cream-coloured slip. Unfired painting in colours was also frequently used as decoration on this ware.

748

749

747

750

751

747. Unglazed red stoneware punch-pot, with accentuated crabstock handle and spout (compare fig. 752) and floral design in relief, Whieldon; about 1750. Ht. 7¼ in. (18·5 cm.). Redwares of this sort, in imitation of those from Yi-hsing in China, were made in Staffordshire from the late 17th century until 1765; the material was used thereafter by Wedgwood and others in classicising wares dubbed *'rosso antico'*. Victoria and Albert Museum, London.

750. White salt-glazed stoneware mug, with reliefs representing the Battle of Portobello between two bands of roulette work and inscribed 'THE BRITISH GLORY: REVIV: D BY ADMIRAL VERNON:' and 'HE TOOK PORTO BEL WITH SIX SHIPS ONLY: NOV. YE: 22 1739.' Ht. 6⅞ in. (17 cm.). Similar reliefs of ships, cannon and Admiral Vernon are found on red lead-glazed earthenware. Victoria and Albert Museum, London.

751. White salt-glazed stoneware mug with reeded loop handle; incised decoration filled in with cobalt (scratch-blue) of grotesque birds, acorns and leaves, also '17 Enoch Booth 42' (Enoch Booth of Tunstall 1742). Ht. 4¾ in. (12 cm.). See fig. 758 by the same potter. Fitzwilliam Museum, Cambridge.

748. Drab-coloured salt-glazed stoneware punch-pot; white stamped applied relief decorations; also white crabstock spout and handles; about 1745. 9½ in. (24 cm.). Victoria and Albert Museum, London.

749. White salt-glazed stoneware teapot in the form of a crouching camel with a square structure, presumably some sort of carriage, on its back; about 1745. Ht. 4½ in. (11·4 cm.). Victoria and Albert Museum, London.

White salt-glazed stoneware

At the very end of the 17th century and in the early years of the 18th, 'white' salt-glazed stoneware of a buff-grey colour was being produced, often in the form of mugs characterised by a brown band round the rim, made by dipping them in a ferruginous wash.

Likewise on other articles made of this ware decoration was of the simplest consisting as a rule of a few horizontal lines incised on it or some applied stamped reliefs in the manner of Dwight and Elers. By about 1720, following the general tendency towards refinement which characterises this period of the Staffordshire industry, this drab stoneware became considerably whiter by the application of a surface wash of white Devonshire clay. This is apparent on the broken edges of some shards where the white outer coating contrasts with the darker colour of the body. Shortly after this, ground flint as well as the white Devonshire clay was incorporated into the body of the ware, giving it a whiteness throughout and making

it lighter in weight. Simeon Shaw, author of the *History of the Staffordshire Potteries* (1829), attributes this invention to John Astbury, whereas Josiah Wedgwood gives the credit for it to Thomas Heath. Both potters were Shelton men.

This improved ware, formerly called 'white stoneware' or 'common white', was manufactured throughout the 18th century but particularly between 1740 and 1760 when it was made in vast quantities. Nearly every pottery throughout the country was producing it. Its comparative scarcity today is no doubt due to the fact that it was mostly made for general use; it was cheap and its preservation therefore not considered. It was to a large extent ousted from the market during the 1760s by the growing popularity of creamware (see below, p. 268) which was considered a finer and more serviceable product.

Many pieces of creamy-coloured salt-glaze will be found to be

752

753

752. White salt-glazed stoneware punch-pot with sharply accentuated crabstock handle and spout; enamelled with Chinese figures in various colours; about 1755. Ht. 7⅜ in. (18·5 cm.). A magnificent example of white salt-glaze by reason of both the richness of its modelling and its superb enamelled decoration. Like the unglazed red stoneware punch-pot in fig. 747, this was probably also made by Thomas Whieldon. Victoria and Albert Museum, London.

753. White salt-glazed stoneware teapot with an applied floral decoration in relief and enamelled in various colours; about 1755. Ht. 5 in. (12·6 cm.). Fitzwilliam Museum, Cambridge.

754

755

754. White salt-glazed stoneware teapot in the form of a cabbage, moulded in relief with overlapping leaves enamelled green, yellow and pink. William Littler; about 1760. Ht. 4 in. (10 cm.). The attribution of this teapot to William Littler is made on the strength of its similarity to certain Longton Hall porcelain pieces. Victoria and Albert Museum, London.

755. White salt-glazed stoneware coffee-pot entirely coated on the outside with a lead-glaze strongly coloured with cobalt and further decorated with white enamel painting; about 1755. Ht. 8 in. (20 cm.). Salt-glaze coated with a deep blue glaze, has in the past been attributed to William Littler on the strength of its similarity to the deep blue glaze on Longton Hall porcelain, but it has been found that it was produced by a number of factories and was not only confined to Staffordshire. Victoria and Albert Museum, London.

756. White salt-glazed stoneware group (so-called 'pew group') of two men and a woman between them seated in a high backed settle or pew. Parts of the clothing and the patches on the woman's cheeks are picked out in black. Ht. 6⅛ in. (15·5 cm.); about 1745. The suggestion has sometimes been made that the pew group figures were the work of Aaron Wood. British Museum, London.

757. White salt-glazed stoneware plate, the rim moulded with a trellis pattern between medallions with foliate borders; the centre with a transfer-print in red of a young man and woman, probably after Boucher; probably Whieldon; about 1760. Diam. 9½ in. (24 cm.). A shard with the identical moulded border pattern found on the Fenton Low site is in the Victoria and Albert Museum; the printing was probably done by Sadler at Liverpool although suggestions have been put forward that the printing on salt-glaze plates of this type was done at Battersea. Victoria and Albert Museum, London.

50. Vase of Wedgwood jasper ware, Etruria, Staffordshire; late 18th century. The relief subject, called by Wedgwood 'The Apotheosis of Homer', derives from a Greek vase in the British Museum. The model was prepared for him by the sculptor, John Flaxman. Wedgwood Museum, Josiah Wedgwood and Sons Ltd., Barlaston, Staffordshire.

756

757

51

52

53

758

759

760

758. Creamware bowl spattered with a light brown manganese glaze except for reserved panels decorated in underglaze-blue. Diam. 10 in. (25·4 cm.). Four shield-shaped panels and a circular one on the inside contain figure subjects and two large circular, four small and two scolloped ones on the outside contain flowers, animals and birds; underneath, a scolloped panel contains the inscription, 'E.B. 1743', Enoch Booth of Tunstall. A scratch-blue salt-glazed mug by the same potter is illustrated in fig. 751. British Museum, London.

759. Colour-glazed creamware teapot (tortoiseshell ware) with crabstock handle and spout and upright flower knob, applied floral pattern of roses, buds and leaves connected by curving stems similar to fig. 760, coloured with green and yellow glazes against a deep grey glazed ground. Whieldon; about 1750. Ht. 4¼ in. (10·5 cm.). Victoria and Albert Museum, London.

760. Colour-glazed earthenware figure of a Turk, coated with blue-grey yellow, cream, brown and green glazes. Moulded leaves on the base are the same as on other pieces for which the same mould must have been used. Whieldon; about 1750. Ht 6½ in. (16·5 cm.). Whieldon employed modellers but this is one of his own figures; it is copied from a Meissen model of about 1745 by J. J. Kändler. Victoria and Albert Museum, London.

much smoother than the normal and are in fact lead-glazed as well, this second glaze having filled in the pitting caused by the action of the salt. Lead-glaze on salt-glazed pieces can usually be seen round the foot-ring of a piece where it often shows as a yellowish colour and is usually crazed. The practice of lead-glazing the white stoneware was probably introduced about 1750, no doubt with the purpose of trying to compete with the new creamware. Although the English potters in their attempts to compete with porcelain, especially that from abroad, never succeeded in producing ware that approached it in whiteness, they exceeded it in fineness of potting, much of the salt-glaze being unrivalled for thinness of body and sharpness of detail in the moulded decorations. The hard stoneware body produced results of the greatest refinement when turned on a lathe and vessels were often no thicker than paper. The Staffordshire potters, having mastered their technical difficulties, were able to find in the white stoneware a suitable material in which to express their natural artistry. The new forms invented were legion, and before enamelling as decoration was introduced, the diversity, originality, and delicacy of the relief decoration were beyond all praise.

The same kind of little patterns in relief stamped on from metal moulds that Dwight and Elers used, persisted until the 1760s. Sometimes use was made of this form of decoration to portray or celebrate an event, as on the mug in the Schreiber Collection at the Victoria and Albert Museum, where the reliefs consist of Admiral Vernon (twice), ships, cannon and buildings, the whole representing the Battle of Portobello.

Another delightful use of these reliefs was that of applying them to a grey or drab coloured body, against which the little white ornaments are particularly effective.

The first coloured decoration to be applied to the surface of salt-glazed wares consisted of touches of cobalt. This was sometimes painted on to the small reliefs with charming effect. Cobalt was also used to accentuate an incised decoration. This was probably done with a pad or sponge, the surplus blue being afterwards wiped off, a treatment that had been anticipated by the use at an earlier date of washes of brown clay applied in the same way. This kind of decoration, known as 'scratch-blue', was introduced at an early date. A recorded example is dated 1724. Signed examples of salt-glaze are rare indeed but a scratch-blue decorated mug at the Fitzwilliam Museum, Cambridge, is incised 'Enoch Booth 1742'. Enoch Booth was a Tunstall potter and several pieces are known which are signed either with his full name or his initials and the year of manufacture. A form of decoration traditionally associated with Ralph Shaw consisted of coating the white salt-glaze with brown slip which was then scratched with a tool producing a decoration in white on a darker ground, usually horizontal bands. Sometimes white reliefs were sprigged or stamped on afterwards.

The introduction of plaster of Paris moulds, about 1745, produced an outburst of fanciful modelling such as the teapot illustrated here in the form of a camel. The method employed was to fashion the required object in the solid, usually from alabaster; intaglio moulds were then made from this in common clay by pressing, block or master moulds being then cast from these and glazed with salt. From this hard body a series of intaglio moulds of plaster of Paris could be made and in them the finished articles were cast. The casting process consisted of pouring slip into the assembled plaster mould, whose porosity absorbed the water, leaving a thin lining of clay. This would be repeated until the clay lining was sufficiently thick, when, after it had dried, it would be detached from the mould. In this way an almost limitless number of objects of the same pattern could be obtained, the plaster mould when worn out being replaced from the salt-glaze block-mould.

Enamelling on salt-glaze was first introduced in about 1740 to Cobridge, probably by two Dutchmen who settled there. Cobridge

751

749

750

748

51. Creamware teapot enamelled by David Rhodes, probably at his workshop in St Martin's Lane, London. Ht. 5½ in. (14 cm.). Enamelled in red, black, yellow, green and purple chintz pattern. Cabbage spout, scroll handle and pierced bulbous knob enamelled rose pink. Wedgwood (Burslem), about 1769. Mark, an incised triangle. Donald Towner Collection.

52. Colour-glazed ware teapot in the form of an apple with leaves; coloured with brown, yellow, grey and green glazes. About 1757. Ht. 3½ in. (8·75 cm.). Probably modelled by William Greatbatch for Whieldon during the period when Wedgwood was still Whieldon's partner. Victoria and Albert Museum, London.

53. Creamware jug, deep cream-colour with reeded double handles with elaborate strawberry terminals, moulded bead-and-reel borders and leaves under the lip, enamelled by D. Rhodes & Co. of Leeds. Inscribed 'Ed. Clayton. Leeds, about 1768. Ht. 8 in. (20·25 cm.). The jug shows a man holding a stick with a handle of ram's horn; on the reverse a fanciful house with distant mountains and cows. Donald Towner Collection.

was to become the centre of the enamelling industry for Staffordshire. The work attributed to the Dutchmen is of very high quality, consisting mostly of Chinese figures, flowers, and trees in which the enamel has a jewel-like quality. Conspicuous in a painting of this type is the use of opaque white spots. An early form of enamelling on salt-glaze consisted of the application of colour to applied reliefs. Charming results could be achieved on white salt-glaze in this way.

William Littler of Brownhills and Longton Hall produced salt-glaze, some of which reflected the porcelain vogue for natural forms current at that time (1750–60). Salt-glaze entirely coated with cobalt and sometimes further decorated with white enamel is usually known as 'Littler blue salt-glaze' but it was manufactured by many other potteries as well. Transfer-printing (pp. 271–2) was used to a limited extent about 1760 as a means of decorating salt-glaze. This form of decoration was confined to plates, both octagonal and round, having the same moulded border and a large section of a plate with this identical pattern, now at the Victoria and Albert Museum, was found on the Fenton Low site (p. 269). Much of the later printing on such plates was probably done at Liverpool, but some of the earlier work may have been done in another centre, at present not certainly identified.

Before leaving salt-glaze, mention must be made of the amusing and charming figures made of this ware, many of which appear to have been the production of a single potter, perhaps Aaron Wood. Single figures also occur either in plain white, touched with blue or manganese, or marbled with solid clay of a contrasting colour ('salt-glazed agate ware').

Although vast quantities of white salt-glaze were made in Staffordshire, it should be pointed out that it was produced in quantities at most potting centres throughout England.

761

Creamware

Creamware, which became Europe's greatest contribution to ceramics, evolved from these traditional Staffordshire wares. It was probably first introduced soon after 1720 and in its earliest form was composed of the same ingredients as white salt-glaze—namely, white clay from Devonshire and calcined flint. The ware was low-fired to form an earthenware and glazed with lead instead of being high-fired to form a stoneware and glazed with salt as with the white salt-glazed stoneware from which it sprang. The two wares were thus intimately related and were usually produced by the same potters.

The creamware which was mostly known during the 18th century as 'cream-coloured earthenware' was at first dusted in its unfired

state with dry lead ore in powder-form (galena) mixed with ground flint and given its one and only firing. The glaze produced in this way was extremely brilliant and of a somewhat golden tinge. Unfortunately the dust formed in the process was highly injurious to the potters and between 1726 and 1732 patents were taken out by Thomas Benson for grinding flints under water. About 1740 a fluid glaze was invented, traditionally by Enoch Booth of Tunstall, and both the lead ore and flints were ground under water. The glaze was then applied to ware which had previously been fired to a biscuit, which was then refired. When one considers the beauty of the form and glaze of a bowl by this potter in the British Museum one wonders how such an advanced state of development was

762

763

761. Creamware figure of a cavalryman on horseback pricked out in black slip, the horse coloured with brown slip : the fluted stand mottled with blue, green and brown glazes. Staffordshire. Ht. 7¾ in. (19 cm.). Victoria and Albert Museum, London.

762. Creamware vase of a deep cream-colour with a rich golden glaze and painted with a figure, insect and flowers in brown, blue and green underglaze colours. Whieldon ; about 1745. Ht. 5 in. (125 cm.). This may be the type of painting to which Whieldon refers in the following entry of his notebook—
'Mr. Thomas Fletcher Dr.
Nov. 7. 1749
    1 doz plates Tor—8/-
    2 doz   do   plane—
    1 doz   do   painted 2/-
    1 doz   do   Cream Colr. 1/8'
Victoria and Albert Museum, London.

763. Creamware sugar-bowl with applied and gilded flowers, tendrils and vine in relief on a deep, cream-coloured body. The cover has a bird knob. Whieldon ; about 1750. Ht. 4 in. (10 cm.). The form, knob and reliefs, are similar to those found on the Whieldon site in tortoiseshell ware and to a tortoiseshell ware sugar-bowl in the Victoria and Albert Museum. Donald Towner Collection.

reached at so early a date. It bears reserved panels of figures and animals painted in underglaze-blue against a cream-coloured background lightly spattered with manganese. The glaze used is slightly tinted with cobalt and is therefore a forerunner of the 'pearlware' of a later period (p. 274).

From the early 1740s the creamware was made side by side with

the salt-glazed stoneware and ran a parallel course till about 1760, after which the salt-glaze declined both in quality and quantity though it still continued to be made at least as late as 1780. Most of the other classes of ware described in this chapter also continued to be made to a greater or lesser extent until about this date, but finally gave way before the ascendency of creamware.

The role of Thomas Whieldon

A central position in all these developments was taken by Thomas Whieldon. Born in 1719, Whieldon was a master potter at Fenton Low by 1740. He was working at Fenton Hall in 1754 and also seems to have had a pot-works at Little Fenton, whether at the same time or later is not certain. Various excavations have been made on the Fenton Low site, where a great many different types of stonewares and earthenwares have been found. From entries in Whieldon's note-book it is apparent that part of the works was let to other potters from time to time, so that one cannot ascribe all these wares to Whieldon without some degree of reserve. They include combined slipware; red stoneware; white stoneware (salt-glaze); red glazed earthenware; buff, brown and red glazed earthenware with cream-coloured stamped motifs; black stoneware; black glazed earthenware both plain and with cream-coloured motifs; solid agate ware; creamware both plain and with coloured glazes, including tortoiseshell ware; figures; in fact every kind of lead-glazed earthenware and stoneware of that time except enamel-painted or transfer-printed wares. How many of these types he himself originated may never be known, but he must have been

regarded by most potters of that time as the greatest potting genius of his day, for we find the most promising of the young potters seeking his tuition and employment, and he in his turn seems to have been only too willing to impart his knowledge and methods to them. Amongst those who benefited in this way may be named Daniel and William Greatbatch, modellers of repute; Aaron Wood, blockmaker and perhaps figure modeller; Robert Garner, potter; Josiah Spode, the founder of the well-known firm of that name; and Josiah Wedgwood, who became Whieldon's partner from 1754 to 1759.

Aaron Wood and William Greatbatch were the most noted of Whieldon's modellers. Aaron Wood was of the Wood family of Burslem, which later became renowned for its fine figure-work (pp. 275–6), and he has already been mentioned as the possible modeller of some of the salt-glazed stoneware figures (p. 268). Other figures, however, such as the delightful salt-glaze and earthenware cavalrymen as well as the slip-decorated earthenware soldiers, musicians and others are usually attributed to Thomas Astbury. A salt-glaze mould for a spittoon at the British Museum is inscribed

759
760

761

764. Colour-glazed teapot; hexagonal with six straight-sided panels containing Chinese figure subjects moulded in relief; cauliflower spout and scroll handle, pineapple knob; decorated with brown, yellow, blue, green and grey colour-glazes. Greatbatch-Wedgwood; about 1762. Ht. 4 in. (10 cm.). From the Wedgwood correspondence of 1760 and again of 1764, we learn that William Greatbatch was supplying Josiah Wedgwood with 'Chinese' teapots, believed to be of this type. Victoria and Albert Museum, London.

765. Green-glazed teapot, with applied stamped motifs picked out in gold; wrapped leaf spout and scroll leaf handle, pierced ogee knob. Incised underneath is a bird with large outstretched claws seemingly about to grasp a large and curly worm. Wedgwood; about 1760. Ht. 4½ in. (12 cm.). The incised name 'Josiah Wedgwood' can be read with difficulty, owing to many other markings and scratches, on a jug from the same service. Victoria and Albert Museum, London.

766. Colour-glazed teapot in the form of a cauliflower; upper part cream-colour, lower part, handle and spout covered with a rich green glaze. Greatbatch-Wedgwood; about 1763. Ht. 4½ in. (12 cm.). The Wedgwood correspondence shows that in 1764 William Greatbatch was supplying Josiah Wedgwood with large quantities of 'Colly flower' ware, including one order for '20 dozen teapots and 5 tureens and stands'. Victoria and Albert Museum, London.

766

764

765

767

768

769

767. Creamware teapot, deep cream-colour, with cabbage spout, scroll handle and pierced ogee knob; partially glazed base; transfer-printed in red with Pierrot discovering Harlequin making love to Columbine. On the reverse, a cottage with sheep; flowers and fruit on the cover. Wedgwood, unmarked; about 1763. Ht. 5 in. (12·5 cm.). Engraved and printed by Sadler and Green at Liverpool. Ex Donald Towner Collection.

768. Creamware plate, deep cream-colour, transfer-printed by Sadler and Green of Liverpool with a landscape in soft purple, printed flower sprays and moulded feather edging on the rim. Wedgwood workman's impressed mark. Brick House, Burslem; about 1767. Diam. 9½ in. (24 cm.). Ex Donald Towner Collection.

769. Creamware coffee-pot, marks pale cream, with double handle, flower knob, shell spout and moulded pattern, transfer-printed in black with flower-sprays, enamelled over in two shades of green in imitation of porcelain with gilding. Impressed mark 'WEDGWOOD' in small irregular capitals, also small central turned circle and flower-shaped workman's mark. Etruria; about 1777. Ht. 8½ in. (21·5 cm.). Ex Donald Towner Collection.

'Aaron Wood'. Daniel Greatbatch is mentioned in Whieldon's notebook as father to William, and both were seemingly employed by Whieldon as modellers. A tortoiseshell tea-caddy in the collection of Miss M. Delhom is inscribed 'Daniel Greatbatch 1755'.

Whieldon's influence extended to all English fine earthenware factories. Unfortunately, as with so many potters, his name has become associated with one particular class of ware, namely 'Tortoiseshell'. It is probably true that he produced quantities of this class of ware and that he may have invented it and brought it to its greatest perfection; nevertheless, his powers of invention and output appear to have been so varied that to connect his name with one type of ware only in no way presents a true picture either of the man or his work. Bearing in mind this versatility, it would appear, in fact, from a statement by Wedgwood, that Whieldon was principally a salt-glaze manufacturer.

Whieldon in his notebook refers to his manufacture of creamware both plain and painted. The latter must almost certainly have been underglaze painting of which a little vase at the Victoria and Albert Museum is a probable example. A very fine specimen of underglaze painting of the same type appears in conjunction with solid agate on a teapot, almost certainly Whieldon, in the collection of Mrs Victor Gollancz.

Before enamelling on creamware became popular, a form of decoration that was extensively used and of which Whieldon was one of the chief exponents, was glazing with colours. The teapot illustrated in colour was almost certainly modelled by William Greatbatch, whose correspondence shows that he made apple teapots for both Whieldon and Wedgwood. The form and colouring of this teapot would suggest that it was manufactured during the Wedgwood–Whieldon partnership (1754–9).

763

762

52
(p. 266)

770

771

772

770. Creamware teapot of medium tint, cabbage spout, scroll handle, pierced bulbous knob, enamelled in rose-pink and on each side with a flower spray in black, red, yellow and purple within a scolloped reserved panel against a background of interlacing circles in black and red. Marked with an incised triangle underneath and a circle with a cross inside painted in black both underneath and under the cover. Wedgwood (Burslem); about 1769. Painted by David Rhodes, probably at his

workshop in St Martin's Lane, London. Ht. 5 in. (12·5 cm.). Donald Towner Collection.

771. Creamware plate with ruins and a distant view of Wakefield enamelled in sepia; a frog enamelled green in a shield at the top. Impressed 'WEDGWOOD' and a small circle; '207' painted in sepia. Etruria; 1774. Diam. 9 in. (23 cm.). Made for the Empress Catherine II of Russia for use at the Palace of

La Grenouillière. Victoria and Albert Museum, London.

772. Creamware teapot with cabbage spout, scale handle, and pierced mushroom knob; enamelled on both sides and on the cover, with flowers and fruit in purple monochrome. Marked underneath with an incised V, an impressed C, and the name 'WEDGWOOD' in impressed small capitals. Etruria; about 1775. Donald Towner Collection.

Wedgwood Pottery

When in 1754 Josiah Wedgwood entered upon this partnership he was twenty-four years old. The arrangement was a peculiar one as under its terms he was permitted to carry out experiments on the premises without the necessity of making the results known to anyone. During the five years that he spent with Whieldon he seems to have spent most of his time in the development of coloured glazes.

In 1759 Wedgwood broke off his partnership with Whieldon and set up for himself at the Ivy House, Burslem. William Greatbatch also left Whieldon at the same time under an agreement with Wedgwood to supply him with wares in the biscuit ready for glazing in colour at the Ivy House. Greatbatch set up at Lower Lane and later moved to Lane Delph. The Greatbatch wares benefited Wedgwood by their originality. These included 'Cauliflower', 'Melon' and 'Pineapple' wares as much as teapots in the form of various fruits such as apples and pears. Such wares were not altogether original although they were the first to have been made in lead-glazed earthenware. There was a strong trend towards natural forms in European and English porcelain and Littler was producing

salt-glaze teapots in the form of cabbages, etc. But in addition to fruits and vegetables Greatbatch was moulding wares with scenes and figures on them. The green glaze of which Wedgwood at first thought so highly and of which he was so heartily sick a few years later was also used as a complete covering to his 'green-glazed ware'. This was sometimes heightened with gold. It was discontinued about 1766 and only revived many years later, in different forms.

As we have already seen, by 1740 creamware had become the finest type of earthenware yet produced in England. From 1760 Wedgwood undertook its further refinement, aiming at something at least comparable to porcelain both in fineness of body and lightness of colour. His first creamware had many imperfections but within a year or two it was of a good even deep buff colour. By 1765, however, Wedgwood had produced a creamware of a different body that was light both in colour and weight and had a thin brilliant glaze. In 1764 Wedgwood moved to the Brick House at Burslem, later known as the Bell Works. Here he continued his manufacture of useful ware till 1772. By far the greatest part of this was sent to Liverpool to be decorated with transfer-prints by John

773

774

775

773. Creamware vase and basaltes base, decorated with small brown and blue colour-glazed mottling. Made in imitation of the stone vases of the day. 'Wedgwood and Bentley, Etruria' impressed on the base within a circular stamp. Etruria; about 1771. Ht. 13 in. (33 cm.). Victoria and Albert Museum, London.

774. Creamware tureen and stand enamelled with a blue border pattern and further enriched with brown and gold. Impressed WEDGWOOD. Etruria; about 1785. Ht. 6½ in. (16·5 cm.). Victoria and Albert Museum, London.

775. Creamware dish of deep cream-colour moulded with shell edge and enamelled with flowers in rosy purple. Burslem; about 1764. L. 8 in. (20 cm.). The name 'WEDGWOOD' in compressed capitals as on this piece is the earliest known Wedgwood impressed mark. Ex Donald Towner Collection.

767
768
Sadler. This firm in 1763 became 'Sadler and Green'. Wedgwood took a very personal interest in the transfer-printing of his creamware by selecting suitable engravings from those available in books or print-shops.

The black prints on the buff-coloured ware that Wedgwood was producing in 1760 and '61 looked well. Mugs and jugs sometimes had a red rim and were signed 'Sadler' in the print. It is noticeable that Sadler's signature occurs only for a very short time. Wedgwood's business arrangements with this firm were peculiar, in that the ware was sold to Sadler in the white and bought back after it had been decorated. All the losses due to breakages whether in transit or during the decorating were therefore borne by Sadler, a state of things which could not last long and a fresh arrangement was soon made. In the correspondence between the two men it was agreed that Wedgwood would employ no other printer to decorate his creamware and that Sadler on his part would not print on wares from any other factory, and in the main this seems to have been adhered to. Certainly Wedgwood did not start his own printing till late in the century and then at first it was only outline printing to be filled in with enamel painting. There is no doubt that Sadler did print on the wares of other potters. This may have been when he was out of stock of Wedgwood's ware or indeed some of it may have been sent to him by Wedgwood himself who frequently bought from other potters when he was out of stock.

767
768
By 1763 Sadler was using a dark red as well as a black for printing and a little later some very beautiful landscapes were printed in purple. Sadler died in 1789 and Guy Green, who had worked with him first as a printer only and then as a full partner from 1763, continued as sole proprietor. From the Wedgwood correspondence we learn that in 1777 Green was printing in outline for Wedgwood and filling in with pea-green enamel. The well-known Wedgwood services printed with shells and seaweeds can be cited as examples of

769
this, as well as the coffee-pot illustrated, on which the painting is in two shades of green in imitation of some porcelain decoration.

Enamelling on salt-glaze had been in use since about 1740 but for the next ten years the only painted decoration on creamware had been that of coloured glazes. About that time, however, it was found that creamware also could be very successfully enamelled. Some of Wedgwood's first creamware was enamelled by a certain Curzon at Lane Delph to whom it was taken by Greatbatch. Simeon Shaw, however, says that Wedgwood's creamware was first decorated with enamel painting by Anne Warburton of Cobridge, but there is no evidence to confirm this. The correspondence between the Warburtons and Wedgwood is wholly concerned with the buying and selling of wares and contains no mention of any enamelling. There is, however, a considerable correspondence between Wedgwood and David Rhodes of Leeds concerned with enamelling, gilding and copper scales for glazing. This correspondence dates from 1763, but when it first started is not known. Jasper Robinson and David Rhodes opened their enamelling workshops not far from the Leeds Pottery and were advertising their enamelling activities in the *Leeds Mercury* and *Leeds Intelligencer* of 1760 and 1761. We find the work of this firm not only on Leeds and Wedgwood wares, but also on those of Derbyshire and Liverpool. By 1768 Rhodes had left Leeds and was working in a London studio for Wedgwood continually disregarding all Wedgwood's enticements to have him at Burslem. He then became head of the Wedgwood enamelling workshops at Little Cheyne Row, Chelsea, where in 1770 he was advertising for assistant enamellers. In 1768 Rhodes entered into partnership with William Hopkins Craft, which terminated in 1770 or '71, during which time Craft seems to have been employed in painting the red Etruscan figures on vases. At first Rhodes' painting on Wedgwood creamware was very much in the styles he used at Leeds—freely painted figures, landscapes,

776. Black stoneware vase with figures in red and white after Greek vase painting, 'Etruscan' ware, painted perhaps by William Hopkins Craft in London. Wedgwood impressed. Etruria; about 1770. Ht. 13 in. (33 cm.). Victoria and Albert Museum, London.

777. Black stoneware vase (basaltes ware) moulded with Venus and Cupid in Vulcan's smithy, and inscribed 'Made by H. Palmer, Hanley, Staffords. E.' and signed 'Voyez Sculpt. 1769'. Ht. 12½ in. (31 cm.). British Museum, London.

778. Creamware jug (Fair Hebe), moulded as a tree trunk with a boy and a dog on one side and a girl with a bird's nest on the other, a paper pinned to the tree is inscribed 'Fair Hebe' and on another 'A bumper a bumper'. Inscribed on the bottle between the boy's feet is 'R.G.' and on the tree-trunk is 'I. Voyez'. The inside is coated with a pale bluish glaze. Moulded by Jean Voyez, who once worked for Wedgwood, for Robert Garner of Fenton; about 1788. Ht. 8¾ in. (22 cm.). Victoria and Albert Museum, London.

776

777

778

779

780

779. Jasper ware plaque, with a portrait in white of Sir Eyre Coote in high relief against a pale blue background, framed in ormulu. Impressed 'WEDGWOOD' Etruria; about 1780. British Museum, London.

780. Black stoneware kettle (basaltes) with mythological figures and vine leaves in white relief. Impressed mark 'NEAL & CO' in large letters. Hanley; about 1780. Ht. 14½ in. (43 cm.). British Museum, London.

770
774

flowers, or stripes and chevrons. Then by 1770 we see the introduction of prim little border patterns which had a sedate charm of their own. Rhodes died in 1777.

From the early 1760s enamelling of a different kind was being done at the Brick House, Burslem, under James Bakewell. This consisted of some delightful freely painted flowers on dessert
775 services, sometimes in black and yellow or green, but usually in crimson or purple monochrome, as on the very charming
772 Wedgwood teapot of about 1775 enamelled in purple monochrome, of which the handle is typical of the early Etruria period.

Of considerable renown was the enormous service of more than a thousand pieces which Wedgwood was commissioned to make for the Empress Catherine of Russia in 1774. The finished pieces were
771 enamelled in sepia with English scenes but are not nearly so pleasing

as the polychrome trial pieces. During the 1760s a new decorative movement based on classical themes began to make itself felt, its protagonists in England being the brothers Adam. This new style became immensely popular and Wedgwood was not slow to make full use of it for his pottery, which now underwent a complete metamorphosis. Creamware vases with pseudo-classic ornaments began to be made, at first using the old coloured and marbled glazes. With experience it was found to be possible so to control the decoration as to simulate the stone vases which were being used as an integral part of the architectural themes of the day.

773

It was at Brick House that Wedgwood first produced his blackware, which he then renamed 'basaltes'. This was an unglazed black stoneware and became the basis of his early ornamental ware. This side of the business was particularly associated with Thomas

781. Jasper ware vase moulded with 'the crowning of a Kitarist' in white relief against a pale blue background. Impressed 'WEDGWOOD 1786'. Ht. 17 in. (43 cm.). Presented to the British Museum by Wedgwood in 1786. British Museum, London. See fig. 50 (p. 265).

782. Jasper ware vase with white reliefs against a pale blue background. Impressed 'TURNER'. Lane End; about 1780. Ht. 11 in. (28 cm.). The blue background of this vase is more mauve in colour than Wedgwood's blue. British Museum, London.

783. Biscuit porcelain pedestal with 'Diana and her nymphs' in white relief against a pale blue background. Sèvres; about 1785. Ht. 9½ in. (24 cm.). Accomplished imitations of Wedgwood's jasper ware were achieved at Sèvres. British Museum, London.

781

782

783

Bentley, a Liverpool merchant, whom he took into partnership in 1769 and who was in charge of the London showrooms for ornamental ware, Wedgwood handling the useful wares. Bentley died in 1780. The basaltes was used for some very pleasing busts and portrait and other plaques; elaborate ornamental pieces such as vases and urns; simple domestic teaware, often decorated with rose engine-turning (p. 261). Wedgwood also used basaltes as a background for the figures painted in terra-cotta on his so called 'Etruscan' ware. Black stoneware was soon in general production in Staffordshire. There is a fine basaltes vase inscribed 'Made by H. Palmer Hanley, Staffords E' and signed 'Voyez Sculpt. 1769'. Jean Voyez had formerly worked for Wedgwood but because of a quarrel between them he took Wedgwood's processes to Palmer for whom he then modelled. He also did work for Robert Garner, of Fenton.

Other makers of black basaltes include Elijah Mayer, Spode, and Neale. A charming basaltes kettle made by Neale decorated with reliefs in white is illustrated. At Leeds it was manufactured in vast quantities between about 1880 and 1815, and it was also made at Caughley, in Shropshire.

Another of Wedgwood's productions at Brick House was red stoneware. Most of this was engine-turned, but later he made a further use of it by ornamenting it with applied decoration of either black or white. Following his usual practice of finding for his wares fresh names that would be more in accord with the higher social status they were now to enjoy, he called his red stoneware 'Rosso antico'.

In 1769 the Etruria works (about two miles from Burslem) were opened for ornamental ware, the useful wares still being produced at the Brick House works in Burslem till 1772, when the whole of

Wedgwood's manufacture was moved to Etruria. Here he produced his 'jasper' ware. This was a fine white stoneware capable of being coloured right through the body by means of metallic oxides. Later the ware received only a surface wash, the colours used being pale blue, dark blue, sage green, lilac, yellow and black. Against these colours the white reliefs stood out in contrast. Apart from some very fine portrait plaques in relief, these wares reflected the popular but superficial taste of the day in a false assessment of the antique that was far removed from the true values of the English potting tradition, although from a purely technical point of view they could hardly be surpassed. Many were also eminently suitable to the architectural settings in which they were destined to find a place.

Wedgwood's jasper ware was imitated not only in Staffordshire, where some equally perfect wares were produced by John Turner, but also on the Continent, notably at Sèvres, where finely modelled blue and white biscuit porcelain was produced in the same style.

In the meantime Wedgwood continued to improve his cream-ware, aiming at an even smoother and paler body and glaze. This was the ware that was to become his greatest contribution to European ceramics.

In 1779 Wedgwood first introduced his 'pearlware', which was a very pale creamware glazed with a bluish tint. As we saw earlier in this chapter, creamware with a bluish glaze had been in production since about 1740 and dated pieces show that other factories were producing true pearlware a few years before Wedgwood. Between 1790 and 1820, however, it was being made in enormous quantities everywhere, and was especially useful for the blue-printing that swept the country at that time. Much of it was also enamelled in a porcelain manner which was somewhat out of character.

784. Pearlware tea-caddy, enamelled with flowers in pink, green, blue, purple, red and black. Marked : 'LEEDS POTTERY' Impressed twice, the two stamps crossing each other. Leeds ; about 1790. Ht. 6¾ in. (17 cm.). Ex Donald Towner Collection.

785. Pearlware twig-basket printed with the 'willow pattern' in soft blue. Impressed mark : 'LEEDS POTTERY' stamped twice, the two marks crossing each other. Leeds ; about 1815. Diam. 10⅛ in. (25·7 cm.). Ex Donald Towner Collection.

786. Creamware figures of children, *Winter* and *Spring*. Impressed 'NEALE & CO' Henley ; about 1780. Ht. 5½ in. (14 cm.). *Winter* wears a black coat ; *Spring* a green blouse and blue shoes. Victoria and Albert Museum, London.

784

785

786

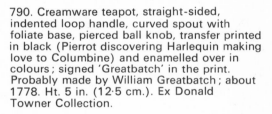

787. Creamware group of Bacchus and Ariadne, enamelled in colours. Bacchus wears a light blue cloak and Ariadne a goat-skin over a yellow robe. Enoch Wood, Burslem; about 1800. Ht. 24¾ in. (62·8 cm.). Fitzwilliam Museum, Cambridge.

788. Creamware figure of a gardener, emblematic of earth, standing before a bocage, enamelled in pink, yellow, green and black. 'WALTON' impressed on the back. Walton, Burslem; about 1825. Ht. 6¾ in. (17 cm.). Victoria and Albert Museum, London.

789. Colour-glazed earthenware figure of a peasant woman, decorated with glazes of soft colours—flesh, green, violet-grey and blue on a cream-coloured base. Impressed mark 'R. Wood' for Ralph Wood the Elder. Burslem; about 1770. Ht. 5½ in. (14 cm.). Victoria and Albert Museum, London.

790. Creamware teapot, straight-sided, indented loop handle, curved spout with foliate base, pierced ball knob, transfer printed in black (Pierrot discovering Harlequin making love to Columbine) and enamelled over in colours; signed 'Greatbatch' in the print. Probably made by William Greatbatch; about 1778. Ht. 5 in. (12·5 cm.). Ex Donald Towner Collection.

791. Creamware punch-pot of a deep cream-colour, undecorated, marked underneath and also under the cover. The handle and knob are unusually elaborate. Leeds Pottery; about 1770. Ht. 8½ in. (21·5 cm.). Some large sized pots of this description are inscribed with the word 'Punch'. Donald Towner Collection.

Other Staffordshire Potters

Wedgwood's influence on contemporary potting in England was enormous, and in Staffordshire a number of potteries became as it were subsidiaries to the Wedgwood factory. Some of these have been termed imitators in a derogatory sense, most unfairly, since in many cases they were supplying Wedgwood with wares which he was selling with his own to meet the enormous demand and it was probably for this reason that so much of the creamware at that time was unmarked. Some potters, however, worked independently of Wedgwood, and amongst these were Turner of Lane End, and Palmer of Hanley who was succeeded by his partner John Neale, when the ware was often marked Neale & Co. In 1802 David Wilson, Neale's manager, became proprietor of the firm, which then traded under his own name of Wilson. All the wares made by this firm were of a very high standard and consisted of the various

types then in demand including creamware, both enamelled and transfer-printed, some very charming figures and basaltes and jasper wares.

John Turner of Lane End, formerly one of Whieldon's apprentices, also produced wares of the highest order, including creamware (much of which was exported to Holland), jasper, basaltes and blue-printed wares; and was particularly famous for his white stoneware. After his death in 1786 his two sons, John and William, carried on the pottery until their bankruptcy in 1806. Even after this William seems to have continued till as late as 1829.

One of the most outstanding contributions to Staffordshire potting was made by the Wood family of Burslem, who were chiefly renowned for their manufacture of figures.

Aaron Wood, as we have already seen, was one of Whieldon's

786

792

793

792. Creamware teapot of a deep cream-colour, enamelled in red and black with a young woman holding some music and the inscription 'Solitude is my Choice', on the reverse some fanciful buildings and trees which also occur on the cover. The terminals and enamelled green, blue, yellow and black. Leeds Pottery; about 1767. Ht. 5 in.

(12·5 cm.). This style of painting can be attributed to the firm of D. Rhodes & Co. at Leeds, which before 1763 was Robinson and Rhodes. Donald Towner Collection.

793. Creamware coffee-pot of deep cream-colour, enamelled by D. Rhodes & Co. at Leeds with a parrot pecking fruit on both sides

in black and red. The terminals are coloured green. Leeds Pottery; about 1765. Ht. 9¾ in. (25 cm.). The subject for the painting seems to have first been published by R. Sayer in a *Drawing Book*, about 1754–56. It was subsequently painted and printed on porcelain and enamels. Ex Donald Towner Collection.

principal modellers, and his brother Ralph (1716–72) produced wares and figures coated with incomparable colour-glazes. The restrained colours subtly merging on his well modelled figures, so often of peasants, produced a most pleasing and artistic result. These lovely colour-glazes had by 1780 given way to enamelling, the work of Ralph's son, also Ralph (1748–95). These enamelled figures, though good in themselves, cannot be said to equal in artistry the work of the elder Ralph.

Enoch Wood (1759–1840), son of Aaron and nephew to the elder Ralph, commenced work on his own account in 1790. Enoch was an extremely able figure modeller and is best known for his portrait busts of famous men and for large-size groups. In addition to figures, Enoch Wood produced some fine reliefs in basaltes, useful ware in creamware, and towards the end of the century was producing porcelain as well.

The Wood and Neale tradition of figure manufacture was continued in Staffordshire by Walton, Salt and others till about 1830 after which the last shreds of artistry had disappeared.

Before discussing other pottery-producing areas, mention must be made of the Staffordshire transfer-printed ware of Neale and Baddeley of Shelton who did a certain amount of black transfer-printing on creamware, enamelled over in colours. Also, some interesting and often amusing prints were engraved by William Greatbatch. It is not certain whether this William Greatbatch was the modeller of that name or another member of the same family, perhaps a son, but it is probable that most of the pieces on which such prints occur were made by the modeller of that name while others are of Leeds and Wedgwood origin. But it was the industry in blue-printed ware that became the chief Staffordshire production in the last quarter of the 18th century and after. The leaders in this activity were Josiah Spode, John Turner, and the Adams family. Wedgwood and many others also took part.

The Leeds Pottery and other Centres

Outside Staffordshire the principal potteries during the second half of the 18th century were centred at Liverpool, Newcastle, Yorkshire, Durham, Bristol and Swansea. But second only in magnitude to Wedgwood's factory at Etruria was the Leeds Pottery at Hunslet, which was worked by the Green family and others.

The first known proprietors were William Green and Henry Ackroyd, whose names appear on a document of 1758 relating to the Pottery. It seems to have been working at least as early as 1750, and at one time or another manufactured most of the Staffordshire types of ware, with the notable exception of jasper ware. Some of these, such as salt-glaze, red stoneware and tortoiseshell ware continued to be made at Leeds until comparatively late in the century, probably 1780. Black stoneware on the other hand was not

manufactured at Leeds until nearly 1800, after which it was produced in vast quantities. But the ware for which the Leeds Pottery was most justifiably famous was its creamware. At first this was a deep cream colour and was either plain, in which case it depended on its form and moulded details for its effect, or enamelled. Some of the early enamelling, from about 1760, was done by the Leeds firm of Robinson and Rhodes. In 1763 David Rhodes became the sole proprietor—Robinson working for him—but as we have already seen, he went to London, where in 1768 he was working for Wedgwood in the Chelsea painting rooms. Much of his painting on Leeds creamware was in black and red and was excellent as decoration for this class of ware. It is probable that the firm broke up when Rhodes left, for we find the same style of painting being used elsewhere after that date, and it is probable that some of the enamellers were employed by the Leeds Pottery itself, while others went further afield.

In 1775 William Hartley became a leading partner in the firm and under his influence the Pottery thrived and a large export trade to the Continent was built up. Some of the ware was exported in the white to Holland, where it was enamelled. The ware was at this time much paler in colour and often elaborately modelled and decorated with pierced openwork. The same high standard was maintained in enamelling. Some fine painting was done in underglaze-blue at this period and transfer-printing was started about 1780 at the Pottery itself. A number of the pieces so decorated are marked 'Leeds Pottery' in the print.

A good quality pearlware was extensively produced from about 1790, and some charming figures were made in this type of ware. The Leeds underglaze blue-printing on pearlware was of a high quality and was produced from about 1810. After 1790 a great many different classes of ware were introduced among which particular mention should be made of a pottery painted with designs in high temperature mineral colours of green, ochre, blue and brown. The example illustrated, however, was actually produced by the Ferrybridge factory in Yorkshire. This type of ware is often referred to as 'Pratt ware' after Felix Pratt, of Fenton, Staffordshire, who probably introduced this kind of colouring, chiefly used by him on designs moulded in relief. In fact, however, the so-called 'Pratt' colouring appears on the wares of a great many potteries, particularly those of Leeds and Bristol.

About 1800 there was a great outburst of new decorative treatments most of which involved the use of coloured slips or 'dips', permitting many different variations including coloured bands, stripes and rectangles; small fragments of coloured clays applied like rough-cast; shining black overpainted with gold lustre; speckled ware; chequered ware; and a return of agate and combed slipware; underglaze and high temperature colours in panels reserved against a background of sepia ('Batavian ware') or pale blue slip, to name only some. Lustre ware, introduced in Staffordshire towards the end of the 18th century, was made at Leeds from about 1815. 'Silver' (from platinum) and pink lustre (from gold) were widely used.

Soon after 1800 most of the original partners of the Leeds Pottery had either died or left, the younger generation were constantly at variance and the export trade was fast declining. William Hartley had left by 1815 and in 1820 the firm of Hartley Greens & Co., was bankrupt, though the pottery continued to work under various new proprietors till nearly 1880.

794

794. Creamware table centre-piece, an imposing item, with four castors for sugar, pepper, oil and vinegar; four hanging baskets and a covered bowl at the top crowned by a figure of 'Plenty'. Pale cream. Leeds Pottery; about 1780. Ht. 24 in. (61 cm.). Ex Donald Towner Collection.

795. Creamware plate, pale cream, with moulded feather edge; enamel-painted in Holland. Leeds Pottery; 1787. Diam. 9½ in. (24 cm.). The portrait is of Prince William V of Orange, in matt black and flesh colour. A Dutch inscription acclaims his return from exile in 1787. Ex Donald Towner Collection.

795

During the last quarter of the 18th century a number of other factories opened near Leeds. Some of these had business or family connections with the Leeds Pottery. The Swinton factory, for instance, was at one time owned by the Green family and run as one concern with the Leeds Pottery. In 1806 it was taken over by members of the Brameld family and finally became the Rockingham China Works. Others in the neighbourhood were the Don Pottery, Rothwell Pottery, Castleford, and Ferrybridge. All these produced creamware, but of a quality inferior to that of the Leeds Pottery.

An important earthenware factory was worked from about 1750 till 1779 at Cockpit Hill in Derby. A few signed transfer-printed pieces of creamware are known. The one illustrated is signed 'Radford fecit, Derby Pot. Works' and 'Pot. Works in Derby'.

796

797

796. Creamware tureen shaped as a melon standing on a leaf, the upper part with pierced openwork; pale cream. Leeds Pottery; about 1780. L. 8½ in. (21·5 cm.). A similar tureen, without the pierced openwork, was also made by the Leeds Pottery at this time. Ex Donald Towner Collection.

797. Creamware tureen, pale cream-colour painted in underglaze-blue with Chinese subjects and flower decoration, surmounted by a fruit knob, and moulded with shell pattern. Leeds Pottery; about 1780. L. 14 in. (35·5 cm.). Donald Towner Collection.

804   There is an enamelled example of Derby creamware, which generally speaking was uneven in quality. Salt-glaze, colour-glazed ware and creamware constituted the principal types of pottery produced.

805   Recent excavations have revealed that a factory at Melbourne, just outside Derby, made a very good quality creamware.

  The English earthenware tradition was continued at Liverpool but the early creamware, salt-glaze and other wares produced there still await identification. The pottery of the Herculaneum factory there, founded during the last years of the 18th century is well known, however, as many of the pieces, largely creamware and pearlware, were marked.

806   From the beginning of the 19th century we find the character and traditions of English potting becoming lost in a vast commercialised industry. Here and there, the flame was kept bright by the genius of individual craftsmen such as W. W. Young at Swansea, whose exquisite painting of birds and butterflies decorates much earthenware made there during the early years of the 19th century. Later still was the charming flower-painting of Fifield on Bristol earthenware, while potteries such as Spode and Davenport produced wares in good style.

798

798. Creamware teapot, pale cream-colour, enamelled in red monochrome with a lady taking tea on one side and a fanciful building on the other. Leeds pottery; about 1775. Ht. 4½ in. (11·5 cm.). Donald Towner Collection.

799. Creamware milk-jug and cover, pale cream-colour enamelled with tulips and other flowers in red, yellow, rosy-purple and green. Leeds Pottery; about 1780. Ht. 6 in. (15 cm.). Donald Towner Collection.

800. Creamware plate, pale cream-colour, transfer-printed with an abbey in red and marked 'Leeds Pottery' in cursive lettering in the print. Leeds Pottery; about 1780. Diam. 9⅞ in. (25 cm.). Ex Donald Towner Collection.

799

800

English-style Pottery in Europe

Towards the end of the 18th century the English export trade to the Continent was seriously affecting the pottery industry there. Neither the maiolica nor the porcelain could compete with the low cost and clean pleasing designs of the English creamware. Wedgwood had agents in most European countries and the Leeds Pottery was exporting a very large proportion of its wares to Germany, Holland, France and Spain. In addition, potters from Staffordshire had started several factories in France for the manufacture of English-style earthenware. The Continental factories were therefore forced in self-defence to turn to the manufacture of creamware themselves, and in so doing they generally copied the English patterns. In France the Pont-aux-Choux factory at Paris was probably the first to

801

802

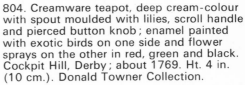

801. Creamware sugar-bowl, pale cream, painted in high temperature mineral colours of blue, green and yellow of the so-called Pratt-ware type. Impressed mark: 'FERRYBRIDGE'; about 1805. Diam. 5 in. (12·5 cm.). Ferrybridge on the river Aire, south of Leeds, near Castleford, sometimes impressed 'WEDGWOOD & CO'. Victoria and Albert Museum, London.

802. Silver lustre dish with two trees, a bird and a five barred gate. Impressed mark: 'LEEDS POTTERY'; about 1819. Diam. 14½ in. (36 cm.). The design on the example shown is in silver resist (for which platinum was used). Patterns could be produced on lustre by the 'resist' process by painting the required design

on the ware with wax or some other resist medium before coating the whole with lustre. On the removal of the resist the design showed as white or cream against the lustre background. Fitzwilliam Museum, Cambridge.

803. Creamware teapot, deep cream-colour, with facetted spout and handle and pierced button knob; transfer printed in black with the tea-party on one side, inscribed 'Radford fecit' 'DERBY Pot Works' and on the other *The Wheel-chair*, inscribed 'Pot Works in DERBY'. Cockpit Hill, Derby; about 1765. Ht. 4⅛ in. (10·5 cm.). The British Museum has an almost similar teapot. Ex Donald Towner Collection.

804. Creamware teapot, deep cream-colour with spout moulded with lilies, scroll handle and pierced button knob; enamel painted with exotic birds on one side and flower sprays on the other in red, green and black. Cockpit Hill, Derby; about 1769. Ht. 4 in. (10 cm.). Donald Towner Collection.

805. Creamware plate, deep cream-colour, octagonal with moulded 'diamond' border enamelled with flower sprays in purple. Melbourne, Derbyshire; about 1770. Diam. 9 in. (23·75 cm.). This plate corresponds to sherds excavated on the Melbourne Pottery site. Judging from the quality of these, it seems that this pottery will deserve notice. Donald Towner Collection.

803

804

805

806

807

806. Pearlware dish of quatrefoil shape, enamelled with a grey wag-tail in natural colours by W. W. Young and with a gold border. Impressed marks: 'SWANSEA' and 'C'. Inscribed in black: 'Motacilla boarula Grey Wagtail'. Swansea; about 1815. L. 9¼ in. (23·5 cm.). The decoration on this piece is by one of the few talented artists surviving in Britain amid growing industrialisation. Victoria and Albert Museum, London.

807. Creamware tureen with moulded floral pattern and modelled fruits, leaves and a bird knob. Pont-aux-Choux, Paris; about 1765. Diam. 10½ in. (26·5 cm.). The colour of this piece resembles that of English salt-glazed stoneware which no doubt influenced its manufacture. In 1772 the Pont-aux-Choux factory advertised itself as 'Manufacture royale des terres de France à l'imitation de celles d'Angleterre'. D. Towner Collection.

808. Creamware coffee-pot with double handle enamelled in polychrome. Impressed mark: 'G.M.' over 'B' (Giovanni Maria Baccin) and a star painted in red enamel. Le Nove, Italy; about 1815. Ht. 10½ in. (26·5 cm.). Scenes in the style of Watteau decorate the sides of this fine piece of Italian creamware. The cover is painted with a seascape. Victoria and Albert Museum, London.

808

manufacture creamware. This was finely modelled in the French idiom but shows a strong English salt-glaze influence. Compared with English creamware, it has a slightly pinkish tinge but is generally of good quality. In 1772 the factory advertised itself as the 'Manufacture royale des terres de France à l'imitation de celles d'Angleterre' (Royal manufactory of French earthenwares in imitation of English ones). Other early French factories were those of Montereau and Creil, which from 1774 were worked by English potters for the manufacture of red ware, black ware, and agate ware. But the class of ware for which these factories are particularly known is transfer-printed creamware. The jet-black prints on a hard white ground are readily distinguishable from English wares and were printed by the Paris firm of Stone, Cocquerel and Le Gros. Staffordshire potters also started factories at La Charité-sur-Loire and at Douai. The latter was formed in 1781 for the manufacture of 'fayence en grès, pâte tendre blanche connue sous le nom de grès d'Angleterre' (fine 'stoneware', soft white ware known by the name of 'English stoneware'). By 1786 creamware, under the name of 'faience fine' (fine earthenware), was being produced at Chantilly and Lunéville, while at Apt in the South of France a yellowish creamware with combed slip decoration imitating English agate and marbled wares was produced. Generally speaking, the French creamware showed greater individuality than that of other Continental factories. Mention has already been made of the fine biscuit porcelain made by the Sèvres factory in imitation of Wedgwood's jasper ware. In Italy some excellent creamware was produced at Le Nove during the early years of the 19th century and earlier. This, though closely resembling Leeds creamware in colour, glaze and texture, possessed individuality of form and detail. Of the many other factories in Europe producing creamware mostly with border patterns in imitation of Wedgwood's Queen's ware, mention should be made of the Holitsch factory in Hungary and the Rendsborg factory in Denmark, where black basaltes was also produced. An inferior creamware was made in Holland, but large quantities of English wares were imported in the 'white' and then enamelled there. Alcora in Spain (see p. 210) and Marieberg in Sweden (see p. 203) produced good creamware in which strong national characteristics are apparent.

808

VIII The Modern World

Pottery in an industrial age
(from 1830)

With the industrial revolution and its aftermath the history of ceramics becomes increasingly complex. The development of industrial pottery, described in this section, is contrasted with that of modern porcelain in the section which follows. Thereafter two further sections deal on the one hand with the development of the modern idea of industrial design, and, on the other hand, with the work of the artist-potter, which may be considered in some respects as a reaction against the products of industry.

It was in Britain that the effects of the industrial revolution had been first apparent, and it will be appropriate, therefore, to consider first the Early Victorian style of printed wares, which following on the popularity of the creamwares were to achieve an almost equally wide dissemination. The main interest of the transfer-printed pottery was its use for purely pictorial purposes. In the second and third decades of the century, when the trade in this ware was being built up, the printed scenes seem nearly always to have been copied from existing engravings intended for printing on paper. In the 1830s, however, the emphasis was shifting towards the use of scenes which had been composed specifically for the decoration of pottery. The first novelty of pictures on pottery was by this time exhausted, and a new generation of designer-engravers were prepared to design as well as adapt engravings for the pottery industry.

The work of the new designers in the mid-century period covered a wide field of contemporary interests and attitudes. There were scenes of classical inspiration, such as were produced on several occasions by the Glasgow firm of J. & M. P. Bell. There were English rustic scenes, and scenes which consisted largely of tasteful arrangements of vases. There were still many copied topographical scenes. But probably the commonest were scenes of pure fantasy, and these incorporated very frequently a view over water overhung by trees and romantically conceived buildings. The buildings appear as caricatures of buildings, almost as follies, with an exaggeration of Gothic crockets or the roof decorations of a Chinese pavilion. Often there are figures and ornamental vases in the foreground with steps leading down into the water and bridges and boats in the middle distance. The borders surrounding such scenes varied from the revived rococo patterns of the 1830s and early 1840s to a bewildering variety of eclectic and original motifs mid-century and later.

On the continent of Europe and in America, the English style of printed wares was widely appreciated, especially in the second quarter of the century, and similar work incorporating copied local views or scenes of fantasy was produced in many of the factories which had been making creamwares in the earlier part of the

century. In France, the associated factories of Montereau and Creil, which had English connections, were particularly concerned with printed wares, as was also that of the Englishman David Johnston established at Bordeaux from 1834 to 1845. From the Paris exhibition of 1839 examples of scenic printed designs have been preserved from the factories of De Boulen at Gien, Utzschneider at Sarreguemines and Fouque Arnoux at Valentine (Haute Garonne). In Germany, two typical factories producing printed wares were those of Damm near Aschaffenburg and Grünstadt in Bavaria. To take a few instances from other countries, in Belgium printed wares came from the factory of Boch Frères at Keramis, La Louvière; in Moravia they came from the factory of Frain near Znojmo (Znaim); Russian examples are to be found from the Gardner factory, near Moscow, and from the factory of Kuznetsoff in Riga, Latvia. In the United States also the American Pottery Company of Jersey City, New Jersey, was producing the first successful American printed wares from 1840. But Sweden was perhaps the country where the English styles were most closely followed and turned to best advantage in the leading factories of Rörstrand and Gustavsberg.

Printed wares were mostly cheap wares, and for this reason the printing remained for the most part monochrome. Blue was the best-liked colour, but by the second quarter of the century many other underglaze colours were possible, notably black and shades of green, red, purple, brown and yellow. Many experiments were, however, being made in multi-colour printing. Of these the most successful seems to have been the method worked out in the late 1840s in England at the firm of F. & R. Pratt, of Fenton, and associated with the artist Jesse Austin. The method was soon picked up by two other Staffordshire firms, T. J. & J. Mayer and John Ridgway, both of whom were showing multi-colour wares alongside Pratt at the Great Exhibition of 1851. The method was used to some extent for tableware, but it was also used for the decoration of pot-lids, which are now of great interest to collectors.

The vogue for decorating pottery with printed scenes died away in the third quarter of the century, but it left behind the long-lasting procedure of decorating simple pottery tablewares with floral designs, either to be left monochrome or to be tinted by hand. Some of the finest floral patterns are relatively early, such as some from the Wedgwood firm in England which stride boldly across the pottery surface. About the late forties a characteristic style of running plant pattern was used by such firms as Minton and Copeland (the successor to Spode), which can also be discerned in other art-forms of the period.

809. (*previous page*). The artist-potter, Bernard Leach, sitting at his wheel in his studio workshop at St Ives, Cornwall, 1959. (Photographed by Brian Seed for *Time* Magazine.)

810. Blue-printed earthenware plate, with the backstamp title 'Versailles', apparently made by Batkin, Walker & Broadhurst, Staffordshire, England; 1840–45. Diam. 10½ in. (26·7 cm.). Such early Victorian scenes of fantasy are attractive both for their content and for the appropriateness of their design. Victoria and Albert Museum, London.

810

54. Two vases from the Rookwood pottery in Cincinnati, Ohio, U.S.A., painted in coloured slips under the glaze. Exhibited in Paris in 1900. Hts. 10⅜ in. (26·4 cm.) and 8¼ in. (21 cm.). Victoria and Albert Museum, London.

55

56

57

811

812

813

814

811. Ewer and basin with printed decoration, made by the firm of David Johnston of Bordeaux. France. Ht. of ewer 10½ in. (26·7 cm.); diam. of basin 12⅜ in. (31·5 cm.). Musée National de Céramique, Sèvres.

812. Earthenware pitcher with black printed decoration depicting (President) W. H. Harrison, made by the American Pottery Company, Jersey City, New Jersey; 1840. Ht. 10½ in. (26·7 cm.). The American Pottery Company was the first to produce successful printed wares in the United States. The Newark Museum, Newark, New Jersey.

813. Earthenware plate printed in black, made by S. T. Kuznetsoff, Riga; about 1850. Diam. 8½ in. (21·6 cm.). A product of one of the Russian Kuznetsoff factories which later dominated much of Russian ceramic production. Victoria and Albert Museum, London.

814. Black printed dish from the Rörstrand factory, Sweden, with view of Gripsholm castle: about 1830–40. L. 16⅞ in. (43 cm.). Rörstrand Museum, Lidköping.

Another ceramic type of the mid-19th century, associated particularly with England, was the slip-cast jug with relief decoration. Jugs of this nature were made widely among the English factories, especially in Staffordshire; the material was usually stoneware, either off-white or coloured, with a smear glaze, but parian porcelain (see p. 296–7) was also used, as well as brown salt-glazed stoneware. A characteristic range of styles became associated with these jugs, which might on occasions be extended to other similar objects such as teapots, but which from their nature could not be conveniently extended to tableware in general. The jugs first appeared as a recognisable type in the 1830s, and from then on were produced with a remarkable freedom of popular design.

One considerable group among those designed in the forties bear 'Gothic' decoration. These were balanced in the forties and fifties by jugs with vaguely classical or Renaissance motifs, such as *amorini* disporting themselves with garlands of flowers. Others again were decorated with contemporary genre scenes such as a group of gypsies or a boy bird-nesting. But the most interesting from an art-historical point of view were the jugs which express in their decoration or their shape the naturalism of the mid-century period. Many of these were decorated with plant motifs growing from a rusticated handle and carefully disposed in running patterns over the surface of the jug; and often the whole form of the jug might be cast to represent a natural object such as a log or a lily-of-the-valley plant. It is interesting to notice that these characteristics became

suddenly less pronounced in the sixties when for a period many of the new designs were restrained, relying for their decoration on formal repeat patterns rendered in shallow relief.

Relief-decorated wares of this sort do not seem to have been produced to any marked extent in the European continental factories, although examples can be found such as, for instance, a jug very much in the English style which was shown by the French Montereau factory at the Paris Exhibition of 1839. On the other hand, an important parallel development of stoneware pottery was taking place in north-west France during the forties. A traditional salt-glazed stoneware industry carried out in the neighbourhood of Beauvais was given a new sense of artistic direction about 1840, apparently due mainly to the influence of a painter named Jules-Claude Ziégler who went into partnership with a manufacturer at Voisinlieu. The newly revived ware was shown at the Paris Exhibition of 1844; here it attracted a good deal of attention, especially for its use of 'running patterns' which appeared in a similar form shortly afterwards on the English relief-decorated jugs. In 1844 a reviewer in the English *Art Union* magazine (later the *Art Journal*) commented upon 'the superiority of the French in the management of what are called running patterns: it can be seen, on examination, that the pattern has a beginning, a middle, and an end, and that it entirely covers the surface it was intended to occupy'.

The United States also saw in the mid-century period an important development of relief-decorated wares in a variety of

816

817

818

819

55. Colour-printed plate, made by F. & R. Pratt of Fenton, England, about 1850. The scene was engraved by Jesse Austin after Thomas Webster's painting 'The Truant'; the surround simulates malachite. Diam. 9½ in. (24·1 cm.). Austin played an important role in the development of colour printing; some of his designs were original, others adaptations of existing paintings. Victoria and Albert Museum, London.

56. Coalport porcelain vase, painted and with applied flower-work, made about 1830. Ht. 11 in. (28 cm.). This English factory, often known as 'Coalbrookdale', was outstanding for its interpretation of the revived rococo style. Victoria and Albert Museum, London.

57. Vegetable dish and plate from a faience service made at one of the twin factories of Montereau and Creil, France, to the commission of Eugène Rousseau with decoration designed by Félix Bracquemond. Ht. (of vegetable dish) 7 in. (17·8 cm.) The service, shown at the Paris exhibition of 1867, early example of renewed Japanese influence in the later 19th century. Victoria and Albert Museum, London.

815

816

817

815. Blue-printed plate from a service by Minton, Stoke-on-Trent, with factory date-mark for 1850 and backstamp entitled 'Passion flower'. Diam. 10¼ in. (26 cm.). The pattern is typical of the loose, but carefully disposed, running patterns of the mid-century period. Victoria and Albert Museum, London.

816. The 'Minster' jug of white stoneware with figures in Gothic niches, made by Charles Meigh of Hanley, England. Ht. 9¼ in. (23·5 cm.). This jug, registered in 1842, was immensely popular and reflects the neo-Gothic taste of the 1840s. Victoria and Albert Museum, London.

817. White stoneware jug moulded in relief with a running pattern of vines; made by Minton, Stoke-on-Trent, England. Ht. 7 in. (17·8 cm.). The design was registered in 1846 and received a prize from the Society of Arts in London. City Art Gallery, Bristol.

materials. The most important production of English-style jugs and related wares in the 1850s came from the Fenton factory in Bennington, Vermont, which was known from about 1853 to 1858 as the United States Pottery Company. Many of the patterns were derived from English designs, but they were mostly rendered in a type of 'parian' porcelain, either uncoloured or else with the white relief pattern clearly defined against a blue pebbled ground. The firm of E. & W. Bennett of Baltimore, Maryland, whose principals were of English origin, were using hard sage-green and blue-coloured bodies for jugs in the English manner, notably a 'marine' jug decorated with relief designs of fishes. The same firm also used earthenware with the deep brown 'Rockingham' glaze for objects of this character, such as a well-known teapot with a relief decoration of 'Rebekah at the Well'; and Rockingham glazed ware was used for relief-decorated jugs by other firms such as the American Pottery Company of Jersey City, New Jersey, and Taylor & Speeler, who initiated the great pottery industry at Trenton in the same State.

The Rockingham glaze, obtained by the admixture of manganese, was apparently originated in the Rockingham factory at Swinton in

England in the early part of the 19th century. It was subsequently much used for cheap ornamental wares, such as toby jugs, *jardinières* and teapots, and its manufacture tended to be associated with 'yellow' or 'cane' ware, which with its transparent glaze was mostly used for kitchen utensils. In Britain this combination was the mainstay of many of the smaller local potteries in the 19th century, and especially of the potteries of the South Derbyshire area. In the United States, Rockingham ware was considerably developed and became one of the most widely used media of American ceramics; it was made by many American factories, but the principal centre for the manufacture of Rockingham, and also of yellow ware, came to be East Liverpool, Ohio. In contrast with the English Rockingham, the American was usually given deliberately a mottled appearance. Rockingham ware of this nature was made at the Fenton factory in Bennington, where, in addition, a more sophisticated form of Rockingham was produced under the title of 'flint enamel' ware. The latter, incorporating a special glazing process with more colouring, was patented by C. W. Fenton in 1849.

The forties saw a renewal if interest in wares directly inspired by

818

819

818. Jug of blue coloured stoneware with hinged pewter lid, made by William Brownfield, Cobridge, England, to a design registered in 1861. Ht. 8½ in. (21·6 cm.). With its formal shallow relief pattern, this jug is typical of many restrained designs of the 1860s. Victoria and Albert Museum, London.

819. Jug of salt-glazed stoneware, with applied decoration of convolvulus sprays and handle in the form of a dragon; made at Voisinlieu, near Beauvais, France, probably to the design of Jules-Claude Ziégler; about 1845. Ht. 10⅝ in. (27 cm.). This ware is an early example of the impact of an easel painter on traditional craft pottery. Victoria and Albert Museum, London.

820. Pitcher of parian porcelain, with pond lily pattern on a blue ground, made by the United States Pottery at Bennington, Vermont, U.S.A., about 1855. Ht. 7¼ in. (18·4 cm.). This pattern apparently follows a similar pattern registered in England by Copeland in 1851. The Metropolitan Museum of Art, New York.

821. Pitcher with Gothic panels in relief and dark brown Rockingham glaze, made between 1838 and 1845 by the American Pottery Co., Jersey City, New Jersey. Ht. 8⅞ in. (22·5 cm.). The Rockingham glaze became especially popular in the United States during the 19th century. The Newark Museum, Newark, New Jersey.

820

821

ancient classical examples, and this was no doubt symptomatic of an increasing tendency to imitate the past whenever this was technically possible. In England the *Art Union* magazine was constantly encouraging work of this sort as though representing the summit of ceramic achievement. The important firm of Copeland, the successor to Spode, was prominent in this activity, which in effect carried on the tradition of Wedgwood's 'black basaltes'. F. & R. Pratt of Fenton, Staffordshire, and Dillwyn & Co., of Swansea were also especially associated with the revival. The model of these wares was the unglazed red-figure pottery of classical antiquity, normally associated with Greece but in the 1840s still described as Etruscan or Etrurian. The apogee of this phase in ceramic fashion was to be found on the stand of Thomas Battam at the 1851 Exhibition, where this London decorating firm mounted a cave decorated with pots and meant to represent an Etruscan tomb.

Wedgwood's jasperware, one of the great achievements of the 18th century, was still being made in the 19th century. The design of this exceptionally hard ware, with its separately moulded relief decoration, was always predominantly classical in inspiration, even though it derived from the Roman cameo-glass technique of the Portland vase rather than from classical pottery. It is interesting to notice, however, that for a short period during the fifties the jasper wares included a proportion of purely contemporary designs. Simple naturalistic plant patterns, such as had become popular on the humble cast-stoneware jugs, were a prominent part of the

823

824

822

822. Lion figure with mottled 'flint enamel' glaze, made by the Fenton factory in Bennington, Vermont, U.S.A., about 1850. Ht. 9¼ in. (23·5 cm.). Flint enamel was in effect an elaboration of the brown Rockingham glaze and was patented by C. W. Fenton in 1849. The Metropolitan Museum of Art, New York.

823. Earthenware vase imitating ancient Greek red-figure pottery, made by Dillwyn of Swansea in Wales about 1850. Ht. 14⅜ in. (36·5 cm.). The 1840s saw a renewal of interest in imitation Greek wares, which were normally known at this time as Etruscan or Etrurian. Victoria and Albert Museum, London.

824. One of a pair of Victorian jasper vases, with separately moulded and applied decoration, made by Josiah Wedgwood & Sons at Etruria, England. Ht. 8 in. (20·3 cm.). Although most of the Wedgwood jasper wares continued in the classical tradition, some were designed during the 1850s with contemporary naturalistic plant patterns. City of Portsmouth Art Gallery Collections.

823

824

825. Ewer of *'Henri Deux'* ware, made by Minton, Stoke-on-Trent, England, for the London Exhibition of 1862. Ht. 15¾ in. (40 cm.). This ware imitated 16th-century *Henri Deux* ware, now called Saint-Porchaire. Victoria and Albert Museum, London.

826. Dish painted in a style reminiscent of Italian Renaissance maiolica, with arabesques and a cartouche with a classical group; made at the Utzschneider factory at Sarreguemines, France; about 1860. Diam. 14¼ in. (36·2 cm.). Victoria and Albert Museum, London.

827. Dish in 19th-century 'Palissy' style, with reptiles in high relief, made by Landais of Tours, France, about 1855. L. 21 in. (53·4 cm.). Wares in the style of the 16th-century French potter, Bernard Palissy, were popular in France, England and Portugal. Victoria and Albert Museum, London.

828. Two vases from a group designed in the spirit of Italian Renaissance maiolica by Alfred Stevens, made by Minton, Stoke on Trent, England. Ht. of larger vase 17 in. (43·2 cm.). Victoria and Albert Museum, London.

827

828

display of Wedgwood wares at the Paris Exhibition held in 1855.

Most of the earthenwares in production, and especially those of the great factories, were moving inexorably towards more and more historicism. The potters were fascinated by their increasing technical efficiency and by their ability to imitate almost every historical style. In this field a great expansion of scholarship was taking place, and this was expressed not only in the production of books but also in the great multiplication of museums. A new self-conscious attention was being given to the decorative arts, and in consequence many new museums appeared in the capitals of the western world devoted wholly to this subject. It was possible for the first time for the manufacturing potter and his public to study at first hand the great works of the past, and they found the experience dazzling.

After the relatively easy conquest of the classical wares they turned with excitement towards more modern themes. Naturally enough, it was the potters of France who first felt the challenge of French Renaissance wares. The work associated with the 16th-century potter, Bernard Palissy, seems to have held an especial attraction for the mid-19th-century public. Its high-relief, almost sculptural, decoration with coloured glazes, could be eerily realistic in its representation of lizards and snakes among dank foliage. The first potter to revive this style was Charles Avisseau of Tours, who began to make Palissy wares in the early forties. He was followed by his son and by his nephew, Landais. In Paris the pottery of Barbizet was making popular versions from about 1850, while the potter, Pull, was making very perfect examples from about 1855.

In England, the Palissy style was taken up by Minton's at Stoke-on-Trent, where close imitations of original pieces were made, but

where the term 'Palissy' was also often used to describe the technical nature of the ware rather than the style. In Portugal, Palissy ware was made skilfully and realistically for many years by Mafra & Son, an earthenware manufacturing firm of Caldas da Rainha which was operating from 1853 onwards.

Another French Renaissance ware which attracted a good deal of attention was the inlaid ware now known as Saint-Porchaire. In the mid-19th century its title was '*Henri Deux*' or '*Faience d'Oiron*'. Its technique implied the careful inlaying of deep brown clays in a whitish body, but something of the same effect could be got by fine painting. French work in this style appeared from the factory at Choisy-le-Roi among others. In England 'Henri Deux' was the medium for some elaborate work by the Minton and Wedgwood factories. French faience of earlier centuries was similarly a subject for much imitative work in the factories and small potteries of France. The factory at Gien made a speciality for many years of the production of wares imitating the old Rouen and other faience styles of the past. Ulysse of Blois and Ristori of Nevers were both imitating the old style of Nevers. However, the Gien factory and Ulysse of Blois were concerned also with versions of the Italian painted maiolica of the 16th century, as were also Joseph Devers, an Italian working in Paris, and the Utzschneider factory at Sarreguemines.

The imitation of painted maiolica was taken up in several other countries. In England it was especially the concern of Minton's in the 1850s and '60s, and one particularly distinguished series, from the artist and designer Alfred Stevens, was shown by Minton's in the London Exhibition of 1862. The Berlin State Porcelain Factory was also concerned in this work, as is seen from some impressive

825

826

827

828

829

830

831

832

829. Dish painted with grotesques in a style reminiscent of Italian Renaissance maiolica; made by Torelli of Florence about 1875. Diam. 15¼ in. (38·8 cm.). Victoria and Albert Museum, London.

830. 'Majolica' *jardinière* and stand, of earthenware with coloured glazes, made by Minton, Stoke-on-Trent, England, in 1850–51. Ht. of *jardinière* alone 14¾ in. (37·5 cm.). This piece, apparently shown at the 1851 Exhibition, can be considered the archetype of the industrial majolica of the later 19th century. Victoria and Albert Museum, London.

831. 'Majolica' sea-horse with cupid, made by Minton, Stoke-on-Trent, England, 1859. Ht. 16 in. (40·7 cm.). Besides ornamental wares, figures such as this were produced in majolica with charming effect. Victoria and Albert Museum, London.

832. 'Majolica' vase with cover, made by the Swedish factory of Rörstrand in 1876. Ht. 15 in. (37·1 cm.). Majolica, in the Victorian sense, with coloured glazes, was widely made in Europe and the United States of America in the latter part of the 19th century. Victoria and Albert Museum, London.

829

examples shown at the Paris Exhibition of 1867. In Italy the painted maiolica of the Renaissance was naturally the main source for much of the decorative earthenware of the latter part of the century. Examples dating from the 1870s have been noted, for instance, from the Ginori pottery at Doccia, from the Torquato Castellani pottery at Rome and from the Torelli pottery at Florence; and in 1878 the most famous of the potteries devoted to the imitation of early maiolica was opened in Florence by Ulysse Cantagalli. In Spain the equivalent source of historicism in pottery was the Hispano-Moresque ware of the 15th and 16th centuries, with its painted lustre decoration on a tin-enamelled ground, reproduced in the later 19th century by firms such as Escofet, Fortuny of Madrid.

Besides the imitative painted work, the term 'majolica', as it was currently spelled, was also interpreted in England to include wares with relief decoration under coloured glazes, and as such it was used to describe a medium which became typically Victorian in character and eminently suited to the production of large domestic objects such as umbrella stands and *jardinières*. This conception of majolica seems to have been worked out for Herbert Minton, the principal of the firm of that name, by Léon Arnoux, a Frenchman who was

already working at his factory. The first pieces of Minton's coloured-glaze majolica were shown at the London Exhibition of 1851, and at the Exhibitions in Paris and London in 1855 and 1862 the ware attracted a great deal of attention. One of the main features of the latter exhibition was a large fountain made entirely of this material. As well as for ornamental vessels the medium was used by Minton's for ornamental figures, often with a charming effect. 'Majolica' in this coloured-glaze sense became immensely popular. Two other Staffordshire firms, George Jones and Adams & Co., were much concerned in its production at a popular level. Wedgwoods were moved to revive their own late 18th-century production of green-glazed ware with an overall decoration of superimposed leaves; a distinguishing feature of the Wedgwood majolica was the use of a translucent glaze over a white body, whereas other firms usually employed a cane-coloured body.

830

831

This industrial majolica spread to fill what was clearly a wide-spread need in the later part of the 19th century. Over a considerable part of Europe its manufacture was commenced, without great artistic pretensions, in the same sort of factories as had embraced first the creamwares and then the printed wares in the

833

834

833. 'Majolica' mug, earthenware with relief decoration and coloured glazes, made by Griffin, Smith & Hill of Phoenixville, Pennsylvania; about 1879. Ht. 3½ in. (8·9 cm.). The firm of Griffin, Smith & Hill was especially associated with the production of this 19th-century style of majolica. Philadelphia Museum of Art.

834. Earthenware flower pot pan, with impressed decoration under a clear green glaze representing a woman with a basket of eggs; made in the factory at Rubelles, near Melun, France; about 1850. Diam. 5 in. (12·7 cm.). An example of the so-called *émaux ombrants* introduced at Rubelles by Baron du Tremblay about 1844; a realistic shaded effect is obtained by running a clear coloured glaze over an impressed motif of varying depth. Victoria and Albert Museum, London.

earlier part of the century. Again the new medium seems to have been taken up with particular enthusiasm in Sweden, where majolica was being made from the late sixties; some impressive products are to be found from the Rörstrand and Gustavsberg factories including *jardinières*, vases, coffee-pots and figurines. In the United States this style of majolica seems to have been made as early as 1853 by E. & W. Bennett of Baltimore, and later the best known producer was the Phoenixville (Pennsylvania) Pottery of Griffin, Smith & Hill. In the nineties it was being made by the Arsenal Pottery of Trenton, which was also, like several English manufacturers, continuing the 18th-century vogue of the toby jug.

Among the coloured-glaze productions of the mid-century a French contribution of some interest was known as the *émaux ombrants* (shading enamels), which were introduced about 1844 by Baron du Tremblay at his factory at Rubelles near Melun. A scenic motif was impressed into the body of a plate or dish which was then covered with a coloured transparent glaze; the deeper portions of the motif would appear darker than those more shallowly covered and a realistic picture could thus be formed of light and shade. This technique was used also in England by Wedgwood in the sixties, for instance, but it was to be considered more a novelty than a generally useful means of decoration. It was in effect the counterpart of the impressed plates of translucent porcelain giving shaded

pictures, known as lithophanes or lithophanies, which were much made in European factories during the middle and later 19th century.

All of the 19th-century earthenwares so far described catered for popular demand, and yet in considering the work of the middle period of the century one is continually aware of a sense of frustration in the decay of individual craftsmanship, of an uncertainty with regard to the manner in which series-produced articles should be designed. The problem was appreciated at an early date in England, where we find the government seeking an answer in the establishment of schools of design in the thirties and forties, and in the establishment of the Museum of Ornamental Art in London in 1852 (later known successively as the South Kensington Museum and the Victoria and Albert Museum). Such efforts represented a joint appeal to the example of past styles and to the standards of artists working in the so-called fine arts of painting and sculpture. A leading spirit in the early Victorian movement of reform was Henry Cole, who was later to be in effect the first Director of the Victoria and Albert Museum. In 1846 he won a prize from the Society of Arts for an earthenware tea service made by Mintons. This led to the short-lived experiment of the 'Felix Summerly's Art Manufactures', Felix Summerly being a pseudonymn which Cole used at this time. The Art Manufactures included objects in all

835. White earthenware teapot with cup and saucer from a tea service designed by Henry Cole (under the pseudonym 'Felix Summerly') and made by Minton, Stoke-on-Trent, England in 1845–46. Ht. 6 in. (15·3 cm.). The success of this service, which won a prize from the Society of Arts, led Cole to commission 'Felix Summerly's Art Manufactures'. Victoria and Albert Museum, London.

836. The 'Hop Jug', designed by Henri J. Townsend and made by Minton, Stoke-on-Trent, England. Ht. 10½ in. (26·7 cm.). Originally commissioned by Henry Cole for his 'Felix Summerly's Art Manufactures' and registered by Minton in 1847, this version of the design, which has coloured glazes, was made during the later 1850s. Victoria and Albert Museum. London.

835

836

837. Earthenware plate with a scene of two figures holding a mirror and attended by cupids, painted by Emile Lessore for Wedgwood, Etruria, England. Diam. 9¼ in. (23·5 cm.). The Frenchman Emile Lessore was painting wares for Wedgwood from the late 1850s, at first in England and later in France, until his death in 1876.
Victoria and Albert Museum, London.

838. Scene of a boy in classical costume with a goat, painted by W. S. Coleman on a Minton plaque about 1870–75.
Diam. 16⅝ in. (42·3 cm.). W. S. Coleman, originally an easel painter, was for a time in charge of Minton's 'Art-Pottery Studio' in Kensington, London. Victoria and Albert Museum, London.

837

838

materials as well as ceramics, and they were all to be designed by artists for production by normal manufacturers. The experiment was short-lived, perhaps because it proved that painters and sculptors cannot necessarily design for techniques of which they are ignorant; but some interesting examples were produced of the Victorian concept of 'suggestive ornament', such, for instance, as the 'Hop Jug' for holding beer which was designed by the painter Henry J. Townsend.

Many instances can be found from the latter part of the century, and indeed from the 20th century, in which manufacturers have sought, consciously or unconsciously, to improve the standard of their wares by establishing working arrangements with 'outside' artists. Often this would be merely a question of commissioning some designs for decorative motifs. In England, for instance, Minton's were using designs from the painter and designer Alfred Stevens in the early sixties and from the painter H. Stacy Marks in the seventies. Perhaps the most interesting example of an independent designer working directly on the ware of a large manufacturer was the painting of the Frenchman Emile Lessore on Wedgwood earthenware. He had originally painted on the ware of the Laurin factory at Bourg-la-Reine near Paris, and, after short spells at Sèvres and Minton's and a period of working at the Wedgwood factory, he continued to paint Wedgwood ware in France from his

return in 1863 until his death in 1876. Although he used the ceramic surface in the manner of a canvas, he nevertheless with his bold sketchy style did much to free ceramic decoration from constricting conventions.

In England and France particularly, the vogue for ceramic painting, and especially pottery painting, spread to amateurs in the sense that it was carried out for the pleasure or interest of the painter rather than of the factory which provided the ware and fired the finished result. Lessore's original work on the ware of the Laurin factory had been of this nature before he was offered a post on the factory's staff. In England a great vogue for amateur ceramic painting was sparked off by an 'Art-Pottery Studio' which Minton's set up in Kensington, London, in 1871. The studio was put under the charge of W. S. Coleman, an easel painter who had been employed for a short time by both Copelands and Minton's. Although the studio was short-lived, it led to the commercial organisation of ceramic painting by amateurs, and, more important, it provided a bridge between commercial production and the newer ideas of decoration which were developing at that time in the London schools of art.

In striking contrast to the more sophisticated ceramic productions, the mid-century period saw the appearance in Britain of the remarkably naive Staffordshire flat-back figures. In the 18th century,

839. A pair of Staffordshire equestrian figures, earthenware sparsely painted, inscribed respectively, 'Duchess' and 'Duke of Cambridge', made about 1854. Ht. of the Duke 14½ in. (36·8 cm.). The representation is probably of the second Duke of Cambridge, the 'Duchess' being Mrs FitzGeorge, who, in fact, never held the title of Duchess of Cambridge. Victoria and Albert Museum, London.

840. Water cistern of earthenware with a yellow glaze, in the form of the bust of a soldier with turban and epaulettes; made by Jean Talbot of La Borne, Henrichemont, near Bourges; about the middle of the 19th century. Ht. 22 in. (56 cm.). In this area of France an ancient 'peasant-art' style of ceramics, such as that of the Talbot family, survived into modern times. Musée départemental des Vosges, Epinal.

839

840

841

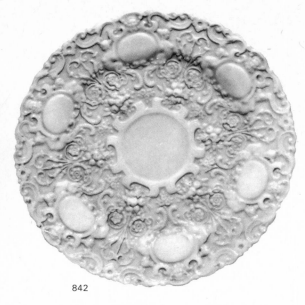

842

843

841. Porcelain vase painted in white on a deep blue ground and gilt; made by the French state factory at Sèvres about 1843. Ht. 11¾ in. (29·9 cm.). Such wares are usually referred to by the title 'Limoges', the technique of decoration being suggested by the Limoges *grisaille* enamels of the 16th century. Victoria and Albert Museum, London.

842. Porcelain plate, moulded in relief with fruit and flowers, scrolls and medallions; made by Jacob Petit, Fontainebleau, France; about 1840–50. Diam. 9⅜ in. (23·8 cm.). Much of Jacob Petit's work was in this style of the revived rococo. Victoria and Albert Museum, London.

843. Covered sugar pot of porcelain, decorated in *pâte-sur-pâte* by Léonard Gély and made by the Sèvres factory, France. Ht. 5 in. (12·7 cm.). This early example of the *pâte-sur-pâte* process was shown at the Paris Exhibition of 1855. Victoria and Albert Museum, London.

and to some extent in the early 19th century, the production of earthenware figures had followed the expensive realistic styles which were natural to the more expensive material of porcelain; but around the middle of the 19th century, groups of earthenware figures were appearing which showed little regard for porcelain styles. The most extreme, and by far the most numerous, were the flat-back chimney-piece figures which were particularly popular in the 1850s and '60s and continued in production throughout the century. These were simply pressed into moulds, avoiding even the expense of casting; they were coloured, often very sparingly, by the use of overglaze or underglaze painting, never by the use of coloured glazes. Many of the figures bear titles which identify them as representations of contemporary celebrities; many reflected the enthusiasms of the period, such as men and women in Scottish Highland dress or scenes from *Uncle Tom's Cabin*. The figures were clearly made in a number of workshops and small factories, including some in Scotland, but the style of the more naive flat-back

figures was closely associated with the firm of Sampson Smith of Longton in Staffordshire.

Although the Staffordshire flat-back figures were echoed slightly in the United States, their style was uniquely British and can be regarded as a unique by-product of the British industrial situation. There are, however, other indications of the continuing vigour of popular art in the field of pottery figures. In France, for instance, one is confronted by the remarkable liveliness and strength of the ceramic figures, and vessels in the form of figures, which were made in the La Borne area near Bourges. One family in particular, the Talbots, dominated the figure-making throughout the 19th century in this ancient pottery-producing region. Here the figures were part of a local craft activity and had little direct connection with the industrial ceramics of France but in the later part of the century at least, many of their purchasers must have been seeking an opportunity for relief from the realism and perfection of ceramics being produced by industrial methods.

Porcelain from 1830

Despite the political disturbances of the Napoleonic wars and their aftermath, the French State factory of Sèvres continued to exercise a great influence, especially in technical matters. Alexandre Brongniart, who abandoned the production of soft-paste porcelain at Sèvres for hard-paste, continued as director for most of the first half of the 19th century. The Empire style of porcelain, with its gilding and its wide areas of painted decoration on classical shapes, persisted for the many prestige productions at Sèvres through the reigns of Louis XVIII, Charles X and Louis-Philippe. Perhaps the most striking evidence of technical perfection coupled with a lack of originality in design is to be found in the emphasis placed on the painted porcelain plaques of Sèvres in the mid-century period which imitated canvas paintings with remarkable accuracy. In the third

quarter of the century careful studies were being made of the implications of the process of casting, and at the Great Exhibition of 1851 in London Sèvres was exhibiting thin pieces of cast hard-paste porcelain in imitation of the Chinese 'egg-shell' wares. The Sèvres Museum had grown up in the early part of the century and the ultimate effect of this was no doubt to encourage a tendency towards historicism. In 1849 Sèvres porcelain played an important part in an exhibition of French Industry in London; the English were not impressed by the Sèvres biscuit figures, but they noted the many imitations of 16th-century Limoges enamels, the imitations of 'old Dresden' and the 'Raffaelle-ware' which was presumably made in imitation of Italian majolica. The revived rococo style, which is described below in connection with the Central European and

839

840

841

844. Biscuit porcelain figure of Mercury about to slay Argus, made by the Royal Porcelain Factory, Copenhagen; about 1870. Ht. 11½ in. (29·2 cm.). The figure is a small-scale copy of a statue made by Thorvaldsen in 1818. Victoria and Albert Museum, London.

845. Rococo officer and campfollower, a pair of painted biscuit porcelain figures on glazed porcelain bases, made by the Prague porcelain factory about 1850. Ht. of officer 9½ in. (24·2 cm.). The use of idealised eighteenth century costume was a characteristic feature of the revived rococo style of the mid-19th century. E. Poche, *Bohemian Porcelain*, Artia, Prague.

845

846

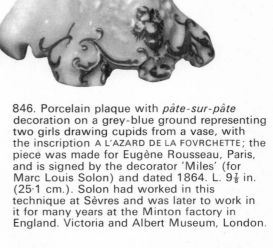

847

846. Porcelain plaque with *pâte-sur-pâte* decoration on a grey-blue ground representing two girls drawing cupids from a vase, with the inscription A L'AZARD DE LA FOVRCHETTE; the piece was made for Eugène Rousseau, Paris, and is signed by the decorator 'Miles' (for Marc Louis Solon) and dated 1864. L. 9⅞ in. (25·1 cm.). Solon had worked in this technique at Sèvres and was later to work in it for many years at the Minton factory in England. Victoria and Albert Museum, London.

847. Porcelain tureen with relief gilding from the 'Thun' service, made at the Klášterec (Klösterle) factory in Bohemia in 1856. Ht. 13⅜ in. (34 cm.). A fine example of the exaggerated swirling motifs of the revived rococo style. E. Poche, *Bohemian Porcelain*, Artia, Prague.

English factories, seems to have made little impact in Sèvres. It was, however, characteristic of other French work and especially of the porcelain of Jacob Petit of Fontainebleau.

In the third quarter of the century the emphasis continued to lie mainly on the solution of technical problems. The most important development was the perfection of the process of decoration by 'pâte-sur-pâte'. By this process the artist builds up the decorative motif by the application of a porcelain slip, usually white on a dark ground; the degree to which the white slip obscures the ground depends upon its thickness, and in this way an interesting possibility is obtained of depicting light and shade. A number of pieces decorated in this technique by Léonard Gély were shown at the Paris Exhibition of 1855. The technique was later developed by artists such as Marc Louis Solon (known until 1870 by the pseudonym 'Miles'), A. T. Gobert and Eléonore Escallier. Solon also worked in Paris with the potter (and glass artist) Eugène Rousseau. After the Franco-Prussian war of 1870 he came to England, where he began to work with great success for Mintons.

In Germany and elsewhere in Central Europe the decorative principles of the Empire style were worked out through several decades. The term 'Biedermeier' is often used to describe the Central European decorative arts of the twenties and thirties and this term may well be used to describe the aftermath of the Empire style in porcelain wares and also in the earthenware table services which followed the porcelain styles.

The first marked change came with the appearance of the revived rococo style which followed in some areas a revival of *chinoiserie*. As its name implies, this style, which was best expressed in porcelain, came from a renewed interest in the work of the mid-18th century. It is important, however, to distinguish it from the more deliberately pastiche styles which were to follow during the 19th century. The revived rococo represented from the start the borrowing merely of a set of motifs which could be exploited to fit a new surge of romanticism and affectation. The revived rococo when expressed in porcelain meant the use of swirling asymmetrical *rocaille* motifs, often in relief and gilded, together with an especial interest in applied decoration of flowers. Although the style represented a marked contrast with its predecessor, it was not adopted everywhere

848. Porcelain vase in the revived rococo style, made at the Imperial Porcelain Factory, St Petersburg, probably about 1850; the decoration, moulded in relief, painted and gilt, is completed by closely-set applied forget-me-nots. Ht. 6⅝ in. (16·8 cm.). The piece was probably fitted originally with a cover. It bears the cipher of Tsar Nicholas I who reigned from 1825 to 1855. Victoria and Albert Museum, London.

849. Figure of a woman in local dress, made in painted biscuit porcelain by the Russian firm of M. S. Kuznetsoff, apparently in the factory at Dulevo; about 1880. Ht. 9½ in. (24·1 cm.). The figure bears the inscription 'Mordovka', i.e. woman from Mordovo, a village some 200 miles S.E. of Moscow. Victoria and Albert Museum, London.

850. Figure of a peasant seated beside a vat, made in painted biscuit porcelain by the Gardner factory, near Moscow, in the mid-19th century. Ht. 5¾ in. (13·6 cm.). Figures with a *genre* interest have been for a long period a characteristic feature of Russian porcelain. Victoria and Albert Museum, London.

851. Part of a porcelain tea service with relief decoration and gilded on a partly green ground, made by the Rockingham factory, England; about 1835. Ht. of teapot 7⅛ in. (18·1 cm.). The revived rococo style brought not only asymmetrical motifs and relief decoration but also the use of low curving shapes. Mrs C. J. Inglis, London.

and the moment of its adoption varied widely from factory to factory. It has been noticed that in Bohemia a phase of interest in *chinoiserie* in the mid-thirties was followed at factories such as Slavkov (Schlaggenwald) and Klášterec (Klösterle) by a whole-hearted adherence to rococo motifs, and yet the more conservative factory of Březová (Pirkenhammer) was still producing some work of an Empire character in the middle of the century.

The revived rococo forms with their curving outlines and relief decoration left very little scope for the porcelain painter. The spirit of the style was essentially one of lightness and fantasy, and it is therefore no accident that, in the Bohemian factories especially, this was a period in which porcelain figure modelling was being intensely developed. Naturally the revival of modelling involved some revival of actual 18th-century models, as is instanced by the use of early Meissen models at the factory of Loket (Elbogen); and, not unnaturally, the early models were a prime concern at the Meissen factory itself in Saxony. An immense number of new models, however, appeared around the middle of the century and in the fifties from such porcelain factories as those at Klášterec and Prague. Although many old ideas were picked up, the range of the subjects and their treatment was distinctively mid-19th-century in character. Figures of gallants in 'rococo' costume, child groups and allegories were common, but there were also figures in contemporary costume, many folk types and even theatrical figures; the bases of

these figures were frequently decorated with rococo scrollwork. The appearance of figures in folk costume is of particular significance, as is also the appearance of figures in rococo costume, a sort of exaggerated and sentimentalised version of mid-18th-century costume which has long continued to have a popular appeal. It is interesting to notice that some of the mid-century porcelain figures were produced in painted biscuit, that is, painted but unglazed, a medium which was to become increasingly popular for cheap figure-work in the latter part of the century.

It may be recalled that Bohemia, now the metropolitan area of Czechoslovakia, was in the 19th century the principal ceramic-producing area of the Austro-Hungarian Empire. The old state factory of Vienna was in decline in the second quarter of the century and finally closed in 1864. The state factories at Meissen in Saxony and Nymphenburg in Bavaria were artistically unimportant at this time, the latter being leased to a private company from 1862. In Denmark the state factory at Copenhagen had similarly fallen upon a period of insignificance, its only notable production being a series of small-scale copies of Thorvaldsen's sculptures carried out in biscuit porcelain.

In Russia, on the other hand, as in France and Prussia, the state factory continued to play a leading role. Known as the Imperial Porcelain Manufactory, it was closely associated with the Court at St Petersburg. Like other state factories further West, it showed

852

853

854

855

852. 'Innocence', a parian porcelain figure made by the Copeland factory at Stoke-on-Trent, England, after an original by the sculptor J. H. Foley. Ht. 16¾ in. (41·6 cm.). The figure was commissioned for distribution by the Art Union of London, and is dated 1847. Victoria and Albert Museum, London.

853. Parian porcelain vase moulded in a vegetable form, apparently representing a group of celery stems, with modelled floral encrustations, made by Samuel Alcock & Co., of Burslem, England; about 1850. Ht. 11¼ in. (28·5 cm.). In this instance the applied flowerwork, usually associated with the revived rococo style, is used on a mid-19th century naturalistic form. Victoria and Albert Museum, London.

854. Compote dish, 'Shakespeare' service, made by Kerr & Binns of Worcester, England; general design by R. W. Binns, the parian figures (of Quince and Flute from *A Midsummer Night's Dream*) modelled by W. B. Kirk and the medallions painted by Thomas Bott. Ht. 15 in. (38·1 cm.). This ambitious service was made for the Dublin Exhibition of 1853. The Dyson Perrins Museum, Worcester.

855. Una and the Lion (from *The Fairy Queen*), a parian porcelain group made by Minton, Stoke-on-Trent, England, after an original by the sculptor John Bell. Ht. 14½ in. (36·8 cm.). This parian group was first made in 1847 for Henry Cole's 'Art Manufactures'. Victoria and Albert Museum, London.

signs of a vested interest in the perpetuation of the Empire style. In the reign of Tzar Nicholas I (1825–55) this was well exemplified in the technically remarkable copies made on porcelain of Old Master paintings in the Hermitage. The revived rococo style was apparently used less for prestige and more for purely ornamental purposes. The reign of Nicholas I had also seen, as elsewhere, the first phase of a period of eclecticism, with imitative wares ranging from Chinese vases to Greek amphorae. Later in the century the Imperial Factory continued to follow the European fashions with, for instance, versions of *pâte-sur-pâte* decoration. It may well be considered, however, that the chief attraction of the factory's output in the 19th century, and indeed the chief attraction of Russian porcelain in general, lay in its production of figures. Catherine II in the 18th century had ordered a series of figures from the Imperial Factory representing the peoples of the Russian Empire, and from this a tradition was developed in figure-modelling which was pleasing by any standards and distinctively Russian in character. The great variety of peasant costume in the widespread provinces of the Empire offered an obvious source of inspiration, and to this was added a *genre* interest in the human types associated with various crafts and occupations. The figures were normally rendered with directness, simplicity and sympathy, and were boldly coloured, often with areas of matt wash. It is interesting to notice that whereas in Bohemia the introduction of the revived rococo style in the making

of porcelain vessels was a determining influence in the development of porcelain figures, in Russia, where the modellers had a very strong tradition of their own, there were only slight signs of using rococo figure-bases and costume.

This pattern of ceramic production in the middle of the 19th century applied not only to the Imperial Factory but also to other prominent Russian factories of the period, notably those of Gardner near Moscow, (see p. 282), Popoff, also near Moscow, Korniloff in St Petersburg and, for the short period 1851 to 1862, Miklaschewski in the Kiev district. Most, if not all, of these factories made porcelain figures in the Russian folk style, together with tableware and vases in a variety of styles among which the revived rococo may be considered basic at this period. The emancipation of the serfs in 1861 seems to have changed the character of some of the Russian production, in so far as the smaller factories on aristocratic estates tended either to disappear or to combine together. A feature of the latter part of the century was the development of the great Kuznetsoff concern. Among its many factories was that of Gardner, which it absorbed in 1891, and by the beginning of the 20th century the Kuznetsoff production of pottery and porcelain was reckoned to represent two-thirds of the whole Russian ceramic industry.

The porcelain factories so far discussed were all concerned in the mid-19th century with the production of the true hard-paste porcelain body, which was developed directly from Meissen's successful imitation of the original Chinese material. The Central and East Europeans had always used the hard-paste material; the French had come to it by the beginning of the 19th century. The British, however, without a state factory and with perhaps a more direct concern in the economics of production and sale, have kept almost exclusively to the soft-paste bone china elaborated by Josiah Spode; in this they have been followed by part of the Swedish and American industry. The dazzling whiteness of bone china and the comparatively low temperature at which it is fired have had inevitably some effect upon the manner in which it has been used, although this has been possibly more apparent in the 20th century than in the 19th.

In England the Empire style was relatively short-lived. It has been noticed already that in providing plain surfaces for painted decoration, the style tended to be especially favoured by state factories needing to produce presentation pieces. It was appropriate, therefore, that the revived rococo style in porcelain should have developed early, and perhaps originally, in the one important porcelain-producing country which did not have a state factory. In factories with a developed system of quantity production the relief decoration of the revived rococo was a far lesser problem than the skilled painting needed by the plain surfaces of the Empire style. Transfer-printing, for all its charm on earthenware, was not thought a suitable substitute for painting on porcelain. It may be noticed also

that the revived rococo was in some sense the first of the imitative styles induced by the industrial revolution; the new factory organisation was tending to destroy the natural spontaneity of design development, in its place substituting an interest in and respect for the achievements of the past. The revival of interest in the rococo may have come originally from silverwork. By 1830 the new version of rococo was fully developed in the porcelain made at such factories as Rockingham, Derby, Davenport and, most especially, Coalport, which is often referred to as 'Coalbrookdale', and it continued as the dominant style of porcelain production in England until about the middle of the forties. From the later 1840s the style shifted to the imitation of the porcelain made at Sèvres in the 1750s and '60s. The English bone china lent itself very well to this latter imitation of the earlier French soft-paste; the imitations were a good deal more precise than those of the revived rococo and some even approximated to forgeries. In this style of work, also, the Coalport factory was prominent, as were the great factories of Minton's and Copelands in the period around the two great London Exhibitions of 1851 and 1862.

In England a revival of porcelain figure-making resulted from the development of the new 'parian' porcelain in the later forties. It seems that this new and relatively hard material was first formulated by Copelands in the course of experiments directed to reviving the old Derby biscuit body. The new material, with an off-white tone and a

851

852

856. Cup and saucer of porcelain, each with two handles inspired by the Greek 'kylix' shape, painted in white enamel on a deep blue ground by Thomas Bott at the Worcester factory of Kerr & Binns in 1859. Diam. of saucer without handles 6½ in. (16·5 cm.). Thomas Bott was a specialist in this so-called 'Limoges' technique from the early fifties until his death in 1870. Victoria and Albert Museum, London.

857. Sweetmeat dish from the Belleek factory (D. McBirney & Co.) Fermanagh, Ireland, probably designed by R. W. Armstrong, 1868. Ht. 5⅜ in. (13·6 cm.). This factory, which first showed its products at the Dublin Exhibition of 1865, used a parian-like porcelain body with an iridescent glaze. Victoria and Albert Museum, London.

858. One of a pair of parian porcelain vases made by Minton, Stoke-on-Trent, England, in 1875, with *pâte-sur-pâte* decoration in white on a blue ground by Marc Louis Solon. Ht. 10¼ in. (26 cm.). The Frenchman Solon brought the technique of *pâte-sur-pâte* decoration to England where the parian porcelain body was found to be particularly appropriate. Victoria and Albert Museum, London.

859. Earthenware vase painted in white and gilt on a deep blue ground, made by the Rörstrand factory, Sweden, in 1882; probably painted by E. H. Tryggelin. Ht. 30¼ in. (77 cm.). A Swedish example of the 'Limoges' technique of decoration in white enamel on a deeply coloured ground. Rörstrand Museum, Lidköping.

856

857

858

859

860

860. One of a pair of porcelain pitchers made by W. E. Tucker of Philadelphia, Pennsylvania, and known to have been bought in his workshop in 1827–28. Ht. 9½ in. (24·1 cm.). Tucker's porcelain was the first to be made in the United States. The Newark Museum, Newark, New Jersey.

861. 'Red Riding Hood' figure made in parian porcelain at Bennington, Vermont, U.S.A. Ht. 6¼ in. (15·9 cm.). Parian figures were made in the Fenton factory at Bennington, which from 1853 to 1858 was known as the United States Pottery. The Metropolitan Museum of Art, New York.

861

slight smear glaze, seemed amazingly like marble and its potentiality for making 'statuettes' was immediately seized upon. Copelands showed examples of the new style of uncoloured porcelain figures at the Manchester Exhibition of 1845–46. In 1847 Minton's were making figures in a similar vein for Henry Cole's 'Art Manufactures' (see p. 290), and they were soon followed by a number of other factories. Contemporary theoreticians were not in the least deterred by the use of one material in imitation of another; indeed they were delighted by the prospect of supplying every home with reduced versions of the finest statuary, and it was in this spirit that the mass of parian figures were put on the market bearing the great names among the mid-19th-century sculptors. On the analogy of marble, the parian figures remained for the most part uncoloured until much later in the century, when the material had eventually ceased to be a novelty.

In the first flush of excitement following the introduction of the new material it was naturally tried for purposes other than the making of statuettes. When the revived rococo style was on the wane in the later 1840s, applied flower-work was adopted for the decoration of parian vases. The firms of Samuel Alcock and Pountneys (of Bristol) were prominent in this work, and examples were shown at the 1851 Exhibition by T. & R. Boote and T., J. & J. Mayer. But this vogue was short-lived; such dust-catching and fragile pieces could only be kept under a glass dome. Because of their lack of colour, the parian flowers had no realism and with their plasticity did not even resemble marble.

More successful, and very characteristic of the more ambitious work of the period, was the integration of parian sculptural elements in important table services made of glazed and painted bone china. A conspicuous example was a Minton dessert service shown at the 1851 Exhibition, which Queen Victoria presented to the Emperor of Austria. This was made basically in the Sèvres style, embellished with small-scale parian sculpture, modelled by the French sculptor, Emile Jeannest, who was at that time working for Minton's. Perhaps even more of a *tour-de-force* was a 'Shakespeare service' made by Kerr & Binns of Worcester for the Dublin Exhibition of 1853. In this instance Shakespearean scenes were realistically modelled in parian by W. B. Kirk to form part of a service which was otherwise of glazed porcelain decorated with Renaissance motifs.

Renaissance motifs, such as chimeras and arabesques, were a characteristic fashion of the 1850s and '60s, and they were used most consistently by the Worcester factory of Kerr & Binns (known as

the Royal Worcester Porcelain Company from 1862). As in France, the 16th-century Limoges painted enamels, mostly in white on a deep blue ground, were considered in the 19th century a reasonable source of inspiration for the treatment of porcelain. The Worcester factory made a speciality of 'Limoges ware' of this sort decorated by the specialist painter, Thomas Bott.

Two more developments of the parian porcelain body should be mentioned. The first was the Irish porcelain of the Belleek factory in Fermanagh which was first introduced at the Dublin Exhibition of 1865. This factory used a parian-like body with a characteristic iridescent glaze, modelled usually into the shape of shells and other marine objects. The second development of the parian body was the use of *pâte-sur-pâte* decoration, which Minton's derived from Sèvres through the employment of Marc Louis Solon (see p. 293); Solon arrived at Minton's in 1870 and immediately began experimenting in the use of *pâte-sur-pâte* decoration with English materials. The parian body was found to be excellent for the purpose, since, while possessing the required degree of hardness, its lower temperature of firing as compared with the normal hard-pastes offered a greater variety in the choice of colours. Solon stayed with Minton's for the rest of his working life until his retirement in 1904. His motifs were mainly human figures depicted in white against a deeply coloured ground. The figures were vaguely Classical or Renaissance in character, rendered with a mixture of playfulness and sentiment in a characteristically late 19th-century spirit. They were clearly related to the style of work in which Solon had been involved in France, and they were related to Thomas Bott's figures on Worcester 'Limoges ware', described above, and to the cameo glass which was being made in the English Midlands from the 1870s onwards; perhaps owing to the current Japanese influence, they were freely disposed without the restriction of enclosing frames. Solon's work for Minton's was a great success and inevitably other English firms followed in this style of work, such as Moore Brothers and George Jones.

Sweden was the only continental country to use bone china, presumably as a result of the particularly strong influence of English earthenware in that country. Of the two great Swedish factories in the second half of the 19th century, Gustavsberg began to make bone china in the early '60s and has continued to use this medium for part of its porcelain production into the mid-20th century. From the early 1860s Gustavsberg was also using parian porcelain for statuettes and other wares which were popular until after the end of

855

856

857

858

853

854

862

863

864

865

862. Footed plate from a 'Belleek' dessert set made by Ott & Brewer of Trenton, New Jersey, in the 1880s. Diam. 9 in. (22·9 cm.). Named after the products of the Belleek factory in Ireland, this finely made ware with a parian porcelain body was widely popular in the United States towards the end of the 19th century. The Newark Museum, Newark, New Jersey.

863. One of a pair of ornamental dishes of earthenware moulded with the figure of a knight on horseback and a border of Gothic decoration, made by Bichweiler of Hamburg in 1880. Diam. 14½ in. (36·9 cm.). Among the many eclectic styles of the late 19th century, this is a Germanic reference to the Middle Ages. Victoria and Albert Museum, London.

864. Earthenware vase painted with flowers, made at Heimberg, Switzerland. Ht. 5¾ in. (14·6 cm.). This piece, in a bright 'peasant' style, was bought from the Paris Exhibition of 1878. Victoria and Albert Museum, London.

865. Earthenware plate painted in polychrome with birds and flowers, made by the firm of Zsolnay of Pécs, Hungary. Diam. 7⅛ in. (18·1 cm.). This piece, acquired from the Paris Exhibition of 1878, is a typical expression of the widespread interest in the 'Persian' style during the latter part of the 19th century. Victoria and Albert Museum, London.

the century. Rörstrand started to make bone china as early as 1857; in the 1870s, however, it began to make some hard-paste porcelain, which gradually became the factory's main speciality. One particularly attractive medium developed by the Swedish factories in the third quarter of the century was the 'Limoges' style of white painting on a deep blue ground, such as that of E. H. Tryggelin at Rörstrand; surprisingly, however, this was carried out, in the case of Rörstrand, at least, on earthenware rather than porcelain.

During the 19th century, the young porcelain industry of the United States of America received influences from various European sources. In the middle of the century, the ceramic material and the style in which it was used depended very largely upon the nature of competing imports from Europe and upon the origin of immigrant operatives. The earliest American porcelain was the so-called Tucker porcelain made in the 1820s and '30s. The production was originated by W. E. Tucker about 1825, and during its short history, until it was discontinued in 1838, the firm was known under various titles, but chiefly as Tucker & Hemphill. The Tucker porcelain was a hard-paste of French type, painted with flowers, portraits or scenes. In the early 1850s Charles Cartlidge & Co., of Greenpoint, Long Island, N.Y., was manufacturing bone-china tea-sets and door-furniture. Hard-paste porcelain was also made by the Union Porcelain Works of Greenpoint, which showed prestige pieces, designed by a German sculptor, Karl Müller, at the Philadelphia Centennial Exhibition of 1876.

In the 1850s and '60s, biscuit porcelain was being used in the style of parian at the United States Pottery at Bennington, Vermont. It is said that true parian was not produced in the United States until after 1875, when it was made by Ott & Brewer of Trenton, New Jersey; but the biscuit porcelain of Bennington and elsewhere of the earlier decades is certainly to be considered as parian in the sense that

its use was modelled on the English parian and it was intended for the same purpose. The production of this version of parian at the United States Pottery was largely due to a certain John Harrison, who had been brought from Copelands in England in 1846 by the earlier Bennington firm of Norton & Fenton. Besides statuettes, the United States Pottery used their parian for making relief-decorated jugs in the English style often emphasising the relief motifs against a pitted coloured ground. The Southern Porcelain Company of Kaolin, South Carolina, was making jugs in a version of parian in the years around 1860; parian was also made in the last quarter of the century by Morrison & Carr of New York, by the Chesapeake Pottery of Baltimore, Maryland, and by Edwin Bennett also of Baltimore, as well as by Ott & Brewer of Trenton.

Perhaps the most characteristic American porcelain, however, of the later 19th century was 'Belleek' or eggshell china. This was introduced into United States production about the middle 1880s by Ott & Brewer of Trenton, and is said to have been achieved by bringing workpeople over from Belleek in Ireland. The new version of Belleek became immediately popular and was soon being made by other Trenton firms, notably the Willets Manufacturing Co., the Ceramic Art Co., and the Columbian Art Pottery. This style of extremely delicate and thinly formed tableware was presumably derived from current late 19th-century imports from the Belleek factory in Ireland and it used a similar parian porcelain body. Another instance of inspiration from a contemporary foreign source is the late 19th-century ware from the Greenwood Pottery of Trenton in the 'Royal Worcester' style. American firms were also involved in this period with the development of the *pâte-sur-pâte* technique. The most notable was the firm of Knowles, Taylor & Knowles of East Liverpool, which exhibited such work at the Chicago Exhibition of 1893.

859

860

861

820

862

866. Earthenware vase with cover and stand, painted with abstract patterns partly suggestive of leaves, designed by Theodorus Colenbrander and made by the Rozenburg factory at The Hague in 1885. Ht. 12 in. (30·5 cm.). Such patterns were apparently inspired by Javanese batik-printed textiles. Hessisches Landesmuseum, Darmstadt.

867. One of a pair of ivory-tinted porcelain vases in the 'Japanese' style, made by the Worcester Royal Porcelain Company, England; about 1872. Ht. 10¼ in. (26 cm.). On each side of the vase Oriental figures engaged in pottery manufacture are represented in imitation of lacquerwork inlaid with ivory. Such pieces, designed by the factory modeller, James Hadley, drew a great deal of attention at the Vienna Exhibition of 1873. Victoria and Albert Museum, London.

868. Jug with relief cast 'Japanese' sprays picked out in blue, made by Pinder, Bourne & Co., of Burslem, England. Ht. 8 in. (20·3 cm.). This design, registered in 1877, illustrates the absorption of Japanese ideas into the manufacture of pieces at a more popular level. Victoria and Albert Museum, London.

866

867

868

Modern Industrial Ceramics
(from 1860)

Shortly after the middle of the century the revived rococo style gave way to styles which incorporated mainly Classical and Renaissance elements. Such styles were characteristic of the 1860s and '70s in Central Europe. The latter half of the century, however, was a period in which many potters and manufacturers were consciously exploring the possibilities of historic and exotic styles. Some followed reminiscent or peasant-art styles, such as are illustrated here in examples from Bichweiler of Hamburg and from the Heimberg wares of Switzerland. In a number of the porcelain factories a further revival of the rococo, known as the Third Rococo, was developed in the last decade or so of the century. Among the exotic influences the Persian and Turkish (or 'Rhodian') styles were prominent in the work of many potteries from Collinot of Paris and Cantagalli of Florence to Zsolnay of Pécs in Hungary. Patterns inspired by Javanese batik-printed textiles were to be found in the 1880s in Holland, in the work of Theodorus Colenbrander at the Rozenburg pottery at the Hague. But all of these influences were subordinate to that of Japan, which can be seen in retrospect to have been of crucial importance, not only in the development of Art Nouveau and modern styles of porcelain and earthenware, but also in the development of modern artist-pottery. Japan as well as China, had had its influence in Europe before; the 'Japan' patterns of the early 19th century, with their angular patchwork motifs, were still current at a popular level in the middle of the century, and indeed

can still be found today. Japanese-style figures in quaint attitudes had been part of the earlier borrowing and were also part of the new. But the new Japanese influence worked more deeply than the mere borrowing of decorative motifs; it implied a whole new approach to the problems of ceramics. In the case of porcelain and industrial pottery, it meant, above all, the freeing of decoration from the formalities of border-patterns and symmetrically arranged motifs; it meant freedom to leave a ground surface unadorned; and it meant eventually the freeing of form from many deeply ingrained conventions of classical origin. Consciously or unconsciously, the basic characteristics of traditional Japanese work were seized upon to become in effect the vehicle of revolt against the ancient classicism of European tradition.

After the long period of Japanese isolation, the first organised showing of Japanese arts to the outside world took place in London at the International Exhibition of 1862. Although the objects shown were insignificant they proved to be the starting point for the new influence in Britain in the following years. Within a decade the Japanese style had affected virtually all the decorative arts including, in Britain especially, the design of furniture. In ceramics the most notable instance was the Royal Worcester factory's work in a popularised Japanese style, which included the use of little modelled figures recessed in panels in the sides of vases. Designed by the factory's chief modeller, James Hadley, they represented a

863

865

866

867

synthesised view of contemporary Japanese crafts, including especially lacquerwork. The ware was first shown at the South Kensington Exhibition of 1871, and it clearly made an impression at the Vienna Exhibition of 1873. At a deeper and less conscious level, the Japanese leaven was working rapidly, to produce, for instance, a charming and quite unambitious stoneware jug registered by Pinder, Bourne & Co. of Burslem in 1877.

In France the Japanese style seems to be as much the concomitant as the inspiration of a determinedly anti-classical tendency on the part of French artists. An important early manifestation of the new Japanese influence on ceramics was to be found in the designs of Félix Bracquemond, an experienced painter and printmaker, who in 1867 conceived a sudden enthusiasm for ceramics. His first practical contact with ceramics was in the studio of the independent artist-potter, Théodore Deck, who at that time was mostly engaged on researches into the nature of Persian and Turkish pottery. About the same time, Bracquemond was commissioned by Eugène Rousseau to design the decoration for a table service in faience. The resulting ware, shown at the Paris Exhibition of 1867 and again at the Vienna Exhibition of 1873, displayed in its decoration a remarkably sensitive reaction to the essential spirit of Japanese design. The vessels were given an enclosing pattern only at the extreme edge; the motifs, such as flower sprays and cocks, with amusing rows of insects, were loosely disposed on the plates against a wide plain ground without apparent regard for the borders. To emphasise the origin of these ideas the motifs themselves were depicted with the hard line and flat colour areas of a Japanese print. Against a background of classical motifs and of crowded decorative arrangements, which even in the rococo style were relatively symmetrical, Bracquemond's sophisticated interpretation of the Japanese spirit must have appeared revolutionary indeed.

Later Bracquemond worked at Sèvres for a short time and was then for many years the principal of the Paris design studio of Charles Haviland's porcelain factory at Limoges. Stylistically, Bracquemond's interpretation of the Japanese spirit was continued at Sèvres by Albert Dammouse, who was concerned with porcelain in the 1870s and later became known for his stoneware (see p. 310). It was mainly from this work by French artists that the modern movement in industrial ceramics can be said to have sprung. In the 1880s, however, the main line of development seemed to pass to Copenhagen and then later to the other Northern European countries.

In Copenhagen the revival of the Royal Porcelain Factory dated from 1883, when its effects were sold to the Alumina earthenware company. That event was followed by a period of reorganisation and conscious experimentation under the energetic leadership of Philip Schou. At the beginning of 1885 Arnold Krog, an architect and painter with some leanings towards the decorative arts, was

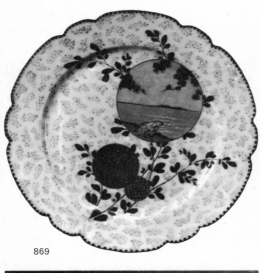

869

870

871

872

869. Porcelain plate painted in 'Japanese' style by Albert Dammouse at the Sèvres factory, France; about 1880. The decoration includes a seascape painted in the larger circular panel. Diam. 9⅜ in. (23·8 cm.). After painting porcelain at Sèvres, Dammouse later became known principally as an artist-potter working in stoneware. Victoria and Albert Museum, London.

870. Wall plaque of porcelain with underglaze painting by Bertha Nathanielsen, made by the Royal Porcelain Factory, Copenhagen; 1901. Diam. 18⅞ in. (48 cm.). This ceramic work betrays for its period a remarkable sense of abstraction. The Royal Copenhagen Porcelain Manufactory.

871. Porcelain vase with underglaze painting of gulls and sea waves by Arnold Krog, made by the Royal Porcelain Factory, Copenhagen, in 1888. Ht. 14 in. (35·7 cm.). An outstanding example of Krog's style of underglaze painting; the wave motif is clearly related to a print by the Japanese artist, Hokusai. Museum für Kunst und Gewerbe, Hamburg.

872. Porcelain vase with *sang-de-boeuf* glaze, made by the Royal Porcelain Factory, Berlin; about 1885. Ht. 8¼ in. (21 cm.). An instance of the growing interest in the use of Oriental forms and glazes. Museum für Kunst und Gewerbe, Hamburg.

873. Dish from the 'Heron' porcelain service, designed by Pietro Krohn and made by the Copenhagen factory of Bing & Grøndahl in 1888. L. 18⅛ in. (46 cm.). With this ambitious and original service, the firm of Bing & Grøndahl embarked on a progressive modern style. Bing & Grøndahl Factory Museum.

874. Porcelain vase streaked with brown and greenish blue and covered with a crystalline glaze, made by the Royal Porcelain Factory, Copenhagen, about 1900. Ht. 8⅞ in. (22·5 cm.). Crystalline glazes appeared in the production of many factories in the period around 1900; at the Copenhagen factory they were first developed in the later 1880s. Victoria and Albert Museum, London.

invited to become an artist at the factory, and almost immediately he seems to have become in effect the art director. Later in 1885 Schou and Krog went on a tour of Holland, Belgium, France and England, and whilst in Paris they met the collector, Siegfried Bing, who had then just returned with many treasures from the Far East. In September of the same year the very first examples of Krog's celebrated underglaze painting came from the kilns in Copenhagen, and by the time of the Paris Exhibition of 1889 the new style was sufficiently developed to win for the factory a Grand Prix and the attention of all Europe's ceramists.

In the course of time Krog attracted to the factory a number of other artists of similar outlook who all used much the same range of subject-matter with the same palette of colours, artists such as C. F. Liisberg, Carl Mortensen, Marianne Høst, V. T. Fischer, Gotfred Rode and Bertha Nathanielsen. Krog seems to have felt that the beauty of the porcelain surface could be adorned only by colours intimately associated with it below the glaze and that areas of unadorned white porcelain should form an integral part of the overall pattern of decoration. His underglaze palette was built around muted blues and greys, which fitted perfectly with his taste for depicting misty Northern scenes. Like the French decorators, he left his dishes and plaques borderless, and like the French Impressionist painters he allowed elements of his design to be cut through by the edge of the vessel. As in the case of the French

decorators the lessons of Japanese art were well-learned but not obvious. Invariably the designs were asymmetrically arranged on surfaces calculated to give the largest possible areas for painting. Generally the subjects were taken from Danish landscapes with birds or other animals, but it has been noticed that a motif such as a sea wave expressed very clearly the impression made on Krog by a print of the Japanese artist, Hokusai. A technical development of the late 1880s was the introduction of painting in coloured porcelain paste to give a relief effect, a technique which was used by C. F. Liisberg and later by Arnold Krog himself. It is interesting to notice that some of the Copenhagen painting implied a sense of abstraction, as in the case of a plaque by Bertha Nathanielsen.

Krog was concerned not only with painted decoration, but also with the shapes of vessels and with the modelling of figures. Although the shapes were of subsidiary importance in the case of the painted vessels, they became inevitably more important in one group of Copenhagen wares which concentrated on the effects of glaze. The use of elaborated glazes represented another facet of the influence from the Far East which in the latter part of the century was affecting not only the great factories, such as Copenhagen, Sèvres and Berlin, but also the small art-potteries and individual artists.

The Oriental glazes which European potters sought to imitate included single-colour glazes, such as the greenish celadon and the red *sang-de-boeuf*, and the *flambé* glazes with variegated and splashed

871

870

875. Figure group of a pair of owls in porcelain, modelled by Arnold Krog and made by the Royal Porcelain Factory, Copenhagen; 1901. Ht. 12¾ in. (32 cm.). This piece by Krog, the art director of the factory, is remarkable for its degree of abstraction and compactness of form. The Royal Copenhagen Porcelain Manufactory.

876. Rörstrand vase in the *Art Nouveau* style, probably designed by Alf Wallander; about 1900. Pansies modelled in slight relief form the rim of the vase. Ht. 8⅜ in. (21·3 cm.). Like other factories, the Rörstrand factory in Sweden followed the lead of the Royal Copenhagen Porcelain Factory in using muted underglaze colours on porcelain. Victoria and Albert Museum, London.

873

874

875

876

877

878

879

877. Porcelain vase with flower painting on a yellow glaze, made in the Sèvres factory, France; 1897–99. Ht. 11¾ in. (30 cm.). This is one of a considerable group of Sèvres vases decorated in a version of the *Art Nouveau* style for the Paris Exhibition of 1900. Kunstgewerbemuseum, Berlin.

878. Vase of earthenware painted with daffodils in blue, green and yellow, made by the Cantagalli firm of Florence (Figli di Giuseppe Cantagalli); about 1899. Ht. 12 in. (30·5 cm.). An Italian expression of *Art Nouveau* feeling for elongated vegetable motifs. Victoria and Albert Museum, London.

879. Porcelain vase from the Rozenburg pottery at The Hague, designed by J. Jurriaan Kok and painted by J. Schellink; 1903. Ht. 10½ in. (26·7 cm.). The Dutch Rozenburg ware expressed the spirit of the *Art Nouveau* not only in its decoration but also in its forms. Collection: Hugh Wakefield.

880

effects; but the most characteristic of the period in Europe were the newly discovered crystalline glazes which incorporated random groups of crystals formed naturally, and often attractively, within the smooth glazed surface. At the Copenhagen factory crystalline glazes were first produced by Clement, the factory chemist, in 1886 and later developed there by V. Engelhardt; in America a crystalline 'tiger-eye' glaze had been already introduced at the Rookwood pottery, Cincinnati, in 1884 (see p. 313). The crystalline glazes were an important innovation in a period when increasing attention was being paid to the use of glaze effects as a sole means of decoration, not only on porcelain, but also on stoneware by artist-potters.

874

The porcelain figures modelled by Krog and by others at Copenhagen under his direction can be said to have initiated a modern style of figure-making. Porcelain figures were no longer thought of as realistic toys or as small-scale versions of monumental sculpture. They were now conceived directly in relation to their medium of slip-cast porcelain with a smooth glazed surface coloured in pastel underglaze shades. In particular the style demanded smooth compact shapes with the minimum of protrusions. In the 1890s, some of the modelling, like the painting on plaques, went through a phase of near abstraction. A striking instance of this is Krog's *Owls* of 1893, which stands in contrast to the more realistic style which was to be continued at Copenhagen in later years.

875

Another Danish firm, Bing & Grøndahl, embarked on a progressive style in 1888 with the 'Heron' service. This was designed by the firm's art director, Pietro Krohn, and is remarkable for its crowded but asymmetrical and austere patterning. Much of the other work of the firm tended to follow in the path of the Royal Factory; F. A. Hallin, who was perhaps the best known of the artists,

873

had been Krog's pupil. In Sweden the Rörstrand factory began to make porcelain in the new style in 1897 under the art-directorship of Alf Wallander. Here the speciality around the end of the century was bold floral decoration modelled in relief and painted in pastel underglaze colours. The decoration was thus given great emphasis and seems often to break into the form of the vessel on which it is placed.

The characteristic international style of the years around the end of the 19th century is well-known as the 'Art Nouveau'. In Northern Europe the manifestation of the style bears the name 'Jugendstil', and elsewhere it has been known as 'Nieuwekunst' and 'Modern Style'. It affected all the decorative arts and all branches of ceramics but it was not adopted universally. It came suddenly for a short period, and it seems now to have flowered a little aside from the main growth of the modern movement. It appeared in much of the work at Rörstrand, for instance, but only slightly in Copenhagen. It was mostly expressed in the decoration of objects, but it was associated with a fashion for tall slender forms and in its fullest development it affected also the details of shaping. The Art Nouveau patterns were essentially derived from plant-like forms and consisted typically of elongated sinuous motifs.

The highpoint of this style was reached at the Paris Exhibition of 1900. For this exhibition the Sèvres factory produced a range of vases decorated in a slightly stiff version of the style. The swirling movement of Art Nouveau was, however, expressed with great sensitivity in a group of figures forming a table decoration, which was designed by Agathon Léonard for Sèvres. Vertical motifs in a somewhat stiff version of Art Nouveau were also seen in Italy on some of the Cantagalli vases of the period. Perhaps the most perfect manifestation of the style was to be seen in the products of the

Rozenburg pottery at The Hague of about 1900 and the years following. The Rozenburg pottery has been mentioned already for its original conception of decoration in the 1880s, but about the end of the century under the leadership of J. Jurriaan Kok a distinctively Art Nouveau style was achieved in porcelain which affected not only the decoration but also the form. Another powerful manifestation of the style came from the Zsolnay firm in Hungary with a series of boldly shaped lustred vases; and about 1900 this firm produced some pieces with striking painted decoration designed by the Hungarian painter, Joseph Rippl-Rónai. Among the English industrial wares the style appeared most prominently at Minton's in an earthenware series, designed by Leon V. Solon and J. W. Wadsworth, mostly decorated with patterning which consisted of flat areas of colour between raised outlines. In its early stages, in the years around 1900, Art Nouveau patterning was to be found more frequently in the works of artist-potters or of small art-potteries (see pp. 310–11), than in the more calculated products of factories concerned with porcelain or with industrial earthenware. In a later phase, however, in the years around 1910, a more stylised and compact version of Art Nouveau became very common in the decoration of new table services.

Apart from a few excesses and affectations, the Art Nouveau was concerned more with decoration than form. The modern movement, on the other hand, was primarily concerned with form. In this process, the most important contributions until the thirties were made by artists and manufacturers in Germany and other Central European countries.

A powerful stimulus towards original thought in the decorative arts came from the artists assembled in the remarkable artists' colony at Darmstadt, which was maintained by the Grand Duke of

880. A dancer, in biscuit porcelain, from the table setting *Le jeu de l'écharpe,* modelled by Agathon Léonard for the Sèvres factory, France. Ht. 12⅜ in. (31·5 cm.). The setting, with its swirling figures, was originally produced for the Paris Exhibition of 1900. Hessisches Landesmuseum, Darmstadt.

881. Straight-sided porcelain dish, designed by Peter Behrens and made by Bauscher Brothers, Weiden, Germany; about 1901. L. 12¾ in. (32·5 cm.). One of two similar services of advanced design by the architect, Peter Behrens. Hessisches Landesmuseum, Darmstadt.

882. Porcelain service designed by Richard Riemerschmid and produced by the Meissen factory, Germany; about 1906. The architect, Richard Riemerschmid, was an active designer working in many media, including both porcelain and stoneware. Staatliche Porzellan-Manufaktur, Meissen.

881

883

882

884

883. Earthenware vase with decoration outlined in trailed slip and filled with coloured glazes, made by Minton, Stoke-on-Trent. Ht. 5⅜ in. (13·5 cm.). Such vases, designed by Leon F. Solon and J. W. Wadsworth in the early years of the 20th century, were among the English manifestations of the Art Nouveau style. Victoria and Albert Museum, London.

884. Porcelain plate from a service designed for the Meissen factory, Germany, about 1905, by Henri van de Velde. Diam. 10½ in. (26·6 cm.). The border of the plate is moulded in relief, with underglaze painting in blue and overglaze gilding. Hessisches Landesmuseum, Darmstadt.

885

886

885. Coffee pot from the 'Donatello' service, designed in 1907 by Philipp Rosenthal and made by the Rosenthal Porcelain factory of Selb, Germany. Ht. 7⅝ in. (19·5 cm.). This example is decorated under the glaze with a motif of cherry branches, but the service was originally designed without decoration. Hessisches Landesmuseum, Darmstadt.

886. 'Masked Lady', modelled by Josef Wackerle and made in porcelain with underglaze painting by the Royal Porcelain Factory, Berlin; about 1911. Ht. 16¾ in. (42·5 cm.). Wackerle modelled figures first for the Nymphenburg factory, where he was art director from 1906 to 1909, and later for the Royal factory in Berlin. Kunstgewerbe-museum, Berlin.

887. 'The Bride as Europa on the Bull', porcelain figure made by the Royal Porcelain Factory, Berlin. Ht. 16⅛ in. (41 cm.). One of the two leading figures from the 'Wedding Procession', a table decoration modelled by the sculptor Adolf Amberg for the wedding of the German Crown Prince in 1905 but not in fact used on that occasion. The models were bought by the Berlin factory in 1909–10. Kunstgewerbemuseum, Cologne.

881 Hesse. The architect, Peter Behrens, and the painter and graphic artist, Hans Christiansen, both designed experimental table services which were shown in Darmstadt in 1901 and were produced respectively by the Bauscher Brothers of Weiden and by Krautheim & Adelberg of Selb. The services by Behrens are of particular interest for their octagonal form and surface designs.

At the Paris Exhibition of 1900, the Meissen factory was showing crystalline glazes and multi-coloured underglaze painting in the Copenhagen style, as well as the older imitative work. A little later the factory began to produce creative work in a modern sense. About 1905, a tea service was commissioned from the architect and 884 designer, Henri van de Velde. At the same time designs were being made for the factory by the architect, Richard Reimerschmid. 882 Besides their work for Meissen, both van de Velde and Reimerschmid were also interesting themselves in stoneware. Van de Velde designed vases for production with figured glazes by Reinhold Hanke of Höhr, Westerwald, and Reimerschmid was one of a number of artists who were concerned with bringing a modern spirit into the production of traditional German stoneware at the pottery of Reinhold Merkelbach in nearby Grenzhausen.

At the Royal Porcelain Factory in Berlin an important period of activity began with the arrival in 1902 of Theo Schmuz-Baudiss, who was to be art director from 1908 to 1926. In his personal work he was interested especially in the use of rich floral patterning and he was responsible for some sumptuous services. This was the period when a number of the leading designers and artists of Germany were achieving a new state of self-consciousness in the 'Deutsche Werkbund' which was founded in 1906. It was also the period when newer firms without any history of state patronage began to come forward. Philipp Rosenthal's important early designs for his 885 'Darmstadt' and 'Donatello' services date from 1905 and 1907 respectively and his 'Isolde' service, which broke away from the attempt to integrate the handle in the general shape, dates from 1910. This service and also the original versions of 'Darmstadt' and 'Donatello' were left white and without decoration, representing a tendency to emphasise form at the expense of decoration which was to become a characteristic of the modern style.

At the same time the art of porcelain figure-making was reaching a high degree of effectiveness in the hands of the German artists and manufacturers. They profited from the earlier discoveries of the Copenhagen factory in the use of underglaze colours, which made the colouring seem truly part of the model, and in their perception of form in its relation to the capabilities of the medium. Unlike the 887

earlier Copenhagen figures, however, the German figures represented more often human than animal subjects, although animal subjects were still common. Perhaps the most characteristic modeller of the period was Josef Wackerle, who was the art director at Nymphenburg from 1906 to 1909, and was responsible for a series of human figures of great charm and personality from about 1905 onwards, first for Nymphenburg and later for the Berlin factory. 886 For the wedding of the German Crown Prince in 1905 the sculptor, Adolf Amberg, designed an ambitious table setting, the 'wedding procession', which included among other items sixteen exotic figure subjects. The design was not, in fact, used for the wedding but was later produced by the Berlin factory and was a subject of great interest when it was shown at the Berlin art exhibition in 1911. 887

The sculptor, Ernst Barlach, was also represented by a number of

strange powerful figures, in white glazed porcelain without any colouring, which were produced from about 1908 to 1913 by the *Schwarzburger Werkstätten für Porzellankunst* at Unterweissbach in Schwarzburg-Rudolstadt. Russian subjects among these figures reflected the Russian journey made by Barlach in 1906; shortly after his return from Russia Barlach had modelled similar figures for production in stoneware at Richard Mutz' studio in Berlin (see p. 311). The *Schwarzburger Werkstätten* had been founded in 1908 by Max Adolf Pfeiffer, who continued as manager until the workshops were associated with another factory in 1913. After the first world war in 1918, Pfeiffer took charge of the Meissen factory and from the following year date the first significant Meissen figures of modern times. A number of artists were concerned, notably Paul Scheurich and Max Esser to mention two who had also modelled for Pfeiffer before the war at the Schwarzburg workshops. Paul Scheurich modelled figures in the post-war period not only for Meissen but also for Nymphenburg, and with the finest effect, for the Berlin factory.

The theoretical determination of the modern style, in its synthesis of handicraft and engineering, was the achievement of Walter Gropius. In 1919 he opened the remodelled Weimar Art School, known as the 'Bauhaus', in which architects, painters and craftsmen were to reach a unity of outlook and effort. The ultimate implications of functionalism, and of the architectural approach to the decorative arts were consistently explored during the decade or so of the school's existence, in Weimar and then in Dessau and Berlin, until it met the displeasure of the Nazis in the early thirties. So far as ceramics was concerned, the effect of Gropius' ideas was worked out and conveyed to the world through the work of several artists

associated with the school, notably Gerhard Marcks, Otto Lindig, Theodor Bogler and Margarete Friedländer (Marguerite Wildenhain). Such work was not only important for its own time but it also set the terms for important designs made since the second world war.

The early 20th century was equally a period of great activity in the Austro-Hungarian Empire. The 'Sezession' movement in Austrian architecture of the later 1890s had proved an important stimulus to the Austrian decorative arts. In 1903 the '*Wiener Werkstätte*' was founded, under the influence particularly of Josef Hoffmann; and in 1905 the '*Wiener Keramik*' workshop was established by Michael Powolny and Berthold Löffler, later to be amalgamated in 1912 with the workshop of one of Powolny's pupils Franz Schleiss, under the title '*Wiener und Gmundener Keramik Werkstätte*'. The products of the *Wiener Keramik* workshop included 'black-and-white majolica', usually decorated with geometric patterns in a style associated with Cubism, from designs by artists such as Michael Powolny, Josef Hoffmann and Dagobert Peche. Powolny was particularly known for his figures modelled in a highly personal style. In a broadly similar spirit Ernst Wahliss of Turn-Teplitz (Trnovany near Teplice) and Vienna was making the 'Serapis-Fayence' in the years before the first world war, covered with heavy-lined, intricate and near-abstract patterning from the designs of artists such as Karl Klaus. In the strictly industrial field of porcelain manufacture the spirit of Austrian design in these years was manifest in the wares commissioned by the Viennese firm of Joseph Böck. Similar ideas were current in Prague, where an organisation known as Artěl was formed in 1908 by a group of architects and other artists to further the decorative arts. During the following years the products of its workshops included ceramics,

888. 'Daphne', porcelain figure, glazed and uncoloured, forming a pair with an 'Apollo', modelled by Paul Scheurich and made by the Berlin State Porcelain Factory; about 1925. Ht. 15 in. (38·1 cm.). Scheurich earlier worked for Meissen and Nymphenburg. Victoria and Albert Museum, London.

889. 'Russian Lovers', modelled by the sculptor, Ernst Barlach, and made in white porcelain by the *Schwarzburger Werkstätten für Porzellankunst*, Germany; 1908. Ht. 7⅞ in. (20 cm.). The subject was inspired by Barlach's journey to Russia in 1906. Kunstgewerbemuseum, Berlin.

890. Porcelain service designed by Margarete Friedländer (Marguerite Wildenhain) for the Berlin State Porcelain Factory; about 1930. Ht. of coffee pot 6½ in. (16·4 cm.). In services such as this the ideas of the Bauhaus were brought into industrial production. Museum für Kunst und Gewerbe, Hamburg.

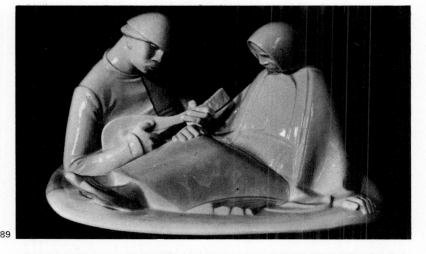

889

888

890

893 designed by the architects, Vlastislav Hofman and Pavel Janák, which expressed a strongly Cubist approach in their geometrical forms.

In later years Austria's influence in industrial ceramics has flowed mainly from the Viennese Augarten factory. Based partly on the simple but significant work of the *Wiener Werkstätte* and partly on older traditions of richness, the Viennese Augarten factory seemed to produce its own version of elegance in the modern style.

894 A service designed by Josef Hoffmann about 1928 is illustrated here, together with parts of a service designed by Ena Rottenberg about

895 1939 in which a chinaman's head is incorporated, somewhat exotically, as the knob on the lid of a smoothly modern teapot.

In France and England new ideas were developing somewhat differently from those of Central Europe during the first thirty years or so of the century. In France a renewed interest in the design and decoration of industrial wares seems to have coincided with the Paris Exhibition of 1925. The most distinguished French work of the twenties and later was probably that produced by the two

896 designers, Jean Luce and Marcel Goupy, both of whom designed decorated tablewares, and also the accompanying glassware, for a limited clientele. It is also noteworthy that the 1925 Exhibition in-

891

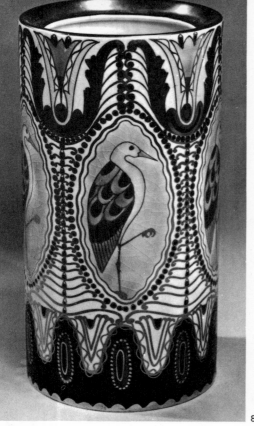

892

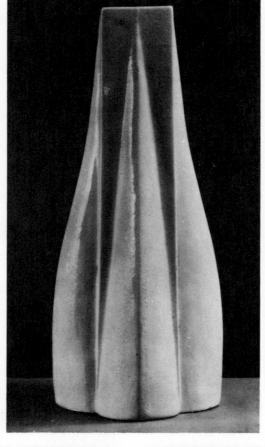

893

891. Figure of a boy riding on a snail, 'black and white majolica' designed by Michael Powolny and produced by the *Wiener Keramik* workshop, Vienna; about 1910. Ht. 7¾ in. (19·7 cm.). Powolny was particularly known for his lively earthenware figures of children. Victoria and Albert Museum, London.

892. Cylindrical vase of earthenware with painted decoration; a style of ware known as 'Serapis-Fayence', designed by Karl Klaus and made by Ernst Wahliss of Trnovany, Bohemia, and Vienna. Ht. 7¼ in. (18·4 cm.). This piece was shown at the Turin Exhibition of 1911. Kungstgewerbemuseum, Berlin.

893. Earthenware vase with yellow glaze designed by Vlastislav Hofman and made by the Artěl organisation, Prague; about 1911. Ht. 11½ in. (29·4 cm.). This Czech organisation was formed in 1908 to produce well-designed articles in various materials. Österreichisches Museum für Angewandte Kunst, Vienna.

894. Porcelain service designed by Josef Hoffmann for the Augarten factory, Vienna; about 1928. Ht. of coffee-pot 7⅛ in. (18 cm.). Hoffmann was for many years a powerful leader of the modern movement in Austria. Österreichisches Museum für Angewandte Kunst, Vienna.

894

895

cluded important work from the Théodore Haviland factory in Limoges with decoration by Jean Dufy, the brother of the painter, Raoul. In England the Omega workshops established by Roger Fry in 1913 provided the occasion, not only for Fry to produce his own handmade pottery, but also for artists such as Duncan Grant and Vanessa Bell to use their loose painterly style in the decoration of ceramics; something of this effect was continued in repetitive indust- rial ceramics during the twenties in the work designed by John and Truda Adams for Carter, Stabler & Adams of Poole, Dorset, and in the designs commissioned from easel painters, such as Paul Nash and Ben Nicholson by the Staffordshire firm of E. Brain about 1937. The most distinguished English industrial work of the thirties, however, came from the firm of Josiah Wedgwood & Sons. In the mid-1930s the firm commissioned from the architect, Keith Murray, a series of distinguished designs, mostly for earthenware vases and bowls, which seemed to be derived directly from his architectural experience. In the later thirties the same firm was seeking to revive the English tradition of printed pottery with designs made by the painter and graphic artist, Eric Ravilious, and from this collaboration came the Persephone earthenware table service. In England and the

United States the work of many small 'art-potteries' in the late 19th and early 20th centuries is related more closely to the work of the individual artist-potters and is considered here in that connection (see pp. 311–14).

Since the second world war almost every major ceramic factory in Europe, America and Japan has produced at least one 'modern' table service which uses in some degree the principle of functional- ism, together with a sculptural sense of elegance. Such services are often sold in plain white, or else with sparse decoration. It should be recognised, however, that these services represent only part of the total output of most of the factories; in an industrial age a remarkable nostalgia is seen in a clinging to traditional elements in ceramic form and decoration. Among the modern work may be mentioned services involving new shapes of some distinction from Castleton China in the United States, designed by Eva Zeisel, and from Copelands in England, designed by Neal French and David White. A service from Richard-Ginori in Italy, designed by Giovanni Gariboldi, expresses an exotic elegance of form. In Western Germany, particularly, the modern style of table service has been firmly established. The most prominent German manufacturer

897

898

899

900

896

897

895. Porcelain service designed by Ena Rottenberg for the Augarten factory, Vienna; about 1939. Ht. of teapot 5 in. (12·8 cm.). A service such as this represents an elegant, although somewhat exotic, contribution to the modern style. Österreichisches Museum für Angewandte Kunst, Vienna.

896. Two plates designed by Jean Luce; about 1925. Diam. about 9⅞ in. (25 cm.). The stylised decoration is typical of its period and of the wares designed by Jean Luce for sale through his own establishment in Paris. Musée des Arts Décoratifs, Paris.

897. Earthenware bowl designed by Keith Murray for Josiah Wedgwood & Sons, Etruria, England. Ht. 6½ in. (16·5 cm.). One of a series of designs commissioned from the architect, Keith Murray, in the mid-1930s. Victoria and Albert Museum, London.

898. Items from a porcelain service designed by Eva Zeisel for Castleton China, New Castle, Pennsylvania, U.S.A.; 1941–5. Ht. of coffee- pot 10⅜ in. (26·3 cm.). The 'Museum' shape, produced in collaboration with the Museum of Modern Art, New York. Victoria and Albert Museum, London.

899. Spode 'Apollo' porcelain service, designed by Neal French and David White and made by Copeland, Stoke-on-Trent, England. Ht. of coffee pot 9⅜ in. (23·8 cm.). The service won a design award in 1960. Victoria and Albert Museum, London.

900. The 'Donatella' service of porcelain decorated with grey and gilt bands, from the Richard-Ginori factory, Milan, Italy. Ht. of coffee-pot 10½ in. (26·7 cm.). This exotically elegant service was designed about 1954 by Giovanni Gariboldi. Victoria and Albert Museum, London.

898

899

900

901

902

901. 'Arzberg 2000' porcelain service designed by Heinz Löffelhardt for the Arzberg factory, West Germany; 1954. Ht. of coffee-pot 6 in. (15·3 cm.). Löffelhardt is one of several German designers who have developed a modern style emphasising ceramic shape. Victoria and Albert Museum, London.

902. Group of vessels, in plain colours and white, from the 'Kilta' range of heat-proof earthenware, made by the Arabia factory at

Helsinki, Finland. Ht. of larger covered jar 4⅞ in. (12·4 cm.). The austere and revolutionary Kilta range was designed by Kaj Franck about 1948 and first appeared on the market in 1953. Victoria and Albert Museum, London.

903. 'Grey Bands', a porcelain service designed by Wilhelm Kåge for the Gustavsberg factory, Sweden; 1944. Ht. of jug 5½ in. (14 cm.). This is a slightly decorated

version of the original 'soft forms' service designed by Kåge in 1940. Victoria and Albert Museum, London.

904. Pieces from a porcelain service, *Det Riflete*, designed by Tias Eckhoff for the Porsgrund porcelain factory, Norway; 1949. Ht. of cream jug 3¾ in. (9·5 cm.). An early design by Tias Eckhoff, who was head designer at the Porsgrund factory from 1952 to 1957. Victoria and Albert Museum, London.

903

904

perhaps has been the Rosenthal firm with its designs from artists such as Wilhelm Wagenfeld and the American, Raymond Loewy, but many others have added to this modern style in which the emphasis is largely upon ceramic shape, notably Heinrich Löffelhardt for the Arzberg and Schönwald factories and Hubert Griemert for the Berlin factory.

In Scandinavia the industrial wares have followed the general tendencies of the modern style, but here a strong craft element has intruded and this is clearly discernible in some of the modern services, which seem to express more clearly than others the nature and limitations of their material. They seem also to have social implications which take account of a need to reduce the distinction between kitchen wares and table wares and to minimise the need for uniformity of pattern throughout a table service. The Scandinavians have more than others furthered the concept of the artist in industry

and have come nearest to the identification of the artist-potter with the ceramic designer.

The most distinctive contribution in this sense has come from Finland, a country with little previous ceramic tradition, whose industrial production is concentrated very largely in the one great factory known as Arabia, near Helsinki. Arabia separated in 1916 from its parent factory of Rörstrand in Sweden, and from the mid-twenties was producing work of importance under the inspiration of Thure Öberg and of artist-designers such as Greta-Lisa Jaderholm-Snellman. Shortly after the second world war a separate design-planning studio was set up under Kaj Franck, who was previously known as a glass and textile designer. Already in 1948 he had designed the revolutionary 'Kilta' service, which appeared on the market in 1953 and has set the general style for many others in Finland and elsewhere. 'Kilta' is a range of heat-proof earthenware

901

902

vessels in several plain colours, which combine many of the functions of cooking, serving and table use. At the Arabia factory this has been followed, for instance, by the deep brown 'Liekki' heat-proof ware, designed by Ulla Procopé in 1957, which is made so that the pieces can be stacked and so that the lids of cooking vessels can be used as serving dishes. Design based on such considerations can be none the less attractive and represents, in fact, a new aspect of functionalism.

In Sweden the industrial wares came mainly from three organisations, the great factories of Gustavsberg, Rörstrand and the Upsala-Ekeby combine, which includes additionally factories in Gävle and Karlskrona. Many outstanding white porcelain services have been produced, a particularly noteworthy example being Wilhelm Kåge's 'soft forms' service designed for Gustavsberg in 1940. But from the middle fifties the most significant design, as in Finland, has concerned services of strictly functional design and composition, usually heat-resisting, and often in plain colours or else decorated with large simple motifs. Such services, or sets of vessels, have been designed by Hertha Bengtson and Marianne Westman for

Rörstrand, by Sven Eric Skawonius for Upsala-Ekeby and by Stig Lindberg and Karin Björquist for Gustavsberg. In Denmark oven-proof ware designed by Magnus Stephensen in 1957 for the Royal Copenhagen factory belongs to the same category. In Norway, in addition to elegant white services, the Porsgrund porcelain factory has produced practical wares with contrasting white or dark-brown elements by Tias Eckhoff and Eystein Sandnes, and the Figgio faience factory has produced heat-resisting earthenware with polychrome decoration by Hermann Bongard.

The Scandinavians, and in particular the Danes, have continued their tradition of figure-making in the great factories. During the interwar years, porcelain was still used for this purpose, as in the figures of Gerhard Henning and Arno Malinowski, who both made figures in a narrative style for the Royal Copenhagen factory. But from the thirties onwards, stoneware was mostly used for this purpose, as in the work of Knud Kyhn, Jais Neilsen and Helge Christoffersen for Royal Copenhagen and of Jean Gauguin (a son of Paul Gauguin) and Mogens Bøggild for Bing & Grøndahl.

Artist-potters from 1860

The richness and complexity of recent ceramic history has been largely due to the interaction of two distinct lines of development. On the one hand the industrial tablewares of the factories have moved from the catalytic influence of Japan, through functionalism, to the standards of modern industrial design. On the other hand, individual artists, inspired by somewhat different aspects of Far Eastern ceramics, have been using the medium for the expression of a personal sense of beauty. In spite of some attempts at synthesis, especially in Scandinavia, the two lines have been largely separate and parallel. The appearance of artist-pottery represented at least in part a reaction against the technical excellence of industrial wares and the lack of personal creativity implied by an extreme sub-division of labour.

The conception of an artist-potter may vary from the 'studio' potter producing the occasional precious object, to the artist craftsman producing everyday wares in series. It may vary, too, from the artist as designer and controller of a workshop of specialists, as was frequently the case in the nineteenth century, to the artist

who, in more modern terms, carries out virtually every process of potting with his own hands in order to establish his whole responsibility for the object produced. Beyond the artist-potter lies the vague conception of the 'art-pottery', which may provide facilities for artist-potters or appeal with its wares to the same public, and some such organisations have already been discussed in this account for their bearing on industrial wares.

A sense of inadequacy, or potential inadequacy, of industrial ceramics belongs most properly to Britain, but it was in France that the artist-potter first appeared and first reacted to Far-Eastern influence. In one sense, men such as Charles Avisseau of Tours and Jules-Claude Ziégler of Voisinlieu, working and experimenting on a personal basis, may be claimed as artist-potters of the 1840s (see pp. 285, 288). But by most reckonings the earliest of the artist-potters in the modern sense was Théodore Deck, who set himself up in Paris to make decorative earthenware in 1856. Deck was greatly successful in his own lifetime; he spent the last four years of his life, from 1887 to 1891, as art director at Sèvres, the first practical potter ever to

905. 'Monkey suckling its young'. A stoneware figure covered with a mottled glaze from the Royal Copenhagen Porcelain Factory, modelled by Knud Kyhn; about 1930–38. Ht. 6¾ in. (17·1 cm.). Victoria and Albert Museum, London.

906. Earthenware plate with decoration designed and painted by Eléonore Escallier for Théodore Deck, Paris. Diam. 23⅝ in. (60 cm.). This early example of painting in the revived Japanese style was shown at the Paris Exhibition of 1867. Mme. Escallier was one of many artists who painted on Deck's faience about this time. Musée des Arts Décoratifs, Paris.

905

906

907

909

907. Earthenware plate with painted decoration on a blue ground, made by Théodore Deck in Paris and shown at the Paris Exhibition of 1878. Diam. 11¾ in. (29·9 cm.). Théodore Deck was especially interested in the effects of Near Eastern wares; in this instance the source of inspiration was 'Rhodian' or Turkish. Victoria and Albert Museum, London.

908. Porcelain vase with *flambé* glaze made by the French potter, Ernest Chaplet. Ht. 15⅜ in. (39 cm.). Chaplet, who died in 1909, did more than any other to develop the cult of glaze techniques among French potters in the later years of the 19th century. Musée des Arts Décoratifs, Paris.

909. Tall six-sided stoneware vase divided by vertical ribbing, with mottled purple glaze, made by the French artist-potter Auguste Delaherche; about 1891. Ht. 26 in. (66 cm.) A fine example of Delaherche's strong sense of form. Victoria and Albert Museum, London.

910. Stoneware vase made by Jean Carriès; about 1890. Ht. 7 in. (17·9 cm.). Principally a sculptor, this French artist was powerfully attracted to ceramics by the possibilities of Far-Eastern glaze techniques. Museum für Kunst und Gewerbe, Hamburg.

910

908

reach that distinction. The chief feature of his work is its remarkable variety, and perhaps for that reason he is now more clearly recognised for the range of his technical innovations than for his personal ceramic style. His first success was in the production of pottery decorated with individually painted scenes, mostly by painter friends. He was particularly inspired by near-eastern and Persian wares and their glazes, and perhaps for this reason he was less affected by the implications of Japanese design than some of those who worked with him such as Félix Bracquemond (see p. 300) and Eléonore Escallier. About 1880, however, he embarked on the making of porcelain and produced some fine *flambé* glazes. In this he was presumably inspired, like other French artists, by the sight of Japanese glazed wares at the Paris Exhibition of 1878.

Deck's work can be considered the starting point of French artist-pottery, but it was Ernest Chaplet who contributed most to a developing cult of glaze techniques among a considerable group of French potters in the later years of the 19th century. In the 1870s Chaplet was concerned in the development of the 'barbotine' method of decoration, first at the Laurin factory at Bourg-la-Reine and later at the Haviland factory in Limoges. This method involved painting in coloured slips, rather in the manner of oil-painting. In the 1880s Chaplet began to attract attention with his stoneware, which he pursued first with the support of the Haviland concern and later in his own workshop at Choisy-le-Roi. From the later

1880s until his death in 1909 he was working with porcelain which he covered with *flambé* glazes, often as fine as any from the Far East.

Mention should be made here of the painter, Jean-Charles Cazin, who, whilst teaching in London in the early 1870s, took part in the early history of artist-pottery in England, producing stoneware with relief decoration in the 'Japanese' style. Auguste Delaherche, Albert Dammouse and Adrien Dalpayrat were all concerned with the elaboration of glaze effects on stoneware or porcelain. Delaherche's work passed through many phases during his long career which extended well into the 20th century; in general, his work is characterised by a remarkable strength of form. Dammouse was above all a decorator: he had worked at Sèvres and had been much influenced by Japanese ideas of pattern (see p. 300). Dalpayrat revealed a sense of form which was perhaps seen at its best in the use of slightly asymmetrical shapes during the *Art Nouveau* period at the end of the century, a characteristic which can also be seen in some of the work of Taxile Doat of Sèvres about 1900. Among the artists in other media who felt the seemingly irresistible attraction of far-eastern glaze technique, was the sculptor, Jean Carriès. As with so many others, his consciousness of this new medium came in the 1880s. Before his early death in 1894, he had used it for expressive sculpture as well as for making vessels. Following Carriès, Georges Hoentschel, Paul Jeanneney and Alexandre Bigot came to pottery in the 1890s and were active around 1900. Jeanneney's stoneware

908

909

910

was very reminiscent of the Far East, whereas Hoentschel sought to minimise this influence with original forms and decorative techniques. Edmond Lachenal produced painted earthenware as well as elaborately glazed stoneware and porcelain, and Félix Massoul was known for a wide range of decorative styles often inspired by his interest in archaeology. Clément Massier, the son of a potter in Vallauris, stood a little aside from the main movement of French artist-pottery centred on Paris. His work, carried out in his own workshop at Golfe-Juan near Cannes, was attractively decorated around the turn of the century with lustre glaze effects.

This remarkable flowering of artist-pottery in France in the decades around 1900 was inevitably reflected elsewhere in Europe. In Germany, individual work of considerable interest was being carried out in the latter part of the 19th century by Maximilian von Heider and his three sons, who worked in Schongau in Bavaria and used lustre glazes. For a long period Max Läuger was influential as a teacher and experimenter in Karlsruhe; he made some remarkable earthenware at the nearby Kandern pottery decorated in *Art Nouveau* and later styles. Another notable artist was Hermann Mutz of Altona, who made a direct study of Japanese collections and was producing around 1900 attractive stoneware with figured glazes. His son, Richard Mutz, set up a ceramic workshop in Berlin about 1904, to produce similar work with flowing glazes. It was to Richard Mutz' credit that he produced so felicitously in stoneware the first of the stark, almost frightening, figures modelled by Ernst Barlach after the return from his Russian journey in 1906 (see p. 305). Julius Scharvogel was yet another German artist-potter who set up a workshop, in this case in Munich, to produce stoneware with thick flowing glazes in the years around 1900. He had been originally with the firm of Villeroy & Boch in Mettlach, and in 1906 he was appointed director of the Grand Ducal Ceramic Factory in Darmstadt, where he was responsible for stoneware with studied glaze effects.

In Denmark the use of ceramics as a medium of expression for the individual artist can be said to have started with the activities of Thorvald Bindesbøll in the 1880s. The medium he used was earthenware and his intention was purely decorative; he was equally concerned with other arts, notably silverwork. By contrast, Herman A. Kähler was entirely a professional potter who took over his father's pottery at Naestved in 1872 and was subsequently well known for his lustre-painted earthenware. Stoneware with high-fired glazes, which was so essentially the medium of artist-potters in France, did not come to Denmark, or indeed to any part of Scandinavia, until comparatively late, and then it was principally exploited through the great factories. In Finland, where this applied equally, the work of the artist-potter, A. W. Finch, is of particular significance. Of English parentage, Finch was born and educated in Belgium, where he was associated with Henri van de Velde. In the late 1890s he went to Finland, where he collaborated with the Swede, Louis Sparre, in setting up the 'Iris' workshop in Porvoo (Borgå) to make Sparre's furniture and Finch's pottery. The latter was practical in spirit and was decorated in a simple linear manner in the *Art Nouveau* style. The workshop was short-lived, but as a teacher at the Central School of Arts and Crafts in Helsinki, Finch was to exert a powerful influence upon the later ceramics of Finland.

Britain was the home of the Arts and Crafts movement, which gave the British arts an unique influence in the world at the end of the 19th century, and made important contributions not only to the theory of handicrafts but also, ultimately, to the concept of industrial design.

Following some earlier attempts to revitalise the industrial arts through designs commissioned from easel painters and sculptors, the full reaction against the effects of industrialism began with the formation of the firm of Morris, Marshall, Faulkner & Co. by William Morris and his friends in 1861. It is interesting to notice that the London International Exhibition of 1862 contained at the same time the first public display of the wares of that firm and also the first exhibition display of Japanese arts. Morris and his circle were chiefly interested in the crafts as they had been in a supposedly ideal medieval state, and they had little use for the influence of Japan and the Far East. By the time that the concept of stoneware with high-fired glazes reached Europe the most active English potters seemed already committed to the limited possibilities of salt-glazed stoneware or painted earthenware.

Perhaps the first English product which can be called artist-pottery was the salt-glazed stoneware decorated in the Doulton factory at Lambeth in London from 1871 by students of the Lambeth School of Art. This peculiar arrangement was made with the firm by the headmaster of the school, and the result was a very great success. The individual artist was responsible only for the choice of shape and for the decoration, but every piece was signed by him, or her, and every one was unique. Among the artists whose work developed in the

911. Stoneware bowl with overrun glaze. made by Richard Mutz, Berlin; about 1905. Diam. 9½ in. (24 cm.). This use of glaze on forms of Far-Eastern inspiration was characteristic of much of the artist-pottery in the early years of the 20th-century. Kunstgewerbemuseum, Berlin.

912. Stoneware vase with mottled overrun glaze, made by Julius Scharvogel in Munich; about 1900. Ht. 4¼ in. (10·8 cm.). Scharvogel had originally worked in the factory of Villeroy & Boch at Mettlach, and was later, for a period from 1906, director of the Grand Ducal Ceramic Factory in Darmstadt. Museum für Kunst und Gewerbe, Hamburg.

913. Earthenware vase with lustre painted decoration, made by Herman A. Kähler of Naestved, Denmark; 1897. Ht. 12⅝ in. (32 cm.). Like many potters of the late 19th-century Kähler made extensive use of lustre painting for the decoration of his work. Kunstgewerbemuseum, Berlin.

911

912

913

914

914. Dish and mug of earthenware, with decoration cut through green and blue slips respectively and with white slip dots, made by A. W. Finch at the 'Iris' workshop at Porvoo (Borgå), Finland; about 1900. Diam. of dish 13⅜ in. (34·6 cm.). Finch, who had been previously associated with Henri van de Velde, became a strong influence in the development of Finnish ceramics. Victoria and Albert Museum, London.

915. Salt-glazed stoneware jug decorated by Emily J. Edwards at the firm of Doulton, Lambeth, London; 1871. Ht. 7¾ in. (19·7 cm.). An early individual piece from the Doulton studio. Victoria and Albert Museum, London.

916. Salt-glazed stoneware vase made by the Martin Brothers of Southall, Middlesex, England; about 1886. Ht. 8½ in. (21·6 cm.). The floral decoration is arranged asymmetrically in the 'Japanese' manner. Victoria and Albert Museum, London.

Japanese manner, and their most effective work around the end of the century was often given vegetable-like texture in a remarkable variety of stoneware colours. [916]

The potter closest to William Morris was William De Morgan, who, like the Doulton artists and the Martin brothers, began his serious production in London in the early 1870s. William De Morgan was the designer of his pottery, but the work of making his pots and tiles, and of decorating them, was usually carried out by others. The medium was earthenware, and it was decorated by painting either in lustre colours or else in 'Persian' colours with blues and greens predominating. [918]

The English art-potteries of the period are of great interest, catering as they did for an intellectual section of the public whose needs had been created by the Arts and Crafts movement. Here one can see most clearly the strength of the reaction against the supposedly soulless technique of the great factories. In the years around 1880, for instance, in the new pottery at Linthorpe near Middlesbrough, Henry Tooth was producing decorative earthenware which combined the interest, novel at that time, of figured glazes, with the highly original forms of the freelance professional

915

916

studio were Hannah Barlow, and her sister and brother, Florence Barlow and Arthur Barlow, George Tinworth, Emily Edwards and Frank Butler. Their style is recognisable at a glance, although the main motifs vary from the representation of animals to almost abstract leafage patterns. Work of this nature was continued in the Doulton studio throughout the remainder of the century and beyond, and very shortly after the initial success the principle of the artist's responsibility for individual pieces was extended to other wares, particularly to painted pottery or 'faience'. The development of artist-pottery in salt-glazed stoneware at Doulton's also led to similar work being carried out elsewhere. About 1872 two artists were experimenting in the possibilities of this medium at the Fulham Pottery, also in London. One of these was the French painter, Jean-Charles Cazin, who already had some experience of decorating pottery (see p. 310); the other was a young English sculptor, Wallace Martin. In the following years Wallace Martin was associated with his younger brothers, Walter and Edwin, in the making of salt-glazed stoneware, at first in London and then for a long period at Southall in Middlesex (whilst a fourth brother, Charles, mostly took charge of their business arrangements). Their pottery was often decorated with loose floral or animal motifs in a

designer, Christopher Dresser. Dresser's designs appeared again a little later in a similar guise in the wares produced in the nineties by William Ault's pottery at Swadlincote in south Derbyshire. Other art wares came from Devon, notably the 'Barum' pottery made at Barnstaple under the direction of C. H. Brannam and the Aller Vale ware made near Newton Abbot. In Somerset, Sir Edmond Elton was making 'Elton Ware' at Clevedon Court over a long period from the early 1880s until 1920; decorated mostly with asymmetrical floral patterns, built up in coloured slips, his work had the character of art-pottery, although in fact it was made under virtually studio conditions. The Della Robbia pottery at Birkenhead in Cheshire, operating from 1894 to 1906, employed for the most part recent art-school students to collaborate in producing their own designs with a combination of painted and *sgraffiato* decoration. In the first decade of the 20th century, however, some of the most popular pottery was decorated solely with elaborate glaze effects. This applied to most of the ware produced by W. Howson Taylor in his Ruskin Pottery at Smethwick, near Birmingham, which was operating from 1898 until 1935. It applied also to the wares produced at the Pilkington factory, near Manchester, under the charge of William and Joseph Burton in 1904 and the following

915

917

years. These included a remarkable variety of scientifically determined colours and effects; from 1906 the firm was also producing pottery with individual lustre-painted decoration designed by artists such as Gordon Forsyth, W. S. Mycock and Gwladys Rodgers. It also applied to much of the output of Bernard Moore, who was the principal of an art-pottery and whose work included individual porcelain pieces with high-fired glazes. In the years immediately before the first world war, the artist-potter Reginald Wells was mainly concerned with the simple effect of glazes in his so-called 'Coldrum' pottery, as was also George Cox in the stoneware which he made in Mortlake.

In the United States of America the art-pottery movement of the 1880s and '90s was of considerable historical importance. It seems that the Centennial Exhibition at Philadelphia in 1876 served to emphasise the shortcomings of American industrial ceramics. Certainly a reaction expressed in the form of artist-pottery gained great momentum during the following years; and the most important centre for the new movement was in Cincinnati, Ohio. In the years immediately after the exhibition, Mary Louise McLaughlin, who was concerned with a group of amateur ceramic painters,

917

917. Earthenware vase with incised decoration and figured glaze, designed by Christopher Dresser for the Linthorpe pottery, near Middlesbrough, England; about 1880. Ht. 6½ in. (16·5 cm.). Dresser, a designer who worked in many media, is here incorporating ideas from pre-Columbian America. Dorman Memorial Museum, Middlesbrough.

918. Earthenware vase made by William De Morgan at Merton Abbey, near London; about 1886. Ht. 12¾ in. (32·4 cm.). The painting is carried out in De Morgan's 'Persian' colours, mainly blues and greens. Victoria and Albert Museum, London.

919. Porcelain vase made by Bernard Moore of Longton, England; 1903. Ht. 7⅞ in. (20 cm.). The vase is covered with a crimson glaze streaked with brown and purple, and like much of the work of the period relies solely on the glaze for its decoration. Victoria and Albert Museum, London.

918   919

worked out a technique for underglaze painting in coloured slips, such as had been shown at the Centennial Exhibition by Haviland of Limoges (see p. 300). Another Cincinnati woman, Maria Longworth Storer (to use her later married name) was similarly concerning herself with ceramic techniques in the later 1870s. In 1880 she founded the Rookwood pottery in Cincinnati, which was to achieve an international reputation in the later years of the century. From 1883 until 1913, this important pottery was under the management of William Watts Taylor. The individual pieces made there were all signed by the decorators, and up to 1900 all were hand-thrown. Like most of the European potteries of the time, the Rookwood style was heavily influenced by Japan, and in the case of Rookwood much of the Japanese influence came directly from the Far East. Mrs Storer had been personally inspired by the Japanese exhibit at Philadelphia, and she imported as one of the pottery's decorators the Japanese, Kataro Shirayamadani. Much of the Rookwood work was decorated with asymmetrical arrangements of flowers painted in coloured slips beneath the glaze on a dark shaded ground. Great attention was paid to the figured grounds and glazes, which included such unique effects as 'tiger-eye', a crystalline glaze introduced in 1884, as well as attractive matt finishes. The Rook-

wood pottery's moment of greatest triumph was at the Paris Exhibition of 1889 when it received a gold medal. It was prominent also at the Paris Exhibition of 1900 when the Japanese style had largely turned to *Art Nouveau*, and from this exhibition Rookwood became widely represented in European museums.

Many other American potters and potteries, however, shared in this movement, which had something of the character of a national revival. Hugh C. Robertson and W. A. Long were two influential potters producing original work towards the end of the 19th century. Hugh C. Robertson was especially concerned with the reproduction of Oriental crackled and high-fired glazes and their use for original designs. He was carrying out work of this nature from 1891 at the Chelsea pottery, Massachusetts, which was moved to Dedham in the same state in 1896. During the 1890s, W. A. Long, working at the Lonhuda Pottery in Steubenville, Ohio, was inspired to use American-Indian shapes with the intention of producing a ware which would be characteristically American. The decorative motifs, however, were similar to those of Rookwood, being loose Japanese-style floral sprays painted underglaze in coloured slips on shaded grounds. One of his decorators at this pottery was Laura A. Fry from Cincinnati, who had been among Mary Louise McLaughlin's

920

921

920. The 'Ali Baba' vase, with decoration painted in coloured slips by Mary Louise McLaughlin of Cincinnati, Ohio, U.S.A.; 1880. Ht. 37¼ in. (94·5 cm.). Miss McLaughlin played an important part in the development of decoration by coloured slip later much used in American art-pottery. Cincinnati Art Museum (lent by Rookwood pottery).

921. Earthenware vase, glazed only on the inside, from the Clifton Art Pottery, Newark, New Jersey, U.S.A. Ht. 6⅛ in. (15·6 cm.). This pottery, established by W. A. Long in 1905, made among other styles an imitative Indian ware; the example shown imitates Pueblo Indian work from Homolobi. Smithsonian Institution, Washington.

group and had also helped to develop the Rookwood glazes by the use of a spraying technique. Later, in 1905, Long established the Clifton Art Pottery at Newark, New Jersey. Here he made, among other styles, an Indian ware which reproduced both the forms and decoration of American-Indian pottery.

921

Another distinct group of American art-pottery wares may be said to have originated with the establishment of the Grueby Faience Company at Boston, Massachusetts, in 1897. The general style was apparently inspired by some works of the French potter, August Delaherche. The decoration consisted of simple hand-modelled leaf-like shapes, well-integrated into the form of the vessels, the whole covered by a matt glaze usually green in colour. The glazes were the work of William H. Grueby; the shapes were designed by George P. Kendrick. Like Rookwood pottery, Grueby Faience was a considerable success at the Paris Exhibition of 1900 and in consequence is to be found in European museums. An early 20th century ware of rather similar pattern was that of the Pewabic pottery, founded about 1900 by Mary Chase Perry at Detroit, Michigan. The relief leaf-forms were highly reminiscent of Grueby's, but the glazes were more flowing and less restricted in range. Teco pottery of Terra Cotta, Illinois, also used mostly matt green glazes but tended to use more organic shapes; one of the main designers here was Fritz Albert, a German with an art training in Berlin.

922

Similar signs of a more direct connection with Europe can be seen in the pottery of Artus Van Briggle made at Colorado Springs, Colorado, and in the Newcomb pottery of New Orleans, Louisiana. Van Briggle was originally a decorator at Rookwood who spent three years studying in Paris in the nineties. He is said to have been concerned with the matt glaze produced by Rookwood in the late 1890s. In 1901 he moved to Colorado Springs, where he set up a pottery and worked until his death in 1904. His work at Colorado Springs can be seen as an integrated expression of the *Art Nouveau* style in modelled pottery, finished with soft matt glazes. The Newcomb Pottery was established by Newcomb College in New Orleans in 1896. Typical products of this pottery in the years

around 1900 were decorated in an international style with *Art Nouveau* motifs coloured and outlined with incising. Characteristic of the United States was the appearance of a number of large commercial art-potteries, notably the Zanesville, Ohio, potteries of S. A. Weller, J. B. Owens and Roseville, which rapidly exploited the original ideas of the American potters and of the international style of the period.

923

So far the story of the artist-potter and of art-pottery has been inextricably interwoven. The idea of the artist taking responsibility for the pot as a work of art is clear. But the idea of subdivision of labour, inherent in the industrial revolution, was still strong enough to ensure that the artist would tend to use the skills of others wherever possible for throwing, turning and firing. In Britain the concept of artist-pottery underwent a remarkable development in the 1920s and '30s. This was the result of a powerful new impact from the Far East acting to strengthen the preconceptions of the Arts and Crafts movement and especially the artist-craftsman's respect for his material. The ideal potter became one who could claim that his pot was uniquely his own creation since he had carried out virtually every process from the digging and pugging of his own clay to the firing of his own personally constructed kiln. The ideal potter was also, more important, a seeker after an impersonal perfection of form and glaze, rather than an artist striving to express the peculiarities of his personal vision. The main group of artist-potters in Britain, and those similarly influenced in Continental Europe and the United States, were now concerned in effect with the integrity of a tradition rather than with contemporary development in either the fine or the industrial arts. The starting point of this change of attitude in Britain was the arrival of Bernard Leach from Japan in 1920.

Leach had been born in China, but was educated in England with a period at the Slade School of Art in London. As a young man, he went to Japan as a teacher of drawing and etching, and it was there that he felt the call to be a potter and learned the potter's craft. It is not surprising, therefore, that he brought to Europe for the first

922

923

924

925

926

922. Vase of earthenware with matt deep-green glaze, made by the Grueby Faience Company of Boston, Massachusetts; about 1899. Ht. 13¼ in. (33·7 cm.). The characteristic decoration of Grueby pottery, with vertical leaf-like motifs modelled in slight relief, is said to be inspired by work of the French potter, Auguste Delaherche (see fig. 909). Victoria and Albert Museum, London.

923. Earthenware vase on base, decorated by Mary Sheerer, Newcomb College Pottery, New Orleans, Louisiana, U.S.A.; about 1897. Ht. 12 in. (30·5 cm.). The decoration clearly reflects the developing style of *Art Nouveau*. Cincinnati Art Museum.

924. Stoneware vase with wax resist decoration made by the Japanese Shoji Hamada; about 1931. Ht. 15¼ in. (38·7 cm.). Hamada came to England with Bernard Leach in 1920. This vase, made after his return to Japan, was exhibited in London. Victoria and Albert Museum, London.

925. Slipware dish with Tree of Life design, made by Bernard Leach at St Ives, Cornwall, England; about 1923. Diam. 16½ in. (42 cm.). In the making of this dish Leach was using the old English medium of slipware, with motifs which are partly personal and partly derived from early Chinese Han dynasty wares. Victoria and Albert Museum, London.

926. Stoneware vase with *'temmoku'* glaze, made by Bernard Leach at St Ives, Cornwall, England; about 1959. Ht. 14½ in. (36·8 cm.). In this mature example of his art Leach derives a fine effect from the black glaze known by the Japanese term *'temmoku'*, which breaks to rust on the angles formed by the decoration. Victoria and Albert Museum, London.

927. Slipware jug made by Michael Cardew at Winchcombe; about 1938. The decoration is carried out in liquid-clay slips under a clear honey-coloured glaze. Ht. 11⅝ in. (29·5 cm.). Cardew, one of the earliest pupils of Bernard Leach, was concerned during the later twenties and thirties in reviving the English tradition of slipware. Victoria and Albert Museum, London.

927

time a complete perception of the meaning and value of Far Eastern ceramics. On his return to England he was accompanied by the young Japanese potter, Shoji Hamada, who, as his pupil and assistant, shared with him the problems of a new environment. Together they set up a pottery at St Ives in Cornwall where they proceeded to experiment in the making of Japenese-style stoneware, with brushwork or wax resist decoration, and the old indigenous English style of slipware pottery. They used natural local materials, as in Japan, for their clays and glazes, and with their characteristic impurities these materials imparted a quality which was largely new and unexpected in England although it fitted well with the outlook of the Arts and Crafts movement. Hamada subsequently returned to Japan, where he became in effect the leader of a parallel revival of craft pottery, involving a number of potters of similar sensitivity and outlook, such as Kanjiro Kawai and Kenkichi Tomimoto.

Although Leach stressed the potter's responsibility for the whole process of pottery-making, he also advocated the sharing of a pottery by a group of potters, especially in the production of pottery for daily use, and it was on these lines that the Leach pottery was organised at St Ives. Many would-be potters came there as pupils, and it was to this that Leach owed a great deal of his influence. One of the first of his pupils was Michael Cardew, who had been already inspired by the slipware of a surviving village potter, Edwin B. Fishley, working at Fremington in Devon. In 1926, Michael Cardew established himself in an old pottery at Winchcombe in Gloucestershire, where he proceeded for many years to make attractive practical wares using the slip technique of decoration. Later he changed to stoneware and has spent long periods as a pottery instructor in Africa on the Gold Coast (now Ghana) and in Nigeria. Two other outstanding pupils of Bernard Leach were Katherine Pleydell-Bouverie and Nora Braden, who worked together at Coleshill in Wiltshire from 1928 to 1936. Katherine Pleydell-Bouverie carried out systematic experiments in glazes made

from various wood and plant ashes and her stoneware is characterised by the beauty of the glazes she obtained. Nora Braden's work was more austere, very strongly formed and sometimes decorated with brushwork. Leach's conception of handmade wares for everyday use was developed in the stoneware medium by Harry Davis who, with his wife, May, was for many years after the second war operating a craftsman's pottery in Cornwall.

Leach's formative influence in Britain between the wars was complemented by that of William Staite Murray. Already before the first war Staite Murray had begun to experiment with pottery. In the early 1920s, as the result of an exhibition, he became aware of Hamada's work with its implications for a fresh approach to the craft. Henceforth he produced a remarkable series of vigorously formed stoneware pots, usually with brush decoration, discernibly different from those of Leach but using basically the same medium. He had no interest in useful wares; he showed his pots with individual titles and high prices in galleries normally devoted to paintings and sculpture. In 1925 Murray became head of the pottery school in the Royal College of Art in London, and as such had a great influence over the following generation of British potters. His pottery career ended in 1940, when he went to Southern Rhodesia. Among his pupils were Henry Hammond, who has subsequently made slipware as well as stoneware, and Sam Haile, who worked for some years in the United States and before his early death had brought a painterly approach to the decoration of both stoneware and slipware.

A British tradition of artist-pottery was thus established between the wars resting firmly on the twin supports of a Japanese conception of stoneware and an early English conception of slipware. The two media are complementary and both can be used for the impersonal expression of a truly ceramic sense of beauty. But they give little scope for the use of colour as such, and their range of form is severely limited. Inevitably potters who are concerned with a personal

928

929

930

928. Stoneware vase made by Katherine Pleydell-Bouverie at Coleshill, England; about 1929–30. Ht. 10 in. (25·4 cm.). A pupil of Bernard Leach, Miss Pleydell-Bouverie has made a careful study of stoneware glazes obtained from wood and plant ashes. Victoria and Albert Museum, London.

929. 'Wheel of Life' vase, of stoneware with brushwork decoration, made by the British artist-potter William Staite Murray; about 1938–39. Ht. 24¾ in. (62·9 cm.). Staite Murray sought the status of fine art for his pots, which were often individually named and were exhibited in galleries normally devoted to paintings and sculpture. Victoria and Albert Museum, London.

930. Stoneware vase formed by coiling and glazed only on the inner surface, made by Dan Arbeid, London; 1959. Ht. 8¾ in. (22·2 cm.). The process of coiling is often used to achieve a more personal interpretation of shape than is possible by throwing on the wheel. Victoria and Albert Museum, London.

58. Wine pitcher of tin-glazed earthenware 'Cavalier sur sa Monture' designed and decorated by Pablo Picasso in the Madoura pottery of Suzanne and Georges Ramie at Vallauris in the South of France, about 1951. Painted in black and brown with scratched detail. Ht. 15½ in. (39·4 cm.). Victoria and Albert Museum, London.

59. Stoneware vase with a red glaze streaked with green, produced by Adrien Dalpayrat in his pottery (Dalpayrat, A. Desbros et Cie.) at Bourg-la-Reine near Paris, France, in 1896. Ht. 20⅜ in. (51·7 cm.). The tall, slightly asymmetrical form illustrates the tendency towards Art Nouveau. Victoria and Albert Museum, London.

60. Two pieces from the Arabia factory studios in Helsinki, Finland, about 1955, both made in the characteristic tall forms of the period. One by Toini Muona is of porcelain asymmetrically formed with a figured deep red glaze; the other by Kyllikki Salmenhaara is of grey glazed chamotte stoneware. Ht. of both 15 in. (38·1 cm.). Victoria and Albert Museum, London.

58

59

60

931

932

934. Bird figure, of earthenware with a black glaze, made by Georges Jouve, Paris; 1951. Ht. 10¾ in. (27·3 cm.). Figures such as this were made by Jouve in a limited series. Victoria and Albert Museum, London.

935. Bird figure of stoneware, made by Jean and Jacqueline Lerat of Bourges; 1964. Ht. 11¾ in. (30 cm.). Jean and Jacqueline Lerat are leading members of the group of French artist-potters working in the ancient pottery-producing area near Bourges. Jean and Jacqueline Lerat, Bourges.

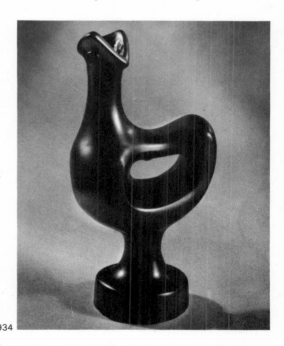

934

935

931. Stoneware vase by Lucie Rie, London; about 1966. Ht. 12⅜ in. (31·5 cm.). Lucie Rie, originally an Austrian potter, has lived and worked in London for many years. Victoria and Albert Museum, London.

932. Two stoneware vases made by the French potter, Emile Decœur, the lefthand in 1910 and the righthand about 1920. Ht. of both 6⅞ in. (17·5 cm.). Decœur was a master of restrained decoration with matt glazes. Musée des Arts Décoratifs, Paris.

933. Covered vase on stand, of salt-glazed stoneware, made by Paul Beyer; about 1935. Ht. 16⅝ in. (42·3 cm.). Paul Beyer was mainly responsible for reviving the use of salt-glazed stoneware among the artist-potters of France. Victoria and Albert Museum, London.

61. Two stoneware pots made by Ruth Duckworth, who has worked both in England and in America. Hts. 14 in. and 21 in. (35·6 cm. and 53·4 cm.). The pots have been formed asymmetrically by coiling, and have been only partially glazed on the outside surface. Both pots are in private collections.

933

936

937

938

939

936. Vase of earthenware painted with two female figures by Georges Rouault and made by the French potter, André Methey; 1907. Ht. 21¼ in. (54 cm.). In the early years of the 20th century Methey was producing many pieces painted by the great easel painters of the Ecole de Paris. Musée National d'Art Moderne, Paris.

937–8. Stoneware vase made by the Spanish potter, José Llorens Artigas, and painted by Joan Miró; 1941. Ht. 11¾ in. (29 cm.). José Llorens Artigas is important for his own work as well as for the work he has produced in collaboration with the easel painters Raoul Dufy, Albert Marquet and Joan Miró. Musée National d'Art Moderne, Paris.

939. Vase made by Gilbert Portanier at Vallauris, France; about 1953–54. Ht. 13¾ in. (34 cm.). Museum für Kunst und Gewerbe, Hamburg.

940. Figure of a woman undressing, earthenware with coloured glazes, made by Leoncillo Leonardi in Rome; 1951. Ht. without pedestal 21½ in. (54·6 cm.). Leonardi has been concerned with ceramics for sculptural purposes and for architectural details. Victoria and Albert Museum, London.

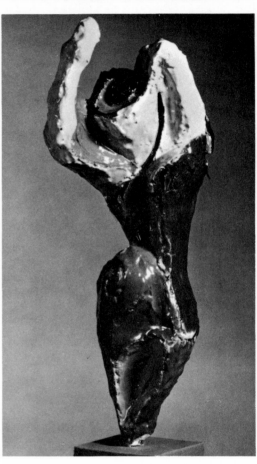

940

approach to pottery or who wish to use it as a means of abstract expression, have turned away to other less inhibiting styles, especially since the second world war. Many of these potters influenced by painting and sculpture have been trained at the Central School of Arts and Crafts in London, including William Newland, his wife Margaret Hine, James Tower, Ian Auld, Dan Arbeid and Ruth Duckworth. Two other potters in Britain of great importance are Lucie Rie and Hans Coper, who came originally from Austria and Germany respectively and who for a time worked together. Lucie Rie's stoneware is elegantly formed, delicate and precise, whilst Hans Coper delights in large vigorous forms.

In France the great period of French artist-pottery, the period of stoneware and of glazes of great beauty, was carried beyond the first world war in the work of Emile Decœur and Emile Lenoble. Decœur used matt glazes with remarkable sensitivity and his restrained surface decoration was always matched meticulously to his forms. Lenoble used incised decoration freely and proved that it could be used with great success on high-fired stoneware. In more recent years his son, Jacques Lenoble, has worked in a somewhat similar spirit. But the twenties and thirties were also the years in

which the scope of French artist-pottery was widening. Potters such as George Serre and Jean Besnard were adopting heavier, more insistent, incised motifs. Potters such as Jean Mayodon and René Buthaud were covering their pottery with theatrical human figures. Paul Beyer revived the use of salt-glazed stoneware and often made up figures from thrown units, allowing the ridges left by the throwing to reveal their origin.

In the years after the second world war many French potters tended to use their medium primarily for figure making and for other purely decorative purposes. Earthenware, especially with a tin-glaze, came rapidly back into fashion for this purpose in the hands of artists such as Guidette Carbonnel, Paul Pouchol, Maurice Savin, Colette Gueden and Odette Lepeltier. Georges Jouve may also be thought of as belonging to this group, since his work was perhaps more that of a ceramic sculptor than of a potter of vessels. On the other hand a vogue for strongly formed stoneware has come from a group of potters who work in the ancient pottery-producing region near Bourges and who have in general been influenced by the work of Paul Beyer. These include such artists as Jean and Jacqueline Lerat, Vassia Ivanoff, Elizabeth Joulia and Ives Mohy.

930
931
932
933
934
935

936

937–8

939

940

Another style of stoneware of great accomplishment comes from Francine Delpierre, whose vessels are thinly coiled in delicately formed shapes.

Artist-pottery in France has undoubtedly been influenced by the great interest which easel painters, and to some extent sculptors, have taken in ceramics. Painters in France seem always to have been fascinated by the performance of ceramic colours as compared with those on canvas. On the other hand, if the painter is to achieve the result he intends he will usually need the intermediary of a professional potter. Much of Théodore Deck's early fame was gained by means of the pottery decorated by his painter friends (see p. 310). The painter Paul Gauguin's ceramics were produced by Chaplet. In the early years of the 20th century, André Methey, who was later to produce on his own account a great deal of attractive colourful pottery, was the producer of pieces painted by many of the great artists of the Ecole de Paris. At one exhibition, the *Salon d'Automne*

on the work of another, much younger, Vallauris potter, Gilbert Portanier.

The tendency for some French artist-pottery to take the form of sculpture or decorator's objects has appeared in a much more exaggerated form in Italy. The modern Italian school of artist-pottery, which appeared in the 1930s, has used very largely the medium of brightly coloured earthenware for pieces which are either purely sculptural or else formed into exaggerated shapes bearing little relation to practical use. As such the Italian work lies precisely at the opposite pole from the purist and impersonal approach of the Anglo-Japanese school of the twenties and thirties. Lucio Fontana, a leading ceramic sculptor, was one of the first to turn his attention to ceramics in the thirties. The German-trained sculptor, Rolando Hettner, and Pietro Melandri of Faenza are also ceramists of long experience, and their work includes decorative vessels. But perhaps the most successful of the Italian ceramists who

941

942

941. Stoneware dish with crackled 'clair de lune' glaze, made by Jan Bontjes van Beek; about 1961–62. Diam. 6⅛ in. (15·5 cm.). Bontjes van Beek, a German potter of Dutch origin, has been prominent as an artist-potter of great sensitivity since the middle 1920s. Museum für Kunst und Gewerbe, Hamburg.

942. Stoneware vase with bubbled glaze, made by Ingeborg and Bruno Asshoff of Bochum, Germany; 1961. Ht. 8¼ in. (21 cm.). Museum für Kunst und Gewerbe, Hamburg.

943. Stoneware vase made by Antonio Cumella-Serret of Barcelona; about 1961–62. Ht. 4¾ in. (12·2 cm.). Museum für Kunst und Gewerbe, Hamburg.

944. Vase with a purple and turquoise glaze, made by Bert Nienhuis; 1933. Ht. 15⅜ in. (39 cm.). Nienhuis was a leading figure in Dutch artist-pottery until his death in 1960. Museum Boymans-van Beuningen, Rotterdam.

943

944

of 1907, Methey's vases, dishes and plates were to be found decorated and signed by Odilon Redon, Rouault, Vuillard, Bonnard, Maurice Denis, Van Dongen, Friez, Derain and Vlaminck. In the 1920s José Llorens Artigas, a Spanish Catalan potter who worked for a long period in France, began to co-operate with Raoul Dufy, and was later working with Albert Marquet. Artigas is a potter of considerable significance in his own right, making stoneware which relies wholly upon the beauty of precisely controlled glazes and a Mediterranean sense of form. Since about the early forties, he has produced distinguished pottery, ceramic sculpture and tilework in collaboration with his fellow Catalan, Joan Miró.

Jean Lurçat and Edouard Pignon are two other painters who have produced pottery, while Fernand Léger has been responsible for a number of impressive ceramic pictures. The most significant of these excursions into ceramics, however, has been that of Pablo Picasso, who began in 1947 to work in the Madoura pottery of Suzanne and Georges Ramié at Vallauris. Picasso's ceramic work expresses inevitably his strength and originality of purpose, and it is to be viewed as an integral part of his general artistic output. It is interesting, however, to notice his influence, even though superficial,

can be called a potter is Guido Gambone. Until about 1949 Gambone worked alone at Vietri, near Naples; in the early fifties he established a workshop in Florence, where he has worked with a number of assistants producing objects in series production as well as his own unique pieces.

Among the modern Italian ceramic sculptors, Leoncillo Leonardi has produced architectural details as well as figure-work of distinction. Romano Rui has been concerned with tiles and plaques of pictorial interest. Elaborately modelled pottery, manipulated into strange shapes, can be seen in the modern work of most Italian potters, and some, such as Agenore Fabbri and Alberto Diato, have continued the Italian tradition of combining the production of purely sculptural works with that of pottery vessels.

In Germany since the first world war artist-potters have concentrated very largely upon a restrained style of stoneware decorated solely by its glaze. They were subject to the influence of the Bauhaus in the twenties, but the effect on artist-pottery seems to have been mainly in the direction of a thoroughgoing respect for the materials used and for simple natural wheel-thrown shapes. It is of interest to notice that Otto Lindig, who played a formative part in the ceramic

946

947

948

945

945. Earthenware vase made by the Hungarian potter, István Gádor; about 1963. Ht. 11¾ in. (29·8 cm.). István Gádor has played a leading part in the development of Hungarian ceramics with strong local characteristics. Victoria and Albert Museum, London.

946. Vase by the Czech potter, Julie Horová, turquoise-green glaze with scraped decoration; about 1962. Ht. 13 in. (33 cm.). Julie Horová's ceramics are imbued with the rich background of her training in Prague and Paris and a long contact with Slovakian folk ceramics. K. Hetteš and P. Rada, *Modern Ceramics*, Artia, Prague, 1965.

947. Stoneware bowls with matt glaze by Aurora Tippe of the Soviet Union. Ht. 5⅞ in. (15 cm.). These sophisticated asymmetrically formed bowls were shown in the exhibition of contemporary ceramics held in Prague in 1962. K. Hetteš and P. Rada, *Modern Ceramics*, Artia, Prague, 1965.

948. Vase made by the Belgian potter, Pierre Caille; about 1962. Ht. 19½ in. (50 cm.). Since the 1940s Pierre Caille has been a leading artist-potter and teacher in Brussels, and his later work includes stoneware. K. Hetteš and P. Rada, *Modern Ceramics*, Artia, Prague, 1965.

activities of the Bauhaus, has continued to make individual pieces.

A figure of great stature in German artist-pottery has been Jan Bontjes van Beek, who was Dutch by birth and was naturalised as a German through his father. He first became prominent in the mid-twenties, and his work in stoneware both before and after the second world war has been most attractive and influential. Richard Bampi, an adventurous potter, was for a short time at the Bauhaus and was also much influenced by Max Läuger; he was concerned at one time with maiolica, and then turned to stoneware in the late thirties and after the second world war; he died in 1966. A third artist-potter whose reputation dates from the 1920s is Elfriede Balzar-Kopp, who produced ceramic sculpture as well as elegant stoneware. Of the West German potters whose reputation dates from after the second world war, Hubert Griemert has paid especial attention to crystalline glazes, which in varying degrees have attracted many of the German potters. Stephan Erdös, of Hungarian origin and a student under Michael Powolny in Vienna, was making stoneware in Germany from about 1946 until his early death in 1956. Otto Hohlt (d. 1960) made figurative plaques and hand-formed vessels; his son, Albrecht (d. 1960), was also a well-known potter. Other distinguished German potters are Rolf Weber, concerned with architectural ceramics as well as pottery, Ingeborg and Bruno Asshoff, whose stoneware is adventurously formed and includes figures, and Karl Scheid, whose work is excellently decorated and glazed and who worked for a time in the early fifties with Harry Davis in England.

In Eastern Germany some outstanding work has been produced since the second world war by Walter Gebauer and by Wolfgang Henze, including wares decorated, respectively, by painted and lustred glazes. Significant modern pottery is also to be found in Switzerland, especially in the plain glazed work of Edouard and André Chapallaz. In Spain, besides José Llorens Artigas, who has already been mentioned, Antonio Cumella-Serret has produced finely proportioned vessels of distinction.

Holland, a country with an ancient pottery tradition, has played an important part in the artist-pottery movement of the 20th century. Bert Nienhuis, who designed for the 'de Distel' art-pottery about the beginning of the century, was an artist-potter of great influence for many years with his elaborately glazed ware. Harm Henrick Kamerlingh Onnes, with a style which places the greater emphasis on decoration, is another Dutch potter who has been influential over a long period. Dirk Hubers, who went to the United States in 1956, has similarly been concerned especially with decoration. In the later fifties some exciting new experimental work in both form and decoration was being carried out by a group of potters at *De Porceleyne Fles* in Delft, and a group of young Amsterdam potters have been producing vigorous stoneware pottery in cylindrical and box-like forms of great interest. In neighbouring Belgium, Pierre Caille has been outstanding since the forties, not only for his pottery but also as a teacher. He originally used faience, but his later work includes stoneware. He has made

949. 'The Lamb', brown-glazed stoneware figure by Dmitry Golovko of the Soviet Union. Ht. 9 in. (23 cm.). This figure, shown in the Prague Exhibition of contemporary ceramics in 1962, illustrates an interest in folk traditions. K. Hetteš and P. Rada, *Modern Ceramics*, Artia, Prague, 1965.

950. Vase with sculptured relief decoration, made by Axel Salto for the Royal Copenhagen Porcelain Factory, Denmark; 1937. Ht. 10¼ in. (26 cm.). Salto, who died in 1961, was using here his 'budding' style which expresses powerfully the relationship of material and glaze. Kunstindustrimuseum, Copenhagen.

951. Vase of 'Farsta' ware made by Wilhelm Kåge at the Gustavsberg factory, Sweden; 1953. Ht. 7 in. (17·8 cm.). An example of individual studio work by the man who was for many years art director of the Gustavsberg factory. Victoria and Albert Museum, London.

952. Stoneware vase with figured glaze made by the Saxbo pottery, Denmark; about 1951. Ht. 6 in. (15·3 cm.). An example of the classic Saxbo ware, designed by Eva Staehr-Nielsen and glazed by Nathalie Krebs. Victoria and Albert Museum, London.

949

950

951

952

figures and decorative panels as well as pottery decorated in a modern style. Also important as a teacher in Belgium is Oliver Strebelle, who is concerned especially with ceramic sculpture.

As in the case of the Bauhaus in Germany, the Wiener Werkstätte in Austria was a powerful influence on both industrial and artist-pottery. Following on the work of Michael Powolny, Robert Obsieger was for many years an important teacher. Among his more noteworthy pupils are Kurt Ohnsorg and Gunda Schihan. In Hungary characteristic styles of artist-pottery and figure-work have emerged, particularly in the work of István Gádor, Margit Kovács and Géza Gorka, all developing their styles between the wars. Here the influence of folk art has been particularly strong and has largely contributed to a continuing style of pottery which is brightly coloured and often asymmetrical. The history of artist-pottery in Czechoslovakia has followed a similar course. Václav Markup has been known since the 1930s for his pottery figures. The potter Otto Eckert, with a family tradition in the craft, is an important teacher in Prague. One of the best-known potters, Julie Horová, was trained partly in France and, living subsequently in Slovakia, acquired an intimate experience of folk ceramics. A similar tendency to find virtues and inspiration in the work of surviving traditional potters has been shared by artist-potters in other Eastern European countries, notably in Poland and Jugoslavia. Little has been known until recently of the activities of artist-potters in the Soviet Union. In the Prague Exhibition of contemporary ceramics in 1962, however, Russian potters made a substantial contribution. Besides sophisticated stonewares such as those by Aurora Tippe, the animal figures of artists such as Dmitry Golovko showed a further interest in folk traditions. It is interesting, too, to notice an unmistakably East European approach to the human figure in work by Elinor Piipun.

The Scandinavians have tended, partly through deliberate policy, to produce artist-pottery in the industrial factories, no doubt to the benefit of the industrial wares. An outstanding instance in Denmark was the distinguished work of Axel Salto, which was produced mainly by the Royal Copenhagen Porcelain Factory. In some of his

finest pieces the stoneware body seems to be 'budding' outwards through the glaze. In the great Swedish factories of Gustavsberg, Rörstrand and Upsala-Ekeby, the artists employed have produced their own personal works, as well as designs for industrial production. Many fine pieces have come from Wilhelm Kåge, Stig Lindberg or Berndt Friberg at Gustavsberg and from Gunnar Nylund or Carl-Harry Stålhane at Rörstrand. In Finland, the great factory of Arabia has arranged to provide studios, materials, firing facilities and a salary for individual artist-potters. This scheme has undoubtedly proved a great success, although some possible limitations are apparent. Almost all the outstanding modern Finnish potters have worked in this manner in the Arabia factory—Toini Muona, Kyllikki Salmenhaara and Raija Tuumi working in thrown stoneware, Aune Siimes and Friedl Kjellberg in delicate porcelain, Birger Kaipiainen (who went to Rörstrand in the late fifties) and Rut Bryk making painterly decorative objects and Michael Schilkin sculptural figures.

Besides the artist-pottery from the factories, however, there have been many art-potteries and artist-potters working in Denmark, Sweden and Norway. In Denmark the Saxbo pottery, founded in 1929, is of particular interest. In its classic form the Saxbo ware was precisely shaped and decorated only by its figured glaze effects; its production was mostly a collaboration between Nathalie Krebs, the principal of the pottery, and Eva Staehr-Nielsen. Since the mid-fifties, however, the range of the Saxbo work has greatly widened to include new decorative techniques and materials. Among the many individual potters in Denmark, Christian Poulsen is one of the few using stoneware; his simply modelled vessels are covered with very thick glaze in carefully calculated colours. In Sweden, Edgar Böckman has been known for many years for his pottery which concentrates on form and material. Erich and Ingrid Triller have made restrained finely glazed stoneware since the mid-thirties. Tyra Lundgren has produced coloured sculptural work in stoneware, and Tom and Grete Möller have made lively practical and decorative wares. In Norway, Erik Pløen's strongly modelled stoneware is

945

946

947
949

950

951

60
(p. 317)

952

955

954

955

956

957

953. Earthenware wall-vase, finished with platinum colour over an orange glaze and with an area of black checks, made by James Melchert, Oakland, California; 1966. Ht. 10 in. (25·4 cm.). An example of the influence of 'Pop Art' in ceramics; the vase is shaped as though made of leather and is decorated with an imitation zip-fastener. Miss Susan Newman, New York.

954. Unglazed stoneware vessel of thrown and coiled construction, made by Peter Voulkos, Berkely, California; 1964. Ht. 25 in. (63·5 cm.). Since the later 1950s Voulkos has been the prominent leader in the American movement towards abstract pottery. Peter Voulkos, California.

955. Stoneware vase with incised decoration, made by Erik Pløen, Norway; about 1959. Ht. 6½ in. (16·5 cm.). Pløen's forms are characteristically strong and austere, often with interesting glaze effects over incising. Nordenfjeldske Kunstindustrimuseum, Trondheim.

956. Stoneware jar of slab construction, unglazed on the exterior, made by Daniel Rhodes, Alfred Station, New York; 1966. Ht. 12⅜ in. (31·5 cm.). A characteristic example of modern American pottery in its strength of form and in its abstract qualities. Daniel Rhodes, New York.

957. Stoneware pot, partly splashed with a pale green glaze, made by Ruth Duckworth in England, 1966. Ht. 12¼ in. (31 cm.). This pot, of an abstract quality, is by a potter who has worked both in England and in the United States. Victoria and Albert Museum, London.

outstanding, as is also the stoneware, often with painted decoration, by Dagny and Finn Hald.

The modern development of artist-pottery in Japan has been already mentioned. In recent years surprising and beautiful pottery has come from the Argentine and Venezuela and from Australia and New Zealand. The South American potters have been greatly influenced, as might be expected, by the local pre-Columbian styles; the Australian and New Zealand potters were influenced initially by artist-pottery in Britain.

But perhaps the most significant pottery of all in recent years has come from the United States of America. The inspiration of American artist-pottery is derived inevitably from many differing sources. Strands of influence can be recognised coming from the Bauhaus, from the Orientalising artist-pottery traditions of Britain and the continent of Europe and, not least, directly from the Orient itself. In these styles, or combined elements of them, are to be found the finely glazed and formed decorative wares of Gertrud and Otto Natzler of California, of Frans Wildenhain of New York, who was originally a Dutchman trained in the Bauhaus, and Fong Chow of New York, an American of Chinese origin; into the same category would come Karen Karnes of New York who makes practical

stonewares for everyday use. A new movement towards abstract pottery has, however, been evident in the United States since the later fifties, which seems to be partly analogous to the sculptural style of some of the Italian pottery. The prominent leader in this movement has been Peter Voulkos of California, with his sculptural use of thrown or slab units. Many other potters in all parts of the country have developed in the same direction, such as Daniel Rhodes of New York, Rudy Autio of Montana or Jerry Rothman of California. The massive and powerful stoneware of the English potter, Ruth Duckworth, who has worked in the States, also reflects this tendency. In general, the work of such potters, although not intended for practical use, is to be described as abstract pottery rather than ceramic sculpture, since it has visibly or by implication an interior as well as an exterior shape.

In California, the process has even been taken a stage further in the ceramic mode which owes much to 'Pop Art' painting and graphics. In this sense, an artist may use clay merely as a convenient material to convey his purpose, without regard for the proprieties normally associated with pottery, as in the instance illustrated here of a wall-vase by James Melchert which is shaped as though made of leather and decorated with an imitation zip-fastener.

954
956
61 (p. 318)
957
953

IX The Primitive World

Pre-European America

Until the 16th-century conquests of the Spanish, there flourished in the New World a remarkable series of civilisations previously unknown to Europeans, who were astonished and excited by the discoveries of the conquistadors. Some of the splendid gifts presented by the Aztec leader Montezuma to Cortes were shipped to the Emperor Charles V in the Low Countries and examined by Albrecht Dürer who wrote: 'In all my life I have never seen anything that rejoiced my heart so much. I have found an admirable art in them and I have been astonished by the subtle spirit of the men of these strange countries.' In spite of most Spaniards' preoccupation with the gold and silver of the Americas, Cortes found room in his reports during the advance on the Aztec capital to note that the pottery was as fine as any he had known in Spain. In fact, pre-European ceramics constituted one of the major art mediums of this continent, attaining a complexity of form and design seldom rivalled at comparable cultural levels.

Because of the limited extent of written records, this variety of ceramic types provides the basis for reconstructing the development of Ancient American civilisations, establishing the sequence and interplay of the immense number of cultures that rose and fell from the time of the earliest occurrence of pottery so far known late in the 4th millennium BC. But a study of the detailed figurative decoration of pre-Conquest pottery takes us still further, for it supplies direct information about the way of life of these peoples—their activities in war or peace, their appearance, costume, habits and pastimes, even something of their social structure and beliefs. For some areas a surprisingly complete picture can be reconstructed in this way

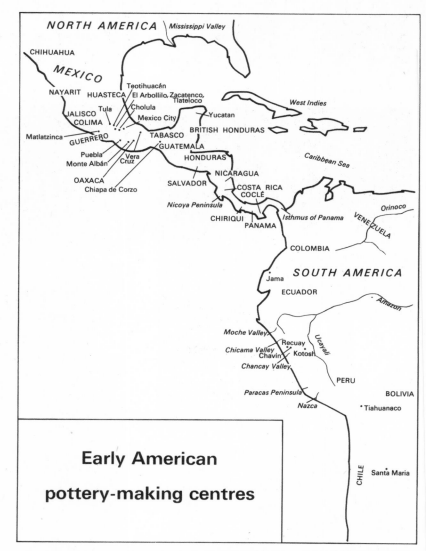

Early American pottery-making centres

959

960

958 (*previous page*). A Zambezi Tonga potter of the Gwembe (Kariba) valley, Zambia, burnishing her pots, decorated with red ochre and graphite, each powdered and mixed with water or fat and applied with the finger. The areas of colour are separated by bands of stamping or by incised lines. Zambia Information Services. (For African pottery, see pp. 334–42.)

959. Cream-slipped 'teapot' vessel, painted in black and modelled in the form of an animal, the head providing a spout. Huasteca, Gulf Coast of Mexico. Post-Classic Period. Ht. 8 in. (20·5 cm.). A number of specialised domestic vessels are found in Mexico: a suggested purpose for the 'teapot' was to serve hot chocolate. British Museum, London.

960. Black-slipped bottle with a square base incised with curvilinear decoration and burnished. Caddoan. Central Louisiana, U.S.A. Ht. 5½ in. (14 cm.). Curvilinear designs, incised or painted, were as characteristic of south-eastern wares as the painted angular patterns were on south-western pottery until European 18th-century penetration. Museum of the American Indian, New York.

961. White-slipped bowl decorated inside with a pair of stylised insects painted in black. Mimbres Valley, New Mexico, U.S.A. About AD 1000–1200. Diam. 9 in. (22·8 cm.). Warping due to faulty firing is typical of this ware but not of south-western pottery as a whole which reached a high standard. Peabody Museum, Harvard University.

962. Glazed Plumbate ware vessel in the form of an animal. Middle America. Post-Classic Period. Ht. 5 in. (12·5 cm.). Immense skill in the use of simple techniques was the basis of American ceramic achievement. Probably manufactured in western Guatemala. Horniman Museum, London.

961

962

963

964

965

966

963. White-slipped hollow figurine of an infant with the characteristic drooping mouth of the Olmec Culture. Mexico. Formative Period. Ht. 14⅛ in. (36·6 cm.). The figurine was recovered from the site of a lakeside village at Tlatilco on the outskirts of Mexico City, indicating the extensive influence of this first great Middle American art style that originated in the Olmec religious centres on the Gulf Coast of Mexico. Private collection, Mexico City.

964. Buff pottery 'laughing head' of a figurine with usual scroll decoration. Central Vera Cruz, Gulf Coast of Mexico. Classic Period. Ht. 5⅞ in. (15 cm.). The few complete figurines found show them to be boy and girl dancers treated with a vivacity normally absent in American pottery. Musée de l'Homme, Paris.

965. Red-slipped tripod jar, highly polished, shaped like a gourd, with feet in the form of birds. Colima, Western Mexico. Ht. 10¼ in. (26 cm.). Tripod legs in a variety of forms are one of the most recurrent features of Middle American pottery. In other respects pottery of the Western Region of Mexico tended to follow a separate line of development. Museum of the American Indian, New York.

966. Cylindrical bowl of Thin Orange ware, on three slab supports, with polychrome painted plaster decoration applied after firing. From vicinity of Teotihuacán, Central Mexico. Classic Period. Ht. 3½ in. (9 cm.). Cylindrical tripod vessels were among the most characteristic products of the economic empire centred on the great city of Teotihuacán and even influenced Maya ceramic development far to the south at a time when there was general harmony between the major pottery-producing areas. Dumbarton Oaks, Harvard University, Washington D.C.

through analysis of the painted scenes or modelled figures.

Pottery was put to many different uses in the New World. An extensive range of domestic vessels was developed for storing, preparing, cooking and serving food or drink; some for American specialities such as hot chocolate, tortillas or grated chili peppers. The spinner relied on exquisitely designed spindle whorls to weight the spindle which in the case of the Aztecs rested on a beautiful little cup to facilitate the spinning. Textiles and the person were ornamented with designs in paint or dye applied by flat or cylindrical clay stamps. Indeed in the lower Amazon modest pottery 'tangas' provided the equivalent of a fig leaf for female attire in a tropical region where clothing was limited. Musicians employed pottery drums, rattles, flutes, panpipes, whistles and trumpets! For the builder, clay was important in many regions, sometimes fired into bricks as well as sun-dried, sometimes fashioned into roof-ornaments for great buildings or to provide caps for protecting the roof apex of simple thatched huts. Nevertheless, outside the domain of the housewife, religious demands led to the largest production of pottery. Besides representations of innumerable deities, requirements often included incense-burners, braziers and other ritual vessels. Funerary practices differed considerably but nearly all involved the use of pottery vessels to furnish burials and thousand upon thousand of the finest examples of Ancient American ceramics have been retrieved from the dead.

High standards in both design and fabric were achieved by the simplest means. Except for a limited application in children's toys, the principle of the wheel remained unknown. Study of surviving practices in Mexico makes it probable that vessels were sometimes rotated on unpivoted turntables during construction but three basic building processes were employed either singly or in combination. Coiling, hand-modelling and moulding. Clays ranged from poor to excellent and tempering materials were equally varied including,

for example, pulverised rocks, volcanic ash, sand, mica, shell, potsherds, bone ash and siliceous ash from bark. Firing techniques exploited the use of both the oxidising flame to produce red to brown wares and the reducing flame to secure a grey to black finish. Slips were used extensively while decoration was undertaken with pigments of both mineral and vegetable origin and could run to as many as eight colours on individual Nazca vessels from Peru. Burnishing was common, unlike glazing which was confined to two modes of decoration: a black to brown-green lead-glaze paint was applied as linear decoration on wares in the south-west United States and in Middle America a vitrified slip covered the 'Plumbate' ware, so called because of its lead-like greyish and lustrous appearance.

The peoples who first crossed the Bering Strait from Asia were nomadic hunters, fishers and food-gatherers. Many millennia elapsed before the emergence in Middle America and the Andean regions in South America of centres of intensive agriculture that provided the basis for the rich pottery-producing civilisations encountered by the Spanish conquistadors. Understandably, these centres saw most of the early advances and the greatest achievements in pre-Conquest ceramics; yet many of the lesser known peoples of the Americas evolved striking styles of their own after the spread of farming economies favourable to the development of pottery. On the other hand, numerous groups remained at a simple cultural level and over extensive areas pottery never replaced containers of stone, wood, bark, skin or other materials.

Chronology remains uncertain in many parts of the New World and the picture changes rapidly as archaeological research continues. At present, the earliest known pottery comes from the coastal site of Valdivia in Ecuador which has yielded a radio-carbon date of about 3200 BC. While it has proved feasible to establish a simplified framework of periods such as Formative, Classic and Post-Classic

959

62
(p. 335)

962

for the major centres of cultural development, the terms differ in significance as applied to the Middle America (see map) and the Central Andes as well as to the regional sub-divisions. Broadly speaking, therefore, the Formative Period was marked by the introduction of pottery commencing at different points in the second millennium BC in the various main areas of Peru and Mexico. The foundations were layed for the ensuing Classic Period that occupied the greater part of the first millennium AD and is widely regarded as the high point of achievement in the arts. During the Post-Classic Period, down to the Spanish Conquest in the 16th century, the principal development in ceramics was in the direction of greater production rather than further aesthetic advance although artistic genius remained undiminished to the end in parts of Central Mexico.

967

968

969

968. Bowl of orange ware, supported on a tripod, painted inside with an eagle and concentric rows of ornament in grey-black. Aztec III. Mexico City. Post-Classic Period. Diam. 8 in. (20·5 cm.). This open bowl represents the first of two stages in the evolution of Aztec pottery from earlier Chichimec and, probably, Puebla wares. University Museum of Archaeology and Ethnology, Cambridge.

969. Grey pottery head, on a damaged funerary urn, possibly belonging to the category known as the 'Goddess with the Regional Coiffure of Yalalteca'. Zapotec. Monte Albán, Oaxaca, Southern Mexico. Classic Period. Ht. 12⅘ in. (32·5 cm.). The loss of part of the figure reveals the method of construction with the cylindrical urn behind. British Museum, London.

967. Highly polished polychrome vase, painted with a design of shields and skulls, of the Mixteca-Puebla ware known as Cholula Polychrome after a main centre. Mexico. Post-Classic. Ht. 10 in. (25·5 cm.). Museum of the American Indian, New York.

North America

In the frozen lands of the Arctic there is archaeological evidence of only scattered pottery distribution. Pottery of poor quality found among the Eskimos of Alaska is probably an intrusive trait from Siberia. To the south a vast sparsely-populated zone, free of pottery, stretched across Canada from the Pacific to the Atlantic, with extensions in California and the Plains. Frequently the diverse hunting and fishing peoples had vigorous artistic traditions, but a life of movement of a largely nomadic group of peoples favoured the elaboration of non-ceramic containers, often beautiful as well as ingenious.

The Indians of the eastern forest areas of the United States bordered by the Mississippi valley, were agriculturists increasingly exposed to influences radiating from the higher cultures of Middle America. Pottery showed real accomplishment in a number of painted, modelled and incised forms found in the Mississippian culture that developed late in the first millennium AD with Middle American features such as sizeable towns and massive temple mounds, notably the Monk's Mound (Illinois) over a hundred feet in height and sixteen acres in extent.

In spite of the arid nature of the south-western United States, a major pottery tradition arose among the ancestors of the Pueblo Indians, so called because they lived in *pueblos* (villages) with houses sometimes rising several storeys high, built of unfired clay termed *adobe*. Middle American influence was again apparent among these peaceful agriculturists, who excelled as potters; nevertheless, pottery of the three main groups—the Hohokam, the Anasazi and the Mogollon—developed its own forms, with an early emphasis on angular painted decoration. Pottery of the Hohokam was devoid of decoration until AD 600–900 when red on buff painted bowls and jars carried animated, human and animal outlines. Among the Anasazi, after AD 1300, there was an increasing use of polychrome painted decoration and the introduction of stylised animal and human forms. A beautiful variety of Anasazi pottery was 'Sikyatki Polychrome', exceptional for boldly painted, sweeping designs in black and red on yellow. Pottery of the third group, the Mogollon, remained undistinguished until the delicate black on white style of the Mimbres valley. Bowl interiors portrayed human beings, birds, animals, fishes, insects and abstract forms. The Mimbres style lasted from AD 1000–1200 and may, in turn, have influenced the later beautiful black-and-red on buff wares of Chihuahua in North Mexico. In the south-west, traditional pottery survived the first Spanish contacts which caused such disruption in Mexico and Peru; even in the present century, field studies have yielded valuable data on techniques.

960

961

Middle America

Highlands and lowlands, tropical forests and deserts underline the geographical diversity of the regions known archaeologically as Meso America or Middle America (see map), starting with Mexico in the north and even embracing at its greatest extent prior to the Spanish Conquest part of north-west Costa Rica. Many aspects of Middle America point to a common heritage underlying an apparent multiplicity of cultures and civilisations, the majority with imposing temples and pyramids, complex calendars, hieroglyphic writing, and an impressive degree of refinement in their arts and crafts. But broad cultural unity did not lead to uniformity in the field of ceramics: although an exchange of ideas can be distinguished in many instances, archaeological excavation has recovered a wealth of distinctive pottery styles in the different regions.

At the outset small hand-modelled figurines associated with crop fertility rites are found all over Mexico and are best known from lakeside villages like El Arbollilo, Zacatenco and Tlatilco in the upland Valley of Mexico. However, the earliest yet discovered permanent village (about 1500–1000 BC) was situated far to the south at Chiapa de Corzo, where dishes and storage jars were made with a sophistication that argues a well-established ceramic tradition. Features of Formative Period pottery such as the stirrup-spout and decorative rocker stamping (achieved by rocking a tool along to form a zig-zag pattern) have been used as evidence for connections between Middle America and South America at this time.

On the Gulf Coast of Mexico in the hot, forest lowlands of Tabasco and Southern Vera Cruz arose the first great art style of Mexico, usually termed 'Olmec', which was Formative in period but Classic in its refinement. The civilisation responsible for this art is usually known as Olmec although this is really the name of the people who occupied the area at the time of the Spanish Conquest. The naturalistic hollow pottery of this culture (as well as the better known colossal stone heads and jade figurines) were characterised by mouths drooping at the corners. Influences from this non-urban culture with temple centres dedicated to a jaguar god, were fundamental and widespread, revealed in such pottery as some figurines from Tlatilco and vessels engraved with jaguar claws besides Olmecoid faces on Monte Albán pottery in Oaxaca.

963

In the following Classic Period another tradition developed on the eastern seaboard further to the north in Central Vera Cruz, where the Spaniards encountered the Totonac nation. While some relationships were apparent with the more formal pottery of highland centres, especially Teotihuacán, this lively Classic Period pottery was notable for an unusual freedom of expression.

964

On the opposite coast, bordering the Pacific, the extensive western region of Mexico remained for longer at a Formative level. Some Olmecoid affinities have been detected in pottery figurines from Guerrero, but much of the pottery of this scarcely explored region, with its flourishing village communities, shows a secular line of development different from that of the peoples to the east with their religious hierarchies. In the Jalisco and Colima areas a pre-occupation with daily life can be seen in the vigorous portrayals of dogs, plants, women and men. A similar tradition flourished to the North in Nayarit where figures were modelled impressionistically as groups in everyday scenes, or robustly treated in individual studies.

965

Separated by mountains from the coastal regions to east and west, the high central plateau occupies the greater part of Mexico. Forbidding desert conditions account for the absence of pottery in the north, but fertile lands suitable for dense permanent settlement enabled central Mexico to play a leading rôle in the evolution of Middle America. After steady but unspectacular progress during the Formative Period, the heavily populated region became the

970. Tripod vase in the form of a jaguar painted in black and red on a brownish ground. Nicoya style, Nicaragua. Ht. 12 9/16 in. (32 cm.). Few parts of the New World rivalled the region linking Middle and South America, in the variety of its vessel shapes and decorative styles. Koninklijk Instituut voor de Tropen, Amsterdam.

970

971. A pedestal dish painted with crocodile heads in black, purple and red on white. Coclé, Panama. Diam. 11½ in. (29 cm.). Coclé polychrome developed from designs with narrow lines and circular scrolls to bolder linear effects in a wider colour range with the scrolls flattened or oval. University Museum of Archaeology and Ethnology, Cambridge.

972. Whistle figurine in the form of a man (with feet broken off) bearing traces of blue paint on his necklace and loin cloth. Maya. Style of Jaina Island, Yucatán, Mexico. Classic Period. Ht. 5⅞ in. (15 cm.). These figurines were made by modelling and partial or complete moulding. Musée de l'Homme, Paris.

971

972

centre of the only three unifying forces in Mexico before the arrival of the Spaniards, who recorded their wonder, amounting almost to disbelief, at the sight of the Valley's numerous lakeside towns with abundant maize fields and stone causeways leading over the lakes to the gardens and buildings of the Aztec island capital, topped with soaring temples, 'rising from the water, all made of stone, like an enchanted vision from the tale of Amadis' (Bernal Díaz).

The impetus towards unification first became evident when Teotihuacán, expanded into a great city in Classic times, the centre of an economic empire trading its pottery even with the Maya far to the south. Its growth was reflected in the evolution from simple Formative pottery figurines produced by hand-modelling to elaborate Classic types mass-produced by moulding. The most typical vessel was the tripod vase with slab or cylindrical feet supporting a cylindrical body often with gently flaring sides. Ornamentation was achieved both by incision and *champlevé* but the most remarkable technique was decoration with coloured stucco applied like *cloisonné*. Vessels and effigies were also made at this time of a fine ware known as 'Thin Orange'.

After the destruction of Teotihuacán by fire about AD 600, a confused period ensued with successive invasions by initially backward warrior peoples from the north, amongst them the Toltecs. With the progressive collapse of Classic civilisation, there was a permanent alteration in the character of Middle America from relatively peaceful societies dominated by priests to agressive states ruled by a military class with a religion that demanded human sacrifice on a growing scale. Pottery once again reached high standards but reflected this fundamental change. By the start of the Post-Classic period, the Toltecs, established their powerful city of Tula and produced several varieties of pottery including a red on cream ware called Matlatzinca and, the most characteristic, an orange on buff ware painted with parallel wavy lines called Mazapan, both named after their respective sites. A unique pottery head found at Tula, covered with mother-of-pearl mosaic, was made of the Plumbate ware mentioned earlier (p. 327). The city succumbed before further barbarian invaders, the Chichimecs. With the decline of the other power-centre of Cholula in western Puebla, a series of city-states arose with their own developments in pottery before they finally came under Aztec domination.

Although they preserved an aggressive vigour and religion,

apparent in the expansion of their power within two centuries from their capital of Tenchtitlán in the valley of Mexico to both sea coasts, the Aztecs rapidly assimilated much from earlier cultures. This explains some of the contradictions in pottery which revealed on the one hand the ferocious extremes of their religious beliefs and on the other displayed considerable beauty and refinement in many of the wares made or favoured by them. Earlier pottery continued local traditions, bearing stylised or abstract decoration, but at the time of the Spanish Conquest sensitive designs—in black on red or orange—portrayed birds, butterflies and other forms of wild life, with particular success on the inside of bowls that were often supported on tripod feet. One of the followers of Cortés, Bernal Díaz, gave some idea of the scale of pottery production in his description of the vast, thriving market of Tlateloco where the Spaniards saw every sort of pottery made in a thousand different forms from great water jars to little jugs. The range of pottery available was increased by the Aztec system of exacting tribute in goods from conquered peoples as well as through the enterprise of the Aztec merchant class.

In the mountainous region of Oaxaca in Southern Mexico, the Mixtecs and Zapotecs resisted complete Aztec domination. The early centre of Zapotec civilisation in the valley of Oaxaca, Monte Albán, had a long existence, commencing in the Formative Period when Olmec influences were apparent in the pottery of its inhabitants, perhaps even then Zapotecan-speaking. In the Classic Period, chamber-tombs were furnished with increasingly elaborate funerary urns composed of cylinders behind dignified representations of divine, human and animal figures. Occupation of Monte Albán was interrupted about AD 900 and the Mixtecs, spreading from their mountainous home became the dominant Post-Classic people in Oaxaca. Subsequently Mixtec influence was so strong that as far north as Cholula in Puebla, a hybrid Mixteca-Puebla style was established, becoming responsible for the finest later pottery of Mexico—highly polished and with a brilliant use of polychrome painting.

In many respects the Maya were the most advanced people of Ancient America with unrivalled achievements in astronomy, mathematics, writing, art and architecture in the great ritual centres of south-east Mexico, British Honduras, north-west Honduras and the Guatemala highlands. Their ceramics alone constitute a major

966

968

969

967

973. Double whistling jar, with a spout and connecting bridge handle, in the form of an animal playing a set of panpipes (concealing the whistle). Negative painted in black over red. Quimbaya style. Colombia. Ht. 5⅛ in. (13 cm.). The vessel is an interesting combination of the Peruvian style of double

whistling jar with the 'mammiform' type of feet typical of Central America. Negative painting extended from Peru to Mexico. Horniman Museum, London.

974. Grey-black pottery head from a broken figurine, showing a typical domed cap and

elaborate ear-ornaments. Jama, Manabí Province, Ecuador. Bahía Phase, Regional Development Period. Ht. 2⁷⁄₁₀ in. (7 cm.). The long pottery sequences on the coast commenced by 3000 BC, significantly earlier than in Peru or Mexico. Horniman Museum, London.

973

974

study because of the quality and variety of styles in both highland and lowland regions. Already in the Formative Period finely made monochrome wares were coming to be supplemented by poly-chrome pottery which reached a brilliant level in the Classic Period, above all in the narrative painting on the sides of cylindrical vases, suited to continuous designs such as processional or ceremonial scenes. Other important classes of vessels were effigy incense-burners, plates, open bowls and tripod vessels with slab feet of Teotihuacán inspiration, once again underlining the close relation-ships in Middle America at this time. Everyday scenes from hunting to food preparation were delicately modelled and moulded in the form of figurines and plaques, many incorporating whistles. In the Post-Classic period, following the abandonment of many Maya ceremonial centres in the southern lowlands and the domination of Yucatán by Toltecs or Toltec-related peoples, there was a decline in pottery standards. Even with the absorption of the conquerors, the Maya failed to regain their artistic genius, and mass production, as in standardised incense burners, became general.

South of the Maya regions, the lands narrowing down to the Isthmus of Panama were subject to varying influences from both Middle and South America. An absence of more advanced political and religious organisation did not prevent the evolution of some of the most distinctive pottery of the New World among the warlike tribes, which also produced work of remarkable beauty in gold, jade and other media. 'Nicoya Polychrome' is the name given collectively to Post-Classic pottery types from the peninsula in north-west Costa Rica, typical vessels being egg-shaped or pear-shaped with ring-bases on tripod feet, usually painted black, red or orange on a white to cream slip. Incorporating elements that point to the Maya or beyond, they were frequently transformed into effigy vessels by the addition of heads modelled in full relief and stylised limbs, mostly painted or in low relief, to portray turkeys, macaws, jaguars and other fauna. Even more arresting is the polychrome pottery from the province of Coclé in Panama. Plates, dishes and jars were brightly painted in black, red, purple, blue, brown or green with fanciful representations of crocodiles, monkeys, snakes, deer and sea creatures surrounded by an extraordinary variety of scrolls to produce superb fluid designs. Development of the style probably occurred over at least two centuries before the Spanish Conquest. By contrast, an earlier unslipped Panamanian ware from Chiriquí was a biscuit colour with delicately modelled animal ornamentation on thin-walled bowls, dishes and vases of fine proportions, often with pedestal bases on tripod supports.

63
(p. 336)

972

970

971

975 a)

c)

b)

d)

975. Four stirrup vessels. On the north coast of Peru, a persistent ceramic tradition can be traced from the dark monochrome of Cupisnique in the Chavín style of the Formative Period a) ht. 7¾ in. (19·5 cm.) through the bichrome painted Formative b) ht. 6¾ in. (17·1 cm.) and Classic Mochica c) ht. 11¾ in. (29·9 cm.) to the mould-made burnished black pottery of the Post-Classic Chimú state d) ht. 8¼ in. (21 cm.). For over 2,000 years the stirrup shaped handle, serving as a spout, remained. British Museum, London.

South America

Over the greater part of South America's seven million square miles, material progress was limited by environment. In the extreme south, the harsh climate of Tierra del Fuego and the adjacent Chilean mainland permitted only a wretched existence for the primitive inhabitants, who remained unacquainted with pottery. Further north, in much of Argentina, simple forms of pottery appeared among the hunting and food-gathering peoples of the grasslands. The interior plains reach their greatest extent in Amazonia, a vast expanse of tropical forest where communication was mostly confined to the rivers. From early in the first millennium BC pottery spread along the Orinoco and Amazon systems; then from the Caribbean coast out through the West Indies in the first millennium AD. None of these regions could rival the quality or quantity of wares produced in the narrow belt of Andean lands bordering the Pacific. To wrest prosperity from the challenging environment demanded a greater concentration on material techniques than in Middle America, where efforts were devoted more to religious ends. West of the massive mountain spine of South America, thriving urban centres developed, with a maximum concentration in the central Andes; spectacular irrigation schemes in the Peruvian coastal valleys and endless terracing in the highlands made possible the pattern of intensive agriculture that supported a dense population long before the Inca Empire. This confident technical mastery is clear in the high achievements of Peruvian pottery in the Formative and Classic Periods; equally it accounts for some of the artistic limitations of Post-Classic wares.

At the northern extreme of the Andean system, Colombia failed to conform to many of the features typical of the more advanced peoples to the south. The inhabitants of the legendary land of El Dorado (the 'Gilded Man' of the Chibcha), were gifted craftsmen in gold rather than pottery. Among the separated highland chieftain-ships, the Quimbaya were more open to outside contact and had a correspondingly varied range of pottery, probably late in period, although chronology remains uncertain in Colombia and sub-division is likely with increased fieldwork. *Champlevé* ornament on a red ware was a local development, yet vessels and figurines were often decorated by the 'negative painting' technique found to the south in Ecuador and Peru as well as to the north. In this process parts of the surface are masked with a resistant ('resist') material, such as wax, and then the vessel is immersed in the colouring medium.

973

Firing fixes the colour but burns away the resist material, exposing the uncoloured areas below. The only people to achieve a confederation, the Chibcha, remained potters of limited outlook who produced stereotyped figurines.

Ecuador fell within the final area of Inca expansion but pre-Inca pottery shared more elements with the regions to the north. Indeed, Asiatic influence—by way of marooned fishermen or other sorts of accidental voyages—has been postulated to explain some features of coastal wares. Highland pottery from the Andean basins cannot rival the impressive sequence established for the Coastal Plain, where Formative Period pottery appeared about 3200 BC, thus preceding both Peru and Mexico. The following Regional Developmental Period from about 500 BC–AD 500 saw a number of distinct styles besides widespread distribution of negative and white-on-red wares. Both the Guangala and Bahía Phases of the Period produced important figurines and polychrome wares, with painted pelican designs prominent on the especially fine Guangala black-and-red on yellow. Pottery of the long Integration Period that lasted until the Conquest during a time of growing urbanisation, displayed a convergent trend and an emphasis on vessels soberly coloured in grey or brown, including the face jars of the Manteño Phase.

In Peru and Bolivia pre-European ceramics reached a second peak, in some respects surpassing Middle America. The character of the many flourishing cultures that succeeded each other over the centuries was strongly affected by the geography of the region which can be subdivided into three main cultural areas on the coast —north, central and south—with corresponding areas in the highlands. Between the Andes and the Pacific, the desert of the long narrow coastal plain was broken at intervals by fertile river valleys. At times the physical barriers were overcome by powerful unifying influences seen in the wide geographic distribution of Chavín, Tiahuanaco and Inca pottery. But during the intervening periods, the physical isolation of the coastal communities, dependent primarily on the cultivation of maize in the irrigated valleys, made communication with the highland interior less difficult than with neighbouring coastal areas, thus favouring a recurrent separatism expressed in markedly different pottery styles able to survive over long periods.

Although the farmer-fishermen who lived from about 2500 BC on the coast produced fine textiles, first pottery recorded in Peru is from the northern highlands and only of about 1800 BC. This grey ware from Kotosh, marking the start of the Formative Period, was decorated with incised geometric designs painted red after firing, or sometimes yellow and white. At the same site about 1000 BC, striking incised red pottery was painted with graphite after firing. Some features foreshadowed the pure Chavín style that emerged two centuries later, named after the massively constructed north highland temple of Chavín de Huantar, devoted to a feline cult and, it has been suggested, having other possible Middle American ceramic connections. Whether or not it reveals any movement towards political as well as religious unity, the art style of Chavín was the first to surmount Peru's geographical barriers, affecting the pottery of the northern highlands and spreading through the coastal areas as far as the south coast where the early Paracas wares were also influenced. Its north coast expression, Cupisnique, is best known for flasks with incised decoration and dark monochrome stirrup-spouted vessels with strong relief-modelling of such subjects as felines. With the wane of pure Chavín influence from about 400 BC, new elements appeared among the inhabitants of the north coast, whose inventiveness has gained them the title of the Experimenters. The end of the Formative Period saw the beginnings of the Mochica Culture developed in the Moche and neighbouring valleys by a dynamic people who were responsible for some of the finest Pre-Columbian pottery. Many of their activities, both peaceful and war-like were represented on stirrup vases with excellent relief-modelling or vivid narrative scenes skilfully drawn in red on a cream background. As a result of this realism, more is known about the Mochica than any other people before the Incas, when written post-Conquest records fill out the picture. In the long course of the Classic Period, stylistic changes took place yet a sure touch was

64
(p. 336)

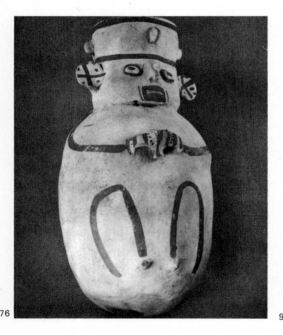

976

977

976. Effigy jar modelled in the form of a man holding a cup, with black on white painted decoration. Chancay style. Central coast of Peru. Later Post-Classic. Ht. 15⅜ in. (39·2 cm.). Central coast pottery was overshadowed by the originality of northern and southern Peruvian wares. Horniman Museum, London.

977. The pottery on Peru's south coast contrasted strikingly with that of the north. Instead of limited colour and emphasis on modelling, it relied on polychrome painting from the time of Paracas Cavernas in the Formative Period (right; ht. 6½ in., 16 cm.) through the naturalistic early Nazca style of the Classic Period (centre; ht. 6⅞ in., 17·5 cm.) to the brilliant stylised designs later in the same period (left; ht. 5⅞ in., 15 cm.). Kemper Collection, London.

978. Bowl with geometric ornament derived from a textile pattern, painted in brown, black and white. Ica style. South coast of Peru. Later Post-Classic Period. Diam. 5½ in. (14 cm.). Kemper Collection, London.

978

979

980   981

979. Polychrome painted aryballus ornamented with birds and geometric decoration. Inca. Peru. Late Post-Classic Period. Ht. 15⅜ in. (39 cm.). This type of vessel was carried as a water jar on the back by means of a rope passed through the handles and over the knob in the form of an animal head. Inca pottery was of excellent construction but still failed to revive the artistic achievements of Peruvian potters in earlier periods. Kemper Collection, London.

980. Head of a feline modelled on a square flange from the rim of a large vessel, painted in red, ochre and black. Tiahuanaco. Bolivia. Classic Period. Ht. 6¼ in. (16 cm.). Kemper Collection, London.

981. Varnished bowl with geometric painted decoration in black on white. Ucayali River, Montaña of Peru. Ht. 4⁷⁄₁₀ in. (12 cm.). This vessel was collected in the present century on the eastern slopes of the Andes but the use of the broad lines outlined by fine lines is reminiscent of the pre-Conquest style of Marajó at the mouth of the Amazon. Horniman Museum, London.

982. Urn used for child burial, painted in red-brown on white, with geometric ornament to represent a textile pattern below a stylised human head on the neck of the vessel modelled in low relief. Santa Maria, Calchaquí, Northwest Argentina. After AD1000. Ht. 23¼ in. (59 cm.). Musée de l'Homme, Paris.

982

retained: moulding was known but did not lead to any degeneration. During the same period Recuay pottery of the North Highlands developed the negative painting tradition of the Experimenters, revealed the continued effect of the Chavín feline cult and gave distinctive treatment to modelled figures often grouped on globular vessels. After the period of Tiahuanaco expansion from the south, there was a resurgence of north coast traditions in the later Post-Classic pottery of the Chimú kingdom. To meet the needs of expanding city populations, mass-produced wares, exploiting the moulding process, revived something of the form but failed to recapture the spirit of Mochica pottery in a range of predominantly black vessels fired in a reducing atmosphere.

In terms of ceramics, at least, the central coast and highlands of Peru were overshadowed by the originality of their northern and southern neighbours. The most distinctive style called Chancay, dates from the later Post-Classic Period when the state of Cuismancu arose. White-slipped bowls and ovoid jars with black painted decoration or rudimentary modelling, followed an earlier black-white-red style.

In contrast to the mainly bichrome styles of the North Coast with their emphasis on realistic modelling and refined draughtsmanship, the polychrome pottery recovered from the cemeteries of the south coast relied on the bold use of brilliant colour and a minimum of sculptured form. At the outset, Chavín influence was strong in the Formative Period pottery of Paracas Cavernas, with feline faces prominent in the incised designs that provided an outline for a range of bright, resinous colours applied after firing to such vessels as double-spout jars and open bowls. Before the appearance of the Classic Nazca style, direct Chavín influence had declined and permanent fired colours were already in use. Nazca pottery was attractively painted, without incision, in as many as eight colours

on a background slip. Among the mythical beings, animals and plants portrayed, the frequency of feline representations again demonstrates the enduring nature of Chavín inspiration. At the end of the Classic Period, local traditions lost their strength and, after the expansion of Tiahuanaco came to an end, there was no south coast equivalent to the revival of earlier pottery forms that took place on the north coast. In the final Post-Classic development, geometric designs derived from textile patterns were painted in black, white and red: this Ica style persisted into Spanish Colonial times. As the spread of Chavín influence from north Peru had found expression in a distinctive art style, so the expansionist character of two powerful movements in the southern highlands led successively to the dissemination of Tiahuanaco and Inca styles. A stiff formality in pottery design was in keeping with the bleak plateau environment of Tiahuanaco, the great religious centre in Bolivia, which entered on an expansionist phase at the end of the Classic Period—perhaps religious or economic at first and military later. Some basic elements of the Tiahuanaco style had been established in the later Formative Period, but the Classic Period led to a refinement of earlier features such as the modelled feline heads on the edge of polychrome painted bowls. Beautifully proportioned beakers or *keros* were a Classic Tiahuanaco innovation.

Further changes occurred with the spread of Tiahuanaco influence via Huari to the coastal regions. After the development of regional varieties, Tiahuanaco's influence finally declined giving way to renewed individual styles by the 13th century. Less than a century before the Spanish Conquest, the period of Inca military expansion began from Cuzco, continuing unchecked until their system of fortifications, roads and bridges united an empire more than three thousand miles in length from north to south. Inca accomplishments in administration, engineering and warfare were not repeated in the

978

980

arts. In ceramics their disciplined outlook can be seen in a range of vessels that exhibit good taste and devotion to decorative detail, yet betray a limited vision. The most typical vessels were the aryballus, bowls, beakers and shallow plates often with bird-head handles. Ultimately the style spread in the wake of Inca armies not only northward into Ecuador, but southward into Chile and north-west Argentina which had both been the home of unusual ceramic styles.

Under the impact of the Spanish Conquest, native traditions were undermined in the Andes as they had been in Middle America. Only in the remoter parts of South America, less attractive to European settlement, did ceramic traditions persist unaffected for any length of time. In recent years, field studies of present-day ethnographic pottery-making have been supplemented by filming but little time is left to record techniques which are dying out and certain sociological aspects which can only be guessed at by the archaeologist.

Africa

Pottery has long occupied an important position in the traditional cultures of the peoples of Africa. An evaluation of its true rôle and importance must, however, take into account the level of these cultures, the modes of life of the peoples and, most important, their environment.

African cultures are basically simple and are linked with a subsistence economy. For the most part the people are hoe cultivators with a knowledge of the simpler techniques of iron and other metal working, and of the utilitarian manufacture for domestic purposes of pottery, basketry, matting and cloth; in the preparation of skins and the carving of wood, however, they often excel. Except in North Africa, where Islamic influence is extremely evident, the wheel was unknown; until the arrival of Europeans the absence of this important device, particularly among the wandering Bushmen, Hottentot and Bantu-speaking peoples of Central, East and Southern Africa has had an important effect in helping to restrict the material cultures to a very simple level and in emphasising the direct dependence of the peoples on their immediate natural environment and the resources in raw materials that it offers. In the treatment of

African pottery-making centres

983. Kabyle, near Fort National, Algeria. An attractive, painted vessel with two handles that was collected in the 19th century. The decorated exterior, painted in red, white and black, provides an interesting contrast to those Bantu vessels already illustrated. British Museum, London.

984. Ain Drahm, Fernana in Kroumir country, Tunisia. A large shallow platter, unfortunately damaged, that was collected at the beginning of this century; it was intended for holding *kouskous*. The upper surface of the platter is decorated with a painted black design on a sandy-red background. Pitt Rivers Museum, Oxford.

985. Riff, North Africa. Detail of a delightfully intricate design in black, brown and cream, painted on a flat dish with a pierced lug. The care with which this complex pattern has been executed should be contrasted with that of the Tonga woman potter (see fig. 958, which appears on p. 325). On her pots it is unlikely that the lines of paint and incision and bands of chevrons that encircle the pot are properly planned; the end is unlikely to marry with the beginning of each line. On this dish, however, the potter has skilfully worked out his almost geometrical pattern to avoid such errors. Minor flaws occur but are not too obvious. British Museum, London.

984

983   985

62. Polychrome painted vase with a double spout connected by a bridge. Nazca. South coast of Peru. Classic Period. Compare fig. 977 on p. 332. The decoration is a design of demons above a row of trophy beads, pointing to the warlike nature of these gifted artists. British Museum, London.

63

64

these materials, only the simplest tools and equipment are used; often they themselves are made from local resources. This lack of machines and complex equipment is again an essential part of these cultures. The finished ware reflects this simplicity in the often crude geometric designs with which it is decorated.

Clay, with timber, iron ore, grasses and reeds, and animal products, is one of the major local resources available to the African villager, a resource of which he makes full use. Throughout Africa the walls of houses, granaries and other buildings are constructed of or coated with clay. For these purposes it is usually sun-dried but in some cases partial or accidental firing occurs—for example, with grain bottles and smelting furnaces.

Except in a very few instances, fired clay objects in Africa have a definite functional value. As is common in most societies living at or near subsistence level there is little room in the material culture for waste, for luxuries, for any ornaments other than those used directly on the body. Any artistry finds expression in the form these functional objects take and in their decoration, which is usually either incised or painted with a simple design, although more elaborate treatment is sometimes given to the shaping, as in the case of mouths of vessels, so as to resemble animal faces.

The variety of uses to which fired clay is put is considerable: spindle whorls and sinkers for fishing nets, cattle figurines and ritual objects for initiation and other ceremonies, moulds for beads and bracelets, pipes and pipe bowls, tuyeres, drums and whistles, children's animal toys, dolls and latterly wheels and motor cars. Its most important use is, however, in the form of vessels, actual pots.

The use of pottery is, moreover, widespread in Africa. All sedentary people possess the necessary knowledge for its manufacture whilst the Hottentots and even the Bushmen knew how to make it, though the latter probably gained their rudimentary knowledge from their Hottentot or Bantu-speaking neighbours. Often they had to barter goods and meat in exchange for a vessel. This practice still occurs and, indeed, since suitable clay is not always present in a locality, even some Bantu communities, where

986

987

988

63. Painted scene from the side of a cylindrical vase (taken by a peripheral camera) showing presentations to a dignitary. Maya. Nebaj, Guatemala. Classic Period. Depth 6½ in. (16·5 cm.). Besides masterly narrative painting, the Maya employed carving, incision, moulding and modelling with comparable skill. British Museum, London.

64. Stirrup vase in the form of a man's head painted in red, cream and white. Mochica, Chicama Valley, North Coast of Peru. Classic Period. Ht. 11⅝ in. (29·6 cm.). Heads of this type are designated portrait-vases because of the striking degree of realism. British Museum, London.

986. Ibo, Osisa on the Niger, Southern Nigeria. This intricate Kwale Ibo piece consists of a pottery pedestal surmounted by a modelled group of figures representing a chief with his wives and courtiers. The chief is seated; flanking him are two musicians, one beating a drum, the other an iron gong. The elaborate work, successfully executed, shows a high degree of technical competence. This is not to be found in the southern, south-central and eastern parts of Africa. British Museum, London.

987. Ashanti, Ghana. An exquisite little pipe bowl of black pottery, shaped in the form of a chair. The actual bowl rests on the seat of the chair whilst the stem, into which a mouthpiece would be fitted, forms the back. This pipe bowl is richly decorated with incised patterns and is a very fine specimen of its kind. Pitt Rivers Museum, Oxford.

988. Ashanti, Ghana. Pottery pipe bowl in the form of a bird. The pipe is polished red; in the incisions white chalk or ash is also present. The pipe is heavily decorated with carefully worked incised patterns. The bowl itself is in the form of a bird perched on the stem. The bird, perhaps a goose, appears to be sleeping with its beak tucked into the feathers of its back. This example is included to emphasise the general similarity of treatment and decoration that is to be found over wide areas of Africa. Whilst there are obvious differences between the Ila pipe bowls illustrated here, on the one hand, and the Ashanti ones, there are also many points of similarity. Pitt Rivers Museum, Oxford.

989

990

991

989. Twa, Lake Kivu, Ruanda. Red pottery bowl on a tall stem and flared foot. Such vessels (*ichotero*) were made by the Twa pygmies for their rulers, the Tutsi. Fire was placed in the bowl and dry twigs of the *umugwavu* tree were dropped on the flame. Skins intended for use as clothing were then held in the smoke to scent them. The shoulder is decorated with a carefully executed pattern of incisions. Pitt Rivers Museum, Oxford.

992. Luzira, Uganda. Pottery figurine from an archaeological site at Zusira. The decoration and other features of pottery play a valuable part in establishing sequences and distributors of Iron-Age culture over wide areas. The figure is unusual in the treatment of the hair, the prominent chin, the wearing of neck rings and particularly the treatment of the eyes and nostrils. British Museum, London.

990. Zezuru (Shona), Wedza, Rhodesia. Zoomorphic vessel used in the *mhondoro* cult of the Shona. The vessel is in red with burnished graphite triangles of black set within lines incised in the clay. Such vessels may depict lions, tortoises, birds or other creatures. Livingstone Museum, Rhodesia.

993. Nyoro, Bunyoro, Uganda. A fine specimen of coiled and burnished ware that shows to good effect the neat, incised patterns of cross-hatching so common throughout southern, eastern and central Africa. The graphite, powdered and mixed with oil, is applied before firing and is burnished with a stone and later with bark cloth (made from the fibrous inner bark of a tree). The Nyoro have long been famed for their burnished ware. Pitt Rivers Museum, Oxford.

991. Msumba (Nkolongwe) District on the eastern shore of Lake Nyasa, Moçambique. Again a most attractive vessel in its neatness and simplicity of line and decoration. The body and interior of the rim are burnished with ochre to a deep red but the tall neck is in natural fired clay. Decoration of the shoulder and neck is by careful incision in bands around the latter and in patterns on the former. Pitt Rivers Museum, Oxford.

994. Azande, North-East Africa. This head, which forms the neck and rim of a globular water vessel, is a delightful example of Azande craftsmanship. It is carefully executed and is dark brown in colour. The facial marks represent tatoos. British Museum, London.

992

993

994

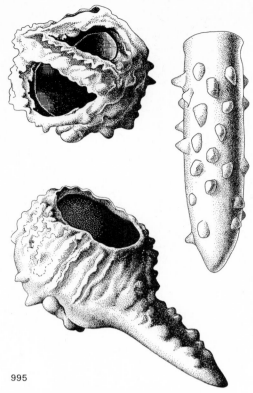

995

996

997

995. Bemba, Northern Province, Zambia. Drawing of three ritual initiation figurines (*mbusa*) of fired coarse clay. These figurines play an important part in the female initiation ceremonies (*chisungu*) of the Bemba, the Bisa and other peoples in north-east Zambia. Each of the figurines symbolises some precept of moral or similar behaviour or some aspect of the future life of the adolescent girl. Livingstone Museum, Rhodesia.

996. Ila, Kafue River, Zambia. Simple clay pipe bowl on reed stem. In use the foot rests on the ground. The bowl is made from fine clay and is first modelled in solid form. The interior of the bowl is then cut out with a knife and the decoration applied. The ware is burnished red, with ochre, or black, with graphite. Such pipes are used throughout Ila and Tonga country. Pitt Rivers Museum, Oxford.

997. Luvale, Barotseland, Zambia. Drawing of a clay tuyere used in smithing to protect the tips of the bellows' nozzles, which are usually of wood or horn, from being charred by the fire. Whereas many peoples use roughly shaped tuyeres, poorly fired, the Luvale produce very fine pipes and decorate them with incisions. Their workmanship can be very good. Livingstone Museum, Rhodesia.

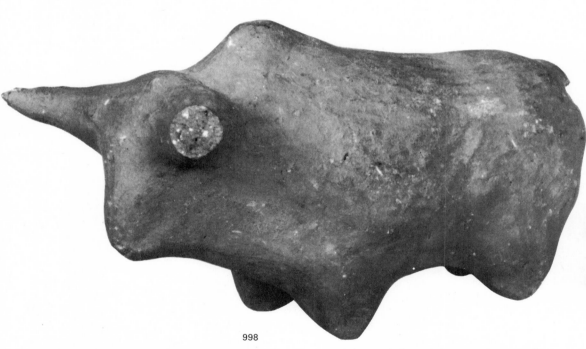

999

998

1000

998. Ndebele, Rhodesia. Fired clay oxen and other animals are to be found in many parts of Africa, fashioned as toys by children, particularly boys. They have also been found in many archaeological excavations, in association with other Iron Age material, throughout southern and central Africa. The Hehe of Tanzania, the Tonga of Zambia, the Suto of Lesotho and the Ndebele are but a few tribes that know how to make them. One of their values lies in their simplicity; they are unsophisticated copies of the beasts of the community. Thus the various strains of cattle in different parts of Africa are reflected in the children's models. These models are not always fired; even when they are the

result is not fully satisfactory. As a result horns and other extremities are easily broken off, as in the present example, or the whole animal may crack and crumble. Other animals as well as cattle are modelled whilst dolls and, nowadays, even motor cars are to be found. British Museum, London.

999. Ila, Kafue River, Zambia. A zoomorphic pipe bowl of the same type as the above but with particularly interesting decorative features. The bowl rests on a buffalo which is being attacked by a leopard. Complex pipe bowls such as this are not common. The painted graphite surface of the specimen has been highly polished. Pitt Rivers Museum, Oxford.

1000. Ila, Kafue River, Zambia. Zoomorphic pipe bowl, made by the Ila (who are also known as the Mashukulumbwe by their Barotse neighbours) the Zambezi Tonga and related peoples. These pipe bowls, like the simpler specimen illustrated above, are modelled by men who take great care and pride in their work. The actual bowl of this specimen rests on the shoulders of an eland. Again incised cross-hatching is employed to provide patterns on the bowl itself. The pipe bowl has been painted with graphite which has been burnished on the upper parts. The three foot reed stem is inserted into the hole at the back of the pipe, in the trunk of the eland's body. Pitt Rivers Museum, Oxford.

1001

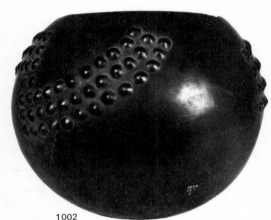

1002

1001. Hottentot, Orange River, Namaqualand, South Africa. A simple, undecorated vessel of coarse type with two bosses at the shoulder. The method of manufacture was usually coiling and any decoration normally consisted of lightly scratched hatching or parallel lines. The rounded conical base (which has been repaired) is similar to that found among a number of Bantu peoples too in the south-western region as far north as the southern part of Angola. South African Museum, Cape Town.

1002. Zulu, Zululand, Natal, South Africa. A wide-mouthed spherical pot burnished black and ornamented with two extended chevrons consisting of parallel rows of pellets of clay. This pot illustrates two unusual features of Zulu pottery. The polished black exterior is obtained not from graphite but from a form of varnish consisting of a mixture of soot and pulp. The second feature is the pellet decoration. Nowadays, the Zulu, like other Bantu, merely press the clay pellets on to the surface of the pot before firing. Formerly, however, the pellets were provided with little stalks that were taken right through the wall and burred over on the inside. British Museum, London.

1003. Ovambo, extreme north of South-West Africa, just south of the Angola border. A simple vessel of coarse texture, decorated at the neck with a few lightly scratched groups of parallel lines. The similarity between this pot and the Hottentot one above is obvious; so too is the rounded conical base. This vessel closely resembles the leather or skin bag from which it has been copied, even to the pierced lugs at the shoulder by means of which, like a bag, it is suspended. South African Museum, Cape Town.

1004. Lovedu, Transvaal, South Africa. A wide-mouthed spherical pot with a very thin rim. The pot is dull red in colour, the colour of the fired clay, and is decorated at the shoulder with a wide bank of burnished graphite. This is flanked by neat bands of incised lines and cross-hatching. The neatness and simplicity of this vessel are typical of the standard of ware common among many peoples in southern Africa. South African Museum, Cape Town.

1003

1004

one may normally expect the skills to be known, have to buy their vessels from perhaps distant neighbours.

The shape, the finish, the workmanship and the quality of African pottery is again determined very largely by the intended function though environmental and other influences play their part. Unlike their European counterparts most African households do not depend so much on flat and level surfaces. Pots stand on the ground, hang in slings or balance on shelves made of sticks. For carrying on the head a rounded base to a pot can be an advantage whilst even more pointed bases sit well in light sandy floors. One finds, too, that the shape may be borrowed from other containers, such as gourds, calabashes or leather bottles. Pots intended for cooking purposes are usually coarse and unpainted but durable. Water vessels, since they are most in the public eye, receive more care and attention in their finish and are, except in North Africa, usually painted in reds and black and made to look attractive. They must also be well balanced, for they are destined to be borne each day on the heads of their owners over perhaps long distances. They are the vessels that the visitor to a village first notices and the ones that will long remain in his memory as typical of the culture of the people. The water pots of a particular group are usually remarkably uniform in size and shape, a tribute to the accuracy of the eye of the potter.

Beer and grain pots are often merely larger versions of water pots and bear most of their characteristics. They range in size up to forty or fifty gallons and even larger and must be very carefully constructed and fired if they are to give good service. Drinking cups

and food dishes, on the other hand, are often, as their names may show, diminutives of water pots, though perhaps a little finer, a little more attractive.

Some peoples (the Shona of Rhodesia afford a good example with their burnished graphite ware) take a particular pride in the vessels they use for bathing. It is with pottery intended for ritual purposes, however, that one finds vessels assuming unusual shapes and forms. In some areas of the Congo, and again among the Basuto of South-East Africa, ordinary domestic vessels are sometimes unusual in shape or even anthropomorphic but, in most regions, it is only in ritual pottery that one finds odd forms appearing. The anthropomorphic ware of the Zezuru *mhondoro* cult of Rhodesia, the initiation *mbusa* of the Bemba and the *cinamwali* pottery objects of the Neenga of Zambia, all are thought-provoking specimens that arouse speculation as to the history of their development and interest in the importance of their rôle in the ceremonies.

The absence from much of Africa of the potter's wheel has meant that most of its peoples depend on simple hand techniques. The three methods most commonly employed are: modelling from the lump or from a 'saucer' of clay; true coiling; and modelling from a 'quoit' or, for larger vessels, from a number of quoits placed one upon the other. The wide distribution of these techniques and the uniformity of processes throughout the sub-continent are startling: the 'quoit' technique has been observed in South Africa, the Middle Zambezi Valley and on the shores of Lake Tanganyika; modelling from a 'saucer' or 'cup' has also been observed in South Africa and

990

995

the Middle Zambezi Valley and again in Nubia, whilst coiling has been reported from the Hottentots of South-West and the BaGanda of East Africa.

Moulding is another method commonly employed, either around another pot (Hausa) or inside a basket (Nyika). Building with flattened slabs of clay (Kikuyu) is also employed. More unusual techniques are the beating of the clay into a stone mould as do the Hausa or the beating out of the clay with a stone, observed among women on the Blue Nile.

The shaping of the body of the vessel, the smoothing and scraping of the walls and the shaping of the neck and rim are carried out with the simplest of tools: a mussel shell, a pebble, a calabash fragment or a grass stalk. The pot itself is set on a sherd or a flat surface and, therefore, as the final task in the shaping the potter, unless he has built up from the rim or has begun by shaping the base, must lift his vessel from its dish, turn it upside down and complete the unfinished bottom, scraping away the excess material and skilfully closing the gap to produce a surface that is smoothly rounded. The decoration of pottery before firing takes the form of incision, stamping, combing, rouletting or other marking to provide geometric patterns in the clay. Extra clay may also be applied to give additional decoration: a broken frieze, shoulder pellets, lugs, handles, or even anthropomorphic figures.

A slip is commonly applied and usually consists only of clay particles in suspension. BaNyoro, however, apply a slip of powdered graphite in a mixture and the sap of a shrub. This is polished with a stone both before and again after firing in order to produce a silvery black lustre. The Kabyles of North Africa use both a red and a white slip, the former from clay and haematite and the latter from kaolin. Designs are then applied in black using iron oxides. A light yellow resin varnish is sometimes applied in order to enhance these designs. Other peoples too are known to apply gum varnishes. The Zulus, however, prefer to use a mixture of soot and a pulp of leaves in order to waterproof their ware. Others, such as the Ila of Zambia and the Hausa of Nigeria smoke their vessels with the same object.

In many regions colour is applied and is usually red, black or brown, for the range of colours in most African communities is again strictly limited to what may be gleaned from the neighbouring countryside. Such colours, from powdered ochres or graphite mixed with water or oil, are usually applied before firing. The ochres would, of course, have a matt finish but the graphite is often burnished with a stone in order to provide a glossy finish. The Zambezi Tonga and many other peoples of southern Africa thus decorate small areas between incised lines or between bands of ochre to produce lozenge, chevron and other designs. Others such as the Ngoni burnish most or even the whole of the exterior of the pot. The incised and stamped areas on a newly fired vessel may be emphasised by dusting with ash or chalk though, of course, this has only a temporary effect.

Throughout Africa, pot-making is primarily women's work. This is appropriate for the main use of pottery occurs in the domestic field. Again, broadly speaking, the division of labour between the sexes in an African community allocates the more mundane chores that entail routine dull labour to the woman. Felling trees and hunting are activities that are usually the work of men; digging and transporting clay, either for pottery or for house walls, are the work of women. This division is not, of course, absolute. One finds, for example, that some Luvale men of Angola and Western Zambia make pottery, and fine ware too. Again ritual vessels or objects associated with masculine pursuits, such as tuyeres in smithing or pipe-bowls, may be made only by men. These are, however, the exceptions.

In very few areas does one find pot-making being practised on anything other than the domestic scale. The potter works at her own house, or more probably outside it, and practices her craft in the intervals between her daily chores. Indeed, many restrict their craft-work to the idle season of the year when the gardens are less demanding of their time. Their equipment is of the simplest, their practices informal and again sufficient pottery is normally made for the use only of themselves and their immediate circle. In North and West Africa particularly, however, this is not the case for large quantities of new pottery are made for sale in the markets. Corporations or guilds are to be found and the production and sale of pots form an essential part of the economies of many families. In the non-market communities to the south, however, this is not the case. The potter, behind whose skills there is sometimes a background of ritual inheritance and ancestral approval, is recognised as a leading member of the community for this is often the leading craft for women. It still occupies only a minor part of her time, however, and is not usually the primary basis of the economy of her household. There is, therefore, little direct incentive or opportunity to improve the techniques she has learned from her mother or the older women.

1005. Suto, Lesotho. The fired clay vessel is vase-shaped, with a narrow base and a wide mouth. A skin membrane is stretched tightly over the latter and tied onto the vessel. These pottery drums have a restricted distribution. A similar Suto (Basuto) drum, used by Bushmen, Hottentot and other peoples in South Africa, is also recorded from the middle Zambezi valley. British Museum, London.

1006. Suto, Lesotho. Pottery bird, possibly a guinea fowl. The head is separate and roughly made; the body is sandy in colour but with red paint on the wings and legs. As a result of the expansion of the Zulu kingdom a considerable movement of peoples occurred in southern Africa. A group of Sotho fugitives, under the name of Kololo, conquered the Lozi kingdom of Barotseland, in what is now Zambia, and ruled for some generations in

the last century. They left behind a number of interesting cultural traits particularly their pottery traditions. British Museum, London.

1007. Suto, Lesotho and Orange Free State, South Africa. Amusing pottery chickens, the smaller collected in Lesotho, formerly Basutoland, in 1891, the larger at Harrismith in the Orange Free State in 1914. The wings, tail, comb and wattles of the latter are painted red. South African Museum, Cape Town.

1005

1006

1007

The intrusion of Western European culture, particularly in the 19th and 20th centuries, has had two major effects: firstly, the African villager has in most regions, shown a strong preference for mass-produced iron cooking pots, enamel ware and paraffin tins and, secondly, urbanisation and the education of girls in schools has withdrawn them to a great extent from ordinary village life, where they would have learned pot-making, among other traditional skills, in the course of their everyday work. Hand-made village pottery is often more expensive, less durable and—perhaps most important in developing communities—less acceptable socially than factory-made ware; indeed, with fewer girls learning the craft, it is, over wide areas, losing ground rapidly or even dying. In some regions this problem has been recognised and, as in Nigeria, government encouragement has long been given and attempts made to modernise the techniques of the potter. Most newly independent states have a keen interest in developing or where necessary resurrecting their village crafts as part of their cultural heritage. Lack of funds combined with the need to handle more pressing problems of health and general education have so far, however, proved a considerable handicap and it is only in those countries where there are already flourishing communities that we may expect African pottery to continue and to develop.

1008. Suto, Ladybrand, Orange Free State, South Africa. Pottery lion. This sophisticated specimen, with its hollow body and standard of finish, is clearly modern and the work of an adult. British Museum, London.

Oceania

The distribution of pottery-making in Oceania presents a complicated pattern with elements of technology and artistic decoration being combined and recombined in endless profusion. It seems, however, that pottery vessels in the larger island land masses nearer to Asia, such as Indonesia, Philippines and the Carolines, have much clearer associations with their Asiatic homelands than have the more distant Oceanic islands such as the Solomons, New Hebrides, New Caledonia and Fiji. Throughout the latter, however, some elements are still apparent which are suggestive of an ancient pottery tradition in south-east China. Traces of geometric style found in the early Chinese and associated cultures include cord marks, mat and basket patterning, lids for vessels, paddle and anvil use for manufacture and the carved paddle for decoration. In general, it could be said that amongst women potters in Oceania the use of the wheel was unknown, that slips were rarely used and that coiling perhaps formed the usual method of manufacture, together with the 'paddle and anvil' technique. In this technique the vessel was beaten into shape by a wooden 'paddle' or beater with the potter's hand or an 'anvil' of stone or some other material supporting the inside of the pot.

Only archaeological pottery has been found in Polynesia and excavations in the Marquesas, Samoa and Tonga show that it was introduced there considerably more than two thousand years ago. Any discussion of Oceanic pottery then, must focus on Fiji since there is in these islands the most southerly survival of living potters still using traditional methods and Fiji pottery shows the greatest range in form and function to be found anywhere in the scattered pottery communities which lie outside the larger continental islands. This description of Oceanic pottery will, therefore, concentrate on Fiji, as representative, even if in part only, of all the pottery traditions which together make up the complete picture of pottery diffusion throughout the Pacific.

It is this marked variety and excellence of craftmanship that helps to distinguish Fijian pottery. Although the humble cooking pot, the world's first portable pressure cooker, was usually left plain, some had limited geometric decoration around the shoulder and rim, applied with a shell, or incising the damp clay with the middle of a coconut leaf. For practical purposes the cooking pots were left unvarnished but in more modern times they have been coated with gum from a pine tree after the pot has been fired. This is merely to

give what the potters imagine to be, greater aesthetic appeal for the European collector. In form, Fijian cooking pots varied from the spherical pots of Malolo Island to those having a pointed base in Sigatoka, while those from Nakoro had a markedly elongated body. On Kadavu Island, the potters made some of the most gigantic cooking pots in Oceania, huge things standing three feet high and fully two feet in diameter. Most rims were out-turned with decoration on the upper surface and notches or grooves around the lip. Occasionally, double rims were formed and *appliqué* buttresses applied round the neck line or inner margin of the rim. Because of their bulk and brittleness, cooking pots rarely had handles while

1009

1014

1017

1010

1011

1012

1010. Unvarnished cooking vessel or ai vakariri. Rewa district, Viti Levu, Fiji. Probably about 1920. Diam. 11 in. (28 cm.). Everted rim and smoothed body above shoulder with zones of incised triangles infilled with impressed units. Appliqué nubbins around sections of shoulder. Fiji Museum Collection.

1011. Varnished earthenware water vessel or saqa ni wai. Rewa district, Viti Levu, Fiji, probably mid-19th century. Diam. 11 in. (28 cm.). Moulded and appliqué relief on upper half of vessel with flanged and impressed mouth. Typical of ornate Rewa relief pottery. Fiji Museum Collection.

1012. Earthenware cooking vessel of cauldron shape known as ai vakariri. Ra Province, probably Malake Island, about 1925. Diam. 9 in. (23 cm.). Upper part of body scraped and varnished, lower section plain. Grooved rim with impressed outer lip and moulded pouring spout. Possibly influenced by European vessels. Fiji Museum Collection.

their pointed or rounded bases meant that clay stands were made to support the pots. In early forms these were quite sophisticated with cut-outs and wing-like projections extending from them but in modern times these free-standing supports merely became clay cylinders with simple paddle marks over their surface.

The most ornate vessel in Fiji was the water container which was often made for chiefs and used in various ceremonials, particularly during the mixing and drinking of *kava*. The shape of these jars varied from large spherical ones with small upright neck which served as a spout, to smaller ones of the same shape with a stirrup handle. Others were shaped rather like a rugby ball with a central vertical spout while others had a stirrup handle and spout at one end. In the Rewa district during the last century these vessels took the form of small canoes, each with a handle. In some cases, they were joined together in pairs or even units of three and four. Similarly, in the same district, potters produced what are now called 'fruit clusters' or small pottery spheres joined at the body in units of three or four and linked also by a three- or four-part handle. Although each connected sphere had its own filling hole there was usually only one spout for the composite vessel. Early European writers state that

both the canoe and the 'fruit cluster' forms were drinking vessels for children and sick people but there is no indication as yet about how old these forms really are; some scholars believe them to be a result of European influence.

The most unusual water container was one shaped like a turtle, complete in detail even to the head, flippers and segments of the shell. As in most of the other water jars, the lower half was left plain and the potters decorated the upper section most lavishly. They used *appliqué* strips of clay to form graceful curves or twisted bands forming a rope-like pattern, thought by some people to be derived from coconut-shell water-containers which had plaited fibre covering them to serve as a carrying aid. Shell and stick-incised designs bordered the clay relief patterns, relieved at intervals by knobs or nubbins placed singly or in continuous vertical and horizontal bands. This form of decoration was carried to an extreme on the canoe and fruit clusters although a very old water container recovered from a temple in 1851 shows the same decorative motif used to achieve fine effect with perfect control of the medium. In the Malolo Group the water containers were noted for their absence of relief decoration on the body and instead there was an incised

1009

1015

1018

1015

1016

1009. Unvarnished earthenware water jar or saqa ni wai. From temple at Muanisau, Rewa district, Viti Levu, Fiji abandoned about 1840. Diam. 11½ in. (29 cm.). A fine example of type with pouring spout and central filling orifice. Decoration on upper part of body consists of moulded ridges, shell-impressed zones and appliqué bands. Used in ceremonial mixing of yaqona or kava. Fiji Museum Collection.

1013. Varnished earthenware water vessel or saqa ni wai, in form of turtle with appliqué relief bands forming plates of carapace. Ra Province, Viti Levu, Fiji, about 1928. L. 12 in. (31 cm.). Single orifice at top centre. Head, tail and limbs formed from body of vessel, underside plain. Fiji Museum Collection.

1014. Lightly burnished terra cotta bowl. Bushman's Bay, Santo, New Hebrides, about 1925. Diam. 8 in. (20 cm.). This cooking vessel was probably coil-made and has both moulded relief and impressed decoration characteristic of Santo pottery on the upper section of the body. Typically everted rim and relief frill around junction of base and body. Fiji Museum Collection.

1013

1014

1015. Varnished earthenware drinking vessel or drua—tolu. Rewa district, Viti Levu, Fiji, early 20th century. Ht. 6¾ in. (17 cm.). Three spheres joined, with spout and filling hole. Moulded ridges and appliqué nubbins on upper part of spheres and triple handle. Typical of Rewa 19th-century forms varying from single to as many as four spheres. Used by children. Fiji Museum Collection.

1016. Varnished earthenware drinking vessel or drua in form of double canoe with stirrup handle. Rewa district, Viti Levu, Fiji. Typical of mid-19th century examples. Diam. 6 in. (15 cm.). Hand moulded linear relief ridges with appliqué nubbins along line of body and handle. Single orifice. Used for invalids and children. Fiji Museum Collection.

1015

1016

herring-bone motif which is the distinguishing feature of these vessels. In bowl forms too, there was variety in shapes. One of the most common was a simple but elegant basin with a flattened rim decorated by shell impressions. Made by using paddle and anvil on round clay slabs which had been first punched with a stone to give a rough bowl shape, they ranged from small examples to ones fully two feet in diameter. These large ones were commonly used for preparing kava and for some of the Fijian desserts. In antiquity, the footed vessel with a ring-stand having cut-outs in it, was formerly present in widely separated places such as the Philippines and Tonga but only a single, modern example is known for Fiji. This specimen has four supports between stand and bowl and is highly decorated around the rim. Some traditional potters are going back to the footed vessel, probably to meet demands from European collectors.

Finger bowls, used for washing hands at meals, were well represented in Fiji. Well-finished and pleasant pieces, they were usually given a marked shoulder angle to form an in-turned rim. These bowls were small enough for the potter to spin in one hand while using a paddle with the other to create the angle at the line of the shoulder. That section of the bowl above the shoulder was decorated with incised or shell impressed chevrons, herring-bone patterns or cross-hatching. Other finger bowls had relief nubbins all over the body or were simply small basins without any shoulder angle. Other rare ones again had sharp vertical ridges rather like an extension of those seen at one end of a coconut.

The last form to be described from Fiji was a specialised one and

was intermediate between a pot and a basin. It was rather like a cauldron with an extremely wide mouth almost the width of the body and had almost a flanged rim and a pouring lip. The body was fairly plain and oval to spherical in outline but others had a slight shoulder angle marked by *appliqué* nubbins and zones of incised designs above this. Like many cooking pots they were dyed red with juice from the mangrove bark but, unlike the majority, which were set at an angle on their clay or stone stands, these cauldrons were placed upright on the fire. While being functional, their appearance is not without appeal and their soft pink surface with restrained body decoration, make them a satisfying object to view.

New Hebrides pottery differs from modern Fijian in giving bold relief to the body of a pot by using semi-circular loops of clay. These form scallops around the bowl rim but on Espiritu Santo, this motif was limited to a single raised ridge running unevenly round the body. Often these were associated with rectangles and dots pricked into the clay and such decoration always seemed to cover the upper coil-made section which was attached to the base. The north coast of New Guinea, and Papua, are regions where there is extensive pottery-making. Among the Motu peoples located near Port Moresby, the remarkable *hiri* or canoe expedition, sees the annual export of thousands of plain, spherical cooking pots across the two hundred odd miles of water in the Gulf of Papua. Formed by a combination of hand-moulding and paddle and anvil techniques, the pots of the Motu industry are merely one example of an extensive series of pottery technologies found in many parts of New Guinea.

1017

1017

1018

1019

1017. Varnished earthenware water vessel or kitu. Yanuya Island, Malolo Group, Fiji with date of manufacture incised, November 8, 1952. L. 13 in. (33 cm.). Form typical of Malolo with end spout and filling orifice centre top. *Appliqué* strips and nubbins separate plain underside from decorated upper section. Fiji Museum Collection.

1018. Earthenware drinking vessel, unvarnished. Muanisau, Rewa district, Fiji. Probably mid-19th century. L. 7½ in. (19 cm.). Canoe shaped with end spout and central filling hole to rear of handle. Moulded relief strip separates decorated zone which is shell-impressed. Used by children and invalids. Fiji Museum Collection.

1019. Unfired brown clay bowl from Lae district, New Guinea made by male potter for South Pacific Commission meeting in 1965. Diam. 7⅛ in. (18 cm.). Impressed lip edge with single rows of gouged and impressed units around neck of bowl. *Appliqué* handles in form of fruit bat. Fiji Museum Collection.

Glossary of Terms

alabastron (Greek) Elongated piriform vessel with narrow neck and usually two lug-handles, for holding perfumes.
amphora (Greek) Jar, primarily for storage, with ovoid body and two handles reaching from mouth or neck to the shoulder.
aryballos (Greek) Oil-bottle with narrow neck, usually with globular body, used by athletes at the bath.
berettino see *bianco-sopra-bianco*.
bianco-sopra-bianco (It.) Decoration in white glaze-mixture.
blanc fixe (Fr.) Decoration in white glaze-mixture on a slightly tinted tin-glaze. *Berettino* or *bianco-sopra-azzurro* (It.) was used specifically of white on a blue glaze (cf. *bleu persan*).
biscuit Fired body without glaze.
bleu persan (Fr. = 'Persian blue') Tin-glazed ware with blue glaze painted in white, and sometimes yellow, glaze-mixtures (cf. *bianco-sopra-bianco*).
bocage (Fr. = 'little wood') A background of modelled leaves and flowers forming part of a ceramic figure or group.
camaieu (Fr.) Painting in different tones of the same colour.
chatironné (Fr.) Style of painting (usually flowers, often in the oriental style) with normally black outlines.
china clay (*kaolin*) A very refractory white clay formed by the decomposition of granite rocks, and an essential element in the making of true 'hard-paste' or 'felspathic' porcelain, of which it forms the body; the other element being china-stone (*petuntse*), a fusible stone also of granitic origin, which fuses with the *kaolin* at about 1300–1400°C. to make the substance of the porcelain, which is glazed with *petuntse* fused with lime or other fluxes.
china stone (*petuntse*) See china clay.
clay, preparation of On being dug from the ground, clay (which sometimes requires to be weathered before use) is mixed with water and allowed to stand so that the grosser particles sink, and the finer can be strained off (*levigation*), the water then usually being driven off by heat. The clay must be thoroughly mixed, and before throwing must be cut and beaten to drive off air-bubbles (*wedging*).
'cloisonné' (Fr.) A term derived from enamelling on metal, to indicate the separation of glazes in cells formed by relief outlines.
combing A technique of making incised patterns with a toothed instrument, or drawing slip lines into arcade- or feather-patterns (see slipware).
crackle Fine fissures in a glaze, deliberately induced, sometimes with a finer crackle within a coarser network.
crazing Fine cracking in a glaze, normally unintentional.
cream-coloured earthenware / **creamware** A light-bodied earthenware with transparent (mainly lead-based) glaze, evolved in England from about 1740 onwards: called in French '*faience fine*'; in German '*Steingut*', and in Italian '*terraglia*'.
crystalline glazes Glazes which are not amorphous, like glass, but contain small crystals of various substances which have separated out as the glaze cooled.
cuenca (Span.) A method of keeping glazes apart by stamping with raised outlines.
cuerda seca (Span. = 'dry cord') A method of keeping glazes apart by outlines drawn in a mixture of manganese and grease, which burned away in the firing.
'Delftware' Dutch tin-glazed earthenware named after the town of Delft: 'delftware' is the English derivative. See Chap. V.
Deutsche Blumen (Germ. = 'German flowers') Flower-painting in the European manner, usually on German porcelain and faience (cf. *fleurs fines*).
enamel A pigment (usually on a lead base) firing at a temperature lower than the glaze on which it is used, and fixed in a subsequent firing in a covered (or 'muffle') kiln.
faience (Fr.) or **Fayence** (Germ.) Tin-glazed earthenware. See page 139.
faience fine (Fr.) Usually used to denote cream-coloured earthenware (*q.v.*) of English type, but sometimes merely for faience of fine quality.
famille jaune (Fr. = 'yellow family') Class of Chinese porcelain, essentially of *famille verte* (*q.v.*) palette, in which the yellow predominates, often as a ground colour.
famille noire (Fr. = 'black family') Class of Chinese porcelain, essentially of *famille verte* (*q.v.*) palette, in which black is used as a ground colour.
famille rose (Fr. = 'pink family') Class of Chinese porcelain with enamelled decoration in which opaque pink and purple tones (based on gold) and white supplement the colours of the *famille verte* (*q.v.*), normally replacing the iron-red and aubergine of the latter.
famille verte (Fr. = 'green family') Class of Chinese porcelain with enamelled decoration in combinations of green, yellow, blue, aubergine and iron-red.
felspathic glazes These are glazes containing felspars (a group of alumino-silicates found as natural rocks) which only fuse at high temperatures. See also china stone.
fleurs des Indes (Fr. = 'India flowers') Flower-painting of vaguely Oriental character, based on Kakiemon or *famille rose* styles and usually *chatironnées* (*q.v.*).
fleurs chatironnées (Fr.) Style of flower-painting in enamel-colours with outlines, usually black.
fleurs fines (Fr. = 'fine flowers') Flower-painting in the European manner with careful shading, usually of recognisable species, and in enamel colours (cf. *Deutsche Blumen*).
fluxing agent A substance which reduces the temperature necessary to bring the fusion of a glaze.
frit A half-fused siliceous mass used in the making of soft-paste porcelain (*q.v.*); also used of a siliceous body fused with natron (see glazed quartz fritware).
galena A lead sulphide (PbS) frequently used by early potters to make lead-glazes.
gilding The process of fixing gold (or a substitute) on the surface of a pot. Unfired gilding used gold-leaf on a size or lacquer base, but this was impermanent. Honey-gilding was practised by using ground gold leaf or precipitated gold powder in honey, and then firing it. This process was replaced in the late 18th century by mercury-gilding, an amalgam of gold and mercury being painted on and the latter then driven off by heating. In the 19th century these methods were replaced by the use of the cheaper 'liquid gold', giving a thin film.
glazed quartz fritware A pottery made of a powdered quartz body made plastic by addition of water and natron, usually coloured turquoise with copper, blue with cobalt, or purple with manganese.
gloss A smooth shining surface given to a pot by surface-dressing of certain clays of small particle-size (see illite).
glost kiln A kiln used for firing the glaze on a ware.
grand feu colours (Fr. = 'great fire') Pigments which can stand the firing-temperatures of the glaze in or under which they are used; normally, in faience, cobalt-blue, manganese-purple, iron-red, copper-green, antimony-yellow; in hard-paste porcelain, underglaze-cobalt-blue and copper-red.
graphite A form of carbon also known as plumbago or black-lead, sometimes used as a surface-dressing on pottery.
haematite Mineral form of ferric oxide (Fe_2O_3) producing a red colour.
hard-paste porcelain See china clay.
high-temperature colours See *grand feu*.
illite A naturally occurring clay particularly suitable for the production of 'gloss' wares (*q.v.*).
'India flowers' See *fleurs des Indes*.
kaolin See china clay.
krater (Greek) Deep wide-mouthed vessel for mixing wine or water, with two handles of varying shapes.
kwaart (Dutch) A clear lead-glaze used over a tin-glaze to give a brilliant surface.
kylix (Greek) Two-handled drinking-cup with shallow bowl, high foot and two horizontal handles.
lambrequin (Fr.) Formal pendent ornament of 'vandyke' character.
levigation See clay, preparation of.
lustre-decoration Ornament achieved by painting on the surface of a pot a metallic pigment which is fired in a reducing atmosphere to produce a fine metallic film, often with iridescent effects. Copper and silver were used for coppery and lemon tones, gold for pink, platinum for 'silver' lustres.
luting Use of slip (liquid clay) to affix reliefs etc. to the surface of a pot.
maiolica Tin-glazed earthenware. See page 139.
majolica Misuse of the word 'maiolica' (*q.v.*) to denote colour-glazed wares (normally lead-glazed) of the mid-19th century.
moulding Clay may be moulded in a number of ways, the process offering obvious advantages in series production. Vessels may be formed by pressing clay into a single open mould with *intaglio* ornamentation, or into two half-moulds similarly decorated, the two moulded clay components being then joined by luting together. Relief ornaments may similarly be taken from moulds and luted to the surface of the pot. Porcelain figures were formed by moulding individual sections and joining them together. (See also slip-casting.)
muffle-skin See enamel.
oxidising atmosphere A clear bright flame in the kiln has a decisive effect on the colours of the ceramic materials being fired, most clays firing red under oxidising, but grey or black under reducing (smoky), conditions. In glazes iron tends to yellow or brown tones under oxidising, green under reducing, conditions, etc.
paddle and anvil technique A method of shaping a pot by beating it on the outside with a paddle-shaped piece of wood while holding a flat stone as an anvil inside the pot.
'parian' ware A fine-grained porcellanous body deriving its name from its resemblance to marble. Usually unglazed, but sometimes with a fine 'smear' glaze.
'peach bloom' An effect of a Chinese copper-red glaze producing pale red and brownish tones.
petit feu colours (Fr. = 'little fire') Enamels (*q.v.*).
petuntse See china clay.
porcelain See china clay, soft-paste porcelain.
porcellanous stoneware A stoneware approaching the character of a felspathic porcelain.
pricking See *sponses*.
reduction See oxidising atmosphere.
refractory A substance resistant to heat (e.g. sand, calcined flint), sometimes added to a ceramic body to give it stability.
repairer The workman who assembled the components of a porcelain figure and added the accessory details (flowers, etc.).
resist A medium (e.g. a wax) by means of which a pattern may be produced on the surface of a pot, which is then dipped in a glaze-mixture, surface-wash, lustre-pigment, or the like. During firing the resist burns away leaving the design in reserve?
rose-engine turning When a pot is 'leather-hard', it may be turned on a lathe and either smoothed or patterned. The 'rose-engine' produced an ornament of waved parallel lines, or basket-work.
sagger (saggar, seggar, supposedly a corruption of 'safeguard') A refractory fire-clay container in which ware can be fired but protected from direct contact with the fire.
sang-de-boeuf (Fr. = 'bull's blood') A deep copper-red glaze.
scyphus (Latin, from Greek *skyphos*) Deep cup usually with low foot and two handles.
sgraffiato (or *sgraffito*, It. = 'scratched') Decoration incised with a point, usually through a layer of slip (*q.v.*).
slip-casting Moulding by means of multipartite plaster-of-Paris moulds with internal *intaglio* decoration. The mould is assembled and liquid clay 'slip' poured into it, the plaster rapidly absorbing the water and leaving a thin film of clay adhering to the mould, which can then be dismantled and the vessel freed. This method permits sharp ornamental detail and thin vessel-walls. See also moulding.
slipware Pottery (normally lead-glazed) in which slip—clay reduced to a more or less liquid consistency—is used for decoration, usually white on a red body. The slip may be painted or trailed on with a spouted can; or designs may be drawn with a point through the slip to reveal the body beneath (*sgraffiato*).
'smear' glaze A glaze laid on the sagger containing the ware, to which it is transmitted in a fine film when volatilised in firing.
soft-paste porcelain An imitation of true ('hard-paste') porcelain produced essentially by the admixture of white clay with a ground frit (*q.v.*) or other substance, e.g. bone-ash, steatite.
sponses (Dutch) Papers on which a design has been pricked out with a point. The paper was then laid on the ware and pounced with a black powder which thereby (the paper being removed) furnished the outlines of the design for subsequent painting over.
'sprigging' Application of small moulded relief-motifs luted on to the pot, the connecting stems etc. being sometimes modelled by hand and applied.
Steingut (Germ.). See cream-coloured earthenware.
stoneware A ware made of refractory clays which vitrify but do not collapse at temperatures in the range 1200–1400°C., thereby becoming impermeable by liquids. Stonewares may be glazed by means of wood-ashes, volatilised common salt, etc., of left unglazed.
style rayonnant (Fr.) Style popular in French faience and porcelain in the late 17th and early 18th centuries, using radiating ornaments of *lambrequins* (*q.v.*) and other lacy designs, scroll-work derived from ironwork, swags of flowers, etc.
terraglia (It.) See cream-coloured earthenware.
terre de Lorraine (Fr. = 'Lorraine clay') Hard pipe-clay compositions used like biscuit porcelain in eastern France.
throwing The process of making a circular clay object on a rotating wheel. Centrifugal force and the pressure of the potter's hands control the form into which the plastic clay is squeezed. On drying, a pot may further be turned on a lathe or the original wheel to give a smoother surface-texture or to modify the profile.
trailing See slipware.
transfer-printing Method by which an engraved design may be transferred from the plate or block to the surface of a pot. At different times thin papers or gelatinous 'bats' have been used for this purpose, depending on the effect required. They were 'inked' with a mixture of metallic oxide in an oily medium, or sometimes with a greasy substance on to which metallic oxide could be dusted. Transfer-printing may be overglaze or underglaze.
trek (Dutch) Outline in blue, manganese-purple or black, usually as employed in blue-painting on Delftware.
turning See throwing and rose-engine turning.
wasters Pots, or fragments of them, which have been spoiled and discarded.

Glossary of Marks

Chinese

Reign-marks of:
Yung Lo (1403-1424) (In archaic script)

Yung Lo (1403-1424)

Hsüan Tê (1426-1435)

(In seal characters)

Ch'êng Hua (1465-1487)

(In seal characters)

Chêng Tê (1506-1521)

Chia Ching (1522-1566)

Wan Li (1573-1619)

K'ang Hsi (1662-1722)

(In seal characters)

Yung Cheng (1723-1735)

(In seal characters)

Ch'ien Lung (1736-1795)

(In seal characters)

European

Netherlands tin-glazed wares (Delftware)

Drie Klokken (The Three Bells)

De Roos (The Rose)

De Paauw (The Peacock)

De Grieksche A (The Greek 'A')
Samuel van Eenhoorn
Adriaenus Koeks

't Jonge Moriaenshooft (The Young Moor's Head)
Rochus Hoppesteyn
Lieve van Dalen

De Starre (The Star)
Albertus Kiehl

De Klaeuw (The Claw)

Het Bijltje (The Axe)

De Lampetkan (The Ewer)

French tin-glazed wares (Faience)

Moustiers
Olerys, Joseph
Laugier, Jean-Baptiste

Fouque, Joseph
Pelloquin, Jean-François

Ferrat, Jean-Baptiste

Féraud, Jean-Gaspard

Marseilles
Leroy, Louis

Fauchier, Joseph

Veuve Perrin

Savy, Honoré

Robert, Joseph-Gaspard

Bonnefoy, Antoine

Strasbourg
Hannong, Paul
Hannong, Joseph

Niderviller
Beyerlé, Baron Jean-Louis de

Custine, Comte de

French Porcelain

Saint Cloud
Chicaneau, Pierre
Trou, Henri

Chantilly
protected by the Prince de Condé

Mennecy
protected by the duc de Villeroy

Vincennes & Sèvres
Vincennes before 1753

Sèvres or Vincennes

mark of 1781

First Republic, 1793-1804

Limoges
protected by the Comte d'Artois

mark on wares made for Sèvres decoration

Paris factories
Clignancourt

Faubourg Saint-Denis

Hannong, Pierre Antoine

Charles-Philippe, Comte d'Artois

La Courtille

rue de Bondy

rue Amelot

rue Thiroux
protected by Queen Marie-Antoinette

Italian porcelain

Florence
mark depicting the cathedral of Florence on rare 'Medici' porcelain

Venice
Vezzi, Francesco

Cozzi, Geminiano Nove

Antonibon, Giovanni

Doccia
Ginori, Marchese Carlo

Capodimonte (also on Buen Retiro)

Charles III, King of Spain

Naples
'Fabbrica Reale Ferdinandea'

'N' mark found on German copies

German Porcelain

Meissen
Königliche Porzellanmanufaktur

'crossed-sword' mark adopted 1723

'A.R.' mark, ownership monogram of 'Augustus Rex'

'Dot period', 1763-74
'Marcolini' period, 1774-1813

Vienna
Vienna shield mark much copied by other 19th-century factories

Höchst
wheel-mark from the arms of Mayence

Frankenthal
lion from arms of the Palatinate. 'Paul Hannong'

Karl Theodor shield

Carl Theodor monogram

Nymphenburg
impressed shield 'hexagram mark'

Fürstenberg
Duke Carl I of Brunswick

Berlin
Gotowski factory

Sceptre from the arms of Berlin

Cassel
'HC' (for Hesse-Cassel)

Kelsterbach
'HD' (for Hesse-Darmstadt)

Ludwigsburg
Charles Eugene, Duke of Würtemberg

Ansbach
arms of Ansbach

Volkstedt
hayforks, sometimes confused with swords

Switzerland

Nyon
Jakob Dortu

Zürich
1763-1790

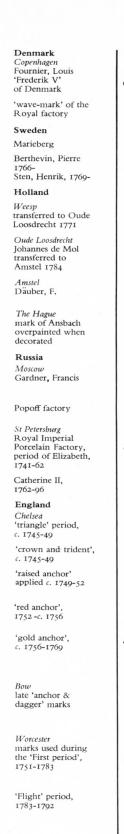

Denmark
Copenhagen
Fournier, Louis 'Frederik V' of Denmark

'wave-mark' of the Royal factory

Sweden

Marieberg

Berthevin, Pierre 1766-
Sten, Henrik, 1769-

Holland

Weesp
transferred to Oude Loosdrecht 1771

Oude Loosdrecht
Johannes de Mol transferred to Amstel 1784

Amstel
Däuber, F.

The Hague
mark of Ansbach overpainted when decorated

Russia
Moscow
Gardner, Francis

Popoff factory

St Petersburg
Royal Imperial Porcelain Factory, period of Elizabeth, 1741-62

Catherine II, 1762-96

England
Chelsea
'triangle' period, c. 1745-49

'crown and trident', c. 1745-49

'raised anchor' applied c. 1749-52

'red anchor', 1752-c. 1756

'gold anchor', c. 1756-1769

Bow
late 'anchor & dagger' marks

Worcester
marks used during the 'First period', 1751-1783

'Flight' period, 1783-1792

'Flight and Barr' period, 1792-1807

Caughley
Turner, Thomas 1772-
marks used on copies of Worcester

Examples of Caughley disguised numerals

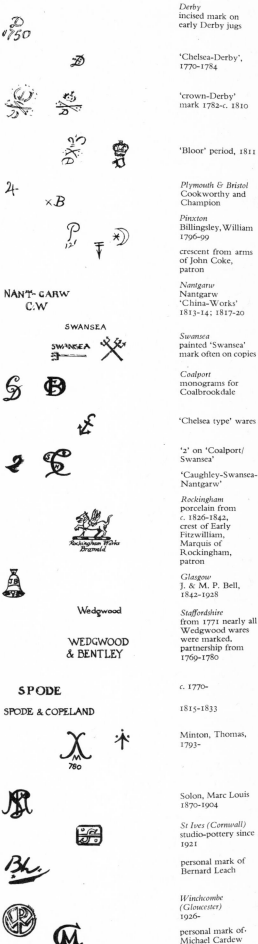

Derby
incised mark on early Derby jugs

'Chelsea-Derby', 1770-1784

'crown-Derby' mark 1782-c. 1810

'Bloor' period, 1811

Plymouth & Bristol
Cookworthy and Champion

Pinxton
Billingsley, William 1796-99

crescent from arms of John Coke, patron

Nantgarw
Nantgarw 'China-Works' 1813-14; 1817-20

Swansea
painted 'Swansea' mark often on copies

Coalport
monograms for Coalbrookdale

'Chelsea type' wares

'2' on 'Coalport/Swansea'

'Caughley-Swansea-Nantgarw'

Rockingham
porcelain from c. 1826-1842, crest of Early Fitzwilliam, Marquis of Rockingham, patron

Glasgow
J. & M. P. Bell, 1842-1928

Staffordshire
from 1771 nearly all Wedgwood wares were marked. partnership from 1769-1780

c. 1770-

1815-1833

Minton, Thomas, 1793-

Solon, Marc Louis 1870-1904

St Ives (Cornwall)
studio-pottery since 1921

personal mark of Bernard Leach

Winchcombe (Gloucester)
1926-

personal mark of Michael Cardew

Index

Italic numbers in this index refer to black-and-white illustrations; numbers in bold type refer to illustrations in colour.

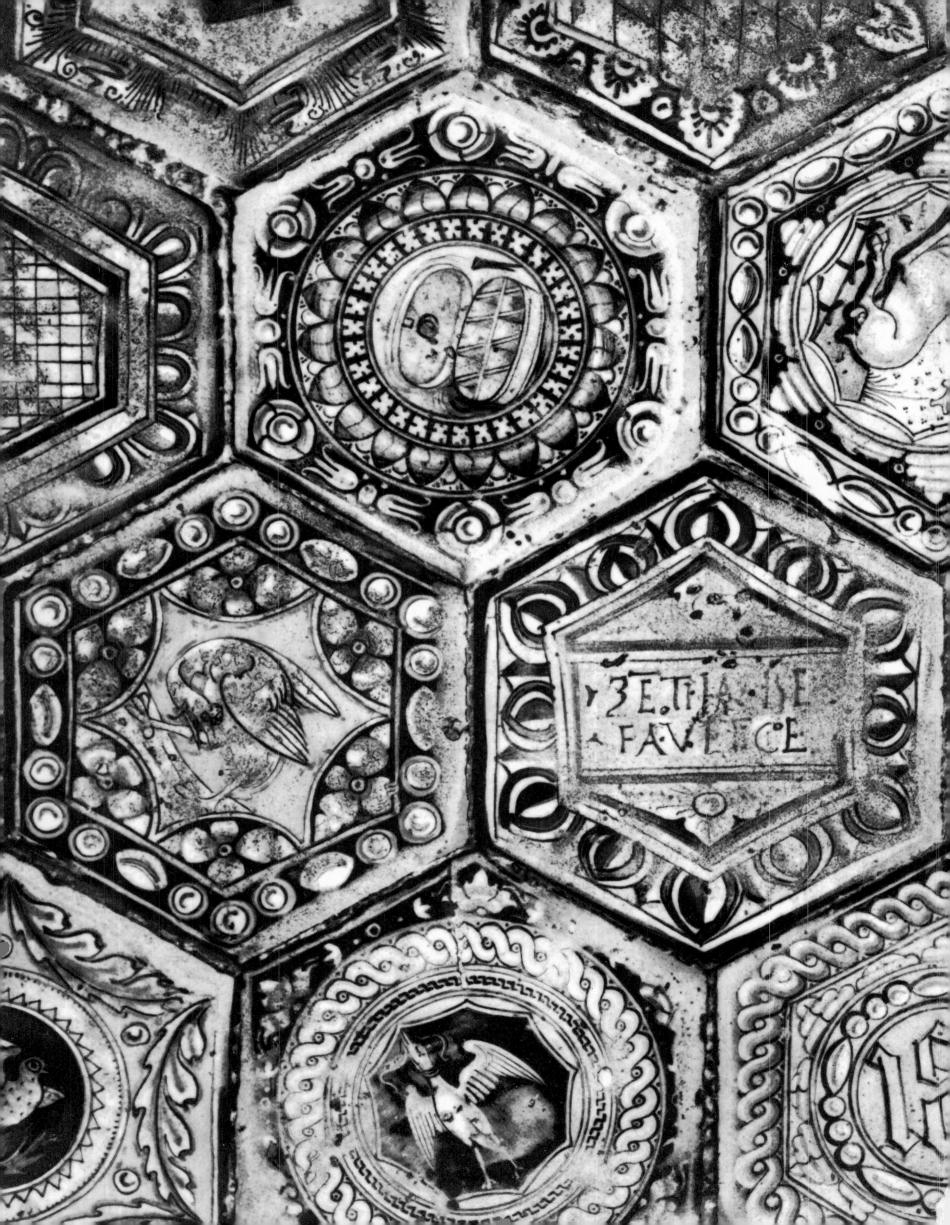